DATE DUE

DEC 0 9 2008	
Dec 17, 2009	

JUVENILE
DELINQUENCY
Mainstream and Crosscurrents

John Randolph Fuller

PEARSON

Prentice
Hall

Upper Saddle River, New Jersey
Columbus, Ohio

Library of Congress Cataloging-in-Publication Data

Fuller, John R.
    Juvenile delinquency : the mainstream and crosscurrents / John R. Fuller.
        p. cm.
    ISBN 0-13-114945-8 (978-0-13-114945-8)
        1. Juvenile delinquency.   2. Juvenile justice,
    Administration of.   I. Title.
        HV9069.F85 2009
        364.36—dc22   2007048233

Editor in Chief: *Vernon Anthony*
Senior Acquisitions Editor: *Tim Peyton*
Development Editor: *Elisa Rogers*
Editorial Assistant: *Alicia Kelly*
Production Coordination: *Linda Zuk, WordCraft LLC*
Project Manager: *Holly Shufeldt*
Cover photo: *PhotoEdit Inc.*
Senior Operations Supervisor: *Patricia A. Tonneman*
Director of Marketing: *David Gesell*
Executive Marketing Manager: *Adam Kloza*

Marketing Assistant: *Alicia Dysert*
Creative Director: *John Christiana*
Art Director & Designer: *Kathryn Foot*
Cover Designer: *Kathryn Foot*
Director, Image Resource Center: *Melinda Patelli*
Manager, Rights and Permissions: *Zina Arabia*
Manager, Visual Research: *Beth Brenzel*
Manager, Cover Visual Research & Permissions: *Karen Sanatar*
Image Permission Coordinator: *Fran Toepfer*
Photo Researcher: *Diane Austin*

This book was set in Janson Text by S4Carlisle. It was printed and bound by Courier Kendallville Inc. The cover was printed by Phoenix Color Corp.

Part-Opener and Chapter-Opener Photo Credits: Pages 1, 2–3: © Iris Coppola/zefa/CORBIS; pp. 2, 34–35: © Brooklyn Museum/CORBIS. All Rights Reserved; pp. 1, 64–65: Spencer Grant, PhotoEdit Inc.; pp. 1, 96–97: Juergen Schmidt/Das Fotoarchiv, Peter Arnold, Inc.; pp. 127, 128–129: © Lynsey Addario / CORBIS. All Rights Reserved; pp. 127, 158–159: www.istockphoto.com; pp. 127, 194–195: Trish Gant © Dorling Kindersley; pp. 127, 226–227: Tom Prettyman, PhotoEdit Inc.; pp. 257, 258–259: Corbis Digital Stock; pp. 257, 290–291: © Goodshoot / CORBIS. All Rights Reserved; pp. 257, 326–327: Dwayne Newton, PhotoEdit Inc.; pp. 257, 360–361: Marc D. Longwood, Pearson Education/PH College; pp. 393, 394–394: © Lynsey Addario / CORBIS. All Rights Reserved; pp. 393, 430–431: AP Wide World Photos; pp. 393, 460–461: David Kennedy, Creative Eye/MIRA.com; pp. 393, 496–497: Joe Sohm/Chromosohm, The Stock Connection

Pearson Education Ltd.
Pearson Education Singapore, Pte. Ltd.
Pearson Education Canada, Ltd.
Pearson Education—Japan

Pearson Education Australia PTY, Limited
Pearson Education North Asia Ltd.
Pearson Educacion de Mexico, S.A. de C.V.
Pearson Education Malaysia, Pte. Ltd.

10 9 8 7 6 5 4 3 2 1
ISBN-13 978-0-13-114945-8
ISBN-10   0-13-114945-8

The book is dedicated to the memory of my parents

Clark B. Fuller
Carol J. Fuller

And to my siblings

Thomas
Susan
Bonnie
Randy

I am happy to say there is not a juvenile delinquent in the family.

(Unless, of course, you count who Bonnie married.)

Brief Contents

Contents

Part II   Theories of Delinquency   127

CHAPTER 5   Theoretical Foundations of Crime and Delinquency   129

CHAPTER 8   Critical, Life-Course, and Integrated Theories   227

CHAPTER 14   The Juvenile Court   431

CHAPTER 15   Juvenile Corrections   461

CHAPTER 16 The Future of Delinquency and Juvenile Justice 497

Preface

Who is responsible for the actions of a child? If the child is intelligent, kind, creative, talented, or industrious, then there is a long line of people ready to own up to having a hand in the child's development, including parents, teachers, coaches, pastors, friends, relatives, and siblings. And this is likely true. In recent years, it has been said that "It takes a village to raise a child."

But what about the "bad kids?" Who claims the responsibility for a child who has broken the law? Is society obligated to claim credit when a child misbehaves? Often, too often maybe, only the child bears the responsibility. If the offense is serious enough, or even heinous, the legal system can treat the youth as an adult. If the offense is less serious, then the youth is treated as a juvenile delinquent. It might take a village to raise a child, but the juvenile delinquent is not only a social orphan, but also considered morally corrupt, intellectually deficient, and behaviorally beyond control. Over the years many approaches to stemming delinquency have been tried, but there remains little consensus on the best response.

The current attitude toward delinquency is both harsh and sympathetic, often depending on the crime rate and the political climate. The very use of the word "delinquent" reflects this. Its usage to describe lawbreaking youths was coined early in the 20th century, a time of vigorous social reform.

The Oxford English Dictionary defines *delinquency* as "failing in, or neglectful of, a duty or obligation... guilty of a misdeed or offense." This is an interesting way to describe youths who break the law. Why didn't the founders of the juvenile court simply call wayward youths "juvenile criminals" or "juvenile offenders?" Instead, youths who broke the law got their own designation of "delinquent." This isn't the same as "criminal," which has far more serious connotations. "Criminal" is "having the nature of a grave offense," and a "crime" is "an act punishable by law." Why did lawbreaking youths get a much more lenient term than lawbreaking adults?

This distinction is at the heart of the study of juvenile delinquency. That is, youths who stray out of society's legal boundaries, whether they participate in something as minor as spray-painting graffiti or as heinous as homicide, are considered to be less morally responsible than adults. In the process of growing and learning, young people make mistakes. They aren't considered to have the life experience to know the consequences of their behaviors. A young child who deliberately touches a hot stove will get far more sympathy (and probably a lecture from mom or dad) than an adult, who will get little or none at all.

In our society, life experience is considered to be key, and it is related to another issue, control. Youths aren't allowed much control in our society, and often for good reason: they have little life experience with which to make wise decisions. Adults, then, have the task of controlling children's experiences and environments in the way that will benefit them most. Unfortunately, however, adults sometimes fail in this responsibility and not only neglect youths, but also victimize them, using the naiveté of youngsters to their own advantage. This is when the state steps in.

The purpose of this book is to explore the nature of delinquency, as well as the closely related issue of youth victimization. The text does this in two ways. First, the mainstream approach helps the student to understand what issues are currently believed to be at the basis of juvenile delinquency, as well as the mechanisms that society has created to deal with delinquency. Second, the crosscurrents approach takes an analytical point of view of what we currently believe to be true of juvenile delinquency and how society should deal with it.

Juvenile Delinquency: Mainstream and Crosscurrents gives students a fresh look at the behavior of young people and why it's often classified as delinquent. This book highlights not only the conventional wisdom found in traditional texts, but also includes a critical component that helps students understand not only what is, but also why things are the way they are, and how they might be different. This mainstream versus crosscurrents approach provides a healthy balance to the tensions between holding children accountable for their behavior and providing the necessary prevention and treatment strategies that can make them productive citizens. Professors and students alike will find this approach stimulating and thought-provoking. Ultimately, the mainstream and crosscurrent approach leads the reader to consider the many causes of delinquency, as well as effective and humane ways of dealing with problem youths.

OUTLINE OF THE BOOK

In Part I, we will define what a juvenile delinquent is and how the definition was developed. Chapter 1 explores how we define juvenile delinquency. Chapter 2 discusses social control and how we apply it to youths. Social phenomena must be measured in order to be understood, and Chapter 3 is a look at how we measure delinquency. Chapter 4 deals with the legal control of youths in other countries and how they compare with the United States.

In Part II, we'll turn to theories of juvenile delinquency, that is, ideas about what makes youths break the law. Chapter 5 examines the theoretical foundations of crime and delinquency, whereas Chapters 6, 7, and 8 delve into the specific theories, including biological, psychological, and sociological, as well as critical, life course, and integrated theories.

Part III analyzes the place of delinquency in society. Chapter 9 discuss delinquency in girls, and Chapters 10 and 11 look at delinquency within the family and schools, respectively. Chapter 12 examines the role that youth gangs play in juvenile delinquency,

Finally, Part IV examines the juvenile justice system, with coverage of the roles of the police, the juvenile court, and juvenile corrections in Chapters 13, 14, and 15. Chapter 16 looks forward to trends in juvenile delinquency control.

SUPPLEMENTS

Instructor's Manual	0131149512
Instructor's Manual* (download only)	0135008549
PowerPoints on CD	0131149520
PowerPoints* (download only)	0135008530
TestGen* (download only)	0131149539
Test Item File for WebCT* (download only)	0135008522
Test Item File for Blackboard/Course Compass* (download only)	0132079054
Companion Website www.Prenhall.com/fuller	

To access supplementary materials online, instructors need to request an instructor access code. Go to **www.pearsonhighered.com/irc,** where you can register for an instructor access code. Within 48 hours after registering, you will receive a confirming e-mail, including an instructor access code. Once you have received your code, go to the site and log on for full instructions on downloading the materials you wish to use.

Acknowledgments

Many people have contributed to the success of this book. I would first like to thank the following reviewers and focus-group members who made many wonderful and substantive suggestions for improving the text's scope and focus. Any remaining shortcomings should be attributed to me alone.

Frank Alberico, *Joliet Junior College*
John Ambenge, *Middlesex Community College*
John Augustine, *Triton College*
Gai Berlage, *Iona College*
Bonnie Black, *Mesa Community College*
Peggy Bowen, *Alvernia College*
Kevin Breault, *Middle Tennessee State University*
Christine Broeker, *Seminole Community College*
Deborah Burris-Kitchen, *Tennessee State University–Nashville*
Mary Ann Czarnezki, *University of Wisconsin-Milwaukee*
Patrice Davis, *Essex County College*
Robert Doyle, *Daytona Beach Community College*
Roger Dunham, *University of Miami*
Patrick Faiella, *Bridgewater State College; Massasoit Community College; U Mass Boston*
Gail Gehrig, *Lewis University*
Nicky Jackson, *Purdue University*
Angela Gardner Johnson, *Vance-Granville Community College*
Mark Jones, *Atlantic Cape Community College/ Community College of Philadelphia*
Marshall Jones, *Florida Institute of Technology*
Hee-Jong Joo, *Sam Houston State University*
Kimberly Kempf-Leonard, *University of Texas, Dallas*
Ann Koshivas, *North Shore Community College*
Ellen Lemley, *Arkansas State University*
Ruth Liu, *San Diego State University*
Miriam Lorenzo, *Miami-Dade Community College-North Campus*

Dennis MacDonald, *Saint Anselm College*
Mary Ellen Mastrorilli, *Boston University*
Robert Michels, *Santa Clara University*
Jill Miller, *Missouri Western State College*
Thomas Mosley, *University of Maryland*
David Mueller, *Boise State University*
Rebecca Nathanson, *Lake-Sumter Community College*
Jerome Neapolitan, *Tennessee Technological University*
Everette Penn, *University of Houston*
Edward Powers, *University of Central Arkansas*
Cynthia Robbins, *University of Delaware*
Robert Rush, *University of Delaware*
Barbara Russo, *Wayne Community College*
Lawrence Scott, *Bunker Hill Community College*
Jo Ann Short, *Northern Virginia Community College*
Robert Sigler, *University of Alabama*
Rebecca Stevens, *University of Akron*
Roy Sudipto, *Indiana State University*
Stephen Sullivan, *Normandale Community College*
Gail Truitt, *Lincoln Land Community College*
Chad Trulson, *University of North Texas*
David Uhler, *Southwestern Illinois College*
Freddie Vaughns, *Bowie State University*
Eve Waltermaurer, *State University of New York–New Paltz*
Betsy Witt, *Tarleton State University*
Bernard Zant, *Bradley University*

A number of other individuals have greatly assisted me in writing this text. At Prentice Hall my editor, Tim Peyton, has been a source of encouragement and guidance. Elisa Rogers has been a joy to work with, and her attention to detail is appreciated. My colleagues at the University of West Georgia have been generous with their advice and in letting me borrow their books. I hope I have returned them all. Specifically, I acknowledge Jane McCandless, Marc LaFountain, Catherine Jenks, David Jenks, Mike Johnson, Christopher Williams, and Lisa Gezon. My student assistants, Heather Kelly and Tracy Carroll, worked hard and I would like to thank them for all their efforts at keeping me supplied with relevant materials to draw upon as I wrote each chapter. Thomas Blomberg of Florida State University provided me with numerous materials that opened my eyes to contemporary ways of understanding the relationship between education and delinquency. Jordan Riak, of *Parents and Teachers Against Violence in Education (PTAVE)*, graciously allowed me to include his insightful article "Facing Down a Drill Sergeant Dad." Others who provided ideas or helped me clarify perspectives are Robert McNamara, Rob Mutchnick, Bruce Berg, Eric Hickey, and Jackie Fillingim.

The person most responsible for this text, however, is Amy Hembree. She is my first editor, constant critic, best friend, brightest inspiration, and loving wife. If not for her, I would still be spending all my time sitting in my recliner watching football and eating ice cream. Hmmm?

About the Author

John Randolph Fuller has been a professor of criminology and sociology at the University of West Georgia for more than 25 years. He brings both an applied and theoretical background to his scholarship. He served as a probation and parole officer for the Florida Probation and Parole Commission in Broward County, Florida, where he managed a caseload of more than 100 felons. He also served as a criminal justice planner for the Palm Beach Metropolitan Criminal Justice Planning Unit. In this capacity, he worked with every criminal justice agency in a three-county area writing and supervising grants for the Law Enforcement Assistance Administration.

Dr. Fuller has received awards for both his scholarship and his teaching. The Textbook and Academic Authors Association bestowed on him its prestigious TEXTY Award for his book *Criminal Justice: Mainstream and Crosscurrents*. Additionally, he was given the first "Distinguished Scholar Award" by the University of West Georgia College of Arts and Sciences.

In 2006, the Institute of Higher Education and the Center for Teaching and Learning at the University of Georgia named Dr. Fuller a Governor's Teaching Fellow. Additionally, he was chosen as Honors Professor of the Year, 2000-2001, by the students of the University of West Georgia's Honors College.

Recognized as an accomplished scholar, teacher, adviser, and mentor, Dr. Fuller is committed to the ideals of fairness and justice for all for victims, offenders, and practitioners in the juvenile and criminal justice systems.

In addition to reading widely and watching too many sport programs on television, Dr. Fuller enjoys playing golf and painting, neither of which he does well.

What is a juvenile delinquent?

How do rites of passage
define adulthood?

Why do we have
a separate juvenile
justice system?

CHAPTER 1

What Is a Juvenile Delinquent?

adolescence
The period between puberty and adulthood in human development that typically falls between the ages of 13 and 19.

juvenile delinquency
A legal term used to describe the behavior of a youth that is marked by violation of the law and antisocial behavior.

Making the transition from child to adult is a risky business in any society. It involves a change in status, rights, responsibilities, and self-concept. It isn't done overnight, and it isn't done easily. The road from childhood to adulthood passes through the exciting and dangerous landscape of **adolescence,** "where there be dragons" in the forms of puberty, drugs, driver's licenses, dating, and first employment. This transition of only a few years can completely alter the sociological and psychological outlook of young people. The fact that this journey is often precarious and that many young people lose their way makes the study of **juvenile delinquency** necessary.

What complicates the study of juvenile delinquency is the observation that the journey from childhood to adulthood not only varies across cultures, but is also very different from one generation to the next.[1] If a single body of knowledge about growing up could be applied to the United States, Russia, China, and Europe, it could be useful in predicting trends and controlling antisocial behavior. However, each of these societies is very different, and even within these societies there are such vast variations that no single body of knowledge can comprehensively explain and control the behavior of young people. Each society has its own set of problems, ranging from the trivial to the deadly. The culture and history of each society are different, yet the problems of gaining acceptance and identity are present in each and must be solved in different ways.[2]

The problems of growing up differ not only across geographic locations, but also across time. Each generation faces new problems and obstacles. Although many of the issues (dating, driving, drugs) are similar, the resources to deal with these issues and the pressures and temptations to deviate can be very different. When parents say, "My dad wouldn't let me have a car until I was 21, and I learned to deal with it and so will you," they fail to realize that this universal issue affects children of different generations in different ways. How far is it from home to school? Where do their friends live? Is public transportation available? Does the youth need a car to get to a job, a sports practice, a religious study group, or a probation officer? Modern society makes demands on children that might not have been as acute in the parent's younger years, and it can be difficult for older generations to appreciate the stresses under which young people operate.

Adolescence is an exciting time of change and growth, as children are transformed into adults. Part of growing up is testing boundaries and breaking rules, and sometimes this trouble can lead to acts of juvenile delinquency. *(Courtesy Will & Deni McIntyre, Photo Researchers, Inc.)*

It can be difficult for older generations to appreciate the stresses that affect the lives of many youths. *(Courtesy Lynsey Addario, CORBIS-NY)*

This struggle between generations is nothing new. The conditions have changed, and one might argue that the consequences are more serious because, in some places, the public arena has become more dangerous. However, the conflict between youngsters and their elders has been a consistent feature of society for many generations. Some issues might have changed in their details, but the central problem remains: How does one pass from the status of a child to that of an adult? The answer to this question is "slowly." Growing up isn't an event, but a process. It involves trial and error, fights and disagreements, mistakes and great accomplishments, but most of all it involves the gaining of trust and respect. Sometimes the passage is never completed, and the youth ends up without the respect of parents and teachers, working at a low-wage job with no future, in prison, or dead.

Most people successfully pass from childhood to adulthood. Those who don't successfully make the transition often end up as clients of the juvenile justice system. Sometimes, those who go on to be lawyers, corporate leaders, or university professors aren't much different from those who end up as murderers, drug dealers, or white-collar offenders.[3] A bit of luck here or some parental influence there, and things might have been different for many youths who find themselves in the clutches of the law. Understanding the sometimes-capricious ways in which the legal system operates requires that we examine this process. To do this, we must understand how the concept of childhood is developed and defined and also what the term *delinquency* means in the juvenile justice system. For example, teenagers did not always exist. See Crosscurrents 1.1 to learn why.

SOCIAL CONSTRUCTION OF CHILDHOOD

Sociologists talk about social status as being either "achieved" or "ascribed." By this, they mean that people either earn their place in society or it's given to them. For instance, one is either male or female, and social status is ascribed accordingly. There is little one can do about ascribed status. People are assumed to have certain characteristics, orientations, or abilities based on gender. Often as not, these assumptions are wrong, but the fact remains that, to a great extent, these ascribed statuses will be acted on by society, and individuals will be treated thusly. In contrast, achieved

CrossCurrents

1.1

The Invention of Teenagers

There haven't always been teenagers. Adolescents have always been around, of course, but the teenager is a 20th-century American phenomenon that emerged from a national surplus of wealth and free time and a culture focused on growth instead of survival.

Prior to the late 1930s, the ages between 12 and 20, what we now call the "teens," existed only as numerical ages. Of course, adolescence held much the same physical and emotional difficulties as it does now, but adolescents weren't considered to be a social group, just children at a difficult age. Prior to the 1930s, many adolescents became adults long before they were out of their teens. When the United States was primarily agricultural, adolescents on farms took on adult work and responsibilities well before the age of 18. This changed little even when the country turned to industry and many young adolescents went to work in factories.

During the early 20th century, adolescents met each other only while on the job, at church, in small schools, or at chaperoned social functions. Relatively few attended school, and even fewer earned high school diplomas, with education largely being the province of the upper classes. During the Great Depression, many families became impoverished, and children and adolescents who would have gone to school instead had to go to work to help feed their families. Many more children died.

As the United States emerged from the Great Depression in the late 1930s, more families had enough money to keep their children in school. Schools were the perfect environment for adolescents to form and reinforce social groups. With the expectation that adolescents only had to attend school, and not hold down a job, came large amounts of free time. American parents expected their children to concentrate on school and other activities, such as sports and clubs, instead of doing backbreaking work.

Popular music had much to do with the formation of the new teen identity. By 1937, adolescents discovered swing music, spending what their parents believed was an inordinate amount of time and money dancing, listening to music, and buying records and clothes. By 1939, 80 percent of American adolescents went to high school, forming a powerful, new demographic. Advertisers, taking note of how much adolescents spent on nonessentials, invented the word *teenager* in 1941 as a way to get a handle on this new market.

With the start of World War II, the teen lifestyle was put on hold as teenagers joined the military. The grave responsibilities of war pushed an entire generation into early adulthood, as adolescents as young as 15 and 16 (many lied about their ages to enter military service) began to fly bombers and storm beaches. As they grew up, America's first generation of teenagers eventually became its "Greatest Generation."

Think About It

1. There will always be adolescents, but will there always be teenagers?
2. Should advertisers direct so many of their messages to young people? Are any of these messages destructive?
3. Will you (or do you) miss being a teenager?

Source: Grace Palladino, *Teenagers: An American History* (New York: Basic Books, 1996), xv–xvii, 5, 50–52, 60–61, 83.

---

statuses are given according to accomplishment. For example, wealth, physical fitness, grade-point average, or number of children are subject to the individual's intentional behavior.

Because we think of ascribed characteristics as basically unchangeable, we believe we shouldn't discriminate against people because of their race, gender, or disability. However, achieved characteristics such as test scores and grade-point averages are used to make decisions about what university a student can attend; education and training decide what occupation one can pursue, and the speed of a pitcher's fastball determines whether he can pitch for the New York Yankees. Therefore, *what people do* seems like a perfectly valid reason to allocate rewards and punishments.

But what about age? Is age an achieved or ascribed characteristic? It is certainly something one can't control. As much as we would like to look older or younger depending on whether we are an adolescent trying to buy beer or a middle-aged actor trying to win a part in a movie, we are pretty much stuck with our age. The trouble is that society discriminates according to age. Americans can't vote until age 18, drink alcohol until age 21, become president until age 35, or receive Social Security until age 62. Therefore, we can safely say that age is an ascribed characteristic because individuals are treated according to a status they can't control. Certain 16-year-olds might be better educated about political matters and be exactly the type of informed voters we would want to trust the future of the country to, but they are not allowed to cast a ballot. Certain 60-year-old men might routinely drink too much beer and pose a threat to society when they drive, but we still allow them to buy alcohol. Discrimination according to age is socially constructed. We agree through the legislative process to accord certain rights and privileges based on age because we believe that, on average, there are appropriate points to set restrictions based on developmental maturity.

A number of criteria are used as a basis for treating juveniles differently than adults. These criteria are used by various institutions and agencies, as well as by families and schools. It is useful to consider how and why this differential treatment is justified:

- **Physical development**   Children don't spring into the world fully developed. They start out as roughly 7 pounds of dependent and needy darlings and develop into adults with their own needs, wants, and ideas. As children grow, they are able to perform increasingly complicated tasks, lift more weight, and better defend themselves from harm. As they increase in size and strength, they receive more opportunities. For instance, some amusement parks post signs by the particularly exciting rides stating that customers must be a certain height to ride. This is a clear case of discrimination based on physical maturity. For safety reasons, based on the engineering of the ride, those who don't measure up to the standard aren't allowed to participate. Although age-graded divisions are used often (schools are the best example), there aren't that many divisions based on height. Occasionally, youth football leagues will compose teams based on weight to give smaller youths an opportunity to play against those of their own size. This difference in physical maturity is important when considering the separation of juveniles from adults in the penal system. Larger adults could take advantage of smaller, weaker juveniles. Therefore, a separate corrections system has been designed to keep youths from the clutches of predatory adults.[4]

- **Intellectual development**   From the earliest age, children are tracked into classes and programs based on their intellectual capacities. Certain children are fast-tracked to allow them to master material without having to wait for the teacher to explain concepts to other children who don't grasp new concepts as quickly. Conversely, other children are placed in special classes or schools that present the material at a much slower rate than in traditional classes. Each of these strategies is designed to group children based on intellectual ability.[5] Although age is a rough indicator of intelligence, a percentage of youths at either end of the continuum require differential experiences if they are to progress. The juvenile justice system takes extra precautions to protect juveniles, because they don't have the intelligence or maturity to comprehend what is happening to them in court.[6] Although it could be argued that adults also don't understand the workings of the criminal justice system and therefore need attorneys, the problem is more acute with juveniles, because not only do they not understand the system, but they also often have little idea that they did anything wrong.

- **Emotional development**   Individuals require adequate time to develop emotional maturity. Children, especially adolescents, are constantly struggling to deal with life's challenges and to find their emotional equilibrium. This struggle is complicated by biological changes resulting from the onset of puberty. Children aren't permitted to engage in a wide variety of functions because they lack the emotional maturity to make good decisions.[7] A good example of this is driving laws. Although 14-year-olds might have excellent hand–eye coordination and can score astronomically high scores on video games, they lack the emotional maturity to make responsible decisions while driving an automobile. Young people are more likely to drive at excessive speeds, take risks, and not anticipate what other drivers might do. Although they might make better racecar drivers than the average 70-year-old, motorists would much rather deal with the slow-driving, but more predictable, elderly motorist than with the adventurous adolescent.

Is it really fair to discriminate against individuals based on their age? We certainly don't make such legal decisions based on gender or race. The best answer to this question is yes, under certain circumstances. These circumstances, according to our laws, are when it's in the best interests of the child. The intent isn't to be punitive toward children, but to protect them from the risks and dangers of the adult world, both for their own sakes and the protection of society.

When Boys Were Men

When discussing juvenile delinquents, as well as crime in general, it's useful to make distinctions between males and females. The intent isn't to minimize female culpability or victimization, but to recognize how crime, particularly street crime, is very much a young man's game. As of 2004, 1,947,800 men were incarcerated in state, federal, and local facilities compared to 183,400 women. For a breakdown by age and sex, see Figure 1-1. Later, we will extensively discuss female delinquency, but for the purposes of presenting the historical development of delinquency, we discuss how young men are involved in law-breaking.

Many observers agree that American society still has well-defined roles for men and women. Although it's true that these roles are starting to dissolve and that sex-role differentiation is less prominent, gender expectations of behavior, temperament, and occupation still exist to some degree. There is considerable disagreement about the desirability of different role expectations for males and females. Feminist scholars argue

Street crime is very much a young man's game. *(Courtesy Jim Corwin, Getty Images Inc. - Stone Allstock)*

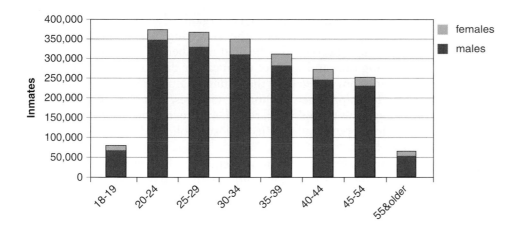

Figure 1-1   Number of Inmates in State and Federal Prisons and Local Jails as of 2004 *Source:* Paige M. Harrison and Allen J. Beck, *Prison and Jail Inmates at Midyear 2004* (Washington, DC: U.S. Department of Justice Bureau of Justice Statistics, 2005), 11. Online at www.ojp.usdoj.gov/bjs/pub/pdf/pjim04.pdf.

that rigid role expectations place women at a competitive disadvantage and force them into second-class jobs.[8] Those who support a more traditional philosophy believe there is an appropriate division of rights and responsibilities for women as opposed to men and that society functions best when females accept a subservient role. The goal here isn't to debate the relative merits of these contrasting positions, but rather to recognize that they exist and to point out that there is a history of sex-role differentiation that still influences how we think about the relationship between women and men.

Young men have always had greater latitude in many activities than young women.[9] This results in greater opportunities, but also in greater danger and risk. Young men are required to become independent earlier and to a much greater degree than young women. To a large extent, men are measured by how well they can take care of themselves physically, financially, and emotionally.[10] Young men traditionally have been expected to strike out on their own and start new families, join the clergy, enlist in the military, or otherwise get out of their parents' homes and stop draining resources. In the past, boys were forced to grow up quickly and fend for themselves, while girls were closely supervised and often went directly from the home of the father to the home of the husband without a period of relative freedom to develop their own interests and abilities.[11]

This enhanced freedom for boys comes at a price, however. Young men have been subjected to a broader range of problems in terms of unsafe working conditions, exploitation from older men, and lack of continued nurturing by the family. Boys often make mistakes that bring them into conflict with authorities. The emphasis on being able to defend oneself in a fight has put a premium on the willingness to use physical violence that can result in charges of assault or bullying.[12]

In some ways, socializing boys in this manner has been considered instrumental to their development. Society has long favored those who test the boundaries of appropriate behavior and rewarded the risk takers. In a society based on competitive capitalism, little distinction is made between those who test the rules in order to succeed and those who are caught breaking the rules and are doomed to fail. In short, the quest to become a man has been problematic. Society has a number of rules, some of them invisible, that dictate how boys grow into men. In the past, these rules were more clear and were represented by distinct ceremonies that marked the passage. Today, such ceremonies are no longer part of the formal culture and are often neglected and not adequately replaced. It is worth considering these ceremonies, often called **rites of passage,** to understand how they affect the likelihood of delinquency.

rites of passage
Ceremonies that serve to mark the passage from one stage of life to another, especially the entry of a youth into adulthood.

Rites of Passage

The issue of boys attaining manhood is as old as organized society. Throughout time and across civilizations, there has been the recurring problem of young men attempting to find ways to become full-fledged members of society.[13] There are a number of ways of doing this, and some of them can be disruptive. One need only to observe the animal kingdom to see how the young, maturing males in animal packs challenge the leader for supremacy. In human societies, this challenge can quickly turn deadly and damage the group's welfare. Therefore, alternative means of attaining manhood were developed that satisfied the symbolic and cultural needs of the boys and the society.[14]

Rites of passage are elaborate initiation ceremonies that transform people, especially young people. In the eyes of society, and especially in his own self-concept, the boy obtains the status of adult through a system of trials and tribulations that include a range of sanctions:

> By using any or all of these techniques—seclusion, hazing, tests of fortitude, genital operations or other forms of scarification, the changing of names—an initiation ritual during the transition phase redefines the physical, social, and spiritual existence of its participants. When the designated period of transition is over, the young men are ready to be initiated formally into their society as adult males.[15]

These rites of passage might include some sort of quest in which the boy is required to live alone in the wilderness for a period of time, fasting or eating only foods with religious connotations. Such rites are designed to test the boy's character to see if he is brave, willing to sacrifice for the group, and able to sever the apron strings, so to speak.

Such rites of passage can be observed to a degree in the practices of several modern-day groups. Fraternity hazing, scouting merit badges, and the treatment of rookie baseball players are all examples of how male groups socialize new members into the organization's value structure.[16] Although many of the half-hearted attempts to make life less comfortable for new members are trivial, the overall reasoning behind these traditions is deeply rooted in the way societies have long dealt with the issue of socializing new members. One could almost argue that there is a cultural need for these initiation rites for groups to function in a healthy manner. However, most modern societies don't have specific initiation ceremonies or rites of passage to assist young men in becoming fully functioning members of society. Why is this so?

- **Long period of adolescence**   One feature of the 21st century that we take for granted is the long period of dependency that children exert on their parents. For many families, it seems like their children never leave home or never stop needing financial support. In the not-so-distant past, children were hurried out of the home to start their own families and lives. Now they linger while they obtain more education or save money for the down payment on their first house. It isn't that young people are lazier these days; it's just that the financial barriers of entry into independent life have become very expensive and out of reach for many young people who are just starting out. Compounding this dependence is the high cost of health care and the practices of the credit industry. Young people with no credit history must rely on the security of their parents' good names to receive a cosigned loan, and unless they get a very good job, they must try to stay on their parents' health care. As a result of this long period of dependency, children, especially young men, have a difficult time demarcating the obtainment of adulthood. It can seem as if they will never escape their parents' financial shadow. Because there is little in the way of cultural ceremonies that can help distinguish young men as adults, this problem becomes acute for the criminal justice system. Drugs, violence, gang activity, and sexual aggressiveness are all things that struggling young males might use to attain their identities.

- **Blurring of male and female roles**   Becoming a man used to be much easier. You simply did the things that women were not allowed to do. Many occupations, sporting events, social clubs, smoking in public, and numerous other activities were reserved for men. Women were forced into roles that were ancillary, supportive, inferior, and less powerful. It was truly a man's world, and the saying "Behind every good man is a good woman" described the highest attainable status for females. This rigid sex-role differentiation allowed boys to gain status and self-esteem as soon as they were able to separate themselves from the accomplishments of women. This wasn't difficult when the entire society was geared toward the advancement of males at the expense of keeping talented and motivated females in supporting roles. The women's movement of the 20th century has essentially eroded many of the stark divisions between what is considered masculine and feminine. Occupations such as lawyer and physician were historically overwhelmingly male. Today, however, at least half of the students in law and medical schools are female, and women are making great strides in other occupations, ranging from law enforcement to academia. There are women boxers, soldiers, and stockbrokers. One would be hard-pressed to find an occupation in the United States that could be considered exclusively male. The workplace is no longer an arena where men can feel superior to women. Today, a man is as likely to be reporting to a woman as he is to be supervising her.[17]

- **Legal issues**   Well into the 20th century, the law worked against the empowerment of women. They weren't allowed to vote, own property, make decisions about their children, or divorce their husbands. A man was the king of his castle and women had little legal recourse to his decisions. This institutional discrimination is now a thing of the past. Women have essentially obtained complete legal equality (despite the defeat of the Equal Rights Amendment) and have had their interests upheld by the courts across a wide range of issues, including employment discrimination, sexual harassment, child-care issues, and equal pay for equal work. Although it can be reasonably argued that much remains to be done in terms of granting full access to women to the reins of power, for our purposes here, it's fair to say that the legal system is no longer totally controlled by men and no longer supports the assumptions of male privilege.[18]

- **New concepts of manhood**   Becoming a man in today's society has become more difficult because the cultural definitions of manhood are a moving target. Men are now encouraged to be more sensitive, nurturing, supportive, and cooperative. The New Age male is required to use his intelligence, people skills, and empathy, rather than brute force, intimidation, and subterfuge, to motivate others.[19]

So how does one become a man in today's society if all the things we have discussed are true? If our society no longer has identifiable rites of passage and the entire nature of manhood has changed, how can young boys ever progress into manhood? The answer to these questions is complex and incomplete, because the whole categorization of man versus woman, male versus female, young versus old, and powerful versus powerless has changed. Relationships are no longer strictly dichotomous, and the roles one plays in a lifetime are multiple, fluid, ephemeral, and of diminished importance. One's self-concept is no longer strictly tied to being a father, daughter, worker, or boss, and one's social status is no longer determined solely by occupation. This makes the development of an identity extremely difficult, especially for young men who used to have more well-defined methods for being considered an adult. Yesterday's wimpy computer geek is today's entrepreneurial multimillionaire, while the all-American high-school quarterback might even have trouble finding a job.

We would be mistaken, however, to think that some of these old cultural methods for specifying when one becomes a man have disappeared altogether. Sometimes, old ways linger even after they have outlived their usefulness. In a time when domination and privilege no longer are effective in the workplace or the home, they continue to be utilized because they might be instrumental in other venues. For young men who have difficulty competing in modern society, crime and delinquency offer ways of obtaining not only money and objects, but also a certain level of self-esteem.[20]

DEFINING THE TERMS

juvenile

An age-related status that has legal ramifications. The U.S. legal system generally considers anyone under 18 years of age a juvenile.

It is time to develop a couple of concrete definitions to guide our understanding of the legal and social implications of juvenile delinquency. The word **juvenile** refers to an age-related status that has legal ramifications. *Juvenile* is applied to those who aren't yet adults. In the United States, we generally draw this line at 18 years of age. This is the age at which one can vote; however, for other privileges, such as drinking alcohol, the line is set at age 21. Some credit-card companies won't extend unsecured credit until the individual is 25. According to the 2000 U.S. census, the population contained over 80 million people under age 19 (see Figure 1-2).

Although this distinction might appear to be a moving target, we will use the legal definition of a juvenile as being someone under age 18. We select this age because, for the most part, this is where the juvenile justice system has decided it should be drawn. In most states, those under 18 are processed by the juvenile justice system, and those over 18 are processed by the criminal justice system. Although there are many exceptions to this rule, including juvenile waiver, which we discuss in Chapter 14, it's a useful distinction for our discussions.

juvenile delinquent

A person, usually under the age of 18, who is determined to have broken the law or committed a status offense in states in which a minor is declared to lack responsibility and who may not be sentenced as an adult.

A **juvenile delinquent** is a juvenile who has violated the law. However, we must be careful when we employ this term because it has a specialized meaning in the juvenile justice system. When the court determines that a youth has violated a law, the youth isn't "found guilty," but rather is "adjudicated a delinquent." This definition is more restrictive than that used in general conversation and is therefore a bit misleading. For our purposes, we will use a less restrictive meaning of the term *delinquent* to include those who have broken the law but might not have been caught and adjudicated.

The study of juvenile delinquency involves more than identifying and controlling those who break the law. Within the field are children with other issues that must be considered. We will deal with these complexities in greater detail later, but they are worth mentioning now so that the reader can put the following chapters in context. In addition to youths who cause trouble by breaking the law, the study of juvenile delinquency includes young people as victims. The term *victim* is used here in an inclusive

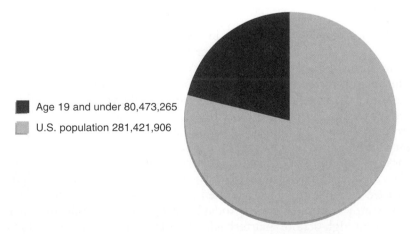

■ Age 19 and under 80,473,265
■ U.S. population 281,421,906

Figure 1-2   Number of Juveniles (age 19 and under) in the U.S. Population as of 2000. *Source:* U.S. Census Bureau, Census 2000 Summary File 1, Matrices P13 anc PCT12. Available online at factfinder.census.gov.

sense. Youths aren't simply victims of other youths who might beat them up or steal their property. They are also victims of the various entities that are supposed to be working on their behalf. Parents, teachers, scoutmasters, clergy, and babysitters have victimized children. Schools that leave children behind, communities that don't provide safe parks and programs, states that fail to provide adequate health care for children in poverty, all in some way victimize youths who are largely powerless to control their own fate.

Juvenile delinquency also includes those youths who violate rules that pertain only to youths and wouldn't be considered an offense if committed by an adult. These **status offenses** include drinking under age, running away from home, truancy, and being incorrigible. There are no corresponding rules for adults, and youths who engage in these actions can find themselves before a juvenile judge. Finally, the study of juvenile delinquency includes children who are neglected, **dependent,** physically or psychologically abused, or caught between warring parents. The juvenile justice system looks out for the welfare of youths regardless if they are perpetrators or victims. The juvenile delinquency field considers a wide range of problems encountered by youths and offers a variety of theories, programs, and options.

status offense
An act considered to be a legal offense only when committed by a juvenile, and one that can be adjudicated only in a juvenile court.

dependent
A term describing the status of a child who needs court protection and assistance because his or her health or welfare is endangered due to the parent's or guardian's inability to provide proper care and supervision.

TRANSITION OR REBELLION

One doesn't obtain adulthood overnight. It isn't a status that can be easily granted with a ceremony in front of family and friends where presents are given, toasts made, and everyone wears special costumes purchased for the occasion. Adulthood is earned through accomplishments, financial independence, and the exhibiting of mature judgment. It's a process that requires years and happens gradually without clear indicators. It requires some false starts, partial victories, and practice behavior. There is tremendous pressure from peers, family, and self to demonstrate the attainment of adulthood. To do this, juveniles occasionally engage in deviant behavior. These deviant behaviors can range from smoking tobacco, using illicit drugs, experimenting with sexuality, and skipping school to more dangerous actions, such as robbing liquor stores, selling drugs, engaging in prostitution, or joining a gang. (For a statistical look at some of these behaviors in high school students, see Figures 1-3 and 1-4.)

It would be inaccurate to argue that all delinquency and crime are directly the result of children attempting to short-cut the route to adulthood, but there is ample evidence that this issue is at least a contributing factor in a great deal of youthful indiscretion.

Adolescents and very young adults are pressured to demonstrate the attainment of adulthood, which sometimes leads to acts of questionable judgment. *(© Mark Peterson / CORBIS All Rights Reserved)*

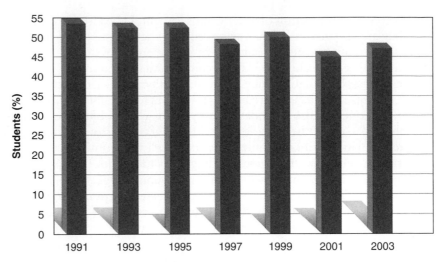

Figure 1-3   **Sexual Intercourse, Ninth- to Twelfth-Grade Students, 1991–2003.** *Source:* National Youth Risk Behavior Survey: 1991-2003, Centers for Disease Control and Prevention. www.cdc.gov/HealthyYouth/yrbs/pdfs/trends-sex.pdf.

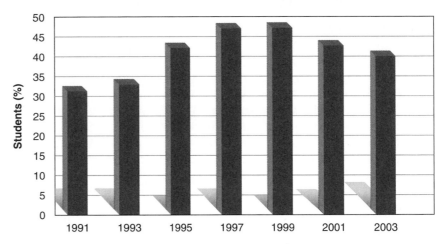

Figure 1-4   **Marijuana Use, Ninth- to Twelfth-Grade Students, 1991–2003.** *Source:* National Youth Risk Behavior Survey: 1991-2003, Centers for Disease Control and Prevention. www.cdc.gov/HealthyYouth/yrbs/pdfs/trends-drugs.pdf.

When considering the types of youths who wind up in trouble with the law, some social and psychological themes can be linked to their attempts to display adulthood:

- **Autonomy from adult control**   Young people desire to depart from the control of their parents as soon as possible. They see their peers as their new primary group and are eager to adopt the norms and values of adolescents, while struggling to be free from the traditional sources of social control, such as the family and the church.[21] For many, this is a necessary, if not exactly desirable, process. However, the power over the child that is lost by the parents is found by the clique, the group, or the gang. Young people have an almost pathological desire to fit in somewhere and will go to great lengths to be accepted by their peers. Shoplifting sprees, drug use, and gang violence are often nothing more than adaptations to the desires of youths to be free of parental influence. What could be more liberating to the middle-class honor student than smoking dope or having sex? Although these activities are considered status offenses, they serve a purpose in demonstrating to parents and authorities that a certain level of autonomy has been obtained. For example, there is a generations-old struggle between parents and children in deciding how late they can stay out. The controversy has gotten so beyond the control of parents that many communities have had to enact curfew laws that place the state in the role of parent to

You Can't Go Home Again

Once upon a very long time ago I was a freshman at college. I loved my new-found freedom to stay out as late as I wanted, to drink beer without worrying about my parents finding out, and to live in a state of disorder and filth in which my bed was never made, there were two piles of clothes on the floor (one dirty, the other not quite as dirty), and I could play poker with my buddies instead of studying for tests. Yes, I was the king of my dorm room, and I answered to no one but myself about when I could sleep, eat, or party. It was a great life . . . for one semester. Then I went home for the holidays.

The trouble started the first night I was to go out with all my high school friends. We had returned from universities from across the country and were ready to party, drink, brag about new girlfriends (real and imagined), and reorder our social hierarchy of who was the coolest of the cool.

Unfortunately, I hit a brick wall as I walked out the door when my mother asked, "What time will you be home?"

"Late," I replied.

"How late?" she said.

"Very, very late. Don't bother to wait up for me," I said as I walked to the car, proud of my independence from parental control. I could always bluff Mom, and I knew I had it made if I could just get to the car.

It was at this point that my father stuck his head out of the door and said, "The car has a midnight curfew. Have it home by then."

I couldn't tell my friends that I had to have my Dad's car home by midnight. Embarrassed enough that I didn't have my own car, I was mortified to have to admit to my friends that I had to beg permission to drive my Dad's new Mustang. I walked back into my house to begin the education of my parents.

"Mom, Dad, let me tell you about what happens when a young man goes to college," I began in what now has become known as my professorial tone.

"Oh, we know what happens," my father replied. "Your brother Tom told us four years ago when he came back from his first semester at college. You remember, John. That was right before he flunked out and joined the Navy."

I knew I had to tread carefully here because my grades were not going to be all that spectacular. Especially, in my fencing class, which I had not attended for the last four weeks. Or English, where I never completed two of the six writing assignments.

"That was different," I said. "Tom didn't apply himself like I have. I'm much more mature than he was. I'm a man now and I have everything under control. You can trust me."

At this point my father uttered the words that every college freshman hears from their parents on that first holiday vacation. "While you are sleeping under my roof, eating my food, going to school on my dime, and driving my car, you will obey the rules of my house."

I won't bore you with the rest of the conversation. You have heard it, or you will, from your parents. What is important to note here is that this is a universal conversation. In one form or another, nearly all children have this talk with their parents. There is an age-old struggle going on here as children attempt to quickly grow into the role of adult while parents try to slow the pace and ensure that the youth is prepared for new responsibilities. It is at this first holiday vacation that their worlds collide, because the youth tends to believe that the attainment of adult judgment is an event, in this case going to college, whereas the parent sees maturing as a process, one that will take years, rather than one short football season.

While each family has its own dynamics, the issues of curfew, drinking, drug use, sexual activity, and respect for family norms will have to be worked out in one manner or another. A certain level of conflict is inevitable, maybe even healthy, as families confront these issues. In some families, these issues will become insurmountable and cause children to leave home before they are financially or psychologically ready, cause parents to terminate support, and cause heartbreak for both. In other families, this conflict will bring the parents and children closer together as they interact on a more equal basis. Is there a right way to do this?

Think About It

1. Have you seen this conflict happen in your family or others as teenagers who have left home for college or jobs come back and struggle with obeying the rules of their childhood?
2. What suggestions do you have for young people who are going to experience this conflict?
3. Should parents use financial support as a club to get their children to follow their rules?

Postscript: In the interest of full disclosure, I must admit that my parents were right and I was wrong. I went back to college after that first holiday and promptly flunked out, got drafted, and was sent to Vietnam.

ensure that children return home at a reasonable time.[22] See Crosscurrent 1.2 for an example of how parents and adolescents negotiate for control.

- **Displays of masculinity**   Young men (and in some cases young women) find it hard to be taken seriously as emerging adults without displaying various aspects of the hyper-masculine role. These displays can be seen in behaviors such as steroid-using weight lifters who don't compete but simply want to look large, or in the aggressive demeanor that some youths employ on the street to keep from feeling (or being) disrespected. This demeanor has been deemed the "code of the street" by sociologist Elijah Anderson.[23] Under this code, a male youth must challenge those who look at him too intensely and be willing to fight to save his honor, even when no words have been exchanged or aggressive behavior exhibited. In other contexts, young men act aggressively toward females as a way of getting attention or get large tattoos as evidence of their ability to withstand pain. The list of ways in which young men display their masculinity can go on and on, but the important point here is that these displays can often be associated with unlawful behavior.

- **Female adaptations**   The way that young people construct their identities varies greatly according to a number of factors, including gender. Because there are limited opportunities for females to break the law, some scholars argue that young girls will use sexual promiscuity as a way of demonstrating their rebellion against parents and equality with young men. This is a controversial point that in many ways unfairly stereotypes women, but it's worth noting that some observers contend that promiscuity is a way for some girls to assert control over their bodies and lives.[24] Sex, it's argued, becomes a way that young women can get some leverage over the double standard that defines American culture.

- **Economic independence**   It can be embarrassing and even humiliating to have to ask parents constantly for money. Many families have little or no money for the discretionary spending habits of their teenagers. Yet, the economy is geared toward wringing every last dollar out of those who have the least to spend. The costs of clothes, shoes, cars, dating, and fast food can quickly exhaust the savings of teenagers working entry-level jobs. This peer pressure to spend lavishly is evidence of Thorstein Veblen's sociological term "conspicuous consumption."[25] It takes little imagination to see how this temptation to acquire beyond one's actual needs can be translated into deviant behavior. Shoplifting is epidemic among some adolescents, and larceny from automobiles and thefts from homes and businesses are how some youths afford to keep pace with their peers. The juvenile justice system has little to combat the intense pressure that is exerted on children and adolescents by the media. The temptation to sell drugs or rob liquor stores is intense for young people with cheeseburger budgets and caviar dreams.

- **Willingness to take risks**   Finally, the theme of willingness to take risks is ever-present in youth culture. We need only to look at the extreme sports that some youths engage in to see how status is allocated to those who perform feats of daring that have little utility other than showing the youth isn't afraid of injury or death. One wonders how the first guy to ride his skateboard on a metal railing ever came up with the idea and might be flabbergasted that kids continue to try this stunt after so many painful failures have been recorded on tape and shown repeatedly on television. Adults question why their children would attempt such feats when the result is broken ankles, wrists, legs, skulls, and worse. Why is this behavior perpetuated? The answer is that risk taking is its own reward. As a theme of adolescence, its utility is demonstrating that life is valuable to the extent one has breathtaking experiences. Unfortunately, it's sometimes one's last breath that is taken.

This list of themes isn't exhaustive, merely illustrative. Other themes apply, and certainly some of these themes could also be attributed to adult offenders. These themes are presented here, however, as a method of alerting the reader to the problems of

Youths often take risks to show others that they are not afraid and to gain status among their friends and peers. *(Courtesy Dallas and John Heaton, The Stock Connection)*

dealing with young people who don't always act in their own best interests. Juvenile delinquents are seldom rational beings who calculate the consequences of their actions against the possible benefits should they succeed. The juvenile justice system is charged with handling these often-irrational youths. To make matters worse, the juvenile justice system must do this without sufficient resources or, all too often, supportive parents. Let us begin by looking at the state's legal authority to deal with the problems of delinquent juveniles.

PARENS PATRIAE AND THE LAW

The concept of ***parens patriae*** can be traced to medieval England where, under the auspices of the chancery court, the state could provide care and protection for a child instead of the parent. This concern for children's welfare was primarily directed at the upper class, which had complicated issues of position and property to be resolved. The chancery courts were not concerned with the criminal conduct of children, which was handled in the same manner as adults, but rather with protecting the economic interests of wealthy children so that they were not victimized by greedy relatives and advisers. The concept of *parens patriae* provided the legal foundation for the state to intervene in the lives of families for the protection of children and gradually grew to concerns other than financial ones. Today the courts rule on a wide range of issues dealing with the children's welfare.[26] (See Case in Point 1.1).

The U.S. justice system extended *parens patriae* to deal with juveniles of more modest means for two primary reasons. Not all parents exerted adequate control over their children, and the state needed to step in and remove some youths from their homes to preserve community order. A second reason the state intervened in families was to protect children from abusive and neglectful parents. Although the idea that parents are responsible for their children still resonates, it has long been observed that some families are so dysfunctional that a youth's physical safety requires removing

parens patriae
Latin for "father of his country," the philosophy that the government is the ultimate guardian of all children or disabled adults.

1.1 CASE IN POINT
COMMONWEALTH V. FISHER

THE CASE	THE POINT
Commonwealth v. Fisher, 213 Pa. 48; 62 A. 198; 1905	*This case, which affirmed the philosophy of parens patriae, was used against similar challenges to the state's power to act as a parent until the 1960s.*

Frank Fisher, age 14, was indicted for larceny and pleaded not guilty. The juvenile court committed Fisher to a house of refuge. Fisher appealed, contending that the law was unconstitutional because he wasn't taken to court with due process, he was denied a jury trial, the court was an unconstitutional body and without jurisdiction, similar offenses received different punishments according to the offender's age, and the law contained more than one subject.

   The Pennsylvania Supreme Court affirmed the lower court's decision, holding that that law's purpose wasn't to punish children but to protect them. The protections that applied to adults in criminal proceedings didn't apply to informal juvenile proceedings because the state's intent was to act as a parent (*parens patriae*) in preventing the child from further law-breaking and possibly becoming an adult offender.

him or her from the home. (Unfortunately, the state often doesn't have viable substitutes for the home, and children go to institutions that do little to ensure their welfare and are sometimes so deleterious to their safety and development that leaving them with abusive parents looks like a good idea.) The courts also intervened in family affairs by holding fathers responsible for the offenses committed by their children. Today, states have juvenile and family courts that handle a wide range of problems and deal with children and families in an attempt to provide systematic and comprehensive solutions to delinquency, abuse, abandonment, child support, and divorce.[27]

ADOLESCENTS AND DELINQUENCY

Juvenile delinquency isn't a new problem. However, in the United States, particularly in the late 20th and early 21st centuries, the problem seems particularly acute. The transition to adulthood can be very difficult for both parents and children. We can use the sociological concept of the generation, that is, the total number of people born and living at about the same time, as a tool to better understand why the age range of 13 to 19 can be so problematic. Two aspects must be considered separately when considering the idea of generation.

- **Adolescence is a period in the life course**   Everyone is allocated one lifetime and, as we pass through the life course, certain events, pressures, opportunities, and occurrences affect everyone and represent a shared experience. Parents talk about their children going through the "terrible twos," where they first began to challenge authority and develop a sense of self. This is a predictable stage that children go through, and it's necessary for the healthy development of the child's self-concept. The onset of puberty can bring a different set of predictable issues for parents. Leaving home for the first time represents another life event that almost everyone must face. Adults must negotiate their adolescent years, and much of what happens in that important time is universal experiences that are shared by parents, grandparents, and children. Although each youth might think his or her problems are unique, they learn later when they have children of their own that the first date, first sexual experience, and first run-in with the law aren't unique to themselves.

- **A generation is a cohort**   Although every generation must endure adolescent years, they do so at different times in history, which can make a big difference. The sociologist C. Wright Mills encourages students to develop an appreciation for the difference between public issues and personal troubles. Mills argues that individuals must understand how they live out their lives within a historical context that exerts unique social forces on their generation. Although people have a great deal of control over their life decisions, political, economic, and social forces exert different effects on people based on where they are in their life course. This **cohort** aspect of generations causes much tension between parents and children. Parents believe that their children's adolescent years are similar to their own and want to use their acquired wisdom to help make their children's situation safer and more productive. Children, on the other hand, see the historical forces affecting their generation as distinctly different from what their parents experienced and feel frustrated by their parents' lack of understanding. Of course, what makes this tension particularly acute is that adolescents are struggling for more control and responsibility over their affairs, while parents are reluctant to let go too soon.

cohort
A set of people who share a particular statistical or demographic characteristic.

Unraveling the differences between the relative effects of life-course events and historical cohort events in one's particular situation is difficult. It's worthwhile, however, to use C. Wright Mills' **sociological imagination** to identify a few of each type to illustrate how complicated it can be to appreciate one's circumstances.

Life-course events that almost every teenager confronts include wresting control of his or her affairs from parents. This includes determining what classes to take in school, whether to work part-time, whom to date, dealing with money, dealing with transportation issues by borrowing the family car or getting his or her own automobile, and deciding what religion to practice or whether to follow a religion at all. Teenagers and parents resolve these issues to varying degrees depending on the strength of their bond, the trust the teenager has been able to build, and, sometimes, the family's experience with older siblings who previously negotiated these issues.

sociological imagination
The idea that one must look beyond the obvious to evaluate how social location influences the way one considers society.

Cohort events are unique to each generation. The "Greatest Generation" that came of age during the Great Depression of the 1930s and fought in World War II had a very different outlook on life than did the baby-boom generation that came of age in the 1960s with the civil rights movement, war in Vietnam, and the assassinations of Martin Luther King, Jr. and the Kennedy brothers. Although it's easy to look back and identify the historical events that shaped a generation, it's more difficult to look around and determine the events and historical forces that are shaping today's teenagers. More particularly, how are these events going to affect the chances of today's teenagers in getting involved in the juvenile and criminal justice systems? What is offered next is speculation. Each student should revisit this exercise and add to or delete from this list depending on how they see history unfolding.

- **War**   At the time of this writing, the United States is still embroiled in wars in Iraq and Afghanistan, and it's reasonable to expect that the United States will be involved in the Middle East for decades to come. The threat of continued international terrorism and the commitments we have made to many countries will likely require the continued stationing of troops overseas for the foreseeable future. For adolescents today, this could mean the possibility of military service. It will mean that tax money for social services that might benefit them will be hard to wrest from military demands, and it will mean the economy will remain in a state of flux. This could affect the juvenile and criminal justice systems as more resources are devoted to homeland security.[28]

- **Technology**   The economic engine of the United States is now greatly based on technology. As consumers, adolescents will have more and cheaper computers, video games, and electronic gadgets, but it will also mean that they will need to continually refine their skills to accommodate technological change.

Finding a high-paying, stable job will continue to be problematic, and workers will need to continually retool to remain competitive. Also, technology has already changed many of the ways that offenses are committed and the ways in which the criminal justice system responds.

- **Economic shifts**   The old saying "The rich get richer and the poor get poorer" is all too true, and we can speculate that it will continue to be true. Although political parties will debate which has the best prescription for what ails the economy, it's likely that adolescents will be among the last to experience any improvement. Those who have entry-level jobs will continue to find themselves struggling to make ends meet on the current minimum wage. The U.S. health-care system is among the best of the industrialized nations for the wealthy, but among the worst for the impoverished. Over 40 million citizens, the majority of them children, lack health insurance. One need not have much imagination to speculate how a continued weak economy will affect young people and their likelihood to break the law.

1.3 *CrossCurrents*

On the Bright Side

Despite what the media might have us believe, adolescents certainly aren't out of control. In fact, when it comes to risky behaviors and criminal activity, they are generally better off now than they have been since 1980. Juvenile violent crime arrests peaked in 1994 and have dropped ever since. Between 1994 and 2002, the juvenile arrest rate for the Violent Crime Index offenses fell 47 percent. In 2005, 2.1 million juveniles were arrested, which is 25 percent fewer than in 1996 (see Figure 1). Today's adolescents appear to be smoking less, engaging in less illicit drug use, and getting arrested less. Juvenile females are also getting pregnant less: the nation's adolescent birth rate fell 30 percent between 1991 and 2002.

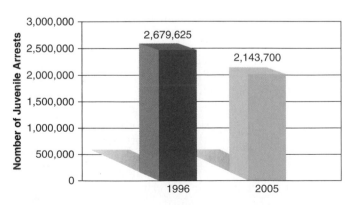

Figure 1

Source: OJJDP Statistical Briefing Book, March 2007. http://ojjdp.ncjrs.gov/ ojstatbb/crime/ qa05101.asp?qaDate=2005. Adapted from Howard N. Snyder, *Juvenile Arrests 2005,* [Forthcoming] (Washington, DC: Office of Juvenile Justice and Delinquency Prevention).

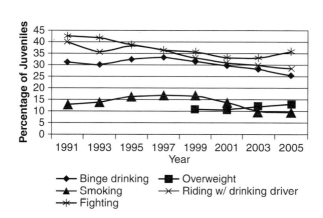

Figure 2

Source: Centers for Disease Control and Prevention, Youth Risk Behavior Surveillance System, http://www.cdc.gov/HealthyYouth/yrbs/index.htm.

A Centers for Disease Control study of students in grades 9 through 12 found that one of the few adolescent risk factors that had risen was that of being overweight. Other indicators, including frequent cigarette smoking, binge drinking (five or more drinks of alcohol in a row), riding in a car in which the driver had been drinking alcohol, and getting into physical fights, had dropped between the years of 1991 and 2005 (see Figure 2).[2]

Between 1992 and 2002, law-breaking behaviors dropped, as well. In 2002, juvenile arrests for violence were the lowest since 1987, and juvenile property-crime arrests were the lowest in about 30 years.

Such issues will certainly affect American teenagers to some degree. These historical circumstances aren't the worst any generation has had to face, but they do promise to be challenging and will require adjustments by government, schools, parents, and adolescents themselves. For those interested in juvenile delinquency and the welfare of children and families, these concerns promise to challenge our ability to suggest new and innovative ways to prevent crime and reduce the suffering of victims. Crosscurrents 1.3 discusses the actual incidence of juvenile delinquency. In many ways, things are not as bad as conventional wisdom tells us.

Art of Graduated Responsibility

C. Wright Mills says that, in addition to the broad historical forces that shape the lives of young people, each of them has an opportunity to write his or her autobiography.[29] By understanding the difference between our personal troubles and public issues, each of us can better position ourselves to meet the challenges of the future. Perhaps professional hockey player Wayne Gretzky said it best when a reporter asked him what made him such a great player. Gretzky replied, "Because I skate to where the puck is going to be." The question that should be asked of those interested in juvenile delinquency is how young people can position themselves to succeed in contemporary society. Further, what policies, programs, and incentives ensure that adolescents make good decisions?

One method being used to help young people make wise decisions is to give them responsibility for their own affairs on a graduated basis. Although this seems like an obvious idea, it's surprising how parents, schools, and the government hold on to decision-making authority until it's too late to release it on a gradual scale. The result is often disastrous, with youths overdosing on drugs, binge drinking, driving at incredible rates of speed, and engaging in unsafe sex. The "just say no" philosophy of risky behavior is ignored by too many young people and is in need of modification. One solution that is beginning to attract attention is that of *graduated responsibility*.

Graduated responsibility is already practiced in society and in the family. Youths are not allowed to drive until they are 16, vote until they are 18, or drink alcohol until they are 21. Many families establish bedtimes based on the age of the children and assign more demanding chores and responsibilities to older children. However, some youths are given discretion over aspects of their lives with little or no preparation. Binge drinking in college is the result of many factors, but certainly one of them is the sudden freedom to drink that accompanies leaving parental supervision. With little or no prior exposure to alcohol, many young people not only drink to excess, but also engage in dangerous drinking games, drive under the influence, and drink such extreme amounts that they sometimes die from alcohol poisoning. Are there better ways to introduce young people to alcohol? Would they be more likely to drink responsibly if they were first exposed to limited amounts under the supervision of parents or other responsible adults?

Many states are experimenting with increasing the transition period for driving automobiles. For many years, young people could get a learner's permit at age 15 that allowed them to drive with parents and then a driver's license at 16 that allowed them to drive without adult supervision. However, the high rate of fatal accidents for young drivers has inspired several states to rethink how much freedom should be granted to inexperienced drivers. Many states now place special curfews on young drivers (see Table 1-1). Although exceptions might be granted to drive to and from a job, what the states are trying to avoid is the situation in which a 16-year-old is speeding in a car

Many states have adjusted the amount of freedom they allow to young drivers. *(Courtesy Jose Carrillo, PhotoEdit Inc.)*

Table 1-1   **States with Graduated Licensing Systems**

State	Minimum Entry Age	Duration of PM Restriction	Unsupervised Driving Prohibited	Passenger Restriction
California	15	12 months	12 AM–5 AM	First 6 months: none up to age 20
Delaware	15, 10 months	6 months	9 PM–6 AM	No more than two
Florida	15	Until age 18	Age 16: 11 PM–6 AM Age 17: 1 AM–5 AM	None
Georgia	15	Until age 18	1 AM–5 AM	No more than three up to age 21
Illinois	15	Until age 17	11 PM–6 AM Sun–Thurs 12 AM–6 AM Fri–Sat	Until age 18: only one in front and no more rear passengers than belts
Indiana	15	Until age 18	1 AM–5 AM Sat–Sun After 11 PM Sun–Thurs	First 90 days: none unless supervised by 21-year-old driver
Iowa	14	12 months	12:30 AM–5 AM	None
Louisiana	15	Until age 17	11 PM–5 AM	None
Maryland	15, 9 months	18 months	12 AM–5 AM	None
Massachusetts	16	Until age 18	12 AM–5 AM	First 6 months: none up to age 18 unless supervised by 21-year-old driver
Michigan	14, 9 months	6 months	12 AM–5 AM	None
New Hampshire	16	Until age 18	1 AM–5 AM	None
New Jersey	16	12 months	12 AM–5 AM	One only
North Carolina	15	6 months	9 PM–5 AM	None
Ohio	15, 6 months	Until age 17	1 AM–5 AM	None
Rhode Island	16	12 months	1 AM–5 AM	None
South Carolina	15	12 months	6 PM–6 AM 8 PM–6 AM	None
South Dakota	14	Until age 16	8 PM–6 AM	None

Source: Saving Teenage Lives, National Highway Traffic Safety Administration. www.nhtsa.dot.gov/people/injury/newdriver/SaveTeens/append_b.html.

packed with friends late at night. Experience has shown that this type of situation is more likely to cause fatal accidents than daytime driving. Some states have even restricted cell-phone use by adolescent drivers; as of 2005, Colorado, Connecticut, Delaware, Maryland, Maine, and Tennessee didn't allow drivers under a specified age or those with provisional licenses to use cell phones while driving.[30] Therefore, some states restrict the time of driving, number of passengers, and purpose. As the youths get older, they receive full driving privileges.

These are but two examples of how graduated responsibility can work to lower the risk of young people getting into trouble. It is important to add that not all young people present the same level of risk, and it isn't fair to paint with too broad a brush. However, a number of risk factors at the individual child, family, peer group, school, and neighborhood levels are amenable to intervention.

Risk Factors and Delinquency

Not all youths are equally susceptible to becoming delinquents. A number of factors make juveniles more likely to engage in delinquent behavior. Many of these factors, such as poverty, are well known and require massive amounts of attention and resources that are difficult to deliver. Poverty is a national and global concern that can be addressed only by significant shifts in trade patterns, tax structures, and corporate and government spending patterns. Although the amelioration of poverty would greatly affect delinquency, as well as many other problems, there is a more modest set of risk factors about which it's realistic to fashion solutions. The list is divided into five levels of concern that represent identified shortcomings in the lives of delinquents: the child, family, school, peer-group, and community levels.

CHILD LEVEL   At the individual level, delinquent children possess some factors at a greater rate than do nondelinquent children. Although we typically blame delinquency on poor choices made by youths or on their simply being "bad kids," we should not overlook the individual traits of delinquents when fashioning solutions to their behavior.

- **Substance abuse**   Substance abuse is both a delinquent activity and a symptom of delinquency. Those who use drugs exhibit two types of concerns. First, there is something lacking in the youths' lives that makes them turn to drugs for escape or fun. Healthy, well-adjusted children don't need to take drugs to feel good, fit in with peers, or escape problems.[31] The second concern with youths using drugs is that getting drugs puts them into an environment in which other types of delinquency are more prevalent. Therefore, if the problem of substance abuse can be successfully addressed, many types of delinquency might be averted.

- **Mental-health problems**   Many youths have untreated mental-health problems. Part of the failure of the nation's health care system is that 40 million people don't have health insurance. Many children with mental-health issues won't get adequate treatment until they come into contact with the juvenile justice system. Timely treatment provided before and instead of court sanctions might be more effective and less costly than that available in detention centers.

- **Impulsiveness**   All children are impulsive to a degree. Part of growing up is learning to tame one's compulsions and develop restraint, empathy, and respect for others. For some children, the only thing that seems to work is selfish, impulsive behavior. Their environments did not reward taking turns, sharing, or deferring gratification. Impulsiveness is a risk factor that can be remedied. Placing youngsters in situations in which more appropriate types of behavior are functional can be a positive first step. This might be done through effective parenting classes, foster homes, and better schooling.

- **Poor social problem-solving skills**   It seems almost unnecessary to say that delinquent youths have poor social problem-solving skills. Would they be in trouble if they could effectively solve their social problems? This question is more complicated than it appears. Most youths learn to solve a wide range of problems as they mature. Many issues are addressed with the aid of parents, schools, and peers. Other problems are personal and sensitive, and many youths successfully deal with them by themselves. However, the real problem is that many youths have only minimal insight and judgment with which to address their problems. In a culture in which the popular media celebrate violence and domination, it isn't surprising that some youths consider violence as an effective first step in solving their problems.[32]

FAMILY LEVEL   Some problems are located in the way young people are socialized by their parents and the dynamics of the family. Certain risk factors at the family level are amenable to informed social policy. These risk factors aren't necessarily issues that can be affected by legislation, but they are ones in which education, advocacy, and clear guidelines can make a difference.

- **Low parental warmth**   It is generally assumed that all parents love their children unconditionally. It's also assumed that this love is manifested in the creation of a warm and supportive family environment. This isn't always the case, however. For a variety of reasons, some parents are not home often enough to develop this warm and supportive environment for their children. Some parents work multiple jobs to make ends meet. They have neither the time nor the money to give a great deal of attention to their children. Other parents are absorbed in their own activities and entertainments. They might have worked hard and now feel entitled to enjoy the golf, gambling, and glamour that money can provide. Their children are provided with all that money can buy but are denied the attention and support of their busy and successful parents. Finally, some parents don't show warmth to their children because they believe that children must become psychologically self-sufficient at an early age. Being distant and tough with their children is looked on as a parenting method that will prepare the youths for the competitive "real" world.

- **Poor parental supervision**   Some parents don't provide adequate supervision for a number of reasons.[33] Many parents aren't present in the home to provide this supervision because they must spend so much time at work. This is partly due to the fact that having a full-time job doesn't always mean having a living wage. Many low-paying jobs don't include benefits such as health insurance or day-care services, so parents are forced to work more jobs. The circumstance of dad going to work and mom staying home with the children is no longer the norm in the United States (and maybe never was). For numerous reasons, both parents in many homes go to work each day, leaving *latchkey kids* who spend their after-school hours unsupervised.

- **Ineffective or harsh discipline practices**   The way that parents discipline their children greatly influences their behavior. Parents might be authoritarian, indulgent, or indifferent.[34] Without consistent, positive, and helpful guidance from parents, children might develop behavioral problems. The idea that physical discipline is required to raise well-behaved children has come under fire in recent years. In fact, a growing body of literature argues that corporal punishment is counterproductive.[35] Hitting children teaches them that violence is the means that powerful people use to get their way.

SCHOOL LEVEL   Not all schools are equally able to meet their students' needs. One underlying problem is that funding for schools is obtained by local governments taxing citizens based on property ownership. This results in wide variations of school funding both across and within states. In many ways, the crisis of school funding is a result of a clash of values. To maintain local control of schools, the funding is vested at the local municipal or county level. Therefore, neighborhoods that are a few miles apart might have vastly different levels of resources committed to the schools. This results in differences in how schools address the following risk factors.

- **Untreated learning disabilities**   Children who are unable to perform in school at their designated grade level are at a real disadvantage. Not only will they not be able to receive the full range of school resources, such as music, art, and extracurricular programs, but they also suffer from low self-esteem, negative labeling, and embarrassment. When this inability to compete is based on untreated learning disabilities, the damage done to the child is particularly unfortunate. A great deal of progress has been made in diagnosing and treating learning disabilities, but unfortunately, not all school districts can afford to address these issues in an optimal way.[36]

- **Low academic achievement**   Low academic achievement is another risk factor that can be addressed. Sometimes the school doesn't receive adequate funding. Some schools track early achievers toward college preparatory classes and early underachievers toward classes designed to place the students in a trade school or directly into the work force. Whatever the reason, the fact remains that schools don't or can't provide the necessary resources to educate each student to his or her full potential.

- **Alienation from school**   Children who don't excel in school are in danger of becoming alienated from learning. Schools foster a culture that rewards top students but doesn't necessarily help lower achievers. Many students believe that schools reward the "chosen ones" and drop out because the policies aren't designed to help them catch up and thrive.[37]

- **Truancy**   Truancy is a sign of extreme alienation. When children find little in terms of reward from school, it isn't surprising that they skip classes. Many schools have developed counterproductive truancy policies. For example, some schools suspend students who skip class. Additionally, some schools place alienated students in programs that isolate them from the rest of the student population and make future truancy a foregone conclusion.

PEER-GROUP LEVEL   An additional set of risk factors operates at the peer-group level. Children are influenced by their friends in deciding what type of behavior is fun. Although parents are often concerned about their child's friends, they seldom locate the source of delinquent behavior in their own child.

- **Association with delinquent peers**   It can be difficult for parents to decide if their children's friends are exerting a positive influence. Because juvenile court records are private, parents might not know that the kids across the street are ruffians. Further, the friend's parents might have little knowledge of what their child is really up to. Often, it's difficult for parents to know the exact identities of their children's friends. When students take the bus to school and interact with their friends outside parental supervision, it can be next to impossible to get

Gangs encourage the rejection of positive values, inevitably leading youths down a road to delinquency and, often, an adult life of crime. *(Courtesy A. Ramey, PhotoEdit Inc.)*

1.1   PROGRAMS *for* CHILDREN

SECOND CHANCE YOUTH PROGRAM

Established in 1989 by a group of community members who lived in East Salinas, California, the Second Chance Youth Program was formed to address the cries for help from youth involved in violence and gang activity. Along with several community leaders, executive director Brian Contreras also recruited individual gang members to help with the development of Second Chance's services.

Gang violence in Salinas has its roots in the prison gang war of the 1970s. In late 1988, a group of adolescents murdered a young man walking home from night school. The incident alerted the community to the needs of youth and the reality of the gang problem.

Lacking office space, Second Chance began outreach on the streets and counseled clients at their homes. Second Chance received its initial funding from private groups and individuals but later began to receive public funding. The agency, originally dependent on volunteers, now has a full-time professional staff.

Source: Second Chance Youth Program, www.scyp.org/.

a clear idea of the ideas, motivation, and role models that children communicate to each other.

- **Gang membership**   Being a member of a gang is an open invitation to a life of delinquency. Whether the gang revolves around the sale of drugs or protecting its perceived turf, gang membership requires certain types of delinquent behavior and encourages a philosophy of rejection of traditional and conventional values.[38] Gang suppression relies primarily on two strategies. The first is based on law enforcement and involves police agencies dedicating special resources, such as gang intelligence units.[39] The second way to deal with gangs is to provide members with effective and realistic alternatives, such as good schools, afterschool programs, and jobs. These two strategies are not mutually exclusive and are most effective when used in tandem. Nevertheless, in certain cities, gang activity is a serious problem, and youths who are dedicated gang members are particularly difficult to deal with outside the juvenile and criminal justice systems. (For example, see Programs for Children 1.1.)

COMMUNITY LEVEL   Some communities experience very little delinquency, and others are crime ridden. The type of community a youth lives in can have a great effect on the chances that he or she will engage in delinquent behavior. Even when factors such as poverty and joblessness are considered, other delinquency risk factors must be addressed.

- **Exposure to violence**   How much violence is historically normal for a community? The answer to this question is an important indicator of the chances of a youth committing delinquent acts. Additionally, communities that have many incidents of family violence will be breeding grounds for delinquent behavior.[40]

- **Exposure to drug dealing**   Communities that have a high incidence of drug sales are prime areas for delinquent behavior. Many drug dealers sell directly to young people who must somehow come up with the funds to pay for their habits. Additionally, many drug dealers will employ youths in the drug trade, because the penalties for youths who get caught selling drugs are substantially less in the juvenile justice system than in the criminal justice system. Finally, communities where drug sales are rampant are often socially disorganized, and drug sales and delinquent street behavior aren't subject to formal or informal controls by parents and neighbors. Often, these neighborhoods are in transition or border on major transportation arteries where the presence of strangers is routine, and the residents don't particularly know one another. A number of strategies can be utilized to address drug dealing in such communities that include a number of community-policing tactics, as well as drug treatment efforts.[41]

- **Access to firearms**   There is considerable debate about the role of firearms in the creation and prevention of crime, but what is clear is that when firearms are used, the violence is more deadly than when other weapons are used. Every state has existing laws that make the possession of firearms by juveniles difficult, but this doesn't stop delinquents from finding guns. There is a healthy black market for firearms that juveniles can tap into, and some parents don't properly secure their weapons.

These risk factors aren't the only concerns of the juvenile justice system. Other factors put juveniles at risk of delinquent behavior, but this list represents factors in which informed social policy can make a difference.

SYSTEM OF LAST RESORT

Critics of the juvenile justice system who say that the system fails to keep children from committing future offenses might not take into consideration just how difficult this task is for a system that has little control over who enters it and how much money it has. Many programs and agencies have substantial control over whom they serve. For instance, universities set standards for admission and for graduation. Schools exclude those most likely to fail by setting standards for entry. Those who do get admitted and then asked to leave because of poor performance are considered to have failed personally, rather than its being the institution's fault.

The juvenile justice system doesn't have this type of control over its charges. Law enforcement agencies, parents, and schools all have a hand in deciding who enters the juvenile justice system. Although schools can flunk out their lowest-achieving students, the juvenile justice system must keep its most recalcitrant and difficult clients. This is what is meant by "the system of last resort." It can't pass its failures on to other institutions. Therefore, we should be tolerant of a certain amount of ineffectiveness in the juvenile justice system. Unless we are willing to provide a great deal more funding for the system, we shouldn't expect it to succeed where other systems have failed. If the schools, whose mission is teaching, can't get a child up to the desired reading level, why do we expect the juvenile justice system, whose mission is social control, to be successful? If a child's family cannot provide the love and support that allows a child to feel wanted and valued, how can we expect the juvenile justice system with its foster homes and detention centers to do the job?

GROWING UP TOO SOON

Are childhood and adolescence more precarious today than in the past? Are families more fragile, and are children more violent? Is it tougher to be a child today?

The answers to these questions are important for our study of juvenile delinquency. The public's perception of the dangers posed by wayward youth has led us to enact a number of laws that treat juvenile delinquency in a more serious manner than in the recent past. Our study of juvenile delinquency must take into consideration the changing context of our perceptions of crime. When we take an absolutist view of delinquency and deviant behavior, we fail to appreciate the nature and history of growing up in the United States.

A certain amount of deviant behavior might actually be beneficial for both the individual youth and society in general. The line between deviance and acceptable behavior is often fuzzy, and sometimes its crossing is rewarded. Social change requires that individuals test the boundaries of approved behavior, and laws that were enacted for the benefit of certain individuals might need to be challenged. For instance, the leaders of the civil rights movement purposefully violated laws that preserved the privileges of those in power. Further, nonviolent social protest has exposed differences of opinion concerning wars, women's rights, and trade policies. What juvenile delinquency issues might be a signal of possible change? For instance, in the 1960s, youth protested the government's ability to draft young men to fight in a war but not allow young people of that same age to drink alcohol or to vote.

Are We Waging a War on Children?

Few people will dispute the goal of making the world safer for children. Adults can look back at their formative years and see points of conflict, missed opportunities, and outright mistakes in judgment and say to themselves that, if only someone had alerted them to the problems, they might have made better choices. Although this is undoubtedly true, it misses a vital point. To learn, people sometimes need to make their own mistakes. There's a fine line between parents letting go of the apron strings and letting go of their responsibilities to provide guidance and support.

When families, churches, schools, and recreational programs fall short of socializing young individuals to become productive citizens, there is a tendency to look to

The principal's office is the traditional disposition for those who break school rules, but many schools' zero-tolerance policies suspend students from school for long periods of time, expel them, or send them straight to the police. *(© Will & Deni McIntyre, CORBIS. All Rights Reserved)*

zero-tolerance policies

School regulations that give teachers and administrators little to no discretion in dealing with rule infractions.

the government, particularly the juvenile justice system, to fill the gap. There are some things, however, that the juvenile justice system is ill equipped to do. The state-raised youth has never been a particularly successfully one. Delinquents, it has been determined, generally do better when kept in families, traditional schools, and the juvenile justice system as opposed to the criminal justice system. Yet, as we enter the 21st century, there is a decided movement to "get tough on crime" that is affecting youth in negative ways. Parents who practice "tough love," schools that adopt **zero-tolerance policies,** and a legal system that gives up on its most challenging juvenile cases and routinely sends them to the criminal justice system are all testaments to a society waging war on its children.

The remainder of this book will attempt to put the history of dealing with juvenile delinquents in a context of mainstream practices and crosscurrent concerns. Much of what has been and is being attempted in forging a productive life for youth has been remarkably successful. However, mistakes have been made repeatedly and, to a great extent, are being perpetuated by the war on crime. This book, then, can be considered not simply as a rote rendition of facts about delinquency and the juvenile justice system, but rather as an occasion for students to think about not only why the system functions as it does, but also how it might be improved. The crosscurrent subtheme, along with the cross-cultural and critical focus, will provide the reader with much to ponder and much to discuss.

SUMMARY

1. The word *juvenile*, which refers to an age-related status that has legal ramifications, is applied to those who are not yet adults. In the United States, this line is generally drawn at age 18.

2. A *juvenile delinquent* is a juvenile who has violated the law. Juvenile delinquency also includes youths who violate rules that pertain only to children, or *status offenses.*

3. Age is an ascribed characteristic, and society discriminates according to age. Many criteria are used as a basis for treating juveniles differently from adults because of physical, intellectual, and emotional development.

4. Making the transition from child to adult is difficult in any society; it involves changes in status, rights, responsibilities, and self-concept.

5. The journey from childhood to adulthood not only varies across cultures, but differs from one generation to the next. The problems of growing up differ across both geographic locations and time.

6. Young males are responsible for most crime and delinquency. One sociological reason for this is the modern lack of rites of passage for boys. Rites of passage are elaborate initiation ceremonies that transform people, especially young people.

7. Although society has rules that dictate how one makes the transition for boyhood to manhood, in the past these rules were represented by distinct ceremonies. Modern rites of passage can be observed in the practices of groups such as fraternities, scouting organizations, and sports teams.

8. The reason that most modern societies don't have specific rites of passage include a long period of adolescence, the blurring of male and female roles, legal issues, and new conceptions of manhood.

9. Some social and psychological themes that can be linked to attempts to display adulthood include autonomy from adult control, displays of masculinity, economic independence, and willingness to take risks.

10. The concept of *parens patriae* can be traced to medieval England. *Parens patriae* provided the legal foundation for the state to intervene in families to protect children.

11. Not all youths are equally susceptible to becoming delinquents. The five levels of concern that represent shortcomings in the lives of delinquents are the child, family, school, peer group, and community.

12. The juvenile justice system is a system of last resort. It receives only those youths who have failed or been failed by other societal institutions.

REVIEW QUESTIONS

1. What is responsible for the lack of formal rites of passage in modern societies?

2. In the United States, is there a set age separating juveniles from adults for all activities?

3. Is there an adult version of the status offense?

4. What social and psychological themes are linked to juveniles' attempts to display adulthood?

5. What is *parens patriae*?

6. What two aspects of the idea of generation must be considered separately?

7. What is graduated responsibility? How does it apply to juveniles?

8. What are the five levels of concern that represent identified shortcomings in delinquents' lives?

9. Why is the juvenile justice system a system of last resort?

10. Is it more or less difficult to be a child today than 100 years ago? 50 years ago? When you were a child?

ADDITIONAL READINGS

Bilchik, Shay. *Violence after School* (Washington, DC: U.S. Department of Justice, 2004).

Davis, Nanette. *Youth Crisis: Growing Up in a High Risk Society* (New York: Praeger, 1998).

Males, Mike A. *The Scapegoat Generation: America's War on Adolescents* (Monroe, ME: Common Courage Press, 1996).

Raphael, Ray. *The Men from the Boys: Rites of Passage in Male America* (Lincoln: University of Nebraska Press, 1988).

Reiman, Jeffery. *The Rich Get Richer and the Poor Get Prison*, 7th ed. (Boston: Allyn and Bacon, 2003).

Wilkinson, Rupert. *American Tough: The Tough-Guy Tradition and American Character* (New York: Harper and Row, 1986).

ENDNOTES

1. William Strauss and Neil Howe, *Generations: The History of America's Future, 1584 to 2069* (New York: William Morrow, 1991). The book gives an excellent analysis of the concept of generations. It's filled with research and is theoretically sophisticated.

2. See Chapter 4 for an analysis of how each country has different youth crime issues and different systems for dealing with them.

3. The point here isn't to be facetious, but to emphasize that criminals share many characteristics with successful and prominent people. Often, it's the luck of not getting caught as a youth that makes the difference. See Edwin Schur, *Radical Non-Intervention: Rethinking the Delinquency Problem* (Upper Saddle River, NJ: Prentice Hall, 1973).

4. Anthony Platt, *The Child Savers: The Invention of Delinquency* (Chicago: University of Chicago Press, 1969).

5. Joel Spring, *American Education*, 11th ed. (New York: McGraw-Hill, 2004).

6. *In re Gault*, 387 U.S. 1, 87 S.Ct. 1428 (1967).

7. James M. Kauffman, *Characteristics of Emotional and Behavioral Disorders of Children and Youth*, 8th ed. (Upper Saddle River, NJ: Prentice Hall, 2005). See especially Chapter 3, "The History of the Problem: Development of the Field and Current Issues."

8. Marie Richmond-Abbot, *Masculine and Feminine: Gender Roles over the Life Cycle* (New York: McGraw Hill, 1992).

9. Barry Thorne, "Girls and Boys Together . . . but Mostly Apart: Gender Arrangements in Elementary School," in Michael S. Kimmel and Michael A. Messner, eds., *Men's Lives*, 4th ed. (Boston: Allyn and Bacon, 1998), 87–100.

10. Robert E. Gould, "Measuring Masculinity by the Size of a Paycheck," in Joseph H. Peck and Jack Sawyer, eds. *Men and Masculinity* (Upper Saddle River, NJ: Prentice Hall, 1974), 96–100.

11. For a fascinating example of this, see, H. W. Brands, *The First American: The Life and Times of Benjamin Franklin* (Garden City, NY: Doubleday, 2000), 9–34.

12. Geoffrey Canada, "Learning to Fight," in Michael S. Kimmel and Michael A. Messner, eds., *Men's Lives*, 4th ed. (Boston: Allyn and Bacon, 1998), 122–126.

13. Joseph F. Kett, *Rites of Passage: Adolescence in America 1790 to the Present* (New York: Basic Books, 1977).

14. For more on this point see, Desmond Morris, *The Naked Ape?* (New York: Dell, 1967). The chapter on fighting, pages 153–162, explains how animals and humans use physical force to obtain status in their society.

15. Ray Raphael, *The Men from the Boys: Rites of Passage in Male America* (Lincoln: University of Nebraska Press, 1988), 6.

16. Judi Addelston and Michael Stirratt, "The Last Bastion of Masculinity: Gender Politics at Citadel," in Michael S. Kimmel and Michael A. Messner, eds., *Men's Lives*, 4th ed. (Boston: Allyn and Bacon, 1998), 205–220.

17. Ibid., p. 216.

18. William G. Doerner and Steven P. Lab, *Victimology*, 4th ed. (Cincinnati. OH: Anderson 2005). Pages 188–190 provide an overview of the history of spousal violence that shows how women were not given full legal rights.

19. National Organization for Men Against Sexism, *Statement of Principles*, in Michael S. Kimmel and Michael A. Messner, eds. (see note 16), p. 591.

20. Ronald D. Hunter and Mark L. Dantzker, *Crime and Criminality: Causes and Consequences* (Upper Saddle River, NJ: Prentice Hall, 2002), 157.

21. Strauss and Howe (see note 1), pp. 433–454.

22. David McDowall and Colin Loftin, "The Impact of Youth Curfew Laws on Juvenile Crime Rates," *Crime and Delinquency* 46 (2000):76–92.

23. Elijah Anderson, *Code of the Street: Decency, Violence, and Moral Life of the Inner City* (New York: Norton, 1999).

24. Leora Tanebaum, *Slut!: Growing Up Female with a Bad Reputation* (New York: Seven Stories Press, 1999). See especially pp. 129–130.

25. Thorstein Veblen, *The Theory of the Leisure Class* (New York: Penguin, 1994).

26. Douglas S. Rendleman, "Parens Patriae: From Chancery to the Juvenile Court," *South Carolina Law Review* 23 (1971):205.

27. Elizabeth Pleck, *Domestic Tyranny: The Making of Social Policy Against Family Violence from Colonial Times to the Present* (New York: Oxford University Press, 1987).

28. Russell D. Howard and Reid L. Sawyer, *Defeating Terrorism: Shaping the New Security Environment* (Guilford, CT: McGraw-Hill, 2004), 42. See "Prospects for the Future," in which the authors warn that the war on terrorism will be with the United States for a long time.

29. C. Wright Mills, *The Sociological Imagination* (New York: Oxford University Press, 1959).

30. Associated Press, "States bar teen drivers using cell phones," MSNBC.com, June 26, 2005, www.msnbc. msn.com/id/8367960/.

31. Although we might argue this point, for a good discussion of theories of drug use, see *The Sociology of American Drug Use* by Charles E. Faupel, Alan M. Horowitz, and Greg S. Weaver (Boston: McGraw-Hill, 2004), Chapter 4, "Theoretical Explanations for Drug Use and Addiction," pp. 107–134.

32. Rita Wicks-Nelson and Allen C. Israel, *Behavior Disorders of Childhood*, 5th ed. (Upper Saddle River, NJ: Prentice Hall, 2003), "Aggression as a Learned Behavior," pp. 210–11.

33. Ibid., pp. 223–24.

34. Robert M. Regoli and John D. Hewitt, *Delinquency in Society*, 6th ed. (New York: McGraw-Hill, 2006), 311–312.

35. Murray A. Straus, *Beating the Devil out of Them: Corporal Punishment in American Families and Its Effects on Children* (New Brunswick, NJ: Transaction, 1994).

36. Kauffman, note 7. See, particularly pp. 215–227, "School's Contribution to Emotional and Behavioral Disorders."

37. Alfie Kohn, *No Contest: The Case Against Competition* (Boston: Houghton Mifflin, 1992). See Chapter 10, "Learning Together," for an alternative way to run schools that might not alienate children.

38. Terence Thornberry et al., "The Role of Juvenile Gangs in Facilitating Delinquent Behavior," *Journal of Research in Crime and Delinquency* 30 (1993): 55–87.

39. Irving Spergel et al., *Gang Suppression and Intervention: Problem and Response, Research Summary* (Washington, DC: Office of Juvenile Justice and Delinquency Prevention, 1994).

40. Robert J. Meadows, *Understanding Violence and Victimization*, 2nd ed. (Upper Saddle River, NJ: Prentice Hall, 2001), 57.

41. Gordon Bazemore and Allen W. Cole, "Police in the 'Laboratory' of the Neighborhood: Evaluating Problem-Oriented Strategies in a Medium-Sized City," *American Journal of Police* 13, no. 3 (1994):119–147.

Why is there a separate juvenile justice system?

What are the justifications for treating male and female juveniles differently?

How were delinquents handled in the past?

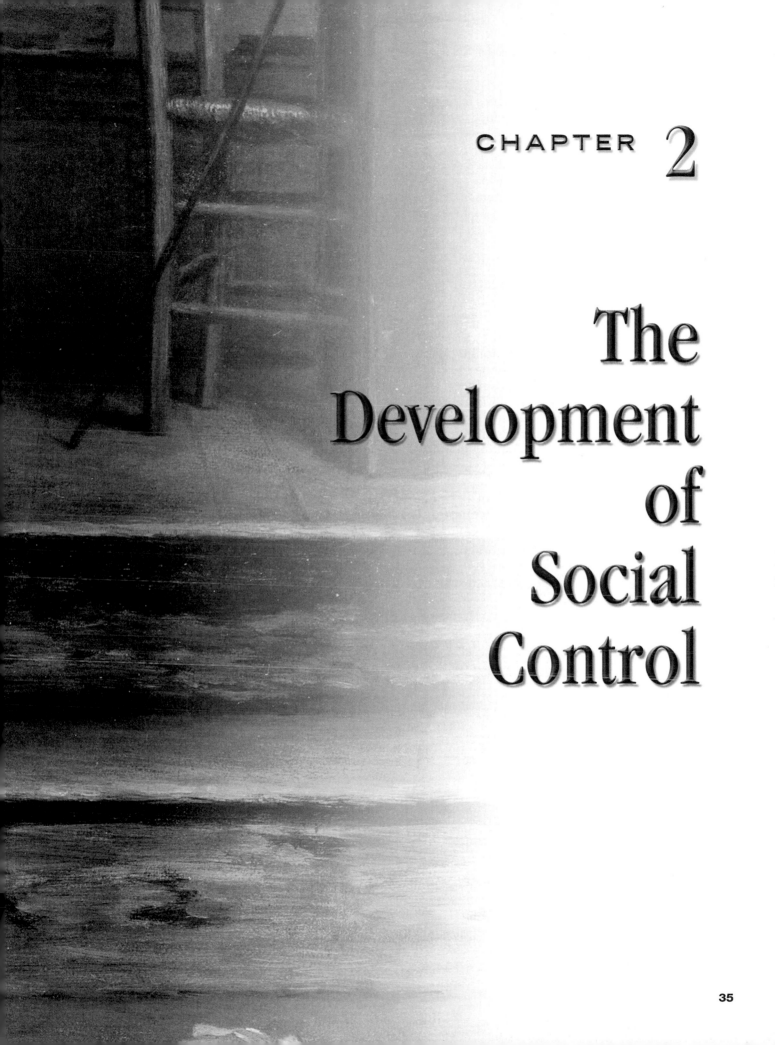

CHAPTER 2

The Development of Social Control

All societies have the task of socializing their young members to become functioning and productive adults. The rhythms of life demand that the young eventually come into their own and assume the roles that enable a society to survive from one generation to the next. We would be mistaken, however, to assume that past societies accomplished socialization as we currently do in the Western world. For many reasons, the long period of youth dependency, which ranges up to age 21, is relatively recent in human evolution. Modern, industrialized societies protect, nurture, help, or discriminate against the young to such a degree that many still live in a state of financial dependency long after their forebears would have been fully functioning members of society. The youth of past generations assumed adult responsibilities sooner than youth do today for three important reasons.

- **Longevity**   Because people live longer today, we can afford to invest more time in preparing children for adulthood. Back when one's life expectancy was 30 to 50 years, it was impractical to devote half of it to preparation for adult roles and responsibilities (see Figures 2-1 and 2-2).

- **Economic pressure**   At a time when most of the population was engaged in working the land, the labor of young people was vital to a family's economic survival. Very young children were assigned chores that increased in skill and sophistication as they grew older. Young boys were trained in hunting and/or agriculture and were expected to do a man's work by the time they were in their middle teens. As the division of labor became more sophisticated and the work required more skill, older and more mature craftspeople became necessary. Consequently, the work force became older, and young people remained in states of economic dependency for longer periods. However, we should note that not all societies develop at the same rate. In many developing countries today, children work long hours in lieu of having what we would consider a normal childhood.

- **Cultural pressure**   Western civilization has changed so radically over the centuries that young people need a great deal more training, education, guidance, and support to function in society. In early agrarian societies, where life

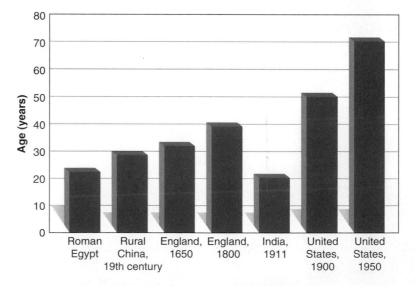

Figure 2-1   **Life Expectancy at Birth in Various Societies Throughout History** *Sources:* James Z. Lee and Cameron Campbell, *Fate and Fortune in Rural China: Social Organization and Population Behavior in Liaoning, 1774–1873* (New York: Cambridge University Press, 1996), 62; John Landers, *Death and the Metropolis: Studies in the Demographic History of London, 1670–1830* (New York: Cambridge University Press, 1993), 158; Kingsley Davis, *The Population of India and Pakistan* (New York: Russell & Russell, 1968), 36; National Center for Health Statistics, *Health, United States, 2004 with Chartbook on Trends in the Health of Americans* (Hyattsville, MD: U.S. Department of Health and Human Services Centers for Disease Control and Prevention, 2004), 143. www.cdc.gov/nchs/data/hus/hus04trend.pdf#027; Roger S. Bagnall and Bruce W. Frier, *The Demography of Roman Egypt* (New York: Cambridge University Press, 1994), 109.

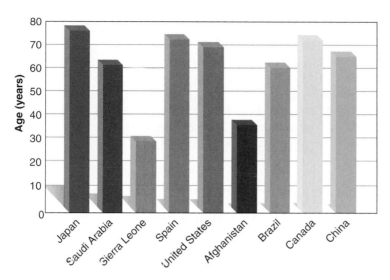

Figure 2-2   **Life Expectancy at Birth in Various Societies, 2002** *Source:* Robert Beaglehole, Alec Irwin, and Thomson Prentice, *The World Health Report 2004* (Switzerland: World Health Organization, 2004), 132–135. www.who.int/whr/2004/en/report04_en.pdf.

In many developing countries, children work long hours at difficult jobs. In this brickyard in Colombia, a boy heaps a load of bricks on a girl's back. *(Courtesy J.P. Laffont, ZUMA Press – Gamma)*

revolved around the land and the seasons, young people had only to learn a finite skill set before cultivating their own homesteads. The primary requirement was physical strength, which meant that older adolescents were encouraged to strike out on their own and start families. However, in mature societies in which land was at a premium, it became dysfunctional for all the sons to receive a piece of the family estate. Therefore, a system of **primogeniture** was established in which the eldest son received the entire estate, and the younger ones were forced to move or join the military or church. Given this lack of land, many young men couldn't afford to start families until their parents died.

primogeniture
A system of inheritance in which the oldest son receives the entire estate.

Consequently, boys stayed home for longer periods to put off the hardships of starting out on their own.

As we can see, the period of children's dependency has lengthened throughout history for a number of reasons. What is most fascinating about this process, however, is how Western concepts of childhood have evolved. Despite the fact that the economic and cultural landscape has changed, the concept of childhood has undergone such a radical transformation that it deserves special treatment if we are to fully comprehend the development of the social control of youth.

DEVELOPMENT OF THE CONCEPT OF CHILDHOOD

When we consider childhood, we think of innocent and dependent children who must be protected from the forces of nature, predatory adults, and their own curiosity. However, some past cultures didn't consider children as a distinct class in need of special protection and nurturing. For example, according to Neil Postman, there is little evidence that the ancient Greeks considered children special.[1] They practiced infanticide and, except for emphasizing education, showed very little interest in the specialized care of children.

This isn't to say that parents had no concern for children; rather, the state didn't accord children particular rights or protections. In fact, much of the treatment of children during the time of the ancient Greeks would be considered child abuse today.[2] Postman emphasizes the effect of the collapse of the Roman Empire on Europe. He states that the Romans developed an idea of childhood that surpassed that of the Greeks. However, along with literacy and education, the concept of childhood disappeared from Europe during the period after the Roman Empire disintegrated.[3]

According to Neil Postman, the Greeks accorded children few special rights or protections. This ancient Greek bronze statue depicts a very young boy, who is probably a professional jockey, racing a horse. *(Courtesy Dagli Orti, Picture Desk, Inc./Kobal Collection)*

What is especially interesting about Postman's analysis is the role of education in the development of childhood. Without education, the socialization process is informal, haphazard, and nonsequential, and the line of demarcation in the transformation from child to adult is vague or even nonexistent. Without a period of formal education to differentiate children from adults, there is little need for the concept of childhood.

As we move to medieval times, we find that the English had a concept of childhood by at least the 12th century, and the Church and common law clearly distinguished between adults and children. Scholar Nicholas Orme states that by 1250 most of the English had at least had contact with literacy, with literate parents teaching literacy skills to their children.[4] Children also received special foods and living accommodations, as well as clothes designed specifically for them. (For an extended discussion about whether the concept of childhood existed in medieval times, see Crosscurrents 2.1.) Orme states that in some cases, however, medieval children were treated more like adults than they are now. For instance, it was possible for those under the age of 12 to marry or enter a religious order.

In the late 1700s, German parents began recording systematic observations of their children's physical and linguistic milestones.[5] These "baby biographies" encouraged observers of children, experts who might now be called pediatricians and child psychologists, to quantify the age at which children developed motor and cognitive skills. This information helped to establish the norms that we now use to gauge the development of biological, psychological, and social maturity.

Acquiring Adulthood

Because children require many years to mature into adults, rights and responsibilities are accorded to them slowly. Parents, teachers, court officials, and legislators believe that children must be protected not only from others, but also from their own impulsive and immature behaviors. Although we might legitimately argue about the exact age at which adult rights and responsibilities should be granted, there is general agreement that chil-

The lives of children in medieval times resembled those of children today in many ways. The painting *Children's Games* by Brueghel shows 16th-century children playing games in town. *(Pieter Brueghel, The Elder (c.1525–1569), "Children's Games," 1560, Flemish. Kunsthistorisches Museum Vienna, Austria/SuperStock)*

The Modern Myth of Medieval Childhood

Once upon a time, no one questioned the idea that childhood is nearly as precious as children themselves. The two were considered inseparable, one almost as magical as the other. Then, in 1960, French historian Philippe Ariès stated flatly that, although children had certainly been around forever, childhood had not. The concept of childhood, he wrote, with clothing, food, rules, games, education, and literature made just for children, was basically a 17th-century invention.

In medieval society the idea of childhood did not exist; this is not to suggest that children were neglected, forsaken, or despised. The idea of childhood is not to be confused with affection for children; it corresponds to an awareness of the particular nature of childhood, that particular nature which distinguishes the child from the adult, even the young adult. In medieval society this awareness was lacking. That is why, as soon as the child could live without the constant solicitude of his mother, his nanny or his cradle-rocker, he belonged to adult society.[1]

This seemed to be a logical idea. Brutal eras like the European Middle Ages would have had no time for childhood as modern folk knew it: a magical time between birth and the late teens in which children were expected to do nothing but grow, learn, and bear little to no responsibility for their actions. In a way, Ariès's grim revelation served proof of the modern era's superiority over the Middle Ages. Courts of the Dark Ages might have given wayward children the short drop (a particularly brutal method of hanging), but it took the modern age to give them reformatories.[2]

Since the 1960s and Ariès's harsh pronouncements, the idea of childhood as a sort of enchanted island seemed to grow, becoming a sort of postmodern paradise lost. Once you leave, you can never return. In *L'Enfant et la vie familiale sous l'ancien regime*, translated in 1962 as *Centuries of Childhood: A Social History of Family Life*, Ariès based much of his assessment on the depiction of children in pictures and art. He noted that medieval children were often represented with the physical features of adults and dressed in adult clothing. He wrote, "Medieval art until about the twelfth century did not know childhood or did not attempt to portray it. It is hard to believe that this neglect was due to incompetence or incapacity; it seems more probable that there was no place for childhood in the medieval world."[3]

Europe's Middle Ages certainly did give children a rough time. Many children didn't survive their first year, and it was not uncommon for a husband and wife to have several children and bury them all before any of them reached adolescence. Ariès argued that because children were about as likely to die as they were to live, parents couldn't emotionally afford to get too attached to them, so they didn't. Ariès's ideas about the medieval disregard of childhood took deep root in nearly every discipline that dealt with childhood, including juvenile justice.

Now many medievalists say that Ariès was wrong. One historian who makes this case is Nicholas Orme in *Medieval Children*. According to Orme and other experts, medieval European adults didn't simply treat children as younger versions of themselves and, much as we do, they considered childhood to be a separate phase of life. Orme stresses that the Church, a primary source of law and social custom, "made a clear distinction between adults and children, at least by about 1200." Also, "The English common law . . . identified a number of ages of majority, varying from twelve to twenty-one, at which young people acquired the right to administer their own affairs and property, and the duty of shouldering adult responsibilities."[4] Orme, who researched paintings, documents, nursery rhymes, play, education, and family life, came to the conclusion that medieval English children were treated very much like modern Western children. Although many laws and customs were different—for instance, medieval children might be sent away to work or marriage at a very young age—medieval adults gave their children an age of their own, much like the one that modern adults give theirs.

Think About It

1. Which historian do you believe is correct about medieval childhood?
2. In what ways would the concept of childhood contribute to the development of the social control of children?

1 Philippe Ariès, *Centuries of Childhood: A Social History of Family Life,* Robert Baldick, trans. (New York: Random House, 1962), 128.

2 The "short drop" refers to the evolution and eventual perfection of execution by hanging. Early on, the condemned had a rope placed around their necks and were dangled only a few feet, resulting in death by slow suffocation. Later, executioners adopted the "long drop" method of hanging, allowing the condemned to fall several feet and die quickly by snapping of the neck. (Robert M. Bohm, *Deathquest: An Introduction to the Theory and Practice of Capital Punishment in the United States,* (Cincinnati, OH: Anderson, 1999), 73.

3 Philippe Ariès (see note 1), p. 33.

4 Nicholas Orme, *Medieval Children* (New Haven, CT: Yale University Press, 2001), 7–8.

dren need socialization, protection, and time to develop a mature perspective. Societies grant adult status based on history, customs, and economic needs. Despite the fact that children (including teenagers) mature gradually, laws, by their nature, set cutoff points at which rights and responsibilities change suddenly. In several states, this age is 18.

One issue that affects the granting of adulthood is that of **patriarchy**. Patriarchy can be defined as situations in which men hold power and authority in political, religious, legal, educational, military, and domestic areas.[6] Patriarchy is exerted over children not only in the families in which the father seeks to exert final authority over decisions concerning the children (often with mixed success), but also over the child-serving institutions of society, such as religion, school, and the juvenile justice system.

Another issue that affects the granting of adulthood is self-discipline. Self-discipline is pervasive in society and exerts a surveillance and conforming function on all of us, especially children.[7] One indication of successful **socialization** is the self-discipline that compels members of a society to believe in and conform to that society's rules. The better that children acquire self-discipline, the more they are allowed discretion, flexibility, control, and self-direction.

But what happens when a youth doesn't demonstrate the acquisition of self-discipline and defies the rules of parents and society? This is a central question in the development of juvenile justice systems. In the early North American colonies, the General Court of Massachusetts Bay created a law that provided for the execution of children who disobeyed their parents (see A Closer Look at Juvenile Issues 2.1). Derived from Biblical language, the *stubborn child law* developed two features that are currently utilized in juvenile justice. First, it directed families to control their children in the interests of society. Second, it sought to limit conflicts and maintain established authority. Although deviance was regarded by the Puritans as an innate flaw in the individual, this law extended the problem to everyone. Grace was a mysterious and elusive thing, and temptation was everywhere. What was needed was a systematic

patriarchy
A social system in which males have authority and fathers are considered the absolute head of the family.

socialization
The process by which people learn the norms, values, and culture of their society.

2.1 A CLOSER LOOK at JUVENILE ISSUES

THE ORIGINAL ZERO-TOLERANCE LAW

In 1646 the General Court of Massachusetts Bay passed this law:

If a man have a stubborn or rebellious son, of sufficient years understanding (viz.) sixteen years of age, which will not obey the voice of his Father, or the voice of his Mother, and that when they have chastened him will not harken unto them: then shall his Father and Mother being his natural parents, lay hold on him, and bring him to the Magistrates assembled in Court and testify unto them, that their son is stubborn and rebellious and will not obey their voice and chastisement, but lives in sundry notorious crimes, such a son will be put to death.

This law is almost identical to Deuteronomy 21:18–21 (King James Version):

If a man have a stubborn and rebellious son, which will not obey the voice of his father, or the voice of his mother, and that, when they have chastened him, will not hearken unto them: Then shall his father and his mother lay hold on him, and bring him out unto the elders of his city, and unto the gate of his place; And they shall say

unto the elders of his city, This our son is stubborn and rebellious, he will not obey our voice; he is a glutton, and a drunkard. And all the men of his city shall stone him with stones, that he die: so shalt thou put evil away from among you . . . .

The Massachusetts Bay law, which was added to the colonial laws of Connecticut, Rhode Island, and New Hampshire, remained on the books in Massachusetts until 1973. According to John Sutton, author of *Stubborn Children*,[1] the law was a forerunner of modern social control in two ways. First, it used families to further the society's values. The second strategy stemmed directly from Puritan religious philosophy. The Puritans believed that no one was free from sin. Children who were wild and undisciplined were especially subject to temptation. The survival of Puritan society, then, depended on how well and how early children were disciplined.

Fortunately, according to Sutton, it appears that none of the children of the Massachusetts Bay colony ever received the death penalty for misbehaving.

1 John R. Sutton, *Stubborn Children: Controlling Delinquency in the United States, 1640–1981* (Berkeley: University of California Press, 1988), 10–13.

social control

The framework of rules and customs that a society collectively applies to the individuals within it to maintain order.

external discipline, such as the stubborn child law, to ensure that the state augmented and supported the family in the **social control** of children.[8]

Leaving Home at an Early Age

How do children gain control over their affairs? Ideally, they gradually earn the trust and confidence of the adults responsible for them. As children take on ever more complex and responsible duties, they are given more freedoms, more opportunities to use their judgment, and more chances to make mistakes. Parents hope their children learn from many little mistakes and seldom make big ones. There are times, however, when this graduated sense of responsibility isn't instilled in children. Sometimes children must grow up fast and assume roles for which they have not been prepared. Although this might seem to be a recipe for disaster for many youths, there are countless cases in which young people who were thrust into adult roles at an early age not only survived, but also prospered.

An important example of this phenomenon from U.S. history is Benjamin Franklin. Although Franklin is generally recalled as a scientist and icon of the American Revolution, his early life is informative to the study of juvenile delinquency. His childhood wasn't easy for a number of reasons, but it does show how a bright and determined youth could negotiate the perils of becoming an adult without the benefit of much parental authority. At the age of 12, Franklin was apprenticed to his older brother's printing shop. Franklin chafed under his brother's poor treatment, and at the age of 15 he ran away from Boston to Philadelphia. Amazingly self-reliant, he sought to better himself by self-education and hard work and became one of the most accomplished men of his era.[9]

Franklin is but one example of someone who was successful, despite leaving home at an early age. There are many more examples, but the fact remains that they aren't

Benjamin Franklin became very successful in business and politics, despite leaving home as a very young man. In this painting, a young Franklin is depicted selling ballads or poems on a street in Philadelphia. *(Courtesy Corbis/Bettmann)*

the norm. In fact, history is replete with stories of individuals who failed because they didn't have the proper guidance. Poverty, crime, prostitution, and destitution have been the fates of many children who found themselves without supportive and nurturing families.

Does society have an obligation to care for those youths who for one reason or another are without a support network? Regardless of how we answer this question, it's in society's interest to ensure that its children have an opportunity to thrive. In a highly competitive world in which the losers are left without the means to survive, only bad results can be expected. People don't suffer the pains of poverty and desolation alone and sometimes attempt to compete, or even survive, through illegitimate means, such as robbery, extortion, burglary, or worse.

CHILD REFORM MOVEMENT

American society has evolved quickly since its inception and, as a result, has seen many major and minor social upheavals brought on by social catalysts, such as repeated waves of immigration, industrialization, technology, economic collapse, war, and the expansion of civil rights. One era of social upheaval that extended from the late 19th to the early 20th centuries was marked simultaneously by lucrative economic opportunities, urban expansion, extensive European immigration, industrialization, and the movement of large clusters of the U.S. population from farms to cities.

All this turmoil left many people better off than before as they pursued new opportunities, but it also left many people in worse straits. Impoverished and disoriented, immigrant parents began to lose control of their Americanized children, and rural American parents who had moved to the cities to look for work began to lose control of their urbanized children. With child-labor laws still developing, many children spent long days in factories doing hard labor. The general result of this disarray was crime, delinquency, and the large-scale abuse and neglect of youths. During this time, several social reform movements arose in an attempt to improve social conditions for children.

One example of how society attempted to ease the burdens of impoverished youth is the **orphan train** of the late 19th century.[10] Large eastern cities such as New York and Boston found themselves with an influx of population from both rural areas and overseas, particularly Europe. Although these teeming cities profited from the supply of cheap labor, they also found themselves with many social problems, including large numbers of orphaned, abandoned, and poverty stricken children from large families. Social service agencies were stretched thin to provide shelter and food for these children. From 1850 well into the 20th century, over 200,000 children were sent west on orphan trains. This *placing-out* served two key purposes.

orphan trains
The practice of 19th- and early 20th-century child-welfare societies of placing many orphans, impoverished children, and young adults on trains to less populated parts of the United States, primarily the West.

- **Removing impoverished children from big cities**   By taking unconnected or loosely connected youth from the cities and resettling them in rural areas, social service workers kept their caseloads manageable. Financial resources, institutional bed space, and low-wage jobs didn't exist for the vast numbers of poor youth. By placing them out, it was believed that the social problems of crime, poor education, and health issues were, if not overcome, then at least transferred so far away that they became someone else's problem.

- **Labor**   The expanding West constantly needed labor to work the farms and ranches, as well as the small businesses in the towns. The chores were endless, and farmers whose children had grown to adulthood and started farms of their own required young people as replacements. It was considered good, honest, healthy outdoor work that was suitable for the children of the cities. By being sent to work on western farms, children got a chance to escape the social problems of the cities and learn skills. Although the process was somewhat similar to indentured servitude, for the most part, it did allow many children to be placed with kind families who took a sincere interest in their welfare and didn't exploit their labor.

house of refuge
An early form of the reformatory during the mid- to late 19th century that housed impoverished and delinquent children and status offenders.

Instant Recall
from Chapter 1
parens patriae
Latin for "father of his country." Refers to the philosophy that the government is the ultimate guardian of all children or disabled adults.

The practice of placing-out ended at the close of the 1920s, when two major societies, the New York Children's Aid Society and the New York Foundling Hospital through the Sisters of Charity, halted their programs and directed their resources toward local foster homes and children's aid programs. There were also allegations that placing-out was not the panacea it was thought to be. Inevitably, some children ended up in bad homes and others with employers who wanted only to exploit their labor and provided no education or family life. Some children lost total contact with their biological families, while others behaved just as badly in their new homes as in their old. Although some of these things probably happened, the most likely reason the brake was put on the orphan trains was that the West no longer needed people. In fact, some urbanized western areas were being quickly introduced to the very problems in the East that had created the orphan trains.[11]

What happened to those who were not placed out? Only a relatively small percentage of youths were sent west to serve as labor on the developing frontier. Those left behind often suffered a worse fate. **Houses of refuge** were created in the larger cities such as New York, Philadelphia, and Boston. These institutions were started by wealthy philanthropists who financed them as vehicles for rescuing and reforming youths from squalid slums. Further, these houses of refuge, in the philanthropists' view, got children off the streets and helped to curb social disorder among the poor and recently arrived immigrants.[12]

The stated intent of houses of refuge was to provide a safe environment where youths could be trained and educated in a trade. The legal authority for placing them in such an institution came from the principle of *parens patriae*. In 1839, *Ex parte Crouse* (see Case in Point 2.1) established the justification of the state's intervention in the life of a young girl placed in a Philadelphia house of refuge.

Not all orphaned children were put on orphan trains. In 1869, the Sisters of Charity opened the New York Foundling Asylum to take in babies abandoned after the Civil War. This photograph of a nun and orphaned children was taken in 1888. *(Photograph by Jacob A. Riis, The Jacob A. Riis Collection, Museum of the City of New York)*

2.1	**CASE IN POINT**
	EX PARTE CROUSE

THE CASE	**THE POINT**
Ex parte Crouse, 4 Whart., Pa. 9 (1839)	*This case reinforced the doctrine of parens patriae and the increasing power of the juvenile court.*

Mary Ann Crouse, age 16, was committed to a Philadelphia county, Pennsylvania, house of refuge by her mother. The county justice of the peace stated that Mary Ann's mother had proved to him "that the said infant by reason of vicious conduct, has rendered her control beyond the power of the said complainant. . . ." By writ of habeas corpus, Mary Ann's father tried to reclaim her from the house of refuge, contending that she was under detention without a jury trial, which was unconstitutional. In denying the motion, the state Supreme Court responded that the house of refuge was a school, not a prison. The court also stated that "the right of parental control is a natural, but not an unalienable one," and that the community's need for productive members superseded a parent's right to raise a child "when unequal to the task of education, or unworthy of it."

The Child-Savers

An important step in the development of social control of youth came about at the end of the 19th century with the work of the **child-savers**, whose activities coincided with and were partly responsible for the eventual development of the juvenile justice system. The term *child-savers*, according to sociologist Anthony Platt, describes the loose coalition of philanthropists, feminists, and social reformers who "helped create special judicial and correctional institutions for the labeling, processing, and management of 'troublesome' youth."[13] For the past century, the juvenile justice system has labored under the philosophy of child-saving that was established by reformers who sought to make the world a better place for unfortunate children. However, the ambiguity in these reformers' motivations is inherent in the development of the juvenile justice system.

> The term "child-savers" is used to characterize a group of "disinterested" reformers who regarded their cause as a matter of conscience and morality, serving no particular class or political interest. The child savers viewed themselves as altruists and humanitarians dedicated to rescuing those who were less fortunately placed in the social order.[14]

However, Platt faults the child-savers for being naïve and even disingenuous. For instance, although they professed to represent the best interests of children, their criteria for what was good for children were embedded in their own value systems. The child-savers wanted to save troubled youngsters by ensuring that they adopted middle-class values. Given the child-savers' rural, Protestant values, it isn't surprising that, because of their different cultural backgrounds, immigrant, Catholic, and urban children often found it difficult to accept the standards set by the state. When snared in legal difficulties, children were subjected to treatment that the juvenile court, not the children or their parents, determined was in the best interests of both society and the child. Let's look at the court's philosophy in terms of reformatories.

- Young offenders must be segregated from the corrupting influences of adult criminals.
- "Delinquents" must be removed from their environment and imprisoned for their own good and protection. Reformatories should be guarded sanctuaries, combining love and guidance with firmness and restraint.
- "Delinquents" should be assigned to reformatories without trial and with minimal legal requirements. Due process is not required because reformatories are intended to reform and not to punish.

child-savers

People at the end of the 19th century who were instrumental in creating special justice institutions to deal with juvenile delinquents and troubled youths.

- Sentences should be indeterminate so that inmates are encouraged to cooperate in their own reform and recalcitrant delinquents are not allowed to resume their criminal careers.

- Reformations should not be confused with sentimentality. Punishment is required only insofar as it is good for the punished person and only when other methods have been exhausted.

- Inmates must be protected from idleness, indulgence, and luxuries through military drill, physical exercise, and constant supervision.

- Reformatories should be built in the countryside and designed according to the "cottage plan."

- Labor, education, and religion constitute the essential program for reform. Inmates should not be given more than an elementary education.

- The value of sobriety, thrift, industry, prudence, "realistic" ambition, and adjustment must be taught.[15]

It is easy to see how these principles of incarceration were designed to serve the interests of society far more than the interests of children. An elementary education prepared the youths for little more than menial occupation, and they were encouraged to develop only "realistic" ambitions. The whole program was designed around the assumption that delinquent behavior could be changed by placing children in their proper place as defined by the values of the dominant society. This plan did not attempt to elevate wayward children above their predetermined place on the social continuum. See Programs for Children 2.1 for the 19th-century view of delinquent and neglected children.

2.1   PROGRAMS *for* CHILDREN

"EXPOSURES, TEMPTATIONS, AND PERILS!"

The reformatories of the 19th century were filled with delinquent, neglected, and dependent children who exhibited a broad range of problems. E. C. Wines, one of the leading authorities on delinquency at the time, described these children in 1880 with the following fascinating language.

I refer the condition and surroundings of these children before their commitment. More than half of them were orphans by the loss of one or both parents, and more than a moiety of the rest worse than orphans by the intemperance, brutality, and crimes of their parents. Nearly one half were wholly or virtually illiterate; the major part were living in idleness, either vagrants or truants; three-fourths were neglecters of church and Sunday-school, and more than three fourths addicted to profanity; more than half were frequenters of theatres, and more than a third habitual chewers or smokers of tobacco; a moiety had been arrested more than once; a large proportion were homeless, or otherwise out of the normal family relations, not simply by orphanage, but by having step-parents, or parents who had separated or were in prison; and almost all were

the children of neglect, of ignorance, of poverty, of misery, of the street, of the dock—in a world of evil surroundings and evil influences whose name is legion, and their power well-nigh omnipotent. What a catalogue of exposures, temptations, and perils! How few and faint the chances for victory in such a battle! How almost certain the issue of disaster, defeat, and ruin! Numbers of these homeless, outcast, beleaguered children came to the reformatories with the impression burned into their souls, "Nobody cares for me!"[1]

Think About It

1. By today's standards, how serious were the actual crimes described by Wines?

2. In a time when the government provided little or no help for children, how precarious was their plight?

3. What resources are available today for the type of children Wines describes?

1 E. C. Wines, *The State of Prisons and of Child-Saving Institutions in the Civilized World* (Cambridge, MA: John Wilson & Son, 1880), 132.

The institution of the juvenile justice system formalized the practice of treating children differently, but it also did much more. It brought a wide range of behaviors that were not considered criminal offenses under the control of the state. By acting in the best interests of the child, the juvenile court didn't have to wait until the child actually broke the law but could intervene whenever it was suspected that there was a problem brewing with the child's situation. Many behaviors for which a juvenile could be placed under court supervision were (and are) called **status offenses**, because it's only the young age of the child, his or her status as a juvenile, that renders such behaviors illegal. Adults who commit the same acts are not subject to sanctions. See A Closer Look at Juvenile Issues 2.2 for a detailed explanation of modern status offenses.

status offense

An act considered to be a legal offense only when committed by a juvenile, and one that can be adjudicated only in a juvenile court.

2.2 A CLOSER LOOK at JUVENILE ISSUES

STATUS OFFENSES

Status laws exist out of a legitimate concern for children's welfare. Young children can be neglected and exploited by adults, and these statutes are designed to protect children until they develop the maturity to make decisions for themselves.

- **Running away** Regardless of the suitability of the home, children are not free to leave. They are legally under the control of their parents and must submit to legal restrictions. Although some children might have legitimate reasons for wanting to leave home, such as abuse and neglect, they are required to get official court approval for leaving and for making sure that their new living conditions are satisfactory. Running away and living on the streets or at the homes of friends is not permitted without court investigation and approval. For a look at the first case of a child successful in legally separating himself from his parents, see Kids in the News 2.1, page 58.
- **Curfew violations** Some jurisdictions require adolescents to be off the streets at certain times of the night. Communities do not want youths roaming the streets after businesses have closed and there are few legitimate activities for young people. Although the children might simply wish to hang out with their friends, many communities believe that wandering youths pose significant public safety concerns. Some jurisdictions relax the curfews for youths who have a reason for being out late, such as employment.
- **Sexual behavior** Young people are restricted from engaging in certain sexual conduct. Depending on the jurisdiction, the age at which someone may engage in sexual relations differs, but as a general rule children are prohibited from having sex.
- **Alcohol and tobacco consumption** Children may not drink alcohol or use tobacco products until a certain age. Usually, alcohol use requires someone to be 21 years old and tobacco 18, but this can vary by state law. Protecting children from these addictive substances is considered appropriate until they attain the necessary maturity to make an informed decision about the consumption of physically harmful drugs.
- **Incorrigibility** Children are supposed to obey their parents. Although there are always conflicts when parents draw boundaries, sometimes

children simply refuse to adhere to these limits, and the court is forced to intervene to protect the child and society.
- **Truancy** Children are required to attend school. In most states they cannot drop out until they are 16 years old.

Although these status laws are intended to protect youths, they might have the unintended consequence of stigmatizing juvenile delinquents or making prohibited behaviors appear more desirable. For instance, smoking cigarettes can appear to be the mark of adulthood to children, so the mere restriction based on age might make it more likely that some youngsters will desire to smoke. More problematic, however, is what happens to those who are caught up in the system after being caught in a status offense. A youth who is discovered while engaging in an illegal activity and is processed by the court might end up with a stigma of deviance that could make later life difficult. Schools, families, and the juvenile justice system might treat the youth more harshly because of the status offense. Some critics believe that, because children often outgrow deviant behavior, the best thing that society can do is to ignore many of their transgressions. However, in a study of girls who committed status offenses, about half of abused and neglected girls who committed status offenses were arrested when they became adults, as well as 36 percent of girls who had not been abused or neglected.[1] A related issue is that authorities are more likely to hold females than males for status offenses, which, according to some critics, is a sign of gender bias and paternalism in the juvenile justice system.[2]

The Juvenile Justice and Delinquency Prevention Act of 2002 does not allow status offenders to be confined in secure facilities. However, accused status offenders may be held in secure juvenile facilities for up to 24 hours following initial contact with law enforcement or the court.[3]

1 Cathy Spatz Widom, "Childhood Victimization and the Derailment of Girls and Women to the Criminal Justice System," *Research on Women and Girls in the Justice System* (Washington, DC: U.S. Department of Justice, 1999), 29. Online at www.ncjrs.org/pdffiles1/nij/180973.pdf.

2 Melissa Sickmud, *Juvenile Offenders and Victims National Report Series: Juveniles in Corrections* (Washington, DC: U.S. Department of Justice, 2004), 14. Online at www.ncjrs.org/pdffiles1/ojjdp/202885.pdf.

3 Ibid., p.17.

The problems of children in the early United States were substantial and of concern to individuals who saw the debilitating effects of poverty and rapid social change. Because the urban poor couldn't or wouldn't care for their children according to middle-class standards, a number of institutions, charities, and philanthropies were established to partially fill the gaps. Families of immigrants and the poor allowed their children to roam the streets, avoid school, and work in dangerous occupations. Although these conditions were business as usual for the impoverished, those in the established, and often wealthy, social classes considered impoverished children to be neglected, abused, and out of control.

Just how bad was this situation? By today's standards we would be appalled by the lack of health care, education, family support, and delinquency. Children were unsupervised and often found themselves abandoned or forced out of their large families at a very early age to make their own way in the world. This situation alarmed those who saw the ills of urbanization as harmful to society and children. What we must realize is that these concerned individuals viewed the world through their own class-based perspective and failed to understand that much of what they considered deviant was, in fact, normal behavior for those in desperate circumstances.

According to C. Wright Mills, many early sociologists considered the process of urbanization to be evil and judged it against the values they brought from their small, rural societies, where life was ordered and predictable and children were taught a strict moral code.[16] They saw social disorganization in the city and worked with philanthropists to develop charities and child-saving agencies that would apply their own sense of order and control to the lives of those they considered to be less fortunate. It was in this environment that the idea for the juvenile court and ultimately an entire juvenile justice system was envisioned.[17]

JUVENILE COURT

The juvenile court is an important step in the development of the social control of American youths. Although we will discuss the juvenile justice system in detail later, we need to become familiar with the juvenile court now because it's critical to the way that we control and protect youngsters.

Before the juvenile court, children and adolescents were treated much like adult offenders. The juvenile court, which is just one aspect of the larger social reform movement of the late 19th and early 20th centuries, changed all that. Youths now had a legal system of their own designed to protect them from predatory adults, abusive parents, and social and economic hardships, as well as from themselves and each other. This same legal system also established formal civil control over youths, and to a limited extent over their parents, simply by designing laws that pertained especially to them. At the time, this dual endeavor of protection and control was something new in legal history because it came from the government. Throughout history, the protection and control of youths came from parents and to a lesser and informal extent from religion and social networks. The establishment of the juvenile court represented the first time that a political government utilized a separate legal system to insert itself on a regular basis between youths and their parents, their religious institutions, and their social networks in order to deal with the youths for their own good.

History of the Juvenile Court

The first juvenile court was established in Chicago, Illinois, in 1899. Reformers and child activists had struggled for a decade to create a court to separate the cases of children from adults. The new court ushered in a philosophy of helping children instead of punishing them, but the child-savers didn't get all they wanted in the new juvenile court because several entrenched interests were working against them to preserve the status quo. For example, the law that created the juvenile court, An Act to Regulate the Treatment and Control of Dependent, Neglected and Delinquent Children, applied only to Cook County, Illinois, leaving the rest of the state to deal with delinquent children in the usual manner.[18] There were two significant differences between urban Chicago and the rest of Illinois. First, the city was swamped with the problems of a rapidly changing environment. Immigration, poverty, crime, and unemployment made Chicago a vastly different place from the agricultural rural areas and small towns. The second significant difference was the presence of activist, and primarily female, reformers who saw it as their civic duty to rescue children from the problems of the city.[19]

In a backlash to curtail the range and scope of the proposed legislation, opponents inserted several items that blunted the full reforming effect sought by the child-savers.

- **Secret hearings**   The reformers wanted the hearings of the new juvenile court to be closed to the public and the press. The bill's opponents contended that this would rob the public of its right to appreciate how the new institution operated. Although modern juvenile hearings have restrictions about revealing the names of youth, the original legislation provided for a more open court.

- **Foster homes**   The legislation prevented the court from paying adults to take children into their homes under foster-care agreements. This legislation was the result of the influence of the industrial (reform) school lobby that lost the labor of children who went into foster care. As a result, Illinois continued to institutionalize dependent children at a very high rate.

- **Jurisdiction**   The bill prevented the juvenile court from controlling those who were committed to a state industrial or training school. Additionally, the court lost jurisdiction over children committed to private institutions. This was done primarily to prevent Protestant state officials from influencing Catholic institutions. The bill went so far as to recommend that children be placed with custodians who were of the same faith. Catholic and Jewish supporters of the bill used this provision to ensure that the new court did not use the legislation to steal the child's faith.[20]

Further reforms chipped away at the original structure and scope of the first court. In spite of these limitations, the first juvenile court went a long way toward ensuring that the welfare of juvenile and delinquent children was considered and that punishing them was not the state's first goal. The history of the passage of the bill demonstrates that it was a highly political process and that the vested interests that had profited from the plight of neglected or delinquent children were quick to protect their turf.

The juvenile court heard its first case on July 3, 1899. Henry Campbell, an 11-year-old boy accused of larceny, appeared before Judge Richard Tuthill. It was a public event, and spectators and the press packed the courtroom to hear Campbell's mother plead for his freedom. She contended that Henry wasn't a bad boy but that he had been led into trouble by others and that she and her husband didn't want Henry institutionalized. They offered an alternative plan in which Henry would be sent to Rome, New York, to live with his grandmother, away from the corrupting influences of Chicago city life.[21] The disposition handed down by the court, which sent Henry to his grandmother, was consistent with the philosophy of the new institution as articulated by its first chief probation officer, Timothy Hurley:

> Instead of reformation, the thought and idea in the judge's mind should be formation. No child should be punished for the purpose of making an example of him, and he certainly cannot be reformed by punishing him. The parental authority of the State should be exercised instead of the criminal power.[22]

The juvenile court took over a decade to mature into the institution envisioned by its proponents. Several intractable issues had to be considered and solved before the court could provide the type of justice its designers envisioned. We will see in later chapters how some of these issues continue to be problematic:

- **Probation officers**   Although the judge is the head of the juvenile court and exercises great discretion in the disposition of cases, the probation officer is in a more pivotal position. The court has always struggled with defining how probation officers should be trained and what their role should be. At its inception, the juvenile court was concerned with the religion of probation officers. Within a decade, probation officers were evenly divided between the Protestant and Catholic faiths, and there was tension concerning how far the court should intervene into the lives of families. Catholic supporters of the juvenile court were suspicious of the court's interventionist tactics and feared that a Protestant, middle-class standard was being applied to all cases.

- **Minority children**   Chicago was undergoing a radical transformation in the early part of the 20th century with unprecedented immigration from Europe and the southern United States. Like many U.S. institutions, the juvenile court struggled to integrate these new arrivals into mainstream society. This problem became particularly acute for black people who were moving into cities like Chicago. Many social institutions, primarily private ones that had discriminated mostly upon religion, started to discriminate by race, as well. Consequently, probation officers soon found that they had few treatment options available for black children who were neglected, dependent, or delinquent. The court was forced to keep minority children under much more severe constraints than youths who could be placed in alternative situations because they were white.[23]

- **Girls**   Young women also presented challenges to the new juvenile court. The first was that parents used the courts to help them control sexually adventurous daughters who were demanding more control over their lives. Fearing that these girls would turn into promiscuous women who would become prostitutes, the courts tended to incarcerate girls at a higher rate than boys.[24]

- **Private hearings**   One problem of having public juvenile court hearings is the frequent exchange of sensitive personal information that is embarrassing to the youth. This was particularly true of cases concerning the sexual behavior of young women. Having a male judge questioning a young girl about her sexual experiences, however necessary to determine an appropriate outcome for the case, was problematic in an open court. In fact, at the time, having a middle-aged man exploring the sex life of girls under any circumstances was deemed questionable. In 1913, the Chicago Juvenile Court hired attorney Mary Bartelme to act as a "referee" on behalf of female defendants (see A Closer Look at Juvenile Issues 2.3 for an overview of her career). By 1920, many of the hearings involving sensitive female sexual information were closed to the public.[25]

The juvenile court reforms took place over a period of time. As with any new enterprise, it took time to develop the court's new procedures and to overcome vested interests and inappropriate, counterproductive policies. Such a major reorientation of the philosophy of handling problem children required experimentation with policies and procedures in light of the prevailing political environment.

Boys, Girls, and Bias: The Double Standard

There has always been a double standard in how males and females are accorded rights, responsibilities, and protections. This double standard is an especially sensitive issue in both the juvenile and criminal justice systems, because many of our principles and methods of social control are based on it.

Across a broad range of concerns, including the right to vote, to own property, to file for divorce, to choose one's marriage partner, and to work in certain occupations, men have, until very recently, enjoyed discretion, whereas women's choices were restricted.

2.3 A CLOSER LOOK at JUVENILE ISSUES

MARY BARTELME (1866–1954)

Mary Bartelme was a pioneer in both the practice of law and juvenile advocacy. The first woman judge elected to the circuit court of Cook County, Illinois, she started her career in 1894 as a probate and real estate lawyer. Her work with juveniles began in 1897 when she was the first woman to be appointed as Public Guardian of Cook County. As Public Guardian, she dealt with custody issues and minors who were wards of the state. In 1899, she and other reformers established the juvenile court of Chicago, as well as a detention home where juvenile delinquents could be held instead of in an adult jail.

As Chicago headed into the 20th century, the court found itself dealing with increasing numbers of young females. Judge Merritt W. Pinckney decided that it would be best for a woman to hear these cases, and in 1913 he appointed Bartelme as his assistant judge. Bartelme applied her philosophies of juvenile justice by holding closed hearings and ensuring that all the personnel, from bailiff to court reporter, were female. In adjudicating these

cases, Bartelme found that many involved only slight infractions of the law and that, while traditional sentencing was inappropriate, the girls' situations at home were also often unacceptable. To remedy this, from 1914 to 1916 she established a series of three Mary Clubs, the first one in her home, where girls could be supervised while waiting to be placed in foster care. Bartelme, who believed that poverty was the main cause of delinquency, also collaborated with local women's organizations to provide clothing and toiletries for girls who appeared in her courtroom.

In 1923, Bartelme was elected juvenile court judge in the Cook County circuit court. There she continued her reforms in the treatment of juveniles. She utilized social scientists during hearings and sentencings and rejected the adversarial practice of law, disallowing attorneys' objections and talking directly to the children. She also believed that legal reforms and public services could help prevent delinquency; in one instance, she supported a law making the age of 16 the lowest age at which a woman could be employed. Re-elected to the bench in 1927, she became the court's presiding judge and heard both boys' and girls' cases.

Like the child-savers, Bartelme, herself the daughter of immigrants, believed that white, middle-class American values were the best for children and encouraged the immigrant children and parents appearing in her court to speak English. Bartelme also practiced racial separation. Two of her Mary Clubs were for white girls, and one, established with the help of black women reformers, was for black girls. She assigned black probation officers to black children. However, she was deeply concerned for children of all races. In the late 1920s, she ordered the creation of the Department of Child Placing to help place black children with foster families. But with the Depression eroding social services, as well as the very fabric of social life, the department couldn't keep up with the influx of children. In 1932, Bartelme appealed to local religious organizations to help provide care for the children but made little headway. The deepening Depression made her efforts increasingly difficult. Group homes closed, funding and support dried up, and the state refused to pick up the slack, turning out scores of children.

In 1933, when her term was up, Bartelme retired to Carmel, California, where she lived with her brother. She died at the age of 88.

Chicago History Museum

Sources: Gwen Hoerr McNamee, *Women Building Chicago, 1790–1990*, Rima Lunin Schultz and Adele Hast, eds. (Bloomington and Indianapolis: Indiana University Press, 2001), 66–70; Mary Bartelme Papers, University of Illinois at Chicago, www.uic.edu/depts/lib/specialcoll/services/rjd/findingaids/MBartelmeb.html.

This double standard also applied to boys and girls. Boys were prepared for positions of leadership in society and families, while girls were prepared to raise children and take care of the home. (See Focus on Ethics 2.1 for a more detailed look at modern double standards.) The early juvenile justice system applied this same double standard to the rehabilitation and protection of youths. Delinquent and needy boys were prepared for trades, and delinquent and needy girls were instructed in home arts and trades based on these skills, such as cooking, sewing, and child care. Let's look at some of the common reasons for differential treatment of males and females throughout history.

- **Biological**   Because females bear children, human societies tend to divide labor between males and females so that males ensure the livelihood of the family while females care for the children and attend to domestic duties. It seems obvious to many that this arrangement grows naturally out of the biological differences between males and females and that one has only to observe patterns in the animal kingdom to conclude that this is a naturally occurring arrangement. This is a contested argument, but it's still used to account for this disparity.

- **Physical**   Related to the biological argument is the physical justification for treating males and females differently. Because males are typically bigger and stronger than females, females have been considered to need protection. Because of the aggressive nature of males, females are often the victims of rape, assault, and intimidation. Therefore, females were considered to need to be constrained in the activities in which they engaged. (In some cultures, they still are.)

- **Religious**   Many religions prescribe that rigid social roles for males and females are supernaturally ordained. Religious texts specify a broad range of behaviors appropriate for one gender, but not for the other. These are particularly persuasive arguments for many people. Religious doctrine provides people with what Alvin Gouldner calls "domain assumptions."[26] Domain assumptions are those ideas that seem so obvious to us that we don't question whether they are true; we simply assume they are true. Many individuals follow religious teachings that specify rigid, precise roles for males and females.

- **Economic power**   Because males have dominated societies for so long, they have been able to control the educational, religious, and social systems that provide what can be called *conventional wisdom*. Much conventional wisdom places males in a privileged position, and many critics point out that this state of affairs between the sexes is self-serving. Power is seldom given up lightly, and it's interesting to observe the intense struggle of women who want to be treated equally in societies in which men are unwilling to give up power and share decision-making authority with women.

Because of the successes of the women's movement, numerous laws have been rescinded and new legal protections for women have been enacted, and, most significantly, there have been changes in the collective way that women consider themselves and the way that girls are treated.

However, despite advances in equal treatment under the law, males and females, as well as boys and girls, are still treated differently by the justice system, which is often necessary. This brings us to a controversial issue that is made even more sensitive because we live in a society that seeks to equalize opportunity and social treatment between males and females. For a variety of biological, political, and social reasons, many of which are unknown, males break the law more than females. There are more men in prison than women, and more boys enter the juvenile justice system than girls. Let's look at some statistics.

- In 2001, just 7 percent of all prison inmates were women.[27] As of 2003, females accounted for only 15 percent of juveniles in residential placement.[28]

- According to the FBI Uniform Crime Reports, in 2005, males represented 76.2 percent of all arrestees (both adult and juvenile), 82.1 percent of violent-crime arrestees, and 68.0 percent of property-crime arrestees.[29]

- In 2005, 897,305 males under 18 were arrested as opposed to 381,643 females under 18. To be fair, the 10-year arrest trend, 1996–2005, shows that the number of male arrestees decreased 7.6 percent, while the number of female arrestees increased 7.4 percent; but the gulf between the number of males and females within the justice system is still very wide.[30]

FOCUS *on* ETHICS

BOYS WILL BE BOYS. GIRLS WILL BE HOME BY 11.

You are a parent with 16-year-old twins. Your daughter, Eve, has been dating the captain of the basketball team for several months and thinks she's in love. This young man, a high school senior, has a reputation as a great basketball player and a good student. He has been accepted at a university with a major basketball program and seems to have a bright future as either a professional athlete or a medical doctor.

Recently, you and your spouse have had concerns about how late Eve stays out with this boy. You both believe it necessary to lay down the law and establish an 11:00 P.M. curfew on weeknights and a midnight curfew on weekends. Eve is furious with you because she says the seniors' parties last much later and that her boyfriend will ensure that nothing bad will happen.

Eve's twin, Riley, just got his driver's license and is constantly out with his friends. Riley is responsible, and you haven't yet thought it necessary to establish a curfew for him. He has recently started dating a girl in his math class, and they stay up very late studying for tests at her house. He is getting his best grades ever, and you believe his girlfriend is having a positive influence on him.

Eve says that you treat her differently because she is, as she says, "a girl." Because she and Riley are exactly the same age—actually she's older by five minutes, a fact she never lets you forget—she demands equal treatment. You say that because Riley is male, and therefore bigger and stronger, he can better take care of himself in dangerous situations and that, for the most part, his late nights have been devoted to studying rather than partying. You tell Eve that, although you trust her, her boyfriend is two years older and, although he seems to be nice, he's at a stage in life when he can take more risks than you are prepared to let her take. You tell her if she were dating someone her own age and not partying so much, you might consider treating her like Riley.

This conflict is causing a lot of friction in the family, and you wonder if you're doing the right thing.

Think About It

1. Should age determine how late teenagers stay out?
2. Is it fair that the child who stays out late studying gets more latitude than the child who stays out late partying?
3. Should gender be considered? Are boys really better able to physically protect themselves than girls?
4. As long as you believe your children are safe, do you really care what they think of your rules?

This disparity between male and female offenders of all ages means that both the juvenile and criminal justice systems process more males than females and more boys than girls.

This is both good news and bad news for females. They are not involved in crime as much as males, nor are they processed by the justice system in high numbers. However, because females are such a minority in criminal and juvenile justice systems, the facilities to handle them aren't always adequate. Consequently, like male facilities, they are often overcrowded. In many ways, the criminal and juvenile justice systems serve females less effectively than males and are forced to divert females because of a lack of space.

For Their Own Good

Protecting neglected, dependent, and delinquent children is a delicate task that requires constant evaluation. Because there is no consensus on what is in the best interests of children, the court must tread lightly in developing policies that incarcerate, treat, and divert those who fall under its purview. Although the court is philosophically committed to acting in the best interests of children, it must still observe a fine line in balancing these interests with the protection of society and the expectations and demands of parents, schools, and community standards. The historic pressures under which the early juvenile courts operated reflected the political, social, economic, and religious sensibilities of the time. It is important to understand some of the issues that shaped the evolution of the juvenile justice system. When discussing designing programs for the benefit of children, it's important to remember that this task is always accomplished according to the values of powerful adults. Although well-meaning, some of these programs, reforms, or initiatives might have detrimental consequences for problem children.

The invention of the juvenile court was accompanied by a new philosophy of helping, rather than punishing, young lawbreakers. Because the court had the best interests of children in mind, there was no need to protect the children from court processes and decisions. Children didn't need legal protection because the court was helping them, not punishing them. This was the underlying philosophy, but several problems emerged in practice. First, a person who's confined might have trouble telling the difference between treatment and punishment. Confinement can be harsh, restrictive, perceived as unfair, and lacking in rehabilitation. Calling the confinement "treatment" is a semantic sleight of hand that doesn't alter the hardships of detention. Today juvenile delinquents are accorded more due-process rights than they were at the inception of the juvenile court. Joseph Sanborn and Anthony Salerno list five reasons for the denial of juveniles' rights at the court's inception:

- **Juvenile rights were deemed unnecessary**   Because the juvenile court was benevolent and rehabilitative, young lawbreakers didn't need due-process rights as found in the adversarial criminal justice system. This philosophy was exemplified in the 1905 case *Commonwealth* v. *Fisher* (see Case in Point 2.2). The state was viewed as a friend of the youth, not the enemy.

- **Juvenile rights were deemed inappropriate**   The juvenile justice system's goal was to correct the underlying problem that caused the delinquency, not to punish the youth. A partisan defense attorney or a jury that knew little about childhood development or youth culture was ill-equipped to diagnose the problem and prescribe adequate treatment.

- **Juvenile rights were deemed harmful**   In addition to being costly and time consuming, providing due-process rights to delinquents might enable them to escape treatment. If the case the police presented was flawed or the juvenile court process was faulty, the youth might be able to use due-process rights to challenge the legality of the proceedings and have the charges dismissed. By not allowing due-process rights, the court could intervene when it saw a problem regardless of evidence that an offense had been committed.

- **Juvenile rights were undeserved**   Adults had a citizen's full constitutional rights. Juveniles were considered to be too immature to exercise these rights

---

2.2   CASE IN POINT

COMMONWEALTH V. FISHER

THE CASE

Commonwealth v. Fisher, 27 Pa. Super. 175 (1905)

THE POINT

This case reinforced the state's power to commit juveniles to houses of refuge and similar institutions without due process.

Fourteen-year-old Frank Fisher pleaded not guilty to a charge of larceny. The district attorney certified that prosecution was unnecessary, and a court of quarter sessions sitting as a juvenile court committed the boy to a house of refuge. Fisher's counsel argued that the court of quarter sessions was improper and that the commission of Fisher without a jury trial violated his constitutional rights.

The superior court responded that not only was the court of quarter sessions proper, but that, as in *Ex parte Crouse,* the purpose of committing Fisher to the house of refuge "is to save, not to punish; it is to rescue, not to imprison; it is to subject to wise care, treatment and control rather than to incarcerate in penitentiaries and jails; it is to strengthen the better instincts and to check the tendencies which are evil; it aims, in the absence of proper parental care, or guardianship, to throw around a child, just starting in an evil course, the strong arm of the *parens patriae.*"

It was not until the U.S. Supreme Court's decision in *In re Gault* (1967) that such strict application of *parens patriae* was questioned.

and so were kept under the control of their parents and the state. Only when they reached the age when they could become productive members of society were they entitled to constitutional rights.

- **Juvenile rights were inapplicable**   Theoretically, what happened in juvenile court was so different from what happened in criminal court that giving rights to juveniles was considered a bad idea. Juveniles were not arrested, tried, and punished. The vocabulary of the juvenile court process facilitated helping children, so due-process rights were not considered to apply to the juvenile court experience.[31]

As can be determined from this list, those who developed the concept of the juvenile court didn't see the necessity or desirability of providing legal rights to juveniles. This philosophy guided the juvenile court until the 1960s, when a series of groundbreaking cases affected not only the juvenile court, but also a vast number of criminal justice issues, ranging from offenders' protections from police searches and seizures to the rights of prison inmates.

Modern System

In an effort to improve crime response, the United States has a separate juvenile justice system. Although this system shares many features and resources with the criminal justice system, it has a different philosophy, personnel, and organizational structure. Later we will discuss moves to combine the juvenile justice system with the criminal justice system, but for now, we will talk about the differences between the two systems and specify how they affect the quality of assistance and justice received by juveniles. However, a caveat is necessary. The juvenile justice system is even more fragmented than the criminal justice system, because the level of variation among the states' juvenile justice systems is so great that there is no typical system. Therefore, what is presented here may be somewhat imprecise when compared to the juvenile justice system in any particular state.

LANGUAGE AND TERMINOLOGY   When police officers respond to an incident, they don't know in advance if the suspect they will be dealing with is an adult or a juvenile. Consequently, the police are the first agency that's confronted with differentiating between delinquency and criminality. The police arrest an adult suspect but "take into custody" a juvenile. The action might look very similar, but the terminology is important. To avoid imposing the stigma of "criminal" on a juvenile, the juvenile justice system uses an alternative vocabulary. A convicted adult is an "offender," but a juvenile offender is considered a delinquent. The adult is served with an **indictment**; the youth, with a **petition**. The adult has a trial; the youth, a fact-finding **hearing**. The adult is convicted of a crime; the youth is **adjudicated**. The adult is sentenced; the youth receives a **disposition**. The list of different terms for similar actions goes on, but the point has been made here for our purposes. The terms are different because language is important, and softer, less stigmatizing terms are employed to limit the negative connotations of the juvenile proceedings.

PROCESS   Although police officers who arrive on the scene of a crime might detain youths, adults, or both, once it's determined that a suspect is a youth, a separate process is initiated. Often officers who specialize in juvenile delinquents will assume the case. At the very least, the case will be referred to juvenile intake at a detention center. Every effort is made to separate youths from adults and to ensure that youths are treated according to the juvenile law. However, in serious cases, juvenile suspects might be bound over to criminal court for trial as most states have several provisions for doing this.[32]

In addition to referral by the police, a youth may enter the juvenile justice system by other avenues. Parents who are unable to control a child may petition the court to intervene and impose restrictions. A youth doesn't have to break the law before the court can specify a treatment plan and limit the youth's freedom and autonomy. Likewise, a

indictment
A formal written statement that charges a person or persons with a serious offense, usually a felony.

petition
In juvenile court, a document that alleges that a juvenile is delinquent and that asks the court to assume jurisdiction over the juvenile or asks that an alleged delinquent be waived to criminal court to be prosecuted as an adult.

hearing
A session that takes place without a jury before a judge or magistrate in which evidence and/or argument is presented to determine some factual or legal issue.

adjudicate
The act of arriving at a judicial decision. To pass judgment.

disposition
The final determination of a case or other matter by a court or other judicial entity.

school can alert the court to problems, including truancy, that will allow the court to take action. Abused or neglected children can also enter the court's protection. Individuals in some positions, such as a nurse or teacher, who suspect child abuse are required by law to report it to the proper authorities even if there is no complaint by the child.

CHANGING NATURE OF CHILDHOOD

The way that we have responded to the concept of childhood over the centuries reveals much about the progress of Western civilization. As adults took more care to nurture and develop the capabilities of children and protect them from the social and economic realities of adulthood, children were able to develop better skill sets with which to finally take their place in society. One way to trace the development of the concept of childhood is to consider the media. Typically, throughout early history, learning and knowledge were controlled by a child's parents and, to a somewhat lesser extent, by the child's extended family and community. Parents taught their children in a personal manner, for example, "at father's knee," and the child's exposure to knowledge was tightly controlled. The media, which began in earnest with the invention of the printing press, changed that.

Neil Postman argues that children benefited from the invention of the printing press because for the first time the masses could learn exactly what the elites learned.[33] The printing press was responsible for transmitting religion, politics, social etiquette, child-rearing advice, and education. The first schools divided students according to ability, but as more children started going to school, they were separated into classes according to age. This age gradation facilitated the development of different rules and responsibilities for children.[34] With the development of the idea of childhood came the demand to explain how children were different from adults and how they should be treated in order to maximize their potential to learn and become productive members of society. According to Postman, Sigmund Freud and John Dewey were especially influential in how we have come to think about children, with the publication of Freud's *The Interpretation of Dreams* and Dewey's *The School and Society*, both of which appeared in 1889.[35]

The contribution Freud made to understanding children's minds was the dismissal of John Locke's notion that children's brains were a *tabula rasa* or blank slate.[36] Freud argued that children possessed psychological drives and sexuality and that they needed to overcome their instinctive passions and learn to control their behavior. If they didn't repress and sublimate these passions, according to Freud, then they couldn't conform to the civilized world. John Dewey considered the development of children and asked, "What is it that the child needs now?" By addressing what the child is, rather than what the child will become, he determined that it was easier to meet children's mental needs and enable them to become constructive participants in the community.

Modern Childhood

Although the existence of a generation gap has long been taken for granted, the pace of social change has accelerated to such a degree that many parents' adolescent experiences are irrelevant for today's youngsters.[37] This is because, although each generation goes through a somewhat predictable cycle of life crises (puberty, first love, first car, first pregnancy), each generation experiences these crises differently because of the broad social forces that affect individuals based on their age location. For instance, September 11, 2001, and the wars in Afghanistan and Iraq have different effects on those of fighting age than those of retirement age, just as the latter generation was affected differently by the war in Vietnam than their parents, who were affected by World War II.

It is important to remember that one's age at which major events happen is an important filter by which these events are interpreted. Therefore, although parents and teachers were once teenagers themselves, they had different pressures and temptations, as well as different guidance, support, and nurturing to prepare them. Consequently, if we are to appreciate what childhood means for today's youngsters, we must use what C. Wright Mills calls **sociological imagination** to take ourselves out of our own social

**Instant Recall
from Chapter 1**
sociological imagination
The idea that one must look beyond the obvious to evaluate how social location influences the way one considers society.

Understanding the current generation of children and teenagers means taking an objective look at their lives and how they must live them. (© Gandee Vasan/Getty Images, Inc.)

location and view young people from a more open and objective paradigm.[38] This challenge to view the young people of today from an objective and neutral appreciation of their social world brings us to the task of describing the historical forces and social pressures that today's children are forced to confront. For an example, see Kids in the News 2.1 about Gregory Kingsley, a child who successfully "divorced" his birth parents at the age of 12.

It is in this new reality that the juvenile justice system, as well as other institutions in society such as religion, school, and family, must attempt to control and socialize children. Because of the rapid rate of social change, especially in technology, much of the fabric of society is being challenged anew. As technology progresses and societies change to accommodate, adjust to, and take advantage of this progression, the parents of each generation will have to struggle to understand the pressures and temptations that their children are experiencing.

Trends in Thinking about Delinquency and Juvenile Justice

The nature of childhood (the period before puberty) and adolescence (the period after puberty and before adulthood) in the United States has changed in the past century. This is especially true in small towns and rural areas. Schools, day-care centers, and recreational facilities are no longer considered the safe havens they once were. Children have cell phones so that parents can keep track of them, and many homes have security systems. It is less common these days for children to roam their neighborhoods looking for fun and to organize their own games. Parents schedule their children's playdates and enroll them in structured activities and sports to fill the hours they aren't at school.[39] What do these features of contemporary American life mean for the nature of childhood?

At the very least, changes in American society mean that the social control exerted on children has drastically changed. Paradoxically, a great deal more control is placed on youngsters' freedom, as well as on many areas in which they have considerably more freedom. How can this be? One explanation is that social control in the United States has, in many ways, shifted from social accountability to personal accountability. This is an important phenomenon, so we will consider it in detail here.

In the past, social expectations of individuals' actions and appearances were far more regimented than they are today. Throughout history, up until the 1950s, males

2.1 K I D S *in the* N E W S

Kingsley v. Kingsley

In 1992, 12-year-old Gregory Kingsley made history by being the youngest child ever to "divorce" his birth parents. Gregory was born in 1980 to Rachel and Gregory Kingsley, Sr. The couple separated when Gregory was a very small child, and Ms. Kingsley took custody of Gregory. After moving from Missouri to Florida in 1990, she placed him in foster care.

After spending a year with the family of George and Lizabeth Russ, who had eight other children, Kingsley decided to stay with them. George Russ, a lawyer, assisted Gregory in preparing a lawsuit to separate him from his mother. (Gregory Kingsley, Sr., who didn't contest the suit, died shortly after the decision.)

During the televised bench trial, numerous witnesses testified about Ms. Kingsley's poor efforts at parenting, and Gregory Kingsley described how his mother would often come home drunk. Between the years of 1983 and 1991, he had been in and out of four foster homes and had spent a total of only eight months with his mother.

After two days of testimony, Orange County Circuit Judge Thomas S. Kirk "found by clear and convincing evidence that Rachel had abandoned Gregory and that termination was in the manifest best interests of Gregory." Ms. Kingsley's parental rights were terminated. Soon after his adoption by the Russes, Kingsley changed his name to Shawn Russ.

Think About It

1. Should a child be able to "divorce" his parents if they are neglectful and abusive?

2. Why do you think Gregory sued to terminate his mother's rights, rather than the Russes suing for custody of him?

3. At the time, conservative Pat Buchanan predicted that Kingsley's successful lawsuit would provoke a rash of frivolous copycat lawsuits by children unhappy with their parents' strict rules. Did it?

Sources: "A Child Asserts His Legal Rights," *Time* 140, no. 14 (October 5, 1992): 2; www.time.com/time/archive/preview/0,10987,1101921005–157970,00.html; Mark Hansen, "Boy Wins 'Divorce' from Mom," *ABA Journal* 78 (December 1992): 16; *Rachel Kingsley* v. *Gregory Kingsley, et al.*, 623 So. 2d 780; 1993 Fla. App. LEXIS 8645; 18 Fla. L. Weekly D 1852.

and females were expected to dress a certain way, obey a specified etiquette, engage in a specific set of activities, and meet social expectations. For example, until the early 1960s, U.S. men generally didn't appear in public without a hat, and many American women wore gloves to go out on even minor errands. Men went to work and earned money, while women took care of the home and children. The place of children was equally as regimented: they went to school and dressed and acted in a manner specified by their parents. A common scenario in impoverished families was that the children quit school, often before their middle-school years, and went to work. Divorce was relatively rare, considered socially improper, and single parents, latchkey children, and blended families were unheard of as demographic classes. Consider, for example, pre-1970s movies and television shows about families in which one parent is missing. The absent parent is almost always dead, not divorced.

Until the mid-20th century, American society expected its citizens, including children, to act and appear in certain ways, and they generally did so or risked censure or even ostracism. Because of the level of social accountability, the level of personal accountability was somewhat less, especially for youths. Children were treated less as individuals and more as extensions of their parents and of society. For example, much of the work of the child-savers involved separating children from their families, religions, and neighborhoods. They were not considered to be individuals who needed these institutions; children, it was expected, could grow wherever they were planted.

This changed during the 1960s, when many of these informal, but strict, social rules were dismantled. Women and minorities were no longer restricted to specific roles and social levels, and people were not only allowed to express more individuality and flout social conventions, but expected to. After the 1960s, divorce rates went up, as did the crime rate (although it has dropped since the 1990s), with the nuclear family being considered endangered, if not already extinct.[40]

Since the 1960s, personal expression has expanded in all directions for all ages. This can be observed, for example, in the form of tattoos, piercings, plastic surgery, extreme sports, consumer-product choice, music, and cars and in such Web vehicles as blogs and social networking sites.[41] The expectation of strict obedience to a set of social standards encompassing all aspects of life and allotted according to age, race, and socioeconomic status has withered. To replace it, it can be argued, is a greater expectation of personal accountability, not only for adults, but also for youths. A person might have as many tattoos as he or she wishes, but if he or she breaks the law (the ultimate set of social standards), then, increasingly, the blame isn't placed on society or family, but on the individual. The individual, unless a very young child, is expected to be responsible for his or her actions and to bear the consequences. This isn't to say that individuals were not held accountable for and punished for lawbreaking before the 1950s—they most certainly were—only that now the offenses of youths (and adults) are considered to be more a product of individual choice, rather than family, religion, or society.

What does this have to do with delinquency and juvenile justice? Basically, youths are now considered less a subset of society and more as individuals who are expected to be responsible for their own actions, almost regardless of age. A product of this philosophy can be observed in the increased waiver of juvenile cases to criminal (adult) court. Oddly, this move toward greater juvenile accountability can be considered to stem from the juvenile justice system. The U.S. juvenile justice system was the first time that a civil government came between youths and their parents (and other social institutions) for the youth's sake. Even in the midst of the child-saving movement, which, as you will recall, shipped whole classes of children off to the West, the government began the practice of treating problematic youths as individuals who needed individualized treatments. In its treatment of individuals, then, the juvenile justice system diverged from its child-saving roots, giving rise to many of our current ideas about youth.

Currently, youngsters are more free than ever to express themselves. However, in many ways it's this individualized focus and expectation of personal accountability that has abbreviated the tolerance of their growing pains as they experiment with the

Today's youngsters have more freedom than ever to express themselves. *(© Gary Parker/Photofusion Picture Library / Alamy)*

boundaries of appropriate behavior. Some parents drug-test their children; schools adhere to zero-tolerance policies for trivial behaviors, sometimes calling the police instead of the parents if there's a problem; and communities demand curfews to keep children home at night. (See Kids in the News 2.2 for more insight into the effects of extreme adherence to zero-tolerance laws.)

Some teenagers work minimum-wage jobs that require them to drive and stay out late. Younger children are home alone in the afternoon with only the television, Internet, and video games for entertainment and guidance, and very young children must negotiate the politics of preschool with other children. In these examples, youngsters are moving toward some aspects of adulthood at a much faster pace than they have for a couple of generations. This illustrates the paradox: youngsters are freer to express themselves, but they must often make difficult personal decisions concerning drugs, violence, and values that their grandparents didn't have to make until they were adults. Prior generations typically assumed the adult responsibilities of their respective eras sooner, but social regimentation left fewer personal choices and, in many ways, made these responsibilities simpler to assume.

For instance, a young rural man in 1900, having little formal education, might have left his father's home to get married and start his own farm and family. So, although he assumed adult responsibilities, he had few decisions to make concerning lifestyle, values, and self-expression, and he had already learned all the skills he needed to run a farm.

Now imagine a young rural man of 17 today. He will probably finish high school having already negotiated decisions on whom to hang out with, how to dress, what music to listen to, what drugs to try (or not to try), how to deal with his parents' divorce, how to get along with his step-parents, whether he should stick to the religion in which he was raised (if any) or seek out a new one, and what career he wants to pursue. This is the short list. He must also decide if he wants to attend college and, if so, where. Does he live at home? Does he get an apartment? A job? A significant

2.2 KIDS in the NEWS

One Little Mistake

In Houston, Texas, a 12-year-old boy ran out of his house without his jacket. He was almost at the bus stop when his mother caught him and insisted it was too cold to go out without a jacket. When he got to school, he discovered a 3-inch pocket knife that he had taken to his Boy Scout meeting the night before. He put the knife in his locker and told his friend about the mistake. The friend promptly turned him in to the school authorities, who had the boy arrested and taken to a juvenile-detention center without telling his parents. The boy was expelled for 45 days and enrolled in an alternative school for juvenile delinquents. The boy, who had won an outstanding student award, was also a model student, a Boy Scout, and a church youth leader. His father said that by the end of the ordeal the boy was contemplating suicide.

Have zero-tolerance policies gone too far? Violence at schools is a real concern, but there is a disjuncture between the highly publicized shootings at Columbine High School in Colorado, the Red Lake, Minnesota, case, and the zero-tolerance policies that schools across the country have adopted. While it's useful to be aware of the potential for violence, it's questionable that school zero-tolerance policies make schools any safer. These policies do, however, remove the discretion of teachers and school administrators and force them to invoke severe sanctions even when the infraction is trivial, innocently enacted, and potentially harmless.

Why have zero-tolerance policies become so popular? The answer is threefold:

- *Objectivity.* By following zero-tolerance policies to the letter, school officials can't be accused of bias or discrimination. When everyone is treated alike regardless of the infraction, and the letter of the law is strictly enforced, the school can claim it has equitable procedures.
- *Deterrence.* By enforcing zero-tolerance policies, the school sends a clear message to students and parents that no infractions will be permitted. Presumably, this sensitizes students and parents to the potential dangers of troubled students.
- *Accountability.* Schools face legal liability when violence happens. Questions are raised about the school's ability to prevent crime. By strictly enforcing rigid zero-tolerance policies, schools can demonstrate that they have taken every precaution imaginable. These policies can be useful in defending against a lawsuit.

Think About It

1. What is your opinion of zero-tolerance policies? Do they go too far, or are they necessary?
2. If you were the school principal, what would you have done with the boy?

Source: Kris Axtman, "Why Tolerance Is Fading for Zero Tolerance in Schools," *Christian Science Monitor*, March 31, 2005. www.csmonitor.com/2005/0331/p01s03-ussc.html.

---

other? Does he instead join the military? Or does he pursue none of the above and remain in his parents' basement working a minimum-wage job?

As you can see (and have probably experienced for yourselves), the young man's personal options are myriad and complicated, far more than the young farmer's of a century before. The modern teenager has to make many life-altering decisions but gets a long, graduated transition into adulthood. This long transition allows more chances for contact with the juvenile justice system simply because of the number of critical decisions that must be made so early.

Finally, we tend to forget that in many ways American youngsters are better off now than ever in terms of longevity, justice, medical care, social mobility, and the chance to get an education. In the United States, it's no longer typical for poor children to be pulled out of school to go work in the fields, and no American child today would be placed on an orphan train. Thanks to improvements in medicine, the rate of infant deaths has dropped from 58.1 percent per 1000 live births in 1933 to 7 percent in 2002.[42] The chance for a child born today in the United States to live to see adulthood is greater than it has ever been.

SUMMARY

1. All societies socialize their young members into functioning and productive adults.

2. The period of children's dependency has increased throughout history, and young people even as recently as 50 years ago became adults sooner than today's children due to longevity and economic and cultural pressures.

3. Children require many years to mature into adults, and societies grant adult status based on history, customs, and economic needs.

4. Two issues that affect the granting of adulthood are patriarchy and discipline. A central question in the development of juvenile justice systems was what to do with a youth who didn't demonstrate self-discipline and defied the parents' rules.

5. In the early American colonies, the General Court of Massachusetts Bay legislated the execution of children who disobeyed their parents. The stubborn child law directed families to control their children for society's sake and sought to limit conflicts and maintain authority.

6. During the 19th century, juvenile authorities attempted to ease the burdens of impoverished youth by placing out children on orphan trains. Others were placed in state and local houses of refuge where they could be educated and trained to work. The legal authority for placing them in such an institution came from the *parens patriae* principle.

7. Platt credits the child-savers with establishing the modern juvenile justice system. Although the child-savers had good intentions, these intentions stemmed from their own value systems. The child-savers sought to ensure that juveniles acted in accordance with the values of the dominant society.

8. The early juvenile justice system formalized the practices of treating children differently and brought a wide range of behaviors that were not considered crimes under the state's control (status offenses).

9. The first juvenile court was established in Chicago, Illinois, in 1899, with the philosophy of helping children, instead of punishing them. Some of the court's problematic issues included probation officers, minority children, and girls. The early court disregarded juveniles' due-process rights.

10. Western society's response to the nature of childhood has changed over the centuries. According to Postman, Dewey and Freud contributed much to modern thinking about childhood and children.

11. The modern U.S. juvenile justice system is separate from the adult criminal justice system, with a different philosophy, personnel, terminology, and organizational structure. Each state has its own system. A youth need not have committed a crime to enter the system.

REVIEW QUESTIONS

1. In what ways is childhood different than it was in past centuries?

2. If you were forced to leave home now, where would you go? What social support agencies are there today that were absent in the past?

3. The juvenile justice system treats boys and girls differently. Is this gendered justice fair?

4. Who were the child-savers? What were their motivations for helping children? Was there any downside to their help?

5. What is the difference between criminal offenses and status offenses?

6. How has technology changed the way we think about childhood?

7. What are the differences between the juvenile justice system and the criminal justice system? How are these differences reflected in the language of each?

8. In what ways do young people have more freedom than they did in the past?

ADDITIONAL READINGS

Ashby, LeRoy. *Endangered Children: Dependency, Neglect, and Abuse in American History* (New York: Twayne, 1997).

Gittens, Joan. *Poor Relations: The Children of the State in Illinois, 1818–1990* (Urbana: University of Illinois Press, 1994).

Graham, Phillip. *The End of Adolescence* (New York: Oxford University Press, 2004).

McCarthy, Kathleen. *Noblesse Oblige: Charity and Cultural Philanthropy in Chicago, 1849–1929* (Chicago: University of Chicago Press, 1982).

O'Connor, Stephen. *Orphan Trains: The Story of Charles Loring Brace and the Children He Saved and Failed* (Boston: Houghton Mifflin, 2001).

Rothman, David. *The Discovery of the Asylum* (Boston: Little, Brown, 1971).

ENDNOTES

1. Neil Postman, *The Disappearance of Childhood* (New York: Random House, 1982), 5–8. See especially Chapter 1.

2. Lloyd deMause, "The Evolution of Childhood," in Lloyd deMause, ed., *The History of Childhood* (New York: Psychohistory Press, 1974).

3. Postman (see note 1), p. 10.

4. Nicholas Orme, *Medieval Children* (New Haven, CT: Yale University Press, 2001), 5–9, 238.

5. Robert S. Feldman, *Child Development*, 3rd ed. (Upper Saddle River, NJ: Prentice Hall, 2004), 11.

6. Nijole V. Benokraitis, *Marriages and Families: Changes, Choices, and Constraints*, 5th ed. (Upper Saddle River, NJ: Prentice Hall, 2005), 114.

7. Michel Foucault, *Discipline and Punish: The Birth of the Prison* (New York: Random House, 1979).

8. John R. Sutton, *Stubborn Children: Controlling Delinquency in the United States, 1640–1981* (Berkeley: University of California Press, 1988), 10–13.

9. H. W. Brands, *The First American* (Garden City, NY: Doubleday, 2000).

10. Marilyn Irvin Holt, *The Orphan Trains: Placing Out in America* (Lincoln: University of Nebraska Press, 1992).

11. Ibid., 162–163.

12. Barry Krisburg and James F. Austin, *Reinventing Juvenile Justice* (Newbury Park, CA: Sage, 1993), 14.

13. Anthony M. Platt, *The Child Savers: The Invention of Delinquency* (Chicago: University of Chicago Press, 1969), 3.

14. Ibid.

15. Ibid., 54–55.

16. C. Wright Mills, "The Professional Ideology of Social Pathologists," *American Journal of Sociology*, 49:165–180.

17. Maureen A. Flanagan, *Seeing with Their Hearts: Chicago Women and the Vision of the Good City* (Princeton, NJ: Princeton University Press, 2002). See Chapter 1.

18. David S. Tanenhaus, *Juvenile Justice in the Making* (New York: Oxford University Press, 2004), 16.

19. Victoria Getis, *The Juvenile Court and the Progressives* (Urbana: University of Illinois Press, 2000), 10–22.

20. Tanenhaus (see note 18), pp. 33–54.

21. Ibid., 23–24.

22. Ibid., 23.

23. Barry C. Feld, *Bad Kids: Race and the Transformation of the Juvenile Court* (New York: Oxford University Press, 1999), 23–28.

24. Anne Meis Knupfer, *Reform and Resistance: Gender, Delinquency, and America's First Juvenile Court* (New York: Routledge, 2001). See Chapter 6.

25. Tanenhaus (see note 18), pp. 51–52.

26. Alvin W. Gouldner, *The Coming Crisis of Western Sociology* (New York: Basic Books, 1970), 29.

27. Paige M. Harrison and Allen J. Beck, *Prisoners in 2004* (Washington, DC: U.S. Department of Justice, Bureau of Justice Statistics, 2005), 1. Online at www.ojp.usdoj.gov/bjs/pub/pdf/p04.pdf.

28. Howard N. Snyder and Melissa Sickmund, *Juvenile Offenders and Victims: 2006 National Report* (Washington, DC: U.S. Department of Justice, Office of Justice Programs, Office of Juvenile Justice and Delinquency Prevention), 207. Online at www.ojjdp.ncjrs.gov/ojstatbb/nr2006/downloads/NR2006.pdf.

29. Federal Bureau of Investigation, *Uniform Crime Reports: Crime in the United States 2005*, www.fbi.gov/ucr/05cius/arrests/index.html.

30. Ibid., Table 33: Ten-Year Arrest Trends, www.fbi.gov/ucr/05cius/data/table_33.html.

31. Joseph B. Sanborn, Jr., and Anthony W. Salerno, *The Juvenile Justice System: Law and Process* (Los Angeles: Roxbury, 2005), pp. 24–25.

32. Snyder and Sickmund (see note 28), p. 111.

33. Postman (see note 1), pp. 24–27.

34. Philippe Ariès, *Centuries of Childhood: A Social History of Family Life*, trans. Robert Baldick (New York: Random House, 1962), 57.

35. Postman (see note 1), p. 62.

36. Locke forwarded this idea in his 1693 book *Some Thoughts Concerning Education*.

37. William Strauss and Neil Howe, *Generations: The History of America's Future, 1584–2069* (New York: Morrow, 1991), 43–58.

38. C. Wright Mills, *The Sociological Imagination* (New York: Oxford University Press, 1959), 11.

39. Ann Hulbert, "The Paradox of Play: Are Kids Today Having Enough Fun?" *Slate*, June 20, 2007, www.slate.com/id/2168764.

40. Claudia Wallis, "The Nuclear Family Goes Boom!" *Time*, Oct. 15, 1992, www.time.com/time/magazine/article/0,9171,976754,00.html.

41. As of 2007, the most popular of these sites included MySpace, Facebook, YouTube, Flickr, and LiveJournal.

42. Kenneth D. Kochanek and Joyce A. Martin, "Supplemental Analyses of Recent Trends in Infant Mortality," Centers for Disease Control and Prevention, National Center for Health Statistics, Table 1, www.cdc.gov/nchs/products/pubs/pubd/hestats/infantmort/infantmort.htm.

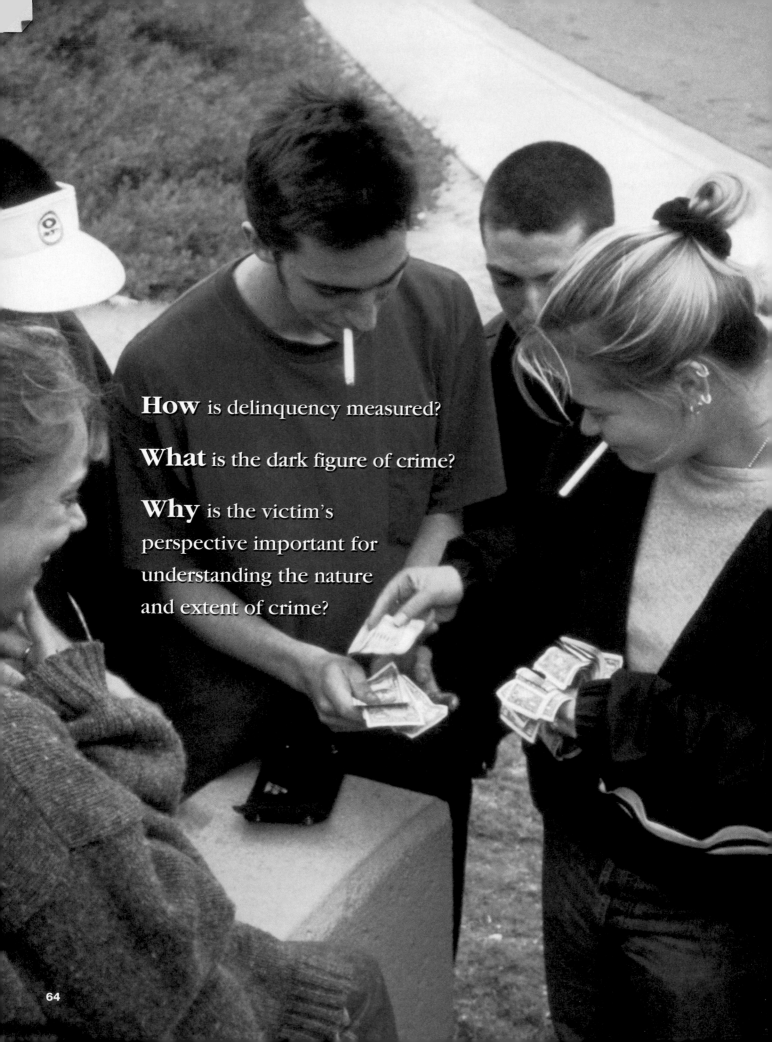

How is delinquency measured?

What is the dark figure of crime?

Why is the victim's perspective important for understanding the nature and extent of crime?

CHAPTER 3

Measuring Delinquency

How do we actually know how much crime there is in our communities? Do all communities define and measure crime in the same way? Is juvenile delinquency measured in the same way as adult offenses? These and other stubborn questions have long concerned those who try to accurately assess the amount of crime in society.

Despite a falling crime rate, the media continue to present stories about crime epidemics and juveniles who appear to be committing more serious offenses at younger ages.[1] Crime is certainly a major social problem, but getting a handle on its actual prevalence (how many people it affects) and seriousness is an ongoing challenge.[2] Scholars and researchers have developed numerous techniques to try to accurately measure the incidence and effects of crime and delinquency. In this chapter, we will review some of the major issues in assessing the level of crime and explain the strengths and shortcomings of some of the popular measurement tools.

DEFINING CRIME

Not all undesirable behaviors are offenses of the criminal law. Many transgressions of manners, etiquette, good taste, and civil demeanor might be offensive to some of us and yet aren't considered criminal offenses. The reason is that criminal offenses are violations of the criminal law. In a democracy, laws are made by representatives of citizens who are concerned about specific behaviors they believe should be prohibited. Often, there isn't a complete consensus on what behaviors should be considered crimes, but once the legislature passes a law, we are all obliged to obey it. We can't pick and choose which laws to obey and which to violate.

On a continuum of social control, crime occupies an extreme position at the serious end. Other behaviors are arranged on the continuum based on their perceived seriousness.

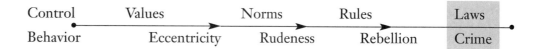

Control	Values	Norms	Rules	Laws
Behavior	Eccentricity	Rudeness	Rebellion	Crime

There might be ramifications to violating a norm or rule, but these ramifications aren't supported by the criminal justice system. Spitting in the classroom will almost certainly draw a rebuke from your professor and the disgust of other students, but it won't get you arrested by the police and brought before a judge. Your grade might suffer, and your classmates might ostracize you, but your liberty won't be curtailed. Informal means of social control are usually enough to keep us from committing undesirable acts. Laws are used when the acts are dangerous, when certain groups have the political muscle to get their values codified, or when there is a strong consensus that informal means don't effectively control the undesired behavior.

Once the government's legislative branch has defined the offenses, the executive branch is charged with enforcing the laws, and the judicial branch with trying the accused, as well as punishing the convicted. The actions of each of these branches of government are crucial to the measurement of crime because each plays a role in mediating how undesirable behavior is answered by the criminal and juvenile justice systems. One such government agency is the Office of Juvenile Justice and Delinquency Prevention, an important source of juvenile statistics (for more, see Programs for Children 3.1).

3.1 PROGRAMS *for* CHILDREN

OFFICE OF JUVENILE JUSTICE AND DELINQUENCY PREVENTION (OJJDP)

The Juvenile Justice and Delinquency Prevention Act of 1974 led to the creation of the federal Office of Juvenile Justice and Delinquency Prevention in 1974. An important source of juvenile statistics, the OJJDP also provides leadership and resources to prevent and respond to juvenile delinquency and victimization. The OJJDP helps states and communities develop and implement prevention and intervention programs and improve the juvenile justice system to protect public safety and provide treatment and rehabilitative services for juveniles and their families. The office's programs include youth courts, delinquency prevention, tribal

programs, and mental health initiatives. The office publishes a number of products concerning juvenile justice, including newsletters, journals, reports, videotapes, and bulletins, such as the children's Youth in Action Series with information about peer mentoring, the arts, crime prevention, and vandalism. The OJJDP also helps to train and deliver technical assistance to justice practitioners, elected officials, and citizen advocates through the National Training and Technical Assistance Center.

Source: Office of Juvenile Justice and Delinquency Prevention, ojjdp.ncjrs.org/.

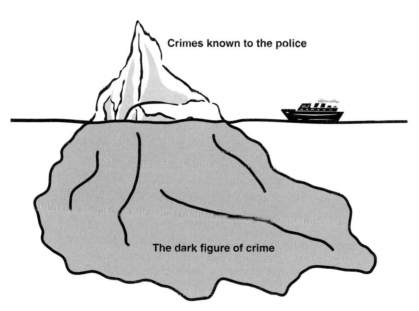

Crimes known to the police

The dark figure of crime

Figure 3-1   The Dark Figure of Crime

The Dark Figure of Crime

When measuring crime and allocating resources to control it, the differences between reported and unreported crime have substantial significance. We can make educated guesses about the amount of unreported crime that exists in any jurisdiction, but we can't know for sure its actual incidence.[3] This is called the **dark figure of crime** (see Figure 3-1).

For example, if a 16-year-old hits a 14-year-old because of a disagreement over a holding call in a flag football game, is it a criminal offense? If the game went on and the two youths maintained their friendship, was any social harm done? Should this assault be considered a criminal offense or even an assault?

If a 16-year-old punches a 14-year-old in the mouth while waiting at the bus stop, should that be considered a criminal offense? If the parents of the 14-year-old called the police, reported the incident to the school, and obtained a lawyer, should the case be treated differently than the flag football example?

By examining these two types of physical violence, we can see how a behavior's context can determine whether it's defined and measured as a criminal offense. Many

dark figure of crime
Crime that goes unreported to police and criminal justice officials and is never quantified.

The intentions of children are less clear than those of adults and are treated differently by parents, school administrators, and the juvenile justice system. Are these boys playing, fighting out of anger, or is one bullying the other? *(Courtesy Bonnie Kamin, PhotoEdit Inc.)*

behaviors (presumably very many) don't make it into the official crime statistics for a number of reasons. This dark figure of crime isn't quantifiable but must be considered when making criminal and juvenile justice policy.

One element of the dark figure of crime is unreported crime. A victim might not report an offense for a number of reasons.

- **The victim might not understand or believe an offense has been committed.**   Like the example of the boys' fight in the flag football game, some victims might not define a behavior as a criminal offense. A child who's being abused by his or her parents probably doesn't know that the parents' behavior is illegal and thinks that the beatings are because he or she is "bad."

- **The victim might lack faith in the system.**   Many victims don't report an offense because they don't believe the police will be successful in apprehending the offenders. Many thefts and larcenies go unreported because the value of the stolen goods is not significant enough to deal with the criminal justice system. This is particularly true if the value of the goods is less than one's insurance deductible. This is also true if the victim is a child. The child's parents might not consider the child's stolen item valuable enough to bother reporting the theft to law enforcement. Some parents might even consider the theft to be a valuable lesson to the child, saying, for example, "If you hadn't left your bicycle so close to the road, it wouldn't have gotten stolen!"

- **The victim might wish to protect the offender.**   Many violent offenses happen at home. Usually, it's cases of spouses assaulting one another and parents abusing their children. In each of these examples, the victims have an interest in keeping the crime a secret. If the unlawful behavior were to be fully prosecuted, the victim, especially a child, could suffer as much as the offender.

- **The victim might be guilty.**   When a drug deal goes bad, what can the victim do? The victim, maybe a teenager, paid good money for a pound of marijuana only to discover later that it's the common household spice oregano. Police officers aren't sympathetic to the victims of such fraudulent transactions, so they largely go unreported.[4]

- **Some offenses reported to the police don't get recorded as offenses.**   Police officers have discretion in deciding if a behavior constitutes a crime or is a serious enough offense to record.

These are but a few examples of why many offenses go unreported. The important thing to keep in mind, however, is that even unreported crime has negative consequences for society and that crime-control policy must fashion solutions that address unreported crime. Historically, rape is an underreported offense because the criminal justice process is so intrusive and embarrassing for the victim.[5] Those who observe criminal offenses also sometimes decline to report the offense, often because they don't want to go to the trouble of reporting it to police. Other reasons include these:

- Distrust of the police
- Recognition of a cultural code that demands that honorable people don't snitch or report crimes
- Fear of reprisals from the offender
- Involvement in an offense while observing the commission of another, possibly unrelated, offense

Although the actual dark figure of crime is unknowable, the criminal justice system has attempted to make reporting crime easier, more nonintrusive, and even patriotic. Many agencies have set up anonymous tip lines that allow callers to report crimes without becoming personally involved.[6] Further, researchers use a variety of methodologies that attempt to measure crime in different ways to correct for underreporting. Let's now examine the primary methods of measuring crime.

UNIFORM CRIME REPORTS

The best-known method for reporting crime in the United States is the ***Uniform Crime Reports*** (UCR). This is a highly coordinated effort in which almost every legal jurisdiction (over 17,000) reports the number of offenses, arrest statistics, and the characteristics of its agency to the Federal Bureau of Investigation (see Figure 3-2). This system of reporting crime, initiated in the 1920s by the International Association of Chiefs of Police, was designed to provide a comparative picture of the level of crime across jurisdictions, cities, and states. Collecting crime data in a consistent and uniform manner is a big step in providing lawmakers and criminal justice officials with the information they need to assess the nature and prevalence of crime.[7]

The strength of the UCR data is that each jurisdiction reports offenses according to a single set of parameters and a uniform set of definitions. Prior to 1930, each jurisdiction used its own criteria for defining offenses, and it was difficult to compare crime data among jurisdictions. Now crime data are collected according to two categories that are used to construct a comparative picture of crime.

The most important category is Part I offenses, which constitute what is referred to as *index crimes*. These eight offenses are murder and nonnegligent manslaughter, forcible rape, robbery, aggravated assault, burglary, larceny–theft, motor vehicle theft, and arson. The first four of these offenses are violent personal crimes, and the latter four are property crimes. Together they form the crime index used to compare offenses across jurisdictions. One way in which the UCR displays crime data is by the raw number of incidents of each offense. In this collection, cities with large populations will appear more dangerous than sparsely populated small towns or rural areas simply because more offenses are happening there. Therefore, to correct for population size, another measure is presented: the *crime rate*. Here the population is

Uniform Crime Reports
An annual publication from the Federal Bureau of Investigation that uses data from all participating U.S. law enforcement agencies to summarize the incidence and rate of reported crime.

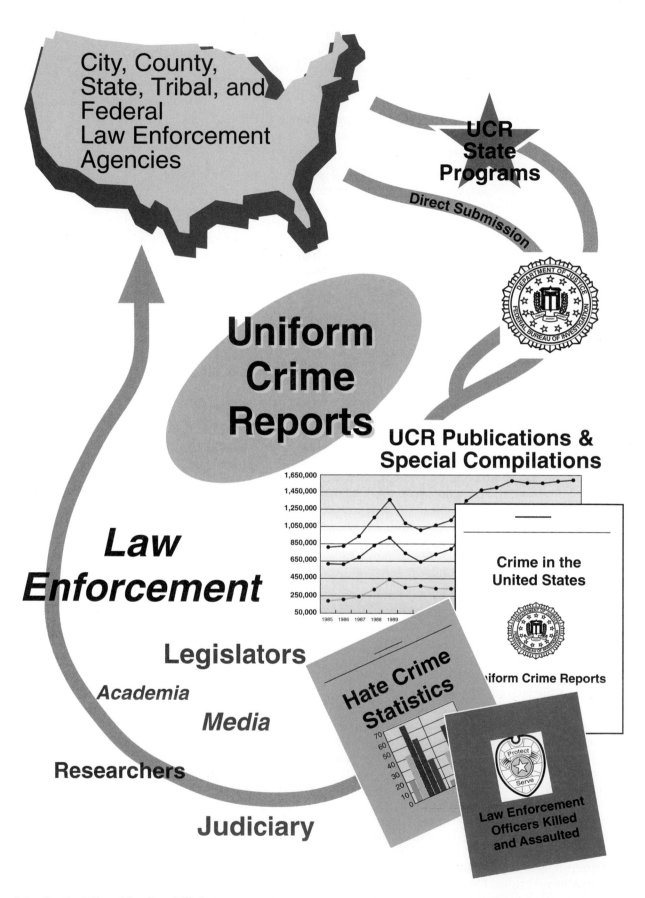

Figure 3-2 **How the *Uniform Crime Reports* Works**

Jurisdictions report statistics to state programs, as well as directly to the FBI, which compiles them into reports and publications. These are distributed to the public, including the reporting jurisdictions. *Source:* U.S. Department of Justice Federal Bureau of Investigation, *Uniform Crime Reporting Handbook,* www.fbi.gov/ucr/handbook/ucrhandbook04.pdf.

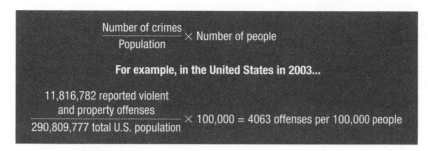

$$\frac{\text{Number of crimes}}{\text{Population}} \times \text{Number of people}$$

For example, in the United States in 2003...

$$\frac{11{,}816{,}782 \text{ reported violent and property offenses}}{290{,}809{,}777 \text{ total U.S. population}} \times 100{,}000 = 4063 \text{ offenses per } 100{,}000 \text{ people}$$

Figure 3-3   **How to Calculate a Crime Rate** *Source: Federal Bureau of Investigation, Crime in the United States, 2003* (Washington, DC: U.S. Government Printing Office, 2004), 71. Online at www.fbi.gov/ucr/cius_03/pdf/03sec2.pdf.

divided into a constant number (100,000) to come up with a comparative rate of crime (see Figure 3-3).

It is impossible to know with any certainty how many of these offenses were committed by juveniles. For many of the offenses, no perpetrator could be identified and, consequently, no one was arrested. We must also recognize that police departments are more likely to handle juveniles informally than they are adult offenders. Also, juveniles are more likely than adults to be caught, as they tend to commit their offenses publicly, in sight of patrolling police officers, and are less accomplished than adult offenders. These differences between adults and juveniles help to skew the statistics on juvenile delinquents.

Part II offenses capture an additional 21 offenses, ranging from forgery and counterfeiting to vagrancy and curfew violation. Some Part II offenses apply only to juveniles, such as runaways, curfew violations, or some loitering laws. Although more information is collected on Part I offenses, Part II offenses give a broader picture of illegal behavior for less serious and less dangerous offenses. Taken together, Parts I and II provide a picture of crime that can be monitored across jurisdictions and from year to year. There are, however, some concerns about just how accurately the numbers reflect the true incidence and rate of crime.

- **The hierarchy rule**   The UCR records only the most serious incident in a set of incidents. This means that if someone breaks into your home, kills your husband, beats your son, steals your car, and sets fire to your garage, only the killing of your husband is recorded in the UCR. The exception to the hierarchy rule is arson. For example, if one offense is arson in a set of offenses that also includes homicide, the arson must be recorded along with the homicide.[8]

- **Follow-up procedures**   The nature of a crime might change over time, and it's important that all jurisdictions adjust their crime figures according to the same procedures. For instance, an aggravated assault might turn into a murder if the victim dies from the injuries a month or two later. There is no way of knowing how diligently each reporting agency follows up on such cases. Although one agency might change the crime to a murder, another might leave it as an aggravated assault.[9]

- **Variations in definition**   Although the UCR attempts to get every agency on the same page when it comes to defining crime, there's a substantial amount of variation in local statutes. For instance, there might be ambiguity in how "carnal knowledge" is defined when dealing with rape cases. Some jurisdictions limit it to actual sexual intercourse, while others might use a more inclusive definition that covers other types of intimate behavior. Additionally, the definition of rape might vary across jurisdictions depending on whether the victim–offender relationship is restricted to strangers, whether they are acquaintances, or whether they are married.

- **Attempted offenses**   How do various jurisdictions code offenses that aren't completed? For example, a burglary in which a teenager breaks into a building and runs away before taking anything when an alarm goes off could be coded differently in different jurisdictions. Some might code it as a simple breaking and entering or as a case of vandalism, while others would code it as a burglary.

As we can see from these examples, the UCR is subject to some variation. Given these qualifications, the UCR is a wonderful tool for criminal justice practitioners, researchers, and the public in understanding crime and the workings of the criminal justice system. It represents a massive, nationwide, coordinated system dedicated to tracking crime. No other entity has been able to launch such an effort and, as imperfect as it is, the UCR is instrumental in the nation's efforts to understand and control crime.

Uniform Crime Reports and Juvenile Delinquency

clearance rate
The number of offenses that are cleared or "solved" by at least one offender being arrested, charged, and prosecuted.

arrest rate
The number of arrests made in a given year divided by population, to produce a measure that can be compared to other jurisdictions.

clearance by exceptional means
A special condition used by law enforcement to generate a clearance in the case of an offender who cannot be formally charged and prosecuted.

It isn't always possible to know the ages of those who break the law, but it is possible to know the ages of those who are arrested. UCR data capture the age of arrestees and make it possible to talk with a small degree of confidence about juvenile delinquency. Although many delinquents are never caught, and some delinquents get arrested repeatedly for multiple violations, there is reason to be confident in the juvenile delinquency figures. Basically, the rates of juvenile delinquency remain fairly constant from year to year. If they swung widely, we would be concerned about measurement errors and have less confidence. Because they seem fairly stable, we have some faith that changes in the rate of juvenile lawbreaking are what is actually being measured. For an in-depth look at the interpretation of statistics, see Crosscurrents 3.1.

There are some built-in limitations to the information that the UCR captures on juveniles. In many ways, the UCR is an excellent measure of what our criminal justice agencies do and a less reliable measure of the actual nature and frequency of crime. Some crimes are reported at a much greater rate than others. For instance, murder is reported at a very high rate. Why? First, there is usually a body lying around somewhere, and people tend to notice a dead body after a while. Although perpetrators might attempt to hide the body, there is still the likelihood of a great deal of physical evidence, such as bloodstains, hair fibers, and odors, which can bring inquiry. Second, the dead person is likely to be missed by family members, co-workers, or bill collectors. People can vanish into thin air, but someone usually notices the absence and notifies the authorities to the possibility of foul play.

Other offenses, such as vandalism and drug sales, can go virtually undetected. Vandalism, such as spray-painting a wall, can be fairly easy for youths to commit without getting caught. Offenses in which there's no direct victim, such as drug sales, are underreported because, when both seller and customer are satisfied with a transaction, there's little incentive to report anything to the police.[10]

Finally, UCR data can't give a comprehensive picture of crime because the data are heavily skewed toward street crime. There are other types of serious crime, such as white-collar crime, environmental crime, corporate crime, and organized crime, that the UCR doesn't adequately capture. Many of these types of crime never become known to the police and therefore never show up in the UCR figures. For what it's designed to do, the UCR does a commendable job. However, as students of the criminal and juvenile justice systems, we must be cognizant of the flawed and biased picture presented by the UCR. To this end, we now turn to other ways of measuring crime that can supplement the picture presented by the UCR.

Why Crime Statistics Don't Tell the Truth

Statistics are complicated. Collecting them is complicated, and interpreting them is even more complicated. Crime statistics are no exception. In fact, they may be some of the most cantankerous social statistics to deal with. This is because they don't represent reality but only vaguely reflect a small portion of it. So why does the government bother to collect crime statistics at all? Because they are the best and only way we have to understand crime. Crime statistics depict movement, not specifics. The statistics are inexact and loaded with errors, not because law enforcement agencies and researchers are bad at math or wish to be inaccurate, but because it's difficult to design a mathematical model to describe what can best be described as chaos. Society isn't a machine, and the larger a given social group, the less predictable it is. You might be able to collect enough data on two people to mathematically represent a set of their activities, such as lawbreaking behavior, but 296 million people present a different challenge.[1]

Collecting data on and correcting for every nuance in a human activity such as lawbreaking behavior would be an infinitely difficult and expensive task. Therefore, data-collection endeavors such as the *Uniform Crime Reports* take shortcuts. No one expects the UCR, or even the NIBRS, to accurately reflect crime. What we can gather from these data, however, is a sense of how people break the law and how often. Ironically, statistical efforts measure this by making the same intentional errors and taking the same shortcuts every time data are collected, giving researchers a set of stable numbers whose rise and fall is logical in that context.

For example, as you have learned from the chapter, the UCR only records data on the most serious offense in a set of offenses. Although it seems like the UCR is missing a lot of data this way—and it is—this method simplifies data collection and reporting. It also ensures fairly good data on the most serious offenses. Homicide is the most serious offense and will nearly always be recorded, so the UCR homicide data are about as reliable as such data get. The other factor contributing to reliability is that the UCR will always drop the less-serious offenses. Crime scholars know this and expect the data on, say, vandalism to represent somewhat less vandalism than there actually is. What is important here is, again, the movement of the numbers. In 1996, there were 320,900 recorded arrests for vandalism as opposed to 273,431 in 2003. Although the numbers don't represent absolute reality, we can assume that there was generally more vandalism in 1996 because more arrests for it were recorded. So crime data are still important, even if they are inexact and vague. For example, if homicide statistics were to jump sharply between the years of 2010 and 2015, law enforcement, crime scholars, and legislators would know that something in society was broken and take steps to address it.

This brings us to the difference between **arrest rates** and **clearance rates**. Arrest rates are the number of arrests made in a given year. Even if it's a case of mistaken identity and the person is out of jail two hours later, the arrest would still be counted. Arrest rates aren't the number of separate individuals arrested, because some individuals are arrested more than once a year. If Tom, John, and Randall were arrested in May 2000, then John was arrested again in October 2000, these would count as four arrests, although only three individuals were arrested. Arrest rates don't represent the number of offenses committed, because a series of offenses committed by one person may result in one arrest, and a single offense may result in multiple arrests. The latter situation is relatively common for juveniles because they are more likely than adults to offend in groups.

UCR clearance rates count the number of offenses cleared, or "solved," not the number of people arrested or prosecuted. The UCR accepts a clearance only if at least one person is arrested, charged, and prosecuted. This is usually noted in statistical publications as "cleared by arrest." Again, the arrest of one person may clear many offenses, and the arrest of several people may clear only one offense. If six people are arrested and prosecuted for one robbery, this counts as one clearance, not six. Clearances recorded in one calendar year may include offenses that occurred in prior years. For a clearance to enter the UCR, there doesn't have be a conviction and punishment, only a prosecution.

If an offender cannot be formally charged and prosecuted, an agency can sometimes still send the statistic to the UCR as a clearance. This is called **clearance by exceptional means**. The reasons that the police can't arrest, charge, and prosecute a suspect include the suspect's death (shot in a gun battle), the victim's refusal to cooperate, or the suspect's not being extradited from another jurisdiction because he or she is being prosecuted for an offense committed there.

The situation becomes more complicated when juveniles are involved. Any time a juvenile delinquent appears before authorities, it's counted as a clearance, even if the juvenile was never physically arrested. Also, if a clearance involves both adults and juveniles, for instance, a trio of vandals comprising two 16-year-olds and a 20-year-old, the clearance is counted as an adult clearance, and the two juveniles don't show up in any clearance statistics.

Juvenile offenses are more likely to be cleared than adult offenses, and juveniles are more likely to be caught and arrested than adults. Because

(Continued)

(Continued)

juveniles tend to commit single offenses in groups, clearance statistics better indicate the proportion of juvenile offenses than arrest statistics. For instance, if six juveniles spray paint a wall with graffiti, the incident results in six arrests, but the vandalism is treated as one offense and one clearance. (It gets better: if the six juveniles have been arrested before for vandalism, that would count as 12 juvenile vandalism arrests and two clearances, although the same six juveniles are responsible.) Adults, however, are less likely to offend in large groups, so there are more cases of one arrest leading to one clearance. The different behaviors of juveniles and adults are a good example of factors that skew crime statistics.

For example, the figure shows that in 2003 people under age 18 accounted for 30 percent of all burglary arrests and 17 percent of all burglaries cleared. So can we assume that juveniles were responsible for 17 percent of the recorded burglaries in the United States? No. Juveniles tend to be caught more easily than adults. This means more adjudications (remember that the juvenile justice system does not prosecute) and therefore more clearances. Many burglaries are committed for which there are no arrests and therefore no opportunity for clearances. Many of these burglaries were probably committed by adults who, because they were never caught or tried, never produced a clearance to be entered into the adult clearance statistics. This makes it look like juveniles are responsible for a higher proportion of burglaries and adults are responsible for a lower proportion of burglaries than is actually the case. However, recall our discussion of how the UCR counts a clearance involving both adults and juveniles only as an adult clearance. This statistical quirk, then, underestimates juvenile offenses, because, in this case, there are many juvenile offenses that never enter the clearance statistics because an adult was involved.

This tour of the statistical funhouse illustrates why it's important that the individual numbers in any given statistical report on crime can't be assumed to reflect absolute reality. It is the relationship between the numbers and the relationship between those numbers from year to year that are important. Time is also very important. The longer the span of time one considers when comparing data, the better idea one has of how offenders break the law and how often they do it.

Sources: Federal Bureau of Investigation, *Uniform Crime Reports: Crime in the United States, 2002* (Washington, DC: U.S. Government Printing Office, 2002), 222–223. Online at www.fbi.gov/ucr/cius_02/pdf/02crime.pdf; Federal Bureau of Investigation, *Uniform Crime Reports: Crime in the United States, 1996* (Washington, DC: U.S. Government Printing Office, 1997), 214. Online at www.fbi.gov/ucr/Cius_97/96CRIME/96crime4.pdf; Federal Bureau of Investigation, *Uniform Crime Reports: Crime in the United States, 2003* (Washington, DC: U.S. Government Printing Office, 2004), 270. Online at www.fbi.gov/ucr/cius_03/pdf/03sec4.pdf; Howard N. Snyder, *Juvenile Arrests, 2002* (Washington, DC: U.S. Government Printing Office, 2004), 2. Online at www.ncjrs.org/pdffiles1/ojjdp/204608.pdf.

1 As of November 2007, the Census Bureau estimated the U.S. population to be over 303 million. For current estimates, see the population clock at www.census.gov/.

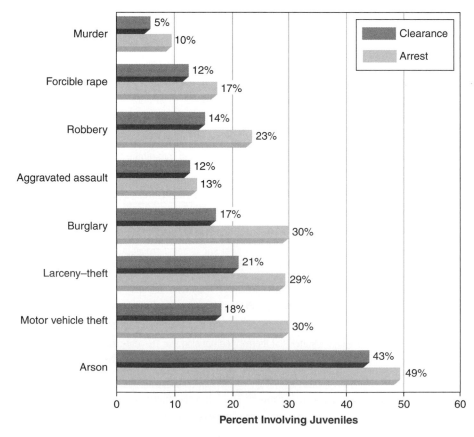

Source: Howard N. Snyder, *Juvenile Arrests, 2002* (Washington, DC: U.S. Government Printing Office, 2004), 2. Online at www.ncjrs.org/pdffiles1/ojjdp/204608.pdf.

SELF-REPORTED CRIME AND VICTIMIZATION SURVEYS

In the *Uniform Crime Reports*, law enforcement agencies report what they know about the amount and seriousness of crime. This gives us measures of arrests and offenses known to the police. The major weakness of the UCR is that the many offenses not known to the police, the dark figure of crime, aren't counted. However, researchers have developed some techniques for tapping into the dark figure of crime. The first technique we will discuss is self-report studies.

Self-report studies ask participants to tell researchers what offenses they have committed. These can be offenses for which they were caught and punished or offenses in which they were smart enough or lucky enough to escape detection.[11] Immediately, we can see some concerns of self-report studies. Why should respondents admit to offenses they have gotten away with? Presumably, offenders reporting their own offenses would be worried about giving away enough information so that they could be caught.[12] The reason that researchers can be fairly confident that respondents will report their own offenses is because the studies are anonymous. That is, respondents answer written questions without having to put their names on the answer sheet. The researchers, who are only interested in the types and levels of offenses committed, are then left with a hundred answer sheets and no way to link them to the respondents. Respondents are assured that the information they give won't be made available to law enforcement agencies and that the police won't come knocking.

Self-report studies give criminal justice scholars a different angle on the measurement of crime. Rather than having data filtered through law enforcement agencies, researchers are able to go directly to offenders and delinquents. The major presumed advantage is that these self-report studies will reveal crimes that aren't known to the police. However, the researchers can never know if the crimes they are capturing with self-report studies were ever reported to the police or not.

A Note on Method

The primary problems with self-report studies are the same as with any form of survey research. According to Clayton Mosher, Terance Miethe, and Dretha Phillips, two basic questions must be asked about survey research to determine its validity and reliability.[13]

1. Were the right people asked the right questions?

2. Did they answer truthfully?

The first question is difficult to deal with when measuring crime because of the issue of generalization. If the researcher were interested in drug use in a particular high school, taking a random sample of students from that school and asking them questions would be sufficient. However, if the researcher were interested in drug use in high schools in the United States, taking a sample from a single school wouldn't be adequate.

There are untold sources of possible measurement errors when a researcher collects information from a single school and tries to use the limited data to make statements about all the schools in the country. Schools vary by racial and ethnic composition, by the social and economic composition of the school district, by the availability of drugs in the community, and by the rules and cultures of each particular school.[14] It is unfair and inaccurate to say that schools in New York, California, and Texas have a drug problem just because a researcher found a high degree of self-reported drug use at a high school in Bremen, Georgia.

Often the sample for a research project is obtained because it's convenient. Students in a research methods class developing instruments such as questionnaires will often use their classmates to field-test the adequacy and clarity of the questions.

However, classmates won't provide an adequate test of the questions, because often they aren't competent to evaluate the underlying logic and structure of the questionnaire. They often know even less than the researcher about what questions to ask.

For instance, suppose students in a criminal justice research methods class are required to develop a self-report questionnaire on some aspect of crime, and one of them decides to study serial murder. This student reviews the literature and comes up with 20 questions that ask serial killers about their motivations for killing and their feelings of dominance and erotic excitement and then asks classmates to fill out the questionnaire. Presumably, none of the classmates is, or ever was, a serial killer, therefore rendering all of them incompetent to provide feedback on the questionnaire's validity. The trick is to get the questionnaire to people who are likely to provide good information. Doing a drug survey in an elite prep school will provide a certain type of information, maybe even a high level of drug use, but this information can't be generalized to all schools in the United States because the elite prep school isn't representative.

How does one go about finding a representative sample? First, the researcher must be clear about how far the results will be extended in terms of generalizability. If one wants to claim that the results are particular to a single school, it's permissible to sample within that school. However, if one wants to generalize to the city, state, or nation, one must have a representative sample drawn from that population. The problem quickly becomes one of time and resources, and trying to get a nationwide picture of crime can be cumbersome and expensive. Often researchers will select specific cities and then say that, for the purposes of the research, they will assume no large systematic differences exist between the chosen cities and other cities. Survey research involves compromises. The goal is to get as representative a sample as possible within the budget and resources available. Additionally, the researchers should specify how their sample was chosen and resist making claims that the data can't support.

As we can see, asking the right people the right questions can be challenging. However, the problem of getting people to tell the truth can be even more difficult. This is especially true when dealing with questionnaires that request information about crime and delinquency. The problems of truth-telling on self-report studies can be of two varieties.

1. **Underreporting of crime.**   Individuals have many reasons to underreport their deviant acts.

   - **Fear of arrest.**   If delinquents believe they might be arrested for admitting to unlawful behaviors, they won't report them in self-report studies. Although researchers might go to great lengths to assure confidentiality, some youths will suspect a law enforcement trick and under-report their delinquent activities.

   - **Embarrassment.**   Some youths have committed unlawful behaviors and are reluctant to acknowledge their acts to anyone, including themselves. They are embarrassed and ashamed of their behavior and are unwilling to have it recorded anywhere.

   - **Fear of action.**   Someone who has a thriving business dealing drugs at school is unlikely to report that the school has a problem. If the truth were known, all kinds of bad things could happen, including police officers working undercover and drug dogs brought in to sniff lockers and students. Some students, therefore, don't want the truth to be known.

2. **Overreporting of crime.**   Some students will purposely overreport deviant acts.

   - **As a joke.**   Students might think it funny to make the school look like a haven for drug addicts. They decide to have fun with the researchers by giving wild and unsubstantiated claims. Unfortunately, the researchers have little way of knowing the students are being playful and might report the exaggerated responses as evidence of a drug problem in the school.

- **As posturing.**   Some students will use the self-report study to give classmates the impression that they are much more involved in a criminal lifestyle than is actually true. Although these studies are anonymous to researchers, these wannabe criminals might try to earn a reputation among their friends by telling them that they reported several crimes on the self-report study. (For an ethical exercise concerning this, see Focus on Ethics 3.1.)

3.1   FOCUS *on* ETHICS

THE DOPE ON SCHOOL

You are finishing your master's degree in criminal justice at a large Southern university, and you suddenly find yourself in a real pickle. Your major professor has just resigned from your thesis committee because she has accepted a job to be a dean at another university. The person she has recommended to replace her is a bright, young, untenured assistant professor who has been at the university for only four years. You are ready to collect the data for your project comparing drug use by high school freshmen against that of high school seniors. You plan to track the temptations, opportunities, and attitudes of students as they progress through their high school years.

All the groundwork has been laid for your research. You have had it approved by the university's institutional review board, you have secured funding from a prestigious foundation, and you have the blessing of the school board. You are clearly the star of the graduate program, and your former major professor who helped you design the research project wants you to follow her to her new university, which has a top-flight doctoral program. Everything seems to be on the fast track until you get a call to meet with the university president.

"Young lady," the president says to you, "I'd like you to do me a big favor."

"Certainly," you reply, wondering what you are getting yourself into.

"I've heard about this research project that you plan to do for your master's thesis, and I want you to reconsider. I don't think this project fits with the best interests of the university so I'm asking you not to do it."

"Excuse me?" you say. "It's a bit late to stop now. I've already been approved by my major professor, my department, the IRB, my funding agency, and the student government. They all think it is a wonderful project. Why would I want to shut it down now?"

The president explains that she has received a phone call from the mayor. Apparently, the high school has been recently declared by the state to be a model high school and is now part of a statewide model school project that channels funds to schools that receive the distinction. For this high school, the money has already been earmarked for a study-abroad student exchange program. Next year's seniors are set to go to Spain, and some Spanish students are ready to visit the town's high school. The mayor tells the university president that if any drug use is exposed at the school for any reason, the school is certain to lose its model distinction and its funding, and no students will get to travel anywhere.

"I'm asking you to voluntarily discontinue this project," the president says.

"And if I don't?"

"You don't want to put me in that position. I'm asking you politely to do something for the good of the high school and this town. If you want to put your own selfish, limited agenda first, then we will have to see what happens."

You leave the president's office stunned. You can't believe what has just happened, and you quickly go to your department and find your new major professor. When you tell him what the president demanded of you, your professor informs you that he has already spoken with the president and that he will resign from your committee if you continue your research. He says that he is going up for promotion next year and that the president hinted that your project could be a factor in the school's decision. Because your professor has a wife and three children to consider, he claims that he does not want to get involved in such a high-level political firestorm.

You go to your former major professor and tell her your problem. She is outraged by the president's behavior and promises to help you fight the decision. However, as she is leaving the school when the term is over next month and moving across the country to her new school, she warns you that her political clout is negligible. She says the best thing she can do for you is to help you get into the master's program at her new school, where you would need to take several classes before you could do a thesis.

What Do You Do?

1. Stay and fight to do the research project knowing it will be an uphill battle against the president. You know that it will put the president in an awkward position to try to stop you and that if you call her bluff, you might win.

2. Negotiate with the president and your new major professor for resources to do another research project. If they want you to do the high school a favor, then they should cough up a grant to allow you to embark on a different, but equally significant project.

3. Follow your former major professor to her new university although it will cost you an extra year of graduate work.

4. When you get your doctorate, you plan to specialize in juvenile justice and work with young people both inside and outside the juvenile justice system. Your research may result in some good for the nation's juveniles, but it could possibly hurt the kids who go to high school in your town. Do you stay and pursue the research even though it could hurt the very people you are trying to help?

These sources of measurement error based on under- or overreporting of crime on self-report studies are difficult to gauge. Researchers will try to prevent them as much as possible by using tactics such as internal consistency checks, in which the same question is asked in several slightly different ways to see if the respondent provides the same answer. Sources of error other than purposeful lying are difficult to evaluate. Perhaps the greatest is the reliance on the respondent's memory. When asked questions such as "How many offenses have you committed in the past six months?" it might be difficult for respondents to remember exactly when an offense was committed. It is hard for anyone to remember the exact date of conversations, events, or disputes. Other problems relating to the respondent's quality of recall depend on the gravity of the offense. A respondent might describe an aggravated assault in which a weapon was used and the victim suffered substantial injury as nothing more than a minor fight.

What Do Self-Report Studies Report?

Self-report studies are extremely valuable because they give us insight into the picture of crime that isn't captured by UCR data. For the most part, self-report studies verify some of the conclusions that researchers have already drawn. For instance, boys report a substantially greater number and variety of offenses than do girls. Additionally, and not surprisingly, older adolescents report more offenses than younger adolescents. This isn't simply because the older adolescents have had more time to commit the acts, because that issue is controlled for by asking only about recent behavior. Rather, it appears that older youths commit more offenses because they are willing to take more risks.

Perhaps the most significant finding from self-report studies is that delinquency is more evenly spread throughout the socioeconomic classes than it appears

Teenagers break the law more often than young children because they are willing to take more risks. *(Courtesy Gabe Palmer, CORBIS-NY)*

from UCR data alone.[15] Because self-report studies focus on more types of crime than the UCR's street crime-laden Part I Index offenses, they are able to tap into a greater variety of criminal behavior. Much of the crime reported by self-report studies is trivial. Rapes and armed robberies aren't generally found, but this is because these events are rare, especially among the types of school-age populations that are generally selected to participate in self-report studies. This type of research is especially effective in measuring offenses without direct victims, such as drug use and underage drinking. By doing youth self-report studies annually, researchers can follow trends in deviant behavior. By sampling high school seniors over decades, it's possible to detect changes in the ebb and flow of drinking and drug-use patterns.

Victimization Surveys

In addition to law enforcement agencies and offenders, there is another set of informed individuals who can shed light on the amount and seriousness of crime. Crime victims can provide an entirely different picture. This picture is valuable because it taps into some very important dimensions that the other two miss. Perhaps the most important aspect of crime that victimization surveys capture is the actual effect that lawbreaking has on victims. By giving voice to crime victims, we can learn something about the human costs that the numbers and percentages miss.

Compared to the *Uniform Crime Reports*, victimization surveys are rather new, having been around for less than 50 years. However, they have become an instrumental part of drawing the picture of crime. Criminologists William Doerner and Steven Lab have traced the development of victimization surveys through four generations of improving their sophistication and comprehensiveness. These four generations of victimization surveys reveal a great deal about not only the level of crime, but also about our ability to measure it.[16]

- **First-generation victimization surveys** Victimization surveys started out in the mid-1960s as efforts to assess if citizens could be asked about sensitive information concerning their experiences as crime victims. One of the first surveys, conducted by the National Opinion Research Center (NORC), found that the *Uniform Crime Reports* underreported many offenses, especially rapes and burglaries.

- **Second-generation victimization surveys** The most important step in second-generation surveys was the attempt to verify the respondents' information by checking the offenses that individuals claimed they were victims of. According to Doerner and Lab, victims recalled less about their crimes as time passed. Respondents were able to remember events that happened three months ago much better than events that happened a year ago. Victims also tended to telescope events, meaning that they unconsciously moved up their recollections of when events happened to more recent dates.

- **Third-generation victimization surveys** Third-generation surveys are best illustrated by the 1972 National Crime Survey, in which over 12,000 households were surveyed multiple times. The third generation of surveys also tried to tap into the victimization of businesses. These efforts provided some useful data but were eventually discontinued because the results were deemed not to be worth the expenditure of resources.[17]

- **Fourth-generation victimization surveys** These surveys are now called the National Crime Victimization Survey. One of the most visible improvements has been the introduction of computer-assisted telephone interviews (CATI), which help the interviewer avoid miscoded data and assist in the selection of the correct questions for individuals based on their answers to other questions.[18]

MEASURES OF YOUTHS AS DELINQUENTS AND VICTIMS

Adults commit more offenses than youths. Although this might be surprising, it shouldn't be. The reason that adults out-offend youth is because there are so many more adults to get into trouble. Additionally, youths, especially the younger ones, are subject to a great deal more supervision than are adults and don't have the opportunity to get into trouble at the same rate. What is apparent is that the adults who do violate the law are clustered around the lower end of the age scale, and their offenses seem to be an extension of juvenile delinquency. As Figure 3-4 shows, lawbreaking is still a young person's game, peaking in the late teens and early twenties and dropping off steeply after that. However, what needs to be kept in mind is that, for many offenders, crime is cumulative. The earlier that youths start to participate in criminal activity, the more likely they are to become heavily involved.

When discussing juvenile delinquency, we must remember that all offenses aren't equal. When raw statistics are considered, it isn't so apparent that most delinquent acts are property offenses as opposed to violent offenses. Although juveniles account for 16 percent of all arrests, they account for 15 percent of the arrests for violent crimes and 29 percent of the arrests for property crimes (see Figure 3-5).

Homicide, forcible rape, and aggravated assault rank among the lowest incidences of juvenile delinquency. The types of offenses (that aren't **status offenses**) most often committed by juveniles are arson and vandalism. In 2005, people under age 18 accounted for 49 percent of those arrested for arson and 37 percent of those arrested for vandalism. Offenses for which juveniles comprise the lowest proportion of arrests are driving under the influence (1 percent), prostitution (2 percent), fraud (3 percent), and drunkenness (3 percent).[19] These figures aren't unusual when we consider the limited opportunities that youths have to participate in these types of behaviors. For instance, to be arrested for fraud, one must have a certain level of financial sophistication. Youths are unlikely to enter positions in which they are given the responsibility to safeguard money, so they have few occasions to engage in fraudulent activity. By contrast, youths have ample time and opportunity to engage in vandalism.

What the statistics don't show us, however, is that these offenses aren't evenly distributed over age, gender, and geographic location. For instance, we know that boys commit more offenses than girls, older teens more than younger teens, and urban neighborhoods experience more unlawful behavior than small towns or rural areas. One example of this uneven distribution of crime can be seen in the arrests of

Instant Recall from Chapter 1

status offense

An act considered to be a legal offense only when committed by a juvenile, and one that can be adjudicated only in a juvenile court.

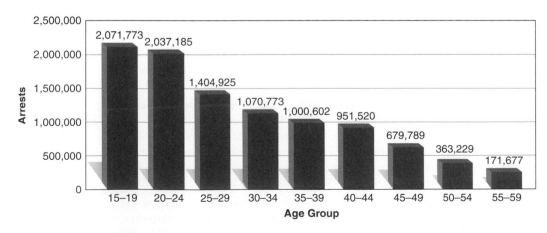

Figure 3-4   Number of Arrests by Age, 2005

These data represent the number of people arrested. It's important to remember that some people might be arrested more than once in a a year, so some of the statistics represent multiple arrests of the same person. *Source:* Federal Bureau of Investigation, *Crime in the United States, 2005: Uniform Crime Reports,* www.fbi.gov/ucr/05cius/data/table_38.html.

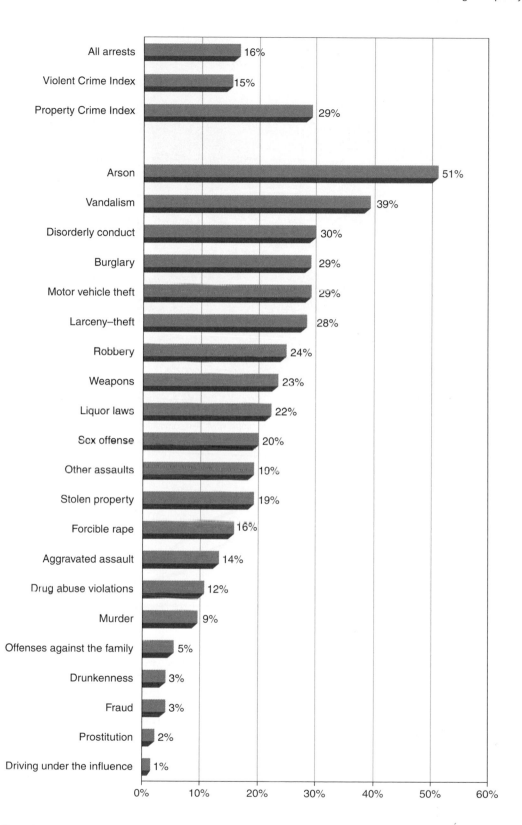

Figure 3-5 **Juvenile Proportion of Arrests by Offense, 2003** *Source: OJJDP Statistical Briefing Book,* February 28, 2005, ojjdp.ncjrs.org/ojstatbb/crime/qa05102.asp?qaDate= 2005022. Adapted from Howard N. Snyder (forthcoming), *Juvenile Arrests 2003* (Washington, DC: Office of Juvenile Justice and Delinquency Prevention).

Youths have more time and opportunity to break the law in simple ways, like committing vandalism, than they do to engage in more serious and sophisticated offenses like white-collar crime. *(Courtesy Stephen Frisch, Stock Boston)*

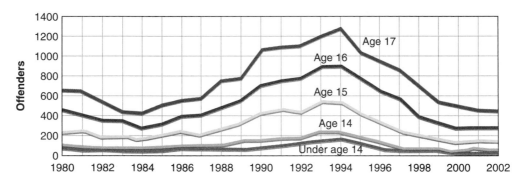

Figure 3-6   Known Juvenile Homicide Offenders by Age, 1980–2002 *Source: OJJDP Statistical Briefing Book, September 30, 1999, ojjdp.ncjrs.org/ojstatbb/offenders/ qa03104.asp. Adapted from Howard N. Snyder and Melissa Sickmund, Juvenile Offenders and Victims: 1999 National Report (Washington, DC: Office of Juvenile Justice and Delinquency Prevention, 1999), 53. Data Source: Federal Bureau of Investigation, Supplementary Homicide Reports for the Years 1980–1997 [machine-readable data files], Washington, DC: FBI.*

juveniles for homicide. Figure 3-6 shows how arrests of juveniles accused of homicide varied over the years between 1980 and 2002. The difference between 14-year-old juvenile arrestees and those 17 years old is dramatic. There is a consistent pattern of older juveniles being arrested for homicide more than those who are a year younger. For example, 15-year-olds are always arrested for homicide more than 14-year-olds, even as the general number of arrests rises and falls.

Youths as Victims

Who are the victims of these youth homicides? For the most part, youths kill other youths. The number of juvenile homicide victims peaked in 1993 at 2,880 and declined to 1,610 victims in 2000. Figure 3-7 shows the number of juvenile homicide victims from 1980 to 2002. In addition to showing how the victimization rate peaked in the mid-1990s, Figure 3-7 shows that the greatest number of victims are those between the ages of 15 and 17. At this age, teenagers are outside the home, away from adult

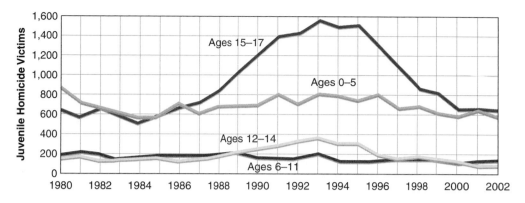

Figure 3-7 **Juvenile Homicide Victims** *Source:* Howard N. Snyder and Melissa Sickmund, *Juvenile Offenders and Victims: 2006 National Report* (Washington, DC: U.S. Department of Justice, Office of Justice Programs, Office of Juvenile Justice and Delinquency Prevention, 2006), 21. Online at ojjdp.ncjrs.org/ojstabb/nr2006/downloads/NR2006.pdf.

Table 3-1 **Acquaintances of Murder Victims**

Gender and Age	Percent of Offenders		
	Family	Acquaintance	Stranger
Males	32%	51%	18%
0–11	66	29	5
12–17	8	66	26
Females	50%	40%	10%
0–11	67	28	5
12–17	19	63	18

Source: Paul D. Harms and Howard N. Snyder, *Trends in the Murder of Juveniles: 1980–2000* (Washington, DC: Office of Juvenile Justice and Delinquency Prevention, September 2004), 7. Online at www.ncjrs.org/pdffiles1/ojjdp/194609.pdf.

supervision. Much of the increase in juvenile homicide was due to gang activity and the emergence of the crack-cocaine market.[20]

For younger children, problems with family or friends led to their homicides. Regardless of age, children are more likely to be killed by a family member or an acquaintance than by a stranger. Between 1980 and 2000, 26 percent of the offenders who killed juveniles were unknown. However, an interesting pattern is observed in those homicides of juveniles in which the offender is known. Table 3-1 shows that for juvenile females 50 percent of their killers were family members, while only 32 percent of juvenile males were killed by family members. These percentages suggest that young males are outside the home more often, where they have more opportunities than females to engage in risky behaviors with strangers.[21] The reason that females are killed by family members so often is because they are under the control of older family members so much of the time. Again, we must be careful when discussing crime levels using only percentages. Because so many males are killed in relation to females, the fact that many males are killed by family members is masked when looking at raw percentages. The home is just as dangerous for males as it is for females; it's just that the streets are even more precarious.

When discussing victimization rates and numbers, there is a tendency to forget the tragedy of youth victimization. Children are truly victims because they don't participate in creating the conditions or environment that encourages crime. Homicide cases in which the victim is the first to use violence are called **victim-precipitated** homicides.[22] Gang violence, drug deals gone wrong, and barroom brawls can produce victims that don't engender sympathy from the police or public. The feeling is that the victim "asked for it" or "got what was coming." There is an entirely different attitude toward child victims, however. No child asks to be victimized. Children are under the control of parents, teachers, older siblings,

victim precipitation
A situation in which a crime victim plays an active role in initiating an offense or escalating it.

or others who are charged with protecting their welfare. When these responsible others make mistakes that harm children or, worse, cause that harm themselves, it's especially unfortunate. Children can get into trouble and engage in dangerous behaviors, but society's attitude is that it's the responsible adult who's problematic, not the wayward child.[23]

SEXUAL VICTIMIZATION   The sexual victimization of children is a major concern for parents, law enforcement, school administrators, and the media. Sexual assaults account for just over half of the juvenile violent-crime victims known to police, with age 14 being the most frequent age of female victims of sexual assault and age 5 being the most frequent age for male victims (see Figure 3-8).

Children are powerless to prevent their victimization when the offender is older, stronger, more worldly, and in a position of responsibility. Although we suspect the number of sexual assaults on children is substantial, official crime records don't clearly represent the problem. The *Uniform Crime Reports* is reasonably good at reporting rapes that are known to the police, but it doesn't gather information about other types of sexual assaults, such as forcible sodomy, sexual assault with an object, and forcible fondling. Victimization surveys reveal a good bit more about how children are sexually victimized, but they don't provide an adequate reflection of the relationship between the child and the offender.

National Incident-Based Reporting System

A crime reporting system in which each separate offense in a crime is described, including data describing the offender(s), victim(s), and property.

A more recently developed system of reporting crime provides a better estimate of the sexual victimization of children. The **National Incident-Based Reporting System** (NIBRS) comprises participating law enforcement agencies that report crime in a different and more detailed way than the UCR. The UCR reports only the most serious offense in any incident. However, the NIBRS records every offense that happens in any criminal incident, so it provides a better picture of the prevalence of the less-serious offenses that the UCR misses. The NIBRS captures a wide range of information, including demographic information on all victims; the level of victim injury; victims' perceptions of offenders' ages, gender, and race; and victim–offender relationships. Additionally, the NIBRS collects information on the location of the offense, weapons used, and dates and times of the offense.[24]

Relatively few law enforcement agencies participate in the NIBRS, so although it provides a more detailed picture of crime, it can't provide a comprehensive one.

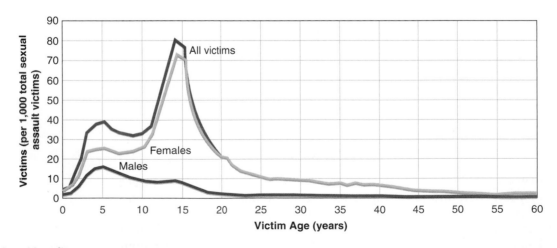

Figure 3-8   Sexual Assaults

Of sexual assaults that were reported to police, 67 percent of female victims and 88 percent of male victims were under age 18. *Source:* Howard N. Snyder and Melissa Sickmund, *Juvenile Offenders and Victims: 2006 National Report* (Washington, DC: U.S. Department of Justice, Office of Justice Programs, Office of Juvenile Justice and Delinquency Prevention, 2006), 31. Analyses of the FBI's National Incident-Based Reporting System master files for the years 2000 and 2001 [machine-readable data files]. Online at ojjdp.ncjrs.org/ojstatbb/nr2006/downloads/NR2006.pdf.

Because the NIBRS represents less than 10 percent of the U.S. population, it's difficult to generalize its results with any confidence.[25] However, with these qualifications clearly stated and understood, the NIBRS can provide a valuable angle from which to view the problem of child sexual victimization.

Table 3-2 shows the age profile of victims of sexual assault. It is most informative to look at the percentage of youths who are victims of forcible rape compared to adults. Those under 18 years of age account for 45.8 percent of the rapes. However, when other sexual offenses are considered, the percent of juvenile victims skyrockets: forcible sodomy (78.8 percent), sexual assault with an object (75.2 percent), and forcible fondling (83.8 percent). The single age that showed the greatest risk of sexual victimization was 14. However, for some offenses, such as sexual assault with an object, the age of greatest risk was much younger, as shown in Figure 3-9.

When considering the sexual victimization of children, another feature that jumps out of the data is the prevalence of female victims. At every level of the age profile, juvenile females stand a greater risk of victimization than do juvenile males. Figure 3-10 shows that, although both males and females show a greater risk of victimization at age 4, for females age 14 there is a substantially greater incidence of sexual assault.

The NIBRS provides an alternative look at the crime picture. It shouldn't be thought of as a replacement for other types of reporting efforts, but rather as a

Table 3-2   Age Profile of the Victims of Sexual Assault

Victim Age	All Sexual Assault	Forcible Rape	Forcible Sodomy	Sexual Assault with Object	Forcible Fondling
Total	100.0%	100.0%	100.0%	100.0%	100.0%
0 to 5	14.0%	4.3%	24.0%	26.5%	20.2%
6 to 11	20.1	8.0	30.8	23.2	29.3
12 to 17	32.8	33.5	24.0	25.5	34.3
18 to 24	14.2	22.6	8.7	9.7	7.7
25 to 34	11.5	19.6	7.5	8.5	5.0
Above 34	7.4	12.0	5.1	6.8	3.5

Source: Howard N. Snyder, *Sexual Assault of Young Children as Reported to Law Enforcement: Victim, Incident, and Offender Characteristics* (Washington, DC: Bureau of Justice Statistics, July 2000), 2. Online at www.ojp.usdoj.gov/bjs/pub/pdf/saycrle.pdf.

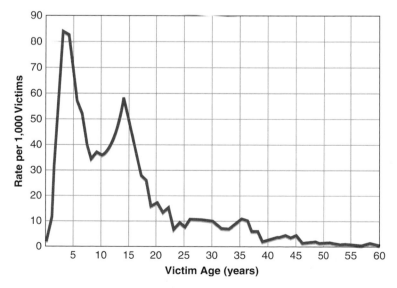

Figure 3-9   Sexual Assault with an Object *Source:* Howard N. Snyder, *Sexual Assault of Young Children as Reported to Law Enforcement: Victim, Incident, and Offender Characteristics* (Washington, DC: Bureau of Justice Statistics, July 2000), 3. Online at www.ojp.usdoj.gov/bjs/pub/pdf/saycrle.pdf.

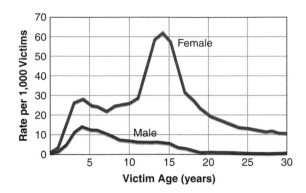

Figure 3-10   Age Distribution of Sexual Assault Victims by Gender *Source:* Howard N. Snyder, *Sexual Assault of Young Children as Reported to Law Enforcement: Victim, Incident, and Offender Characteristics* (Washington, DC: Bureau of Justice Statistics, July 2000), 4. Online at www.ojp.usdoj.gov/bjs/pub/pdf/saycrle.pdf.

supplement. Because it's costlier and more labor intensive, it's unlikely that it will ever obtain the status and funding of the UCR. However, it might not need to in order to be a useful tool. Even though it has limitations—it gathers samples that aren't representative of the country—it does help to shine a light on the dark figure of crime, because it includes all the offenses that occur in any single criminal event, rather than simply the most serious offense, as is the case with the UCR. For the purposes of this chapter, this feature of reporting every offense is important, because it reveals a great deal more about the victimization of children than would normally be captured.

EFFECTS OF YOUTH VICTIMIZATION   The victimization of young people is a major concern for several reasons. Although the intent here isn't to argue that adults don't significantly suffer from crime, it's worth noting that youths, especially children, can suffer in different ways, aside from not precipitating their victimization.

- **Ignorance of victimization**   Children, especially young children, might unknowingly be crime victims. They don't know what constitutes criminal behavior, so they don't know that it should be reported. When friends or family members sexually or emotionally abuse them, children might mistake the attention for nurturing and love. Often, it's only after children become adults that they are able to identify and label the actions as abuse.

- **Long-lasting harm**   The violation of trust in those who are supposed to be responsible for their welfare can have a deep and long-lasting effect on child victims. Often, the criminal behavior of adults can be traced back to the abuse and neglect they experienced as children. Trauma resulting from childhood victimization can lie dormant in a child's psyche and not be manifested for years until it emerges in one of a variety of forms, ranging from aggressive and violent behavior to being submissive and withdrawn.

- **Guilt**   Children can be convinced that the offenses committed against them are actually their own fault. When a father is incarcerated for sexual abuse, the child might interpret, sometimes with the help of the mother, the event as the child's fault for reporting the offense.

- **Permanent physical injuries**   Because children's bodies aren't fully developed, any physical injury can become permanent. Some parents might slap their child's hand as opposed to spanking in the belief that it's less harmful. However, the carpal bones in a child's hand aren't fully developed, and the punishment can cause arrested development. Children who are spanked violently on the buttocks might suffer damage to nerve endings, bladders, and pelvic bones. While perhaps well-meaning, this type of punishment can have greater ramifications than envisioned by parents.[26]

- **Family devastation**   When a child is the victim of a homicide, the effect on the family can be more severe than if the loss is of another member of the family. Parents invest hopes and dreams in their children and can feel particularly guilty when the child is lost as the result of crime.

These are but a few reasons why the victimization of children is detrimental to their development; however, these harms are all at the individual level and directly affect specific children. There is another factor in how children are affected by crime that isn't on the list. To some extent, the nature of how children interact with their environment has changed. Many parents are so concerned about their children's safety that they seldom let them out of the sight of responsible adults. A couple of generations ago, children would freely roam their neighborhoods or play unsupervised with other children. Today, many parents, who are often criticized as "helicopter parents," schedule their children's playdates and send them to supervised after-school programs or day care instead of letting them freely play and explore.[27] The nature of childhood might be undergoing subtle but fundamental changes because of parental perceptions of juvenile crime and victimization.

A Typology of Juvenile Delinquents

All juvenile delinquency isn't caused by the same factors and isn't equally serious. A **typology** of juvenile delinquents is useful in understanding the differences in types of juvenile delinquency. A typology is simply a conceptual grouping of items into categories so that they can be considered separately and compared. The creating of typologies is one of the first steps in the scientific method, and a good typology should be mutually exclusive and exhaustive. *Mutually exclusive* means that an item should fit into one and only one category. *Exhaustive* means that every item fits into a category. Sometimes, researchers will add the category of "other" to capture all the cases that don't fit neatly into their schema.

typology
A systematic classification of types.

Our typology of juvenile delinquents is neither mutually exclusive nor exhaustive. Many delinquents could fit into more than one category, and some delinquents wouldn't fit anywhere. However, this doesn't mean that our typology isn't useful in differentiating among the types and seriousness of juvenile delinquency. On the contrary, it provides a starting point from which to evaluate the seriousness of delinquent behavior and can point the way toward appropriate treatment or punishment. The typology presented here is designed to illustrate the major categories of juvenile delinquents.

STATUS OFFENDERS   Status offenders are youths who have done things that aren't criminal offenses but are considered undesirable for young people to do. If these behaviors were committed by an adult, the state wouldn't intervene. Therefore, status offenses are activities that are specified as offenses strictly because of the offender's age. Status offenses include underage drinking, curfew violations, underage smoking, running away, truancy, and being incorrigible. How serious are these offenses? Considered individually, each offense might appear to be trivial. However, when they occur in combination over a long period of time, they can signal the onset of more serious delinquency.

Although a juvenile might have a legitimate reason to run away from home, such as an abusive parent, where the juvenile goes is important. Juveniles whose destination is the street are in danger of becoming involved in more serious offenses. Status offenses are enacted for the welfare of the child, rather than the protection of society. They are considered the least-serious offenses but might actually be an indicator of

Status offenses, such as these young girls smoking cigarettes, can often draw a youth into the juvenile justice system.
(Courtesy Mark Peterson, Corbis Bettmann)

future criminality. There is a legitimate debate about what to do with status offenders so that they aren't drawn into the juvenile justice system.

PROPERTY OFFENDERS   Juveniles are responsible for a significant percentage of property offenses, which include arson, vandalism, burglary, larceny-theft, and motor vehicle theft (refer back to Figure 3-5). This is because these are the offenses that juveniles have the opportunity to commit. For instance, it's easier for them to break into cars and steal audio equipment rather than to embezzle money from a bank.

DRUG USERS AND ABUSERS   Drug and alcohol use by juveniles is a concern that has plagued parents, teachers, and juvenile justice officials for decades. Youths typically begin to test the boundaries of appropriate behavior during the adolescent years. In some ways, they are simply mimicking adult behavior, and in other ways they are rebelling against conventional norms and seeking a thrill by breaking the law.

The actual danger of drug use varies according to the drugs used and the context in which they are consumed.[28] Although it can't be argued that any recreational drugs are good for children, there is a consensus that some drugs are worse than others. For instance, beer, wine, and marijuana aren't considered to be as harmful as vodka, crack cocaine, and heroin. Parents have real concerns, however, if their child drinks a six-pack of beer and gets behind the wheel of an automobile. The dangerousness of drugs and alcohol is difficult to define without considering the context. Many young people have violated these laws and gone on to lead productive lives as college professors, doctors, business executives, and politicians, including presidents.

GANG MEMBERS   Gang membership is highly correlated with delinquent behavior. This isn't surprising, since involvement with illegal activity gives gang identity much

Some gangs specialize in activities such as selling illegal drugs. *(Courtesy Spencer Grant, PhotoEdit Inc.*

of its meaning. Whether it's a traditional street gang that struggles to define and protect its turf from other gangs or a gang that deals in drugs, prostitution, and gambling, gangs are almost by definition criminal organizations. Joining a gang often requires breaking the law as an initiation rite and, in some neighborhoods, gang membership is inevitable, because being unaffiliated leaves one open to exploitation from every gang. Gangs are involved in a wide range of illegal activity. Although some will specialize in particular offenses such as motor vehicle theft or drug sales, many other gangs engage in opportunistic criminal behaviors ranging from assault to drug dealing to larceny.[29] Some scholars have argued that the majority of delinquent acts are committed by gang members.

CHRONIC AND VIOLENT JUVENILE DELINQUENTS   The final category is that of chronic and violent delinquents. Some youths commit an inordinate number of offenses. They are repeat offenders who are continually in and out of juvenile training facilities. Some of these youths are violent delinquents who start as school bullies and graduate to assault and robbery.[30] Some are disturbed children who commit specialized offenses such as arson. Finally, some are extremely violent youths who kill others for a variety of reasons, such as revenge against parents, hatred of schoolmates, or terrorizing minority groups. These youths might have long criminal histories or commit heinous offenses with little or no warning. It is these types of delinquents who have their cases waived to the adult court system.

The juvenile justice system, which is designed to work in the best interests of the child, is ill equipped to deal with serious delinquents who commit high-profile offenses that the public wants to see punished. This is the type of offender who draws negative publicity to the shortcomings of the juvenile justice system and has politicians calling for get-tough-on-crime legislation.

PREDICTING DELINQUENCY

It should be clear by now that measuring crime, especially juvenile delinquency, is an inexact science. Because of the dark figure of crime, which can only be estimated, and the way the UCR documents only the most serious offense in a law-breaking incident, the official statistics must be used carefully. Although various attempts to measure crime require a great deal of effort and expense, they can only approximate the actual level of crime. If measuring crime is so difficult, what about predicting it? Law enforcement policy-makers are charged not only with responding to crime, but also with trying to prevent it. How successful are they in forecasting illegal behavior? The short answer to this question is they aren't that successful. Therefore, it's extremely useful to examine the problems of attempting to forecast delinquency.

Here Come the Superpredators

superpredator

A term coined by John Dilulio in 1995 to describe a cohort of children who were supposed to grow up to be particularly violent juvenile offenders because of poverty, maternal drug abuse, and other factors.

In the mid-1990s, several prominent criminologists made frightening predictions about an imminent juvenile crime wave.[31] They forecast that a new wave of **superpredators** was growing up and would soon enter their crime-prone years and wreak havoc.[32] These criminologists based their predictions on a number of assumptions that proved to be elusive. Although the superpredator scare made for exciting news stories, it didn't inform juvenile justice policy in a healthy way. The get-tough-on-juvenile-crime movement can be blamed, in part, for this faulty prediction that we were in for a new, dangerous, and large increase in juvenile crime.

The crime wave never arrived (see Figure 3-11 to see that juvenile arrests actually decreased and leveled off somewhat between 1995 and 2003), and there is very little talk these days about superpredator youths who are committing thousands of heinous crimes. Where did these predictions of superpredators come from? On what data and assumptions were they based? Why were they so inaccurate? A review of the superpredator scare reveals that predicting delinquent behavior is only partly science, and that luck and politics also entered the equation.

- **Cohort size** Population rises and falls in every society. For example, during the Great Depression of the 1930s and World War II of the early 1940s, the

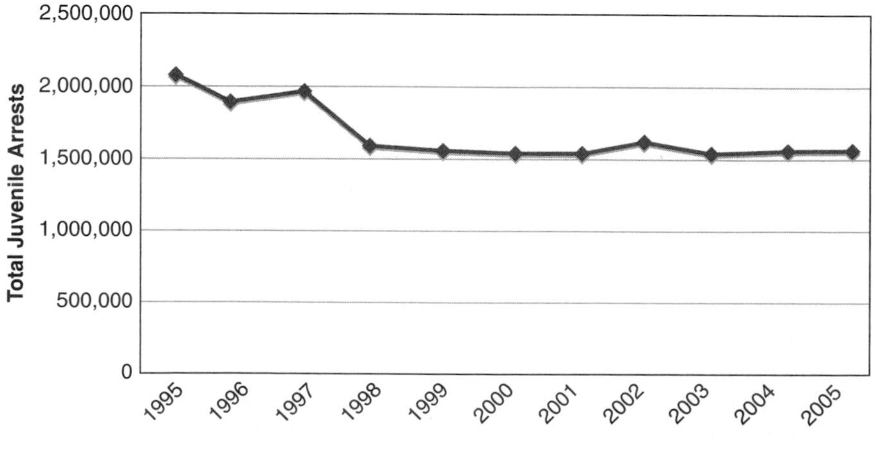

Figure 3-11 **Number of Arrests of Suspects under Age 18, by Year** *Source:* Federal Bureau of Investigation, *Uniform Crime Reports: Crime in the United States* (Washington, DC: U.S. Government Printing Office). Years 1995–2005. Online at www.fbi.gov/ucr/ucr.htm#cius.

3.1 A CLOSER LOOK at JUVENILE ISSUES

PHILADELPHIA BIRTH COHORT STUDY

The Philadelphia Birth Cohort Study is a **longitudinal study** in which researchers followed the nature and pattern of delinquency and criminality in two groups of males, one born in 1945 and the other in 1958, who lived in Philadelphia, Pennsylvania, from their tenth to their eighteenth birthdays. The 1945 cohort comprised 9,945 males, and the 1958 cohort comprised 13,160 males. Researchers derived information from school records, delinquency records, and interviews with some of the participants when they became adults. The study collected basic demographic information on each participant: sex, race, age, date of birth, religious affiliation, and socioeconomic status. Then the study collected information on the offenses (if any) committed by the participants when they were juveniles and when they were adults. The study collected information about each offense, including the offense location and date; the complainant's sex, age, and race; number and age of victims; number of victims killed or hospitalized; weapon involvement; and court disposition.

Here are some of the findings from the study.

- Thirty-three percent of the 1958 cohort and 34.9 percent of the 1945 cohort had at least one police contact before their eighteenth birthday.
- The 1958 cohort committed more offenses and much more serious offenses than the 1945 cohort. Only a few youths were responsible for most of the delinquent acts.
- More than 60 percent of first offenses were non-index crimes. Delinquency was more prevalent among non-whites and youths of lower socioeconomic status.
- Delinquency was associated with residential instability, poor school achievement, and failure to graduate from high school.

Source: Robert M. Figlio, Paul E. Tracy, and Marvin E. Wolfgang, *Delinquency Careers in Two Birth Cohorts* (New York: Plenum Press, 1990).

---

number of new births was depressed for economic and social reasons. After World War II, a baby boom occurred, and these children reached their crime-prone years in the late 1950s and 1960s. Demographers have tracked similar large **cohorts** of young people, and criminologists suggested that the group entering its crime-prone years in the early 2000s would produce a crime wave.

- **Chronic delinquents**   One of the most well-known and well-respected studies of juvenile delinquents is the Philadelphia Birth Cohort Study (see A Closer Look at Juvenile Issues 3.1). One important finding of this landmark research was that 6 percent of the youths committed a disproportionate number of offenses. If 6 percent of all juveniles continued to be chronic offenders, the superpredator proponents stated that it could be predicted that there would be a great deal more crime because of the larger proportion of crime-prone youth.

- **Younger serious delinquents**   The superpredator predictors assumed that delinquents would turn to serious crime at a younger age than had normally been the case. This didn't occur to any great degree.

- **Crack babies**   With the epidemic of crack cocaine in the 1980s came the worry that women who used crack were giving birth to thousands of babies who were addicted to crack at birth and who would suffer long-term deleterious consequences. Today, we hear very little about the crack-baby syndrome, and it appears as if the phenomenon was more media hype than actual problem. It certainly didn't result in a wave of superpredator youths 16 years later.

- **Get-tough-on-crime politics**   How do politicians respond to voters' fear of crime? One way is to talk about being tougher on crime than your opponent. So many politicians have made the get-tough stance a major part of their campaign that there is a perception that crime is out of control and will continue to escalate. These exaggerated predictions have resulted in the incarceration rather than the treatment of mentally ill juveniles (see Kids in the News 3.1.)

longitudinal study
A type of study or survey in which the same subjects are observed over a usually lengthy period of time.

Instant Recall from Chapter 1
cohorts
A group whose members share a particular statistical or demographic characteristic.

So many variables influence predictions of delinquency that it's almost impossible to be accurate in the long term. Changes in school policies, involvement by parents, economic conditions, and numerous other factors that are unforeseen by predictors will confound any forecast. Yet, it's useful and desirable to anticipate how the factors that appear now might influence future crime rates. However, policy-makers can't continually look in the rearview mirror when planning the allocation of resources.

3.1   K I D S in the N E W S

Sick and in Jail

Incarcerating the mentally ill isn't a new strategy in social control. Throughout history, the mentally ill and mentally retarded have been imprisoned for everything from offending social mores to breaking the law. This solution was common in pre-20th-century societies, and unfortunately, it seems that not much has changed. Americans are still unsure of what to do with or how to treat the nation's mentally ill offenders. Too often, the mentally ill are incarcerated, not out of cruelty, but because there is no other recourse.

A 2004 study prepared for Democrats on the House Committee on Government Reform found that nearly 2,000 mentally ill juveniles were housed in the nation's jails. To make matters worse, some mentally ill juveniles didn't require detention: they were being held in jails while waiting for treatment or because they had nowhere else to go. This is common in many states. For example, according to a 2004 report from New Jersey's Office of the Child Advocate, not only are mentally ill juveniles being held in facilities that are not equipped or staffed to deal with them, but whether a mentally ill juvenile receives treatment "is largely subject to the discretion of county administrators, the individual philosophy of detention directors, and resources available in that particular county."

The report also found that 21 percent of juveniles who enter the state's juvenile justice system have a "serious emotional disorder," a percentage that the study states is consistent with the number of mentally ill juveniles in detention throughout the United States. The study reported over 90 suicide threats or attempts from juveniles in detention centers during an 8-month period in 2004. The detention of mentally ill juveniles has led to crowding problems as well, with 11 detention centers stating that they held more juveniles on any given day than they were rated to hold in a year.[1]

One problem arises from the fact that criminal behavior can be a symptom of mental illness and those responsible for controlling such behavior, primarily the police, aren't mental health specialists. If someone is breaking a law, then it's the police's job to ensure that this person stops breaking the law, and it's the job of corrections officials to detain those who are sent to them. Also, the justice system's treatment of mentally ill offenders has never been codified or even formalized. The Bill of Rights and legal precedent specify the basic treatment of suspects, and the United States created a separate justice system for juveniles in the early 20th century; but mentally ill offenders have always been in legal limbo. The mentally ill have no separate legal system or right to treatment.

Many mentally ill offenders are juveniles, and although as juveniles they are protected somewhat by the juvenile justice system, this hasn't kept them from ending up in jails rather than hospitals. The problem finally got some federal attention in 2004 with the Mentally Ill Offender Treatment and Crime Reduction Act. The act authorized a $50 million federal grant program for states and jurisdictions to establish more mental health courts, expand inmate access to mental health treatment, and fund training for police and mental health personnel.[2]

Think About It

1. Should mentally ill offenders have a "bill of rights"?

2. What should be done with mentally ill juveniles who have nowhere to go? Is jail the proper place for them?

1 Office of the Child Advocate, *Juvenile Detention Center Investigation: An Examination of Conditions of Care for Youth with Mental Health Needs*, Executive Summary, November 2004, p. 4. Online at www.state.nj.us/childadvocate/publications/PDFs/1FINAL_JJ_Mental_Health_Exec_Sum.pdf.
2 Kevin Rothstein, "Feds: Mentally Ill Kids Consigned to Confinement," *Boston Herald*, July 8, 2004, p. 4.

SUMMARY

1. Not all undesirable behavior is crime. Criminal offenses are violations of the criminal law and occupy the extreme end of social control. Violations of norms and rules aren't supported by the justice system.

2. Scholars and researchers have developed numerous techniques for trying to accurately measure the incidence and effects of crime and delinquency.

3. The legislative branch of the government defines offenses, the executive branch is charged with enforcing them, and the judicial branch determines both guilt and punishment.

4. The differences between reported and unreported crime are significant. We can't know for sure the actual incidence of unreported crime. This is the dark figure of crime.

5. The context of a behavior can determine whether a behavior is defined and measured as a criminal offense. A victim might not report a crime because he or she might not understand an offense has been committed, lack faith in the system, wish to protect the offender, or be guilty also.

6. Researchers use a variety of methodologies that attempt to measure crime in different ways to correct for measurement errors.

7. The best-known method for reporting crime in the United States is the *Uniform Crime Reports*. Almost every legal jurisdiction reports the number of offenses and its agency's characteristics to the FBI.

8. The strength of the UCR data is that each jurisdiction reports offenses according to a single set of parameters and a uniform set of definitions.

9. The UCR Part I offenses are murder and non-negligent manslaughter, forcible rape, robbery, aggravated assault, burglary, larceny–theft, motor vehicle theft, and arson.

10. Part II offenses capture an additional 21 offenses. Some Part II offenses apply only to juveniles, such as running away, underage drinking, curfew violations, underage smoking, truancy, and incorrigibility.

11. UCR data can't give a comprehensive picture of crime because they are heavily skewed toward street crime.

12. Other methods of crime measurement try to reveal the dark figure of crime. Self-report studies use anonymous questionnaires to ask participants what offenses they have committed. Victimization surveys ask respondents about their experiences as crime victims.

13. Adults commit more offenses than youths. The ages of adult offenders are clustered around the lower end of the scale, and their offenses seem to be an extension of juvenile crime.

14. In the National Incident-Based Reporting System, participating law enforcement agencies report crime in a different and more detailed way than in the UCR.

15. The victimization of children is a major concern for several reasons: children don't precipitate their victimization, they might not be aware of their victimization, they might suffer life-long mental and physical harm, they might harbor guilt for being victims.

16. A typology of juvenile delinquents includes status offenders, drug users and abusers, gang members, and chronic and violent juveniles.

17. Predicting delinquency is problematic. An example would be the mid-1990s idea of superpredators.

REVIEW QUESTIONS

1. What is crime?

2. Why would a victim choose not to report an offense?

3. What makes the *Uniform Crime Reports* so useful? What are its drawbacks?

4. What are self-report studies?

5. What are victimization surveys?

6. How do scholars determine the validity and reliability of survey research?

7. In what ways might crime affect youths differently than adults?

8. Can juvenile offending be accurately predicted?

ADDITIONAL READINGS

Benard, Thomas, "Juvenile Crime and the Transformation of Juvenile Justice: Is There a Juvenile Crime Wave?" *Justice Quarterly* 16 (1999):336–356.

Binderman, Albert, and James Lynch, *Understanding Crime Incidence Statistics* (New York: Springer-Verlag, 1991).

Hagan, John, *Crime and Disrepute* (Thousand Oaks, CA: Pine Forge, 1994).

Satcher, David, *Youth Violence* (Washington, DC: U.S. Department of Health and Human Services, 2002).

Seidman, David, and Michael Couzens, "Getting the Crime Rate Down: Political Pressure and Crime Reporting," *Law and Society Review* 8 (1974):457–493.

Paul Tracy, Marvin Wolfgang, and Robert Figlio, *Delinquency in Two Birth Cohorts, Executive Summary* (Washington, DC: U.S. Department of Justice, 1985).

ENDNOTES

1. Vincent F. Sacco, *When Crime Waves* (Thousand Oaks, CA: Sage, 2005), 92–93.

2. James C. Howell, *Preventing and Reducing Juvenile Delinquency: A Comprehensive Framework* (Thousand Oaks, CA: Sage, 2003), 15–19.

3. Paul Tappan, "Who Is the Criminal," *American Sociological Review* 12 (1947): 96–102.

4. Paul Brantingham and Patricia Brantingham, *Patterns in Crime* (New York: Macmillan, 1984), 49.

5. William G. Doerner and Steven P. Lab, *Victimology*, 4th ed. (Cincinnati, OH: Anderson, 2005), 160–165.

6. Greenwich Police Department, Greenwich, CT, www.greenwichpolice.com/tips.htm.

7. Federal Bureau of Investigation, www.fbi.gov/.

8. U.S. Department of Justice, Federal Bureau of Investigation, *Uniform Crime Reporting Handbook*, www.fbi.gov/ucr/handbook/ucrhandbook04.pdf.

9. Clayton J. Mosher, Terance D. Miethe, and Dretha M. Phillips, *The Mismeasure of Crime* (Thousand Oaks, CA: Sage, 2002), 65–69.

10. Robert Meier and Gilbert Geis, *Victimless Crimes: Prostitution, Drugs, Homosexuality, Abortion* (Los Angeles: Roxbury, 1997).

11. Terence Thornberry and Marvin D. Krohn, "The Self-Report Method for Measuring Delinquency and Crime," in *Criminal Justice 2000: Measurement and Analysis of Crime and Justice* (Washington, DC: U.S. Department of Justice, 2000), 33–83.

12. Gordon Waldo and Theodore G. Chiricos, "Perceived Penal Sanction and Self-Reported Criminality, a Neglected Approach to Deterrence Research," *Social Problems* 19 (1972):522–540.

13. See note 9, pp. 102–106.

14. Gary Kleck, "On the Use of Self-Report Data to Determine the Class Distribution of Criminal and Delinquent Behavior," *American Sociological Review* 47 (1982):427–433.

15. Charles R. Tittle, Wayne J. Villemez, and Douglas A. Smith, "The Myth of Social Class and Criminality: An Empirical Examination of the Empirical Evidence," *American Sociological Review* 43 (1978):643–656. It should be noted, however, that this finding is disputed. See John Braithwaite, "The Myth of Social Class and Criminality Revisited," *American Sociological Review* 46 (1981):36–57.

16. See note 5, pp. 31–51. This section is devoted to summarizing Doerner and Lab's excellent discussion of victimization surveys.

17. Ibid., 37–38.

18. Ibid., 39–42.

19. Federal Bureau of Investigation, *Crime in the United States 2005*, Arrests by Age (Table 38), www.fbi.gov/ucr/05cius/data/table_38.html.

20. John Conklin, *Why Crime Rates Fell* (Boston: Allyn and Bacon, 2003.)

21. Kathryn Graham and Samantha Wells, "'Somebody's Gonna Get Their Head Kicked in Tonight!' Aggression Among Young Males in Bars—A Question of Values?" *British Journal of Criminology* 43, no. 3 (2003):546–566.

22. For a good discussion of the research on victim precipitation, see Doerner and Lab (see note 5), pp. 11–13.

23. John Wright and Frank Cullen, "Parental Efficacy and Delinquent Behavior: Do Control and Support Matter?" *Criminology* 39 (2001):691–693.

24. Michael Maxfield, "The National Incident-Based Reporting System: Research and Policy Implications," *Journal of Quantitative Criminology* 15 (1999):119–149.

25. David J. Roberts, *Implementing the National Incident-Based Reporting System: A Project Status Report* (Washington, DC: U.S. Department of Justice, 1997).

26. Murray A. Straus, *Beating the Devil Out of Them: Corporal Punishment in American Families and Its Effects on Children* (New Brunswick, NJ: Transaction, 2001).

27. Valerie Strauss, "Putting Parents in Their Place: Outside Class," *Washington Post*, March 21, 2006, p. A08. Online at www.washingtonpost.com/wp-dyn/content/article/2006/03/20/AR2006032001167.html.

28. Erich Goode, *Drugs in American Society* (New York: McGraw-Hill, 2004).

29. Randall Shelden, Sharon Tracy, and William Brown, *Youth Gangs in American Society* (Belmont, CA: Wadsworth, 2004).

30. Tonja Nansel et al., "Bullying Behaviors among U.S. Youth," *Journal of the American Medical Association* 289 (2001):2094–2100.

31. John J. Dilulio, Jr., "The Coming of the Super-predators," *Weekly Standard*, November 27, 1995, p. 23.

32. James Alan Fox, "The Calm before the Crime Wave Storm," *Los Angeles Times*, October 10, 1996, p. B9.

What is ethnocentrism?

How does culture affect how
children are treated by the law?

Why is globalism an important
factor in producing delinquency?

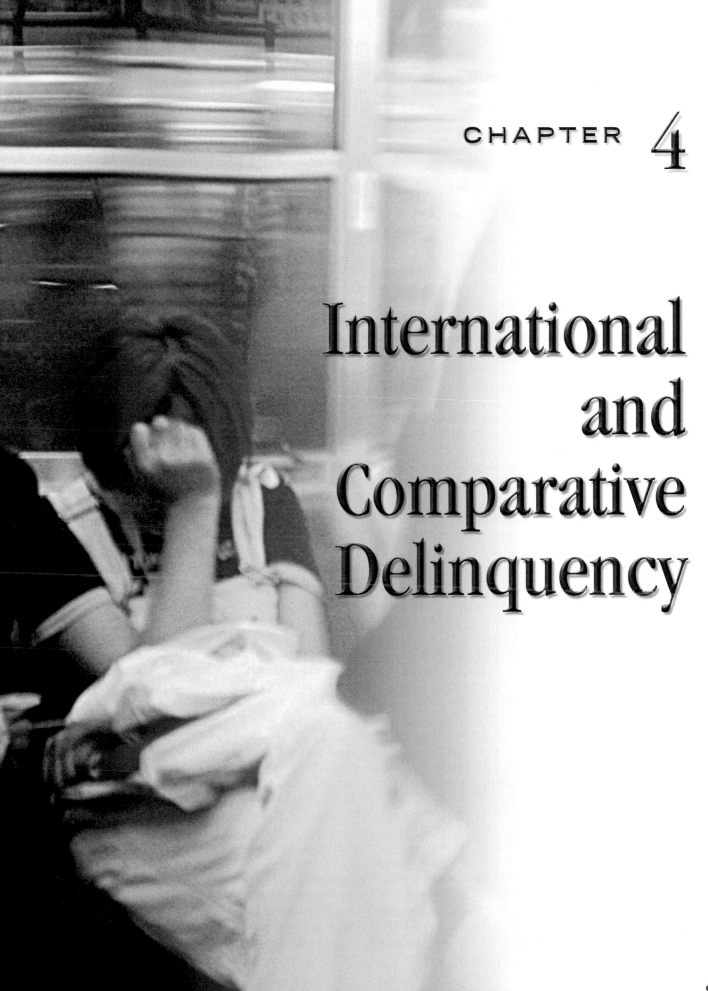

CHAPTER 4

International
and
Comparative
Delinquency

If we are to appreciate why young people break the law and learn how to effectively respond, we must look beyond our borders at how other societies handle youth justice. First, let's review the reasons why we seldom consider other cultures.

- **Cultural isolation**   To a large extent, the United States is culturally isolated from the rest of the world, primarily because of the size of the country. Because the United States is so large and can meet the needs of so much of its population, Americans tend to look inward. The term *isolationist* was used to describe the United States prior to both of the world wars in which European countries fought for years before the United States got involved. U.S. isolation can also be observed in the relatively small number of Americans who speak a language other than English. In contrast, in a small European nation such as Switzerland, many people are multilingual because they have the opportunity to interact with individuals from many different cultures.[1]

- **Ability to affect**   Another reason the delinquency experiences of other countries are seldom considered is because we have little opportunity to make changes in other countries. Although other countries might do things differently, and perhaps even better, we often ignore them because we can't reproduce some of the underlying conditions that make their ways different. For example, because of cultural history, youths in other countries might have completely different experiences with alcohol. Countries that have embraced Islam have radically different laws, customs, and penalties for alcoholic consumption.[2] It is unlikely that the cultural and religious traditions of Islamic countries can be reproduced in the United States as a way to handle adolescent drinking.

- **Ethnocentrism**   Sometimes there is a tendency to consider variations of behavior around the world and conclude that the way one's own culture does things is the best way. **Ethnocentrism** means that individuals believe that their own laws, religion, schools, and family practices are the right way, the natural way, or "God's chosen way."[3]

- **Globalism**   **Globalism** refers to the shrinking of the world. Many cultures are losing their distinctiveness and are becoming homogenized. Because the United States is the world's only remaining traditional superpower, its culture is quickly spreading around the world. The English language has become the international language of trade, and with advances in satellite technology, American culture, including MTV and CNN, is available almost everywhere. Why learn about other cultures when they are becoming so much like our own?

From health care to education to the control of juvenile delinquency, some countries appear to have developed superior responses to their youth problems. Although many of these solutions aren't readily feasible in the United States because of political, cultural, or societal reasons, it's worth considering how other countries' experiences might better inform some of the policies of the U.S. juvenile justice system.

Before we consider other youth justice systems, we should discuss how a nation's particular culture affects not only how a government responds to youth crime, but also the reasons that young people break the law. To do this, we must consider the concept of culture (for another look at how cultures differ, see Focus on Ethics 4.1). For instance, Singapore has different expectations of youths' behavior than the United States, as well as a very low crime rate. Is it fair to expect Americans in Singapore to be cognizant of the cultural differences? For more on this, see Crosscurrents 4.1.

ethnocentrism
The belief in the natural superiority of one's particular ethnic group or culture.

globalism
The philosophy or act of placing the interests of the world above those of individual nations.

4.1 FOCUS *on* ETHICS

NO WAY TO TREAT A LADY

You have a problem. As a manager of your university's basketball program, you have befriended an international student who was recruited because he is a 6-foot 10-inch power forward with a great 3-point shot. You introduced this student to a friend of yours from your hometown, and now they have become close friends and have moved in together. Your friend has been showing up for classes with bruises on her arms, and today one of her girlfriends has come to you and told you that she has a cut over her eye and a swollen lip.

After going to your friend's apartment, you confirm that she has injuries, and you also observe that your basketball-playing international student has scratches on his neck. You demand an explanation, but the ballplayer tells you to mind your own business.

"You Americans don't know how to make your women behave. They have to learn that the man is the boss and to do what I say."

You turn to your female friend, and she says, "Please stay out of this. We will work this all out. I love him and plan to go back with him to his homeland, so we will have to establish our own way of dealing with problems. I can't expect him to suddenly adopt American culture. I'm sure I can educate him on how to have a mutually supportive relationship, but it's going to take some time."

You are not sure what to do. Over the next several weeks, you notice even more evidence of physical abuse, and the girlfriends of your friend are pressuring you to confront the basketball player, tell the coach about the problem, or somehow solve the problem before something really bad happens. In the meantime, the international basketball player is lighting up the court and leading the team to a conference championship.

What Do You Do?

1. Stay out of the middle of this essentially domestic dispute. It is none of your business, and you can only lose two friends by butting in.

2. Tell the coach. You have a responsibility to the team, and this is a potential problem that could blow up and force the coach to suspend the player.

3. Tell your friend's parents. You have known them for years, and you feel an obligation to them because they are neighbors of your family.

4. Get some of your friends and confront the basketball player and tell him that in the United States we don't beat women. Threaten to rough him up if he doesn't stop physically abusing his girlfriend.

CULTURE AND THE DISCONTENTED

Culture consists of art, technology, customs, laws, artifacts, and the special bond that makes individuals believe they are connected and qualitatively different from others outside the culture.[4] Sometimes we are blind to culture and its effects. Like fish in water, we don't realize that a sea of culture surrounds us until we are plucked out and placed in a different culture. Then we flop around, trying to acclimate to a new environment and figure out how to communicate, find our way around the city, drive on the correct side of the road, and order a beer. We don't fit in because all our cultural reference points are gone, and we haven't deciphered the new cultural code.

To understand other cultures, we must first appreciate the limitations of our own perspective. We must use C. Wright Mills' **sociological imagination** to consider delinquent behavior and understand what part of it is peculiar to a particular culture and what part applies to all cultures.[5] Do other societies raise their children in ways that avoid the problems of American delinquency? Are there better ways of socializing children? Our attempts to answer these questions won't be conclusive. The influence of culture, although pervasive, is difficult to pinpoint in rapidly changing societies. The goals of this chapter are more modest and will highlight several of the pertinent and important issues of attempting cross-cultural comparisons and offer some examples of how other countries respond to delinquent behavior.

**Instant Recall
from Chapter 1**
sociological imagination
The idea that one must look beyond the obvious to evaluate how social location influences the way one considers society.

4.1 CrossCurrents

Punished in Singapore

In October 1993, Singapore police arrested nine youths for vandalism, one of whom identified 18-year-old Michael Fay, an American living in Singapore with his parents, as one of the perpetrators. Fay was arrested at his parents' home and charged with 50 counts of vandalism. In March 1994, after agreeing to a plea bargain in which he admitted the offense, which Fay later said was coerced by torture, Fay was convicted on two counts of vandalism and possession of stolen property. He was sentenced to four months in prison, six lashes from a cane, and a fine of about $2,000.[1]

The situation touched off an uproar in the United States, but not because many Americans believed caning to be a brutal and inappropriate punishment. The sentence seemed to have as many supporters as detractors, if not more. Many Americans professed to be ashamed of the U.S. juvenile justice system, which they criticized as coddling spoiled, violent, and entitled juvenile delinquents. Caning, went much of the popular opinion, was a perfectly just punishment and should be instituted in the United States. Even Fay's hometown of Dayton, Ohio, granted him little quarter. According to the *Nation*, Ohio Representative Tony Hall received loads of mail supporting the caning, and the Dayton newspaper reported wide public support for it as well.[2]

The admiration of so many Americans for Singaporean justice didn't extend to the White House. President Bill Clinton criticized Singapore and wrote to President Ong Teng Cheong on Fay's behalf. The strategy was partially successful. Fay's sentence was reduced from six cane strokes to four, which he received in May 1994.

Many Americans equate the idea of caning with the swats their parents might have given them with a willowy tree branch, flyswatter, or belt. In Singapore, however, judicial canings are administered by a martial-arts expert, whose 4-foot, half-inch-thick cane is soaked in water to make it stronger. The canings are reported to cause open wounds and scarring, and recipients are reported to require treatment for shock afterward. Caning is not an unusual punishment in Singapore, where it has both supporters and critics. Its supporters point to the harsh punishment as being at least partly responsible for the country's remarkably low crime rate, while its critics say the sentence is used too much and sometimes for political purposes. Some offenders are exempt: the unhealthy, women, and men over the age of 50 or under the age of 16.[3]

Fay told *Newsweek* that he shook the hand of the man who caned him, "To show that I'd kept my pride. He works for the government; that's his job."[4] But did the caning encourage Fay to stay out of trouble? Or, given the possibility that his confession was coerced, did it warp a good kid? In 1994, *People* reported that a month after returning home to Dayton, Fay got into a physical fight with his father. He eventually became addicted to sniffing butane gas, a habit he had acquired in Singapore, and by September 1994, he was in a Minnesota drug-rehabilitation facility. In 1998, while living in Winter Park, Florida, he pleaded guilty to possession of marijuana.[5]

Think About It

1. Do you believe Fay when he says he was tortured into confessing? Another boy was reportedly beaten until his eardrum ruptured.
2. The paint that Fay and the others were accused of spraying on the cars was easily removed, leaving no permanent damage. Should this have had a bearing on their treatment?
4. Why do you think Fay continued to get into trouble after his experience in Singapore?
5. Did Fay deserve what he got?

Michael Fay, accompanied by his father, leaves the Queenstown Prison in Singapore following his release in 1994. *(Courtesy Tan Ah Soon, AP Wide World Photos)*

1. Kerry A. Flatley, "Boy Caned in Singapore Makes News Again," *Christian Science Monitor*, April 9, 1998, 18.

2. "No Mercy," *Nation* 258, no. 16 (April 1994):543.

3. Joel Hodson, "A Case for American Studies: The Michael Fay Affair, Singapore–US Relations, and American Studies in Singapore," *American Studies International* XLI, no. 3 (October 2003):7.

4. Melinda Liu, "'I Tried to Ignore the Pain,'" *Newsweek* 124, no. 1 (July 1994):36.

5. "Michael Fay," *People* 42, no. 26 (December 1994):60.

Comparative Delinquency

Before actually considering the problems of youth offending in other societies, we must consider how culture greatly determines what is acceptable behavior and what is unacceptable behavior. The cultural context in which behavior occurs dictates how a particular society will respond. For instance, premarital sex can be punished with a death sentence in some Islamic societies, but it's considered pretty normal in the United States, although it's frowned on by some segments of society. So what components of culture determine whether behavior is rewarded or punished? At the most basic level, the list would include the following:

- **Religion**   Religion is a powerful social institution. It's the absolute social authority in some countries, while others marginalize it. In the United States, religion has an uneven history as an influencing force. Because of the constitutional provisions for the separation of church and state, religion doesn't play as important a part in the justice system as it does in some other countries. Nevertheless, the proper place for religion in public life, especially in the justice system, continues to be contested.[6] From the controversy of displaying the Christian Ten Commandments in local courthouses, to the struggles to get federal judges who have specific views on abortion confirmed by the U.S. Senate, to the federal funding of faith-based rehabilitation programs, religion has once again demanded a seat at the table of criminal justice policy. In societies dominated by a single religion, there's little or no controversy about religion playing a dominant role in the justice system. As we discuss later, other justice systems are tied much more directly to the prevailing religion in some countries.

- **Gender**   Although the women's movement of the 20th century has made great strides in improving the level of gender equality in the United States, the struggle continues because of entrenched interests in maintaining distinct roles for women and men. Some other societies haven't been as progressive in breaking down the barriers between the rights of women and men.[7] Therefore, any examination of the justice system must account for how women's issues are handled. In countries where women can't vote, enter into legal contracts, own property, or choose their husbands, it isn't surprising to see gender inequities encoded into the criminal law.

- **Economic development**   One of the most significant factors that makes the social environment of countries different is the level of economic development. There is a great deal of difference between a fully developed, industrialized, Western nation like the United States and a developing nation such as Sudan. Comparing delinquency rates between these countries isn't only impossible, but also fruitless. The differences in what influences children's lives in each country are so great that it's pointless to even make such an attempt. In Sudan, where the daily concerns are genocide, famine, and political turmoil, the most pressing issues of youths are survival, not delinquency. Therefore, the stage of development can tell us more about the conditions of childhood in a country than can just the rate of delinquency.

With this understanding that culture is a determining force in how delinquency is defined, measured, and recognized, we can now consider youth offending and victimization throughout the world. Although this chapter can't cover all the circumstances that affect youths, we can highlight and compare certain youth issues, including laws, police treatment, rehabilitation, and detention. The United Nations has adopted a set of rules concerning juvenile detention. For a selection of these rules, see A Closer Look at Juvenile Issues 4.1.

As we skip around the globe in this section, our goal is simply to indicate patterns of youth crime and victimization and not to present a comprehensive view.

4.1 A CLOSER LOOK at JUVENILE ISSUES

SELECTED UNITED NATIONS RULES FOR THE PROTECTION OF JUVENILES DEPRIVED OF THEIR LIBERTY

The juvenile justice system should uphold the rights and safety and promote the physical and mental well-being of juveniles. Imprisonment should be used as a last resort.

The rules should be applied impartially, without discrimination of any kind as to race, colour, sex, age, language, religion, nationality, political or other opinion, cultural beliefs or practices, property, birth or family status, ethnic or social origin, and disability.

A juvenile is every person under the age of 18. The age limit below which it should not be permitted to deprive a child of his or her liberty should be determined by law.

The deprivation of liberty should be effected in conditions and circumstances that ensure respect for the human rights of juveniles.

Juveniles deprived of their liberty shall not for any reason related to their status be denied the civil, economic, political, social, or cultural rights to which they are entitled under national or international law and which are compatible with the deprivation of liberty.

Juveniles who are detained under arrest or awaiting trial ("untried") are presumed innocent and shall be treated as such.

Juveniles should have the right of legal counsel and be enabled to apply for free legal aid, where such aid is available, and to communicate regularly with their legal advisers.

No juvenile should be received in any detention facility without a valid commitment order of a judicial, administrative, or other public authority.

As soon as possible after the moment of admission, each juvenile should be interviewed, and a psychological and social report identifying any factors relevant to the specific type and level of care and program required by the juvenile should be prepared.

In all detention facilities, juveniles should be separated from adults unless they are members of the same family.

The design of detention facilities for juveniles and the physical environment should be in keeping with the rehabilitative aim of residential treatment, with due regard to the need of the juvenile for privacy, sensory stimuli, opportunities for association with peers, and participation in sports, physical exercise, and leisure-time activities.

Every detention facility shall ensure that every juvenile receives food that is suitably prepared and presented at normal meal times and of a quality and quantity to satisfy the standards of dietetics, hygiene and health and, as far as possible, religious and cultural requirements. Clean drinking water should be available to every juvenile at any time.

Every juvenile of compulsory school age has the right to education suited to his or her needs and abilities and designed to prepare him or her for return to society.

Juveniles above compulsory school age who wish to continue their education should be permitted and encouraged to do so, and every effort should be made to provide them with access to appropriate educational programs.

Every juvenile should have the right to a suitable amount of time for daily free exercise, in the open air whenever weather permits, during which time appropriate recreational and physical training should normally be provided.

Every juvenile should be allowed to satisfy the needs of his or her religious and spiritual life, in particular by attending the services or meetings provided in the detention facility or by conducting his or her own services and having possession of the necessary books or items of religious observance and instruction of his or her denomination.

Juvenile detention facilities should adopt specialized drug abuse prevention and rehabilitation programs administered by qualified personnel.

The family or guardian of a juvenile and any other person designated by the juvenile have the right to be informed of the state of health of the juvenile on request and in the event of any important changes in the health of the juvenile.

Every juvenile should have the right to receive regular and frequent visits, in principle once a week and not less than once a month, in circumstances that respect the need of the juvenile for privacy, contact, and unrestricted communication with the family and the defense counsel.

Every juvenile should have the right to communicate in writing or by telephone at least twice a week with the person of his or her choice, unless legally restricted, and should be assisted as necessary to effectively enjoy this right. Every juvenile should have the right to receive correspondence.

The carrying and use of weapons by personnel should be prohibited in any facility where juveniles are detained.

All disciplinary measures constituting cruel, inhuman, or degrading treatment shall be strictly prohibited, including corporal punishment, placement in a dark cell, closed or solitary confinement, or any other punishment that may compromise the physical or mental health of the juvenile concerned.[1]

1 Abridged from United Nations Rules for the Protection of Juveniles Deprived of Their Liberty, adopted December 1990. Online at www.ohchr.org/english/law/res45_113.htm.

JUVENILE DELINQUENCY AND JUVENILE JUSTICE IN OTHER COUNTRIES

Comparing foreign youth crime and youth justice systems to the United States' juvenile justice system is interesting because a great variety of responses to problems can be seen, and it's always possible to find a better way. Remember, however, that major differences among cultures, justice systems, and data collection make direct comparisons difficult. We have already discussed how religion, gender roles, and level of development can affect the cultural conditions in which young people must negotiate their respective legal systems. Now let's turn to some features of youth justice systems to get a sense of why it's difficult to compare youth justice statistics.

The first major hurdle that comparative researchers confront is language.[8] Although some researchers might speak two or three languages fluently enough to do comparative research, few, if any, criminologists speak all the western European languages, much less those of the rest of the world. Therefore, one must either find a common language in which to communicate with officials from other countries or hire an interpreter. Luckily, many scholars study abroad, and the United States is the recipient of graduate students from around the globe who can provide a picture of their nation's justice systems.

In addition to the language barrier, there are certain definitional barriers. Offenses vary from country to country, and an activity that is considered a felony in one country might be considered a misdemeanor in another and legal in a third. The terms *felony* and *misdemeanor* are problematic as well, because not all countries categorize seriousness of crime in this manner. Countries report and record crime data in a variety of ways. Resource constraints, political agendas, accuracy, and technology can make it difficult to compare criminal and youth justice data. For example, the nation of Oman collects delinquency statistics on males but not on females.[9]

It might be tempting to conclude that, with all the differences between countries in terms of culture and reporting procedures, attempting to do comparative analysis on crime and delinquency is a fruitless endeavor. If one wants a neat set of statistics that can easily be accurately coded into a dataset and analyzed by a statistical computer program, this might be the case. However, even given the differences in culture, definitions of crime, and reporting practices, the comparative method can yield valuable information. In fact, by highlighting the differences, researchers can obtain insights not only on how criminal and youth justice systems compare, but also on how these differences might provide ideas and suggestions for the improvement on how juvenile justice is meted out in the United States.[10]

It is beyond the scope of this book to provide a comprehensive overview of youth justice around the world. Rather, the goal is to present some representative examples of the differences not only of justice systems, but also of the cultures in which these systems operate. Because there is as much variation among the types of systems within regions of the world as between them, this material is organized based on the population size of the country. As we move from the larger countries to the smaller ones, we will demonstrate the richness and ramifications of cultural differences as reflected by a variety of systems of youth justice.

China

China is a great place to start our investigation of other youth justice systems because it's so different from the United States and because it is undergoing extremely rapid social change. The cultural dynamics in China are so fluid that it is difficult to assume with any confidence what its future holds. It is quickly being transformed from a state-controlled economy to a market economy, and its people are demanding greater freedoms and more control over their daily lives. Here are some of the major issues pressing on China.

- **Population**   China has over 1.3 billion citizens.[11] When you consider that the United States has about 300 million people, it becomes clear that the extra billion people that China must support present immense challenges.[12] Family planning is a matter of government policy, and a one-child-per-couple rule is enforced. Because of its large population, there are restrictions on where people might live. China's citizens must obtain permission to move from one province to another because the government can't allow everyone to move to already-crowded urban areas. Population size is China's primary concern, and it influences not only government policy, but also the entire range of China's cultural issues.

- **Government**   China is one of the few remaining communist countries in the world. It became communist in 1949 under the leadership of Mao Zedong, and, like the Soviet Union, it attempted centralized economic planning, which failed to provide for its people's needs. China's Cultural Revolution, in which all things Western were rejected, plunged the country into cultural isolation and poverty. China fell far behind the rest of the world in terms of industrialization and world trade and is now trying to modernize. Its economy is currently a changing mixture of capitalism and **communism** as its leaders compete on the world's economic stage without letting the marketplace dictate cultural and political change.

- **Religion**   China has no official religion. The government has a policy of atheism but is becoming somewhat tolerant of individual religious practices. Historically, the religion of China was Confucianism, with Buddhism and Taoism also practiced. Western missionaries introduced Christianity, and the northern Xinjiang province is almost completely Muslim. After years of repressing all religions, China now has a more tolerant policy, but the government is far from supportive of religious freedoms.[13]

communism

A system of social organization in which the ownership of property is ascribed to the community or to the state.

It is within this context of cultural change that China's youth justice system is emerging. In comparison to the United States, China doesn't have a formal juvenile justice system, so other societal institutions handle the less significant cases.[14] Schools, families, and neighborhood organizations deal with many minor instances of deviant behavior with the idea that these problems can best be solved without police involvement. When there are youth suspects in serious cases of homicide, rape, or robbery, the adult court and corrections programs handle them. In such cases, provisions are made to separate young children from adults, but the legal mechanisms are essentially the same.

The youth crime rate in China is difficult to measure because most available statistics are those of official agencies. China didn't even disclose its crime statistics to the public until 1986, and like the *Uniform Crime Reports*, China's official statistics can't reflect the vast dark figure of crime.[15] The differences in how crime is handled informally in China make comparisons with the United States even more inaccurate.

Although the age of criminal responsibility in China is 16, a youth between the ages of 14 and 16 who commits a serious offense such as homicide, an injurious assault, robbery, arson, or habitual theft, is considered to bear full criminal responsibility. Usually, however, the severity of the punishment is lighter than it would be for a person over the age of 16, and the death penalty isn't specified for youths under the age of 18. Youths under the age of 16 who aren't punished by the state are sent home, and the head of the family is ordered to discipline the youth.[16]

In 2003, according to official statistics, authorities arrested 69,780 youths, which represented 9.1 percent of all suspects arrested that year, as well as an increase of 12.7 percent over the number of youths arrested in 2002. According to official statistics, 317,925 youths were arrested from 1998 to 2003, comprising 7.3 percent of the criminal suspects arrested during these five years.[17] A youth delinquency prevention office survey reported that most young suspects were between the ages of 15 and 16, although an increasing number of youths under the age of 14 have been arrested in recent years.

According to the China Youth and Children Research Center, the main youth crimes were robbery, theft, assault, and rape. Gang crimes accounted for 70 percent of delinquency, and about 85 percent of the country's drug addicts are youths.[18] Youth crime in China is almost exclusively male. Although females comprise only 2 percent of those arrested for youth offending, their numbers are on the rise.[19] As China continues to modernize, it can be anticipated that female delinquency will start to catch up with female delinquency in other countries while continuing to be only a small proportion of delinquency in China.

Although China still has no youth justice system, in 2004, the southern municipality of Guangzhou began the establishment of the nation's first dedicated youth court. In 1984, Shanghai opened China's first youth courtroom in which youths were differentiated from adult offenders. Currently, China has more than 7,200 judges who hear delinquency cases.[20] As of 2004, about 19,000 youths were incarcerated in "education centers," which are separate from adult detention facilities. The adult system has provisions that specify how youths are to be processed, but there's no statutory authority to guide the development of a separate system as is found in the United States. As in the adult system, the primary disposition available to young offenders who are sent to court are fines and incarceration. Although minor offenders are treated outside the system to a much greater extent than in the United States, once the offense is considered serious enough, the youth is inserted into a system that hasn't yet evolved well-defined processes and programs for the prevention and rehabilitation of young offenders.

This might be changing, however, as China has adopted an official policy of rehabilitation for young offenders, rather than punishment. In 2003, Shanghai and Beijing launched a program in which young offenders convicted of minor offenses worked in communities, instead of serving a jail term. This disposition might even be more critical in China than it is in the United States. Ding Shouxing, chief justice with Shanghai's Changning district court, has explained that, because most Chinese families have only one child, "Imprisonment would not only leave a scar that stains the young, but also makes their parents despair, and thus might change the life of a child and his family completely."[21]

In China a police officer leads juvenile inmates to a class at the Chongqing Juvenile Offender Correctional Center. The center has a nine-year compulsory education program for inmates age 18 and under. To encourage the youths to earn their diplomas, the center commutes up to five months of their sentences. *(© China Photos/Getty Images, Inc.)*

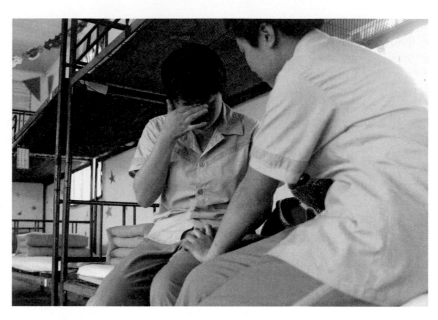

A female juvenile inmate at the Hubei Juvenile Correctional Center in China cries because she misses her mother. *(© China Photos/Getty Images, Inc.)*

4.1   K I D S *in the* N E W S

China's New Youth Party

China thinks it has a youth problem. It is difficult to compare crime statistics across countries—in fact, differences in culture, legal systems, definitions of offenses, and modes of collection render statistical comparisons almost meaningless—but China has reported a spike in youth crime: 12.7 percent in 2003, to be exact. The communist country is notorious for strict control over its citizenry, as well as the high recruitment of young people into the Communist Party. What's going on?

"Long hair, decadence, punks and hip-hop," Hung Huang, the publisher of the Chinese edition of *Seventeen*, told the *Los Angeles Times*.

China really appears to be worried. As of the summer of 2004, the government banned all new foreign films and firmed up restrictions on foreign textbooks, cell-phone text messages, the Internet, and teen magazines. The "youth palaces," state-funded afterschool community centers, are getting more money, too. Chinese youths are still joining the Communist Party, but many consider it a networking opportunity, rather than a patriotic act. One young college graduate told the *Los Angeles Times* that joining the party was more about getting a good job than "believing in communism."

How worried are Chinese officials? The national media administration has issued guidelines directing TV anchors to stop coloring their hair, wearing "bizarre" clothes, speaking in Hong Kong or Taiwan accents, and displaying navels, cleavage, or too much leg.[1]

Think About It

1. Does China have a youth problem?
2. Is the rise in Chinese youth crime related to displays of navels, cleavage, or colored hair?

Three Chinese teenage girls show off their Western-style hair-dos, piercings, and clothes. The Chinese government is worried about losing control over its youth. *(Courtesy Richard Nowitz/National Geographic Image Collection)*

1. Mark Magnier, "China's New Fear Is Green Hair and Hip-Hop," *Los Angeles Times*, July 4, 2004, Sunday final edition, p. D4.

Although one might be tempted to conclude that China has a long way to go before it catches up with the United States in its youth-offending response, this is a precarious conclusion, because so little is known about the comparative virtues of each system, given the wide gap in cultural conditions and quality of data.

Like Americans, the Chinese point to bad parenting as a cause of juvenile crime. In Shanghai, youths charged with minor offenses are urged to do volunteer work during their probationary periods, and both the youth and the youth's parents are counseled. In discussing the program, a district court official said, "Many juvenile crimes are related to the youngsters' parents, who are either too busy to take care of them or have spoiled them. We're hoping to help them better educate their kids."[22]

The one statement that can be made with certainty about China's delinquency issues and its response to youth offending is that these will certainly change in the years ahead. China is undergoing sweeping reforms in its economy and in the freedoms that its citizens expect. As Western culture via satellite television becomes available, China can expect more challenges to its society, which emphasizes conformity (see Kids in the News 4.1). Movement toward democracy will also bring more scrutiny of China's legal system.

India

With close to a billion people, India is the world's largest democracy. Like China, it's an old country that has been plagued for centuries with overpopulation and poverty. Unlike China, India was exposed to Western-style government as a British colony. India gained its independence in 1947 and has been a self-governing democracy for as long as China has been a communist state. Part of the process of separation from Britain involved dividing traditional India into two countries, India and Pakistan, based on religion.[23] After a massive transfer of population, India is now 80 percent Hindu and 12 percent Muslim. By contrast, Pakistan is now a predominantly Muslim state. Although this division settled growing tensions within India that threatened to escalate into civil war, it left the two countries with conflicts over disputed property, such as the Kashmir, as well as religious and ethnic tensions for the minorities who remain in each country.[24]

India was heavily influenced by British colonization. It based its legal institutions on the British model, and many of its lawyers and judges, such as Mohandas K. Gandhi, were educated in England. Once India gained independence, there was a relatively seamless transition in legal apparatus involving youths, because the British had already granted broad authority to India for a wide range of concerns.

The modern foundation of India's approach to juvenile delinquency was created in 1986 by the Juvenile Justice Act. The act's primary objective was to protect, care for, rehabilitate, educate, and give vocational training to delinquent children, as well as to make services available to neglected children. This program provides for a number of aftercare homes for children, many of them run by voluntary organizations. Formal introduction into the juvenile justice system occurs only after other alternatives have been explored. Additionally, the Juvenile Justice Act seeks to address the family's problems before employing detention. Prior to 2000, the age below which males were considered to be juveniles was set at age 16. Males over the age of 16 were considered to be adults. In 2000, the legislation was amended to raise the age to 18 (which is also the juvenile cutoff age for females).

In India, the age of criminal responsibility begins at 7. However, children between the ages of 7 and 12 aren't held responsible for criminal acts if it can be proved that the child doesn't understand what he or she has done. India has special courts to deal with young offenders.[25] In 2003, official statistics state that 33,320 youths were arrested and sent to court. At year's end, a large percentage were still awaiting trial, but of those who were adjudicated, most were placed under the care of their parents or guardians (see Figure 4-1).[26]

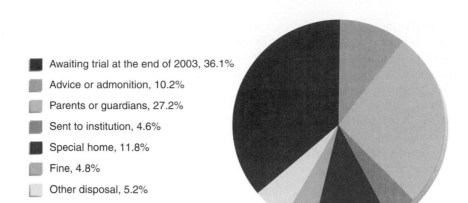

- ■ Awaiting trial at the end of 2003, 36.1%
- ■ Advice or admonition, 10.2%
- ■ Parents or guardians, 27.2%
- ■ Sent to institution, 4.6%
- ■ Special home, 11.8%
- ■ Fine, 4.8%
- ■ Other disposal, 5.2%

Figure 4-1   Juvenile Adjudications (Disposals) in India, 2003 *Source:* National Crime Records Bureau, *Crime in India 2003*, 393. Online ncrb.nic.in/crime2003/cii-2003/CHAP10.pdf.

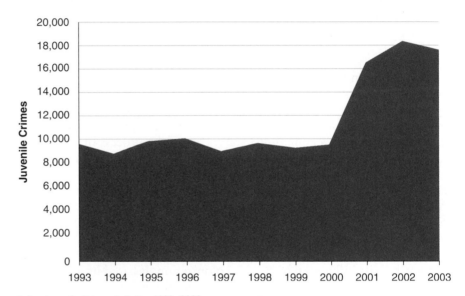

Figure 4-2   Juvenile Crimes in India, 1993–2003
The rise in crimes from 2001 on can probably be attributed to a revision of the juvenile age of responsibility for males from under age 16 to include those under age 18. *Source:* National Crime Records Bureau, *Crime in India 2003*, 394. Online at ncrb.nic.in/crime2003/cii-2003/Table%2010.1.pdf.

The proportion of offenses committed by youths, defined as those under the age of 18, was a little over 1 percent of all crimes committed in 2003.[27] This means that, statistically, about 99 percent of the crime in India is committed by those over 18 years of age (see Figure 4-2). Although it's important to remember that these data don't account for unreported crime, it's striking that India has such low levels of reported youth offenses compared to the United States. In 2003, there were 1,563,149 arrests in the United States in the 18-and-under age group, comprising 16.3 percent of all U.S. arrests.[28] Another interesting fact is that, of the youths arrested in India in 2003, 93.5 percent lived with parents or guardians; only 6.5 percent were homeless children.[29]

Because of the large population living in poverty, India places a special emphasis on street children. The aim is to prevent the destitution of children and to help them off the streets. In addition to getting these children into alternative living situations, the program aims to ensure that they have access to adequate nutrition, drinking water, education, and recreational facilities. Further, addressing abuse and exploitation of children is considered a primary objective. Street children are likely to fall victim to those who traffic in child slavery and prostitution.

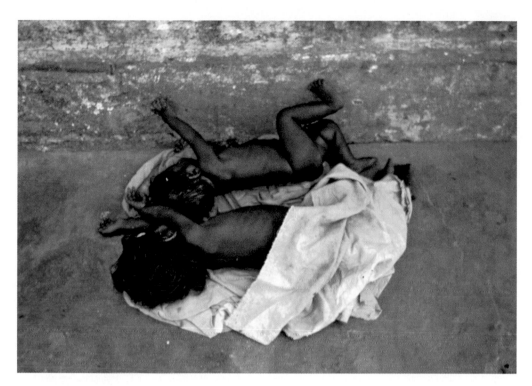

India has a very large population of impoverished, homeless people, many of whom are children. In the city of Madras, two small children sleep on the sidewalk. *(Courtesy Paul W. Liebhardt)*

Russia

Like China, Russia is a large and diverse country that is undergoing rapid social change. As an emerging democracy, it's experiencing the growing pains of a free-market economy and the demands of greater social freedoms by its citizens. Geographically the largest country in the world, Russia has close to 150 million people spread out over 21 republics, six territories, and 49 provinces.[30]

Russia is a very old country, but its present government is very new. For centuries, it was ruled by monarchs who were part of the royal families of Europe. In 1917, a workers' revolt led by Vladimir Lenin overthrew the czar and instituted a communist government that lasted for approximately 70 years.[31]

Everything changed in Russia in 1989 when the Soviet state collapsed, and many of the countries under its control claimed independence. Russia struggled with the new market economy and plunged into economic turmoil as many of the assets of the old Soviet state were acquired by capitalists, many of them former high-ranking members of the Soviet party.[32] The economy quickly changed from one controlled by the government to one in which private citizens controlled the major industries. Conditions in Russia are slowly changing as it develops democratic institutions and a capitalist economy. However, it's a rocky road, and this can be readily seen in the problems of crime, especially organized crime.[33]

Along with a new and problematic capitalist economic system, Russia is struggling with introducing democratic institutions. Along with its newfound freedoms is a growing youth delinquency problem. The former Soviet government controlled street crime with its repressive criminal justice system. Now, with democratic institutions struggling to develop interdisciplinary and interagency approaches to crime, Russia must address the causes of youth crime that stem from social upheaval, poverty, and individuals' rising expectations.

In 1994, Russia adopted a new criminal code that defines criminal responsibility and other legal aspects that pertain to young offenders. The code specifies that youths be afforded both punishment and compulsory measures for re-education.

Three street children stand near an empty lot in Saint Petersburg, Russia. According to UNICEF estimates, between 1 and 5 million Russian children live on the streets, with 50,000 more children going to live on the streets every year.
(Courtesy Jens Kalaene/DPA/Landov)

Re-education in Russia is roughly equivalent to rehabilitation and is used when it's deemed that young offenders would benefit from further training, treatment, or schooling. Punishment options include a range of possibilities that are alternatives to imprisonment. Age is considered a mitigating factor, and those who recruit others into criminal activity can expect to be treated more harshly than those who are recruited.[34]

Russia's criminal code divides youths into three groups of responsibility based on age. The age of criminal responsibility is 16, and youths age 14 and over are considered responsible only for offenses such as murder, major bodily injury, rape, kidnapping, larceny, robbery, burglary, and the theft of firearms and drugs.[35]

Under 14	Not criminally responsible
14 to 16	Criminally responsible for certain serious acts
16 to 18	Criminally responsible for all acts
18 and over	Adult

Thefts and robberies comprise more than half of youth offenses, with the most common offense being the theft of mobile telephones.[36] In 2005, Sergey Manakhov of the Interior Ministry's Investigation Commission gave a news conference in which he outlined a number of facts about rising youth crime in Russia.

- One in eight known offenders in 2004 was a minor.
- Youth crime was 6 percent higher in 2004 than in 2003.
- In 2004, the total known number of youth offenses was over 154,000, with 1,500 homicides.
- In 2004, one in six young offenders was intoxicated at the time of the offense.
- In 2004, young offenders were the subject of 79,000 criminal investigations, 72,000 of which went to court. Cases might be dropped if victims are compensated, if all parties agree to drop the case, or if the offender is remorseful.[37]

Like youth justice systems in many other countries, Russia attempts to use informal or alternative dispositions whenever possible. The law allows youth justice administrators to consider the circumstances of each case when fashioning a disposition. This individualized justice is consistent with efforts in the United States and recognizes that the effective treatment or education of the offender needs to be imposed with an appreciation of the youth's personal limitations as well as the resources available for changing the delinquent behavior. Two other facets of the Russian youth criminal code deserve mentioning at this point. First, capital punishment can't be applied to those under the age of 18. Second, a minor can't be incarcerated for more than 10 years.

In an effort to develop alternative means of handling young offenders, Russia instituted a number of educational-labor colonies. Some are similar to the U.S.-style boot-camp programs in which the offenders undergo an intensive regimen of work and discipline in an effort to develop conforming behavior. Some of these colonies have more mild regimens and are geared toward providing youths with workplace skills that they can use upon release.[38]

South Africa

South Africa has unique youth-offending issues that are a direct result of its tumultuous history. Few Western-style nations have experienced the kind of social turmoil and disruption that South Africa has, and few nations have as many natural resources that can ultimately be brought to bear on its issues of economic inequality.

Originally colonized by the Dutch in 1652, South Africa has had a history of suppressing black Africans. The Dutch and the British fought the Boer War to establish dominance in the region, and black South Africans were seldom considered as having claims of their own to the land and natural resources.[39] After World War II, the British granted independence to South Africa, and the white British and Dutch descendants established an **apartheid** system of government that disenfranchised all the black citizens. Rigid racial segregation relegated black Africans to shantytowns from which they commuted back and forth to work as low-paid laborers.[40]

The plight of children in the shantytowns was harsh. Children were caught up in the struggle for equality, and many were incarcerated along with adults. Adults who had committed common offenses and children who were being held for political purposes were incarcerated together, and little was done to separate these children from each other or from adult inmates.[41]

South Africa was transformed, relatively peacefully, into a constitutional republic in 1996. The South African legal system is still being developed, and at this point, young offenders have no separate statute. The laws that govern the treatment of youths in the criminal justice system are distributed throughout a variety of other laws, including the country's constitution. These laws specify that the government must consider the age of the child and that detention should be used only as a last resort.

South Africa has no courts specifically designed for young offenders. Their cases are heard by the same judges that preside over adult cases, and court personnel aren't specially trained to deal with youth cases. Some court personnel have a great deal of experience dealing with youths, but they end up spending most of their time dealing with adult cases. Although a youth has a right to legal counsel when substantial injustice is possible, such as incarceration, many families can't afford it. Many youths decline the offer of representation by court-appointed attorneys. Less than 50 percent of those who appear before the court are represented by counsel.

South Africa is undergoing rapid social change as a result of its move from apartheid to democracy. In addition, there's the problem of vast income inequality between whites, who are losing political control, and blacks, who are gaining it. The country is in such flux that it's difficult to forecast how the legal system will eventually handle young offenders. Until some of the underlying problems of crime, such as poverty, illiteracy, and gangsterism, are successfully addressed, South Africa's legal system will continue to struggle with issues such as due process. The new government

apartheid
An official policy of racial segregation involving political, legal, and economic discrimination against nonwhites.

has yet to establish laws that create a separate system for youths, but as the entire relationship between citizens and the state is newly specified, one can expect that South Africa will address the issues of justice for children.

Japan

Japan is an ancient country with a fascinating history. Its first constitution was written in 604 C.E. and has undergone many changes since. The most recent change happened after World War II when the allied nations forced Japan to institute a democracy. Its criminal code was patterned after the U.S. system to guarantee due process, while its fundamental framework was similar to the legal models found in most of western Europe.[42]

Japan's juvenile law might best be described as following the welfare and rehabilitation models. However, there has been strong pressure from the ministry of justice and prosecutors to amend the law to give them more power to be tougher on young offenders. In the 1990s, there were some sensational cases in which children murdered other children and, in one case, a youth put the severed head of a classmate on the gate at school. These cases, along with a growing victims' rights movement, led the media to advocate harsher sentences for youths who committed heinous crimes.[43] In 2004, police arrested 219 children younger than 14 for serious offenses such as murder, robbery, and arson. Up 3.3 percent from 2003, this was the highest such figure in the last decade according to Japan's National Police Agency.[44]

Generally, Japanese tradition favors avoiding disputes. Although the number of lawsuits has increased, informal resolutions, such as mediation and arbitration, are still preferred. People younger than 20 are considered juveniles, and juvenile cases go to the district's family court. Adjudications include probation and commitment to a training home or training school. Juveniles might be prosecuted in the criminal court when the offense is very serious. The death penalty is prohibited for anyone under age 18.[45] Offenders under age 14 are typically not held criminally responsible and are subject instead to Japan's Child Welfare Law.[46] In 2000, the nation's youth law was revised to reflect the following concerns:

- At the hearing, the youth should reflect on his or her offense and, along with the parents, realize their responsibility for the deviant behavior.

- The input of the victim is considered in the case. However, the victim isn't allowed to be present at the hearing. The court makes the name of the offender known to the victim and provides reasons for his or her disposition.

- In serious cases, the prosecutor can appear in court to provide judges with the pertinent facts as long as there is a legal representative also appearing for the young offender.

- The law is concerned with accountability. Offenders as young as 14 can face charges for homicide or other serious offenses. However, offenders as old as 19 who haven't committed heinous crimes will be kept in family court, which hears their cases.[47]

One interesting feature of Japan's efforts to deal with potential juvenile delinquents is the resources it puts into prevention activities. These activities take many forms and are found in various parts of Japan's culture. For instance, one prevention activity not found in the United States is the company-police conference. In the 1960s, corporations brought many teenagers from rural areas to the cities to work in factories after they graduated from junior high school. The police and the corporation cooperated in having a police officer assigned to the company to counsel and direct these young people as they adjusted to living away from home and learned to negotiate the challenges and temptations of living in the city. Today, Japan's companies do not employ as many young teenagers, but there are still 300 company-police conferences each year.

In urban Japan, koban, or police boxes, are important crime-prevention measures. *(Courtesy Annebicque Bernard, Corbis/Bettmann)*

Another prevention activity is the school-police conference, which is aimed at the high delinquency rate in high schools that began to appear right after World War II. By 1998, there were about 2,400 school-police conferences that reached 90 percent of all students in elementary, junior high, and senior high schools. These prevention activities place a police officer in the school to learn the concerns of students and present a positive role model. It is somewhat similar to the Officer Friendly programs that have been tried in some U.S. jurisdictions.

The police also participate in community prevention efforts. They have developed police boxes (*koban*) in urban areas and police houses (*chuzaishos*) in rural areas to facilitate prevention activities. Of special concern for these officers are the amusement areas where juveniles gather and are most likely to engage in delinquent behavior. These prevention efforts are very similar to the community-policing movement in the United States.

The police in Japan also actively engage volunteers in organized prevention efforts. In 1998, approximately 51,000 guidance volunteers assisted the police in preventing youth crime. There are three types of police volunteers: the guidance volunteer, the police helper for juveniles, and the instructor for juveniles. Each specializes in a different kind of prevention activity, and each is credited with helping to provide an environment where juveniles are under constant control and surveillance by families, schools, the police, and community volunteers.

Although Japan is a densely populated country, it isn't overwhelmed with young people as is the case in some of the developing countries of Africa and Asia. In fact, the proportion of teenagers to the rest of the population has been declining for a number of years. So much attention is being paid to the children that some fear they are becoming excessively protected, guided, and supervised.

England and Wales

The juvenile justice system in England and Wales is separate from those in other parts of the United Kingdom. The countries were united by the 1536 and 1542 Acts of Union, and their common legal systems are adversarial in all courts, including the juvenile courts.[48] Northern Ireland and Scotland have juvenile justice systems that operate under different laws and circumstances, so it would be confusing and misleading to lump them together. What makes England and Wales so interesting is the long history of attempts to deal with delinquency and the declining status of the country as a world power.

England was once the world's foremost industrial and economic power. Now the country struggles with immigration, economic stagnation, and unemployment. Consequently, it has fashioned a juvenile justice system that has been subject to wide fluctuations in philosophy as it tries to respond to changing political conditions and the new challenges of racial animosity and ethnic tensions.[49] The age of criminal responsibility in England and Wales is 10, and offenders between the ages of 10 and 17 appear before a youth court. Youth court sanctions are more restricted than those for adult courts; also, the court might impose fines that parents must pay, and youths might receive supervision or attendance-center orders.[50] The youth crime culture of England and Wales is distinctive in three ways. The use of drugs is pronounced, the stealing of cars for joyriding is of concern, and the existence of the "yob" culture is unique. Each of these issues is worth further exploration.

DRUGS   Like the United States, illegal drug use in England and Wales is a major social issue. It is estimated that half of young males and a third of young females have used illegal drugs at one time.[51] Further, there's a growing trend for younger children to experiment with drugs. Much of the drug use is restricted to marijuana, but other drugs are readily available. There is a clear link between drug use and crime among young people. Those who use drugs are more likely to engage in other types of deviant behavior. Many of those who use drugs become addicted, require substantial financial resources to pay for their habit, and turn to stealing or selling drugs.

JOYRIDING   Car crime accounts for about a quarter of the offenses committed by young males in England and Wales. Notice in Figure 4-3 that motoring offenses far outstrip most other offenses. Breaking into cars and stealing radios or personal effects, as well as the car itself, are perceived as problems committed by young urban males. The taking of the car for a joyride is a popular youth offense. The car isn't stolen to be kept as personal property or broken down and sold for parts. Rather, the car is driven, often at high speeds, and later abandoned, sometimes with considerable damage. The purpose of the offense is excitement. For working-class young men who are unemployed and lacking in ways to demonstrate their masculinity and bravado, joyriding represents an opportunity to don the mantle of manhood.

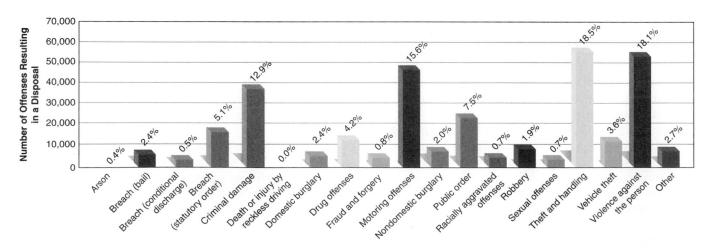

Figure 4-3   A Look at Offenses in England and Wales, 2005–2006. These figures do not represent all offenses committed by juveniles, but only those that resulted in a disposal. *Source:* Youth Justice Board for England and Wales, *Youth Justice Annual Statistics 2005/06*, p.7. Online at www.yjb.gov.uk/Publications/Resources/Downloads/Youth%20Justice%20Annual%20Statistics%202005-06.pdf.

YOB CULTURE   The growing public concern over the yobs is a facet of juvenile crime that isn't familiar to observers in the United States. The term *yob*, which is usually used to describe a young, male hooligan, comes from the backward spelling of "boy."[52] These young urban males, typically age 16 to 24, are common features of delinquency, especially victimizing the elderly and those who live in low-income areas. Rosalind Coward gives us one way of considering yobs:

> Yobs is a species of young white working class male which, if the British public is to be believed, is more common than ever before. The yob is foul-mouthed, irresponsible, probably unemployed and violent. The yob hangs around council estates where he terrorizes the local inhabitants, possibly in the company of his pit-bull terrier. He fathers children rather than caring for them. He is often drunk, probably uses drugs and is likely to be involved in crime, including domestic violence. He is the ultimate expression of macho values: mad, bad and dangerous to know.[53]

It is difficult to estimate how much the yob culture contributes to the delinquency problem in England and Wales. In 2005, after a group of about 20 youths beat and severely injured a man who had chased them after a rock was thrown at his car, local legislators instituted a crackdown, vowing punishments of up to three months' detention or a £5,000 fine.[54] Business owners have also complained about yob crowds making shopping areas unsafe. In 2003, the Anti-Social Behaviour Act was created to address the problem, with many of its provisions aimed directly at yob activities (see A Closer Look at Juvenile Issues 4.2).

It is tempting to speculate that if the economy in England and Wales were to improve drastically, especially in the industrial sectors, yob behavior would diminish. However, economic conditions are only one factor that contributes to yob culture. In 2005, there were reports of well-to-do undergraduate students engaging in yob-style behavior at Oxford University. School officials even worried publicly that the bad behavior of the school's rich students would discourage impoverished ones from attending the university.[55]

Whatever its prevalence and real harm, media reports make yob behavior appear to be epidemic. In 2003–2004, England's government reported that crime had fallen by 39 percent, down from a peak in 1995, and the risk of being victimized had fallen from 40 percent in 1995 to 26 percent, the lowest recorded level since 1981.[56] Also, the proportion of people believing that crime had increased over the past two years had dropped, compared to the previous year. Table 4-1 shows that the public's perception of antisocial behavior fell, also. And despite the public's

---

4.2 A CLOSER LOOK *at* JUVENILE ISSUES

ENGLAND'S ANTI-SOCIAL BEHAVIOUR ACT

The Anti-Social Behaviour Act was passed in 2003 as part of the government's "Together" campaign, which gave local councils, police, environmental health officers, housing officers, and officials new powers to address antisocial behavior. The act's provisions include the following:

- Powers to disperse groups in designated areas suffering persistent and serious antisocial behavior
- Extended powers to deal with aggravated trespass
- Restrictions on the use of air weapons and replica guns and bans on air-cartridge weapons that can be converted to firearms

- New mechanisms for enforcing parental responsibility for children who behave in an antisocial way in school or in the community
- Banning the sale of spray paints to youths under 16
- Powers for landlords to take action against antisocial tenants, including faster evictions
- Improved powers to deal with public assemblies and aggravated trespass
- Penalty notices for parents in truancy cases[1]

1. Home Office, Anti-Social Behaviour Act, June 2005, www.homeoffice.gov.uk/crime/antisocialbehaviour/legislation/asbact.html.

Table 4-1   **Antisocial Behavior Indicators in England and Wales**

The level of perceived antisocial behavior has fallen in England and Wales. The proportion of people reporting high levels of disorder in their jurisdiction fell from 21 to 16 percent between 2002/03 and 2003/04.

| | Percentage Saying Very or Fairly Big Problem in Their Area | | | | | | | |
	1992	1994	1996	1998	2000	2001/02 Interviews	2002/03 Interviews	2003/04 Interviews
High level of perceived antisocial behavior	n/a	n/a	n/a	n/a	n/a	19	21	16
Abandoned or burnt-out cars	n/a	n/a	n/a	n/a	14	20	25	15
Noisy neighbors or loud parties	8	8	8	8	9	10	10	9
People being drunk or rowdy in public places	n/a	n/a	n/a	n/a	n/a	22	23	19
People using or dealing drugs	14	22	21	25	33	31	32	25
Teenagers hanging around on the streets	20	26	24	27	32	32	33	27
Rubbish or litter lying around	30	26	26	28	30	32	33	29
Vandalism, graffiti, and other deliberate damage to property	26	29	24	26	32	34	35	28

Source: Tricia Dodd et al., *Crime in England and Wales 2003/2004* (London: Communication and Development Unit, July 2004), 18–19. Online at www.homeoffice.gov.uk/rds/pdfs04/hosb1004.pdf.

reported fear of yob behavior, the most likely victims of violent crime were also most likely to be yobs.[57]

What are the processes for dealing with young offenders? The English system of juvenile justice is very similar to that of the United States, making for some interesting comparisons and contrasts. Before 2000, one of the first steps was the *police caution*, which was a formal warning from a senior police officer to someone who admitted an offense that could have led to prosecution. Cautioning was intended to give minor offenders, traditionally juveniles and first-time offenders, a chance to reform and avoid a criminal record. The offender had to admit guilt and agree to a caution in order for one to be given. However, in 2000, the Crime and Disorder Act replaced the use of cautions for offenders under 18 with reprimands and final warnings.

Reprimands are also given to first-time offenders for minor offenses, except that any further offenses lead to either a final warning or a charge. A youth who receives a final warning is referred to a local *youth-offending team*, which assesses the youth and prepares a rehabilitation program to address his or her behavior. This assessment usually involves contacting the victim to determine whether victim–offender mediation or reparation to the victim and/or community is appropriate. Older youths are more likely than younger ones to receive final warnings rather than reprimands.[58]

Young offenders between 10 and 17 are sent to youth courts. The youth court, introduced in 1992, replaced the juvenile court, which was established in 1908 and handled young offenders only up to age 16. Youth courts have specially trained judges, and no one is allowed in youth courts except for court officers, the parties to the case, parents or guardians, the youth's legal representatives, witnesses, and specified media representatives. The press can report on proceedings but can't identify the offender. For a closer look at the adjudication (or disposal) of cases in England and Wales, see Figure 4-4. The following are circumstances in which a youth is tried in the adult criminal court (the Crown Court) instead of youth court.

- A youth is charged with homicide (either murder or manslaughter).
- An offender between the ages of 10 and 18 is charged with indecent assault, dangerous driving, or a "grave crime," an offense for which an adult could be incarcerated for at least 14 years. Such a case might go to the Crown Court if a judge decides that the appropriate sentence would be more than the youth court is allowed to give.
- A youth is charged jointly with another person age 18 or over. Both offenders are sent to the Crown Court.[59]

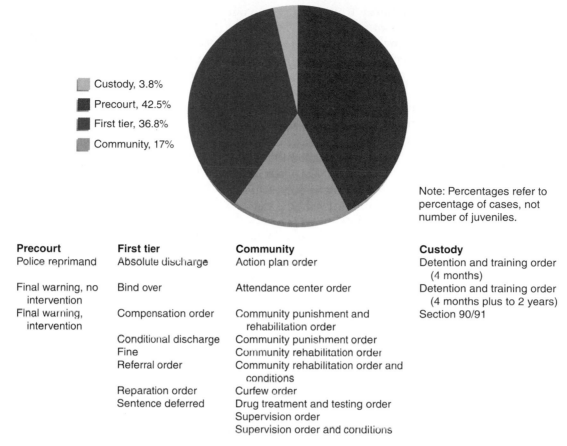

Custody, 3.8%
Precourt, 42.5%
First tier, 36.8%
Community, 17%

Note: Percentages refer to percentage of cases, not number of juveniles.

Precourt	**First tier**	**Community**	**Custody**
Police reprimand	Absolute discharge	Action plan order	Detention and training order (4 months)
Final warning, no intervention	Bind over	Attendance center order	Detention and training order (4 months plus to 2 years)
Final warning, intervention	Compensation order	Community punishment and rehabilitation order	Section 90/91
	Conditional discharge	Community punishment order	
	Fine	Community rehabilitation order	
	Referral order	Community rehabilitation order and conditions	
	Reparation order	Curfew order	
	Sentence deferred	Drug treatment and testing order	
		Supervision order	
		Supervision order and conditions	

Figure 4-4   **Court Disposals, England and Wales, 2003–2004**

The disposal (adjudication) of juvenile cases in England and Wales consisted of pre-court disposals, first-tier disposals, community disposals, and custody disposals. Each disposal covers a variety of sentences. For example, a juvenile receiving pre-court disposal might get a police reprimand. Another juvenile receiving a community disposal might be the subject of a curfew order. Source. Youth Justice Board, Youth Justice Annual Statistics, 2003/2004, 52. Online at www.youth-justice-board.gov.uk/Publications/Downloads/Annual%20Statistics%200304%20full.pdf.

As for detention, some young offenders are held outside the government's Prison Service. Secure Training Centres hold young offenders up to age 17 and are run by private contractors. Local Authority Secure Children's Homes generally accommodate offenders ages 12 to 14, girls under age 16, and boys ages 15 to 16 who are considered to be vulnerable.[60]

Hong Kong

The final place in which we examine juvenile delinquency is Hong Kong. Although not a country anymore (in 1997 it reverted to China after 155 years of British control), Hong Kong has such a fascinating history and is such a unique city that it's worth considering.

Hong Kong has always been very much a Chinese city. Although the British ruled for a century and a half, the culture was predominantly Chinese. The administrative governing procedures and the capitalist economy were patterned after England's, but many cultural aspects were unaffected by British control. Most importantly, for the purposes of discussing juvenile delinquency, we must appreciate the strong emphasis on family that exists in China and Hong Kong. Traditionally, Chinese society was organized on the Confucian principle that individuals were to act according to the duties imposed on them by their social status. A person was bound to obey all forms of authority, and most issues of delinquency were handled within the family. However, other influences within Hong Kong upset the traditional social structure that emphasized social control within the family. Since World War II, industrialization and urbanization have changed how families control their children. With both parents working away from home and youths in school with their peers, the socialization functions of the past have shifted.[61]

In the 1960s, Hong Kong experienced many incidents that raised the profile of youth crime. With youths staying out late at night and disobeying parents, the media began to report on young offenders at a greater rate. The result was a public concern about a perceived growing youth crime rate. In truth, the rate wasn't much different, although the public had become more concerned based on the expanded media coverage.

In 1964, the media reported on the *ah fei* (teddy boy) problem. In Hong Kong, *ah fei* referred to young hooligans, usually under the age of 23, who engaged in petty offenses and were visible on the streets in the form of loose-knit gangs. Further, organized crime groups know as *triads* were highlighted in the press, and there was widespread concern that young people with no jobs and little parental control would end up being recruited into organized crime. In the years since the triads first concerned law enforcement officials, they have grown into Hong Kong's most troubling problem for young people. What used to be considered normal schoolyard bullying is now suspected to be triad activities.[62]

Hong Kong has some features that make it a unique city and give it a different relationship with its young people. First, Hong Kong is a culturally and linguistically homogeneous city with 96 percent of the population being Chinese. Hong Kong has virtually no racial or ethnic minorities. Because of widespread economic development, Hong Kong has had a powerful surge in building and wealth. Hong Kong has virtually no ethnic ghettos and no underclass. All this presents an environment in which youth crime is a concern but, in terms of frequency, isn't as severe as in many other countries.

The youth crime that does exist in Hong Kong might be overstated. Hong Kong is basically one of the safest cities in the world. In 2005, the overall crime rate in the first quarter fell 6.6 percent over the same period in 2004, and the number of young offenders was down 32 percent compared to the same period.[63] The minimum age of criminal responsibility is 10. In 2000 and 2001, 721 children age 10 to 13 were prosecuted for crimes such as wounding, serious assault, and robbery.[64] Because of the media's amplification of the problem, the government has instituted a number of diversion programs to identify and prevent youth crime. This has brought an increased number of adolescents under the control of authorities and led to **net widening**, in which youths who, under normal circumstances, would be released are now introduced into some type of diversion program. Although this type of intervention might preclude future offending, it makes the situation appear more serious because so many youths are under state control.

net widening
Measures that bring more offenders and individuals into the criminal justice system or cause those already in the system to become more involved.

What is the future of youth justice in Hong Kong? There will be more changes in the government structure. Even though the city reverted to China in 1997, it retained much of its independence and administrative structure. It is now considered a special administrative region and continues to enjoy a high degree of autonomy. As part of the agreement to return Hong Kong to China, the law provides for the existing justice system to be maintained for the next 50 years. This means that the rule of law and existing policies of treatment and rehabilitation will be preserved.

Fifty years from now, China will be a much different place also. Given China's move toward capitalism, it might be that when the time comes for Hong Kong and China to fully integrate, the differences between the two will be much less than they are today. Already, Hong Kong is showing the rest of China the benefits and principles of capitalism, and in a sort of tail-wagging-the-dog scenario, Hong Kong might show China the way to other Western features of culture such as democracy.

INTERNATIONAL VICTIMIZATION OF CHILDREN

Other aspects of youth justice require a broader scope than the study of individual countries can provide. Two of these are the use of children as soldiers and as prostitutes.

Although these international problems have more to do with juvenile victimization than juvenile delinquency, they illustrate the context of childhood in some countries. These two pressing issues also emphasize the mutable definitions of youth crime. In the United States, a child who shoots and kills a person is considered a juvenile delinquent. In Afghanistan, this child might be valued as a soldier. In the United States, children who are forced into prostitution are considered victims and taken under the wing of the state, and their parents or guardians are prosecuted. In some Asian countries, child prostitution is common and sometimes has the tacit approval of the authorities because of the thriving sex-tourism trade.

The use of children as soldiers and prostitutes in some countries sheds some light on the United States' status offender laws. Regardless of the society, children don't control their place in it. Children don't get a say in how laws are made, how their status as children is considered, and how their societies restrict, enable, or use them as children. If a society requires that a child under the age of 16 attend school, then that child attends school. If another society requires a child to be a soldier as soon as he or she is physically able, then that child becomes a soldier. This is a power that practically every country in the world uses, regardless of its modernity or style of government. As mentioned earlier in the chapter, in the 1960s, young men could be forced into military service at age 18, although they could neither drink alcohol nor vote. Although legally considered to be adults, they were still subject to juvenile status laws. The U.S. government, at this time, used the status of young people to serve its needs.

The status of *youth* is subject to a society's dictates like no other status. This is one reason that *status* is such an important concept in the study of delinquency. Children, and most adolescents, are physically, intellectually, and psychologically inferior to

In some developing countries, boys are valued as soldiers. In Liberia, a boy soldier poses with his automatic rifle.
(Courtesy P. Robert, Corbis/Sygma)

adults. This is fundamental to their status. Children are vulnerable and can be both nurtured and controlled. The issue is control that becomes abuse.

Americans generally believe that it is society's responsibility to nurture and protect children and to keep them from harming themselves and others. In the United States, when a child strays too far from control, he or she is considered delinquent. Both the control and the delinquency are circumscribed by laws. Most of these laws are the same ones that govern adults, but some are created especially for juveniles. In the United States, the laws that apply to everyone protect society, and status offender laws exist mainly to protect children from themselves and predatory adults.

It can be argued that delinquency doesn't exist in many developing countries. Just as without laws, there's no crime, there's also no juvenile delinquency, only varying degrees of child victimization and victimizers, abuse, and neglect. To be fair, the United States has taken a hundred years to develop its juvenile justice system and specify the rights of youths. Some juvenile rights are still under contention. Only relatively recently, in 2005, did the U.S. Supreme Court exempt juveniles from capital punishment.[65] Ideally, rights accompany laws. This is one reason that the framers of the U.S. Constitution attached the Bill of Rights. However, none of the world's governments or constitutions has a children's bill of rights to balance the laws it uses to control them.

Children at War

Traditionally, the role of warrior was reserved for only the strongest men. Women and children were excluded not only from the ranks of soldiers but, in many societies, were also considered off-limits in terms of inflicting casualties.[66] In some ancient societies, it was considered wrong to kill an enemy's animals or destroy crops. War was strictly an affair between soldiers.

This has changed in modern times. Now it is common to wage war on civilian populations. Children are targeted as victims and used as warriors: in Afghanistan, children as young as 5 have fought in battles, and a 14-year-old killed the first U.S. soldier there.[67] Modern wars with high-altitude bombing have ravaged civilian populations since World War II, and the introduction of "smart bombs" has encouraged governments to place schools and hospitals next to military targets in the vain hope that the military targets will be spared. Being a civilian is no longer a guarantee that one won't be sought out for killing. In fact, it can make one an even more attractive target when military organizations desire to break their enemies' will.

Children used to be excluded from war for a variety of reasons. Aside from their being considered too valuable to risk losing, children were also considered too fragile to wield arms. It was considered a man's work to engage in warfare, and children were relegated to minor supporting roles, such as herding cattle, blowing bugles, or carrying supplies, if they were allowed on the battlefield at all. Boys who longed to prove their manhood on the battlefield were told to wait their turn.[68]

Today, these rules are being violated in underdeveloped countries around the world. As traditional societies break down in the wake of rapid social change, breaking the rules against targeting civilians and children or using children as soldiers has become commonplace. For example, in the aftermath of the demise of communism in the former Yugoslavia, a civil war broke out involving several ethnic groups. In an effort to destroy the enemy's will to fight or to avenge past atrocities, Serbian snipers would target children walking between parents.[69]

In other parts of the world, children are recruited as soldiers and forced to kill wounded or captured prisoners in order to harden them to the realities of being on the battlefield. For example,

> Children's presence as fighters also affects the norms of good behavior in war. The protections typically afforded to wounded soldiers and prisoners of war are often ignored in lieu of indoctrination needs. Rebel groups with child soldiers tend not to take prisoners. Instead, they typically kill the POWs on the spot or

bring them back to camp to kill as instructive victims. Likewise, even the force's own wounded children are subject to being executed by their fellow fighters, as leaders see them as needless drains on the organization and easily replaced. One survey in Colombia found that more than a third of former child soldiers admitted to having directly participated in out-of-combat killings.[70]

Child Prostitution

There is a well-known worldwide scandal involving the sexual exploitation of children. Citizens from some of the world's wealthiest nations, including the United States, travel to other countries to have sex with children.[71] Child prostitution laws are overlooked because of the money brought in by sex tourism. (For a look at organizations that work to save children from sex tourism, see Programs for Children 4.1.) Although many of these sex tourists consider themselves to be stellar citizens of their own countries, they adopt different attitudes when visiting Thailand, the Philippines, Cambodia, Indonesia, Sri Lanka, or Vietnam.

Prostitution is often considered a victimless crime. When two people agree on a transaction that includes a specific service for a specific price, it's considered to be consensual sex. Prostitution is legal in some countries and, if well regulated, isn't considered a social problem.[72] However, some forms of prostitution are considered social problems and are subject to arrest, prosecution, and imprisonment. The most obvious of these activities is the use of children as sexual partners. Few people (although there are some) would argue that it's appropriate for adults to engage in sexual relations with children. Even some who engage in the sexual exploitation of children in other countries would not deem it permissible in their home countries. Although children in Western, industrialized countries might be deemed innocent and out-of-bounds, those in impoverished developing countries are often considered to be

---

4.1 ## PROGRAMS *for* CHILDREN

PREVENTING PROSTITUTION

The problem of child prostitution in Southeast Asia is pervasive. In addition to Thailand, Cambodia is a country that has not been able (or willing) to control the sexual exploitation of children. However, some privately funded non-government organizations (NGOs) try to ease the circumstances that propel children into being exploited. One such NGO is M'lop Tapang, which is located in the seaside community of Siahnoukville, a favorite destination of pedophiles from many countries.

Established in June 2003, M'lop Tapang operates on an annual budget of about $60,000 and has a staff of 23 workers, including a full-time nurse. The program identifies young children who are on the street, using drugs, and in danger of falling victim to crime, disease, and exploitation. Each morning, the program takes the children to a center where they are fed breakfast and given medical care and entered into education programs. The program has helped more than 250 children and even provides services to older sisters and mothers who might be likely to be recruited by the sex industry.

Recruiting children from life on the street in Cambodia can be difficult. The M'lop Tapang centers will not allow children to attend if they are carrying knives or if they are inebriated. An inexpensive amphetamine in

the form of crystal methedrine, known as Ya Ma or "crazy medicine," sells for less than a dollar. A tube of glue that can keep the child intoxicated for a day costs about 12 cents.

An important part of the program is attempting to reintegrate the children into their families. Poverty can make difficult demands on families, and the children who are left to fend for themselves on the street are often denied support and family bonding. By educating the parents through the children on issues such as health care, sanitation, and AIDS, the centers are able to help maintain some of the connections between children and parents.

Thousands of NGOs serve children around the world, filling in the gaps where government services are lacking. In some countries, they are the major providers of youth services. Funded by churches, charities, anonymous benefactors, or foundations, nonprofit, non-government organizations are sometimes the only resource that stands between poor children and a short, nasty, and brutal life.[1]

1. Lisa Smith, "Suffer the Children," *Weekly Standard*, June 18–19, 2005, www.Thestandard.com.hk/stdn/std/Weekend/GF18Jp03.html.

legitimate sex partners because the authorities of these countries often welcome this type of commerce.

Thailand is ground zero for the sex-tourism industry. Although accurate numbers of child prostitutes are impossible to find, trade has long been aimed at foreigners. In the 1960s and early 1970s, thousands of U.S. servicemen were stationed in Thailand. The airmen, along with thousands of soldiers who went to Thailand on R&R (rest and recreation), provided a ready market for prostitution, a market that has survived and prospered. Young Thai women are pictured in advertising brochures as smiling and compliant. Typically, they are from the poorer northern provinces and are sent to Bangkok to earn money for their families. Sometimes their parents sell them to a brothel, where they are forced to work off the price of their room and board, as well as the money paid to their parents. However, the young women are never able to earn their freedom. The very young ones service foreigners in grand hotels, but as they age, they slip down the hierarchy of prostitutes until they have to work on the street.[73] Because of rural Thailand's poverty, even poorly paid prostitutes earn more than a typical police officer, so corruption within law enforcement is prevalent.[74]

SUMMARY

1. To appreciate why young people commit crime and learn how to effectively respond, we must look beyond our borders at how other societies handle juvenile justice.

2. The cultural components that determine whether behavior is rewarded or punished include religion, gender, and development.

3. It is sometimes difficult to consider other cultures and to compare them with one's own because of cultural isolation, ability to affect, ethnocentrism, and globalism. Major differences between cultures and justice systems make direct comparisons difficult and unproductive.

4. The major hurdles that researchers of comparative juvenile justice confront are the language barrier, definitional barriers, and the fact that countries report and record crime data in a variety of ways.

5. China is undergoing extremely rapid social change and does not have a formal juvenile justice system. The adult system provides for the treatment of juveniles, but there is no statutory authority to guide the development of a separate system.

6. Some of China's major, pressing issues include population, government, and religion.

7. Other institutions in Chinese society, such as schools, families, and neighborhood organizations, handle most minor cases.

8. India was heavily influenced by British colonization and based its legal institutions on the British model.

9. Youth crime is a relatively small problem in India and isn't the foremost concern. Because of the large population that lives in poverty, India places a special emphasis on street children.

10. Russia's new democratic institutions are struggling to develop approaches to crime and to address the causes of youth crime that stem from the family, poverty, and individuals' rising expectations.

11. Russia attempts to use informal or alternative dispositions whenever possible. The law allows youth justice administrators to consider the circumstances of each case when creating a disposition.

12. Capital punishment in Russia can't be used against persons under the age of 18, and a minor can't be incarcerated for more than 10 years.

13. After years of apartheid, South Africa was transformed into a constitutional republic in 1996. The legal system in South Africa is still being developed, and currently there is no separate statute for young offenders.

14. In South Africa, laws that govern the treatment of youths in the criminal justice system are distributed throughout a variety of other laws, including the country's constitution. These laws specify that the government must consider the age of the child and that detention should be used only as a last resort.

15. Japan's juvenile law can be described as following the welfare and rehabilitation models.

16. Japan devotes many resources to youth crime prevention. A prevention activity that isn't found

in the United States is the company-police conference. Another prevention activity is the school-police conference, which does have an analog in the United States in the form of Officer Friendly–type programs.

17. The police in Japan actively engage volunteers in organized prevention efforts. There are three types of police volunteers: the guidance volunteer, the police helper for juveniles, and the instructor for juveniles.

18. The youth justice system in England and Wales is separate from those in other parts of the United Kingdom, as well as similar to that of the United States.

19. The youth crime culture of England and Wales is distinctive in three ways: the use of drugs, the stealing of cars for joyriding, and yob culture.

20. In England and Wales, offenders under 18 might receive reprimands and final warnings. A final warning means that a youth is referred to a local youth-offending team, which assesses the youth and prepares a rehabilitation program.

21. English and Welsh juveniles between 10 and 17 are sent to youth courts, which were introduced in 1992.

22. A youth in England and Wales might be tried in the adult criminal court for homicide, indecent assault, dangerous driving, or a "grave crime" or if the youth is charged jointly with another person age 18 or over.

23. Hong Kong is a special autonomous region under the control of China. It does have more youth crime than it did a few decades ago but is still one of the safest cities in the world. Still, the government has instituted diversion programs to identify and prevent youth crime.

24. Two international issues concerning childhood emphasize the mutable definitions of youth crime: child soldiers and child prostitutes. Both activities utilize children in ways that would give them the status of delinquents and/or victims in the United States, but in other countries they are considered economic or military necessities.

REVIEW QUESTIONS

1. Why are direct comparisons between international juvenile justice systems difficult and generally unproductive?

2. What are some of the major hurdles confronting comparative juvenile justice scholars?

3. What are some of the major issues pressing on China? How do these affect its methods for handling young offenders?

4. How do the Chinese handle minor cases?

5. What is India's foremost youth concern? Does India have a serious youth crime problem?

6. How is the youth crime culture of England and Wales distinctive?

7. What unique political issues in South Africa affect its youth crime policy?

8. What is the status of juvenile capital punishment in Russia?

9. What models does Japan's juvenile law follow?

10. Does Hong Kong have a youth crime problem? What is the government doing about it?

ADDITIONAL READINGS

Findlay, Mark, *The Globalization of Crime: Understanding Transnational Relationships in Context* (New York: Cambridge University Press, 1999).

Human Rights Watch, "*'You'll Learn Not to Cry': Child Combatants in Colombia,*" September 2003, pp. 4–5.

Ignatieff, Michael, *The Warrior's Honor: Ethnic Wars and the Modern Conscience* (New York: Holt, 1998).

Pilkington, Hilary, *Russia's Youth and Its Culture: A Nation's Constructors and Constructed* (New York: Routledge, 1994).

Save the Children, "Children of the Gun," Children in Crisis Project Report, www.savethechildren.org/crisis.

United Nations Center for International Crime Prevention, www.uncjin.org/CICP/cicp.html.

ENDNOTES

1. For a classic example of a work that speaks to the cultural isolation of the United States, see *A Nation of Sheep* by William J. Lederer (New York: Norton, 1961).

2. Nagaty Sanad, *The Theory of Crime and Criminal Responsibility in Islamic Law* (Chicago: University of Illinois at Chicago, 1991).

3. Martha Crenshaw, "Why Is America the Primary Target? Terrorism as Globalized Civil War," in Charles W. Kegley, Jr., ed., *The New Global Terrorism: Characteristics, Causes, and Controls* (Upper Saddle River, NJ: Prentice Hall, 2003), 160–172.

4. Ruth Benedict, *The Chrysanthemum and the Sword: Patterns of Japanese Culture* (Rutland, VT: Charles E. Tuttle, 1946). Although dated now, this book is considered a classic on how culture affects a society. Of particular interest to students of juvenile delinquency is Chapter 11 on self-discipline.

5. C. Wright Mills, *The Sociological Imagination* (New York: Oxford University Press, 1959).

6. Michael Braswell, John Fuller, and Bo Lozoff, *Corrections, Peacemaking, and Restorative Justice: Transforming Individuals and Institutions* (Cincinnati, OH: Anderson, 2001). See especially Chapter 8, "Toward Restorative and Community Justice," 141–153.

7. Alice Walker and Pratibha Parmar, *Warrior Marks: Female Genital Mutilation and the Sexual Blinding of Women* (New York: Harcourt Brace, 1993). This remarkable book includes interviews with young women who have undergone painful surgery that alters their genitals. The reasons are varied but are bound up in the cultures that practice this procedure.

8. Graeme Newman, "Problems of Method in Comparative Criminology," *International Journal of Comparative and Applied Criminal Justice* 1, no. 1 (1977):17–31.

9. United Nations (1990), *Prevention of Delinquency, Juvenile Justice and the Protection of the Young: Policy Approaches and Directions* (A/CONF.144/16). Vienna: U.N. Crime Prevention and Criminal Justice Branch.

10. Piers Beirne and Joan Hill, *Comparative Criminology: An Annotated Bibliography* (New York: Greenwood Press, 1991.)

11. *CIA World Factbook: China*, www.cia.gov/library/publications/the-world-factbook/print/ch.html.

12. *CIA World Factbook: United States*, www.cia.gov/library/publications/the-world-factbook/print/us.html.

13. Liling Yue, "Youth Justice in China," in John A. Winterdyk, ed., *Juvenile Justice Systems: International Perspectives*, (Toronto: Canadian Scholar's Press, 2002), 103–126.

14. Lening Zhang et al., "Crime Prevention in a Communitarian Society: Bang-Jiao and Tiao-Jie in the People's Republic of China," *Justice Quarterly* 13, no. 2 (1996):199–222.

15. Jianan Guo et al., *World Factbook of Criminal Justice Systems: China*, 1993. Online at www.ojp.usdoj.gov/bjs/pub/ascii/wfbcjchi.txt.

16. Ibid.

17. Stacy Mosher, "Juvenile Crime Fact Sheet," *China Rights Forum: Growing Up in China* 4 (December 18, 2004):39. Online at www.hrichina.org/fs/view/downloadables/pdf/downloadable-resources/JuvenileCrime4.2004.pdf.

18. Ibid.

19. See note 11, pp. 110–111.

20. Xinhua, "China's First Juvenile Court to Open in Guangzhou," January 28, 2004.

21. Xinhua, "Community Service Gets Offending Minors Back on Track," July 25, 2003.

22. "Youth Offenders Get Voluntary Service," *China Daily*, April 16, 2005, p.2.

23. Robert Payne, *The Life and Death of Mahatma Gandhi* (New York: Smithmark, 1994), 517–580.

24. Tapan Chakreborty, "Juvenile Delinquency and Juvenile Justice in India," in John A. Winterdyk, ed., *Juvenile Justice Systems: International Perspectives*, (Toronto: Canadian Scholar's Press, 2002), 265–296.

25. R.K. Raghavan, *World Factbook of Criminal Justice Systems: India*, 1993, www.ojp.usdoj.gov/bjs/pub/ascii/wfbcjind.txt.

26. National Crime Records Bureau, *Crime in India 2003*, 393. Online at ncrb.nic.in/crime2003/cii-2003/CHAP10.pdf.

27. Ibid., 389.

28. Federal Bureau of Investigation, *Uniform Crime Reports: Crime in the United States* (Washington, DC: U.S. Government Printing Office, 2004), 280. Online at www.fbi.gov/ucr/cius_03/pdf/03sec4.pdf.

29. Ibid.

30. Dmitry A. Shestakov and Natalia D. Shestakova, "An Overview of Juvenile Justice and Juvenile Crime in Russia," in John A. Winterdyk, ed., *Juvenile Justice Systems: International Perspectives* (Toronto: Canadian Scholar's Press, 2002), 127–151, 411–440.

31. Aleksandr I. Solzhenitsyn, *The Gulag Archipelago 1918–1956* (New York: Harper and Row, 1973), 3–73.

32. Seymour M. Hersh, "The Wild East," *Atlantic Monthly* (June 1994):61–86.

33. Joseph Serio, "Organized Crime in the Soviet Union and Beyond," *Low Intensity Conflict and Law Enforcement* 1, no. 2 (Fall 1992):127–151.

34. Shestakov and Shestakova (see note 30), p. 418.

35. Ilya V. Nikiforov, *World Factbook of Criminal Justice Systems: Russia*, 1993, www.ojp.usdoj.gov/bjs/pub/ascii/wfbcjrus.txt.

36. Ivan Novikov, "Juvenile Crime Rate on Rise in Russia," ITAR-TASS, April 18, 2005.

37. Interfax/BBC, "Russian Police Spokesman Reports Rise in Juvenile Crime," March 15, 2005.

38. Shestakov and Shestakova (see note 30), p. 435.

39. Thomas Pakenham, *The Boer War* (New York: Random House, 1979).

40. Nelson Mandela, *Long Walk to Freedom: The Autobiography of Nelson Mandela* (Boston: Little, Brown, 1994). See especially Part Three, "Birth of a Freedom Fighter," 93–140.

41. Ann Skelton and Hennie Potgieter, "Juvenile Justice in South Africa," in John A. Winterdyk, ed., *Juvenile Justice Systems: International Perspectives* (Toronto: Canadian Scholar's Press, 2002), 477–501.

42. Geoffery Perret, *Old Soldiers Never Die: The Life of Douglas MacArthur* (New York: Random House, 1996). Perret credits MacArthur with writing the Japanese constitution. "It was the most important single achievement of the occupation. The new constitution put Japan on the path to becoming a truly free and democratic country in a part of the world where freedom and democracy had never existed before. It helped make Japan a country that was the envy, not the scourge of East Asia," pp. 506–507.

43. Minoru Yokoyama, "Juvenile Justice and Juvenile Crime: An Overview of Japan," in John A. Winterdyk, ed., *Juvenile Justice Systems: International Perspectives* (Toronto: Canadian Scholar's Press, 2002), 322–352.

44. Kyodo News Service/Japan Economic Newswire, "Serious Crimes by Juveniles under 14 on Rise," February 3, 2005.

45. Tadashi Moriyama, *World Factbook of Criminal Justice Systems: Japan 1993*, www.ojp.usdoj.gov/bjs/pub/ascii/wfbcjjap.txt.

46. See note 41.

47. Yokoyama (see note 43), pp. 327–328.

48. Corretta Phillips, Gemma Cox, and Ken Pease, *World Factbook of Criminal Justice Systems: England and Wales*, 1993, www.ojp.usdoj.gov/bjs/pub/ascii/wfbcjeng.txt.

49. Loraine Gelsthorpe and Vicky Kemp, "Comparative Juvenile Justice: England and Wales," John A. Winterdyk, ed., in *Juvenile Justice Systems: International Perspectives* (Toronto: Canadian Scholar's Press, 2002), 127–169.

50. See note 47.

51. Helene Raskin White, Robert Padina, and Randy LaGrange, "Longitudinal Predictors of Serious Substance Use and Delinquency," *Criminology* 25 (1987):715–740.

52. BBC, " 'Yobs' Not a Banned Police Word," October 2, 2006, news.bbc.co.uk/2/hi/uk_news/england/london/5400184.stm.

53. Rosalind Coward, "Whipping Boys," *Guardian Weekend*, September 2, 1994, p. 5, as quoted in Gelsthorpe and Kemp (see note 49), p.161.

54. Mark Blacklock, "Being Soft on Yobs Just Doesn't Work," *The Express*, May 19, 2005, UK first edition, p. 9.

55. Sarah Cassidy and Richard Garner, "Public School Yobs Deter Bright Pupils from Applying to Oxford, Says Patten," *The (London) Independent*, February 4, 2005, first edition, p. 16.

56. Tricia Dodd, Sian Nicholas, David Povey, and Alison Walker, *Crime in England and Wales 2003/2004* (London: Communication and Development Unit, July 2004), 1. Online at www.homeoffice.gov.uk/rds/pdfs04/hosb1004.pdf.

57. Ibid., 67.

58. *Criminal Statistics England and Wales 2003* (London: The Stationery Office, 2004), 23, 91. Online at www.archive2.official-documents.co.uk/document/cm63/6361/6361.pdf.

59. Ibid., 95.

60. Ibid., 54.

61. Harold Traver, "Juvenile Delinquency in Hong Kong," in John A. Winterdyk, ed., *Juvenile Justice Systems: International Perspectives* (Toronto: Canadian Scholar's Press, 2002), 208–234.

62. Ibid., p. 213.

63. Financial Times Information, "Hong Kong: First Quarter Crime Down 6.6%," May 1, 2005.

64. Polly Hui, "Groups Urge Change in Criminal-Age Law," *South China Morning Post*, February 6, 2004, p. 3.

65. Warren Richey, "Juvenile Death Penalty Abolished," *Christian Science Monitor*, March 2, 2005, sec. USA, p. 01.

66. P.W. Singer, *Children at War* (New York: Pantheon Books, 2005), 3–8.

67. Paul J. Nyden, "Modern Warfare Lighter Weapons, Non-State Armies Have Led to a Limber and Teachable Worldwide Pool of Killer Recruits: Children at War," *Charleston Gazette* (West Virginia), March 20, 2005, p. P1E.

68. Singer (see note 66), p 9.

69. Ibid., 5.

70. Ibid., 102.

71. Sarah Shannon, "The Global Sex Trade: Humans as the Ultimate Commodity," *Crime and Justice International* 17 (2001): 5–7.

72. Robert Meier and Gilbert Geis, *Victimless Crime? Prostitution, Drugs, Homosexuality, Abortion* (Los Angeles: Roxbury, 1997).

73. Alex Renton, "Learning the Thai Sex Trade," *Prospect* 110 (May 2005). Online at www.prospect-magazine.co.uk/article_details.php?id=6889.

74. Ibid.

Why is understanding theory important to understanding delinquency?

What are the classical and positivist schools of criminology?

How has religion influenced our view of delinquency?

CHAPTER 5

Theoretical Foundations of Crime and Delinquency

One of the most fascinating features of juvenile delinquency that students quickly discover is that whatever they think the solution to crime is, someone else has thought of it already. Students are sometimes surprised to discover that their original ideas are actually well-established explanations for delinquency and have been used to develop laws, policies, and programs in the juvenile justice system. These established explanations are generally situated within one of two schools of criminological thought: the classical school and the positivist school.

The classical and positivist schools were developed by scholars, researchers, thinkers, philosophers, sociologists, and early criminologists who were looking for rational explanations for crime and deviance. A third way of thinking about crime and deviance, **spiritual explanations**, is one that's been developed by everyone who has ever wondered why another person breaks the law or violates the rules or norms of society. The classical and positivist schools go back to the 18th and 19th centuries; spiritual explanations probably reach back to the dawn of humanity.

This chapter will explore these three ways of thinking about crime and deviance because they are the most important to the creation of the criminal and juvenile justice systems. Although developed in the past, these systems of thought still influence our current system and ideas of justice, and none have truly fallen out of favor.

- Many people still suggest spiritual explanations for deviant behavior and lawbreaking. As a social institution, religion continues to influence social control in the United States.[1] Spiritual ideas are embedded in our popular culture and are at the foundation of the modern criminal justice system.
- The **classical school of criminology** is fundamental to our understanding of crime. Although classical criminology was developed during the Enlightenment, it's still an important part of our laws and criminal justice system.
- The **positivist school of criminology** focuses on the offender, rather than on the offense. The positivist school seeks the truth about human nature through science, rather than religion or philosophy.

At the bases of the classical and positivist schools are theories, and to understand these two schools, we first have to know what a theory is. The important work of the juvenile justice system is based on theory, and the study of theory is crucial to all academic enterprise, including the study of juvenile delinquency.[2] We will devote the next four chapters to considering many of the theories that seek to explain why some youths break the law and how the juvenile justice system responds. First, however, we need to understand why theories are important, how they are constructed, and how to evaluate them so that we can compare and contrast the various explanations of juvenile delinquency.

WHAT GOOD IS THEORY AND WHAT IS GOOD THEORY?

The word **theory** has a dubious connotation for some people. Many people think of theory as little more than an educated guess. This isn't true: a **hypothesis** is an educated guess (see A Closer Look at Juvenile Issues 5.1). Theories are based on real-life observations and data and are important tools for understanding the world.[3] We use theories and hypotheses every day whether we realize it or not. For example, you are driving your car and following a loaded pickup truck from a construction site. After a few miles, you hear a loud bang and begin to have trouble controlling the car. You develop a quick hypothesis that you have a flat tire. Upon halting the car and seeing the nails sticking out of the flat tire, you develop a theory that some nails fell out of the pickup truck; you ran over them, and they punctured your tire. You don't know this for sure, but based on the evidence, you theorize it to be true.

Some theories are simple, such as our flat-tire theory, and some are complicated, such as Albert Einstein's theory of general relativity. Although textbook definitions of

---

spiritual explanations
Explanations for crime and deviance that stem from religious belief.

classical school of criminology
A school of thought that employs the idea of free will to explain criminal behavior.

positivist school of criminology
A school of thought that considers the causes of crime and delinquency to be external to the offender and uses scientific techniques to study crime.

theory
A set of interconnected statements or propositions that explain how two or more events or factors are related to one another. [Daniel J. Curran and Claire M. Renzetti, Theories of Crime, 2nd ed. (Boston: Allyn and Bacon, 2001), 2.]

hypothesis
An untested idea that is set forth to explain a given fact or phenomenon. An educated guess.

5.1 A CLOSER LOOK *at* JUVENILE ISSUES

NOT JUST A THEORY

Contrary to popular belief, a scientific theory isn't an educated guess. That would be a hypothesis, which is a tentative explanation for an observation or phenomenon. Hypotheses have their place in science—they are an early step in the scientific method—but when some people refer to scientific theories, be it the theory of evolution or the theory of general relativity, as "just a theory," they're actually confusing "theory" with "hypothesis."

In science, a theory is a way to organize facts and explain data. In the social sciences, theories use facts and data to explain human behavior, and in criminal justice, theories seek to explain human deviance. A theory offers an intellectual framework for discussion and investigation but is also subject to refinement. If another theory comes along that offers a better explanation for a given issue, the old theory might be discarded.

theory might differ slightly, they consistently address similar issues. In this text, we will use the definition developed by sociologists Daniel Curran and Clair Renzetti: "A theory is a set of interconnected statements or propositions that explain how two or more events or factors are related to one another."[4]

For example, if we say that the crime rate decreases as educational level increases, we're considering two factors, crime rate and educational level, and specifying their inverse relationship. By specifying the direction of the relationship, we can then conduct observations to determine the theory's validity. Within Curran and Renzetti's simple definition is the potential to specify how any two clearly stated factors are related to each other. According to criminologists Ronald Akers and Christine Sellers, some criteria must be addressed when evaluating theories.[5]

- **Logical consistency** Does the theory make sense? For example, Akers and Sellers state that the theory must have propositions that are logically stated and internally consistent. They contend that if a theory argues that offenders have biological reasons for what they do, then it makes no sense to claim that family socialization is a basic cause of criminal behavior. It would make more sense to claim that the cause of criminal behavior is a gene that is passed from the parents to the children.

- **Scope** The amount of deviant behavior that a theory can explain depends on its scope. A theory that addresses only shoplifting is useless for explaining violent offenses. Although good theories attempt to explain a broad range of behavior, some theories overreach. There can be a trade-off between the broad scope of a theory and its ability to produce strong and consistent results.

- **Parsimony** In terms of theory, parsimony refers to the economy of an explanation. Parsimonious theories explain a good deal of behavior using straightforward language. Parsimony and scope are related, and some of the best theories carry a great deal of meaning with carefully selected words.

- **Testability** A good theory should be stated in such a way that the propositions and their relationships can be scientifically tested. According to Akers and Sellers, a theory might not be testable for a number of reasons. First, it might be based on a tautology, or circular reasoning.[6] If we say that low self-control is measured by a failure to refrain from crime and then say that crime is caused by low self-control, we haven't offered a testable theory.[7] The key to developing testable theories is to start with observable criteria. If we say, "The devil made me do it," we must then find some way to observe the actions of an individual called the devil. Because belief in the devil, like the belief in a supreme being, is considered a matter of faith, it's difficult to observe such factors with any scientific certainty. Finally, Akers and Sellers point out that it's not sufficient to simply construct theories that can be supported, but that a good theory can also be rejected or falsified.[8] If the facts of a case are continually reinterpreted to support a theory, the theory can never be rejected.

- **Empirical validity** Empirical validity is evidence that an instrument is measuring what it has been designed to measure. By repeatedly testing a theory with different populations or in different geographic locations, researchers can collect data about a theory's reliability and empirical validity. For example, several small-scale treatment programs that appeared to be successful didn't succeed when tried on a larger scale or in different locations. It became evident that the earlier positive results stemmed from the determination of a staff who was dedicated to a new and innovative program.[9] Once the program became routine and subject to staff who considered the program as just a job, the positive results vanished. So, in this case, it was repeated testing of a program's features in other locations that helped researchers determine if the program worked.[10]

- **Usefulness and policy implications** The criterion that divides criminological theory between an abstract academic exercise and practical application is the degree to which it can guide policy. Crime and crime control are pressing concerns, and the theories that scholars develop can have far-reaching ramifications. For instance, a theory that demonstrates that youths who are exposed to alcohol at an early age are more prone to drinking problems as adults would suggest that parents should protect their children from alcohol for as long as possible. However, some theories suggest policy changes that are unreasonable, impossible, or unethical. Imagine that a researcher develops a theory that left-handed children are at a greater risk of becoming delinquent than right-handed children. Should we force all left-handed children to use their right hand? What would be the unintended consequences of such a policy? Policies suggested by theory must be considered in the light of ethical and professional guidelines to ensure responsible public policy.

- **Ideology** Finally, Akers and Sellers suggest that a theory must be considered based on its ideological underpinnings.[11] Theories can be derived from the agendas of reformers or the world views of those in charge, with the explicit purpose of forwarding a particular political or social purpose. For instance, those concerned with the modern, Western-style nuclear family will most likely reject theories that suggest that an intact nuclear family isn't absolutely required for the development of healthy children. Regardless of the veracity of theories, it's useful to know the ideology of those responsible for them. Although it's possible for someone to have a slanted ideological perspective and still develop an objective theory, it's intellectually honest to reveal ideological bias.[12]

It is easy to see from these criteria for evaluating theory that a lot of thought and research goes into constructing explanations of crime and society's response to it. Few theories fall out of favor in criminology. Like flotsam and jetsam on a beach, theories wash ashore and are added to the theories that came before them. Some remain in use, while others are only half-used or only occasionally considered.

One of the first concerns we will observe in our study of theory is that no single theory completely explains all the issues that are important to the study of juvenile delinquency. Many theories might reveal the truth but still fail to capture the whole truth. This is because crime is complicated and multifaceted. For now, we must be satisfied with partial explanations, conflicting theories, and an incomplete understanding of why people, including juveniles, break the law.

WHAT'S GOTTEN INTO YOU? SPIRITUAL EXPLANATIONS

Spiritual explanations, which are rooted in religion, tend to be favored by many people— "The devil made him do it," "That serial killer is pure evil," or "She was just born bad"—and aspects of the spiritual point of view remain in the formal justice system. One social reason for punishment, especially for heinous crimes, is to satisfy the need of both society and the victim or victims for revenge by symbolically quelling evil. See Crosscurrents 5.1 for more on the concept of evil. The custom of and justifications for seeking revenge come from ancient religious texts. For example, in Leviticus 24:17–22 we can observe one of the origins of the Western idea of **lex talionis,** or the law of retribution.[13]

> 17 And he that killeth any man shall surely be put to death.
> 18 And he that killeth a beast shall make it good; beast for beast.
> 19 And if a man cause a blemish in his neighbour; as he hath done, so shall it be done to him;
> 20 Breach for breach, eye for eye, tooth for tooth: as he hath caused a blemish in a man, so shall it be done to him again.

lex talionis

The law of retribution and/or retaliation drawn from the book of Leviticus.

Religion is a powerful social institution. For much of the recorded history of the Western world, organized religion was vital to political and social control. In western Europe, the Christian church was linked to royalty in that the royal power was considered a reflection of the will of God, a concept also known as the "divine right of kings."[14] This dual system of Christian church and state survived for centuries because the only people who were educated were royalty, aristocrats, and clergy.

Because of the strong influence of the Christian church in western Europe and England, the English legal system, upon which the U.S. legal system is based, is largely derived from Christian ideas of justice and morality. These ideas explained the nature of humanity and social control as a struggle between good and evil, and crime and deviant behavior were considered to be the works of "the devil" or of human beings who deviated from the will of God.

But just how was the "devil" considered to influence people to break the law and young people to misbehave, and how has society traditionally retaliated? According to Stephen Pfohl, demonic explanations of deviant behavior were of two types.

- **Road of temptation** According to the theory of demonic influence, each of us is tempted by the devil to engage in deviant acts. Perhaps the most important

William Blake's painting *The Good and Evil Angels Struggling for Possession of a Child* is a dramatic depiction of the forces that many people believe to be in contention for human beings. *(Blake, "The Good and Evil Angels Struggling for Possession of a Child," ca. 1805. © Tate Gallery/Art Resource)*

5.1 CrossCurrents

Evil

The concept of evil is neither new nor particularly unique to either modern or ancient cultures. Although the practice of criminal justice since the Enlightenment has inched away from official diagnoses of evil, the concept is alive and well. It seems that just when theorists believe they have a handle on what makes the most heinous offenders do what they do, another offender comes along who does something even more inexplicably heinous. For a while it seemed that social surroundings and upbringing could explain the murderous behavior of some offenders. Hormones, physical illness, and brain chemistry were believed to play a key role. However, there are some offenders whose activities seem to be unexplainable by any current theory. The concept of evil, however, is a broad brush that covers a lot of behaviors, so it gets another hearing.

Most recently, the concept of evil has come back in style. Although as of late 2005, violent crime in the United States had been down for many years, some standout cases, such as the BTK killer and the DC snipers, demanded an explanation, for which evil fit the bill.[1]

The dictionary definitions of evil include such words as *harm*, *misfortune*, and *destruction*, as well as *spite*, *ruin*, *injury*, and *pain*. Although anyone can be judged to perform an evil act, be considered evil, or

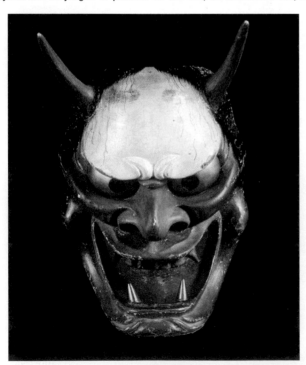

Bad behavior in both adults and children is often thought to be the work of a demon or devil. *(Courtesy of Mitsui Bunko. Pacific Press Service)*

suffer from evil, the word has a strong connection to the religious and is often connected to what some religions deem a spirit, demon, or, in some cases, Satan. Evil makes an appearance within the first few verses of the Quran, the Torah, and the Bible.

The evil that is considered the responsibility of the U.S. justice system is that which is connected to crime. Evil crimes tend to be restricted to rape and murder. Even so, some rapes and murders would probably be excluded from the evil category or at least have been only recently added. For example, not long ago in the United States, a husband who had forcible sex with his wife was not considered to have raped her, and it was considered impossible to rape a man. The assailants in these cases were not considered rapists and therefore were not evil. In another example, murders committed by members of gangs or organized crime against other gang and organized crime members might be considered "business as usual." Murder might still be considered bad in these cases, but not quite evil. In popular thought, the description of evil tends to be restricted to mass murderers (the Manson family), serial killers (John Wayne Gacy), and the occasional one-time murderer who kills in a particularly gruesome or aggravated fashion (Scott Peterson, who was convicted in 2004 of killing his pregnant wife, Laci).

Such cases have led some mental health experts, philosophers, and criminologists to attempt to create a secular definition of evil. Philosopher Claudia Card, author of *The Atrocity Paradigm*, defines evil as "a harm that is (1) reasonably foreseeable (or appreciable) and (2) culpably inflicted (or tolerated, aggravated, or maintained), and that (3) deprives, or seriously risks depriving, others of the basics that are necessary to make a life possible and tolerable or decent (or to make a death decent)."[2] Card further explains that "the nature and severity of the harms, rather than perpetrators' psychological states, distinguish evils from ordinary wrongs."[3]

In 2001, Michael Welner, a professor of psychiatry at New York University, began building the Depravity Scale, using a questionnaire that asked law and mental health professionals the types of behaviors they considered depraved.[4] According to the Depravity Scale website, the idea is "to provide a standardized scale for the justice system to determine with scientific certainty which aspects of a crime represent depravity." In a *New York Times* interview, Michael H. Stone of Columbia University, who studied hundreds of violent criminals to create his 22-level Gradations of Evil Scale, said that it was time for experts to give evil people "the proper appellation."[5] Psychologist Robert Hare, creator of the landmark psychopathy checklist, a test designed to determine an individual's psychopathic tendencies, said that "There is a group we call lethal predators, who are psychopathic, sadistic, and sane, and people have said this is approaching a measure of evil, and with good reason."[6]

Not all mental health experts agree that the term *evil* is useful, pointing out that not only is it subjective, but also that it isn't a medical designation. The problem is that the exact definition of evil varies depending on who is defining it. The scientific method depends on a consistent definition of terms. For example, all physicists define *light* the same way. Many legal and mental health experts would assert that exact terminology and ascertainable criteria are necessary when branding an offender with a term that could get him or her executed. According to Eric Hickey:

In the "hard sciences" such as chemistry and physics, exactness and quantification are necessary requirements; however, the notion of evil is intangible and unmeasurable, and it is often used as a misnomer for inappropriate behavior. [B]oth bad and evil persons may engage in similar types of undesirable behaviors yet be categorized with different labels. Part of the problem in assigning such labels is determining exactly what constitutes good or evil.[7]

Neural research on antisocial and violent people has shown some differences in brain structure. In some cases, researchers have found breakdowns in the parts of the brain responsible for cognition, planning, and impulse control.[8] Other research undertaken by James Blair on serial killers—people whose offenses are often nonimpulsive, well-considered, and planned—has revealed temporal lobe defects affecting emotion and empathy. It appears that at least some offenders' lack of pity has a physical basis in the brain.[9]

In the justice system, the issue of using the label *evil* is not just philosophical. Justice is concerned not only with offenses, offenders, and motivations, but with corrections and, if possible, rehabilitation. The most important question is this: What do we do with someone who does things that many people think are evil? Does the knowledge that some of what we call evil may be the process of brain dysfunction mitigate the evil deed? For example, what do we do with a 15-year-old killer who we know has a damaged or poorly functioning amygdala? Does that make the killer less responsible? Do we punish, execute, or medicate? Is it possible to rehabilitate the youth?

Psychiatrist Sean Spence writes, "As our scientific knowledge expands, it seems that the space for moral evil contracts."[10] Spence goes on to warn that although we might eventually learn exactly where evil sits in the brain, society must still deal with the offender.[11] The debate over evil isn't purely philosophical. It has consequences for everyone involved in the criminal and juvenile justice systems. The debate is especially sensitive when juveniles are concerned.

Generally, offenders under the age of 18 aren't considered to bear the full responsibility for their actions, except in heinous offenses such as rape or murder. (In some states, a juvenile suspected of these offenses will be automatically waived to criminal court.) The mission of the juvenile justice system, however, is to rehabilitate, not punish. If society decides that a delinquent is "born evil" and can't be helped, it's possible that the youth could remain within the confines of the justice system forever.

In August 2005, Mitchell Johnson left a Tennessee detention facility on his 21st birthday, with plans to become a minister and no criminal record. Seven years earlier, in 1998, he and Andrew Golden pulled a fire alarm in their Jonesboro, Arkansas, middle school and hid outside with a cache of weapons. As the students and teachers exited the school, Johnson and Golden shot and killed 4 students and a teacher and wounded 10 others. Survivors of the attack and local residents were distressed at the news of Johnson's release.[12] Is Johnson himself evil, or is the evil confined to what he did? Did he freely choose his destructive course, or was it a product of some physical or social ill?

Perhaps the most interesting thing about evil is that we can't really define it, except when it happens. It is the monster in the shadows that engulfs everything with its presence without revealing itself.

Think About It

1. Should the concept of evil be acknowledged by the criminal justice system?
2. Is evil strictly a religious concept, or can the concept be applied to secular issues as well?
3. Can evil be measured?

1 Shannan M. Catalano, *Criminal Victimization, 2004* (Washington, DC: Bureau of Justice Statistics, 2005). Online at www.ojp.usdoj.gov/bjs/pub/pdf/cv04.pdf. Dennis Rader killed 10 people in the Wichita, Kansas, area from 1974 to 1991. Rader had been a Lutheran church official and Boy Scout leader. Rader, who called himself BTK, which stood for "bind, torture and kill," was sentenced to 10 consecutive life terms in 2005. John Allen Muhammad and Lee Boyd Malvo were convicted in the October 2002 sniper-style shootings that killed 10 people and wounded 3 in the Washington, DC area, as well as in Alabama and Washington state. Malvo, who was 17 at the time of the shootings, was sentenced to life in prison without parole. Muhammad was sentenced to death.
2 Claudia Card, *The Atrocity Paradigm: A Theory of Evil* (New York: Oxford University Press, 2002), 16.
3 Ibid., 4.
4 Online at www.depravityscale.org.
5 Michael H. Stone, *Abnormalities of Personality: Within and Beyond the Realm of Treatment* (New York: Norton, 1993), 458–475; Benedict Carey, "For the Worst of Us, the Diagnosis May Be 'Evil,'" *New York Times*, February 8, 2005, www.nytimes.com/2005/02/08/health/psychology/08evil.html?ex=1265691600&en=42d1894675043979&ei=5090&partner=rssuserland.
6 Carey (see note 5).
7 Eric W. Hickey, *Serial Murderers and Their Victims*, 4th ed. (Belmont, CA: Thomson Wadsworth, 2006), 50.
8 Adrian Raine is considered a pioneer in this field. See Adrian Raine et al., "Reduced Prefrontal and Increased Subcortical Brain Functioning Assessed Using Positron Emission Tomography in Predatory and Affective Murderers," *Behavioral Sciences and the Law* 16 (1998): 319–332. For a brief layman's view, see "Natural Born Killers?" *Psychology Today* 28, no. 1 (January/February 1995): 10.
9 Blair has also done work on the brain function of children with psychopathic tendencies. For examples of this work see R.J.R. Blair et al., "Deafness to Fear in Boys with Psychopathic Tendencies," *Journal of Child Psychology and Psychiatry* 46 (2005): 327–336, and R.J.R. Blair, "The Roles of Orbital Frontal Cortex in the Modulation of Antisocial Behavior," *Brain and Cognition* 55 (2004): 198–208.
10 Sean Spence, "Bad or Mad?" *New Scientist* 181, no. 2439 (March 20–26, 2004): 38–41.
11 Ibid.
12 "Jonesboro School Shooter Free," CNN, August 12, 2005, www.cnn.com/2005/LAW/08/12/jonesboro.shooter/index.html. Andrew Golden was released in May 2007.

5.1   FOCUS on ETHICS

THE DEVIL'S ADVOCATE

As a juvenile court judge, you have always been concerned with treating the whole child. You are renowned for your creative sentences that strike to the heart of the problems affecting children and their families. You have received honors from fellow judges, the press, and the community. Proud of your reputation as a cutting-edge jurist, you are not afraid to impose innovative dispositions that you believe will benefit individual children and the community.

Now you are sitting in judgment on one of the most fascinating cases of your career. A teenage boy has been accused of a series of despicable offenses spanning five years. These offenses range from small matters, such as four-letter-word graffiti, to serious matters such as stalking his girlfriend and killing her pets when she rebuffed him. There is no doubt that this boy is headed for serious trouble and is becoming a real threat to the community. You are prepared to hold him in a detention center until you read the evaluation from your court caseworker. She provides a complete social history of the boy and his family that reveals that they come from a very conservative fundamentalist religion. The parents are adamant that their son is possessed by a demon and that the only hope for him is exorcism.

What Do You Do?

1. Let the boy see the exorcist because you think this might be the best chance to keep him out of trouble. It is possible that because exorcism fits within the religious and psychological framework of the youth and his parents, it might do some good.

2. Remember that you are an officer of the court and that the Constitution has a definitive prohibition against mixing the concerns of church and state. You sentence the youth to detention.

3. Order the youth into temporary foster care. A proceeding such as an exorcism could physically harm the boy and make matters worse, and you fear the parents might try it anyway.

aspect of the road of temptation, and one which we shall see recur in many other theories of deviance, is the idea that humans have a choice between good and evil. The choices that we make determine our character and are used by the criminal justice system to justify punishment. In other words, those who choose to do the crime also choose to do the time.

- **Road of possession**   In demonic theory, choice is less of a factor when someone is considered to be inhabited by an evil spirit. Here a person's body and mind are believed to be possessed, and this person is no longer deemed to be responsible.[15]

Both of these explanations are especially applicable to young people, who traditionally have been considered to be more subject to both temptation and possession due to youth, inexperience, and vulnerability. Some parents who believe their child to be possessed by an evil spirit might resort to supernatural means, commonly known as *exorcism*, to evict the entity they believe is troubling their child. For a look at modern exorcisms, see Kids in the News 5.1.

These early ideas that people who committed crimes were tempted or possessed by an evil spirit are more than historical curiosities. According to Harvard law school professor Alan Dershowitz, U.S. criminal law can be traced back to the book of Genesis.[16] Religion continues to play a part in the justice system, as well as in the way that Americans think about crime and deviance. For example, the Ten Commandments remains an important aspect of the U.S. legal system and, until recently, could be found posted in courthouses around the United States. The existence of the Ten Commandments assumes that people can choose to follow them or not. This idea departs from spiritual theories in that an evil entity is responsible for tempting or possessing people.[17] The offense does not originate with the "devil" but with the offender.

Focus on Ethics 5.1 presents a legal scenario concerning what appear to be common manifestations of evil.

The Devil Inside

Exorcism is a religious ritual that seeks to remove demons who are believed to be occupying or controlling people, places, or objects. Although in the United States it's most closely associated with the Catholic faith, it's an ancient practice and is a feature of many religions. A Catholic exorcism must be performed by a priest who has received the rite of exorcism and has permission from the bishop, so Catholic exorcisms are somewhat difficult to obtain. However, according to Michael W. Cuneo, author of *American Exorcism*, exorcisms in other faiths are performed with astonishing regularity in the United States.[1]

Exorcisms were extremely rare in the United States until they became popularized in the 1970s by the publication of William Peter Blatty's *The Exorcist* and the subsequent 1973 film of the same title. Since then, what had been known only as an arcane Catholic rite has become a "booming business—operating below radar perhaps, invisible to anyone not specifically on the lookout for it, but booming nevertheless."[2] Religious adherents may have their houses exorcised or themselves or sometimes their children. Although the performance of exorcisms isn't unique to children, unfortunately at least three of the publicized fatalities during modern exorcisms have occurred with children.[3]

- In 2003, 8-year-old Terrance Cottrell, Jr., was wrapped in sheets and restrained by members of the Faith Temple Church of the Apostolic Faith in Milwaukee, Wisconsin. Cottrell, who was autistic, had been taken to the church by his mother for an exorcism. According to the medical examiner, Cottrell was asphyxiated by pressure placed on his chest.[4]
- In 1998 in Sayville, New York, 17-year-old Charity Miranda's mother and sister suffocated her with a plastic bag to kill a demon.
- In 1997 a 5-year-old New York City girl was forced by her mother and grandmother to drink a mixture of ammonia, vinegar, and olive oil. The women then bound and gagged the girl with duct tape. After the girl's death, the women said they were trying to poison a demon that had entered the child.

In a nonfatal case, a clinical psychologist who performed an exorcism on a child claimed a constitutional right to do the ceremony. Psychologist and Lutheran minister Kenneth Olson of Phoenix, Arizona, performed an exorcism on a child who was referred to him by the state's Child Protective Services. According to *Olson* v. *Morris*, the child's foster father claimed the boy's biological parents had satanically abused him. Olson, who placed his hands on the boy and prayed for the demons to leave, billed the state for the treatment. Olson was already on probation with the state's licensing board for a 1988 exorcism.[5]

In the United Kingdom, a London man named Malcolm Poussaint, who describes himself as a voodoo priest, says he has performed exorcisms on children, some as young as 6, who parents claim are possessed by demons. Poussaint told the London *Sunday Telegraph* that he performs these rituals in a candle-lit room and that the parents hold onto the child while Poussaint chants and prays. "Sometimes the child is shaking because there's a bad spirit in the child," Poussaint told the *Telegraph*. "The child sometimes cries and I hold onto the child so the child is not able to move. I will get the mother to hold onto the child so I can send the vibrations across to the child."[6]

These examples demonstrate that demonic explanations for delinquency and misbehavior are alive and well in modern times. Because of the respect for religion, there has been little effort to ban these practices except when a child dies.

Think About It

1. Can exorcism work, even if by making a parent and/or child believe that a demon was responsible for his or her behavior?

2. How should the law treat parents who inadvertently cause their children harm with an exorcism?

1 Michael W. Cuneo, *American Exorcism* (Garden City, NY: Doubleday, 2001), xii.
2 Ibid.
3 It is interesting that many of the most popular horror movies about possession and demons depend on child protagonists: *The Exorcist, The Sixth Sense, The Shining, The Omen, Rosemary's Baby,* and *Poltergeist.*
4 Kevin Christopher, "Autistic Boy Killed During Exorcism," *Skeptical Inquirer* 27, no. 6 (November/December 2003):11.
5 Martha Churchill, "Psychologist Wants Constitutional Protection for Exorcism Done in Therapy," *Skeptical Inquirer* 23, no. 5 (September/October 1999): 7–9. Perucci Ferraiuolo, "Exorcism Costs Counselor License," *Christianity Today* 37, no. 14 (November 1993):47.
6 Tariq Tahir, "My Exorcisms Get Results, Says Voodoo Priest of North London," *Sunday Telegraph* (London), June 19, 2005, p. 14.

CLASSICAL SCHOOL OF CRIMINOLOGY

The spiritual perspective has been largely overtaken in the justice system by other ways of envisioning why people break the law and how society should respond. These alternative perspectives are grounded in the changing economic, political, and social conditions of

deterrence
The control of behavior through the fear of consequences.

free will
The ability or discretion to make choices that are unaffected by agencies such as fate or divine will.

heterogeneity
The quality of consisting of dissimilar elements or parts.

capitalism
An economic system characterized by the private or corporate ownership of production and distribution; the prices and production of goods are determined by competition in a market.

their times. The first perspective we will study is classical criminology, which grew out of the ideas that fueled the Enlightenment (see A Closer Look at Juvenile Issues 5.2).

Classical criminology influences the modern criminal and juvenile justice systems with its theories of **deterrence**, emphasis on punishment, and, to a lesser extent, prohibition of torture. Classical criminology is especially present in the continued emphasis on incarceration as a means of deterrence and punishment, as well as the idea that deterrence and punishment are duties of the justice system. Classical criminology uses the idea of **free will** to explain that offenders choose to break the law and that the best way to control lawbreaking is to deter potential offenders.[18] A number of Enlightenment-era social shifts fundamentally changed the administration of justice, all of which encouraged the development of classical criminology.

- **Changes in population**   Scholars have learned that the size, density, and **heterogeneity** of a population greatly influence economic and social policies. The population of Europe changed greatly from the 16th to the 18th centuries as people moved from rural areas and cities began to grow. One of the most prominent ways this affected the social control of deviant behavior is the emergence of anonymity in the cities. In societies where everyone knows each other and where people have strong social bonds, there are pressure and reward for conforming behavior. As more of the population moved to the cities and the old social networks disintegrated, both juveniles and adults had greater opportunities to break the law without detection. As people of different cultures began to live together, they found that they often viewed behavior very differently. Without a shared set of values and history, people were more likely to conflict and less willing to respect one another's privacy, property, and sensibilities.

- **Political and economic changes**   Major political and economic changes happened during the move toward a more rational way of dealing with crime and deviance. The most significant change is the move from feudalism to **capitalism**. The change in the relationship between owner and worker can't be overstated in terms of its effect on social organization and social control. Under feudalism, the workers, called *serfs*, were bound to the land under the protection and control of a vassal, who obtained his rank by birth. When a vassal sold land, the serfs went with it. The arrangement was binding across generations, so serfs labored on the same lands as their parents, as would their children. This form of communal control was weakened by the trade economy of capitalism, in which labor wasn't attached to serf–vassal loyalty, but rather was based on a fixed, impersonal wage. This resulted in an economic individualism in which people fended for themselves and in which young people had the opportunity to determine their own futures for better or worse.

- **Religious and intellectual changes**   As the Protestant Reformation challenged the authority of the Roman Catholic Church, several developments drastically altered the ways in which society controlled crime. Most significantly, the changes in religious life meant that individuals didn't have to go to the clergy to determine right and wrong. No longer was there just one standard of judging deviance, and people were free to develop their own explanations and reasons for crime. Scholars who sought to develop a more rational view of crime created a philosophy in which people were free to choose their own actions.[19]

These social changes had profound influences on how people viewed their responsibilities to obey the law and deal with lawbreakers. The classical school of criminology grew out of these changes, but it took scholars and public officials to translate these societal changes into theoretical underpinnings that informed policy. The two figures that are best associated with the classical school of criminology are Cesare Beccaria and Jeremy Bentham.

This 19th-century illustration depicts German serfs working in the fields for the lord of the manor. In this manner, a family would farm the same land for several generations for the same ruling family. *(Courtesy Corbis/Bettmann)*

Cesare Beccaria

Born in 1738, Cesare Beccaria, an Italian lawyer, became interested in the prison system, which he viewed as repressive, corrupt, and filled with irrationality and injustice.[20] As a reformer, he was concerned with establishing a rational, humane system of social control. His 1764 treatise *An Essay on Crimes and Punishment* influenced many philosophers and early criminologists.[21] In this essay, he laid out nine principles that he claimed would produce a more effective and humane criminal justice system. Beccaria took the complaints and frustrations that many of his contemporaries had with the medieval penal practices and created a new philosophy. Sociologist Stephen Pfohl summarized these principles in the following points:

- Society has an interest in making sure that rational punishment is administered in order to preserve the social contract that individuals make with those in the community. If transgressions aren't punished, then there's little incentive to obey the law and expectations of neighbors. The punishment must make sense to the public and not be arbitrary or tyrannical.

- The law and punishment are to be determined by the legislature and the guilt by the judge. In earlier times, judges had broad discretion in torturing people as part of the fact-finding mission and as part of the punishment. There was little control of overzealous judges who acted in irrational and abusive ways toward defendants, who had few, if any, rights.

- People are presumed to employ a **hedonistic calculus** to maximize pleasure and avoid pain. This simple principle explains a broad range of deviant behavior and serves as a guide to construct punishments designed to prevent crime.

- Rationally calculated punishment is the best form of social control. If people decide to break the law because they deem the pleasure outweighs the possible punishment, then society needs only to alter the statute to make the punishment more certain, faster, and severe.

- Deterrence is the basis for social control. People won't break the law if they think they will get caught and punished.

- The classical school of criminology is more concerned with controlling the unlawful acts of individuals than with controlling the individual. There is no

hedonistic calculus
The idea that potential offenders plan their actions in order to maximize pleasure and minimize pain.

Cesare Beccaria (1738–1794). *(Courtesy The Granger Collection)*

concern for why someone commits an offense, only with making the punishment severe enough to deter potential offenders. All offenders are thus treated equally according to their infractions, and their social class, gender, age, or personal deficiencies have no part in fashioning the sentence.[22]

It is difficult to overstate Beccaria's contributions to the development of modern legal systems. France was the first country to apply Beccaria's ideas. After the 1789 French Revolution, the new government sought to build a new legal system based on justice and rationality and used Beccaria's ideas to create the French Code of 1791. However, French judges soon found that the classical philosophy was too harsh in some circumstances.[23]

In its zeal for justice, the French Code called for treating all offenders, regardless of age, sex, mental ability, or background, in exactly the same fashion. This meant that a 7-year-old boy who stole a loaf of bread would be treated the same way and given the same sentence as a 37-year-old man who committed the same offense. The French realized that they needed more discretion than classical philosophy allowed and altered the code to accommodate the young, as well as other special offenders. Legislators revised the French Code in 1819 to recognize "age, mental condition and extenuating circumstances."[24]

Jeremy Bentham

Another social thinker and reformer who greatly influenced the development of classical criminology was Jeremy Bentham (1748–1832). Bentham developed an

5.2 A CLOSER LOOK at JUVENILE ISSUES

THE ENLIGHTENMENT AND CRIMINAL JUSTICE

The Enlightenment, which roughly spanned the 18th century, was a 100-year interlude of energetic thinking and writing based largely on reason, secular ideals, and sharp criticism of all that had gone before. The Enlightenment is particularly important because it continues to influence modern science, law, and government. Many of history's great documents were produced during the Enlightenment, including the Declaration of Independence and the U.S. Constitution.

Enlightenment philosophy is especially important to the modern U.S. criminal justice system and its treatment of juveniles. The philosophy of Beccaria and Bentham, which emphasized fairness, humaneness, and rationality, was important to the creation of the U.S. juvenile justice system and its laws and legal processes that account for the special needs of children and adolescents.

Jeremy Bentham (1748–1832). *(Portrait of Jeremy Bentham, British jurist and philosopher. Painting by Henry W. Pickenqild, 1829, National Portrait Gallery, London)*

approach that, like Beccaria's, was concerned with the way individuals weighed pleasure and pain when deciding whether to commit deviant acts. Bentham reasoned that deterrence theory is a major part of the way that society should respond to crime.[25]

Sometimes students make the mistake of thinking that deterrence theory involves only the imposition of more severe sanctions.[26] Bentham and Beccaria both remind us, however, that the certainty of punishment is more influential in controlling crime than the severity of punishment. In the modern United States, the certainty of getting caught for many offenses, such as dealing drugs, is relatively low and is offset by the prospect of immense profits. Sometimes the value of the return is subjective. Some youths might consider a $20 return on an offense to be worth the chance that they will get caught. In fact, many youths don't even consider the chance that they will get caught.

What Is Deterrence?

Does deterrence theory as promoted by the classical school of criminology work? At one level, the answer is yes. Most of us most of the time don't break the law partially because we fear being caught and punished. Certainly, there are a number of other reasons that we obey the law, such as being bonded to our community and respecting the rights of others, but we're all aware that bad things might happen to us should we seek illegal pleasure at someone else's expense.

We can also contend that, given the crime rate and institutional overcrowding, deterrence theory isn't working well enough. Even with the prospect of the death penalty—or life imprisonment in the case of juveniles—some offenders still commit heinous offenses.[27] In doing this hedonistic calculus, why do so many people make the wrong decision?

For instance, armed robbery is a first-degree felony punishable by a long prison sentence. In some states, an offense as serious as armed robbery will get a juvenile sent straight to criminal court. This brings up an important issue: How do children and adolescents perceive deterrence? Much of deterrence depends on mental maturity and future-time orientation. An adult can consider an offense, then imagine getting caught and punished for that offense, and then imagine how unpleasant a long prison term would be. Research has shown that youths don't imagine the distant future in the same way that an adult does. A 15-year-old obsessing about the homecoming dance isn't thinking about what he will be doing when he's 60. Nor do youths truly comprehend the permanence of some legal consequences, such as a life sentence.

Deterrence is problematic for those who, because of age, are focused on the short term rather than the long term.[28] There is a good chance that someone might get killed in an armed robbery, which can mean a life sentence for a juvenile. One would think then that anyone contemplating armed robbery would pick a target that would yield a great deal of money to offset the possibility of severe punishment. Yet offenders often pick a target, such as a convenience store that keeps only a hundred dollars or so in the cash drawer, for their risk.

Criminologists have spent decades attempting to determine whether deterrence theory works. This is a difficult task because, in effect, they are trying to measure crime that doesn't occur. Some offending varies by season and weather, and some offending varies by **demographic** variables such as the age ratios, neighborhood conditions, and the presence of illegal drugs.[29] It can be extremely difficult to decide which offenses occurred because of a lack of deterrence and which offenses occurred because of a big shipment of cocaine hitting the streets.

So how do researchers attempt to measure the deterrent effects of laws? One method has been to examine the effect of capital punishment on homicide rates.[30] Deterrence theory contends that the homicide rate would fall after citizens heard about an execution. Because homicide rates might rise or fall anyway, researchers compare a state that executes offenders with a neighboring state that doesn't. If the state with capital punishment showed a significant drop in its homicide rate while the neighboring state without capital punishment showed no change in its homicide rate, researchers could conclude that executing murderers might act as a deterrent.[31]

Another basic concern of deterrence research concerns the accuracy of knowledge of the severity of various sanctions. If we assume that more severe sanctions will deter individuals from breaking the law, we must ensure that we can determine that potential offenders are aware of what the sanctions actually entail. But even this level of understanding can be misleading, because potential offenders don't need an accurate understanding of the sanctions in order to be deterred. All they need is a belief that they will get caught (certainty), get caught swiftly (celerity), and be punished drastically (severity) for deterrence theory to work. Therefore, the perceptions of potential offenders can be as important as their objective knowledge of their situation.[32] In summarizing the deterrent effect of criminal sanctions, Akers and Sellers conclude that certainty of punishment is the most powerful aspect of deterrence theory. Neither the severity nor the swiftness of punishment is as robust as the certainty of getting caught. Imagine a teenager who's planning to shoplift several video games. According to Akers and Sellers, the teenager is more likely to be deterred by the guarantee that she will get caught, rather than by a year-long sentence to a detention center or the expectation that she won't have to wait long for that sentence.

Deterrence and Juveniles

Prior to 1900, juvenile offenders were treated much as adult offenders and subjected to the same punishments. However, youths, according to modern juvenile theory, aren't rational in the ways that adults are, and youths' physically immature brains operate differently.[33] This poses a problem for deterrence theory's hedonistic calculus, which requires a mature, rational mind to perform it successfully.

At the time that much of the basic classical school theory was being formulated, little was known about the neurological differences between children and adults, and even less was known about the brain itself. Early classical theorists expected youths to perform the hedonistic calculus as efficiently as adults. The expectations of the effect of deterrence on juveniles and the way in which juveniles perceive deterrence must be considered differently by criminal justice practitioners.

For example, a small self-report study in Georgia by Richard E. Redding and Elizabeth J. Fuller explored the deterrent effect of juvenile waiver (or transfer) laws,

demographics

The study of the characteristics of human populations.

which are laws that allow juveniles to be tried and sentenced as adults (see Chapter 14 for a complete discussion). Several key points emerged from the juveniles who participated in the study.[34]

- The youths were largely unaware of waiver laws.
- The youths believed that knowing about the law might have deterred them from committing their offenses. They also suggested ways that more youths could be made aware of the laws.
- The youths believed that being tried as adults was unfair. About half in the study did not know why they were being tried as adults. (Many, apparently, were charged with armed robbery, an offense that they did not consider to be serious. When asked to list what they believed were the truly serious crimes, the responses were split between rape and murder.)
- The youths believed that the actual consequences of their offenses were worse than they had imagined. Most of these juveniles had already been through the juvenile system and thought that the sanctions they received there were little more than "a slap on the wrist."
- Other research quoted in the study found that juvenile waiver laws actually weakened **specific deterrence**; that is, **recidivism** among juveniles tried and sentenced as adults increased. The effect on **general deterrence**, however, remained in question.
- Many of the youths who knew of the law did not think it would apply to them. Redding and Fuller give two possible reasons for this. The first is the general immaturity of juveniles, which includes **impulsivity**, limited perspective of time, and willingness to take risks.[35] The other is that the youths' prior experience with the juvenile justice system was too gentle and gave the youths the message that there was little consequence to committing a criminal offense.

In an interesting counterpoint to the last item (this will be covered in more detail in Chapter 15), serving "hard time" in an adult facility appears to have a brutalizing effect on juveniles, possibly making them more likely to offend again. So, although the youths quoted in the study said that knowing about the waiver laws might have deterred them from their offenses, research has found that trying and sentencing them as adults might worsen their rate of recidivism.

Another issue that the study emphasized concerns the fact that deterrence, either specific or general, doesn't work if the target population is unaware of the laws that are supposed to achieve that deterrence. The state of Georgia had produced a video about the waiver laws that was shown intermittently in state schools, in prevention programs, and on television. However, most of the juveniles in the study didn't have a chance to see the video as they rarely or never attended school. They were truant, they had been expelled, or they had dropped out. The law's deterrent effect was lost on youths who had no idea that it existed or why it was being applied to them.[36]

In contrast, most adults are generally aware of the consequences of entering the criminal justice system. For the most serious offenses, there are expectations of long prison terms, life sentences, or even execution. Even civil lawsuits worry many adults because of their expense. Because of the juvenile system's focus on rehabilitation, juvenile penalties can be relatively light and geared toward saving the youth (whether the youth is aware of this or not), so the youth might not perceive them as "serious." However, youths transferred to the criminal justice system can receive decades-long sentences in adult facilities depending on the gravity of the offense.

Classical School of Criminology Today

The failure of researchers to demonstrate the utility of deterrence theory does not mean that the classical school of criminology isn't important to the study of contemporary

specific deterrence
A method of control in which an offender is prevented from committing more offenses by either incarceration or death.

recidivism
Continuing to commit delinquent or criminal offenses after being convicted and sentenced for prior offenses.

general deterrence
A method of control in which the punishment of a single offender sets an example for the rest of society.

impulsivity
The tendency to act quickly without considering the consequences.

rational choice theory
A theory that states that people consciously choose criminal behavior.

shock deterrence
A method of giving minor offenders, often juveniles, an alarming experience with the justice system in order to convince them to obey the law.

criminal justice. Besides setting the framework for many of the rules and procedures used by law enforcement and the courts, the classical school informs new theories of crime and criminal justice system practices. Two of these modern initiatives are **rational choice theory** and **shock deterrence**. Each of these theories is worth examining to see how the present remains firmly entrenched in past ideas and practices.

RATIONAL CHOICE THEORY   Do people choose to break the law or choose to desist from a criminal lifestyle in the same manner that they decide to buy an automobile or join a fraternal organization? In other words, is whether to break the law simply another decision that we make in the context of hundreds of decisions we make every day? Rational choice theory states that the individual decision to offend is susceptible to examination in much the same way as the decision to buy a home. People weigh the costs and benefits of all their decisions and act in their own best interests.

According to Frank P. Williams and Marilyn D. McShane, offenders make two different types of decisions when contemplating an offense.[37] First, they make involvement decisions in which they determine whether they will engage in a particular offense, continue the offense, or desist from it. For instance, in a study of persistent property offenders, Kenneth D. Tunnell found that money was the primary and almost exclusive motivation for the decision to commit the offense.[38]

The other type of decision that offenders consider is event decisions about what tactics to use. If the tactics to successfully commit the offense appear easy, the offender will decide to become involved, whereas if the tactics appear difficult, the offender will desist. At a certain level, this appears to be simple common sense. For example, banks put money in safes to make the tactics of bank robbery more difficult so that potential bank robbers will pass them by.

The difference between rational choice theory and classical criminology is that rational choice theory is rooted in economics. Economists envision the choice to commit an offense as they would any other choice and try to establish mathematical models to explain the behavior.[39] This can be problematic for several reasons.

- The researcher has to assume the variables that the offender considers in choosing to offend can be captured in the model. The expected reward isn't really known before the offender commits an offense. Unlike a decision to buy a car in which the value is well established, a mugger who decides to assault someone is uncertain what the payoff will be.[40]

- Not all individuals bring the same resources to the decision to commit an offense. Some individuals have money, credit, insurance, and a support network that can affect the decision, while others have very few resources and are desperate. These factors seldom enter the decision-making process as envisioned by rational choice models.[41]

- Many offenders don't adequately weigh the risks of getting caught. They falsely believe that they are very good at crime and engage in repetitive and reckless behavior that is sure to draw the attention of police. Their irrational patterns almost guarantee that they will eventually be apprehended.[42]

- It is extremely difficult to factor in variables such as anger, intoxication, boredom, and impulsivity. These variables aren't always available in existing data sets based on official crime reports.[43]

- Even given the difficulty in obtaining information on the variables that offenders use when deciding to commit offenses, there's another conceptual flaw in rational choice theory concerning the assumption that the offender does, in fact, make rational choices. Some criminologists believe that many offenders act irrationally and engage in behaviors directly contrary to their well-being.[44]

It should be noted that these criticisms of rational choice theory don't mean that pursuing this line of research is futile. For certain offenses, such as burglary, in which offenders have the time to plan the event and take precautions against detection, it's useful to attempt to understand what factors they consider. Additionally, when sufficiently large data sets are used, it's possible to observe broad patterns of choice.

Rational choice theory is a relatively new approach, and as more criminologists become familiar with it, we can expect its methodology to become more sophisticated and its applicability more vigorous. Another important question for the study of juvenile delinquency concerns the rationality of the choices that delinquents make. We might find that juvenile delinquents understand their own best interests less than adults understand theirs.

SHOCK DETERRENCE   If offenders are unable to make good choices when considering whether to commit an offense, perhaps they simply lack information on the consequences of getting caught. How much do any of us actually know about the skill of the police in catching offenders, the prosecutors in constructing solid cases that prove guilt, or what life in prison is really like? For the most part, many people get their impressions of the criminal justice system from Hollywood. We watch movies and television and believe they accurately reflect society. How is a 16-year-old youth contemplating robbing a convenience store supposed to have a realistic idea of the costs and consequences of his actions?

The criminal justice system has employed a number of strategies to address this very problem. By giving predelinquents or first-offenders a sobering and realistic look at the consequences of breaking the law, some criminal justice administrators reason that potential delinquents will make better choices. The idea behind this technique is to shock youths with a draconian look at what might happen if they continue to break the law. Basically, three types of shock deterrence programs attempt to address delinquency and change behavior in this way.

SHOCK INCARCERATION   **Shock incarceration** is intended to alter how offenders consider the benefits and costs of breaking the law. Here, offenders are sentenced to long periods behind bars but are released on probation after a few weeks. This experience is intended to demonstrate to the offender how restrictive incarcerated life can be. Presumably, juvenile delinquents will be deterred from further law-breaking and will cooperate with the probation officer, rather than risk losing their freedom again. One can only imagine the relief a youth must feel after spending two weeks behind bars and suddenly being placed on probation and going home. The shock of short-term incarceration is presumed to give the youngster enough information about incarceration to convince him or her that the risks-and-rewards equation doesn't favor breaking the law.

The major, untested assumption here is that the short-term incarceration does indeed shock the youth. Although many people would find incarceration uncomfortable, some juveniles might benefit from the predictable routine and consistent discipline. We aren't suggesting here that youths enjoy incarceration but rather that the short period of loss of freedom might not be that much of a shock and therefore might not have the intended consequence of deterring crime.[45]

SCARED STRAIGHT–STYLE PROGRAMS   In 1975, several inmates serving sentences of 25 years or more in New Jersey's Rahway prison formed the Lifers' Group to give inmates a more sympathetic image. With the help of prison officials, they created the Juvenile Awareness Project to educate juveniles on the consequences of incarceration. Youths under the age of 18 toured the prison and listened to inmates talk frankly about prison life, including "prison violence, including assault and murder, homosexual rape, suicide as a fact of prison life, inedible food, the impersonal atmosphere in which there was no unity between inmates, and the need to live by the bells."[46]

At first, the inmates acted more as counselors, using reasoning and persuasion. Gradually, however, the inmates began to feel they weren't getting through to the youths, and the program escalated to the point that the goal was to "shock" the youths with threats and intimidation and to "scare them straight." The inmates would yell

shock incarceration

The practice of sentencing offenders to a long period of incarceration and then granting them probation after a short time without their prior knowledge.

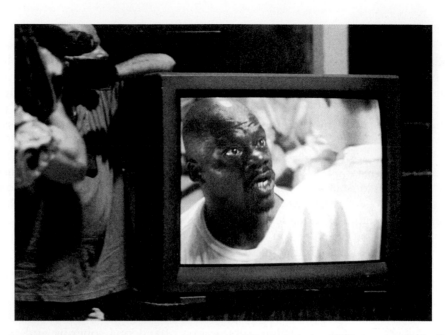

An inmate at East Jersey State Prison appears in *Scared Straight '99*, which aired on MTV in August 1999. The film was an update of the original *Scared Straight! (Courtesy Mike Derer, AP Wide World Photos)*

and tell the youths all the terrible things they would do if the young people ever entered the prison as inmates. Threats of rape and brutal beatings were intended to terrorize the youths so much that they wouldn't break the law anymore because they now had a realistic idea of incarceration.

The Juvenile Awareness Project probably would have been eventually discarded if not for a documentary film that made the program famous and spawned dozens of copycat programs across the country. The documentary *Scared Straight!* (see Programs for Children 5.1 became an instant hit. The program, based on the classical criminology principle of deterrence, was promoted as a way to deliver real information about incarceration that would alter juveniles' calculations about the feasibility and advisability of breaking the law.

However, besides not deterring youths to the degree claimed by its adherents, *Scared Straight*-type programs ignored the various reasons that people engage in deviant behavior. The youths who participated in the program didn't always come from groups who were likely to be serious delinquents but instead tended to be typical middle-class boys. Further, those who were exposed to *Scared Straight* were arrested five times more than a matched sample of those who didn't participate.[47] James O. Finckenauer of Rutgers University conducted a study that compared two groups of youths with similar histories of delinquency. One group of 46 youths had attended *Scared Straight*, while the other group of 35 youths had not. Finckenauer reported that 41 percent of the *Scared Straight* graduates had gotten into trouble again in contrast with only 11 percent of the control group.[48]

BOOT-CAMP PRISONS   The most popular of the shock-incarceration techniques is the **boot-camp prison** strategy in which offenders are subjected to military-style discipline and routine. Hundreds of these types of programs have been set up at both the juvenile and young adult levels. We will discuss boot-camp prisons in greater detail in Chapter 15, but it's worth discussing here to appreciate how it's related to the principles of the classical school of criminology.

Basic training in the military is designed to put enormous physical and psychological stress on recruits to break down their old ways of thinking and to instill the military way of deferring to authority and executing orders. This is necessary to get essentially good teenagers to do something they would not normally consider: kill

boot-camp prison
A short-term prison usually for young offenders that uses military boot-camp training and discipline techniques for rehabilitation.

5.1   PROGRAMS *for* CHILDREN

THE SCARED STRAIGHT! PHENOMENON

The original *Scared Straight* program became popular very quickly. According to a 1978 *Reader's Digest* article, the program, which began with inmates "scaring" one group of youths a week, was soon handling two groups daily, five days a week. With the public becoming increasingly concerned about the rising juvenile delinquency rate, such an unusual program could not remain obscure for long.[1]

In 1978 the documentary *Scared Straight!* debuted on television. The movie was broadcast uncensored in an era when three networks controlled the nation's viewing choices and strict standards and practices controlled the networks. Popular and controversial, *Scared Straight!* spawned heated public discussion on the subject of juvenile delinquency and what to do about it. In 1979, the movie won two Emmys and an Oscar for Best Documentary.[2]

The *Scared Straight* program received overwhelming public support, and many people wrote to their state legislators demanding similar programs in their own states. The spotlight also brought criticism. Although *Scared Straight* initially claimed a success rate of 90 percent, this figure didn't withstand subsequent evaluations. By 1980, with program attendance falling, the prison modified the program, dropping confrontational tactics in favor of counseling. Ironically, a similar program in which inmates counseled youths had been going on at California's San Quentin penitentiary since 1965 without the benefit of a national discussion.[3] Two sequels to *Scared Straight!* followed up on the lives of some of the youths from the original documentary.

Currently, many states still sponsor Scared Straight–style programs, and the original program is still available at East Jersey State Prison. According to the prison's website:

> *Participants must already be involved with a law enforcement agency or the court system and be accompanied by a parent and/or a probation officer. The session begins with a tour of the facility, followed by an intensive face-to-face session with inmates and a discussion of choices and decision making.*[4]

1 Roul Tunley. "Don't Let Them Take Me Back!" *Reader's Digest* 112 (January 1978):96–100.
2 Eileen Keerdoja et al., "Prison Program Gets a New Boost," *Newsweek* 96 (November 3, 1980):16.
3 Aric Press and Donna Foote, "Does Scaring Work?" *Newsweek* 93 (May 14, 1979).131.
4 New Jersey Department of Corrections Division of Programs & Community Services, www.state.nj.us/corrections/structure/html/community.html.

another human being. Once the recruits are broken down, the training is designed to instill a sense of accomplishment, belonging, and pride in being part of a military organization. Additionally, the shock of basic training is followed by years of military service in which any effects of psychological brutalization are negated, controlled, or ameliorated.[49] Military basic training replaces one attitude and way of life with another.

By contrast, the boot-camp prison concept fails to provide the redeeming features of military service. Youths are subjected to 90 days of abuse and humiliation as if there's something restorative in the technique itself. Certainly, the youths can be dominated to the point where they obey the commands of the "drill sergeants," but this experience does little to prepare them for life in civil society. National Institute of Justice evaluation studies have shown that neither juvenile nor adult boot camps reduce recidivism, whether they are programs with a heavy military emphasis or treatment-oriented programs. An Office of Juvenile Justice and Delinquency Prevention study found no significant differences in recidivism rates between boot-camp

A drill sergeant at a boot-camp prison for juvenile delinquents watches four teenage boys lying in a mud hole called the "attitude pit." *(Courtesy David Kennedy, Creative Eye/MIRA.com).*

participants and juveniles who had participated in other programs. In some cases, boot-camp graduates actually had higher rates of recidivism.[50] Criminologists Malcolm Feely and Jonathan Simon have suggested that the one thing boot-camp prison might be good for is developing drug dealers and gang members.[51]

CAN DETERRENCE WORK? Although deterrence is certainly one of the cornerstones of the criminal justice system, programs designed to alter the way offenders measure the risks and rewards of breaking the law haven't been very successful and in some cases have been counterproductive.[52] The reasons for this lack of accomplishment have to do with the complex nature of deterrence.

Although we might think that all that is necessary to alter one's calculation of risk versus rewards is to make the punishment more severe, deterrence theory is more complicated than that. In addition to the severity of punishment should one get caught, deterrence theory postulates that offenders also calculate the chances of getting caught (certainty) and the swiftness of punishment once caught (celerity). These last two facets of deterrence theory are more difficult to produce than severity of punishment. Although police agencies might add more officers and increase security procedures, clever and opportunistic offenders, including juveniles, will adjust their strategies to avoid getting caught.[53] Short of becoming a police state, where everyone's freedoms are curtailed, there are only a limited number of ways that we can increase the perception of offenders that they are likely to get caught. In fact, virtually all offenders believe they have taken the necessary precautions to avoid detection when they commit their offenses.

The swiftness of the punishment following arrest and conviction is also difficult for criminal justice administrators to achieve. Because of a combination of procedural laws and the overcrowding of jails, courts, and prisons, it's almost impossible to punish any offender, either juvenile or adult, in a period of time that could affect the likelihood of deterrence. The most extreme example of the lack of swiftness of punishment is the decades it generally takes for an offender on death row to be executed. Certainly this works against deterrence theory and the idea that potential murderers will think twice about taking a life.

POSITIVIST SCHOOL OF CRIMINOLOGY

The classical school of criminology focused on the offense and treated all offenders as if they had the same motivations. That is, offenders were assumed to possess free will and to break the law for the same reasons. The rate of crime could be affected by altering the severity, swiftness, and certainty of punishment, because all offenders would react to these changes in the same way. If the consequences were unattractive enough, then potential offenders would choose not to break the law.

The positivist school, however, is concerned with the offender's motivations and characteristics. The tracks of positivism can be observed in the statistical study of crime, efforts to rehabilitate offenders, and the initiation of social programs to prevent crime. The positivist school focuses on the offender, rather than the offense or the law, and posits that humans don't necessarily have free will and that human behavior is determined by various external factors.[54] The positivist school considers offenders' motivations and examines their physical characteristics, social background, and moral development to determine why they break the law and what can be done to rehabilitate their behavior.

Positivist criminology considers the circumstances of individuals and states that, as opposed to free will, some people are influenced to offend because of **determinism**. By this, we mean that someone who is impoverished; suffers from racial, gender, or class discrimination; is undereducated; and is mentally challenged is more likely to break the law than someone without these social disadvantages. A combination of internal factors and external environmental conditions can work to limit opportunities for individual success in the conventional way and compel individuals to meet their needs, desires, and fantasies through illegitimate means.[55]

The other major difference between the classical school and the positivist school is the methodologies they use to explain crime. The classical school utilizes philosophy to try to understand why people break the law, while the positivist school uses science. Both are products of the Enlightenment, but the positivists used natural science as a model on which to base their theories of human behavior. By considering the biological, psychological, and social traits of individuals, as well as the conditions of society, positivist theorists believe it is possible to determine the underlying causes of crime and to prescribe complex treatments that go far beyond altering the severity of punishments.

According to positivist theory, the way to eliminate crime is to eliminate what appears to be causing it. This involves adjusting such external factors as biology (diet, exercise, environment, medication), psychology (therapy, medication), and/or environment (attending to poverty, education, security, sanitation, and cultural ills). In short, the positivist school considers crime to be the product of external factors, and to the extent that these factors can be ameliorated or eliminated, so can crime. As such, the positivist school focuses on rehabilitation, rather than deterrence or punishment.

determinism

The philosophical doctrine that human action is determined by external forces and is not a result of free will.

History of the Positivist School

The positivist school of criminology didn't develop all at once. It was a product of an exciting time in science and the arts when a multitude of accomplishments were amassed in Europe and the United States. In 1859, Charles Darwin published *On the Origin of the Species*, in which he argued that human beings were basically highly developed animals who were affected by biology and environment. It is not a coincidence that the positivist school with its scientific perspective on crime and deviant behavior came about during this period. In terms of crime and the criminal justice system, science advanced from several different fronts, and there was considerable error as criminologists developed theories and methods.

ADOLPHE QUETELET   Quetelet, a French mathematician and astronomer who also studied crime statistics, was fascinated by the regularity in property and violent crimes. In what has been called the first true scientific study of crime, Quetelet's

Research on the Propensity for Crime at Different Ages (1831) argued that poverty wasn't the main cause of crime and demonstrated that wealthy neighborhoods showed more crime than poor neighborhoods.[56] He decided that opportunity explained crime rates better than poverty and stated that the government couldn't do much to alter crime rates because criminal behavior was a result of moral defectiveness that was revealed in offenders' biological characteristics.

To deal with the causes of crime, Quetelet recommended that the government institute social reforms that would improve the physical conditions in which people lived and that allowed citizens' moral and intellectual qualities to be fully developed. Quetelet used statistics on offenders' educational levels, gender, and age, as well as the effects of climate and the seasons. According to Quetelet, the primary factor in determining the tendency for crime was age:

> Age is without contradiction the cause which acts with the most energy to develop or moderate the propensity for crime. This fatal propensity seems to develop in proportion to the intensity of physical strength and passions in man. It attains its maximum around 25 years, a period where physical development is pretty nearly ended. Intellectual and moral development, which takes place with more slowness, then moderates the propensity for crime which diminishes still more slowly by the weakening of man's physical strength and passions.[57]

ANDRE-MICHEL GUERRY   Part of the Enlightenment's contribution to science was the development of detailed records that could be studied to find patterns. Guerry, a French lawyer, was appointed as director of criminal statistics for the French Ministry of Justice, where he developed maps of crime rates as they related to other social factors, including poverty and education. Guerry, credited with being the first to use scientific criminology, pioneered the use of crime statistics to graphically represent how social factors contribute to crime rates across jurisdictions.[58]

Both Guerry and Quetelet applied mathematical analysis to explaining and mapping crime rates in relation to other social factors. Although Guerry's and Quetelet's studies aren't sophisticated by today's standards, they are an important part of the development of the scientific method in the study of crime. Modern studies using geographic positioning systems emerged from the work of these two early criminologists.[59]

AUGUSTE COMTE   Comte is credited with being the founder of positivist sociology A French philosopher and social scientist, he championed several important steps in how social scientists should go about their work so that it could be verified and replicated. These steps included developing testable hypotheses, the use of comparative methods, the classification of societies, a systematic approach to the study of social history, and the study of abnormality as a means of understanding normal behavior.[60]

CESARE LOMBROSO   Lombroso is credited with being the founder of positivist criminology based on his work in trying to find the causes of crime from a multifactor approach. Lombroso is also important because he was one of the first to employ the scientific method in the study of crime.[61] (See A Closer Look at Juvenile Issues 5.3 to learn more about the application of the scientific method to social science.)

An Italian physician, Lombroso developed a theory of criminal behavior based on offenders' physical characteristics. Although his later work included a range of variables that he claimed were related to crime, such as climate, rainfall, the price of grain, sex and marriage customs, criminal laws, banking practices, national tariff policies, the structure of government, church organization, and religious belief, he will always be remembered for his initial physiological theory of crime.

Lombroso, like many late 19th-century theorists, was influenced by Charles Darwin's theory of evolution. Lombroso postulated that criminals weren't as highly

5.3 A CLOSER LOOK *at* JUVENILE ISSUES

THE SCIENTIFIC METHOD AND SOCIAL SCIENCE

Science is a methodical way to acquire knowledge, not the knowledge itself. The scientific method is based not on belief but on evidence, and scientists try to avoid bias. The exact steps in the scientific method may vary a little from one scientist to the next, but generally, scientists follow these steps:

1. Identify a problem or ask a question.
2. Develop a hypothesis.
3. Formulate a procedure to test the hypothesis.
4. Collect and analyze data through experimentation or observation.
5. Arrive at a conclusion and communicate the results.

The questions that scientists ask must be answerable. This might require narrowing the terms. For instance, the question, "Why are all juvenile delinquents bad?" is unanswerable. What is bad? Does bad mean evil? What does evil mean? Does bad mean criminal? Does bad refer to an action or a state of mind? The wording also poses a chicken-and-egg problem. Are some juveniles delinquent because they are bad, or are they bad because they are delinquent? It also presupposes that all juvenile delinquents are "bad." This question is highly subjective, so it is unanswerable by the scientific method.

A better question is "What causes some youths to break the criminal law?" First, the terms are easily defined. In the United States, juveniles are

typically defined as people under the age of 18. Unlike the prior question, it doesn't presuppose juveniles as delinquents. The criminal law is the criminal code of the United States. It is known that some people under the age of 18 break the U.S. criminal law. Asking "What causes?" and not "Why?" refines the question even further. "Why?" is a philosophical question that might muddle the issue. "What causes?" looks for measurable, quantifiable concerns that might cause a juvenile to break the law.

Next a scientist forms a hypothesis, which is basically an educated guess. This means that scientists gather as much information as they can, which usually means reading the literature. Hypotheses don't have to be correct; a good hypothesis is also one that can be rejected. There must be a way to test the answers to try to make the hypothesis fail. Also, a hypothesis is never proved. It is either confirmed or not confirmed.

The scientist must then come up with a way to test the hypothesis. In the natural sciences, this usually involves both experimentation and observation. In the social sciences, such as the study of criminology and criminal justice, testing a hypothesis is a little more problematic. A chemist can mix some substances in a flask and place them over a Bunsen burner, and space scientists can crash as many probes into comets as their budget allows. But social scientists can't just dream up a social situation and inject some human beings into it. Good science depends on observation and experimentation; however, there are moral, legal, and ethical issues when dealing with human subjects.

Pharmaceutical companies, for example, which must use human subjects to produce human medications, must be very cognizant of the law. Although in the past some social scientists used humans in experiments—the most famous (or infamous) being Philip G. Zimbardo's 1971 Stanford Prison Experiment—social science typically relies on observation and statistical analysis to gather information. Social science issues, even those involving criminal and juvenile justice, don't involve immediate life-and-death problems (like, say, cancer or AIDS), and the legal and ethical issues inherent in human experimentation are often too great to justify the knowledge that could be gained.

Another problem with human experimentation is that, because of human psychology, it's most useful to observe people who don't know they are being observed. This is difficult enough to do with simple observation. It is nearly impossible to set up social experiments on people so that they don't know they are participating in an experiment, especially given the legal and ethical issues. Even in the Stanford Prison Experiment, the participants were conscious of both the experiment and the observation.

Therefore, testing a criminal justice hypothesis involves gathering data on real-life scenes that already exist and events that have already happened, such as counting arrests or offenses or inmates. It also involves the use of demographic information, such as that gathered in the U.S. Census. Offenders and victims can report their experiences and perceptions in self-report studies, and a well-designed study can refine this information into

Source: Scientific Method Flowchart, The NASA Science Files, whyfiles.larc.nasa.gov/text/educators/tools/pbl/scientific_method.html.

(Continued)

(Continued)

useful, consistent data. Social scientists use statistical analysis to provide a measure of the probability of an answer, although not *the* answer. In the end, there are only two options: reject the hypothesis or don't reject the hypothesis. Proof exists only when the chance for error is zero, and there is always some chance for error.

The conclusion and the communication of the results comprise a statement of how the results relate to the hypothesis, the results that were contrary to the hypothesis, and ideas for further testing. Good scientific method doesn't change the hypothesis or omit results that don't support the hypothesis; it also posits reasons for the difference between the hypothesis and the results of the analysis.

Lombroso thought that criminality was represented in physical features. These sketches of male faces show six supposed criminal types. *(Courtesy Federal Bureau of Investigation)*

atavism

The appearance in a person of features thought to be from earlier stages of human evolution.

evolved as normal people and that they were predisposed to commit crime. Lombroso identified over a hundred supposed physical abnormalities that he called **atavisms**, which he claimed represented the subhuman or primitive features of a biological throwback. The atavisms included a range of measurable physical features such as low cranial capacity and a retreating forehead, as well as features such as tattoos or using excessive gestures. Lombroso's ideas of physical atavisms were based on thousands of precise measurements that he made on Italian offenders. His speculations that individuals who deviated physically from the average Italian were throwbacks to an earlier developed human now seem ludicrous.

Positivism and Juveniles

Unlike the issues concerning rational choice, deterrence, and juvenile delinquents, positivism treats delinquents much as it treats adult offenders. That is, it considers the external factors that affect juveniles, with the factors affecting juveniles and adults being much the same: employment, poverty, family life, culture, health, and so on. Positivism, however, does focus more on the specific ages of youths than it does the ages of adults. The developmental differences between a 16-year-old and a 14-year-old are vast compared with the differences between a 32-year-old and a 30-year-old.

Family life is also a major issue. Positivist studies consider in detail the effects that divorce rates, mixed families (families with stepparents and stepchildren), single-parent homes, and parents' educational levels and religion have on youths. In fact, studies of youths consider the parents almost as much as the children. Research on the neurological differences between adults and children, as well as other physical differences that might affect behavior, originate from positivist theory. Because positivism considers factors external to offenders, positivist theorists depend on research to develop their ideas. However, research on humans, especially on juveniles, is very difficult to do. To learn more about how research is performed with children and adolescents, see Crosscurrents 5.2 box.

Chapters 6 through 8 will deal with positivist ideas in greater detail, fleshing out the many theories of juvenile delinquency that are rooted in positivism. These theories will include biological explanations that were initiated by the early positivists and that continue today as modern science gives researchers increasingly sophisticated tools to examine the reasons for criminal behavior.

5.2 CrossCurrents

Human Experimentation

Any research that uses human subjects must be done very carefully. Although medical research is perhaps the most precarious legally and ethically, human research in the social sciences poses challenges as well. The positivist direction that the study of criminology and criminal justice has taken over the last century demands that the scientific method be followed, which means that experimentation and observation must be undertaken. Until the late 20th century, research on humans was more easily and readily done than it is now because there were few strictures on it.

Perhaps the most famous criminal justice-related experiment is the 1971 Stanford Prison Experiment at Stanford University in California. This experiment, which simulated a prison, recruited young men who had answered a newspaper ad requesting volunteers for a study of the psychological effects of prison. The applicants were interviewed and given personality tests to eliminate those with psychological, medical, or legal issues. The 24 college students chosen for the experiment were paid $15 a day. Half of the group was assigned to be prisoners and the other half guards. Although the experiment was designed to run for two weeks, researcher Philip Zimbardo ended it after six days: "[I]t became clear that we had to end the study. We had created an overwhelmingly powerful situation—a situation in which prisoners were withdrawing and behaving in pathological ways, and in which some of the guards were behaving sadistically."[1]

This experiment is not only controversial; it is nonrepeatable. Given the modern legal environment in which people are much more willing to undertake litigation than they were in 1971, it's unlikely today that a university would let such an experiment proceed and, if it did, it's very likely that lawsuits would follow. Critics point out that the experiment didn't exactly replicate a U.S. prison. The researchers shaved the heads of the "inmates" and made them wear stocking caps and had them endure other humiliations uncommon in U.S. prisons. However, some scholars and journalists have noted the similarities of the Stanford Prison Experiment and the torture that was alleged to have taken place at Abu Ghraib, the U.S. military prison in Iraq.

Procedures for social science research on humans were refined in the latter years of the 20th century. Now informed consent must be obtained as well as the involvement of an institutional review board, along with parental permission if the research involves juveniles. Currently, the National Institutes of Health provide thorough ethical guidelines [2]

Here are some examples of the way that criminologists interested in juvenile delinquency conduct research.

- A study on stress levels in children involved boys between the ages of 6 and 16 who played a short computer game against an opponent. Researchers measured hormones in the boys' saliva. The boys' parents signed permission forms, and the project was explained to the boys, who also signed forms. The boys, who received no money for their participation, got a party at the end of the study.[3]
- A five-year study on the violent behavior of children who witness gun crime used interviews of over 1,500 children from 78 Chicago neighborhoods. The researchers returned to the youths at three points in their adolescence, interviewing them and their caregivers. Data were collected about the youths' families, personalities, neighborhoods, and school performance, and the youths were grouped by their susceptibility to witness gun violence. They were interviewed again two years later to see who had witnessed a shooting. Three years later, the researchers interviewed them again to determine which had participated in violence.[4]

(Continued)

(Continued)

What is an institutional review board?

An institutional review board is a committee of physicians, statisticians, researchers, and community advocates that ensures that a clinical trial is ethical and that the subjects' rights are protected. Federal regulations require that every institution involved in biomedical or behavioral research using human subjects must have an institutional review board to approve and periodically review the research.

Source: Mayo Clinic Glossary of Clinical Trials Terms, clinicaltrials.mayo.edu/glossary.cfm

Think About It

1. Should more research be allowed on human subjects?
2. Should researchers treat young children differently than teenagers?
3. Why do researchers take such special care with children?

1 Philip G. Zimbardo, *The Stanford Prison Experiment: A Simulation Study of the Psychology of Imprisonment,* www.prisonexp.org/slide-37.htm.
2 U.S. Department of Health and Human Services, *Guidelines for the Conduct of Research Involving Human Subjects at the National Institutes of Health* (Washington, DC: U.S. Government Printing Office, 2004), 22. Online at ohsr.od.nih.gov/guidelines/GrayBooklet82404.pdf; *The Belmont Report: Ethical Principles and Guidelines for the Protection of Human Subjects* (1979) provides the basis for federal laws governing research involving human subjects, Title 45 Code of Federal Regulations, Part 46, Protection of Human Subjects. These regulations apply to all research involving human subjects conducted or supported by the Intramural Research Program of the National Institutes of Health (p. 5).
3 Cynthia T. Pegram, "Project Studies Violence in Children," *News & Advance* (Lynchburg, VA), June 5, 2005, www.newsadvance.com/servlet/Satellite?pagename=LNA%2FMGArticle%2FLNA_BasicArticle&c=MGArticle&cid=1031783111435&path=!news!archive.
4 *Medical News Today,* "Children Who Witness Gun Crime More Likely to Commit Violent Crime," May 27, 2005, www.medicalnewstoday.com/medicalnews.php?newsid=25174.

SUMMARY

1. The work of the juvenile justice system is based on theory, and the study of theory is fundamental to all academic enterprise, including juvenile delinquency.

2. Theories attempt to explain the connections between facts so that we can observe patterns, construct policies, and better understand how factors are related.

3. Curran and Renzetti's definition of a theory is as follows: A theory is a set of interconnected statements or propositions that explain how two or more events or factors are related to one another.

4. According to Akers and Sellers, these criteria must be addressed when evaluating theories: logical consistency, scope, parsimony, testability, empirical validity, usefulness and policy implications, and ideology.

5. Three of the most traditional explanations of crime are spiritual explanations, the classical school of criminology, and the positivist school of criminology. Although developed in past centuries, all these systems of thought influence our current system and ideas of justice.

6. The spiritual perspective has been largely overtaken in the justice system by other ways of understanding why people break the law and how society should respond.

7. Classical criminology uses the idea of free will to explain that offenders choose to engage in crime and that the best way to control crime is to deter offenders and make it uncomfortable or unprofitable for them to offend.

8. The two figures best associated with classical criminology are Cesare Beccaria and Jeremy Bentham. Beccaria was concerned with establishing a more rational and humane system of social control. Bentham developed an approach that was concerned with the way individuals weighed pleasure and pain when deciding whether to commit deviant acts.

9. Another basic concern of deterrence research is the accuracy of knowledge of the severity of various sanctions. A belief that one will be caught (certainty) and swiftly and drastically punished (celerity and severity) is needed for deterrence theory to work. Akers and Sellers conclude that certainty of punishment is the most powerful aspect of deterrence theory.

10. According to rational choice theory, people weigh the costs and benefits of their decisions and act in their own best interests. Williams and McShane state that offenders make two types of decisions when contemplating crime: involvement decisions in which they determine whether they will engage in a particular offense, continue an offense, or desist from it and event decisions about what tactics to use when committing an offense.

11. Some criminal justice administrators believe that shock deterrence tactics will influence youths to obey the law and avoid the justice system. Three shock deterrence programs are shock incarceration, *Scared Straight*-type programs, and boot-camp prisons.

12. The positivist school of criminology focuses on the offender rather than the offense and uses science rather than philosophy to explain crime. It considers offenders' motivations and examines their physical characteristics, social background, and moral development to determine why they offend and what can be done to rehabilitate them.

13. Positivism considers the factors that affect juveniles and adults to be much the same: employment, poverty, family life, culture, health, and so on. Positivism focuses more on youths' specific ages than it does on the ages of adults and considers in detail the effects of family issues on youths.

REVIEW QUESTIONS

1. What is a theory? What is a hypothesis?

2. What is evil? Can it be defined? Why or why not?

3. How did the Enlightenment affect criminological theory?

4. Have any of the ways of considering crime been completely discarded?

5. What is deterrence?

6. Where do spiritual explanations of crime come from?

7. According to classical criminology, why do offenders break the law?

8. What does the positivist school of criminology focus on rather than on the offense?

9. What are atavisms?

ADDITIONAL READINGS

Beirne, Piers. *Inventing Criminology: Essays on the Rise of Home Criminals*. Albany: State University of New York Press, 1993.

Beccaria, Cesare. *On Crimes and Punishments* (1764). Trans. Henry Paolucci. Indianapolis, IN: Bobbs-Merrill, 1963.

Dinwiddy, John R. *Bentham*. New York: Oxford University Press, 1989.

Grasmick, Harold G., and Robert J. Bursik, Jr. "Conscience, Significant Others, and Rational Choice: Extending the Deterrence Model." *Law and Society Review* 24:837–861.

Ferracutti, Stefano. "Cesare Lombroso (1835–1907)." *Journal of Forensic Psychiatry* 7:130–149.

Neyhouse, Teresa J. *Positivism in Criminological Thought: A Study in the History and Use of Ideas*. New York: LFB Scholarly Publishing, 2002.

ENDNOTES

1. Peter L. Berger, *The Sacred Canopy: Elements of a Sociological Theory of Religion* (Garden City, NY: Doubleday, 1969).

2. Leslie Stevenson, *Seven Theories of Human Nature* (New York: Oxford University Press, 1994). See also George C. Homans, *The Nature of Social Science* (New York: Wiley, 1967).

3. Thomas J. Barnard, "Twenty Years of Testing Theories: What Have We Learned and Why," *Journal of Research in Crime and Delinquency* 27, no. 4 (1990):325–347.

4. Daniel J. Curran and Claire M. Renzetti, *Theories of Crime*, 2nd ed. (Boston: Allyn and Bacon, 2001), 2.

5. Ronald L. Akers and Christine S. Sellers, *Criminological Theories: Introduction, Evaluation, and Application*, 4th ed. (Los Angeles: Roxbury, 2004), 5–7.

6. Ibid., 6.

7. Ibid., 7.

8. Ibid., 8.

9. C. Garrett, "Effects of Residential Treatment on Adjudicated Delinquents: A Meta-Analysis," *Journal of Research in Crime and Delinquency* 22 (1985): 287–308.

10. David Lester, "Group and Milieu Therapy," in Patricia Van Voorhis, Michael Braswell, and David Lester, *Correctional Counseling and Rehabilitation*, 3rd ed. (Cincinnati, OH: Anderson, 1997), 189–217.

11. See note 5, 12–14.

12. Alvin Gouldner, *The Coming Crisis of Western Sociology* (New York: Basic Books, 1970).

13. King James Version.

14. French bishop Jacques-Benigne Bossuet (1627–1704)

originated the theory of the divine right of kings, which claimed that some kings were chosen by God to rule and were accountable only to God.

15. Stephen Pfohl, *Images of Deviance and Social Control: A Sociological History*, 2nd ed. (New York: McGraw-Hill, 1994), 22–23.

16. Alan M. Dershowitz, *The Genesis of Justice: Ten Stories of Biblical Injustice That Led to the Ten Commandments and Modern Law* (New York: Warner Books, 2000).

17. This philosophy provides an interesting addition to Pfohl's statement that, theologically, humans are bad because Adam and Eve succumbed to temptation to eat the fruit of the tree of knowledge. However, it was God who placed the apparently very luscious tree in the middle of the Garden of Eden with the command not to touch it (Genesis 1–3, KJV).

18. Donald J. Shoemaker, *Theories of Delinquency: An Examination of Explanations of Delinquent Behavior* (New York: Oxford University Press, 2005), 13.

19. Pfohl (see note 15), 64–67.

20. Marcello T. Maestro, *Cesare Beccaria and the Origins of Penal Reform* (Philadelphia: Temple University Press, 1973).

21. Cesare Beccaria, *On Crimes and Punishments* (1764), trans. Henry Paolucci (Indianapolis, IN: Bobbs-Merrill, 1963).

22. Pfohl (see note 15), 71–73.

23. Mark M. Lanier and Stuart Henry, *Essential Criminology* (Boulder, CO: Westview Press, 2004), 78.

24. George B. Vold, Thomas J. Bernard, and Jeffrey B. Snipes, *Theoretical Criminology*, 5th ed. (New York: Oxford University Press, 2002), 20.

25. Jeremy Bentham, *An Introduction to the Principles of Morals and Legislations* (1789) (New York: Kegan Paul, 1948).

26. Daniel S. Nagin and Raymond Paternoster, "The Preventive Effects of the Perceived Risk of Arrest: Testing on Expanded Conception of Deterrence," *Criminology 28* (1991):325–346.

27. Scott H. Decker and Carol W. Kohlfeld, "Capital Punishment and Executions in the Lone Star State: A Deterrence Study," *Criminal Justice Research Bulletin 3*, no. 12 (1988): 1–6.

28. Lisa J. Berlin, Jenni Owen, and Geelea Seaford, eds., *Adolescent Offenders and the Line Between the Juvenile and Criminal Justice Systems* (Durham, NC: Center for Child and Family Policy, 2007). Online at www.pubpol.duke.edu/centers/child/familyimpact/07 BriefingReport.pdf.

29. Helen Taucher, Ann D. Witte, and Harriet Griesinger, "Criminal Deterrence: Revisiting the Issue of Birth Cohort," *Review of Economics and Statistics 76* (1994):399–412.

30. Sam G. McFarland, "Is Capital Punishment a Short-Term Deterrent to Homicide? A Study of the Effects of Four Recent American Executions," *Journal of Criminal Law and Criminology 74* (1983): 1014–1030.

31. Keith Harries and Derral Cheatwood, *The Geography of Execution: The Capital Punishment Quagmire in America* (Lanham, MD: Rowman and Littlefield, 1997).

32. Gordon Waldo and Theodore Chiricos, "Perceived Penal Sanction and Self-Reported Criminality: A Neglected Approach to Deterrence Research," *Social Problems 19* (1972):522–540.

33. Adam Ortiz, "Adolescence, Brain Development and Legal Culpability," American Bar Association Juvenile Justice Center, January 2004, www.abanet.org/crimjust/juvjus/Adolescence.pdf; Bruce Bower, "Teen Brains on Trial," *Science News 165*, no. 19 (May 8, 2004), 299. Online at www.sciencenews.org/articles/20040508/bob9.asp. Carolyn Y. Johnson, "Brain Science v. Death Penalty," *Boston Globe*, October 12, 2004, www.boston.com/news/globe/health_science/articles/2004/10/12/brain_science_v_death_penalty/.

34. Richard E. Redding and Elizabeth J. Fuller, "What Do Juvenile Offenders Know About Being Tried as Adults? Implications for Deterrence," *Juvenile and Family Court Journal 55*, no. 3 (Summer 2004):35–44. Online at law.bepress.com/villanovalw-ps/papers/art29/. Elizabeth J. Fuller isn't related to the author.

35. E. S. Scott, N. D. Reppucci, and J. L. Woolard, "Evaluating Adolescent Decision Making in Legal Contexts," *Law & Human Behavior 19* (1995):221–244; L. Steinberg and E. Cauffman, "Maturity of Judgment in Adolescence: Psychosocial Factors in Adolescent Decision Making," *Law & Human Behavior 20* (1996):249–272, paraphrased in Redding and Fuller.

36. Redding and Fuller (See note 34), 35–44.

37. Frank P. Williams III and Marilyn D. McShane, *Criminological Theory*, 4th ed. (Upper Saddle River, NJ: Prentice Hall, 2004), 240.

38. Kenneth D. Tunnell, *Choosing Crime: The Criminal Calculus of Property Offenders* (Chicago: Nelson-Hall, 1992).

39. Erling Eide, *Economics of Crime: Deterrence and the Rational Offender* (Amsterdam: Elsevier/North Holland, 1994).

40. Eric Johnson and John Payne, "The Decision to Commit a Crime: An Information-Processing Analysis," in Derek B. Cornish and Ronald V. Clarke, eds., *The Reasoning Criminal: Rational Choice Perspectives on Offending* (New York: Springer-Verlag, 1986), 170–185.

41. Daniel S. Nagin and Raymond Paternoster, "Personal Capital and Social Control: The Deterrence Implications of a Theory of Individual Differences in Criminal Offending," *Criminology* 32 (1994): 581–606.

42. Julie Horney and Ineke Haen Marshall, "Risk Perceptions Among Serious Offenders: The Role of Crime and Punishment," *Criminology* 23 (1992): 575–592.

43. Paul F. Cromwell et al., "How Drugs Affect Decisions by Burglars," *International Journal of Offender Therapy and Comparative Criminology* 35 (1991): 310–321.

44. Leslie Kennedy and David Forde, "Risky Lifestyles and Dangerous Results: Routine Activities and Exposure to Crime," *Sociology and Social Research* 74 (1990): 208–211.

45. Doris Layton MacKenzie and Alex Piquero, "The Impact of Shock Incarceration Programs on Prison Crowding," *Crime and Delinquency* 40 (1994): 222–249.

46. James O. Finckenauer, *Scared Straight and the Panacea Phenomenon* (Upper Saddle River, NJ: Prentice Hall, 1982), 69.

47. Ibid., 136.

48. James O. Finckenauer, "Scared Crooked," *Psychology Today 13* (November 1979):6.

49. Gwynne Dyer, *War* (Crown, 1985).

50. Dale G. Parent, *Correctional Boot Camps: Lessons from a Decade of Research* (Washington, DC: U.S. Department of Justice, Office of Justice Programs, National Institute of Justice, 2003), 4, 7. Online at www.ncjrs.gov/pdffiles1/nij/197018.pdf.

51. Malcom Feeley and Jonathon Simon, "The New Penology: Notes on the Emerging Strategy of Corrections and Its Implications," *Criminology* 30, no. 4 (November 1992):449–474.

52. Williams and McShane (see note 37), p. 23.

53. Ernie Thomson, "Deterrence Versus Brutalization: The Case of Arizona," *Homicide Studies* 1 (1997):110–128.

54. Derek B. Cornish and Ronald V. G. Clarke, "Understanding Crime Displacement: Application of Rational Choice Theory," *Criminology* 25 (1987):933–947.

55. Ysabel Rennie, "The Positivist Revolution," in *The Search for Criminal Man* (Lexington, MA: Lexington Books, 1978).

56. Sawyer F. Sylvester, Introduction to *Research on the Propensity for Crime at Different Ages*, by Adolphe Quetelet, trans. Sawyer F. Sylvester (Cincinnati, OH: Anderson, 1984), v, xviii.

57. Adolphe Quetelet, *Research on the Propensity for Crime at Different Ages*, trans. Sawyer F. Sylvester (Cincinnati, OH: Anderson, 1984), 64–65.

58. Gillis J. Harp, *Positivist Republic: Auguste Comte and the Reconstruction of American Liberalism, 1865–1920* (University Park, PA: Pennsylvania State University Press, 1995).

59. George B. Wold, Thomas J. Barnard, and Jeffrey B. Snipes, *Theoretical Criminology*, 5th ed. (New York: Oxford University Press, 2002), 21–23.

60. C. Ray Jeffery, "An Interdisciplinary Theory of Criminal Behavior," in William S. Laufer and Freda Adler, *Advances in Criminological Theory 1* (New Brunswick, NJ: Transaction, 1989), 69–87.

61. Marvin E. Wolfgang, "Cesare Lombroso (1835–1909)" in Hermann Manneheim, ed. *Pioneers in Criminology*, 2nd ed. (Montclair, NJ: Patterson Smith, 1972), 232–291.

Why are psychological theories of criminality important to the study of delinquency?

What role might the brain have in antisocial behavior?

How does the positivist school of criminology shift the focus from the offense to the offender?

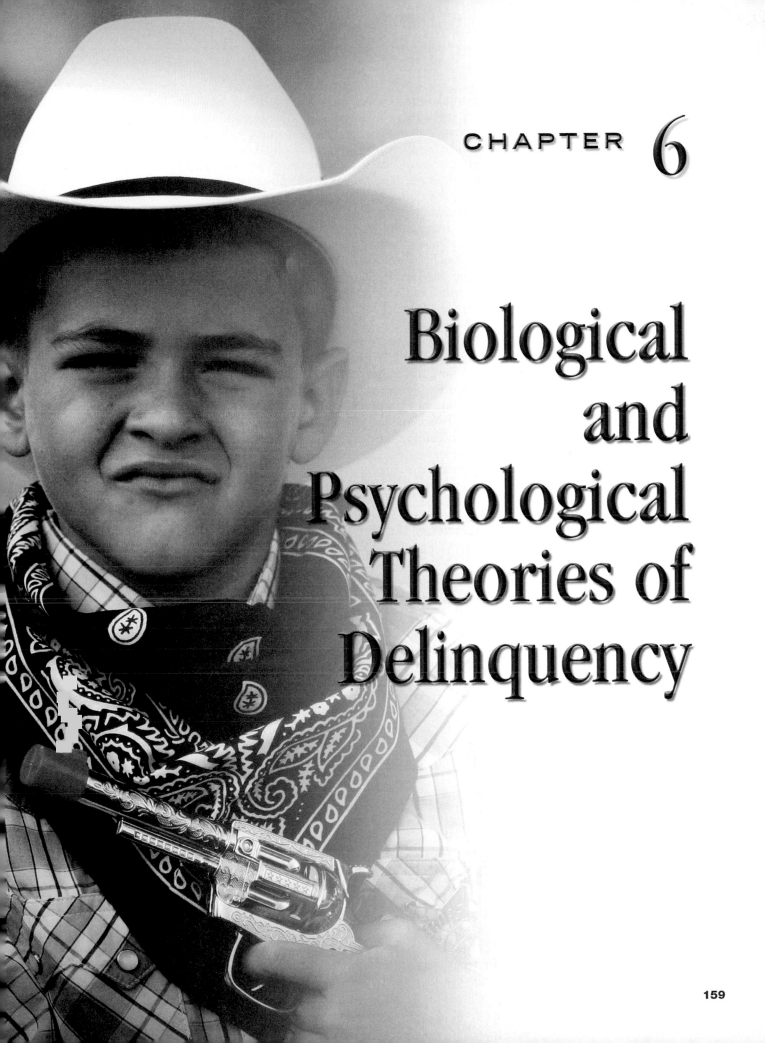

CHAPTER 6

Biological and Psychological Theories of Delinquency

Why do people commit crime? What drives them to break the law and, in some cases, harm others, including their loved ones? The classical school of criminology explanation, that offenders choose to break the law after weighing the risks and rewards of such behavior, can be unsatisfying. The philosophy that those who break the law, including juvenile delinquents and status offenders, are exercising their free will is useful for constructing penalties and designing programs based on deterrence, but there are too many cases in which this explanation appears simplistic and devoid of the policy implications that could effectively address the problems of crime and juvenile delinquency.[1]

The positivist school of criminology shifts the focus from the offense to the offender and is much more interested in the reasons that people violate the law. The positivist school has a long and rich theoretical development, which we will cover in the next three chapters. In this chapter, we will consider biological and psychological theories of crime and human behavior. These theories address the early history of explanations for antisocial behavior, as well as some recent scientific developments in the study of crime and juvenile delinquency. Chapters 7 and 8 will cover established and contemporary sociological explanations of antisocial behavior. In these three chapters, students will find theories that seek to describe and explain human behavior in light of juvenile delinquency.

Students are cautioned, however, against subscribing exclusively to one theory. Crime and deliquency is a multifaceted phenomenon, and no single theory explains all the various behaviors of those who break the law. However, after completing these chapters on criminological theory, the student should have a good idea of the broad range of explanations that criminologists have developed. Although particular attention will be paid to theories that explain juvenile delinquency, it's important to remember that many of the theories don't distinguish between delinquency and adult crime.

BIOLOGICAL THEORIES OF DELINQUENCY AND CRIME

Biological theories of crime seek to provide a physical explanation for the actions of offenders. These theories range from the outdated—atavisms, body types, and phrenology—to today's more advanced theories, which are based on the highly technical study of neurotransmitters, hormones, and genetics. See Table 6-1 for a table of these theories and areas of research. However, they all seek to answer the same question: Can the desire or urge to violate social laws, customs, and mores lie in the body itself? And if it does, what can be done about it?

In this section, we will discuss the history of biological theories of crime, as well as the relationship between juvenile delinquency and theories of heredity, neurotransmitters, hormones, and biosocial theory.

First Biological Theories of Crime

The first real biological theories of crime were developed in the years after the development of modern methods of scientific research and Charles Darwin's publication of *On the Origin of Species* (1859). The idea that the natural world and all that lived in it could be classified, cataloged, quantified, and predicted became very attractive to a number of early social scientists. Ironically, human existence, as well as the societies in which it takes place, seems chaotic to us even as we create it and live it. The need to understand and predict these chaotic behaviors and social processes has always been especially earnest in relation to the study of crime and, more recently, how some children become juvenile delinquents.

CESARE LOMBROSO AND ATAVISMS   Cesare Lombroso's theory of **atavisms** qualifies as a biological theory, although in his later work he also considered sociological factors.[2] Lombroso, an Italian physician who lived from 1836 to 1909, argued that those

Instant Recall from Chapter 5
atavism

The appearance in a person of features thought to be from earlier stages of human evolution. Popularized by Cesare Lombroso.

Table 6-1   **Biological Theories of Delinquency**

Category	Areas of Research	Examples
Genetics or heredity	Heritability	Impulsivity, hyperactivity, aggression, genes that provide for the regulation of behavior, alcoholism
	Evolution	Aggression
Chemical	Pollution	Exposure to lead, toxic metals, dioxins, manganese, mercury, pesticides
	Hormones and neurotransmitters	Low monoamine oxidase (MAO), high testosterone, androgen–estrogen imbalance[a] Dopamine and serotonin disorders
Neurological	Personality disorders	Attention deficit disorder (ADD), antisocial personality disorder, attention deficit hyperactivity disorder (ADHD), conduct disorder, prefrontal cortical dysfunction, bipolar disorder, oppositional defiant disorder, antisocial personality disorder
	Learning disabilities	Low IQ, dyslexia, depression, mental retardation
Illness or trauma	Illness	Brain tumor, schizophrenia
	Physical injury	Premature birth, low birth weight, perinatal trauma, severe head injury; maternal smoking, alcohol, and drug abuse
	Structural brain abnormality	Abnormalities of the frontal and temporal lobes, hypothalamus, and amygdala
Diet	Vitamin deficiency	Junk food, malnutrition; deficiencies of niacin, pantothenic acid, thiamin, vitamin B_6, vitamin C, iron, magnesium and tryptophan[b]
	Food additives	Artificial colors[c]
	Naturally occurring substances	Alcohol, sugar, caffeine, some legal and illegal drugs

[a] C. J. Peter Eriksson, Bettina von der Pahlen, Taisto Sarkola, and Kaija Seppa, "Oestradiol and Human Male Alcohol-Related Aggression," *Alcohol and Alcoholism* 38, no. 6 (2003):589–596. Reprinted by permission of Oxford University Press.
[b] Melvyn R. Werbach, "Nutritional Influences on Aggressive Behavior," *Journal of Orthomolecular Medicine* 7, no. 1 (1995):45–51.
[c] "Synthetic Food Coloring and Behavior: A Dose Response Effect in a Double-Blind, Placebo-Controlled, Repeated-Measures Study," *Journal of Pediatrics* (November 1994): 691–698. Reprinted with permission from Elsevier.

who broke the law were likely to have certain physical features that could be observed by careful examination and would indicate that offenders weren't as fully evolved as nonoffenders. Lombroso's evidence was based on comparing offenders to other individuals. He performed autopsies on 66 male offenders and concluded that they shared features with primitive humans. He also examined 832 living offenders, both male and female, as well as 390 law-abiding Italian soldiers.[3]

Lombroso's theory that offenders are physically different from the rest of us hasn't held up to scrutiny. He is remembered as the founder of positivist criminology because he made a concerted effort to ground his research in the scientific method. The fact that he was wrong about offenders being throwbacks to an earlier form of human causes many criminologists to devalue his contribution to the field.[4] However, because he continually refined his work over a number of years and stressed a scientific approach, his place as a serious criminologist is assured.

WILLIAM SHELDON AND BODY TYPE   Although Lombroso's theory of atavisms failed to gain acceptance, other theories based on physical differences have been created and discarded over the years. Body-type theories postulated a relationship between the physical appearance of the body and the temperament of the mind. These theories of body type were especially popular with criminologists such as William Sheldon (1898–1977), who constructed a physical and mental typology based on the physiology of development.[5] Sheldon's body-type theory had three components (see Figure 6-1):

- **Endomorphic**   Endomorphic body types are soft, round, and fat. They have tapering limbs, small bones, and smooth skin. Endomorphs tend to be extroverts and seek comfort.

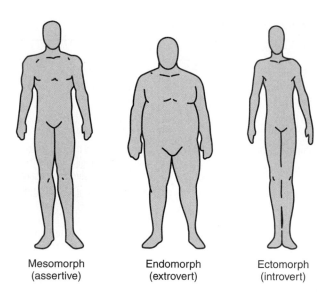

Mesomorph
(assertive)

Endomorph
(extrovert)

Ectomorph
(introvert)

Figure 6-1   **Sheldon's Body-Type Theory**

- **Mesomorphic**   Mesomorphic body types have large muscles, heavy chests, and a hard, lean look. They are active, dynamic individuals who act aggressively and walk, talk, and gesture assertively.
- **Ectomorphic**   Ectomorphs are skinny individuals who appear fragile and have little body mass. They have small features, delicate bones, and fine hair. Behaviorally, they are introverts who shrink from crowds, are sensitive to noise and distractions, suffer from chronic fatigue and insomnia, and have skin problems and allergies.

According to Sheldon, everyone possesses the characteristics of each of these body types to some degree. Sheldon developed a measure using a scale from 1 to 7 for a person's possession of each type. Therefore, someone with a 1–4–7 somatotype would have few endomorphic characteristics, a healthy dose of mesomorphic characteristics, and many ectomorphic characteristics. This theory tried to explain what offenses each type of offender was most likely to commit. For instance, those individuals with primarily mesomorph characteristics can be expected to engage in street crimes that require aggressiveness and muscle, while an endomorphic offender could be expected to be an embezzler or a forger.[6]

When we consider Sheldon's body-type theory of crime today, it appears simplistic and unworkable. To suggest that body type is destiny ignores our experiences with the vast range of offenders of every size and shape who commit a wide range of offenses. The many psychological and sociological variables that require consideration in determining why individuals violate the law can't be reduced to the body type of offenders.

FRANZ JOSEPH GALL AND PHRENOLOGY   Another way the physical body was thought to indicate a criminal personality was related to the size, shape, and topography of the skull. The pseudoscience of **phrenology** was very popular at the beginning of the 19th century and was promoted primarily by Franz Joseph Gall. Physicians have long realized that certain parts of the brain are responsible for certain functions, and phrenologists attempted to create a scientific discipline around these observations. Postulating that the outside of the skull could reveal brain structure, the phrenologist would feel for bumps and suggest what type of personality and behavior could be expected. For instance, phrenologists speculated that their science could uncover a penchant for destructiveness, secretiveness, and philoprogenitiveness (love of offspring).[7] Although we seldom hear about phrenology anymore, some still advocate it as a viable scientific approach.[8]

phrenology

The outdated study of the skull as an indicator of personality.

New students at Braemar High School in 1937 have the bumps on their heads assessed to see what subjects they might excel in. *(Courtesy Harry Todd, Getty Images Inc. -Hulton Archive Photos)*

Phrenology fell into disrepute for several reasons. In addition to limited evidence of effectiveness, phrenology's adherents fought bitter political battles in the press as they attempted to discredit each other. Additionally, phrenology was co-opted by outright quacks and reduced to a parlor game. The development and popularization of phrenology occurred before modern biological research and scientific practices really took hold. However, phrenology is still discussed because it's probably the earliest cohesive attempt to predict human behavior, and criminality, by considering the body.

Heredity

Early attempts to find a physical reason to explain why someone would violate the law are crude, unscientific, and easy for us to ridicule today because they appear so elementary and superficial. Although a number of other early efforts that attempted to find reasons for crime weren't entirely successful, we don't dismiss them lightly because we are still attempting to make these connections with new and improved scientific tools.

One concept that continues to have appeal is the idea that a tendency to break the law can be inherited by children from parents through their **genes**. This isn't a new idea; in fact, it's over a century old. From about 1900 to World War II, the pseudoscience of **eugenics** was vigorously promoted in the United States as the cure to all social and behavioral human ills. For more on the fascinating and alarming history of eugenics, see Crosscurrents 6.1.

With the decoding of **DNA**, we are continually finding new genetic reasons for how our bodies are structured and how they function, as well as evidence of what traits are inherited. Early attempts to link **heredity** and genetics to crime relied on the use of family trees. Researchers noticed that in certain families crime seemed to be a consistent feature and speculated that it might be inherited. For instance, in independent studies of the Jukes family, two researchers found seven murderers, 60 thieves, 50 prostitutes, and many other social deviants and offenders.[9] In comparing the Jukes to another family, the Edwards, the researchers found that, in addition to there being no offenders (actually they were mistaken in this observation), the Edwards had governors, preachers, writers, and judges.[10] See Case in Point 6.1 for *Buck* v. *Bell*, a 1927 case in which the state of Virginia succeeded in sterilizing a young woman whose family had been deemed feebleminded.

genes
Short lengths of DNA that determine the inherited characteristics that distinguish individuals.

eugenics
The idea that humans can be improved by strictly controlled breeding.

DNA
Deoxyribonucleic acid. The substance inside a cell nucleus that carries the instructions for making living organisms.

heredity
The handing down of traits from parents to their offspring.

Eugenics

The first time many people hear the word *eugenics* is in old *Star Trek* episodes, usually in the context of the "eugenics wars" and the subsequent movie *The Wrath of Khan*. Given such an introduction, it's easy to dismiss the idea of eugenics as something created only to add a little science to television sci-fi. But eugenics, the idea that the human race can be improved by strictly controlled breeding, exists and was at one time considered the road to the future in the United States.

The word *eugenics* was coined in the early 1880s by Francis Galton, who based it on a Greek root word meaning "good in birth."[1] Loosely basing its theories on the ideas of Galton and the genetics work of Gregor Mendel, the American eugenics movement became popular in the early 20th century.[2] In 1903, the American Breeders Association (ABA) was founded, and the Carnegie Institution funded the Station for the Experimental Study of Evolution in Cold Spring Harbor, New York. The ABA featured committees with titles like the "Heritability of Feeblemindedness" and "Sterilization and Other Means of Eliminating Defective Germ Plasm." In 1911, while privately funded agencies such as the Eugenics Records Office tried to stamp out undesirable traits in the American "breeding stock," leading geneticist Charles Davenport wrote *Heredity in Relation to Eugenics*, which before World War II was cited in more than a third of high school biology texts. Davenport was worried that the nation's breeding stock would

> *rapidly become darker in pigmentation, smaller in stature, more mercurial, more attached to music and art, more given to crimes of larceny, kidnapping, assault, murder, rape, and sex-immorality . . . than were the original English settlers.[3]*

By 1924, eugenics courses were common in universities, colleges, and high schools.[4] The American eugenics movement, driven by the energy and commitment of its founders and adherents, quickly went international. In the early 1930s, American eugenics luminaries were receiving mail from Adolf Hitler, then just a young German politician.[5]

A major target for eugenicists was criminality. In 1914, a New York prisons committee began documenting "hereditary criminality," and the New York City Police Department established a eugenic investigations laboratory. Inmates at Sing Sing were examined in a search for criminality in family trees.[6] Sterilization of offenders, or those merely deemed offenders, had begun as early as 1899 in Indiana. There, Dr. Harry Clay Sharp, prison physician at the Indiana Reformatory at Jeffersonville, began regularly performing crude vasectomies, with a 19-year-old inmate as his first patient. Although such sterilization wasn't exactly legal at the

A crowd sits watching the Eugenic and Health Exhibit at the Kansas Free Fair in 1929. *(Courtesy Lewis W. Hine, Library of Congress)*

time, Sharp urged his colleagues to push for state laws to restrict marriage and sterilize all male inmates everywhere, "whether it be an almshouse, insane asylum, institute for the feeble minded, reformatory, or prison."[7]

World War II, with its discovery of Hitler's massive eugenics efforts, as well as the aging of American eugenics champions, finally slowed eugenics in the United States. As of 2006, some vestiges remained, however, with some of the state sterilization laws remaining on the books.[8]

Thanks to eugenics, modern genetic research into any aspect of antisocial behavior or criminality is suspect. In his 2003 book, *War Against the Weak*, Edwin Black entitles the final chapters "Eugenics Becomes Genetics" and "Newgenics," in which he points out the various databases that hold the DNA of criminal suspects and arrestees.[9] In 1992, academic outcry halted a planned National Institutes of Health–funded conference called Genetic Factors in Crime. Critics believed that the conference's plan to study the use of biochemical markers and medications for violent behavior would encourage the idea that black people are genetically predisposed to crime.[10]

Despite continuing controversy, the use and study of genetics will probably remain within the fields of criminology and law enforcement. The FBI's DNA database, Combined DNA Indexing System (CODIS), is stocked with genetic samples from prison inmates. However, CODIS is used to match suspects to offenses and to find missing people, rather than to predict who will commit a criminal offense.[11] The use of genetics differs from country to country. As of 2005 in England, the DNA of more than 24,000 juveniles who were arrested, but not charged or cautioned, was included in the national crime database. Despite public concern, the government has refused to dispose of the records of those who weren't convicted.[12]

Think About It

1. Should criminologists consider genetics in their study of crime?
2. What is your opinion of the American eugenics movement?
3. Should the U.S. government use a genetic database like CODIS to try to predict who might commit a criminal offense?

1. Steven Selden, *Inheriting Shame* (New York: Teachers College Press, 1999), xiv.
2. Ibid., 2. Gregor Mendel was a Moravian monk who performed groundbreaking breeding experiments with pea plants and found that specific traits appeared in each generation in predictable ratios.
3. C. B. Davenport, *Heredity in Relation to Eugenics* (New York: Holt, 1911), 219, as quoted in Black, *War Against the Weak,* (New York: Four Walls Eight Windows, 2003), p. 6.
4. *Autobiography of Leon. F. Whitney,* unpublished manuscript circa 1973, APS Manuscript Collection, pp. 204–205, as quoted in Black, p. 75.
5. Black, p. 259.
6. Ibid., 96.
7. Harry C. Sharp, "The Severing of the Vasa Deferentia and Its Relation to the Neuropsychopathic Constitution," *New York Medical Journal* 8 (March 1902): 413–414, as quoted in Black, p. 64.
8. Black., 400.
9. Ibid., 429.
10. Gregory Stock, *Redesigning Humans* (Boston: Houghton Mifflin, 2002), 230; Mark S. Frankel, "Multicultural Science," *Chronicle of Higher Education,* November 10, 1993, B2.
11 John Solomon, "FBI's DNA Database Gets Heavy Use," Associated Press, March 8, 2004.
12 Sue Reid, "Do the Police Have Your Child's DNA?" *Daily Mail* (London), January 21, 2006, p. 26A.

6.1   CASE IN POINT

BUCK V. BELL

THE CASE	**THE POINT**
Buck v. Bell 274 U.S. 200 (1927)	*This infamous case upheld the right of states to sterilize those determined to be mentally incompetent.*

Carrie Buck was a 17-year-old woman in the state of Virginia whose adoptive family committed her to a state mental institution after learning she was pregnant. It was concluded that Carrie, although she had been a good student in school and claimed that the pregnancy was the result of rape, was "feebleminded."

After she gave birth to a daughter, Carrie was sent to the Colony for Epileptics and Feebleminded. Buck's mother had previously been committed to the same institution under the same diagnosis of feeblemindedness. Carrie's infant was soon declared to be "mentally defective," and doctors concluded that the three females represented three generations of feeblemindedness.

Shortly before Carrie Buck was committed, Virginia passed a law allowing the inmates of mental institutions to be sterilized. Shortly thereafter, an institutional hearing determined that Buck should be sterilized. Buck's counsel claimed that she had been denied due process and equal protection under the Fourteenth Amendment, and the case wound its way through the courts, all of which upheld the new law.

The Supreme Court found that the law did not violate the Constitution and that all legal safeguards had been properly followed. In his opinion, Justice Oliver Wendell Holmes wrote that the issue was not the propriety of the sterilization procedure but the substantive law, which had been followed.

In stating the decision of the court to allow Carrie Buck to be sterilized, Holmes wrote, "It is better for all the world, if instead of waiting to execute degenerate offspring for crime ... society can prevent those who are manifestly unfit from continuing their kind. Three generations of imbeciles are enough."

Source: Edwin Black, *War Against the Weak* (New York: Four Walls Eight Windows, 2003), 108–121.

This type of research has two key problems. First, comparing two families doesn't provide a sufficient sample to conclude that genetics produces the observed differences in criminal behavior. Hundreds of randomly chosen families would have to be studied to arrive at such conclusions. The Jukes family was included precisely because of the number of offenses of its members. The second issue has to do with the old problem of separating the influence of genetics (nature) from environment (nurture). If a child is surrounded by family members who break the law, wouldn't it be as likely that they learned to break the law as it would be that they shared criminogenic genes?[11]

So how can we distinguish between inherited behaviors and learned behaviors? To do so, we would have to study individuals with the same genetic makeup but different life experiences. Identical twins provide ideal subjects for such research.

STUDIES OF TWINS AND ADOPTED CHILDREN Certain traits appear to be transmitted from parents to children through genes rather than learning. A series of studies suggests that traits related to repetitive aggressive behavior, such as impulsivity, drug abuse, alcoholism, and cognitive defects are heritable. Other studies have found that personality factors such as extroversion, introversion, cognitive deficits, conduct disorder, and anxiety are both heritable and predictive of substance abuse and aggression.

When considering the differences between fraternal and identical twins, the concept of inherited behavior becomes even clearer. **Fraternal twins** occur when two eggs are fertilized by two sperm. These twins are the same as other siblings, except that they are gestated at the same time and are born within minutes of each other. Identical twins are from the same egg and fertilized by a single sperm and have exactly the same genetic makeup. The presumption is that **identical twins** share more behavioral similarities than fraternal twins.[12]

George Vold and colleagues discussed one significant study that looked at 6,000 pairs of twins to see if criminality in one twin was indicative of criminality in the other. The study reported that this happened 35.8 percent of the time in male identical twins, while in male fraternal twins it occurred 12.3 percent of the time. In female identical twins, when one was identified as engaging in antisocial behavior, the other also did 21.4 percent of the time. This rate dropped to 4.3 percent in female fraternal twins. In a further look at the data, this relationship was shown to be even more robust for serious criminality.[13]

We should be careful, however, before we attribute destiny to heredity. This study didn't separate the effects of heredity and socialization. Although the identical twins

fraternal twins

Siblings produced by the simultaneous fertilization of two egg cells; the twins are only as genetically similar as regular siblings.

identical twins

Siblings produced by the division of a single fertilized egg cell who are genetically identical.

Unlike identical twins, fraternal twins do not share a genetic makeup. Here, the fraternal twins Remee (right) and Kian (left) were born to parents who each had one black and one white parent. It is speculated that Kian inherited all the black genes, and Remee all the white genes. The odds of this happening are a million to one.

(Courtesy of Gary Roberts, www.worldwidefeatures.com)

showed more similarities in committing criminal offenses, we don't know if their environments differed greatly from those of the fraternal twins. One way to study this is to look at twins who grew up in different environments. By studying identical twins raised in separate families, it's possible to examine their differences in behavior and then attribute these differences or similarities to genetics or environment.

The largest obstacle to this type of research is finding twins who were separated at birth. Because this is a relatively uncommon occurrence, these studies suffer from having extremely small sample sizes. Vold and colleagues reported on three studies that used this technique. One study reported on 32 sets of identical twins, and another study reported on eight sets of identical twins.[14] Finally, a study done by Walters used meta-analysis (meaning that a large number of these comparisons were examined), and factors such as sample size, quality of research design, and gender of the twins were controlled for.[15] Vold and colleagues concluded that all three of these studies found some evidence that criminal behavior can be inherited.

A final method for determining the relationship between genetics and environment is to consider the antisocial behavior of adopted children and compare their legal records to those of both the biological parents and the adoptive parents. One would expect to find a similarity to the adoptive parents if environment was the main cause of criminality and a stronger relationship to the biological parents if heredity was more important. The studies analyzed by Vold and colleagues reported a consistent relationship between biological parents and their children in terms of antisocial behavior. This held true more often for property crime than it did for violent crime, but this finding might be deceptive. Property offenders typically commit many more offenses than do violent offenders, so they can be expected to show up in official statistics at a much greater rate. Violent behavior might be as easily transmitted as criminal behavior toward property, but this is less likely to be discovered using crime data.[16]

What can we conclude from these studies?

- Separating the influences of genetics and environment on criminal behavior is difficult.
- The studies that have succeeded in finding research techniques to separate the influences of genetics and environment are limited to very small samples.
- There appears to be a consistent relationship between the antisocial behavior of biological parents and their children.
- This relationship holds true even when adoptive parents, fraternal twins, and separate environments are considered.

HEREDITY AND BEHAVIOR   Are genes indeed responsible for criminality? It is possible to inherit certain diseases from one's parents or even more distant ancestors. Do parents also pass to their children genes that cause them to violate the law? See Focus on Ethics 6.1 for a look at a possible scenario.

We can't answer these questions based on the evidence that we have reviewed thus far. Although there might be some association between the criminality of parents and children, no firm causal link has been identified. What genes or traits could antisocial parents pass to their children? Is it too much testosterone? Not enough of some brain chemical that allows for the child to experience empathy? Are a violent temper, disregard for others' feelings, aggression, and extreme competitiveness inherited? These questions are difficult to answer because something always intervenes between genetics and criminality. The influence of heredity is always indirect and controlled by a host of factors that might include environmental factors.

Because genetic factors don't exist in a vacuum, it's necessary to consider how these factors interact with the many social and environmental factors that also might play a role in the development of criminality. Diana Fishbein, one of the foremost

FOCUS on ETHICS

6.1

THE PERFECT CHILD

The year is 2016, and you and your husband want to become pregnant with your first child. You both would like to have a son. Thanks to genetic engineering, you can choose or strongly direct many of your child's mental and physical traits, including its sex. You pay a $100,000 deposit to a reputable company called FerShur to help you plan your child.

You know you carry a gene for a disease that eventually degenerates brain cells, causing loss of both physical control and intellectual faculties. The disease can strike at any time after the age of 18 and, without extensive treatment, is not only severely debilitating, but fatal. However, as a female, you only carry the gene, and you won't get the disease. You have a male cousin with the disease who has undergone extensive treatment and, although his life is difficult, he might live into his fifties.

Doctors aren't yet able to "turn off" this gene with any consistent success. Therefore, either a prospective son or daughter has a 50–50 chance of inheriting your defective gene. A daughter with the gene will never get sick, but a son who has the gene will.

You have also learned that your husband and his sister both carry genetic components related to the activity of neurotransmitters, hormones, and monoamine oxidase in their brains that encourage violent, aggressive behavior. Your husband is a decent, law-abiding, thrill-seeking guy who plays rugby and skydives. Your sister-in-law, however, has an extremely violent temper. She has severe mood swings and has been arrested three times for domestic violence. Your in-laws still struggle to provide her with help and guidance.

Here is your dilemma. You both really want a son, but chances are even that he will inherit and contract your debilitating disease. If he's healthy, your gene-team suggests, he might become a successful fighter pilot or quarterback or some other type of thrill-seeking professional. Your daughter will be healthy whether or not she inherits your gene, but she might also be antisocial and uncontrollable like your sister-in-law.

Although this scenario sounds improbable now, advances in reproductive technology might make all this possible. The real issue here concerns the ability to choose personal characteristics. In terms of juvenile delinquency, would you select traits for your child that would ensure she or he never committed any aggressive or violent acts? What if that decision affected the child's health in some other way?

Think About It

1. What other implications for juvenile delinquency and society may arise from such technology?
2. Should the government control this technology?
3. As illustrated in the scenario, altering a child's genes will likely be expensive. Should gene therapy be a luxury only for the wealthy, or should society bear the cost through insurance or socialized medicine? What if a future study on gene alteration found that the practice significantly decreased the crime rate?

criminologists studying biobehavioral perspectives, summarizes these issues in the following points:

1. All human behavior has a genetic component.
2. There are no genes for or biological causes of specific human behaviors. Instead, genes help design our temperament and personality and provide a predisposition to behave according to certain patterns.
3. The environment can modify the expression of genetic and biological traits. No one is predestined to behave in a certain way or to break the law.
4. On a global level, social and economic deprivation, deleterious environmental conditions, psychological trauma, and abuse can lead to antisocial behavior. The deterioration of cities and dissolution of social resources are substantially contributory.
5. Vulnerabilities to antisocial behavior cross all boundaries but will be most abundant where social risks are the highest.[17]

It is important to note that even those who are convinced of the importance of the connection between biology and crime don't contend that the relationship is determinative. Although biology plays a significant part in how our behavior is shaped, it's wise to remember that crime is socially defined. For example, killing another person might mean one is considered a murderer or a war hero depending on the context of the behavior. Although certain individuals might have a biological predisposition to be more violent than others, it often depends on the behavior's circumstances before the behavior can be considered either appropriate or criminal.

Before we conclude our discussion of the relationship between biology and deviant behavior, another crucial concern requires examination. Although there is significant evidence of a relationship between biology and deviant behavior, so far little or no solid theoretical connection has been established. Some experts on child and adolescent behavior believe poor nutrition and too much fat-laden, unhealthy food have a negative effect on behavior in school and the ability to learn (see Kids in the News 6.1).

6.1   K I D S in the N E W S

Johnny Eat Good

What we eat affects our personalities and our moods. Caffeine makes us feel energetic and mentally sharp, but too much can make us jittery and nervous. Sugar imparts a quick boost of energy, as do carbohydrates. A big, heavy meal makes some people feel sleepy, while going too long between meals or not eating enough can result in weakness, depressed moods, and other bad side effects. According to some experts, food also has subtle effects on hyperactivity, aggression, depression, and other neurological states, particularly in children.

In 1997, Appleton Central Alternative High School in Wisconsin instituted a program with the bakery company Natural Ovens. Prior to that year, the school, which is attended by students with known behavioral issues, had such serious discipline problems that it employed a full-time police officer. The new meal program did away with all soda and candy vending machines, as well as fast-food-type menu items such as hamburgers, pizza, and french fries. Instead, the cafeteria began serving salads, fresh fruits, whole grain breads, and other minimally processed foods.

According to a teacher on the school's website, "We noticed a change in behavior from the get-go. All teachers reported that students were able to concentrate for longer periods in class. The switchover to healthy breakfast and lunch programs resulted in fewer reports of stomachaches, headaches, and fatigue among students, as well as less tardiness and far fewer disciplinary referrals to the office."

A school district administrator reported that the school didn't have a single expulsion in 2001 and that dropouts decreased dramatically. School officials say their students have exhibited steady good behavior in the decade since the menu changes.

Even the company a child keeps while eating can have an effect on mental and physical health. University of Minneapolis researchers found that as the number of meals a child ate with his or her family increased, the child's risk for tobacco, alcohol, and marijuana usage decreased, as well as the chances of low grades, depression, and thoughts of suicide.

In 2006, an Omaha juvenile court judge began letting some juvenile offenders attend a fitness and nutrition program. In designing the program, the judge referred to studies that he said suggested that good nutrition and regular exercise could improve IQ, attentiveness, and general well-being.

Think About It

1. Are the menu changes at the high school responsible for the improvement in the students' behavior? Why? Why not?

2. Have you tried switching to a healthier diet? If so, did it make you feel better physically?

3. Should programs stressing good nutrition and fitness be instituted in juvenile detention facilities?

Some nutrition experts believe that the quality of food given to children can affect hyperactivity, aggression, depression, and other neurological states. *(Courtesy Cathleen Campbell, Getty Images, Inc – Liason)*

Sources: Appleton Area School District, "Promoting Healthy Lifestyles," www.aasd.k12.wi.us/aca/Promoting%20Healthy%20Lifestyles-CMYK-FINAL2.pdf, p. 2; Joe Dejka, "Fighting Bad Influences with Diet, Exercise," *Omaha World-Herald*, January 16, 2006, p. 01B; Julia Watson, "Good School Meals Can Calm Students," UPI, May 24, 2005; Michael Meacher, "Diet Can Make You Nice," *New Statesman*, February 16, 2004, www.newstatesman.com/200402160019; Rob Zaleski, "Fighting Fat Foods with 'Super Size'" *Capital Times* (Madison, WI), May 28, 2004, p. 1C; UPI, "Family Meals Can Improve Teen's Well-Being," August 3, 2004.

What physical differences exist in the brains of those who engage in criminal or violent behavior as opposed to the brains of those who don't? What parts of the brain should be examined to determine if these differences exist? To answer these questions, researchers are looking at biochemistry, specifically neurotransmitters and hormones.

Neurotransmitters

neurotransmitter

A chemical that transmits information between neurons.

Neurotransmitters are chemicals that transmit information between neurons. This function is at least partially determined by genetics. Therefore, we can safely assume that some human behaviors have a biological basis. Some researchers believe that too little or too much of these neurotransmitters might be responsible for neurological and mood disorders, many of which are related to abnormal aggression, crime, and juvenile development. The two neurotransmitters that have received the most attention in the criminological literature are dopamine and serotonin.

- **Dopamine**   We aren't sure exactly how dopamine works in the human body to control behavior. It has been associated with aggressive and violent behavior in animals as well as humans, and some studies have linked increases in dopamine to psychotic behavior. Although we don't know for sure how much dopamine is necessary or desirable, researchers are confident that once its interaction with other neurotransmitters is better understood, it will be possible to predict with more confidence how this important brain chemical relates to behavior.

- **Serotonin**   Low levels of serotonin have been linked to poor impulse control and ultimately to aggressive or violent behavior. This is a complicated issue, because the link to serotonin levels and aggressive behavior is affected by a person's ability to control their behavior, and this ability is related to other factors. For instance, underlying hostility or negative moods might be more important than serotonin levels, but they might also interact with serotonin to produce aggression. Complicating this relationship even further is the influence of alcohol. Individuals might react differently to the effects of alcohol, and some studies have shown that alcohol can lower serotonin levels. Therefore, there is some confusion as to whether serotonin causes the lack of impulse control that contributes to aggressive behavior or whether alcohol first lowers the serotonin level.[18]

Three additional chemicals in the brain have been found to be related to antisocial behaviors.

- **Norepinephrine and epinephrine**   Norepinephrine and epinephrine are important to the regulation of our reaction to stress. Although not predictive

Photomicrograph of the neurotransmitter dopamine. *(Courtesy Dennis Kunkel, Phototake NYC)*

Photomicrograph of the neurotransmitter serotonin. *(Courtesy Dennis Kunkel, Phototake NYC)*

of particular behavioral outcomes, norepinephrine particularly interacts with factors such as individual predisposition, setting, and circumstances to produce such tendencies as impulsivity, sensation seeking, and high activity levels. Although some studies have found an association between norepinephrine and aggression or violence, the direction of this relationship hasn't been established.[19] This means that aggression and violence are as likely to produce norepinephrine as norepinephrine is to cause aggression and violence.

- **Monoamine oxidase**   The final brain chemical that might affect antisocial behavior is monoamine oxidase (MAO), an enzyme that metabolizes serotonin, dopamine, epinephrine, and norepinephrine. Low levels of MAO have been associated with psychopathy, aggression, violent behavior, alcoholism, sensation-seeking behavior, and impulsivity.[20]

We can see an example of how researchers analyze the relationship between brain chemistry and behavior in a 2002 study that looked at males from birth to adulthood to determine why some abused boys develop behavior problems while other abused boys don't. The researchers found that a variation in the gene for monoamine oxidase A (MAO-A) ameliorated the psychological effects of abuse. Abused children whose genes expressed high levels of MAO-A were less likely to become antisocial in adulthood. The study concluded that there is evidence that genes can moderate the effects of an abusive childhood environment.[21]

Hormones

Another area in which researchers have found a relationship between the human body and aggression or violence is in the study of sex and stress hormones. In males, the hormone testosterone has been linked to increases in aggression and sex drive.[22] Although testosterone naturally occurs in females, the levels are much lower and the effects substantially different. As with other relationships between the body and behavior, there is a chicken-and-egg dilemma. Do testosterone levels rise when a person engages in aggressive behavior, or does testosterone cause people to become aggressive?

Before puberty, boys and girls have about the same amount of sex hormones. As children grow into adolescents, however, both sexes experience a surge in the production of hormones such as testosterone, which brings on the rapid mood swings that are typically associated with adolescence. Both boys and girls might be more angry, while boys might feel more annoyance and girls more depression.[23] Both boys and girls grow bigger and stronger and typically desire to experiment with new behaviors and seek novel or risky situations. This behavior is affected by neurotransmitters which, in turn, are regulated by sex hormones.[24]

Although boys tend to be more prone to wrestling and fighting than girls, boys and girls have about the same amount of sex hormones prior to puberty. *(Courtesy Catherine-Ursillo, Photo Researchers, Inc.)*

The hormone-modulated behaviors of boys and girls part ways here. After puberty, male testosterone levels are roughly 10 times greater than those of females, so adolescent males end up with far more active testosterone than adolescent females.[25] Researchers believe this high amount of testosterone in young men might be at least partly responsible for the differences in antisocial behavior and the different rate of criminal offenses between adolescent males and females, as well as adult men and women.[26]

Although evidence points to a relationship between sex hormones and antisocial behavior and aggression, especially in adolescent males, researchers still have much to learn. A study that examined the relationship between **androgens** and aggression in prepubescent boys who had been diagnosed with severely aggressive and antisocial behavior concluded that adrenal androgen is important to aggression in boys.[27] Another study found similar links in young males who were at risk for antisocial behavior. Significantly higher androgen levels were found in boys but not in girls, with the boys showing the most antisocial behavior having the highest androgen levels.[28]

Those who advocate the inclusion of biological variables in the study of criminal behavior have a difficult task in unraveling the relationship between hormones and criminality.[29] Although there is tempting anecdotal evidence, it remains incomplete, and conclusions can be only provisionally drawn.[30]

Biosocial Theory

Another way to consider the influence of biological conditions on crime is **biosocial theory**, which seeks to explain how environmental conditions interact with the body to produce behavior. Biosocial theory is a relatively new field of study that utilizes a Darwinian theoretical framework to explain why behavior is established and why it continues. For the main theories that reside within biosocial theories, see Table 6-2.

The study of biosocial theory considers the effects of **evolution**, including heredity, on the brain and human behavior. A relationship between delinquency and biosocial theory can be derived from the observation that males, especially adolescent and young adult males, are especially risk-prone, competitive, and violent. Researchers have noted that this male behavior peaks during youth, when there's not only a deluge of testosterone but also when male competition for females (and therefore reproductive success) is at its most intense.[31] Researchers have also observed that male

androgen
A general term for male hormones.

biosocial theory
The study of the effects of Darwinian evolution on brain structure and human behavior.

evolution
A gradual process in which the genetic composition of a population changes over many generations as natural selection acts on the genes of individuals.

Table 6-2   **Three Main Evolutionary Theories of Crime**
These biosocial theories of crime are examples of how evolutionary theory is applied to theories that seek to explain crime.

Cheater theory	The theory relies on the different reproductive strategies of men and women. Men can potentially produce more offspring than women. Women seek to maintain a mate to help raise children. A man can help a sole woman raise his children and have a limited number of children, or he alternatively can trick or force a woman into having his children and then move to the next woman. The alternative strategy is the likelier path of criminal offenders and psychopaths even after adolescence. Cheater theory states that antisocial activity is stimulated by the same traits that stimulate a cheater's sexual strategy.
Control adaptation theory	People pursue various reproductive strategies for environmental reasons. A person will be sexually promiscuous if he or she learned during childhood that interpersonal relationships are ephemeral and unreliable. A person will be more sexually restrictive if he or she has matured with the idea that relationships are permanent. Strategies are not chosen consciously, but subconsciously.
Alternative adaptation theory	Human reproductive effort is represented by a continuum. At one end is promiscuity, or mating effort, and at the other is parenting effort or effort devoted to raising children. Demographically, the best predictors of both reproductive effort and crime or delinquency are sex and age. Males and young people focus on mating; females and older adults focus on parenting. Deceit, impulsivity, and hedonism are useful for focusing on both mating effort and criminal activity. Empathy and altruism are useful for both parenting effort and noncriminal activities. Cultures that emphasize the mating end of the continuum would be considered criminal in modern Western societies. However, these behaviors are adaptive in antisocial cultures and may be adaptive in some modern Western subcultures.

violent behavior decreases as testosterone levels and the drive to reproduce decreases as males advance later into adulthood and old age.[32]

Some researchers have even argued that rape is a way for a male to spread his genes and, at some level, might be biologically encoded.[33] This isn't to say that biosocial theory asserts the existence of "crime genes." From the biosocial standpoint, almost all the effects of genes on behavior are indirect because their messages are processed through the brain. Antisocial behavior is too complex for there to be one gene, or even a group of genes, to act as a direct cause.[34]

There is a great deal of resistance to biosocial theories from criminologists with backgrounds in legal and sociological traditions. Walsh lists five objections to biosocial theories:

1. Biosocial theories are deterministic and socially dangerous.

2. There can't be any genes for crime because crime is socially constructed.

3. If a problem is considered biological, therapeutic nihilism will ensue. That is, society might give up on trying to rehabilitate delinquents and adult offenders.

4. Crime can't have a biological basis because crime rates change rapidly and changes in genes require many generations.

5. Biological theories tend to be insensitive to people's feelings.[35]

The second criticism of biosocial theory, that crime, especially delinquency, is socially defined, is especially interesting. The social definitions can be very narrow: An action that is considered an offense in one state isn't considered an offense just a few miles away across the state line. So how can genes govern a social phenomenon? Biosocial theorists assert that almost every society with a written criminal code criminalizes a basic set of behaviors. These are behaviors that harm other members of society physically (murder, rape) or harm their property (theft, destruction) and that are basically the same from one society to the next.[36] Biosocial theorists also point out that crime itself might be an adaptation that, while harming society, allows the individual to survive and reproduce.[37]

This discussion of the theories that offer physical reasons for antisocial behavior has only touched on the debate. Although some of the explanations, such as Lombroso's atavisms and phrenology, are no longer applicable, other explanations based on studies of the brain and DNA appear to be more promising.

PSYCHOLOGICAL THEORIES OF CRIME

Psychological theories of criminality, although important to the study of crime, are particularly crucial to the study of delinquency. When dealing with adult offenders, a number of assumptions can be made about their level of emotional, cognitive, and moral development. Adults are expected to be able to tell the difference between right and wrong and to curb their temptations and urges to break the law. The principles of deterrence are expected to work better on adults, who are expected to be able to adequately weigh the rewards of lawbreaking against the likelihood of getting caught.

These assumptions can't be safely made about youths. The ability to recognize right and wrong is the result of a long process of socialization that varies with each individual. Further, the bodies and brains of young people are in constant development until they reach early adulthood.[38] Youths are different when it comes to psychological maturity, and the criminal justice system has spun off a separate juvenile justice system to deal with clients who are deemed to require treatment rather than punishment. The remainder of this chapter considers the following concerns of psychological theories of delinquency:

- How do the inner and subconscious experiences of childhood affect behavior?
- At what age do children develop the cognitive ability to comprehend how their behaviors affect others?
- At what age do children develop their moral foundation to determine what is right and wrong?
- Do males and females develop cognitive and moral abilities differently?
- Does intelligence play a part in how children learn and resist delinquency?
- What part does the child's personality play in her or his ability to resist delinquency?

Each of these questions is important and is the focus of significant research. Here only a cursory answer to each question is possible, but we don't mean to minimize the contribution of psychological factors to delinquency. In many respects, these psychological factors are more important to the study of delinquency than they are to the study of adult crime.

In this section, we will look at psychodynamic perspective, cognitive development and delinquency, and moral development, as well as the effects of intelligence, mental retardation, and personality on antisocial behavior.

Psychodynamic Perspective

Have you ever witnessed someone do something really silly and wondered, "Why did they do that?" Or, even more perplexing, have you done something silly and been at a loss to explain your behavior? The first psychological theory to address these questions was Sigmund Freud's psychoanalytic theory, which contends that our behavior is motivated by inner forces, memories, and conflicts of which we have very little awareness or control.[39]

Freud suggested that humans go through a process of psychosexual development as they progress from birth to adulthood (see Table 6-3). Children must successfully pass through a number of stages, or they might develop problems later in life with psychological phobias, relating to others, or severe personality disorders. Freud suggested that everyone passes through these stages—oral, anal, phallic, latency, and

Table 6-3   **Freud's Stages of Psychosexual Development**

Stage	Approximate Age	Focus	Experiences
Oral	Birth to 12–18 months	Mouth	The infant needs to be gratified through sucking, eating, mouthing, or biting.
Anal	12–18 months to 3 years	Anus	Children passing through this stage are concerned with expelling or holding feces and with the process of toilet training.
Phallic	3–6 years	Genitals	At this stage, children are interested in their genitals and come to identify with the same-sex parent. Those who do not successfully negotiate this stage might experience such issues as Oedipal conflicts, in which the son is jealous of his father's sexual access to the mother.
Latency	6–12 years	None	At this stage, sexual concerns are largely unimportant.
Genital	Adolescence to adulthood	Genital	Sexual interests reemerge, and mature sexual relationships are established.

Source: Robert S. Feldman, *Child Development*, 4th ed., © 2007. Electronically reproduced by permission of Pearson Education, Inc., Upper Saddle River, New Jersey.

genital—and that, if an individual has difficulty in any particular stage, behavior problems will manifest themselves either then or at a later stage of life when they can be successfully corrected only by therapy. Although Freud's psychoanalytic theory has its critics, it was the first theory to employ a purely psychological focus. More recent psychological theories have been developed as extensions to psychoanalytic theory or in reaction to it.

For the purposes of the study of delinquency, psychoanalytic theory is no longer a major focus. However, its contributions to the importance of the psychological perspective, as well as much of its vocabulary, have remained consistent features of how human behavior is considered. Further, to understand why various practices in the juvenile justice system have been developed, it's necessary to understand the history of psychology in which Freud is such a dominant figure. We will return to Freud a little later when we discuss personality and delinquent behavior.

Piaget's Cognitive Development

Have you ever watched an infant play with food? For most of us, food has a specific purpose, and our contact with it is limited to preparing it and getting it from the plate to our mouths. For infants, food is more multipurpose. It can be a source of amusement as they see how far it can be flung, what happens when it's applied to the head of the cat, or whether it can stick to the wall. For infants, food is another ingredient to be explored and to learn from.

According to Swiss psychologist Jean Piaget, children learn through two primary processes: assimilation and accommodation. Assimilation is a process by which infants learn according to how they already comprehend the world. When presented with new stimuli, they manipulate it by touching it, chewing it, or banging it to determine its properties and fit it into their existing patterns of thought. Accommodation, on the other hand, occurs when infants encounter new stimuli that don't easily fit into their patterns of thinking, understanding, or behaving. Piaget theorized that infants are limited by their reflexes and that they begin to learn more and more as their motor skills develop and allow them to experiment with stimuli in more sophisticated ways.[40]

Piaget suggested that infants go though six stages of sensorimotor development between birth and age 2. Although there is considerable overlap in the transition from one stage to the next, Piaget argued that each child follows this process at basically the same rate, and the timing of the development is consistent, especially early in their lives. Although later psychological theorists took issue with this tidy timetable of

Swiss educational psychologist Jean Piaget observes a learning exercise. *(Courtesy Wayne Behling with permission of Judith Behling Ford)*

cognitive development, they do credit Piaget with providing a broad outline of sensorimotor development.[41]

What is important to remember is that cognitive development follows the ability of the child to learn from stimuli by achieving greater and greater ability to manipulate, play with, and experience them. Table 6-4 depicts Piaget's conception of how infants acquire these abilities. Following sensorimotor development are three further stages through which Piaget believed individuals must progress along the route to adulthood.

Although Piaget was influential in mapping the processes and stages of cognitive development, his scheme has limitations that become more problematic as children age. Most importantly, subsequent psychologists contend that Piaget greatly underestimated the ages at which children are capable of acquiring cognitive abilities.[42] For our purposes here, it's sufficient to understand that Piaget pioneered the idea that children learn cognitive skills throughout their childhood and that we must appreciate the stages of development when we consider delinquency. Children, especially young children, who have delinquency issues are still undergoing cognitive development and might be having trouble with normal cognitive development, even as they cause problems for their parents, teachers, siblings, peers, and themselves.

Moral Development

When we consider the difference between right and wrong, we assume there's a standard. Right and wrong don't exist in a vacuum, but rather are products of particular cultures that pass values and attitudes from one generation to another. Therefore, when we talk about a "moral compass," we are suggesting that each individual has a culturally learned system of ethics, values, and principles that act as a guide in evaluating behavior."[43]

Where do young people learn these moral values and, more importantly, how are they developed? In dealing with adult crime it's expected that the offender either did know or should have known what types of behavior are socially approved. In dealing with children, this assumption can't be safely made. Children can be ignorant of the correct behavior for a specific situation, confused by competing demands for their loyalty, or even not understand that their actions are their own choices.

Table 6-4   **Piaget's Stages of Cognitive Development**
Intelligence is demonstrated through motor activity without the use of symbols. Knowledge of the world is based on physical interactions and experiences.

Sensorimotor stage (birth to 2 years)

Substage	Age (months)	Description
1. Simple reflexes	0–1	The infant's reflexes are its focus. For example, the infant sucks at anything placed in its lips.
2. Primary circular reactions	1–4	Coordination of separate actions. An infant grasps an object while sucking on it.
3. Secondary circular reactions	4–8	Infants begin to act on the outside world. A child might repeatedly pick up a rattle and shake it in different ways to see how the sound changes.
4. Coordination of secondary circular reactions	8–12	Coordinates several schemes to solve a problem. An infant will push away one toy to reach another toy that is lying partially exposed under it.
5. Tertiary circular reactions	12–18	Conducting experiments to observe the consequences. A child will drop a toy repeatedly, varying the position from which it falls, observing each time to see where it falls.
6. Beginnings of symbolic thought	18–24	Develops symbolic thought. Infants can imagine where hidden objects might be. If a ball rolls under an object, the child can figure out where it might emerge.

Preoperational stage (ages 2–7)

Symbols are used; language use matures, and memory and imagination develop, but thinking is nonlogical and egocentric. From 2 to 4 years, the child can imagine objects that are not present. From 4 to 7 years, the child starts to use reason and ask a variety of questions.

Concrete operational stage (7–11 years)

The child engages in the logical and systematic manipulation of symbols related to concrete objects. Operational thinking develops, and egocentric thought fades. However, the child's ability to apply logic is effective only with concrete objects, not to verbal statements or abstract situations.

Formal operational stage (11 years–adulthood)

The adolescent engages in logical, abstract thinking and can imagine and analyze the possibilities of a situation to determine the best approach. Young adolescents return to egocentric thought early in this stage. Many adults never enter this stage. Even adults capable of higher levels of cognitive thought do not do it all the time. Preoperational thought is present in adult behavior.

Source: Robert S. Feldman, Child Development, 4th ed., © 2007. Electronically reproduced by permission of Pearson Education, Inc., Upper Saddle River, New Jersey.

KOHLBERG'S THEORY OF MORAL DEVELOPMENT   Much like cognitive ability, the capacity to make moral judgments and engage in moral behavior is something that is gradually acquired. Human beings don't develop ethical behavior all at once, but gain it gradually through experience by engaging in different types of behavior, some of it right, some wrong. Children slowly develop the ability to make the correct decisions and, until a certain age, they aren't capable of evaluating situations requiring complex moral reasoning.

Developmental psychologist Lawrence Kohlberg, whose work was based on Piaget's, argued that as humans grow and change, they progress through stages of moral development in which they learn to apply ethical behavior and develop a sense of justice and fairness. At certain ages, human beings are simply incapable of evaluating moral dilemmas because our moral development hasn't caught up with our cognitive development.

Kohlberg contended that until age 13, children aren't cognitively equipped to move beyond conventional morality and thus might have difficulty in making many of the complex decisions that are required to deal with the problems of crime and delinquency. Stage 4 is where most of our law-abiding behavior is resolved because, according to Kohlberg, only about 25 percent of adults are capable of moving on to postconventional morality. An important caveat to Kohlberg's theory of moral development is that just because someone can make moral judgments doesn't mean that he or she will automatically engage in moral behavior.[44] Researchers have found that knowing what is morally correct doesn't always mean that moral actions follow.

Another assertion of Piaget and Kohlberg is that children's peer relationships, that is, their relationships with children their own age, are key to developing pro-social attitudes and relating to others. If children are treated well and treat others well, they learn to see other people as caring and themselves as worth caring for.[45]

DOES GENDER AFFECT MORALITY? Like much research on crime and delinquency, research concerning moral development has been done primarily on males. As more research designs have come to include more females, the conventional wisdom has been modified to explain differing outcomes when the ideas, feelings, beliefs, and behaviors of women and girls are fully considered.

Psychologist Carol Gilligan has studied the moral development of girls and found some additional concerns that Kohlberg failed to consider. Specifically, although boys consider morality primarily in broad principles, such as justice or fairness, girls consider it in terms of compassion and are willing to sacrifice themselves to help specific individuals within the context of particular relationships. According to Gilligan, girls progress through three stages of moral development:

1. **Orientation through individual survival** The concern is what is best for oneself.
2. **Goodness as self-sacrifice** This stage takes into account the needs of others, and the girl might sacrifice her own self-interests to make others happy.
3. **Morality of nonviolence** The most sophisticated form of reasoning according to Gilligan, this establishes a moral equivalence between self and others. Here hurting anyone, including oneself, is considered immoral.[46]

Some researchers contend that the differences between the moral reasoning of boys and girls suggested by Gilligan are too sweeping and that both males and females consider justice and compassion in making ethical judgments.[47] Although this question must be addressed by future research, it's important to credit Gilligan for expanding the range of issues that children consider in their moral reasoning. Further, it's crucial to the study of delinquency to keep an open mind not only about possible differences between the sexes, but also about the fundamental questions concerning the age at which children can make these important decisions. When psychological theories of delinquency are compared to theories of adult crime, age of accountability is a primary concern.

Intelligence and Crime

Are criminal offenders and juvenile delinquents less intelligent than law-abiding people? Are detention facilities, jails, and penitentiaries filled with the stupid and unlucky? At one time, psychologists argued as such. In the early 1900s, American psychologist H. H. Goddard, a proponent of eugenics who is credited with coining the word *moron*, evaluated studies and reported the range of those prison inmates who were "feebleminded" to be from 28 to 89 percent. The median finding was 70 percent, which led Goddard to conclude that most inmates were feebleminded.[48] The following evidence was suggested to support the idea that delinquents and adult offenders were less intelligent than nonoffenders:

- Individuals who lack intelligence can't evaluate or control their behavior. They don't have the mental skills to tell right from wrong and can't rein in their impulses.
- Those with limited intelligence can't compete in the workplace to satisfy their needs through legitimate means. They are compelled to break the law to

achieve financial survival and establish their sense of self-worth. Legitimate opportunities are beyond their abilities, so they turn to crime to compete in a capitalist society that requires individuals to provide for themselves.

- Those with low intelligence aren't able to negotiate the rules and procedures of the justice system as well as those with normal abilities and so are likely to end up incarcerated at a greater rate.

But are these assumptions about the intelligence of offenders correct? To answer this question, it's necessary to consider several issues that make judging the mental abilities of offenders problematic. The history of intelligence testing shows that researchers have had to develop inventive ways to get at the difficult target of objectively comparing the innate intelligence of one person to another.

The intelligence test and the concept of mental age were originated by French psychologist and educator Alfred Binet. He was attempting to identify early in their educational careers those students who weren't succeeding in school and required alternative educational methods. He started with students whom teachers had already identified as "bright" or "dull" and through trial and error devised test items that sorted the students into these categories. The strengths and weaknesses of Binet's efforts are still found in today's intelligence tests.[49]

Binet had no theory as to the nature of intelligence. His approach defined intelligence to be whatever the tests measured. This approach allowed researchers to focus on the differences among individuals. The measure of success on Binet's test was success in school. The tests didn't measure alternative attributes that could be a measure of intelligence but were unrelated to academic proficiency. Finally, Binet linked each test to the child's mental age. Therefore, if a 5-year-old child scored at the average of those who were two years older, the child was assigned a mental age of 7.

Binet's test and formula for determining intelligence were later revised by psychologists William Stern and Lewis Terman, who developed a single score called the **intelligence quotient**. Today, intelligence scores are calculated with more sophisticated techniques, but they are still based on a 100-point average at the center of a bell-shaped curve. Figure 6-2 illustrates this principle. Since Binet's time, intelligence testing has improved considerably.

Intelligence researchers are now relatively good predictors of school performance. However, it's important to note that school performance is but one way to

intelligence quotient (IQ)
A measure of intelligence as indicated by an intelligence test, usually the ratio of mental age to chronological age.

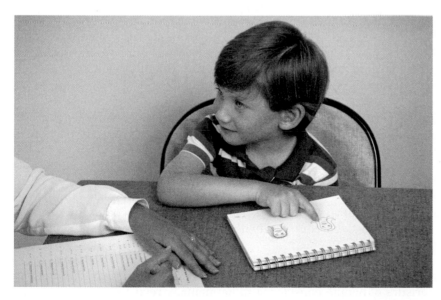

French psychologist and educator Alfred Binet originated the concept of mental age. Here a boy takes the Stanford-Binet intelligence test, which is a popular assessment of intelligence. *(Courtesy Lew Merrim, Photo Researchers, Inc.)*

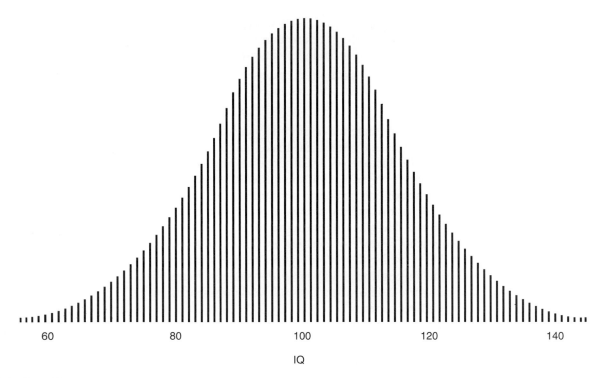

60   80   100   120   140

IQ

Figure 6-2   The Bell Curve Intelligence tests are designed to give normally distributed scores that, when graphed, produce a bell-shaped curve. The intelligence of most people falls within the greater portion of the curve.

assess innate intelligence and that intelligence and school performance aren't the sole indicators of the likelihood of juvenile delinquency or adult criminality. Criminological research has discovered a relationship between low IQ and delinquency.[50] However, although the two factors are related, some researchers say that low IQ doesn't directly cause delinquent behavior, but is a risk factor in that it affects school performance, increases the susceptibility to pressure from antisocial friends, and affects self-control.[51]

Perhaps the most perplexing concern when considering relationships between intelligence and crime is the claim that intelligence tests are culturally biased. According to the critics of IQ tests, to the extent that the tests include items that depend on one's cultural background and experiences, it's problematic when those of differing economic, racial, or social backgrounds are judged according to the tests' assumptions of being from white, upper- or middle-class backgrounds. See Crosscurrents 6.2 for a further look at this controversy.

MENTAL RETARDATION AND CRIME   Another dimension of intelligence and crime requires consideration. Some individuals who don't have the intellectual ability to engage in normal societal activities often become clients of the criminal justice system. One of these conditions is mental retardation. The American Association of Mental Retardation characterizes the condition of mental retardation as "significantly sub-average intellectual functioning, existing concurrently with related limitations in two or more of the following applicable adaptive skill areas: communication, self-care, home living, social skills, community use, self-direction, health and safety, functional academics, leisure and work."[52]

It is difficult to define what is meant by "applicable adaptive skills," and experts vary widely on whom to apply the label of mental retardation to. Consequently, the characteristics of people considered to be mentally retarded range from individuals who can be taught to function and work with very little attention to individuals who are untrainable. Again, the issue of racial and cultural bias is present when we talk

6.2   *CrossCurrents*

Cultural and Racial Differences in Intelligence Testing

One fairly consistent finding of intelligence tests has been that blacks score about 15 points lower than the mean score for whites. There might be a number of reasons for this consistent relationship, and it's a source of debate as to whether it's a product of heredity or environment. Another aspect of the debate concerns the nature of intelligence. Is there only one type of objective intelligence? Or, on the other hand, do intelligence tests simply measure one's immersion in the dominant culture of society and mismeasure the potential of those who are the products of subcultures?

One explanation for these differences in IQ scores is that they are the result of heredity rather than environment. For instance, in their controversial book *The Bell Curve*, authors Richard Herrnstein and Charles Murray not only argue that the lower IQ scores of blacks are due primarily to heredity, but that these intelligence scores are also related to higher rates of poverty, low employment, and use of public assistance.[1] Critics of Herrnstein and Murray are unconvinced by their argument or their interpretation of their data. The performance of middle-class black children on intelligence tests is very similar to that of middle-class white children. Further, critics contend there is little evidence to suggest that intelligence-test scores are related to poverty and other social ills as suggested by *The Bell Curve*.[2]

Does this mean that intelligence-test scores shouldn't be examined for a relationship to crime? The answer is certainly no. The scientific method dictates that we must use objective standards and deal with the data that are produced. Many scientists contend that intelligence tests aren't culturally biased. Anthony Walsh argues that sociologists have been overly reliant on environmental causes to explain crime and have ignored much of the research done by geneticists, psychometricians, and developmental psychologists.[3]

The argument over the possible cultural bias of intelligence tests is political, as well as scientific. If it were generally accepted that minority children didn't possess the same level of innate intelligence as white children, some fear it might be too easy to suggest that individuals of various racial groups should be tracked to specific occupations. This is a sensitive political issue, because the differences within racial groups are as great as the differences between them. Race is a difficult variable to measure, and basing public policy on race is not only difficult; it violates our basic ideals of justice and fairness.[4]

Think About It

1. Do you think IQ tests are culturally biased?
2. Why is intelligence testing such a sensitive subject?

1. Richard J. Herrnstein and Charles Murray, *The Bell Curve: Intelligence and Class Structure in American Life* (New York: Free Press, 1994).
2. R. E. Nisbett, "Race, and Genetics and IQ," in C. Jencks and M. Phillips, eds., *The Black–White Test Score Gap* (Washington, DC: Brookings Institution, 1998).
3. Anthony Walsh, *Biosocial Criminology* (Cincinnati, OH: Anderson 2002). See especially Chapter 2, "Behavior, Genetics, and Criminology," 23–48.
4. Scott Menard and Barbara J. Morse, "A Structural Critique of the IQ-Delinquency Hypothesis: Theory and Evidence," *American Journal of Sociology* 6, no. 89 (1984):1347–1378.

about mental retardation, and minority children are much more likely to be placed in special education classes than are white children.[53]

A related and persistent issue is that of mentally ill, mentally retarded, and learning disabled individuals being funneled into the juvenile justice and criminal justice systems instead of into treatment or education. Between 28 and 43 percent of incarcerated juveniles are estimated to need special education, and researchers have found links between learning disabilities and encounters with the juvenile justice system.[54] The population of students in the criminal justice system who have learning disabilities is estimated to be as high as 50 percent.[55]

Mental health care in the United States, which was a fairly centralized institution in the early to mid-20th century, has become a decentralized system of social agencies that comprise mental health, social services, medical, housing, and law enforcement agencies. This means that one or more agencies might end up with a client who needs the services of another set of agencies. This trend, according to Nancy Wolff, not only makes all agencies appear ineffective and inefficient, but sometimes also deepens the client's problems, including the incidence of disorderly or violent behavior.[56] For more on this issue and its effect on the juvenile justice system, see Kids in the News 6.2.

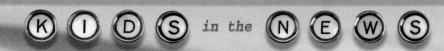

Waiting for Care

Young offenders with emotional and mental disorders are often sent to detention centers instead of to treatment facilities. This isn't unusual; the same often happens to adult offenders, who are sent to jails and prisons instead of hospitals. A common reason for this, aside from jurisdictions showing that they're "tough on crime," is a lack of money and resources.[1] In 2001, the U.S. General Accounting Office discovered that parents surrendered nearly 13,000 children to the government for treatment because they couldn't afford mental health care.[2]

A 2005 investigation into New Jersey's juvenile detention facilities found that foster children, many of whom had mental health issues, had been locked up for long beyond their sentences because they had nowhere else to go. According to a report released the prior year from the state's Office of the Child Advocate, the problem has been ongoing, with juvenile detention centers serving "inappropriately and illegally as placements to confine youth awaiting appropriate placement and treatment."[3]

Ironically, an investigation found that children waiting for social services spent longer in detention than those actually sentenced for an offense. As of 2005 in California, about 250 youths a day were sent to detention while waiting for placement in services. Some youths weren't even suspected of committing an offense, which, a federal study found, was common throughout the United States.[4]

According to government statistics, 16 percent of all adult inmates in U.S. prisons and jails are mentally ill, as are 80 percent of youths entering the juvenile justice system. A 2004 congressional study of three-quarters of all juvenile detention facilities in the United States from January to June 2003 found the following:

- Two-thirds of facilities in 47 states house youths who are waiting for community mental health treatment. In 33 states, mentally ill youths are held in detention without any charges.

- Children as young as 7 were found to have waited for treatment in detention. See Figure A for the youngest ages held by the facilities. Nearly 140 facilities reported housing youths as young as 11 to 12.
- On any given night, nearly 2,000 youths, representing 7 percent of all detained youths, were waiting in detention for placement in mental health programs.
- Two-thirds of the juvenile detention facilities reported that some youths attempted suicide or attacked others.
- Juvenile detention facilities spent about $100 million a year housing youths who were waiting for community mental health services.[5]

Think About It

1. Is placing youths in detention while they await mental health services acceptable? What if it is the only way authorities have to keep them safe?

2. Should a specific set of legal rules be created to handle mentally ill youths?

3. What should be done about the youths who are already in the juvenile justice system who need mental help?

1. Bart Jansen, "States Strand Mentally Ill Children," *Portland Press Herald* (Maine), July 8, 2004, final edition, A1; Nancy Solomon, "Foster Children Languishing in New Jersey Jails as the State Attempts to Reform Its Child Welfare System," National Public Radio Morning Edition, July 21, 2005.
2. Paula M. Ditton, "Mental Health Treatment of Inmates and Probationers" (Washington, DC: U.S. Department of Justice, Office of Justice Programs, Bureau of Justice Statistics, July 1999), 1. Online at www.ojp.usdoj.gov/bjs/pub/pdf/mhtip.pdf.
3. Jonathan Tamari, "Mentally Ill Kids Misplaced in Juvenile Jails, Report Finds," *Asbury Park Press* (New Jersey), November 23, 2004.
4. Wyatt Buchanan, "Mentally Ill Youths Are Jailed," *San Francisco Chronicle*, January 25, 2005, Bay Area final edition, B2.
5. United States House of Representatives Committee on Government Reform, *Incarceration of Youth Who Are Waiting for Community Mental Health Services in the United States* (Washington, DC: Government Printing Office, 2004), i–ii. Online at www.democrats.reform.house.gov/Documents/20040817121901-25170.pdf.

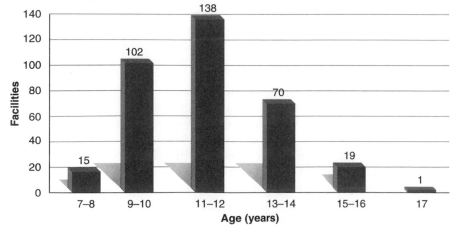

Youngest Age of Youth Waiting for Mental Health Services in Detention

Figure A   *Source:* United States House of Representatives Committee on Government Reform, *Incarceration of Youth Who Are waiting for Community Mental Health Services in the United States* (Washington, DC: Government Printing Office, 2004), i–ii. Online at www.democrats.reform.house.gov/Documents/20040817121901-25170.pdf.

Freud, Personality, and Delinquent Behavior

Individuals have different personalities. A personality is "a set of relatively enduring behavioral characteristics (including thoughts) and internal predispositions that describes how a person reacts to the environment."[57] Personality is one of the major features by which people judge other individuals. However, the concept of personality is slippery because it's difficult to quantify. Psychologists and criminologists have sought to use personality to explain why people break the law and as an insight into how to treat or rehabilitate offenders.

As with so many issues that pertain to psychology, the study of personality begins with Freud. Freud didn't directly write about delinquency or criminal behavior, but he did lay the foundation for conceptualizing the components of personality. According to Freud, the personality comprises three interrelated parts (see Figure 6-3).

- **Id**   The **id** is an unconscious aspect of the personality that is responsible for controlling our two primary instincts: sex and destruction or aggression. The id is present at birth and seeks to maximize pleasure and minimize pain. The id can be thought of as one's natural inclinations that drive behavior prior to socialization. Gradually, as the individual learns the etiquette, norms, rules, and laws of the social group, the id is brought under control, and concern for others is developed. The degree to which the id is controlled varies by individual, and some offenders who are impulsive can be considered as having an underregulated id.

id

In Sigmund Freud's theory of the human psyche, the id represents the most primitive, irrational instincts and is controlled by the pleasure principle.

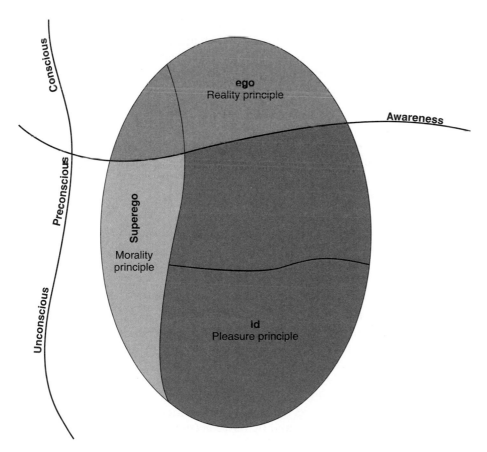

Figure 6-3   Id, Ego, and Superego Freud believed that the id, ego, and superego functioned on all levels of awareness. The conscious represents fully aware thought, the preconscious is awareness (thoughts, memories) that is not too difficult to access, and the unconscious is deeply hidden awareness.

- **Ego**   The **ego** represents the rational part of the personality and responds to the id's drives and instincts in socially acceptable ways. It develops in the first year of life as the individual begins to understand that the needs of others must also be considered. A well-developed ego allows the individual to delay gratification and participate in civil society without always putting his or her immediate concerns ahead of others. The ego operates on the reality principle.

- **Superego**   The **superego** represents the conscience and operates on the morality principle. It can be thought of as that little voice inside your head that helps you decide what is right and what is wrong. The superego is actually an internalization of society's norms and values that must be considered and balanced when considering taking action. The superego produces feelings of guilt when an individual behaves in a way that he or she knows contradicts the values of society and his or her own internalized values.[58]

Freud believed that these three components of the personality work in harmony in a psychologically healthy person. The ego keeps the id in check and also makes sure the superego doesn't make one too rigid or too much of a perfectionist. It is easy to see how Freud's components of the personality can be used to explain a variety of crime. For instance, those who have an underdeveloped superego have never internalized the rules of society, so their ids run amok. Those who have an overdeveloped superego might break the law because they have a deep desire to be caught and punished. They might actually leave clues at the scene of the crime as a way to be detected and to have their feelings of guilt alleviated.

Freud's ideas concerning the personality have become so popularized that it's difficult to distinguish the musings of armchair psychologists from learned and serious psychoanalysts. Psychoanalytic theory is complicated and takes years to fully appreciate, and it has suffered from the temptation of many to simplify it to the point where it's commonly considered as pop psychology. However, many experts have serious reservations about Freud's perspective. There are three issues that those concerned with delinquency ought to keep in mind:

1. Freud's components of the personality are difficult to measure. To evaluate the perspective, we must consider therapists' recordings of treatment sessions and rely on their interpretations of what patients say. This becomes especially difficult when dealing with the subconscious. In addition to whatever bias the therapist might introduce, therapists often disagree on interpretations. For these and other reasons, psychoanalytic theory might be considered as much an art as a science.

2. A second concern that is problematic for the study of delinquency is Freud's contention that personality is fixed in early childhood and never really changes. He considered various attributes of the personality to be products of heredity, which ignores the processes of social learning that can drastically alter how people respond to opportunities and temptations throughout life.

3. Freud's understanding of women is a product of the times and social environment of 19th-century Europe. Given the rigid gender-role expectations of that time, it's understandable that Freud viewed females as passive, inherently jealous, and inferior to men. Today, these views aren't only outdated and misogynistic, but are politically untenable for any application to public policy in a time when gender equality is legally required. Although Freud might be forgiven for being a product of his culture, his ideas about women don't translate to the modern era and have been supplanted by more accurate insight into how personalities are formed.[59]

The intent here has been to place Freud's ideas in a historical context and to emphasize that, despite the major limitations of his perspective, his specific contention that personality is formed in childhood is a major feature of the study of juvenile delinquency. It is useful to compare Freud's ideas to an old song: although the lyrics are dated and no longer sung, we still hum the melody.

Is There a Criminal Personality?

It seems like common sense to assume that personality is related to the propensity to break the law. People, either through the decisions they make or the situations they put themselves in, direct much of their own destiny. Consequently, the aspects of personality that are related to how one interacts with others, handles frustrations, or delays gratification are likely to determine, in large part, the degree to which one will engage in delinquent or criminal behavior. Although there might be agreement that personality should be a clue to an individual's likelihood of engaging in crime, measuring this phenomenon is difficult.

One of the first criminological studies that attempted to understand the link between personality and crime was published in 1950 by Sheldon and Eleanor Glueck. The Gluecks compared 500 delinquent boys against a sample of 500 nondelinquent boys and found that, although each set had the same personality characteristics, the delinquent boys shared an interesting set of interrelated features that not only contributed to their delinquency, but also helped them to survive in more conventional ways. A closer look at the characteristics that were more pronounced in delinquents than in nondelinquents is instructive.[60]

1. **Extroversion** The delinquent boys were found to be more extroverted than those in the control group. This should not be surprising, because the types of crimes boys typically engage in require social interaction. Those who are shy and withdrawn are less likely to engage in fighting, theft, and robbery than those who can confidently interact with others.

2. **Impulsivity** Crime, especially for juveniles, is often a spur-of-the-moment decision. Young boys also tend to be impatient when wanting something. Although everyone can be impatient to some extent, the Gluecks found that delinquent boys were less able to defer gratification and wait for rewards than were the nondelinquent boys. One by-product of impulsivity is that there's less time to plan the offense, so those delinquents who give in to their whims are more likely to be caught by the police and have their offenses recorded.

3. **Hostility** Those who have had contact with the juvenile justice system are bound to be resentful of authority and demonstrate negative attitudes toward society.

4. **Fearlessness** The delinquent boys tended to be less afraid of failure or defeat. Engaging in delinquent behavior takes a bit of nerve. Those who lack confidence and self-reliance are likely to abstain from engaging in risky actions.

5. **Suspicion** Delinquents are suspicious of the juvenile justice system and often of society. Crime and delinquency are viewed as ways of overcoming the inherent inequalities present in society.

6. **Low self-esteem** Some youths who engage in delinquent behavior or crime might consider offending as a way of getting attention or establishing identity. It is understandable that the Gluecks would find that delinquents exhibit feelings of not being recognized or appreciated at a greater rate than nondelinquents.

The size and scope of the Gluecks' study are impressive. They found support for differences in the personality of delinquents and nondelinquents by using three types of prediction tables: one based on social background, one based on character traits as measured by the Rorschach test, and a third based on personality traits as determined in psychiatric interviews. Of particular interest, however, is the Gluecks' observation that not all the differences between the two groups were negative.[61] In many ways, the delinquents were found to be as socially likeable as the nondelinquents and not in some way defective, as was consistently assumed by some biological and intelligence theories.

MINNESOTA MULTIPHASIC PERSONALITY INVENTORY   More recently, psychologists and criminologists have attempted to examine the differences between the personalities of offenders and nonoffenders by studying how they answer questions on personality inventories. The most well known of these instruments is the Minnesota Multiphasic Personality Inventory (MMPI-2), which also has a version for adolescents, the MMPI-A.

The MMPI provides an interesting way of assessing an individual's personality and has been found to be accurate in distinguishing offenders from nonoffenders.[62] This ability is based in large part on the questions that include statements such as "I have never been in trouble with the law." However, these types of statements don't measure personality characteristics but rather the respondents' social circumstances. Therefore, it's unclear whether we can conclude from the MMPI that there are real personality differences between delinquents and nondelinquents.

A study of adolescent male delinquents did find, however, that the MMPI-A could predict some violent juvenile delinquency. Although neither IQ nor MMPI-A scores could predict whether the youths would commit further serious, *nonviolent* offenses, the MMPI-A did predict whether they would go on to commit any *violent* offenses. The delinquents who later committed more nonviolent serious offenses had records filled with nonviolent offenses. According to these results, then, personality is a predictor of violent juvenile delinquency, while past offending is better at predicting whether a delinquent will continue to commit nonviolent offenses.[63]

PSYCHOPATHS AND SOCIOPATHS   Some crimes are so heinous that they seem to have no explanation. Gruesome rapes or murders in which the offender humiliates or tortures the victim and afterward shows absolutely no remorse appear to be so outside the bounds of understandable behavior that we might label these offenders "crazy" or "monster." Psychologists have different labels that attempt to distinguish these types of extreme offenders from others who break the law. The most common of these labels is **psychopath**.[64] However, as Eric Hickey points out in his book on serial murderers, the term *psychopath* is often used interchangeably with **sociopath**.

Hickey builds a typology that he believes unravels many of the definitional difficulties in describing this type of behavior. Hickey considers the relative differences in intelligence and social skills in these personality types.

1. **Sociopath**   The sociopath is antisocial. This individual possesses the demeanor of one familiar with the insides of jails and correctional facilities and also has a history of criminal behavior. In addition, this person has acquired certain attributes that facilitate criminal activity: callousness, anger, indifference, and fantasies of revenge. Average to below-average intelligence is commonly found in sociopaths throughout state prison systems.

2. **Psychopath**   The psychopath usually doesn't have a lengthy history of criminal behavior. That isn't to say that this person is never arrested, but he or she is more careful to avoid arrest. This individual tends to have above-average intelligence and is less obvious to the investigator and therapist because psychopaths are less prone to show their antisocial attitudes. Psychopaths differentiate themselves from sociopaths in that psychopaths tend to display a higher level of skill in their offenses. The psychopath often doesn't physically harm a victim. Remember, the core of psychopathy is power and control over the victim through whatever means necessary to improve his or her status.

psychopath
A person with a personality disorder who behaves without remorse or caring for others. Often used interchangeably with the term sociopath.

sociopath
A person with a personality disorder who behaves without remorse or caring for others and who often has a history of criminal behavior. Often used interchangeably with the term psychopath.

6.2 FOCUS on ETHICS

WHY WAIT UNTIL IT'S TOO LATE?

There has always been something wrong with your son Paul. He failed the fourth, seventh, and ninth grades. He has been arrested for larceny, burglary, robbery, curfew violation, drug use (four times for six different drugs), drug sales (three times, methamphetamine, marijuana, and cocaine), and now for aggravated assault. You are perplexed about what to do with your 17-year-old, and when the prosecutor offers you a special program for violent offenders, you convince Paul that he needs help and should seize this opportunity.

The violent-offender program gives Paul a complete diagnostic workup. It finds him physically fit and in complete control of his emotions. It rules out any type of chemical imbalance, brain disorder, or dietary deficiency. In looking at his social history, it concluded that his parents provided a supportive household; the schools he attended weren't only adequate but expensive private institutions, and his friends were more likely to be drawn into trouble by him than the other way around. Although the program can't find anything to explain his antisocial behavior, it does conclude that things are getting worse rather than better. It finds that Paul is extremely bright but seriously limited in his ability to relate to others.

After extensive psychological tests, the counselors advise you that Paul has a psychopathic personality. Furthermore, the program's director has decided that Paul isn't a good candidate for the violent-offender program, probation, a halfway house, or any of the other options available to the court. Because the woman he assaulted dropped the charges and moved out of state, Paul is due to be released and plans to come live with you because he has nowhere else to go.

You don't want Paul to be released. He has shown no remorse for his actions, and he obeys neither you nor the authorities. Paul has made several statements that are thinly disguised threats on other people and himself. You are afraid that if Paul is released, he will escalate his unlawful acts to the point that he does something really terrible. When you think about school shootings such as the one at Columbine High School in Colorado, you tremble with fear that your son could someday be capable of such an act. You don't want to wait until it is too late to help Paul.

The prosecutor comes to you with a possible solution. Under a new law, it's possible to place Paul in preventive detention for up to three years, even though he isn't presently charged with any offense. It would require you to sign a statement declaring that you fear Paul would do grievous harm if he were released. Paul would spend his time in a prison psychiatric center far from your home, and he wouldn't be allowed to have visitors for at least a year. When this option was discussed with Paul, he was understandably very upset and vowed revenge on you and the rest of the family. Everyone can see that Paul is on the edge, and you're afraid that if nothing is done, he'll do something really harmful.

Think About It

1. Should you allow Paul to be released from jail and come home to live with you and hope that your continued love and support will finally turn him around?

2. Should you allow Paul to be released from jail and tell him that, because of his continued troubles, he's now on his own and not to return until he has learned to obey the law and stay away from drugs?

3. Should you sign the necessary papers to have your son detained against his will to protect yourself, him, and other innocent people?

4. Should you try to get the law changed so that the responsibility doesn't fall on a family member to sign papers allowing for preventive detention? Should the prosecutor or the judge be the one to make this decision?

---

3. **Primary psychopath**   The primary psychopath is also antisocial, but the untrained eye will never see the nature of the true primary psychopath. The victim might even defend his or her predator, believing wholeheartedly in the innocence of this person. Primary psychopaths are social chameleons who can blend into any environment. They range in intelligence from above average to highly intelligent and have developed skill levels far superior to other offenders.[65]

Hickey's typology based on intelligence and social skills is interesting but not exactly useful in identifying these personalities before they offend. Sociopaths are more likely to be incarcerated, and primary psychopaths are almost undetectable except by experts. To have any public policy implications, it's necessary to be able to identify the psychopath before he or she commits the types of gruesome offense that garners the offender this label (for an ethical scenario, see Focus on Ethics 6.2). This is problematic because the various attributes of psychopaths, according to Dr. Robert Hare's 1991 *Psychopathy Checklist Revised*, include the following features:[66]

- Glibness or superficial charm
- Grandiose sense of self-worth, narcissism
- Pathological lying
- Manipulative behavior
- Lack of remorse or guilt
- Shallow affect
- Callousness, lack of empathy
- Failure to accept responsibility for actions
- Need for stimulation, proneness to boredom
- Parasitic lifestyle
- Poor behavioral controls
- Early behavioral problems
- Lack of realistic, long-term goals
- Impulsivity
- Irresponsibility
- Juvenile delinquency
- Revocation of conditional release
- Promiscuous sexual behavior
- Several short-term marital relationships
- Criminal versatility

Most of us might observe some of these features in our own personality. In fact, the majority of these characteristics describe typical teenagers through the normal process of rebellion against parents and authority and formation of their own identities. Applying these features to the psychopath means we must consider not just the term but the level of involvement in the behavior and the duration of the behavior. Perhaps more important, we must recognize that it's a combination of these features, rather than any single one, that constitutes a viable definition of the psychopath.

Once a definition of the psychopath is agreed on, the next concern is finding a way to measure the label and construct ways of identifying those who are likely to commit future offenses. It is easy to use hindsight to label a sociopath or the psychopath who is already in prison or at least who possesses a long criminal record. Finally, there are ethical concerns about what to do with those who exhibit these characteristics.

SUMMARY

1. The positivist school of criminology shifts the focus from the offense to the offender. The term *biological theories of crime* refers to theories that provide a physical explanation for offenders' actions.

2. Body-type theories postulated that there was a relationship between the physical appearance of the body and the temperament of the mind.

3. Lombroso's theory of atavisms stated that those who broke the law were likely to have certain physical features.

4. Sheldon constructed a physical and mental typology based on the physiology of development. Sheldon's body types had three components: endomorphic, mesomorphic, and ectomorphic.

5. Phrenology, popular at the beginning of the 19th century, was promoted primarily by Franz Joseph Gall and was thought to indicate personality by the features of the skull.

6. Certain traits appear to be transmitted from parents to children through genetic makeup rather than social learning.

7. Early attempts to link heredity and genetics to crime relied on the use of family trees. Researchers now study heredity by considering twins and adopted children.

8. Neurotransmitters are chemicals that transmit information between neurons. Four neurotransmitters important to human behavior are dopamine, serotonin, norepinephrine, and epinephrine. Another brain chemical, monoamine oxidase, is an enzyme that metabolizes them.

9. Researchers also consider hormones in the search for relationships between the body and antisocial tendencies. In males, the hormone testosterone has been linked to increases in aggression.

10. Biosocial theory considers the effects of evolution, including heredity, on the brain and human behavior.

11. Walsh lists five typical objections to many biological theories of crime: biosocial theories are deterministic and socially dangerous; crime is socially constructed, so there can't be any genes for crime; the possibility of therapeutic nihilism; crime rates change rapidly, and changes in genes require generations; biological theories tend to be insensitive.

12. The first psychological theory to address questions of criminality was Freud's psychoanalytic theory, which contends that human behavior is motivated by inner forces, memories, and conflicts.

13. Freud suggested that humans go through a process of psychosexual development from birth to adulthood and that humans must successfully complete these stages or develop psychological problems later.

14. Piaget contended that children learn through two primary processes: assimilation and accommodation. Piaget suggested that infants go though six stages of sensorimotor development between birth and age 2, as well as three further stages on the route to adulthood.

15. Kohlberg argued that as humans grow and change, they progress through stages of moral development in which they learn to apply ethical behavior and develop a sense of justice and fairness.

16. According to Gilligan, girls progress through three stages of moral development: orientation through individual survival, goodness as self-sacrifice, and morality of nonviolence.

17. The intelligence test and the concept of mental age were originated by Binet. He had no theory as to the nature of intelligence, linked the measure of success to success in school, and linked tests to the children's mental ages.

18. Critics of intelligence tests say the tests are culturally and racially biased.

19. Some individuals who don't have the intellectual ability to engage in normal societal activities often become clients of the justice system, including mentally ill, mentally retarded, and learning disabled individuals.

20. Freud's contention that personality is formed in childhood is a major feature of the study of juvenile delinquency. According to Freud, the personality comprises the id, ego, and superego.

21. The Gluecks found that delinquent boys shared features that not only contributed to their delinquency, but also helped them to survive. Pronounced characteristics included extroversion, impulsivity, hostility, fearlessness, suspicion, and low self-esteem.

22. Recently, researchers have examined the differences between the personalities of offenders and nonoffenders by studying their performance on personality inventories. The most well known of these is the Minnesota Multiphasic Personality Inventory (MMPI) and MMPI-A for adolescents.

23. Psychologists have labels that attempt to distinguish extreme offenders from others who break the law. Two of these terms, which are used interchangeably, are *psychopath* and *sociopath*.

REVIEW QUESTIONS

1. What does the terminology *biological theories of crime* refer to?

2. How do Lombroso's atavisms and Sheldon's body-type theories qualify as biological theories?

3. What are genes? What is DNA?

4. What are neurotransmitters? Why are they important? What is the role of monoamine oxidase?

5. What is the role of hormones in adolescence?

6. How does evolutionary psychology seek to explain why behavior is established and why it continues?

7. From a biosocial standpoint, how do genes affect behavior?

8. What are Freud's contributions to psychodynamic perspective and the concept of personality?

9. Why did psychologist Alfred Binet create the intelligence test? What are some concerns when considering the relationship between intelligence and crime?

10. What is a psychopath? Why is the terminology controversial?

ADDITIONAL READINGS

Cullen, Frank T., and Robert Agnew, eds. *Criminological Theory: Past to Present: Essential Readings.* Los Angeles: Roxbury, 2003.

Ellis, Lee, and Anthony Walsh. "Gene Based Evolutionary Theories in Criminology." *Criminology* 35:229–275.

Gould, Stephen Jay. *The Mismeasure of Man.* New York: Norton, 1981.

Lanier, Mark H., and Stuart Henry. *Essential Criminology.* Boulder, CO: Westwood Press.

Piaget, Jean. *The Moral Judgment of the Child.* New York: Free Press, 1965.

Rafter, Nicole Hahn. *Creating Born Criminals.* Urbana: University of Illinois Press, 1997.

ENDNOTES

1. Daniel J. Curran and Claire M. Renzetti, *Theories of Crime,* 2nd ed. (Boston: Allyn and Bacon, 2001), 9–11. See especially their discussion on neoclassical criminology for an excellent explanation of the need to expand the view of criminology so that the criminal justice system can develop policies to address crime.

2. Gina Lombroso-Ferres, "Criminal Men," in Joseph E. Jacoby, ed. *Classics in Criminology,* 2nd ed. (Prospect Heights, IL: Waveland Press, 1994), 116–131.

3. George B. Vold, Thomas J. Bernard, and Jeffrey B. Snipes, *Theoretical Criminology,* 5th ed. (New York: Oxford University Press), 32–35.

4. Stephen Jay Gould, *The Mismeasure of Man* (New York: Norton, 1981), 121–143.

5. William H. Sheldon, *Varieties of Delinquent Youth* (New York: Harper, 1949), 14–30.

6. Sheldon Glueck and Eleanor Glueck, *Physique and Delinquency* (New York: Harper, 1956).

7. John van Wyhe, *The History of Phrenology on the Web,* http://pages.britishlibrary.net/phrenology/.

8. *The Phrenology Page,* http://134.184.33.110/phreno/.

9. Richard L. Dugdale, *The Jukes: A Study in Crime and Pauperism, Disease, and Heredity* (New York: Putnam, 1877).

10. Arthur H. Estabrook, *The Jukes in 1915* (Washington, DC: Carnegie Institute of Washington, 1916).

11. David C. Rowe and David P. Farrington, "The Familial Transmission of Criminal Convictions," *Criminology* 35, no. 1 (1997):177–201.

12. Diana Fishbein, *Biobehavioral Perspectives in Criminology* (Belmont, CA: Wadsworth, 2001), 27.

13. Vold et al. (see note 3), p. 40.

14. Ibid., 41–42.

15. Glen D. Walters, "A Meta-Analysis of the Gene–Crime Relationship," *Criminology* 30, no. 4 (1992):595–613.

16. Vold et al. (see note 3), p. 42.

17. Fishbein (see note 12), p. 33.

18. Ibid. Fishbein provides an excellent discussion of how biological factors might be related to crime. This chapter draws heavily on her writings. See Chapter 4.

19. Fishbein (see note 12), p. 40.

20. Lee Ellis, "Monoamine Oxidase and Criminality: Identifying an Apparent Biological Marker for Antisocial Behavior," *Journal of Research in Crime and Delinquency* 28 (1992):227–251.

21. Avshalom Caspi et al., "Role of Genotype in the Cycle of Violence in Maltreated Children," *Science* 297 (August 2, 2002):851–854.

22. J. Martin Ramirez, "Hormones and Aggression in Childhood and Adolescence," *Aggression & Violent Behavior* 8, no. 6 (November 2003):621–645; Alexander McKay, "Testosterone, Sexual Offense Recidivism and Treatment Effect among Adult Male Sexual Offenders," *Canadian Journal of Human Sexuality* 14, no. 1–2 (2005):43–44; Jean King, Washington De Oliveira, and Nihal Patel, "Deficits in Testosterone Facilitate Enhanced Fear Response," *Psychoneuroendocrinology* 30, no. 4 (May 2005):333–340; L.H. Studer, A.S. Aylwin, and J.R. Reddon, "Testosterone, Sexual Offense Recidivism, and Treatment Effect among Adult Male Sexual Offenders," *Sexual Abuse: A Journal of Research and Treatment* 17, no.2 (2005):171–181.

23. C. M. Buchanan, J. S. Eccles, and J. B. Becker, "Are Adolescents the Victims of Raging Hormones: Evidence for Activational Effects of Hormones on Moods and Behavior at Adolescence," *Psychological Bulletin* 111, no. 1 (January 1992):62–107; Benjamin L. Hankin and Lyn Y. Abramson, "Development of Gender Differences in Depression: An Elaborated Cognitive Vulnerability–Transactional Stress Theory," *Psychological Bulletin* 127, no. 6 (November 2001):773–796; Eric Stice, Katherine Presnell, and Sarah Kate Bearman, "Relation of Early Menarche to Depression, Eating Disorders, Substance Abuse, and Comorbid Psychopathology among Adolescent Girls," *Developmental Psychology* 37, no. 5 (September 2001):608–619.

24. J. R. Udry, "Biosocial Models of Adolescent Problem Behaviors," *Social Biology* 37, no. 1 & 2 (1990):1–10; Marvin Zuckerman, "The Psychophysiology of Sensation-Seeking," *Journal of Personality* 58, no. 1 (March 1990):314–345.

25. Buchanan, Eccles, and Becker (see note 23); Udry (see note 24).

26. Anthony Walsh, *Biosocial Criminology* (Cincinnati, OH: Anderson, 2002), 140.

27. Stephanie VanGoozen et al., "Adrenal Androgens and Aggression in Conduct Disorder Prepubertal Boys and Normal Controls," *Biological Psychiatry* 43, no. 2 (January 15, 1998):156–158.

28. Athanasios Maras et al. "Association of Testosterone and Dihydrotestosterone with Externalizing Behavior in Adolescent Boys and Girls," *Psychoneuroendocrinology*, 28, no. 7 (October 2003): 932–940.

29. Alan Booth and D. Wayne Osgood, "The Influence of Testosterone on Deviance in Adulthood: Assessing and Explaining the Relationship," *Criminology* 31, no. 1 (1993):93–117.

30. Fishbein (see note 12), p. 44.

31. Vernon L. Quinsey, "Evolutionary Theory and Criminal Behaviour," *Legal & Criminological Psychology* 7, no. 1 (February 2002):3.

32. Ibid.; Margo Wilson and Martin Daly, "Competitiveness, Risk Taking, and Violence: The Young Male Syndrome," *Ethology and Sociobiology* 6 (1985):59–73; Martin Daly and Margo Wilson, *Homicide* (New York: Aldine, 1988).

33. Lee Ellis, *Theories of Rape: Inquiries into the Cause of Sexual Aggression* (New York: Hemisphere, 1989).

34. Lee Ellis and Anthony Walsh, "Gene-Based Evolutionary Theories in Criminology," *Criminology* 35, no. 2 (May 1997):229; Lee Ellis, "The Nature of the Biosocial Perspective," Lee Ellis and Harry Hoffman, eds. in *Introduction to Crime in Biological, Social, and Moral Contexts*, (New York: Praeger, 1990).

35. Walsh (see note 26), pp. 16–22.

36. Ellis and Walsh (see note 34), p. 230; Lee Ellis, "Conceptualizing Criminal and Related Behavior from a Biosocial Perspective," in Lee Ellis and Harry Hoffman, eds. *Crime in Biological, Social, and Moral Contexts*

(New York: Praeger, 1990), 19; Hans J. Eysenck and Gisli H. Gudjonsson, *The Causes and Cures of Criminality* (New York: Plenum, 1989), 1.

37. Ellis and Walsh (see note 34), p. 255.

38. Robert S. Feldman, *Child Development* (Upper Saddle River, NJ: Prentice Hall, 2004).

39. Sigmund Freud, *A General Introduction to Psychoanalysis* (New York: Boni and Liveright, 1920).

40. Jean Piaget, *The Origins of Intelligence in Children* (New York: International Universities Press, 1952).

41. Robert S. Siegler, "How Does Change Occur? A Microgenetic Study of Number Conversion," *Cognitive Psychology* 28 (1995):225–273.

42. R. Baillargeon, "Object Permanence in 3 1/2- and 4 1/2-Month-Old Infants," *Developmental Psychology* 23 (1987):655–670.

43. William Damon, *The Moral Child: Nurturing Children's Natural Moral Growth* (New York: Free Press, 1988).

44. Lawrence Kohlberg, *The Philosophy of Moral Development: Moral Stages and the Idea of Justice* (San Francisco: Harper and Row, 1981).

45. Ervin Staub, "The Roots of Goodness: The Fulfillment of Basic Human Needs and the Development of Caring, Helping and Nonaggression, Inclusive Caring, Moral Courage, Active Bystandership, and Altruism Born of Suffering," *Nebraska Symposium on Motivation* 51 (2005):33–72; Emma J. Palmer, "The Relationship Between Moral Reasoning and Aggression, and the Implications for Practice," *Psychology, Crime & Law* 11, no. 4 (December 2005):356.

46. Carol Gilligan, *In a Different Voice: Psychological Theory and Women's Development* (Cambridge, MA: Harvard University Press, 1982).

47. C. Perry and W. G. McIntire, "Modes of Moral Judgment among Early Adolescents," *Adolescence* 30 (1995):707–715.

48. H. H. Goddard, *Feeblemindedness: Its Causes and Consequences* (New York: Macmillan, 1914).

49. Feldman (see note 38), pp. 365–367.

50. Donald Lynam, Terrie Moffitt, and Magda Stouthamer-Loeber, "Explaining the Relation Between IQ and Delinquency: Class, Race, Test Motivation, School Failure, or Self-Control?" *Journal of Abnormal Psychology* 102, no. 2 (May 1993):187; Paul D. Lipsitt, Stephen L. Buka, and Lewis P. Lipsitt, "Early Intelligence Scores and Subsequent Delinquency: A Prospective Study," *American Journal of Family Therapy* 18, no. 2 (Summer 1990):197.

51. Jean Marie McGloin, Travis C. Pratt, and Jeff Maahs, "Rethinking the IQ-Delinquency Relationship: A Longitudinal Analysis of Multiple Theoretical Models," *Justice Quarterly* 21, no. 3 (September 2004):624; Lisa M. McCartan and Elaine Gunnison, "The IQ/Crime Relationship: An Extension and Replication of Previous Research," *Journal of Crime & Justice* 27, no. 1 (2004):61.

52. American Association on Mental Retardation, *Mental Retardation: Definition, Classification, and Systems of Support* (Washington, DC: AAMR, 1992).

53. D. J. Reschly, "Identification and Assessment of Students with Disabilities," *Future of Children* 6 (1996):40–53.

54. C. M. Fink, "Special Education in Service for Correctional Education," *Journal of Correctional Education* 41, no. 4 (1991):186–190; D. I. Morgan, "Prevalence and Types of Handicapping Conditions Found in Juvenile Correctional Institutions: A National Survey," *Journal of Special Education* 13 (1979):293–295; R. B. Rutherford, Jr., et al., "Special Education in the Most Restrictive Environment: Correctional/Special Education," *Journal of Special Education* 19 (1985):59–71; B. F. Perlmutter, "Delinquency and Learning Disabilities: Evidence for Compensatory Behavior and Adaptation," *Journal of Youth and Adolescence* 16, no. 2 (1987):89–95.

55. R. Bell, "Tried-and-True Educational Methods Aren't True to the Special Needs of Prison Inmates," *Chicago Tribune*, November 28, 1990, p. 23; Clyde A. Winters, "Learning Disabilities, Crime, Delinquency, and Special Education Placement," *Adolescence* 32, no. 126 (1997):451–463.

56. Nancy Wolff, "Interactions Between Mental Health and Law Enforcement Systems, Problems and Prospects for Cooperation," *Journal of Health Politics, Policy & Law* 23, no. 1 (February 1998):133.

57. Vold et al. (see note 3).

58. Feldman (see note 38), pp. 23–24.

59. Curran and Renzetti (see note 1), pp. 78–79.

60. Sheldon Glueck and Eleanor Glueck, *Unraveling Juvenile Delinquency* (New York: Commonwealth Fund, 1950).

61. Ibid.

62. Gordon P. Waldo and Simon Dinitz, "Personality Attributes of the Criminal: An Analysis of Research Studies," *Journal of Research in Crime and Delinquency* 4, no. 2 (1967):185–202.

63. Jennifer S. Parker et al., "Predictors of Serious and Violent Offending by Adjudicated Male Adolescents,"

North American Journal of Psychology 7, no. 3 (2005):407–418.

64. Steven H. Egger, *The Killers among Us: An Examination of Serial Murder and Its Investigation* (Upper Saddle River, NJ: Prentice Hall, 1998), 25–29.

65. Eric W. Hickey, *Serial Murderers and Their Victims*, 4th ed. (Belmont, CA: Wadsworth, 2006), 81–82.

66. Robert D. Hare, *The Hare Psychopathy Checklist*, revised (Toronto: Multi-Health Systems, 1991).

What distinguishes sociological theories from biological or psychological theories?

How have sociological theories of delinquency changed over time?

Why has the sociological perspective become such a popular way to explain delinquency?

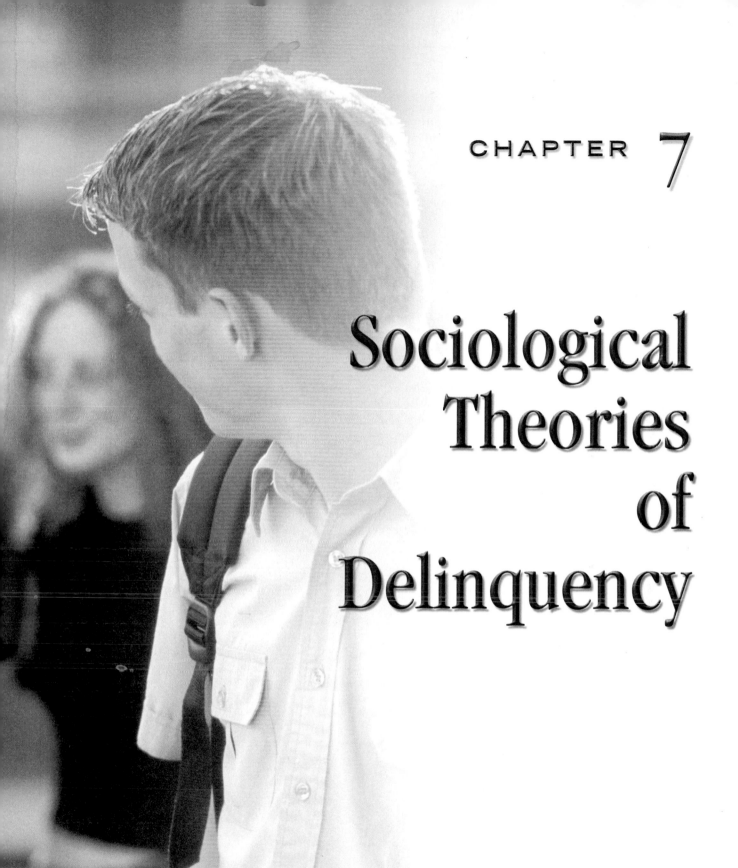

CHAPTER 7

Sociological Theories of Delinquency

In the previous two chapters, we examined how theorists have looked to the individual to explain how and why crime occurs. By considering spiritual, biological, psychological, and other individual explanations, we have seen how people might be compelled or might choose to break the law. These have been some of the most popular theories of crime, and contemporary theorists continue to explore them. Now, however, we will turn to a different level of explanation for crime and delinquency. Instead of considering the individual as the genesis of deviant behavior, we will study factors outside the offender. Sociological theories contend that the interaction of the individual with the social environment can yield powerful explanations of crime that can be observed.

This chapter covers four types of sociological theories: social structure, social process, subcultural, and social reaction. These theories encompass numerous, more detailed descriptions of crime and delinquency that guide the development of social policies designed to prevent deviant behavior.

SOCIAL STRUCTURE THEORIES

At the turn of the 20th century, North America was undergoing a tremendous social change as a result of the Industrial Revolution. The agrarian population was transforming into a more urban population, and the social norms, values, and laws that had served a rural setting didn't translate well into guiding a diverse and crowded urban one.[1]

Sociologists at the University of Chicago were the first to recognize this change in the United States. Building on Ferdinand Tönnies's comparisons in Germany of the close-knit rural communities (*Gemeinschaft*) to the impersonal mass society of urban communities (*Gesellschaft*) (see Table 7-1), the Chicago sociologists sought to understand the human condition, especially crime and deviant behavior, in the light of the social disorganization they saw in the city.[2]

The Industrial Revolution brought thousands of people, many of them children, to work in factories. Here a girl works at a mechanical spinning machine in an early 20th-century mill. *(Courtesy Lewis W. Hine, Library of Congress)*

Table 7-1   *Gesellschaft* and *Gemeinschaft* Compared

Gesellschaft	*Gemeinschaft*
Urban	Rural
Social differences are more striking than similarities.	Similar backgrounds and experiences foster a feeling of community.
Social interactions tend to be impersonal and task-specific.	Social interactions tend to be familiar and friendly.
Self-interest	Cooperation
Tasks are more important than relationships.	Tasks and personal relationships are mingled and inseparable.
Emphasis on privacy	Little emphasis on privacy
Formal social control	Informal social control
Tolerance of deviance	Intolerance of deviance
Emphasis on achieved statuses	Emphasis on ascribed statuses
Social change is evident.	Social change is limited.

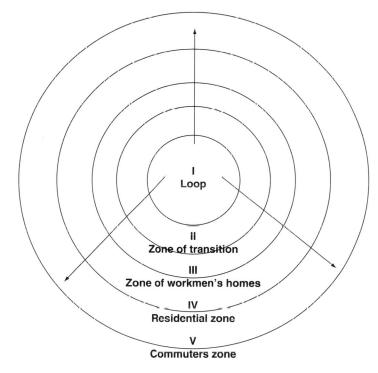

Figure 7-1   **Ernest Burgess's Theory of Urban Growth**

Social Disorganization

At the heart of the Chicago sociologists' analysis is Ernest Burgess's theory of how cities grow (see Figure 7-1). Burgess theorized that cities develop in concentric circles, growing toward outer areas. Each concentric circle represents a zone of development that shares characteristics, and these zones are in constant transition as the city grows. As the urban area expands toward rural areas, each zone develops certain characteristics, such as an area of working-class homes, affluent homes, commuter neighborhoods, and industrial zones.[3]

Clifford Shaw and Henry McKay theorized that if Burgess was right in his explanation of the fluid and changing nature of the growing city, they could use this model to address juvenile delinquency.[4] Shaw and McKay believed that the core values of society would be sorely tested and strained by persistent poverty, rapid population

As urban areas expand toward rural areas, each zone, including suburbs, develops certain characteristics. Here rows of suburban homes extend for miles in northwest San Fernando Valley, California. *(Courtesy Cathleen Campbell, Getty Images, Inc–Liaison)*

growth, population heterogeneity, and population movement. They hypothesized that delinquency rates would be higher in zones that were unstable and lower in zones that were stable. Shaw and McKay's thinking is illustrated by the following quote:

> The development of divergent systems of values requires a type of situation in which traditional conventional social control is either weak or nonexistent. It's a well-known fact that the growth of cities and the increase in devices for transportation and communication have so accelerated the rate of change in our society that the traditional means of social control, effective in primitive society and in isolated rural communities, have been weakened everywhere and rendered especially ineffective in large cities. Moreover, the city, with its anonymity, its emphasis on economic rather than personal values, and its freedom and tolerance, furnishes a favorable situation of the development of devices to improve one's status, outside of the conventionally accepted and approved method.[5]

URBAN INEQUALITY   This social disorganization argument put forth by Shaw and McKay has led others to consider how the social structural issues of the inner city might contribute to the creation of crime and delinquency statistics. For instance, Robert Sampson and William Julius Wilson extended Shaw and McKay's thesis by introducing race into the equation. Sampson and Wilson rejected the claim that the culture developed by the inner city is an easy way to explain crime and that there is little that society can do about it.

Rather, they contended that social disorganization creates different ways of seeing the dynamics of society and different norms based on social position that alter how people view their communities. For instance, in areas where drug use, poverty, and substandard housing are a normal part of everyday life, there is greater tolerance for crime and delinquency as a mechanism for individuals to survive, gain status, and pursue the American dream, albeit in a deviant way.[6]

By looking at the world in this way, residents of these areas separate themselves from the viewpoint of the greater community. This leads to a social isolation that further impedes the ability of these residents to resist the temptations of crime and

High collective efficacy can help make a neighborhood a nice place to live. *(Courtesy Ken Karp, Pearson Education Corporate Digital Archive)*

delinquency. From a policy perspective, the work of Sampson and Wilson argues for reintegrating inner-city residents into the greater society. This would first mean addressing the structural problem of poverty by developing community, governmental, and corporate programs aimed at providing adequate jobs, housing, and schools.[7]

What is it about communities that encourages or discourages its citizens to break the law? It can't simply be poverty, because many economically disadvantaged areas don't have high crime rates. Robert Sampson, Stephen Raudenbush, and Felton Earls studied the social dynamics of the city and envisioned a concept called **collective efficacy,** which they believe is related to community crime rates.[8]

Collective efficacy is a group's shared belief of the extent to which it can successfully complete a task. Collective efficacy occurs at the intersection of two contextual features of a neighborhood. The first of these features is informal social control. This refers to citizens who intervene by stopping others' antisocial behaviors and maintaining public order in the community.[9] For instance, keeping a group of youths on a street corner from harassing others requires only the intervention of a shopkeeper or one of the youths' parents. When others in the community speak up or act, potential delinquency can be averted.

This informal social control varies across communities and is related to the other feature of collective efficacy, **social cohesion,** and/or trust. People are more likely to intervene in situations and attempts to maintain informal social control when they trust their neighbors and can expect them to be supportive and cooperative. Neighborhoods are more than a collection of buildings with people living in them. The relationships among people are an intangible factor in each neighborhood, and those with good relationships are better able to maintain social control. Collective efficacy occurs in neighborhoods where individuals are willing to speak up and act when laws are being violated or the community threatened. This informal social control is highly correlated with social cohesion, and the resulting collective efficacy is what makes meaningful communities possible.[10] This type of social organization is difficult to measure, but for those who live in a location where the *Gemeinschaft* is high, the connectedness between citizens is evident.

collective efficacy
A group's shared belief of the extent to which the group can successfully complete a task.

social cohesion
A condition in which the majority of a given society's citizens respect the law and are committed to social order.

SOCIAL PROCESS THEORIES

Social process theories are concerned not with how society is put together, but rather with how it works. Social processes are the ways that individuals and groups develop rules of behavior and social norms. Additionally, these social processes enable individuals to comprehend the types of behavior that are expected of them.

Learning Theories

Several theories assert that crime is a learned behavior. There are many sources of this learning, which can be quite different depending on the circumstances and the environment the individual confronts. It is common to talk about penitentiaries as "universities of crime," because so many inmates fail to learn the lessons that society envisions that the penitentiary should teach. However, parents will often tell their children not to hang around a certain group of other children because the parents fear a negative influence will be conveyed.[11] Television and the media have also been faulted as providing negative examples for young people to emulate, and this tension has resulted in a classification system for movies, television programs, video games, and music.[12]

DIFFERENTIAL ASSOCIATION   The best known of the learning theories of delinquency, and one of the theories that has had a great deal of influence on crime research, is Edwin Sutherland's **differential association theory.**[13] Sutherland's theory is stated in the form of nine propositions (see Figure 7-2) in which he argues that crime is learned from others, especially close family members and delinquent peers.

Sutherland contended that young people learn two things from their associations with deviant others. First, they learn the attitude that breaking the law is desirable or what Sutherland called "definitions favorable to the violation of the law." Second, Sutherland contended that youths learn techniques of breaking the law from their interaction with others. Focus on Ethics 7.1 has an example of peers who are thought to influence delinquency.

Not all youths turn to delinquency because they have delinquent friends. Clearly, most youths are also influenced to obey the law by law-abiding friends and family members. Sutherland argues that the difference between lawbreaking and law-abiding behavior is affected by four factors that influence the balance between how often youths are exposed to messages that say crime is good versus messages that say crime is bad. These factors—priority, frequency, duration, and intensity—are related to what is learned in interaction with significant friends and family members. For example, if a young person spends all his or her time with a juvenile gang that engages in violence, drug use, and vandalism, this youth will be more likely to learn definitions favorable to the violation of the law than if he or she spent the majority of the time engaged in church activities. The gang experience can be very intense, allowing little freedom for the youth to form other loyalties. If the youth joins a gang early in

differential association theory
A theory by Edwin Sutherland that states that crime is learned.

---

1. Criminal behavior is learned.
2. Criminal behavior is learned in interaction with other persons in a process of communication.
3. The principal part of the learning of criminal behavior occurs within intimate personal groups.
4. When criminal behavior is learned, the learning includes (a) techniques of committing the crime, which are sometimes very complicated, sometimes very simple, and (b) the specific direction of motives, drives, rationalizations, and attitudes.
5. The specific direction of motives and drives is learned from definitions of the legal codes as favorable or unfavorable.
6. A person becomes delinquent because of an excess of definitions favorable to violation of law over definitions unfavorable to violation of law.
7. Differential associations may vary in frequency, duration, priority, and intensity.
8. The process of learning criminal behavior by association with criminal and anticriminal patterns involves all the mechanisms that are involved in any other learning.
9. While criminal behavior is an expression of general needs and values, it is not explained by those general needs and values, since noncriminal behavior is an expression of the same needs and values.

Figure 7-2   **Sutherland's Nine Propositions** *Source:* Edwin Sutherland, *Principles of Criminology*, 4th ed. (Chicago: J. B. Lippincott, 1947), 6–7.

FOCUS on ETHICS

BAD BOYS, BAD BOYS

You have always been proud of your 16-year-old son. Throughout his life, he's given you nothing but pleasure and has been a great source of pride. He has excelled at school and in sports. Now, however, you are experiencing some concern. He has recently gotten his driver's license and has been using the family car to escape your supervision. He is gone every afternoon after school and doesn't come home until late at night. On the weekends, it's even worse. Although you can't be sure of what he's doing, you've noticed that his choice of friends has changed. Instead of hanging out with his old friends and teammates, he now seems to be running with an older crowd whom you don't know and who are rather tough looking and lack basic social etiquette and manners. These boys exhibit several signs that seem like red flags to you, including numerous tattoos, baggy pants, and multicolored hair. One of the boys has so many body piercings that he looks like he fell face-first into a tackle box.

You consider yourself a person who doesn't judge people by the way they look, but your son's behavior is changing, and you think it's because of the influence of these boys. On the negative side, he hardly talks to you anymore. When he's home, he stays in his room and listens to music that you find painful to hear. He plays online poker and video games rather than spending time with you and your spouse and his siblings. He seems not to care how he dresses, and his room has become so messy that you don't even go there anymore. His sense of humor has become

cynical, and he no longer attends religious services with the family. On the positive side, his grades haven't slipped; he hasn't been arrested; you've detected no sign of smoking, drinking, or drug use; and he says he wants to get a job at a mall store that sells funky clothes.

You aren't sure if you should do anything about this situation. On one hand, you realize that children go through phases and that this might simply be part of growing up. On the other hand, you wonder if you're witnessing the early warning signs of a boy going bad.

What Should You Do?

1. Leave him alone. He isn't hurting anyone, and he needs room to find his identity and place in the world. He has to grow up sometime, and you should give him the space he needs.

2. Set a curfew for the car. He can do as he pleases, but the car is yours, and you can demand it be home at a reasonable hour.

3. Insist that he change his set of friends. You don't like the way they look, and you're afraid they will lead him down the path of delinquency.

4. Search his room for drugs or stolen property. Just because he's always been a good kid doesn't mean that he isn't experimenting with bad behaviors. You don't want to be the last one to know that he's making a mess of his life.

Sutherland contended that youths learn how to break the law from others, including their friends.
Peer pressure is often a factor in the behavior of children who become involved in delinquency.

(Courtesy Jim Varney, Photo Researchers, Inc.)

life (priority) and stays in the gang for many years (duration), the chances of becoming a juvenile delinquent increase drastically.

One main concept of Sutherland's differential association theory that is important to remember is that antisocial behavior is learned in the same way that law-abiding behavior is learned. One point that Sutherland failed to clarify concerns the exact meaning of "definitions favorable to the violation of the law."[14] Did he mean that young people actually have values that say crime is permissible, or did he mean that they hold values that are conducive to crime such as fighting, thrill seeking, and toughness? It might be that values favoring crime are applicable only to certain situations. These situations might require young people to find excuses to justify their behavior. One theory that looks at these excuses or justifications is called **techniques of neutralization,** which we will discuss later in this chapter.

SOCIAL LEARNING THEORY   **Social learning theory** is an extension, refinement, and improvement on Sutherland's theory of differential association. According to social learning theory, people learn behaviors by watching other people and mimicking interactions that are rewarded and avoiding those that are punished. Sutherland's eighth proposition states that antisocial behavior is learned like any other attitude or skill, but it doesn't specify exactly how crime is learned.[15] Rather, it's social learning theory that goes on to explain how crime is learned.

Criminologist Ron Akers has spent the better part of his career developing social learning theory well beyond the ideas of differential association. Akers first worked with Burgess to construct a theory that blended the ideas of differential association with the psychological principles underlying **operant conditioning** and **behaviorism.**[16] They were able to combine many aspects of differential association with psychological concepts, such as schedules of reinforcement and behaviors that are voluntary on the part of the respondent, as well as those that are conditioned by involuntary reflex behavior and the principle of rewards and punishment. This advancement on differential association enabled Akers and Burgess to specify how behavior is learned and to develop their theory so that it could be put in the form of testable propositions.

Although Akers and Burgess began with differential association, by the time they applied several aspects of psychological theories to social learning, they ended up with a theory that was "closer to cognitive learning . . . than to the radical or orthodox operant behaviorism of B. F. Skinner." As Akers has moved beyond his earlier work with Burgess, he has developed his social learning theory of crime across four dimensions (see Figure 7-3).

- **Differential association**   Like Sutherland, Akers contends that individuals learn techniques and attitudes toward breaking the law from others. It's important, however, to specify who these others might be. Clearly, family members, especially parents, are an early influence (priority) on the values the youth develops, and peers can exert tremendous pressure (intensity) to conform or not conform to the law. Additionally, numerous other individuals influence young people, including neighbors, churches, teachers, or people in the community, as well as the media. Because of the range of media available to young people today, values and attitudes might be picked up from the Internet, movies, television, and video games, as well as from people on the Internet whom they have never personally met. According to Akers, there is now a greatly expanded range of peer groups from which young people can derive attitudes about the law.

- **Definitions**   Definitions are the value judgments that juvenile delinquents apply to their lawbreaking behavior. Akers's concept of definitions is similar to Sykes and Matza's techniques of neutralization. By excusing unlawful behavior through these accounts, disclaimers, rationalizations, and moral disengagement,

---

techniques of neutralization
A theory that describes how some youths who break the law use rationalizations to explain away their deviant behavior.

social learning theory
The idea that people learn behaviors by watching other people and mimicking interactions that are rewarded and avoiding those that are punished.

operant conditioning
A form of conditioning based on learning from the positive or negative consequences of an action.

behaviorism
A field of psychology that focuses on the study of behavior that is observed.

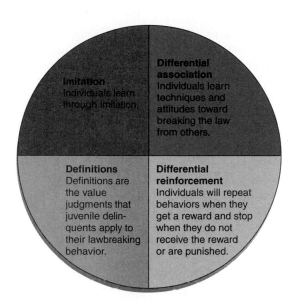

Figure 7-3 The Four Dimensions of Ron Akers's Social Learning Theory

Media, especially television and video games, can exert an especially powerful influence on children. *(Courtesy Pascal Crapet, Getty Images Inc.—Stone Allstock)*

young people are able to maintain positive feelings about their behavior and character. In fact, some of the positive or neutralizing definitions allow the individual to reframe extremely harmful and disreputable behavior. Much like the heroic outlaw of the Old West, Robin Hood, or contemporary international terrorists, juvenile delinquents can cleanse their consciences by defining their harmful behavior as harmless, righteous, deserved, or not their fault.

differential reinforcement
The rewarding of one behavior and not another or the rewarding of one behavior and punishment of another.

negative reinforcement
Avoidance of painful or stressful conditions or events.

- **Differential reinforcement**   Individuals will repeat behaviors when they receive a reward and cease the behavior when they don't receive the reward or are punished. This statement is a simplistic synthesis of operant conditioning, but it captures the commonsense logic that underlies the theory. Akers includes this idea in his concept of **differential reinforcement.** Rewards come in many forms, and it's important to understand what individuals consider to be rewarding. The reward might be money, approval, food, or simply a pleasant feeling. These are all considered positive reinforcement and are likely to increase the behavior. The behavior is also likely to occur if it allows the individual to escape unpleasant consequences. This avoidance of disagreeable events is called **negative reinforcement.** Additionally, the likelihood of the behavior continuing is influenced by punishment, which can be either direct or indirect. Direct punishment occurs when something unpleasant is done to the subject, such as incarceration or corporal punishment. Indirect punishment occurs when a planned reward or pleasant consequence is removed.

- **Imitation**   Akers's social learning theory of crime also includes the idea that individuals learn through imitation. When a person sees someone break a law and escape the negative consequences of punishment, he or she might choose to participate in unlawful behavior as well. Imitation explains how people first decide to engage in crime but has less to do with why they persist or decide to quit.[17]

Social learning theory has remained a popular explanation for crime, delinquency, and deviant behavior for two primary reasons. The first reason that social learning theory is appreciated by many criminologists is because it has withstood the rigors of empirical testing. Social learning theory has consistently been shown to explain delinquency at least as well as other theories, and some studies have shown it to be better than most other theories.[18]

The second reason that social learning theory is popular is because it offers obvious policy implications. For instance, a number of programs use behavior modification techniques that reward the good behavior of inmates or juvenile delinquents. Frank Williams and Marilyn McShane point out that these programs are often referred to as "M&M economies" because they used the popular candy as a reward to promote desired behaviors. By rigidly structuring the rewards and punishments of a behavior modification program, administrators can entice participants to exhibit the types of behaviors that are conducive to successfully completing the program. Unfortunately, these learned behaviors are often merely adaptations to the artificial environments of treatment programs and are quickly discarded when the juvenile delinquent returns to the real world.[19] Despite the popularity of behavior modification programs, there have been several incidents of abusive programs that have impeded rehabilitation efforts.

Although behavior modification programs have earned some negative publicity, the underlying utility of social learning theory is still considered to be useful. The trick is to teach juvenile delinquents that their behaviors have long-term consequences and that the short-term reward isn't always the most desirable choice.

TECHNIQUES OF NEUTRALIZATION   Why do people break laws that they actually believe are good for society? For some adult offenders and juvenile delinquents, it's simply a matter of choosing to engage in behaviors that are contrary to their personal value system. An individual might agree that selling illegal drugs is wrong, but because of the potential to make a great deal of money, she or he might be willing to live with and adjust to this disjunction of values versus behavior. However, many youths break the law without such a cavalier attitude and are forced to reconcile their values with their offenses.

Gresham Sykes and David Matza developed the theory of techniques of neutralization to explain how youths who generally don't approve of delinquency are able to rationalize or justify their own deviant conduct.[20] Young individuals construct these defense mechanisms prior to breaking the law as ways of deflecting moral blame.

- **Denial of responsibility**   According to Sykes and Matza, individuals employ denial of responsibility to mitigate their unlawful behaviors in two ways. The first, and least common, is to claim the offense was an accident. By using this rationalization, the offender can avoid responsibility by denying motivation. The second way the offender can claim denial of responsibility is to assert that his or her actions were caused by some outside force. For example, indifferent parents, bad companions, or a socially disorganized neighborhood can be used as reasons why the offender had little choice but to act in the way he or she did. Harvard law professor Alan Dershowitz wrote a book called *The Abuse Excuse*, which uses this rationale to account for individuals not taking responsibility for a broad range of behaviors. The offender compares the situation to a billiard ball that is helplessly propelled into behaviors over which he or she has no control.[21]

- **Denial of injury**   Often, juvenile delinquents will excuse their actions by claiming that no one was injured. Offenses such as vandalism, even though there is property damage, might be rationalized by asserting that it was done as a prank and that the insurance company will pay for the damages. Additionally, when a youth gets into a fistfight and doesn't brutally beat the opponent, the rationalization is that no real injury was done and that the fight was simply roughhousing. Although the youth might in fact cause substantial injury to property or other people, the behavior is minimized and blame is deflected by denying that real harm was done.

- **Denial of victim**   Some juvenile delinquents attempt to excuse their actions by claiming that the injured party doesn't deserve true victim status. According to the youth, it's permissible to attack some individuals, such as homosexuals or members of minority groups. The youths see themselves as avengers or retaliators for real or imagined slights. Their logic doesn't have to be consistent provided that they are able to put themselves into the role of a modern Robin Hood who preserves street justice. The injured victim is transformed into someone who deserves contempt, and there is no dishonor in dishing out violence to such a person. The denial-of-victim neutralization technique is also applied to a victim who is physically absent or unknown. The victim is an abstraction, and the youth is able to commit delinquent acts without feeling the blame of dealing with someone's tangible loss or pain.

- **Condemnation of condemners**   Young people are quick to spot hypocrisy. When criticized for smoking marijuana, they point to adults who smoke tobacco and abuse alcohol. They believe those who are guilty of deviance themselves unjustly condemn the deviance of young people. The police who arrest them are viewed as corrupt, stupid, and brutal. Teachers are ineffective and give bad grades to students they don't like and show favoritism to those who "play the game" and become teachers' pets. Parents are faulted for condemning in their children the same behaviors they engaged in when they were young. This technique of neutralization works well when youths are encouraged to think critically and find fault with the status quo. It is always much easier for parents and teachers to prescribe the types of behaviors they wish to see, rather than to model them.

- **Appeal to higher loyalties**   Sometimes young people understand the logic behind what society holds up as correct behavior, but they are conflicted because another group is competing for their loyalty. The gang, friendship clique, football team, or cheerleading squad might hold a great deal of influence over the youth who wants to do good but who is bonded to a smaller group by identity or a need to belong. Perhaps one of the best contemporary examples of appeal to higher loyalty is the deeply religious individuals who commit violence against abortion clinics or kill doctors who provide abortion services. These individuals are conforming in other ways but see their duty to their religion and moral code as overwhelming the laws of the country; thus they are able to commit offenses that they would reject under any other context. Unfortunately for them, society doesn't share this distinction and prosecutes them to the full extent of the law. Although their motivation might be pure in their own eyes, it's viewed by society as terrorism and dealt with in the harshest manner. Nevertheless, understanding the appeal to higher loyalties helps us account for the negative behaviors of people who otherwise obey the law. Often, members of youth gangs will cite their loyalty to the gang as a reason why they commit delinquent acts.

Sykes and Matza's techniques of neutralization help answer one of the most interesting questions in criminology. Why do people break laws in which they believe? The answer that Sykes and Matza provide is simple, appealing, and understandable. When people break the law, they are able to provide themselves with excuses that minimize their blame. In this way, they are able to escape the full ramifications of their wrongdoing and provide themselves with at least some degree of justification for their antisocial behavior.[22]

The techniques of neutralization aren't always fully effective. Some juvenile delinquents who employ them will still feel guilty or remorseful even as they commit future offenses, and some delinquents are so isolated from the dominant society that they feel no remorse at all. Yet, according to Sykes and Matza, the techniques of neutralization help lessen the constraints of social control to such a great extent that juvenile delinquents can justify committing a broad range of unlawful behavior, even while they find fault in others for engaging in similar behavior.

The usefulness of this theory has broad appeal for criminologists. It has been employed to explain the actions of child molesters, bad-check writers, and steroid-using athletes.[23] Any time there is a disjunction between the ideals taught to young people and the way society actually works, it can be expected that youths will seize on this discrepancy and use it to justify breaking the law.

Anomie and Strain Theory

anomie

A condition in which a people or society undergoes a breakdown of social norms and values. Also, personal anxiety and isolation produced by rapidly shifting moral and cultural values.

strain theory

The idea that juvenile delinquency is at least partially a result of being excluded from economic rewards.

Another theory highly regarded by many criminologists is **anomie** or **strain theory.** Anomie is personal anxiety or isolation, also called *normlessness*, produced by rapidly shifting moral values. Although anomie and strain theory aren't interchangeable, they do refer to the same social processes. Strain theory refers to the personal strain and anger caused by being excluded from economic rewards. This strain and anger can cause youths to commit delinquent acts. It is useful to think of strain theory as an extension of anomie. Anomie and strain theory are associated with two important sociologists, Emile Durkheim and Robert Merton, along with the contemporary work being done on general strain theory by Robert Agnew.

DURKHEIM AND ANOMIE   Durkheim used the term *anomie* to refer to the sense of normlessness that people feel during times of rapid social change, when the usual ways of relating to each other are confused by impersonalization, detailed divisions of labor, and the breakdown of moral order. Deviant behavior occurs when people feel that the traditional ways of relating to others no longer work. People need clear rules to live by, and when these rules are absent or no longer apply, people might feel dissatisfied and frustrated. Durkheim used the term *anomie* to refer to the conditions of a society and not necessarily to individuals. Perhaps his most famous work in which he utilized anomie is *Suicide: A Study in Sociology* (1897), in which he looked at the suicide rates of several countries and concluded that the breakdown in social norms as a result of social change was responsible for higher rates of suicide.[24]

MERTON AND STRAIN   Merton's strain theory is similar to anomie, but he considers deviance in a slightly different and expanded way. Merton divided social norms into two types of concerns.[25] The first, *social goals*, argued that society teaches individuals to pursue desirable ends. In the United States, the overriding social goal is economic success and accumulating as much wealth as possible. Typically, Americans are socialized from an early age to strive for financial independence. Other societies, however, have different cultural goals. For example, in some traditional Asian societies, getting rich isn't as important as maintaining one's family obligations and showing the required deference to those in positions of authority.

Merton's second cultural norm deals with the means that one uses to pursue cultural goals. Typically, accumulating wealth isn't considered to be legitimate if it's done through force, coercion, violence, fraud, or duplicity. The culturally approved means for acquiring wealth in American society is study, hard work, and creativity. Although we all might agree with the culturally approved goal of getting wealthy through the culturally approved means of working hard, not everyone has equal access to these means. Because of issues such as racism, sexism, or social class bias, some young people find their means to the socially approved goals of acquiring wealth to be blocked. This doesn't mean that these young people give up on their goals, however. Rather, they find other, often illegitimate, means for attempting to get what society tells them they need to have. Merton calls these other means *modes of adaptation*. Merton's five modes of adaptation, explained next, are illustrated in Table 7-2.

- **Conformity**   Most of us, including most young people, fall into Merton's category of *conformist*. We have been so heavily socialized into law-abiding behavior that we still strive for our goals by working hard, even if we think the process isn't fair and that we might spend a long time trying to achieve our goals. Because of family upbringing, religious values, or just common decency, most people choose to obey the law and maintain self-respect and a good name. Therefore, according to Merton, we accept both the goals of society and the culturally approved means to obtain these goals.

- **Innovation**   Those who accept the socially approved goals but employ alternative means for achieving these goals are called *innovators*. There are many ways of innovating, the most relevant here being resorting to crime to obtain financial security. Sometimes there's a fine line between legitimate and illegitimate innovation. Aggressive business practices and consumer fraud are difficult to discern and are often decided after the fact by a court of law. Sometimes illegitimate innovations through robbery, theft, and/or lying are more efficient than culturally approved means, and the temptation is high to take such shortcuts to the goal. Some delinquency is actually innovation, such as selling drugs or stealing items to sell for a profit to allow youths to buy things they couldn't otherwise afford.

- **Ritual**   Some people reject the culturally approved goals but cling tenaciously to the means. These *ritualists* are simply going through the motions of chasing the dream. They long ago gave up on becoming financially successful, but they get a certain satisfaction out of maintaining their positions by doing their jobs in a credible if unimaginative way. These individuals include the professor who never updates classes, the clerk who makes sure every form is filled out

Table 7-2   **Merton's Five Modes of Adaptation**

Type	Accept Goals	Accept Means
Conformity	Yes	Yes
Innovation	Yes	No
Ritual	No	Yes
Retreat	No	No
Rebellion	Creates and substitutes new goals and means	

completely, and the chef who, while preparing good-tasting food, is unconcerned with how the dish is presented. Because young people haven't had much life experience, few could be called true ritualists.

- **Retreat** The American dream is so elusive for some people that they have given up the idea of being successful and no longer pursue the means that would allow them to succeed. These individuals, *retreatists*, represent the vagrants, drug addicts, and alcoholics of society. They retreat to the bottle or needle and have little hope or care of achieving a respectable job or position in society. Historically, this doesn't represent a very large segment of society, but with severe dislocations in the economy, it appears to be more prevalent with the increases of the homeless, unemployed, and incarcerated. As with ritualism, retreatism requires a certain amount of life experience. A young person who is this disillusioned might be a victim of mental illness or clinical depression.

- **Rebellion** Finally, some people reject society's accepted goals and means and substitute new ones. These people, *rebellionists*, are most recently exemplified by the hippies of the 1960s. The counterculture of that period saw getting rich as undesirable or even immoral, given the inequities in society, and therefore attempted to address some of these inequities through social protests and flaunting of the dominant society's values. Other types of rebels might include revolutionaries who advocate the overthrow of governments and the substitution of new leaders who espouse a different set of values. Young people, including juvenile delinquents, are prime candidates to become rebellionists. A majority of the aforementioned hippies, who were members of the baby-boom generation, adopted their attitudes during late adolescence and young adulthood.

Merton's theory can explain the offenses of the lower class better than the crimes of those who have been successful in the current economic structure. Those who can successfully compete in the job market don't need to resort to Merton's adaptations, because socially approved means to their desired goals aren't systematically blocked. Just because the middle and upper classes don't experience the strain or anomie of the lower classes doesn't mean they don't engage in unlawful behavior. Their strain might be of a different variety, being not so much about financial issues as about other concerns, such as reputation among elites, perceived respect, or simple greed.[26]

AGNEW AND STRAIN   Before we leave anomie and strain theory, it's important to consider the theoretical contributions of another criminologist. Robert Agnew has developed general strain theory from a microlevel perspective that attempts to broaden the concept of strain to include more than Merton's disjunction between means and goals. Agnew considers crime and delinquency as adaptations to stress, and his major contribution to strain theory is the expansion of the types of stress that are considered to be sources of strain. Specifically, Agnew identifies three major sources of stress.[27]

- **Strain caused by the disjunction between just or fair outcomes and actual outcomes** This is an interesting point that allows us to consider how the individual views the type of justice that is allocated to his or her acts. People have expectations of outcomes based both on how hard they have worked and how hard they have seen others work. When it doesn't appear that outcomes are allocated on equity, but rather as a result of inside information such as favoritism, family connections, or class bias, the individual feels a certain amount of strain and disillusionment about the fairness of society.

- **Strain caused by the removal of positively valued stimuli from the individual** Stress is produced by events other than failure to achieve goals. According to Agnew, a great deal of literature about aggression suggests that strain is caused by the removal of something that is valued. Examples of events that could cause this type of strain include the loss of a loved one, the divorce of parents, the loss of a job, breaking up with a significant other, or suspension from school. When something valuable is removed from one's life, the individual attempts to fill the void through adaptations that can often include crime and delinquency.

- **Strain caused by the presentation of negative stimuli**   Certain noxious stimuli introduced into an individual's environment can cause strain that results in delinquency. On one level, these noxious stimuli can take a physical form, such as extremely unpleasant odors, disgusting scenes, air pollution, high population density, and/or noise and heat. At another level, these stimuli can be found in the form of personal interaction in which the individual is subjected to physical or sexual abuse, criminal victimization, physical punishment, negative associations with parents or peers, physical pain, or verbal threats and insults.

Agnew's general strain theory has greatly expanded what is considered stressful. Moreover, Agnew and others have subjected this new way of considering strain to a great deal of empirical investigation.[28] Like Akers's social learning theory, general strain theory provides important insights into why juvenile delinquents break the law. It is important to remember that strain theory is concerned primarily with the stresses and concerns of young people.

Social Control Theory

Thus far, the focus of criminological and delinquency theories has been to explain why individuals violate the law. This seems like a straightforward approach that has led to the examination of biological, psychological, and sociological factors that demonstrate differences between delinquents and nondelinquents. However, social control theory approaches the issue of why people break the law from a different perspective. Instead of asking why people break the law, it instead asks why don't we all break the law?

In many ways, social control theories are theories of socialization. They look to see to what extent youths have learned the habits, attitudes, and perspectives of society and try to identify deficiencies in this socialization. All groups socialize their members to conform to the group norms, and the health of each group is monitored by the adherence to these norms. Sociologist Emile Durkheim provided the example of a "society of saints," where although each saint was law-abiding, there would still be group norms that would separate the better saints from the less devoted.[29] Inadequate time spent at prayer, being improperly pious, or violating dietary restrictions are all infractions of acceptable behavior in Durkheim's society of saints.

Here, we will briefly review three types of social control theories: personality-oriented control theories, containment theories, and social bonding theories. These types of theories demonstrate how social control perspective has gained in sophistication and testability.

PERSONALITY AND SOCIAL CONTROL   Yale sociologist Albert Reiss was one of the first scholars to consider the intersection of personality and social control. Writing in the 1950s, he used the then-fashionable perspective of psychoanalysis to examine the effect of personality on delinquency. More importantly, he identified three aspects of social control that interacted with personality that could result in delinquency:

1. **A lack of proper internal controls developed during childhood**   Those who aren't taught to control their temper, defer gratification, or respect the rights of others during childhood are likely to engage in delinquent behavior.

2. **A breakdown in internal controls**   A properly socialized youth might become delinquent because he or she follows deviant peers, is tempted by rewards for delinquency, or is under the influence of drugs or alcohol.

3. **An absence of or conflicts in the social rules provided by important groups such as parents or schools**   Changes in lifestyle, such as an absent parent because of divorce or a change in schools, can result in a weakening of the youth's social control.[30]

Other theorists have refined Reiss's ideas to explain how individuals are socialized to engage in appropriate and law-abiding behavior.

CONTAINMENT THEORY Walter Reckless envisioned individuals as being influenced by both inner controls (or inner containment) based on their self-concept and personality and outer controls (or outer containment) based on the adequacy of their social support systems, such as family, schools, peers. Reckless never clearly delineated what he meant by inner containment but suggested that it was bound up in the self-concept of individuals. He thought that those who possess tolerance for frustration, healthy self-esteem, a sense of responsibility, and self-control were psychologically well-armed to resist the temptations of delinquency. Similarly, outer containment involves family and community advantages, such as proper discipline and effective parental supervision, opportunities for positive social activities, conventional chances for acceptance, and developing a positive identity.[31]

Reckless saw individuals as being pushed because of inadequate inner containment and pulled because of pressures from outer containment, which induced them to commit criminal or delinquent acts. According to Reckless, the more important of these two influences to a youth's self-concept was inner containment.[32]

Containment theory has appeal because it considers both the individual's personality and the societal pressures that can tempt him or her into unlawful behavior. But the crucial question that remained unanswered pertains to what makes a youth believe in the rules of society. The theorist who is credited with answering this question is Travis Hirschi, who developed the idea of the social bond.

HIRSCHI'S SOCIAL CONTROL THEORY Hirschi's social control theory states that individuals are bonded to conventional society and institutions to varying degrees. Youths who have strong and flexible bonds to society won't engage in delinquent behavior, whereas those who have weak bonds will. The signature factor in Hirschi's theory is the manner in which he identifies the characteristics of the social bond. Hirschi envisioned the social bond as having four dimensions:

- **Attachment** Delinquent behavior can be inhibited by the extent to which a youth is attached to conventional society. These attachments can take the form of an emotional bond with parents, concern for the opinions of teachers, or respect for peers.

- **Involvement** Youths who are involved in positive activities have little time and emotional energy to engage in delinquency. Based on the old axiom "Idle hands are the devil's playground," Hirschi saw that keeping youths involved in wholesome activities could prevent bad behavior.

- **Commitment** Commitment deals with the extent to which an individual is already involved in conventional behavior. People who are invested in conventional society have more at stake than those who don't. Basically, those who have nothing invested in conventional behavior have nothing to lose. Those who succeed at school and have a bright future are less likely to take the chance of committing delinquent acts.

- **Belief** People who respect the rules of society are more likely to obey them. If the rules and social conditions are perceived as fair, people will work within the system to advance themselves. Youths who see society's rules stacked against them due to race, class, or gender inequities are more prone to delinquent behavior.[33]

One reason that social control theory became so popular among criminologists is because it could be examined by self-report studies.[34] By asking youths what behaviors they have committed and recording how bonded they are to conventional society, social control theorists were able to measure the relative influence of each of Hirschi's elements of the social bond. Other measures of delinquency, such as official crime statistics or victimization studies, aren't particularly useful for revealing social control theory.

SUBCULTURAL THEORIES

Let's now turn to another set of theories that are used to explain crime in general, but especially to explain juvenile delinquency. These theories have a good deal of utility because they explain why young people engage in delinquent activities as members of gangs. We will examine gangs, especially contemporary gangs, in greater detail in Chapter 12, but it's worthwhile here to observe how criminologists link gang activity to the theoretical development of crime and delinquency.

Subcultural theories of crime and delinquency were among the first explanations of juvenile delinquency offered by American criminologists. Starting in the 1950s and continuing until today, criminologists have observed the nature of group deviance and done considerable research linking gangs to the communities in which they thrived. Here, we will look at five subcultural theories that represent a long tradition of attempting to explain a consistent feature of juvenile delinquency: that youths often break the law in the company of friends.

Delinquent Boys

Albert Cohen was primarily concerned with lower-class males in gangs. He was particularly interested in the reasons that young boys break the law in ways that seem to have so little purpose. He contended that much of their behavior was nonutilitarian, malicious, and negativistic. In other words, the offenses did little to gain the boys any advantage, such as money, and seemed to have little payoff. The boys would hurt others and take pleasure in their suffering, and their behavior was often a statement that rejected the values of the rest of society. Further, the boys lived for the moment and had little regard for the future. This short-term hedonism meant that most of their actions produced very little in the way of useful results. The boys had their own criteria for keeping score and allocating status that were completely at odds with mainstream society.[35]

According to Cohen, children of all social classes compete with each other in school, but all children aren't equally prepared for this competition. For instance, Cohen asserts:

> In a society like ours, however, in which a child might be legitimately compared, in terms of the same criteria, with "all comers" regardless of family background, it doesn't follow that the ability to achieve these criteria is necessarily distributed without regard to family background and social class. Systematic class-linked differences in the ability to achieve will regulate to the bottom of the status pyramid those children belonging to the most disadvantaged classes, not by virtue of their class position as such but by virtue of their lack of the requisite personal qualifications resulting from their class-linked handicaps.[36]

Consequently, youths are judged according to a "middle-class measuring rod" that is difficult for lower-class youths to attain. (For an explanation of the term *middle-class values*, see A Closer Look at Juvenile Issues 7.1.) When lower-class boys fail to measure up to the middle-class school standards, they experience status frustration and react in ways that cause delinquent behavior.[37] According to Cohen, this reaction is a defense mechanism that insulates them from feelings of low self-worth. By rejecting middle-class values, the boys are free to excuse themselves from caring about playing the rigged game of middle-class values.

Differential Opportunity Theory

Richard Cloward and Lloyd Ohlin use their theory of differential opportunity to extend the ideas of strain put forth by Merton and Cohen. When lower-class boys experience problems competing in society, they turn to the delinquent subculture to

7.1 A CLOSER LOOK at JUVENILE ISSUES

WHAT IS MIDDLE CLASS?

Any study of society usually includes a lot of discussion about class. Traditionally, the United States prides itself on being a classless society in that social and economic class isn't a barrier to wealth or social status. It is a deeply held belief of Americans that a person can be born into poverty and become a billionaire CEO or president of the United States or anything that he or she wants to be provided that he or she works at it hard enough.

Class does exist in the United States, however informally, and it's loosely defined by economic status. In fact, Americans consider a broad and strong middle class to be the bedrock of a healthy democratic society. The American middle class is so enduring and ubiquitous that it has its own philosophy, which, not coincidentally, is also pretty much the philosophy of the American dream and its attainment.

So what is this philosophy? According to sociologist Albert K. Cohen, the following nine *norms* are essential to being middle class:

1. **Ambition**   A person who isn't ambitious is maladjusted. Ambition also means an orientation to long-term goals and the determination to get ahead. A parent's first duty is to make his or her children want to be somebody.

2. **Individual responsibility**   The key words here are resourcefulness, independence, and self-reliance. The obligation to assist or share with friends and family is minimal.

3. **Achievement**   Outstanding performance of almost any kind is applauded, including both athletic achievement and academic achievement.

4. **Temperance**   This is the willingness to forgo immediate satisfactions and self-indulgence in the interest of long-term goals.

5. **Rationality**   This refers to forethought, planning, scheduling, and the efficient allocation of resources.

6. **Courtesy and likability**   In the middle class, mastery of certain conventions of speech and gestures is important to success. It is interesting that in the early 21st century as the world of work has become more oriented toward the office, rather than the shop or factory floor, classes for adults on etiquette and table manners are becoming common.

7. **Less physical aggression**   It's important to have good relations with as many people as possible while remaining competitive in an impersonal, nonphysical way.

8. **Educational recreation**   Leisure time should be spent constructively, developing a skill, pursuing a worthwhile hobby, or maintaining physical fitness.

9. **Respect for property**   This is recognition of the property rights of others, as well as carefully maintaining one's own property so that it is not destroyed or wasted.

Source: Albert K. Cohen, *Delinquent Boys: The Culture of the Gang* (New York: Free Press, 1955), 88–92.

Table 7-3   **Cloward and Ohlin's Three Delinquent Subcultures**

Criminal pattern	Boys meet their material needs by stealing. Status is earned by being a good thief.
Conflict pattern	The youth who engages in this pattern is typically the gang member who fights to maintain his reputation and defend the honor of the gang.
Retreatist pattern	The drug addict and the alcoholic are the norm in this pattern.

Source: Richard Cloward and Lloyd Ohlin, *Delinquency and Opportunity* (New York: Free Press, 1960).

help them adapt to their circumstances. Cloward and Ohlin specify three types of delinquent subcultures (see Table 7-3) that are available for these boys to immerse themselves in as ways of combating the strain they experience as a result of their class status.[38]

The first delinquent subculture offered by Cloward and Ohlin is termed the *criminal pattern*. Here, boys meet their material needs by engaging in activities such as theft. Status is earned by being a good thief and making the "big score." The criminal pattern is closely associated with adult criminal activities and can be a stepping-stone for the youth to becoming a career offender.

The second delinquent subculture is called the *conflict pattern*. The type of youth who engages in this pattern is the warrior. He is the gang member who is willing to fight to maintain his reputation and to defend the honor of the gang. This type of juvenile delinquent gains status by being willing to fight at the slightest provocation.

Minor delinquency, such as shoplifting, can at first be merely a way for delinquents to get what they want or need. However, it can pave the way to career offending. *(Courtesy Chuck Savage, Chuck Savage Productions Inc.)*

Displays of physical strength, masculinity, fearlessness, and courage are used to frighten others and to enhance the prestige of the individual and his or her gang.

The third type of delinquent subculture is the *retreatist pattern*. Here, the drug addict and the alcoholic are the norm. These individuals are after the "kick," which is described as the high that is experienced from drug use or as the rush of adrenalin from lawbreaking. Cloward and Ohlin, writing in the parlance of the 1950s, called this type of juvenile delinquent a "cat" and describe another facet of the retreatist subculture that goes beyond simple drug use:

> The successful cat has a lucrative "hustle" which contrasts sharply with the routine and discipline required in the ordinary occupational tasks of conventional society. The many varieties of the hustle are characterized by a rejection of violence or force and a preference for manipulating, persuading, outwitting, or "conning" others to obtain resources for experiencing the kick. The cat begs, borrows, steals, or engages in some petty con-game. He caters to the illegitimate cravings of others by peddling drugs or working as a pimp. A highly exploitative attitude towards women permits the cat to view pimping as a prestigious source of income. Through the labor of "chicks" engaged in prostitution or shoplifting, he can live in idleness and concentrate his entire attention to organizing, scheduling, and experiencing the esthetic pleasure of the kick. The hustle of the cat is secondary to his interests in the kick. In this respect the cat differs from his fellow delinquents in the criminal subculture, for whom income-producing activity is a primary concern.[39]

The main contribution of Cloward and Ohlin's theory is their contention that it's not only the opportunities that youths have to engage in conventional activities that decide their delinquency, but also the opportunities they have to engage in illegitimate enterprises. Just as each youth might have differential access to jobs, mentoring, stable family life, and good schools, so each of them has different exposure to opportunities to know drug dealers and gang members. In many ways, then, youths aren't only pushed toward crime because of lack of legitimate opportunities, but also pulled toward crime by illegitimate opportunities.[40]

Focal Concerns of the Lower Class

Walter Miller is another scholar who locates the source of crime and delinquency in the subculture in which some young people are socialized. According to Miller, the subculture of the lower class emphasizes many middle-class values but also has a different set of focal concerns that often puts them in conflict with traditional society. These focal concerns are rooted in the lifestyle in which low-skilled labor is common, and the traits and characteristics that enable one to succeed in such an environment are rewarded.[41]

Although Cohen saw deviant lower-class youth as flouting the values of the middle class with negativistic behavior, Miller sees their deviance as simply responding to lower-class subcultural standards. These focal concerns of the lower class shape the youth's behavior with the following six concepts:

- **Trouble**   Lower-class youths are used to being "in trouble" with the dominant society. Either by being problem students at school, hassled on the street corner by the police, or being constantly yelled at by their parents, many of these youths live with a dark cloud of trouble hanging over their heads all the time.

- **Toughness**   Boys' status in lower-class neighborhoods is measured by toughness. Boys must be willing to fight to protect their self-esteem and status on the street. Boys must be brave and fearless and not afraid to fight, even when destined through inferior size and strength to lose.

- **Smartness**   The smartness of the lower class isn't the academic intelligence that is rewarded by middle-class values. Rather, it's the ability to be cunning and to live by one's wits. A youth who displays smartness is the one who isn't taken advantage of by others.

- **Excitement**   Like any youth, lower-class youths crave excitement. Seeking thrills by taking risks and engaging in dangerous activities is a way of generating excitement and a sense of living on the edge.

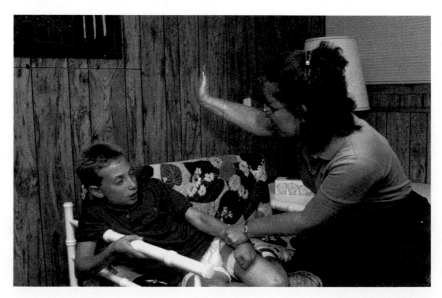

According to Cohen, lower-class youths are accustomed to being "in trouble" with authority figures, including their parents. *(Courtesy Robert Brenner, PhotoEdit Inc.)*

- **Fate**   To justify their relative lack of success in the dominant society, lower-class youths attribute many of the outcomes of their activities to luck or chance, rather than to skill and knowledge.

- **Autonomy**   Autonomy refers to the independence that the youth values. By not having to rely on others and rejecting the values and rewards of the dominant society, these youths are able to isolate themselves from the expectations and demands of middle-class authority figures.

This discussion of focal concerns of the lower class shouldn't be considered as an indictment of the quality of ethical behavior of this subculture. Rather, Miller intended it simply as an explanation of how lower-class youths might find themselves involved with crime and delinquency as a result of the frustration of living up to middle-class standards and the enhanced opportunities they have in lower-class neighborhoods to break the law. This is especially true for gang activities in which the peer group often performs functions of belonging and stability that the youth lacks at home.[42] When a male role model is absent in the household, the gang can provide a learning environment that emphasizes the focal concerns of toughness, street smarts, fighting ability, risk taking, and excitement.

Although these activities might not be criminal acts, they do place the youth in positions in which lawbreaking is likely. However, the youth's intent is simply to engage in the adult behaviors of his class, and the law violations are but an indirect result.[43] For an example of a program designed to help youth find role models, see Programs for Children 7.1.

7.1   PROGRAMS *for* CHILDREN

BIG BROTHER IS WATCHING, LISTENING, TALKING, AND HELPING

Not all children have the supportive social network that can give them the advice, guidance, and encouragement that enable them to become productive citizens. Some children come from families that are fractured by divorce, violence, poverty, and/or crime. Although many of these children can find alternative support networks, others can't. One long-lasting program that has proved valuable for generations of children is the Big Brothers Big Sisters program.

According to the Coalition for Evidence-Based Policy, Big Brothers Big Sisters is a national mentoring program that matches youths ages 6–18, predominantly from low-income, single-parent households, with adult volunteer mentors who are typically young (20–34) and well educated (the majority are college graduates). The youth's parent or guardian applies for the child to be matched with a mentor through a written application and a child–parent interview. Potential mentors are screened by a Big Brothers Big Sisters case worker through a personal interview, home visit, and criminal, background, and reference check to ensure that they are not a safety risk and are likely to form a positive relationship with the youth. Prior to a match being made, the youth and parent meet with the potential mentor; the match's completion requires the parent's approval. The mentor and youth typically meet for two to four times per month for at least a year and engage in activities of their choosing (e.g., studying, cooking, playing sports). The typical meeting lasts 3 to 4 hours.

For approximately $1,000 per child, Big Brothers Big Sisters has served over 200,000 children with 417 programs across the nation. Research conducted by Jean Grossman and Joseph Tierney found that those in a Big Brother or Big Sister program

- Were 46 percent less likely to have started using illegal drugs
- Were 27 percent less likely to have started using alcohol
- Had 32 percent fewer incidents of hitting someone in the previous 12 months
- Skipped fewer school days in the previous 12 months
- Enjoyed a small, marginally significant, positive effect on grade-point average (2.71 vs. 2.63)
- Were neither more nor less likely to steal or damage property

Source: Jean Baldwin Grossman and Joseph P. Tierney, "Does Mentoring Work? An Impact Study of the Big Brothers Big Sisters Program," *Evaluation Review* 22, no. 3 (June 1998):403–426. Online at www.bbbsa.org/site/pp.asp?c=iuJ3JgO2F&b= 14576 and www.evidencebasedprograms.org/Default.aspx?tabid=146.

Subculture of Violence

Crime and delinquency aren't evenly distributed across the population. Antisocial behavior is more common in some neighborhoods, communities, schools, or subcultures than in other areas. This phenomenon is particularly easy to see when violence is examined. Marvin Wolfgang and Franco Ferracuti developed their subculture of violence thesis to explain why certain groups consistently produce violent behavior.[44]

Wolfgang and Ferracuti contend that subcultures in which violence is prevalent don't necessarily reject all the values of the dominant culture. In fact, the violence attributed to the subculture is often just a reflection of violence in the larger culture. The differences are that in the greater society the violence is often deemed legitimate, whereas in the subculture it's considered deviant behavior. Also, the subculture's violence is often more intense, widespread, and frequent. According to the subculture of violence thesis, a violent response is required in more situations and under a greater range of circumstances than in the larger culture. These circumstances include parent–child relationships, domestic quarrels, street fights, gang conflicts, and other types of assaults. Violence is a learned response that allows the individual to survive in a subculture where the conventional ways of resolving conflicts aren't always effective. According to Wolfgang and Ferracuti, the violent response is concentrated in males who are in late adolescence and who retain the violent response until middle age.

One of the more interesting aspects of the subculture of violence thesis is that it doesn't apply to all young men in the same way. A number of personality characteristics that are shaped by the environment mediate how involved in violence the youth becomes. Some of these young men develop an integrated social–psychological approach that habitually requires violence to resolve conflicts, including those in marriage, child rearing, and disputes with neighbors.

The violence that this perspective can best explain is the violence that exists within a subculture or that results from interaction with another violent subculture. Violence, then, isn't considered as something to be avoided but, rather, as a legitimate way of resolving conflict.[45] Status is accorded to those who are willing to use violence for the smallest real or imagined slight, and once one has the reputation as someone who will fight with little provocation, the threat of violence can be sufficient to avoid actual fighting.

It is important to remember that, even in a community that supports the subculture of violence, deadly violence is still rare. Although even law-abiding citizens consider violence to be semilegitimate, there are rules and expectations as to when a violent response is required. People understand what constitutes the need to use legitimate and illegitimate violence. To say that "he had it coming" or "she was asking for it" demonstrates that violence is an expected and, in some ways, functional part of the social order.[46]

We must note that, like many of the sociological theories of crime and delinquency we have studied, the subculture of violence thesis explains only a limited amount of deviance. This perspective is confined only to groups that are either mired in lower-class values or concerned with masculinity rituals. For instance, the environment of the rugby team or the boxing club celebrates the use of violence as an expression of one's masculinity. Likewise, in some single-sex subcultures, such as the youth-detention facility or the adult prison, the readiness to use violence is a personality feature that protects one from becoming a victim of the informal hierarchy of status roles.[47]

The Code of the Street

The subculture of violence thesis has been given new currency by the ground-breaking work of sociologist Elijah Anderson in his book *The Code of the Street: Decency, Violence, and the Moral Life of the Inner City*. In this book, Anderson claims that disadvantaged black neighborhoods promote a violent code of conduct that young men (and to a great degree young women) must obey. Anderson points out that there are both "decent" families and "street" families who vie for respect in the street. The code requires that individuals must feel that they are treated "right" by others, which entails being given proper respect. The quickest way to challenge someone is to maintain eye contact for too long as a means of disrespect. The code requires that person to stand up for him- or herself and insists that the one staring announce his or her intentions or motivation. Anderson contends that because inner-city residents lack faith that the police will respond effectively and protect them from danger, they have to do it themselves and be ready to employ violence to ward off street predators.[48]

The origins of this code come from the street parents who are unable to cope effectively themselves and instill in their children the willingness to use violence as a way of displaying power. Anderson explains it this way:

> In these circumstances a woman—or a man, although men are less consistently present in children's lives—can be quite aggressive with children, yelling and striking them for the least little infraction of the rules she has laid down. Often little if any serious explanation follows the verbal and physical punishment. This response teaches children a particular lesson. They learn that to solve any kind of interpersonal problem one must quickly resort to hitting or other violent behavior. Actual peace and quiet, and also the appearance of calm, respectful children conveyed to her neighbors and friends, are often what the young mother most desires, but at times she will be very aggressive in trying to get them. Thus she might be quick to beat her children, especially if they defy her law, not because she hates them but because this is the way she knows how to control them.[49]

Anderson argues that many of these street mothers are sporadic in the care and discipline of their children. Many of them have problems of their own revolving around trying to earn money and maintaining relationships with husbands or boyfriends and with dependence on alcohol or drugs. The children are left to fend for themselves in a violent world with short-tempered adult role models.

The children grow up in the streets where their primary socialization comes from other, older children. What they learn is "might makes right" and that verbal and physical aggression is the coin of the realm. Anderson says that when these children learn that the social meaning of fighting entails rewards and the esteem of peers, it is likely that the child will internalize this way of adaptation and conflict resolution if it's left unchallenged.

The law-abiding families of the neighborhood provide their children with counteracting role models and messages. The law-abiding families must teach their children the code of the street, lest they fail to pick up on what is happening around them or make a social gaffe that could get them hurt or killed. However, they must also teach their children the values of the dominant society and ingrain in them a sense of ethics and morals that are derived from the church, the extended family, and the middle-class life that they are striving to achieve.

One orienting tenet of the code of the street is manhood. With the idea that someone might attempt to "mess with you" or challenge a youth's manhood, the youth must always be ready to display a willingness to protect himself. The clothes he wears, the way he carries himself, and the way he talks are all indicators of the façade of manhood he is attempting to convey to others. Even when one's self-esteem is low due to an inadequate education, unemployment, and the inability to take care of one's family, one's manhood can be buttressed by displays of temper, violence, or nerve.

Anderson provides an interesting analysis of nerve. Central to the issue of manhood is the widespread belief that one of the most effective ways of gaining respect is to show "nerve." Nerve is shown when one takes another person's possessions (the more valuable the better), "messes with" someone's "woman," throws the first punch, "gets in someone's face," or pulls the trigger. Its proper display helps prevent attacks and also helps build a reputation that prevents future challenges.[50] But since such a show of nerve is a forceful expression of disrespect toward the person on the receiving end, the victim

The ability and willingness to fight and defend one's manhood are very important aspects of the code of the street. Here two angry Filipino gang members confront each other. *(Courtesy Michael Newman, PhotoEdit Inc.)*

might be greatly offended and seek to retaliate with equal or greater force. A display of nerve, therefore, can easily provoke a life-threatening response, and the background knowledge of this possibility has often been incorporated into the concept of nerve.

On a practical level, this code of the street has important implications for life outside the disadvantaged neighborhood and for the juvenile justice system. According to Anderson, the code gives youths a very limited view of life that makes them ready to die rather than to be disrespected. In interactions with middle-class individuals, the youth reared on the code of the street might resort to what is considered unacceptable violence at school, sporting events, concerts, or parks. What is meant to be good-natured teasing by some youth can be considered threats to another's manhood that require instant physical retaliation, often with deadly consequences. When the police deal with these young people, they are often surprised that the youths feel more threatened by their peers' opinions of their toughness than they are by a possible confrontation with police officers that could result in incarceration.[51]

The subculture of violence thesis put forth by Wolfgang and Ferracuti, especially as articulated by Anderson, presents another type of sociological theory that attempts to explain some of the more chronic types of delinquency. Most important is the realization that reforming the youth might require reforming the entire mindset of the disadvantaged community. To do this would require massive resources aimed at reducing poverty, improving schools, and addressing the issues of dysfunctional families.[52] All these concerns will be discussed in greater detail in Part III.

SOCIAL REACTION THEORIES

Social reaction theories consider not only the behavior of people, but also how that behavior is influenced by the reactions of others. The way that parents, schools, and the juvenile justice system react to delinquency affects whether this behavior is repeated by the youth. Here, we look at two types of social reaction theories, labeling theory and the more recent shaming theory.

Labeling Theory

A number of theorists have contributed to the development of **labeling theory,** but the first to use this perspective was Frank Tannenbaum in *Crime and the Community* (1938), in which he discussed how juveniles are "tagged" as deviants and how this tag can follow them through the juvenile justice system, as well as life, and influence how others see them.[53] People react to the tag, and this, in turn, influences the youth's self-concept. Robert Merton called this a self-fulfilling prophecy, in which the individual internalizes the label and subsequently acts the part. Because conventional society determines what behavior is appropriate, those who engage in other types of behavior have their actions termed *deviant* and are subject to what Tannenbaum calls the "dramatization of evil."

An important idea of labeling theory is that no behavior is intrinsically deviant, but it is subject to the label placed on it by those who have the power to have their values adopted by the larger culture.[54] For instance, killing another person is a relative act. In some circumstances, such as war, self-defense, or capital punishment, the killing of another human being is permissible, valued, or rewarded. In other circumstances, such as in the commission of a crime, the killing of another person is punished, often extremely. The difference lies in the context and the values that are attached to the context by those who have power.

Another important idea behind labeling theory is that the actual behavior isn't as important as the perception of the behavior. For instance, a person doesn't have to break the law to be considered a criminal or a juvenile delinquent. Many of us have suffered the consequences at some time in our lives when we were accused of something we did not do and were punished unjustly. Even though we were innocent of the infraction, the label of deviant might have stuck; and perhaps our parents, a school

labeling theory
A theory that describes how a label applied by society can affect an individual's self-perception and behavior.

7.1 KIDS in the NEWS

Did a Label Lead to a Shooting?

Can a single incident ruin a child's life and push him or her into a life of delinquency?

A Chicago shooting has some people wondering just that. In June 2006, Romarr Gipson, 15, and his 18-year-old stepbrother were charged with aggravated battery after they were shown on video shooting two men in a parked car. One victim was treated and released for a minor bullet wound, but the other victim was seriously wounded.

Eight years earlier, Romarr Gipson, then age 7, had the misfortune of being one of the youngest in U.S. history to be prosecuted for murder.[1] Gipson and an 8-year-old boy were falsely accused of killing an 11-year-old girl so that they could steal her bicycle. A month passed before the boys were cleared when tests showed that they couldn't have produced the semen found on the girl's clothing. An adult convicted sex offender was later found guilty of the murder and sentenced to life in prison.

Although Gipson's family received $2 million from the city, many who know him say the experience of being accused at such a young age irreparably damaged him. Gipson's attorney said Gipson wet his bed for several years, chewed his fingernails until they bled, and hid if he saw a police car approach.

The other boy who was accused never got into the legal trouble that Gipson has, but attorneys say he went from a social boy who got good grades in school to a teenager who's afraid to leave his house.[2]

Think About It

1. Did being labeled as a murderer at such a young age cause Gipson's later behavior? What about the other boy?

2. Should special care be taken not to label juveniles, especially in such difficult circumstances as that which Gipson and the other boy faced?

1 Monica Davey, "Falsely Accused of Murder at Age 7, a 15-Year-Old Is Back In Court On New Charges," *New York Times,* June 19, 2006, section A, p. 12.
2 Don Babwin, "Some Wonder If False Murder Accusation Led U.S. Teen Down Troubled Path," Associated Press, June 20, 2006.

principal, or a juvenile court judge applied a punishment that hurt us just as much as if we were actually guilty of the offense of which we were unjustly accused.[55] See Kids in the News 7.1 for an example of how a label might affect a child.

Edwin Lemert added another dimension to labeling theory by distinguishing between primary and secondary deviance.[56] **Primary deviance** is the label that is placed on the delinquent or offender once he or she is caught breaking the law. Primary deviance is a useful tool for society because it identifies offenders or those who are prone to crime. For instance, prison inmates often must wear distinctive clothing so that they can be distinguished from prison staff. Likewise, we keep track of offenders with databases that law enforcement officers can consult when they make contact with citizens. Those with prior records or outstanding warrants can be identified and treated appropriately. Sometimes the effect of primary deviance can appear to be extreme. Those with sex-offense records are subject to having their neighbors and co-workers know about their past. And even though they might have been to prison and "done their time" or "paid their dues," the label of sex offender sticks to them and prevents them from fully reintegrating into society. Howard Becker referred to this process as a "master status" that overwhelms all other statuses of the individual.[57] Regardless of the fact that the individual is a productive worker, good spouse, reliable taxpayer, church official, or PTA president, the label of sex offender means that society will treat him or her as a deviant, pervert, or dangerous criminal.

In many ways, the concept of **secondary deviance** is more problematic than primary deviance because it has a long-lasting effect on an individual's psychology. For instance, children who are told they are stupid, lazy, or ugly might internalize these labels and come to believe them as defining characteristics of their identities. When we say they internalize these labels, we mean that they come to believe them and to begin to act them out. Consequently, the youth who is told he is lazy might quit trying to study, and the one who is told she is stupid might drop out of school. These labels can have long-lasting effects on how young people see themselves, and inaccurate or careless labeling on the part of parents and school officials can be deleterious.

Labeling theory has implications for juvenile justice system policy. By limiting the degree to which young people are inserted into the system and the degree to which labels are applied to them, the degree to which they come to view themselves as deviant can also be limited. Edwin Schur, in his book *Radical Nonintervention*, contends that the best thing that can be done for many minor offenders is to ignore their deviant acts.[58] By not having their behavior treated as serious, the offending youths don't attach their self-concepts to their actions and will often simply outgrow their misbehavior. Just about every person has committed behaviors for which he or she could have been brought into the juvenile or criminal justice systems. By not getting arrested, processed, and punished, many law-abiding adults escaped the primary and secondary deviance processes and have gone on to be respectable citizens.

Labeling theory also recognizes that there are positive labels. The child who is encouraged to excel will sometimes perform to a degree well past previous expectations. The self-fulfilling prophecy concept is subject to such positives that it's unwise to underestimate the potential of those who truly believe in their ability to succeed.

Shaming Theory

Labeling theory forms the foundation for the more recent emphasis on **shaming**. Shaming is an old concept that is concerned with applying a mark or stigma on disgraced individuals. One of the most recognized examples of shaming is from Nathaniel Hawthorne's novel *The Scarlet Letter*, in which Hester Prynne is forced to wear a red letter *A* on her clothing to mark her as an adulteress. The shame is expected to deter not the offender, who has already committed the offense, but others. However, this isn't always the case. According to John Braithwaite, an important

---

primary deviance

A term from labeling theory that describes the label that society places on the offender.

secondary deviance

A term from labeling theory that describes the labels that individuals internalize and come to believe as accurate.

shaming

The act of applying a mark or stigma on disgraced individuals.

distinction must be made about shaming. First, there is stigmatizing shaming, which has a negative effect on the offender's behavior. Those who suffer from stigmatizing shaming might join deviant subculture groups, such as street gangs, who engage in crime.[59]

Stigmatizing shaming has made something of a comeback in recent years, with judges engaging in what they think is creative sentencing by requiring offenders to march in front of the courthouse or in front of an establishment from which they have stolen wearing a sign that proclaims their offenses. The idea behind stigmatizing shaming is to embarrass and humiliate the offenders so that they don't repeat their

---

7.1   *CrossCurrents*

It's a Dirty Shame

The use of shaming in the criminal and juvenile courts has made something of a comeback in recent years. Once used extensively in the colonial period when offenders were placed in stocks and subjected to the ridicule and abuse of other citizens, modern judges now use shaming techniques as a form of creative sentencing in which the punishment is supposed to fit the crime. A few examples illustrate this recurring sentencing practice.

- In Texas in 2003, Judge Buddie Hahn gave an abusive father a choice between spending 30 nights in jail or 30 nights sleeping in the doghouse where prosecutors alleged the man had forced his 11-year-old stepson to sleep.

- In Georgia, Judge Sidney Nation suspended almost all of Brenton Jay Raffensperger's 7-year sentence for cocaine possession and driving under the influence in exchange for his promise to buy a coffin and keep it in his home to remind him of the costs of drug addiction.

- In Ohio, a municipal judge, Michael Cicconetti, cut a 120-day jail sentence down to 45 days for two teens who, on Christmas Eve 2002, defaced a statue of Jesus that they stole from a church's nativity scene. In exchange, the pair had to deliver a new statue to the church and march through town with a donkey and a sign reading "Sorry for the Jackass Offense."

- In North Carolina in 2002, Judge James Honeycutt ordered four young offenders who broke into a school and did $60,000 in damage to wear signs around their necks in public that read "I Am a Juvenile Criminal." One, a 14-year-old girl, appealed, and Honeycutt was reversed.[1]

Judges engage in this type of creative sentencing for a couple of reasons. First, it's cheap. Compared to sending someone to prison, jail, or a juvenile facility, the cost of these alternative sentences can usually be absorbed by the local probation department and treated as an additional condition of probation. A second reason for these sentences is that they are very public and give the rest of society the idea that the criminal and juvenile justice systems are tough on crime. The hope is that the public humiliation of offenders will deter others from committing similar offenses.

Finally, a third reason these are popular forms of sentencing is that they give the judges visibility and notoriety. In jurisdictions that elect judges, these sentences are one of the few ways that judges can get the public's attention in positive ways. For instance, in Texas, Judge Ted Poe has used creative sentencing to such an extent that his sentences are known as "Poe-tic justice," and he is called the "King of Shame." Judge Poe used this sentencing practice so effectively that he's now a member of the House of Representatives.

Although there might be a place for creative sentencing that provides an educative effect, some scholars contend that sentences that emphasize humiliation are counterproductive and undesirable.[2] Certainly, when dealing with juvenile delinquents, the court must be careful to consider how labeling and shaming can have negative effects on youths with few social bonds to conventional society.

Think About It

1. Is shaming an advisable sentencing option?
2. Is there a danger that shaming will backfire and cause the offender to engage in future delinquency because of the humiliation?
3. What shaming techniques do you think would be advisable but not harmful?
4. Is shaming letting the delinquent off easy?

1 Jonathan Turley, "Shame on You," *Washington Post,* September 18, 2005, p. B03. Online at www.washingtonpost.com/wp-dyn/content/article/2005/09/17/AR2005091700064.html.
2 Dan Markel, "Are Shaming Punishments Beautifully Retributive? Retributivism and the Implications for the Alternative Sanctions Debate," *Vanderbilt Law Review* 54 (2001):2157.

behavior.[60] The return of some jurisdictions to making prison inmates wear black and white striped outfits is another example of efforts to employ stigmatizing shaming techniques. Stigmatizing shaming is what Harold Garfinkel terms "status degradation ceremonies" that, although designed to deter individuals from committing future crimes, actually so alienate them from conventional society that they end up pursuing crime as a career.[61] For a discussion of stigmatizing shaming, see Crosscurrents 7.1.

Braithwaite, who is critical of stigmatizing shaming, suggests a more positive way to employ labeling theory to devise policies to reduce crime. According to Braithwaite, shaming can have a reintegrative function. If done right, shaming can help the offender become a productive member of the community again and can help the community accept and forgive the offender. **Reintegrative shaming** is particularly appropriate for youths because it's done in an informal setting. Rather than stigmatizing the youth in an open courtroom with the media recording the event, reintegrative shaming occurs with the youth being confronted by those in his or her social network. Parents, family members, school officials, community representatives, local police officers, and anyone else connected with the youth's problems might be included in the hearing, where all are involved in crafting a solution to the problem. When the youth's input is included in the decision, it's presumed the youth will have a greater commitment to seeing that solution succeed.

Through reintegrative shaming, the offender can truly examine his or her culpability in the unlawful behavior and make restitution, apology, and amends to victims and society. This principle is the basis for the restorative justice programs that attempt to repair the harm that crime does to the relationships between offenders and victims. How effective reintegrative shaming can be in preventing future criminal behavior depends a great deal on other processes, such as the quality of follow-up services. A status degradation ceremony is unlikely to be conclusive on its own. However, there is potential for reintegrative shaming applied at a turning point in a youth's life to be useful and effective.

reintegrative shaming
A form of justice in which an offender is confronted and dealt with by those in his or her social network.

SUMMARY

1. This chapter covers four families of sociological theories: social structure, social process, subcultural, and social reaction.

2. At the turn of the 20th century, University of Chicago sociologists sought to understand crime and deviant behavior in the light of the social disorganization they perceived in the city. The sociologists built on Ferdinand Tönnies's comparisons in Germany of close-knit rural communities (*Gemeinschaft*) to the impersonal mass society of urban communities (*Gesellschaft*).

3. Burgess theorized that cities develop in concentric circles, growing toward outer areas. As the urban area expands toward rural areas, each zone develops certain characteristics, such as an area of working-class homes, affluent homes, commuter neighborhoods, and industrial zones.

4. Building on Burgess's work, Shaw and McKay believed that the core values of society would be strained by persistent poverty, rapid population growth, population heterogeneity, and population movement. They hypothesized that delinquent rates would be higher in zones that were experiencing instability and lower in zones that were stable.

5. Sampson and Wilson extended Shaw and McKay's thesis by considering race. Sampson and Wilson rejected the claims that the culture developed by the inner city is an easy way to explain crime and that there is little society can do about it.

6. Sampson, Raudenbush, and Earls envisioned a concept called collective efficacy, which is a group's shared belief of the extent to which it can successfully complete a task.

7. Some theories assert that crime is learned: differential association and social learning theory (people learn crime from others) and techniques of neutralization (youths who break the law seek to explain away their behavior).

8. Akers developed his social learning theory of crime across four dimensions: differential association, definitions, differential reinforcement, and imitation.

9. The defense mechanisms that youths use in techniques of neutralization are denial of responsibility, denial of injury, denial of victim, condemnation of condemners, and appeal to higher loyalties.

10. A popular social process theory is anomie or strain theory. Anomie is personal anxiety or isolation produced by rapidly shifting moral values. Merton's strain theory refers to the personal strain caused by being excluded from economic rewards.

11. Merton's five modes of adaptation to strain are conformity, innovation, ritual, retreat, and rebellion.

12. According to Agnew, the types of stress that are sources of strain are strain caused by the disjunction between just or fair outcomes and actual outcomes, strain caused by the removal of positively valued stimuli from the individual, and strain caused by negative stimuli.

13. Five subcultural theories deal with how youths often break the law in the company of friends. These theories deal with delinquent boys, differential opportunity, the lower class, the subculture of violence, and the code of the street.

14. Social reaction theories consider how behavior is influenced by the reactions of others.

15. Labeling theory describes how a label or tag applied by society can affect an individual's self-perception and behavior. An important idea of labeling theory is that no behavior is intrinsically deviant, but it is subject to the label placed on it by those whose values have been adopted by the larger culture. A second important idea is that actual behavior isn't as important as the perception of the behavior.

16. Lemert distinguished between primary and secondary deviance in labeling theory. Primary deviance is the label that is placed on the offender. Secondary deviance is the label that individuals internalize.

17. The implications that labeling theory has for juvenile justice system policy concern limiting the degree to which labels are applied to young offenders so that the degree to which they consider themselves as deviant is also limited.

18. Shaming, which is related to labeling theory, is applying a mark or stigma on disgraced individuals. Reintegrative shaming involves the youth being confronted by those in his or her social network who are involved in the crafting of the solution to the problem.

REVIEW QUESTIONS

1. What is the difference between *Gemeinschaft* and *Gesellschaft*?

2. What is Ernest Burgess's theory of how cities grow?

3. How is social cohesion related to collective efficacy?

4. What are microtheories? macrotheories?

5. What two things did Sutherland contend that young people learn from their associations with deviant others?

6. What are the four dimensions of Akers's social learning theory of crime?

7. What defense mechanisms are commonly used in techniques of neutralization?

8. What is normlessness?

9. What are the six issues pertaining to the focal concerns of the lower class?

10. What is shaming? How does it compare to reintegrative shaming?

ADDITIONAL READINGS

Akers, Ronald L., and Christine S. Sellers. *Criminological Theory: Introduction, Evaluation, and Application*, 4th ed. Los Angeles: Roxbury, 2004.

Daly, Kathleen, and Lisa Maher. *Criminology at the Crossroads*. New York: Oxford University Press, 1998.

Moyer, Imogene. *Criminological Theories: Traditional and Non-Traditional Voices and Themes*. Thousand Oaks, CA: Sage, 2001.

Schwendinger, Julia R., and Herman Schwendinger. *Adolescent Subcultures and Delinquency*. New York: Praeger, 1985.

Warr, Mark. *Companions in Crime: The Social Aspects of Criminal Conduct*. New York: Cambridge University Press, 2002.

Williams, Frank P., III, and Marilyn D. McShane. *Criminological Theory: Selected Classic Readings*, 2nd ed. Cincinnati, OH: Anderson, 1998.

ENDNOTES

1. Lincoln Steffens, *The Autobiography of Lincoln Steffens* (New York: Harcourt, Brace, Jovanovich, 1931). Steffens was a muckraking journalist who has colorfully described the social and political upheavals at the dawning of the 20th century. This book can be read profitably on a number of levels. In addition to being entertaining, it provides a detailed picture of the problems and possibilities for youth at the time.

2. Ferdinand Tönnies, *Community and Society* (1887; reprint, Rutgers, NJ: Transaction, 1988).

3. Ernest W. Burgess, "The Growth of the City," in Robert E. Park, Ernest W. Burgess, and Roderick D. McKenzie, eds. *The City* (Chicago: University of Chicago Press, 1925), 47–62.

4. Clifford R. Shaw and Henry D. McKay, "Juvenile Delinquency and Urban Areas" in Francis T. Cullen and Robert Agnew, eds. *Criminological Theory: Past to Present*, 3rd ed. (Los Angeles: Roxbury, 2006), 109.

5. Clifford R. Shaw and Henry D. McKay, "Juvenile Delinquency and Urban Areas," in Francis T. Cullen and Robert Agnew, eds., *Criminological Theory: Past to Present* (Los Angeles: Roxbury, 2006), 109.

6. Robert J. Sampson and William Julius Wilson, "A Theory of Race, Crime and Urban Inequality," in Francis T. Cullen and Robert Agnew, eds. *Criminological Theory: Past to Present* (Los Angeles: Roxbury, 2006), 111–117. See note 5.

7. Ibid., 114–115.

8. Robert J. Sampson, Stephen W. Raudenbush, and Felton Earls, "Collective Efficacy and Crime," in Francis T. Cullen and Robert Agnew, eds. *Criminological Theory: Past to Present*, 3rd ed. (Los Angeles: Roxbury, 2003), 119–123.

9. Robert J. Sampson, Jeffrey D. Morenoff, and Felton Earls, "Beyond Social Capital: Spatial Dynamics of Collective Efficacy for Children," *American Sociological Review* 64 (1999):633–660.

10. Sampson, Raudenbush, and Earls (see note 8), p. 122.

11. Delbert S. Elliott and Scott Menard, "Delinquent Friends and Delinquent Behavior: Temporal and Developmental Patterns," in *Delinquency and Crime: Current Theories* (New York: Cambridge University Press, 1996), 28–67.

12. L. Rowell Huesmann et al., "Longitudinal Relations Between Children's Exposure to TV Violence and Their Aggressive and Violent Behavior in Young Adulthood," *Developmental Psychology* 39 (2003):201–221.

13. Edwin H. Sutherland, Donald R. Cressey, and David F. Luckenbill, *Principle of Criminology*, 11th ed. (Dix Hill, NY: General Hall, 1992).

14. Cullen and Agnew (see note 5), pp. 125–126.

15. Edwin H. Sutherland and Donald R. Cressey, "A Theory of Differential Association," in Francis T. Cullen and Robert Agnew, eds. *Criminological Theory: Past to Present* (Los Angeles: Roxbury, 2003), 132.

16. Robert L. Burgess and Ronald L. Akers, "A Differential Association-Reinforcement Theory of Criminal Behavior," *Social Problems* 14 (1966):128–147.

17. Ronald L. Akers, "A Social Learning Theory of Crime," in Francis T. Cullen and Robert Agnew, eds. *Criminological Theory: Past to Present* (Los Angeles: Roxbury, 2003), 142–153.

18. Ronald L. Akers and Gary Jensen, "Social Learning Theory and the Explanation of Crime: A Guide for the New Century," *Advances in Criminological Theory* 11 (Somerset, NJ: Transaction, 2002).

19. Frank P. Williams III and Marilyn D. McShane, *Criminological Theory*, 4th ed. (Upper Saddle River, NJ: Prentice Hall, 2004), 227.

20. Gresham M. Sykes and David Matza, "Techniques of Neutralization: A Theory of Delinquency," *American Sociological Review* 22 (1957):664–670.

21. Alan M. Dershowitz, *The Abuse Excuse and Other Cop-Outs, Sob Stories, and Evasions of Responsibility* (Boston: Back Bay Books, 2000).

22. Robert Agnew, "The Techniques of Neutralization and Violence," *Criminology* 32 (1994):555–580.

23. John R. Fuller and Marc L. LaFountain, "Performance-Enhancing Drugs in Sport: A Different Form of Drug Abuse," *Adolescence* 22 (1987).

24. Emile Durkheim, *Suicide: A Study in Sociology* (1897; reprint, New York: Free Press, 1951).

25. Robert K. Merton, "Social Structure and Anomie," *American Sociological Review* 3 (1938):672–682.

26. Dorothy Meier and Wendell Bell, "Anomie and Differential Access to the Achievement of Life Goals," *American Sociological Review* 26 (1959):753–758.

27. Robert Agnew, "Foundation for a General Strain Theory of Crime and Delinquency," *Criminology* 30 (1992):47–87.

28. Robert Agnew, "Building on the Foundation of General Strain Theory: Specifying the Types of Strain Most Likely to Lead to Crime and Delinquency," *Journal of Research in Crime and Delinquency* 38 (2001):319–361; see also Velmer S. Burton and Francis T. Cullen, "The Empirical Status of Strain Theory," *Journal of Crime and Justice* 15 (1992):1–30.

29. Emile Durkheim, *The Rules of the Sociological Method*, trans. Sarah A. Solovay and John Mueller (New York: Free Press, 1885), reprinted 1965.

30. Albert Reiss, Jr., "Delinquency and the Failure of Personal and Social Controls," *American Sociological Review* 16 (1951):196–207.

31. Walter C. Reckless, *The Crime Problem* (New York: Appleton-Century-Crofts, 1955).

32. Walter C. Reckless, Simon Dinitz, and Ellen Murray, "Self-Concept as an Insulator Against Delinquency," *American Sociological Review* 21 (1956):744–756.

33. Travis Hirschi, *Causes of Delinquency* (Berkeley: University of California Press, 1969).

34. Frank P. Williams III, *Imagining Criminology: An Alternative Paradigm* (New York: Garland, 1999).

35. Albert K. Cohen, *Delinquent Boys: The Culture of the Gang* (New York: Free Press, 1955).

36. Ibid., 86.

37. Albert L. Rhodes and Albert J. Reiss, "Apathy, Truancy, and Delinquency as an Adaptation to School Failure," *Social Forces* 48 (1969):12–22.

38. Richard A. Cloward and Lloyd E. Ohlin, *Delinquency and Opportunity: A Theory of Delinquent Gangs* (New York: Free Press, 1960).

39. Ibid., 26–27.

40. Roy Fisher, "Borstal Recall Delinquency and the Cloward–Ohlin Theory of Criminal Subcultures," *British Journal of Criminology* 10 (1970):52–63.

41. Walter B. Miller, "Lower-Class Culture as a Generating Milieu of Gang Delinquency," *Journal of Social Issues* 14 (1958):5–19.

42. Wilson R. Palacios, "Side by Side: An Ethnographic Study of a Miami Gang," *Journal of Gang Research* 4 (1996):27–38.

43. Gerald D. Robin, "Gang Member Delinquency: Its Extent, Sequence and Typology," *Journal of Criminal Law, Criminology and Police Science* 55 (1964):59–69.

44. Marvin E. Wolfgang and Franco Ferracuti, *The Subculture of Violence: Towards an Integrated Theory in Criminology* (London: Tavistock, 1967).

45. Michael Smith, "Hockey Violence: A Test of the Violent Subculture Hypothesis," *Social Problems* 27 (1979):235–247.

46. Tom W. Rice and Carolyn R. Goldman, "Another Look at the Subculture of Violence Thesis: Who Murders Whom and Under What Circumstances," *Sociological Spectrum* 14 (1994):371–384.

47. James Gilligan, *Violence: Reflections on a National Epidemic* (New York: Random House, 1996). See especially Chapter 3, "Violent Action as Symbolic Language: Myth, Ritual, and Tragedy," pp. 57–88.

48. Elijah Anderson, *Code of the Street: Decency, Violence, and the Moral Life of the Inner City* (New York: Norton, 1999).

49. Elijah Anderson, "The Code of the Streets," in Francis T. Cullen and Robert Agnew, eds. *Criminological Theory: Past to Present* (Los Angeles: Roxbury, 2003), 162.

50. Ibid., 91–93.

51. Robert J. Sampson and Dawn Jeglum Bartusch, *Attitudes Toward Crime: Police, and the Law: Individual and Neighborhood Differences* (Washington, DC: U.S. Department of Justice, National Institute of Justice, 1999).

52. Charles Murray, *Losing Ground: American Social Policy, 1950–1980* (New York: Basic Books, 1984).

53. Frank Tannenbaum, *Crime and the Community* (Boston: Ginn, 1938).

54. Howard S. Becker, *Outsiders: Studies in the Sociology of Deviance* (New York: Free Press, 1963).

55. Williams and McShane (see note 19), p. 145.

56. Edwin M. Lemert, *Social Pathology: A Systematic Approach to the Theory of Sociopathic Behavior* (New York: McGraw-Hill, 1951).

57. Becker (see note 54), p. 9.

58. Edwin M. Schur, *Radical Non-Intervention: Rethinking the Delinquency Problem* (Upper Saddle River, NJ: Prentice Hall, 1973).

59. John Braithwaite, *Crime, Shame, and Reintegration* (Cambridge, UK: University of Cambridge Press, 1989).

60. David P. Farrington, "The Effects of Public Labeling," *British Journal of Criminology* 17 (1977):112–125.

61. Harold Garfinkel, "Conditions of Successful Degradation Ceremonies," *American Journal of Sociology* 61 (1956):420–424.

What are the major critical
theories of crime and delinquency?

Why are life-course theories
of delinquency so prevalent
in modern times?

How do integrated theories
explain delinquency?

CHAPTER 8

Critical, Life-Course, and Integrated Theories

In Chapter 7, we studied the foundational sociological theories that have been used to explain crime and delinquency. Now let's turn to other, more recent sociological theories that extend the sociological perspective to explain why individuals and groups violate the law. This chapter covers three types of theories. The first type of theory covered is critical theory. We use the term *critical* to include types of explanations that are sometimes called *conflict, Marxist,* or *radical.*[1] Although the significant distinctions among these theories would become apparent with further study, they are presented here as critical theories.

The second type of theory we will examine is life-course theory. These important theories explain not only delinquency, but they also link early crime to the patterns of offending that occur as offenders move through adulthood and into old age. These changing patterns of crime are linked in interesting ways.

Finally, we will study attempts to integrate theories of crime and delinquency. Because most theories explain only a limited amount or type of crime, theorists have sought to combine several theories under an organizing perspective to account for a wider variation of deviant behavior and to give a more holistic view of crime and delinquency.

CRITICAL THEORIES

Many students are uncomfortable with critical theories because the theories have an unfavorable view of economic systems, gender relations, and the way that some groups use their power to control other groups. Critical theories challenge students to examine their lifestyles, values, and histories to understand how crime happens and is dealt with. Critical theories of crime and delinquency do not distinguish between "bad people" (offenders) and "good people" (citizens).

Often, when studying critical theories, students must face the prospect that their behavior and economic and social interests are part of the crime problem. On reflection, some students might remember the axiom "We have met the enemy and he is us." Cullen and Agnew identify five central themes of critical theories that help to differentiate them from other types of sociological theories of crime and delinquency.[2]

1. The concepts of inequality and power are integral to any understanding of crime and its control. The criminal justice system is part of the mechanism of the state that is controlled by powerful interests and used to enhance the benefits of those who control the institutions of society.

2. Crime is not a value-free concept, but a political concept. Those who control the political system define what is and is not considered a crime. The behaviors of the impoverished are more often considered crimes and are dealt with more severely by the criminal justice system than are the actions of the wealthy and powerful.

3. The criminal justice system ultimately serves the interests of the capitalist class by enforcing laws in a discriminatory manner that favors the wealthy and hurts the impoverished. Further, those working in the system will frequently break the law themselves, often with impunity, to protect the interests of the powerful. The corruption of public officials, wiretapping of protestors, and covert actions to undermine other governments are examples of this official misconduct.

4. Capitalism is a system of economics that causes a large degree of crime. The needs of the poor are ignored under capitalism, and the lax government regulation of businesses results in crimes against those without power, as well as the deterioration of the public environment.

5. The solution to crime, according to critical theories, is the creation of a more equitable society. Many critical criminologists believe that they should take an activist role in exposing the contradictions of capitalism and not simply be armchair theorists.

These five themes, although central to the critical study of crime and delinquency, don't encompass all the varied critiques that modern theorists have developed. This chapter will also include some critical theories that are based not so much in economics as they are in culture. Race, age, gender, lifestyle, and many other organizing principles are potential targets for the critical criminologist. Here we will concentrate on a few of the better-known perspectives that have been used to consider crime. Of particular interest is how these critiques of economic systems and culture affect the delinquency problem. Sometimes it's difficult to make the link between the broader concerns of the political, economic, and social structure and the reasons that individual youths end up in the juvenile justice system.[3] Critical theories can help explain why it always seems that the same sort of youngster ends up in trouble.

Marxist Theory

The political philosophy of Karl Marx has had a great deal of influence on economics and politics for the past century. Although we won't deal with the global dislocations caused by communism, such as the rise and fall of the Soviet Union and the changing economic nature of China, these are important aspects of the universal influence that Marxist thought has had on the world. Here the discussion is limited to the implications of Marx's thinking for the problems of crime and delinquency. Although Marx himself wrote very little about crime, his ideas have been extended by many other scholars, and it's fair to say that this line of thinking has made important contributions to our understanding of why people break the law and, more significantly, how society responds.[4]

At one level, Marx's explanation of crime is simple. He divides society into two parts, the **bourgeoisie**, who control and own the means of production, and the **proletariat**, the workers who are exploited by this economic system. A key idea of Marxism is that the working class labors under a **false consciousness**, meaning that they believe that such an unequal economic arrangement is legitimate. According to Marx, only when the workers seize the means of production and establish a socialist state where people "work to their ability and get paid according to their needs" will a fair system of government be established.[5]

Willem Bonger was one of the first scholars to link Marxism and crime. Bonger saw egoism as the reason people broke the law in capitalist societies. Because individuals must look out for their own interests and their family's interests, a certain amount of selfish competition is inherent in the system, and concern for others' welfare is secondary. According to Bonger, impoverished people living in a capitalist state are stimulated to break the law for two reasons. First, the impoverished break the law to survive. Because wealth and resources are unevenly distributed, the impoverished will break the law, particularly committing property offenses, to secure enough resources to meet their immediate needs and provide for their families.[6]

The second reason Bonger believed that impoverished people are more likely to break the law in a capitalist society is because wealth is the measuring rod by which people are judged. In a society such as the United States, individuals' contributions aren't valued so much as what they have acquired. People are thus encouraged to be manipulative and deceptive to accumulate wealth. The drug dealer or stock-market inside trader might live in the same neighborhoods and drive the same model of automobiles as those who are successful in legitimate ways. In a capitalist society that judges people on their possessions, the poker player might be more highly regarded than the nurse, and the pimp might be financially more secure than the teacher.

According to William Chambliss, crime serves to divert our attention from the exploitive nature of capitalism and focus it on the offenses of impoverished people. Because the wealthy and powerful can ensure that their interests are encoded in the criminal law, it's the street crime of impoverished property offenders that gets most of the legal system's attention. Chambliss contends that the inherent inequalities of the capitalist system and the privileged position of the ruling class go unnoticed and

bourgeoisie
In Marxist theory, those who own property and the means of production.

proletariat
In Marxist theory, the working class.

false consciousness
In Marxist theory, the belief that the arrangement of the bourgeoisie owning the means of production and the proletariat working for the interests of the bourgeoisie is legitimate.

Impoverished people sometimes break the law in order to survive, an age-old behavior that wealthy classes often find threatening. This illustration, *Juveniles Stealing Boots*, is from the 1872 book *Dangerous Classes of New York*.

(© Bettmann/CORBIS All Rights Reserved)

that the powerful escape the severe sanctions that are imposed on the lower classes for less harmful behaviors.[7]

Although poverty is linked to crime in capitalist societies, poverty itself is not viewed as the cause of crime. Raymond Michalowski points out that many impoverished societies have low crime rates. Crime becomes common when there is a vast difference between the impoverished and the wealthy. The relative deprivation that is felt by those without means and resources is more important than the actual deprivation.[8] In nations where there is not only a wide gap between the wealthy and the impoverished, but where that gap is visible and celebrated, crime is to be expected. When young people watch television programs such as *Lifestyles of the Rich and Famous* and see ostentatious displays of wealth, it makes their own meager living standard not only seem insufficient, but embarrassing.

Marxist criminology has its critics. The perspective has been faulted on many points by both traditional criminologists and critical criminologists. Traditional criminologists contend that Marxism makes some fundamental assumptions about human nature that don't stand up to scrutiny.[9] People don't always act in their economic interests, and to assume that they do reduces the argument to pure economics.

Another criticism of Marxism is that it suggests a utopian, moralistic society. Could the United States jettison capitalism and adopt the ideal socialist state that Marxism suggests? Would this reduce the amount and severity of crime? Critics of Marxism aren't confident that the devil you don't know is better than the devil you do. Critical criminologists worry that Marxist criminologists romanticize criminals and the idea of a revolutionary class. Additionally, the idea that we all live under a false consciousness and can't recognize the boot of oppression on our neck is problematic according to many critical criminologists.[10]

Our discussion of Marxism and its relationship to crime has been necessarily brief and inadequate. There is a long and rich development of literature in sociological and political science circles that extends the ideas presented here. The primary concern with this discussion has been to point out the contextual nature of crime and

This poster from the Russian Revolution attacks the "Tsar, priest, and rich man" who ride over the bodies of workers. According to Michalowski, crime becomes common when there is a vast difference between the impoverished and the wealthy. *(Courtesy The Granger Collection, New York)*

delinquency. It isn't enough to consider why a young person has broken the law when the reasons might be mediated by broad social forces beyond the youth's recognition. Like a fish that doesn't realize it's in water, a youth might not comprehend that the reasons he or she breaks the law are because of the pressures of living in a capitalist society.

Left Realism

Many critics of Marxist criminology believe that it romanticizes both offenders and the revolutionary nature of the perspective. In many ways, the idea that the powerful control society and use its laws and institutions to benefit themselves is an attractive perspective that tends to portray impoverished people as noble and offenders as Robin Hood–type figures who steal only from the wealthy. Left-realism theory, however, argues that this perspective is not only fundamentally flawed, but is also harmful to the people it seeks to benefit.

Left realism contends that the idealism of Marxist criminology sacrifices the interests of impoverished people for the interests of lower-class offenders.[11] Offenders most often victimize those who are in the same social class. When a lower-class youth burglarizes a home, it's usually a neighbor who is equally as impoverished. The major issue according to left-realist criminologists is that other liberal and critical criminologists are reluctant to blame the offender and instead blame the victim and the system.[12]

left realism
A theory that considers mainstream criminology to underestimate the victimization of the poor and women and is concerned with why the poor commit offenses mainly against one another.

Much of the money on incarceration and juvenile detention might be better spent on alleviating the poverty that contributes to crime. Here children play around a tree trunk in the South Bronx, New York. *(Courtesy C. Vergara, Photo Researchers, Inc.)*

The primary focus of left realists is to ensure that the impoverished aren't further victimized by the criminal justice system and the way that criminologists explain crime. Left realists favor developing social policy over criminal policy. Alleviating the problems of poverty might give impoverished youths fewer reasons to break the law and give impoverished people the means to protect themselves against predators. Left realists believe that empowering impoverished communities helps develop meaningful relationships that can prevent crime and change the outlook of potential delinquents.

Left-realist criminologists argue for short-term but immediate reforms that will reduce class inequality and the problems of those without power. According to Walter DeKeseredy, several activities could help lower poverty and unemployment rates, which, in turn, would curb crime and build stronger communities.[13]

- Job creation and training programs, including publicly supported community-oriented programs
- A higher minimum wage and universal health care
- Government-sponsored day care so that impoverished single parents can work without the bulk of their paychecks going to pay for child care
- Housing assistance, which enables abused women and children to escape their environments without ending up destitute
- Introducing entrepreneurial skills into high school curriculums

A major left-realist concern is that government agencies and the justice system, in their efforts to control crime, further victimize the impoverished people who are most affected by crime. Although impoverished people commit many street offenses, most are law-abiding and are overwhelmingly the victims of crime. By instigating "tough on crime" measures, the government often makes the situation worse for the victims, rather than better. The money spent fighting crime and locking up impoverished children could be better spent on alleviating the poverty that contributes to crime.[14]

Finally, it should be noted that left-realism criminology argues for the support of impoverished women and children. The patriarchal nature of family relations in which the father and husband has financial, emotional, and physical control over

These little girls live in a blighted section of Los Angeles, California. *(Courtesy Joseph Sohm; ChromoSohm Inc., Corbis/Bettmann)*

women and children is deemed problematic, especially when this control is supported by government policies.[15] Left realism deromanticizes the idea of the "revolutionary bandit," primarily because the victims of crime are usually family members or neighbors. For a look at the relationship between wealth and justice, see Kids in the News 8.1.

Critical-Race Theory

Critical criminologists look at the problems of crime and justice through a number of lenses. For example, feminist theorists see gender as problematic (the ideas and theories of feminists will be dealt with in substantial detail in Chapter 9). Those concerned with social class have used left realism and Marxist critiques to examine the issues of crime and delinquency. As we will see, **critical-race theory** focuses on how racial issues have determined the quality of justice that has been available to people of color in North America.

Critical-race theory is an extension of the field of critical legal studies. Critical legal studies consider how the law has allowed those with power to make and enforce statutes that favor themselves and work against the poor.[16] The two perspectives share many characteristics, but critical-race theorists contend that race is a dominant factor in the way many legal systems dispense justice.[17]

For example, the treatment of people of color has moved through several phases, from ownership of human beings to Jim Crow laws to overt and covert forms of discrimination. Race is at the heart of how the legal system treats citizens according to critical-race theorists. One need only look at issues such as racial profiling, interracial dating and marriage, and racial hoaxes such as the Susan Smith case to comprehend how race is a primary determinant of how the legal system treats individuals.[18] One distinguishing feature of critical-race theory, and something that has subjected this perspective to a great deal of criticism, is the types of methodology that support

critical-race theory

A theory that asserts that race is central to law and social justice issues.

The Root of All Justice

The U.S. legal system has done much to separate the need for money from the attainment of justice, or at least a fair trial, but unfortunately the two are still closely related. A defendant with enough money to hire a team of expensive lawyers has a much better chance of never seeing the inside of a cell than a defendant who must make do with the overworked lawyer that the court provides. This isn't to say that there aren't some excellent public defenders, but that lawyers for the indigent and poor are often overworked and underpaid. Sometimes they are subject to the political vagaries of a particular jurisdiction, and sometimes they are just incompetent.[1]

Often the party that suffers from inadequate public defense is the state. In Massachusetts in 2004, impoverished defendants were being released or not tried at all as their appointed lawyers refused the cases because of the low pay. One county was forced to release impoverished defendants who had been jailed for more than seven days without seeing a lawyer.[2]

The situation affects juveniles as much as it does adults, if not more. Some jurisdictions automatically consider juvenile defendants indigent because, as juveniles, they are without an income of their own. In such cases, the judge typically will instruct the juvenile's parents or guardians to find a lawyer or appoint one if the parents or guardians cannot do so.

However, in 2004, an Indiana county public defender's office began turning away indigent juvenile defendants because there weren't enough lawyers to handle the caseload. Juvenile court judges had to appoint private attorneys for indigent youths. A county official said that the public defender's office needed 13 more lawyers to handle the caseload.[3] In 2005, a Tennessee county public defender's office sought to do the same thing but was blocked by a juvenile court judge.[4]

According to a 2006 report from the National Juvenile Defender Center, in Indiana nearly a quarter of the arrested juveniles interviewed for the study had waived their right to an attorney, often because their parents determined that they couldn't afford one.[5] A lack of funding also ensured that the public defender's office was careful about taking up the slack.

The lack of adequate funding in many (Indiana) jurisdictions has clearly had a significant impact upon the practice of routine waiver. In one telling incident, an investigator observed a public defender sitting in a courtroom while child after child waived the right to an attorney. When the investigator approached the attorney about these waivers, the attorney indicated that accepting too many cases from juvenile court would place their public defender program in jeopardy of losing reimbursement funding, as they would exceed (Indiana Public Defender) Commission caseload standards.[6]

The situation varies from state to state. Texas doesn't guarantee a juvenile's right to court-appointed representation, with each county following different criteria for determining indigence. Also, the appointment of a lawyer doesn't relieve the obligation of the juvenile's parents to pay. According to the report, "One county even has a contempt call for parents who are delinquent in their payments to the court, which, according to a court administrator, 'really brings in money for the court; sometimes we even have to put parents in jail.'"[7]

Think About It

1. Should governments commit even more money to provide lawyers for juveniles who can't afford one?

2. Should all jurisdictions automatically consider juveniles as indigent or first consider the parents' ability to pay for legal representation?

1 Kit R. Roane, "When the Poor Go to Court," *U.S. News & World Report* 140, no. 3 (January 23, 2006): 34–35.
2 Tamara Race, "Reluctant Lawyers Worry Court Officials," *Patriot Ledger* (Quincy, MA), August 5, 2004, city edition, News, p. 1.
3 Associated Press, "Marion County Public Defender Stops Accepting Juvenile Clients," July 26, 2004.
4 Brian Lazenby, "Caseload Concerns Public Defender," *Chattanooga Times and Free Press*, May 1, 2006.
5 Ken Kusmer, "Study: Juveniles Routinely Waive Rights under Pressure," *Indianapolis Star*, April 12, 2006.
6 Elizabeth Gladden Kehoe and Kim Brooks Tandy, *Indiana: An Assessment of Access to Counsel & Quality of Representation in Delinquency Proceedings* (Washington, DC: National Juvenile Defender Center, 2006), 30–34. Online at www.njdc.info/pdf/Indiana%20Assessment.pdf.
7 Cathryn E. Stewart et al., *Selling Justice Short: Juvenile Indigent Defense in Texas* (Austin, TX: Texas Appleseed, 2000), 17. Online at www.njdc.info/pdf/TexasAssess.pdf.

its arguments. Critical-race theory makes no claims to be value free. Race, according to critical-race theorists, is a deciding factor in how individuals view justice. One example of how race is related to one's view of the criminal justice system is the reactions of blacks and whites to the outcome of the O. J. Simpson trial.[19] Polls have shown that how one viewed the fairness of the verdict was related to one's race.[20]

Although romanticized in the popular imagination, legends of the "revolutionary bandit" are often far more attractive than the truth. Here, Bonnie and Clyde, two revolutionary bandits of the 1930s, pose with a shotgun. *(Courtesy Corbis/Bettmann)*

Finally, critical-race theory has been faulted for the type of data that are used as evidence. Critical-race theory employs first-person narratives to enhance its arguments. This runs counter to the way many criminologists employ science and statistics to seek the truth. Additionally, critical-race theorists use allegories, storytelling, and imagined dialogues to illustrate important concepts. Critics of critical-race theory claim that these methods make the perspective more of an art than a science. Critical-race theorists would contend that this type of criticism is simply another example of how those with power define what gets counted as evidence and how truth can be revealed.[21]

For our purposes, we won't take a position on the veracity of the claims of critical-race studies or on the objections of its critics. Here we only aim to alert the reader to this interesting way to consider crime and delinquency.

Postmodern Criminology

Postmodern criminology provides a new and different way of considering crime and justice, because it is concerned primarily with change and how that change is perceived. Specifically, Bruce Arrigo invokes Einstein's theory of relativity to illustrate how postmodern thought can be used to explore delinquency and justice.[22] Here we will present a limited analysis of postmodernism in order to understand its relevance to criminological theory. The reader should be aware that in academic circles postmodernism is a powerful perspective that is used by many disciplines, particularly in literary criticism and legal and social theory. To some, postmodernism represents the worst case of academic mumbo-jumbo with its precise meanings and specialized language.[23] For others, postmodernism has opened up new ways of comprehending

postmodern criminology
A theory that considers justice, law, fairness, responsibility, and authority not to be absolute, but to be mediated by personal contexts.

social life in a complex world. Postmodern criminology is worth reviewing for the insights it can provide for a more informed study of crime.[24]

Postmodern thought would have us believe that there is no objective truth. What we think and why we think it depend on the social, political, religious, and economic context in which we live. We order the world according to models or paradigms into which we have sorted the knowledge that we believe to be true. For instance, one well-known ancient paradigm asserted Earth as the center of the universe, and ancient astronomers worked for centuries to prove that the sun is at the center of our solar system and the Earth is the center of little more than the human imagination.[25]

Our social and political life can also be informed by postmodern thought. According to postmodernism, our concepts of justice, law, fairness, responsibility, and authority are all affected by the context in which we live and therefore aren't absolute. To understand how our criminal and juvenile justice systems operate, it's useful to consider some of the ways in which postmodern thought can provide a different angle from which to observe how justice is determined in our era.

According to Arrigo, three key issues inform the postmodern and critical criminological enterprise.

- **The centrality of language**   Our language shapes our reality. That is, without language, we have little appreciation for the world around us. An offender entering prison must learn a new system of language to survive, and knowledge of prison argot (or lingo) is required to protect oneself. The ability to use and comprehend language puts some participants in the criminal justice system at a great advantage over others. In the courtroom, the legal-speak can become unintelligible to those without a law degree or experience watching criminal trials. Defendants are at the mercy of the court or their attorney when it comes to deciphering the legal procedures. The specialized system of discourse can have disastrous effects on those who fail to grasp the fine intricacies of language. Words such as *plea*, *continuance*, *objection*, and *stipulate* have meanings in the courtroom that are unknown to anyone who is unfamiliar with modern legal proceedings. According to Arrigo, the issues of language in criminology don't end at the courthouse.

- **Partial knowledge and provisional truth**   Often in criminal justice system interactions, the participants must act on incomplete knowledge and without the benefit of knowing the whole truth. For instance, when the police stop a girl at a bus station and question her about where she came from and whom she is planning to meet in the city, the police are concerned for the girl's safety and welfare. Because pimps and gangsters pick up many runaways at bus stations, it's reasonable for the police to question, detain, and ensure the girl's safety. This might mean contacting the girl's parents and sending her home. However, the police do this based on incomplete knowledge of the situation. One reason that young girls run away from home is because a relative or close friend is sexually abusing them. Running away is a reasonable response to a dangerous and volatile situation. The interaction with the police at the bus stop, therefore, is likely to be perceived differently by the girl than by the police. The resulting lies, deception, and miscommunication are tragic, because the police and the girl are working toward the same goal (her safety) without one understanding the other's perspective. Postmodern criminology would have us appreciate this dilemma and construct policies that would help train police officers to understand the contextual nature of their interactions with citizens.

- **Deconstruction, difference, and possibility**   Because language can be so problematic, postmodern criminologists argue that it's necessary to deconstruct the meanings and implications of any text (written or spoken) to decode the hidden implications. Deconstruction involves a close reading of situations to uncover what biases, hidden values, or contradictory beliefs lie under the surface of the appearance of fact and knowledge. Postmodern thought requires us to appreciate these differences and negotiate reasonable solutions that work for most citizens. How laws are crafted, why offenders break the law, and how law enforcement and courts respond to crime are all subject to different possibilities. The idea that there is one absolute truth and that everyone embraces it or should embrace it is challenged by postmodern thought. Once we are made aware of the variable nature of our understandings of crime, the better we can seek the multiple justices that might be available.

Postmodern criminology, which has only recently gained a foothold in traditional criminological discourse, is fighting an uphill battle for acceptance, because one must invest a good deal of study before understanding its benefits. Postmodern criminology suffers from the same sort of linguistic inaccuracy for which it faults traditional criminology. According to Arrigo, postmodern criminology has been faulted as nihilistic, pessimistic, and fatalistic.[26] As incomplete and fragmentary as our knowledge might be, the criminal and juvenile justice systems still must process cases and decide what to do with offenders. Justice officials don't have the luxury of teasing out everyone's multiple motivations. From a practical standpoint, postmodern criminology is akin to the old philosopher who muddied the water and then complained he couldn't see.

Cultural Criminology

What we know about crime and what we think we know about crime are the result of either our direct experience or what we gather from our culture and the media. However, a new perspective for considering theoretical criminology considers how the media and popular culture intersect with the lives of offenders and the criminal justice system. This new perspective, called **cultural criminology**, has been led by criminologist Jeff

cultural criminology
A theory that explores the relationships among culture, media institutions, crime, and social control.

8.1 FOCUS *on* ETHICS

ARTIST, REBEL, OR 798?

Your 14-year-old cousin Bryan has recently been arrested for spraying graffiti on the high school. You drove by the school (which you attended 20 years earlier) before the cleaning crews got to work and saw a rather colorful mural adorning the side of the otherwise drab brick wall. Your friend's husband, who is a police officer, tells you that gang symbols were embedded in the mural and refers to Bryan as a 798, which is local police code for gang-related activity. Your aunt says that although Bryan isn't a bad kid, he's been hanging out with the wrong crowd. Bryan has shown you some of his sketchbooks, and you think he was just expressing himself.

Unlike the crude tagging done by gangs, Bryan's mural shows actual skill. In a picture he took of the graffiti—he documents all his graffiti in a scrapbook—he shows you parts of the graffiti that have special meaning to him and his friends, specifically in the color combinations. He has also lifted some characters from the comic-book artist Robert Crumb that also have special meanings for him. You try to explain this to your friend's husband, the police officer, but he insists that "the little 798" is running with a dangerous gang and that the graffiti is proof.

This afternoon, Bryan and his parents returned from court. Since Bryan admitted to the graffiti, his parents waived the right to an attorney,

and the judge adjudicated Bryan delinquent. Bryan and his parents have to pay for the school's cleaning costs, and Bryan's name has gone on a jurisdiction "gang-watch list." He has been expelled and now must attend a school for troubled youths, as well as report regularly to a case worker. Since you have taken several classes in criminology, your aunt calls you to complain that they didn't understand a single thing that went on in court that day, especially all the Latin terminology that the judge and lawyers used.

Think About It

1. Is Bryan in a gang?

2. Which parties in the scenario use a specialized language? What forms do these specialized languages take?

3. What effect, if any, do you think the authorities' labeling of Bryan as "delinquent" and "798" will have on Bryan's self-concept?

4. What do you do? Will you treat Bryan more cautiously because the police believe he's in a gang? Or will you try to encourage Bryan's artistic talents in a more legitimate direction?

Ferrell, who has used a range of tools from media analysis and popular culture studies to give new insight into how crime and delinquency affect everyday life.[27] See Focus on Ethics 8.1 to see how postmodernist and cultural criminology approaches might be constructively applied to a scenario.

In many ways, cultural criminology is an outgrowth of postmodern criminology in that it enables us to deconstruct the images and symbols created by offenders, victims, and criminal justice professionals in order to determine the underlying meanings and values associated with offending. Ferrell contends that the media filters the images they present to fit their version of reality and, perhaps more importantly, to fit their needs to be entertaining as well as informative. According to Ferrell, this results in a view more like a funhouse of mirrors, rather than a straightforward, objective presentation of the news.[28]

The range of subject matter available to the cultural criminologist is unlimited. It spans the continuum from the traditional news presented by television networks and major newspapers to the cultural artifacts left by powerless youths attempting to make political and identity statements by spraying graffiti on walls, trains, and subway cars. Cultural criminology can expose the assumptions behind the lyrics of music from different genres or uncover the intentions and feelings of individuals who construct informal roadside memorials to mark the location of a loved one's death.

Important to understanding all the incidences is the appreciation that there is more to these activities than meets the eye. Cultural criminologists help us understand what lies beneath the surface of some of the most taken-for-granted artifacts in society and, just as important, they help us to uncover the textured layers of meaning involved in the media's coverage of crime and delinquency. A few examples can illustrate the range and complexity of this emerging theoretical perspective.

- **Distortion of crime and justice**   Criminologist Gregg Barak has looked at "news-making criminology" to uncover how the media purposefully present the picture of crime and justice in such a way that it serves their need for ratings.[29] He is particularly critical of television programs such as *America's Most Wanted*, *Unsolved Mysteries*, and *Hard Copy*. These programs focus on the most sensational types of violent crime and have spawned a disconnection in the minds of many people about the nature and extent of serious and violent crime in their communities. Of particular concern is the way these programs indirectly romanticize and glorify violent crime while supposedly reporting and condemning it. For instance, in the infamous case of the Central Park jogger who was raped and severely beaten in New York City, the press used sexually laden accounts to describe an act of brutal violence. Instead of reporting that the woman was grabbed and touched, the press used terms such as *fondling* and *sexually exploring*.[30] In fact, the single-minded focus of the press in reporting this case as a gang rape was revealed years later when the accused youths were exonerated by the confession of a man in prison.

- **Gang fashions**   Clothes are important because they help people present themselves so that others will get a sense of their identity and values. For the most part, this presentation of self is an individualistic concern intended to demonstrate contemporary styles and flattering portrayals of physique. According to criminologist Jody Miller, however, what a gang member in Los Angeles wears can mean a great deal more. Miller interviewed probation officers and was able to construct an idea of how they viewed or "read" the attire of youths immersed in the gang lifestyle.[31] According to the probation officers, gang members wore clothing styles, often oversized, that emphasized team logos and prison symbolism. The large clothes have two functions: to conceal weapons and to make the gang member appear larger and more intimidating. Sport team logos also have specific meanings. Oakland Raiders attire signals "outlaw," while Georgetown University means "gangster." The dress has consequences for the youth and those around him or her. A young man who adopts the clothing associated with gang involvement alerts everyone who can read his attire that he is ready to defend his gang. This makes him and anyone around him targets for the violence of rival gang members. According to the probation officers, gangs aren't intimately acquainted with members of rival gangs and will consider clothing as a valid reason to shoot another youth.[32] In Los Angeles, it's not a good idea to wear or imitate gang styles because of the potentially deadly consequences.

● **Music and crime**   Cultural criminologists might also look at music as a window into the values and attitudes that individuals hold about the reasons people commit crime and society's response. Although it's common today to claim that no one listens to music lyrics, that it's all about the beat, cultural criminologists would dispute this point. Two studies of the effect of music on crime are particularly noteworthy. First, Mark Hamm, an expert on domestic terrorism, has examined the American skinhead subculture and drawn inferences between the white-power heavy metal music of the 1980s and the racist, anti-Semitic, and homophobic attitudes of this subculture.[33] Hamm makes the important point that skinhead music links skinheads to each other in ways that help them communicate values and attitudes, transcend everyday life, and imbue it with a sense of higher purpose that has far-reaching consequences. Hamm says that the shared values, popular music, and subcultural style of skinheads must be organized to be understood. Further, it must be understood to be controlled. Ken Tunnell did a second form of cultural analysis on music. Looking at what he termed the "murder ballads" of bluegrass music, Tunnell addressed the patriarchal nature of the American Southeast and Appalachian regions. The central theme of these murder ballads served to justify violence in a certain fatalistic way that often ended up with consequences that involved the criminal justice system. In short, murder was morally, if not legally, permissible under certain circumstances. One interesting feature Tunnell found in the changing nature of bluegrass music is the emphasis on incarceration. Tunnell speculated that this might reflect a change in attitudes about capital punishment and a growing preference for lengthy prison sentences.[34]

The American skinhead culture has drawn many white, teenage males. Here skinheads pose in front of a Nazi flag.

(Courtesy Mark Richards, PhotoEdit Inc.)

As a new and emerging theoretical perspective, cultural criminology shows substantial promise for helping to understand why young people violate the law. It considers both the influence of a wide range of media on the behavior of young people and how youngsters assign meaning to their behavior by using the media to portray symbols and signs that are significant to them. Cultural criminologists show us how graffiti is not simply vandalism and an eyesore, but rather how it can become a roadmap to explain a wide range of political and symbolic messages designed to enable youths to communicate with each other.[35]

Peacemaking Criminology

Another relatively new perspective emerging in theoretical criminology is peacemaking. Although some might argue that peacemaking criminology contains little that is actually new and that its ideas have been around forever in the teaching of major religions, it's worth considering the recent formulation and organization of these ideas as applied specifically to the questions of crime and delinquency.

In 1991, Harold Pepinsky and Richard Quinney published a book of readings titled *Criminology as Peacemaking*. In this volume, they brought together the work of scholars who wrote about religious and humanist perspectives on crime along with those who used feminist and critical explanations. The book's purpose was to give substance to a new way of looking at crime and delinquency that sought to relieve the pain and suffering caused to victims and, interestingly enough, to offenders.[36]

Peacemaking criminology presents a holistic view of the social and personal effect of crime and affixes responsibility not only to the individuals involved, but also to the social structure that accepts, enables, or encourages the harm that individuals do to others. As such, peacemaking criminology critiques not just antisocial individuals, but also the institutions and cultures that produce the pain and suffering associated with crime.

The peacemaking perspective can be used to examine problems ranging from international conflict and human rights abuses to the interactions of delinquents involved in violence. The idea behind peacemaking criminology is that the same principles apply to conflicts at many levels and that the solutions to these conflicts are grounded in the same philosophical concerns and practical strategies. In 1998, John R. Fuller developed a model called the peacemaking pyramid (see Figure 8-1), which organizes the tenets of the peacemaking perspective and allows individuals to comprehend its far-reaching potential. According to Fuller, solutions to crime and conflict can best be addressed by working through the levels of the pyramid. The higher the level reached, the more the process is considered to be peacemaking.[37]

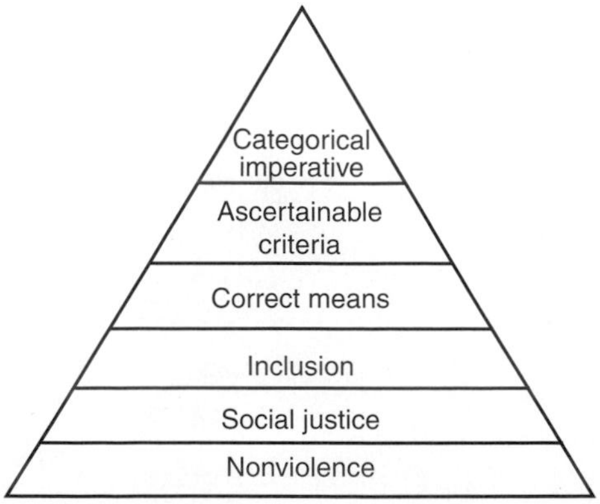

peacemaking criminology

A branch of criminology that considers the social and personal effect of crime as a whole: not only the offender and victim, but also the social structure that accepts, enables, or encourages the offense.

Figure 8-1   Peacemaking Pyramid

Source: John R. Fuller, *Criminal Justice: A Peacemaking Perspective.* Published by Allyn and Bacon, Boston, MA. Copyright © 1998 by Pearson Education. Reprinted by permission of the publisher.

- **Nonviolence** The first underlying premise of peacemaking criminology is nonviolence. This means nonviolence not only on the part of the offender, but also on the part of law enforcement and the state. When the government uses violence in the form of police brutality or capital punishment, it models the very behavior it's trying to eliminate. Peacemaking criminology advocates policies such as increased gun control, rehabilitation, and limits on the state's use of force. The state must use a certain level of violence depending on the circumstances, but violence should be used as a last resort, and the state should help resolve conflicts before employing violence. For instance, although a SWAT team might sometimes be necessary, a law enforcement agency should have trained negotiators to address situations before they escalate. See Programs for Kids 8.1 for a look at a programmatic nonviolent approach in K–12 education and child rearing.

- **Social justice** The next premise of peacemaking criminology is social justice. As a critical criminology, peacemaking criminology is concerned with the overall sense of fairness and equity in society. The criminal justice system shouldn't simply maintain the privilege of those in power but should increase

8.1 PROGRAMS *for* CHILDREN

NONVIOLENCE BEGINS AT HOME

The first premise of the peacemaking pyramid is nonviolence. Much as we might preach this to our children, the way in which we model nonviolence to them will have a more lasting influence. One group of concerned individuals, Parents and Teachers Against Violence in Education (PTAVE), has established a website called Project NoSpank, which provides information to parents and school administrators on the dangers of corporal punishment (see figure).

Project NoSpank is fighting an uphill battle in the United States in attempting to eliminate the hitting of children. Although great strides have been made in calling attention to the issues of hitting children, most people will still argue that there is a big difference between spanking and beating. Project NoSpank doesn't make this distinction and is absolute in its message that hitting children, or otherwise physically and psychologically attacking them, is immoral, counterproductive, and misguided. Project NoSpank has amassed a great deal of literature that supports its claims. Additionally, PTAVE lobbies the government at both the state and federal levels to pass laws forbidding violence against children. The Project NoSpank website is a valuable resource for students writing papers in disciplines such as sociology, psychology, nursing, education, and criminal justice. Although many students will be unconvinced by the antiviolence message of Project NoSpank, they will find that exploring it will make them examine their own attitudes toward spanking in the home and at school.

In classrooms with Internet access or as an out-of-class assignment, it's useful for students to explore this site for several reasons.

Think About It

1. What is the background of the people who developed this site? Why are they so vehement in their arguments against spanking?

2. Does the site present convincing evidence against the use of corporal punishment? Is the site fair and balanced, or does it twist facts to make its case?

3. What does the site propose as ways to remedy the problems of corporal punishment? Are these remedies realistic? Which of the remedies can be accomplished by individuals, and which require the cooperation of the government?

4. Can you find other websites that present opposing viewpoints? Is the evidence used by sites promoting physical discipline more or less convincing than that provided by Project NoSpank?

1. Spanking teaches children two dangerous lessons: hitting people is okay and violence works.
2. Spanking destroys children's self-esteem, damages their ability to learn, and sets the stage for future emotional problems.
3. Children learn good behavior by imitating good behavior and respect by being respected.

Project NoSpank offers a variety of graphic materials from its website to get its message across. *Source:* www.nospank.net/nospanking.pdf.

the rights and welfare of everyone, including those without power. Domestic violence is a good example of an issue in which the criminal justice system has the potential to rectify injustice. Instead of only arresting the one who is violent, the system must protect victims, who are often children, and educate all involved about how to have positive and supporting relationships. The key is to solve the underlying issue, rather than just punish the batterer.

- **Inclusion**   In many ways, justice is in the eye of the beholder. Although the criminal justice system might arrest, try, sentence, and punish an offender, both offenders and victims sometimes feel that the solution isn't really just. The defense attorney, prosecutor, and judge are the experts in dispensing justice, and their decisions about process and results are what usually determine how cases are disposed of. Peacemaking criminology includes other interested parties in the crafting of a just decision. The victim(s) and the offender, as well as representatives from the school, community, religious organizations, and law enforcement, might also be included in arriving at solutions. By bringing the victim and offender together in an environment that is not so adversarial, it's often possible to solicit both input into the decision and the commitment to abide by it from all interested parties. An offender who agrees to a sentence and has had an opportunity to participate in crafting it might be more likely to keep a promise to stay out of trouble.

- **Correct means**   According to peacemaking criminology, the ends don't justify the means. The criminal justice system is limited in terms of procedural law, which requires that the offender be provided with certain rights, as well as an initial presumption of innocence. Even if the offender is guilty of committing horrendous acts, peacemaking criminology argues that he or she should be accorded the legal safeguards that are guaranteed by the Constitution. According to **correct means**, the process of arriving at justice must be done in accordance with the model of justice. This premise is illustrated by a quote from Gandhi: "There is no path to peace, peace is the path."

- **Ascertainable criteria**   One intractable problem with the criminal justice system is the vast network of confusing rules and specialized language that make it almost impossible for those who are new to the system to comprehend how decisions are made. **Ascertainable criteria** means that the language and procedures used to pursue justice must be made clear to all. Similar to the prior discussion of postmodern criminology's focus on the centrality of language, peacemaking criminology is concerned with the problem of participants understanding the legal process. This problem is particularly acute in the juvenile justice system, where young people not only don't understand the specialized language, but aren't yet sophisticated enough to appreciate the nature of the proceeding or the consequences. Those appearing before the juvenile court judge often are terrified of a number of things, including their parents, the judge, the possibility of not returning home, and the likelihood of going to a detention center. Given these immediate concerns coupled with the legal-speak used in the court, youths are often clueless about the decisions that are made concerning their lives.

- **Categorical imperative**   For a system of justice to be perceived as fair and impartial, it must treat similar cases consistently. Although a certain amount of discretion is necessary to fashion effective dispositions for individual cases, the system can't be arbitrary and capricious if it's to maintain the public's trust. The premise of **categorical imperative** is derived from philosopher Immanuel Kant, who wrote that decisions should be made as if the outcome would act as a model for future decisions.[38]

These principles of peacemaking criminology show how this perspective is concerned with reducing the suffering of everyone who is caught up in the criminal and

---

correct means
A term from peacemaking criminology that means the process of arriving at justice must be done in a just manner.

ascertainable criteria
In peacemaking criminology, the concept that the language and procedures used to pursue justice must be made clear to all.

categorical imperative
In peacemaking criminology, the concept that a system of justice must treat cases with similar characteristics consistently if the system is to be perceived as fair and impartial.

juvenile justice systems. In many ways, the peacemaking perspective requires that the system act as a wise parent and not react to antisocial behavior with violence and revenge, but rather with care and compassion designed to enable victims and offenders to repair the harm done by the criminal or delinquent incident.

All critical theories are concerned with broad sociological issues that consider the relationship between the individual and the political, social, or economic conditions that define the way society operates. These theories are important because they extend the inquiry of criminological examination beyond the deficiencies of the individual or the shortcomings of interpersonal relationships to the way that the government and the culture affect the creation and violation of laws. The study of these critical theories forces us to evaluate the taken-for-granted assumptions about capitalism, race relations, gender issues, and how power is used to maintain social control. The one critical theory that has not been covered in this chapter is feminist criminology, which will be covered extensively in Chapter 9.

LIFE-COURSE THEORIES

Sociologists and criminologists have long used the life-course approach to explain many issues.[39] The life-course perspective represents one of the most robust and potentially important ways for explaining delinquency.

The primary issue that life-course theories examine in relationship to crime is age. Age is a central focus of concern for several reasons. One reason are that age is such an accessible variable for research purposes.[40] By that we mean that age is a core piece of data because it's collected in every form and piece of paper that are used to keep track of individuals in schools, hospitals, social service agencies, prisons, and funeral homes. In short, age is a wonderful variable with which to conduct research because it's so stable and so well collected.

Unlike attitudes toward crime, level of education, chemicals in the body, or relationship with parents, age is an easy variable to track. Age is also an important variable because it acts as a reliable proxy for physical development and a somewhat reliable proxy for social development. Rights and responsibilities have always been allocated on the basis of age.[41] One's grade level in school and eligibility to drive an automobile, vote, drink alcohol, and collect social security are all age determined, or at least age related.

How is age related to crime and delinquency? We have long known that young children and elderly adults commit very little crime. Between these two ages is a rising curve that peaks from the late teens to the mid-20s (see Figures 8-2, 8-3, and 8-4). This has been a consistent pattern in societies across time and cultures. It has to do with several factors, including the increase of testosterone in young males, the transition of adolescents to adult responsibilities and opportunities, and the changing cultural pressures and expectations that go along with one's expected social and emotional development. However, even given these consistent features of age-dependent criminal behavior, some interesting questions can be asked. For instance, is this age–crime curve consistent across social conditions? If not, what are the important differences in those social conditions that lead to lower crime rates? Why do most offenders eventually stop or desist from crime?[42] Are there interventions that can be aimed at people of a certain age that can affect their proclivities to break the law? All these questions are considered important areas for research from the life-course perspective.

In this part of the chapter, we will examine the two most promising life-course theories. First, we look at the work of Terrie Moffitt, who differentiates between those whose offenses are limited to adolescence and those who keep breaking the law throughout their lives. Next, we look at the work of Robert Sampson and John Laub, whose work focuses on the transitions and pathways that characterize patterns of delinquency and crime.

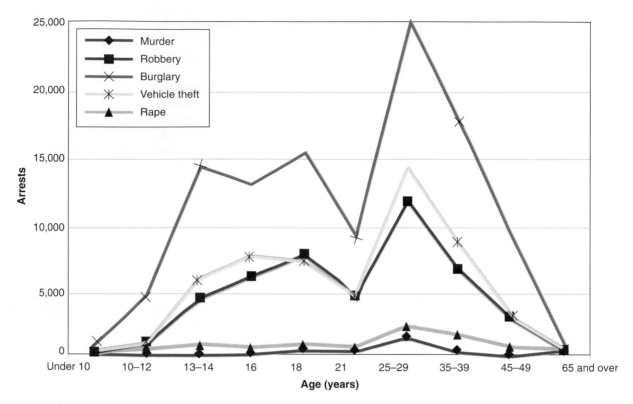

Figure 8-2 **Number of Arrests by Age and Offense, 2005** *Source:* FBI, *Uniform Crime Reports, Crime in the United States, Arrests by Age, 2005,* www.fbi.gov/ucr/05cius/data/table_38.html.

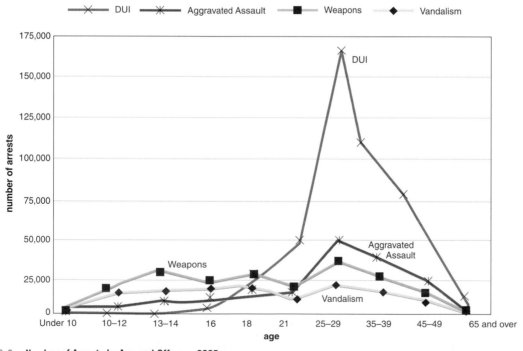

Figure 8-3 **Number of Arrests by Age and Offense, 2005** *Source:* FBI, *Uniform Crime Reports, Crime in the United States, Arrests by Age, 2005,* www.fbi.gov/ucr/05cius/data/table_38.html.

Life-Course Persistent and Adolescent-Limited Crime

Terrie Moffitt developed her life-course perspective of crime by specifying two types of offenders who engage in antisocial behavior in distinctly different patterns: life-course persistent offenders and adolescence-limited offenders.[43] Moffitt has drawn

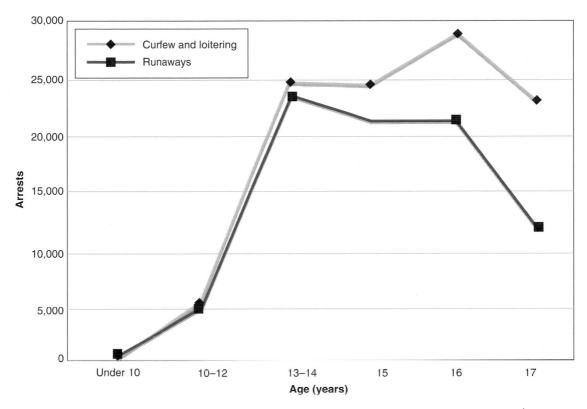

Figure 8-4   **Number of Arrests by Age and Offense, 2005** *Source:* FBI, *Uniform Crime Reports, Crime in the United States, Arrests by Age, 2005,* www.fbi.gov/ucr/05cius/data/table_38.html.

on a vast number of other theories, including biological and psychological, to develop a sociological explanation of the patterns of offending that appear to be persistent features of the problems of crime and delinquency.

We begin the examination of her work with an explication of the life-course persistent offenders. This is the most serious of the two groups, and the theory she uses to explain their behavior attempts to integrate biological, psychological, and sociological variables.

LIFE COURSE PERSISTENT OFFENDERS   **Life-course persistent offenders** begin to engage in antisocial behavior at an early age and continue to commit acts that harm others throughout their lives. The context and situations that elicit this negative behavior change over the life course, as does the type of disapproved behavior. A child that bites other children at age 4, hits others at age 10, rapes at age 17, robs liquor stores at 23, and commits child abuse at age 45 is an example of a life-course persistent offender.[44]

According to Moffitt, these offenders are relatively rare but are capable of harming others a great deal. The life-course persistent offender might have experienced deficits in neuropsychological abilities at an early age that make him or her more susceptible to weak cognitive abilities, as well as more susceptible to detection by authorities, such as parents, teachers, and police officers. Moffitt has found that these neuropsychological deficiencies are manifested in poor scores on tests of language and self-control, inattention, hyperactivity, and impulsivity. These features are consistent with the emergence of antisocial behavior.

Moffitt goes on to discuss the inadequate environment that many of these life-course persistent offenders come from. She contends that those children with neuropsychological issues are disproportionately born into environments that aren't conducive to addressing their problems. When the parents are prone to antisocial behavior, the children will be more likely to exhibit the same attitudes and values.

life-course persistent offender
In life-course criminological theory, an offender who begins inappropriate behavior at an early age and continues to commit antisocial and deviant acts.

Consequently, Moffitt found a cumulative effect in children who are born with cognitive disabilities, poor parenting, impoverished social and economic neighborhoods, and limited opportunities. The interaction of these factors combines to produce the life-course persistent offender.

This happens because these youths have developed a limited behavioral repertoire; they both respond inappropriately in many situations and are unable to capitalize on opportunities in which they might acquire and practice prosocial alternatives. Consequently, these children learn to accept rejection and become defensive and embittered. Moffitt claims that if social and academic skills aren't mastered in childhood, it's very difficult to make up for it later.

adolescence-limited offender

In life-course criminological theory, youths who engage in antisocial and deviant behavior for only a short period of time and only in certain situations.

ADOLESCENCE-LIMITED OFFENDERS   Moffitt's second theory of life-course criminology involves the **adolescence-limited offender**. This group of offenders is much larger than the life-course persistent group and might, in fact, include just about every juvenile. Because most of us, at one time or another, committed acts for which we could have been brought into the juvenile justice system, we could all be called adolescence-limited offenders. The key idea here is that most children engage in this antisocial behavior for only a short period of time and only in certain situations. They are able to distinguish when antisocial behavior might be beneficial to them and when it will cost them dearly if they get caught. They are also able to turn their prosocial behavior on and off as they learn the situations in which it's important to be considered a good child. For example, a child might shoplift, smoke marijuana, and fight with others when he or she is with peers but still earn good grades at school, sing in the church choir, and interact in a positive way with parents. The deviant behavior is not heavily ingrained in their personality, and after they become young adults, they desist from it altogether.[45]

Moffitt's theory of adolescence-limited offenders suggests answers to different questions than does the life-course persistent theory. Neuropsychological disabilities aren't the concern when dealing with adolescence-limited offenders. The reasons for which this group engages in antisocial behavior have to do with mimicry and reinforcement. An interesting thing happens in high school that draws many

Teenagers who participate in risky delinquent behavior, such as drinking alcohol and driving, often move on to mature behavior as young adults. *(Courtesy Richard Hutchings, Photo Researchers, Inc.)*

teenagers into deviant behavior. The life-course persistent offenders who were previously marginalized by teachers and parents now become more interesting to other teenagers because their deviant ways look like fun. Drug use, sexual activity, vandalism, car racing, and fighting now become the path to higher visibility and status. The life-course persistent offenders replace parents, sports heroes, and celebrities as the new role models for a large percentage of youths who never before engaged in delinquent behavior.

Moffitt also claims that many youths are drawn to delinquent activities as a way of proclaiming their independence by flaunting conventional social etiquette. Moffitt claims that there is a social and psychological reinforcement in cutting the apron strings and engaging in new challenges and adventures. In fact, Moffitt argues that "every curfew violated, car stolen, drug taken, and baby conceived is a statement of personal independence and thus a reinforcement for delinquent involvement."

In a time when there are no longer any formal puberty rites to mark the transition to adulthood, adolescents have invented their own deviant ways of marking their change in status. This can be seen visibly by tattoos, body piercings, and cigarette smoking. It can also be detected by the delinquent risk-taking activities such as shoplifting, unprotected sex, drug use, intoxication, and driving fast. Moffitt claims that, although these activities might not look appealing to the middle-aged academic, they are precious resources to the teenager who is attempting to establish independence, acquire status, enhance self-esteem, and have fun.[46]

Finally, Moffitt answers the question, "Why do adolescence-limited offenders stop committing crimes and adopt a conventional lifestyle?" As the young person ages, he or she finds more legitimate opportunities to acquire the resources that formerly were available only through delinquent behavior. Moffitt contends that adolescents have a maturity gap where they aspire to the goods and privileges of adults but are prevented because of their age. As they get older, the maturity gap narrows, and youths are more likely to try to meet their needs through conventional behavior, because the range of conventional behavior is now much wider. For instance, drinking alcohol is no longer a social taboo but has now become the accepted option of an adult. Drinking alcohol is no longer an act of defiance, so the binge drinking and all-night partying are no longer considered radical behavior that should be mimicked but rather poor choices for the person who has to get up in the morning and go to work.[47]

Moffitt's contributions to a life-course theory of crime are significant. Although some might argue that her taxonomy is simplistic, it's useful because it creates a clear demarcation of different types of offending patterns.

Pathways and Turning Points

Another life-course theory of crime and delinquency that has proved to be interesting and informative has been developed by Robert Sampson and John Laub. The strength of their theory is that it brings together the current sociological literature on life-course theory with Travis Hirschi's control theory of delinquency, examining these concepts in light of a powerful data set developed by Sheldon Glueck and Eleanor Glueck. Sampson and Laub, who found the original computer cards used by the Gluecks in the basement of the Harvard library, not only reinterpreted these data, but also did follow-up studies on some of the original subjects.[48] See A Closer Look at Juvenile Issues 8.1 to learn more about the Gluecks' seminal study and Sampson and Laub's revisiting of it.

Sampson and Laub looked at how one's connection to conventional society changes over the life course and how these changes influence one's chances of offending. Life, according to Sampson and Laub, can be considered as a progression of age-related responsibilities and opportunities that are available as one moves from infancy to old age. Certain pathways (working career, parenthood, and criminal behavior) differ for each individual, as do the transition points (graduation from high school, first job, first marriage) that mark changes in status and opportunities. Sampson and Laub

8.1 A CLOSER LOOK at JUVENILE ISSUES

THIS IS THEIR LIVES

In the 1940s, Harvard researchers Sheldon Glueck and Eleanor Glueck began a study of 1,000 males, ages 10 to 17, who had been born in Boston. Five hundred of the subjects had entered a correctional facility as youths. The other 500, who served as a control group, were law-abiding youths who attended public schools. The Gluecks observed the two groups at the ages of 14, 25, and 32 and published the results of their longitudinal study—*longitudinal* meaning that the Gluecks tracked their subjects over an extended period of time—in 1950 in their influential book *Unraveling Juvenile Delinquency*.[1]

Sampson and Laub returned to the study in the 1980s by finding and interviewing 53 of the men over a six-year period. They discovered that offending dropped steeply as the men aged. Between the ages of 17 and 24, 84 percent of the men had committed violent offenses. However, the number of violent offenders dropped to 14 percent as the men entered their 40s and to 3 percent when they were in their 60s. On average, a subject committed his first offense at age 12 and stopped offending in his late 30s. Three of the most important factors in stemming the men's criminal activity besides age were marriage, steady employment, and military service.[2]

The Gluecks' original data set currently resides at the Radcliffe Institute of Advanced Study at Harvard University.

1 Charles Coe, "Twigs Bent, Trees Go Straight," *Harvard Magazine*, www.harvard magazine.com/on-line/030491.html.
2 John H. Laub and Robert J. Sampson, *Shared Beginnings, Divergent Lives: Delinquent Boys to Age 70* (Cambridge, MA: Harvard University Press, 2003).

use these pathways and transition points to examine how individuals' commitment to delinquency and crime changes over the lifespan. They are particularly concerned with the informal mechanisms of social control that happen early in life and connect the individual to conventional lifestyles.[49]

By considering how individuals are bonded to the conventional norms of society and applying an understanding of the life course, it's possible to explain delinquency and crime. Sampson and Laub use Hirschi's social control theory of delinquency and observe how his concepts of attachment, involvement, commitment, and belief are variables that determine the strength of a youth's bonds to peers, family, and school. In looking at adults, the bonds to the labor force, marriage, or parenthood are the factors that determine how much deviant behavior is committed.[50] What is important to Sampson and Laub is how the pathways to crime might be interrupted by significant transitions or turning points. These turning points are so crucial that they can redirect the trajectory of a life that is headed down the road of crime.

For instance, marrying a person with positive values, going to college, joining the military, or getting a first job with exciting opportunities can completely alter the course of one's life. However, most turning points aren't so dramatic and act over time as a process, rather than as a dramatic event. Also, turning points can negatively affect one's life course and result in an early trajectory toward antisocial behavior.

Another important feature of Sampson and Laub's theory is the idea of cumulative disadvantage. Problems with the law or authorities early in life might contribute to difficulties later. Youths who are labeled delinquent are cut off from some of the chances or events that might help them make the leap into respectable behavior. For instance, the military doesn't allow felons to enlist. The military has often been a means of cleansing the record of troubled youths. The philosophy of boot-camp prisons is based on the expected positive transitions that accompany military discipline. (Unfortunately, boot-camp prisons don't clear the arrest record the way that actual military service does.) Sampson and Laub detail how early issues in the family, school, and juvenile justice system can accumulate and send the youth in a negative direction.[51]

For example, in their reconsideration of the Gluecks' data, Sampson and Laub found that the length of incarceration had an important effect on the likelihood of finding stable employment later in life. Even when prior crime and excessive juvenile

Early intervention might prevent young delinquents from becoming life-course persistent offenders and possibly ending up in prison for life. Inmate Therman Jeffron was incarcerated for a murder he committed five decades ago. *(Courtesy Olivier Pighetti/Saola, Getty Images, Inc. –Liaison)*

alcohol consumption were considered, those who spent longer time behind bars had more difficulty entering and remaining in the labor force than those who were incarcerated for shorter periods of time.

A primary strength of Sampson and Laub's theory is that, because of the longitudinal nature of their research (they were able to follow the same set of males for over 60 years), they were able to link juvenile delinquency with adult offending. This provides a better understanding of the effect of life-course events and allows scholars to speculate on how early interventions might profitably alter the propensity of young people growing up to be what Moffitt calls life-course persistent offenders.

The Prediction Problem

One perplexing problem for life-course theories is that they are better at looking backward than looking forward. When the data are analyzed at the end of a criminal career, it's easy to pick out the trajectory that resulted in a life of crime. What is more difficult, however, is identifying those who are early in their antisocial behavior and projecting who will desist from a life of crime and who will continue. The sophisticated nature of life-course theory promises to rectify this problem. Life-course criminology is a relatively new enterprise, and its potential to yield evidence that can produce effective crime-reduction policies is enormous.

INTEGRATED THEORIES

Two issues often frustrate students of criminological theory. First, they want to know which theory is the "right" one. With all the competing perspectives, it's only reasonable to look for the one that really explains why people break the law. This is, of course, an ultimately frustrating search, because these criminological theories deal with different aspects of crime. Crime and delinquency are tremendously complicated and involve social behaviors that people engage in for a multitude of reasons. No single theory can encompass this range of behavior. Once this is understood, students then ask the question, "Can we tie these theories together to come up with a more comprehensive viewpoint?" The answer to this question is a qualified yes.

Although we can't get a complete picture of crime, leading criminologists have tried to integrate theories to expand the scope of explanation. For example, life-course theories draw from other established theories to explain crime and delinquency patterns over the lifetime of individuals. Next we will look at three of the more promising attempts to integrate criminological theory.

Elliott's Integrated Theory of Delinquent Behavior

Criminologist Delbert Elliott has worked with a number of colleagues over the years to formulate his integrated theory. Elliott draws on three leading theories of delinquency: **strain**, social control, and **social learning**. The key to appreciating Elliott's theory is that he doesn't accept these theories in the exact manner in which their creators fashioned them. He borrows important aspects from the theories but changes other aspects to fit them into his concept of integration.[52]

For example, when dealing with strain theory, he actually expands it to include more than lower-class delinquents. Elliott, therefore, argues that middle-class delinquents suffer from a very similar type of strain. Whereas the lower-class youth are chasing the American dream of being financially secure and resort to delinquency when they find their means to success blocked, Elliot argues that middle-class youth are pursuing slightly different goals, such as athletic ability or physical attractiveness. These middle-class youth experience strain when they fail to achieve such goals, which aren't always obtainable by simple hard work. Middle-class boys who have high aspirations are just as susceptible to strain as are lower-class youth, but for different reasons.

Elliott therefore argues that strain theory is not enough to explain delinquency and must be combined with social control and social learning theories. In looking at social control theory, Elliott reduces it to two measures, integration and commitment, and argues that those who experience strain will have their bonds to conventional society tested and will turn to delinquent peers from whom they learn antisocial behavior. The three theories, strain, social control, and social learning, are interrelated and act on individuals in different ways depending on factors such as social class, which can strengthen or weaken one's sense of strain and one's commitment to conventional society.

Thornberry's Interactional Theory of Delinquency

Terence Thornberry draws on two types of delinquency theories to construct the interactional perspective: social control theory and social learning theory. Thornberry emphasizes the reciprocal interaction between the main ideas in the theories. In terms of interaction, Thornberry contends that the attachment one has to parents is variable and changes as parent and child deal with problems. Attachment can't be measured once and treated as if it doesn't change. Thornberry's model accommodates the interaction of youths with attachment to parent, commitment to school, belief in conventional values, and association with delinquent peers.[53] As the youth develops delinquent values because of these interactions, he or she is more likely to engage in delinquent behavior.

Of equal importance to Thornberry is the reciprocal nature of these interactions. Although an association with delinquent peers might make one more likely to engage in delinquent behavior, Thornberry argues that this is not a one-way street. As one engages in delinquent acts, one is more likely to find other delinquent peers to associate with. This might be a function of meeting other delinquents in the juvenile justice system, or it might simply be that those who get in trouble often associate at the same locations. Whether it's the street corner, the shopping mall, or the school, those who are likely to engage in delinquency will find each other. They might share the same circumstances (broken home, failure at school, or unemployment), but as sources of strain these conditions aren't as important to Thornberry as are weak bonds of social control and social learning in peer groups.

An additional function of Thornberry's interactional theory that makes it an attractive integrated theory is his attempt to specify how an individual's attachment to society's conventional bonds might change over the life course. This developmental approach allows Thornberry to consider how changes in the expected path of one's life might radically alter the direction in which one is headed. Therefore, the middle-class youth who gets arrested for selling large quantities of marijuana might begin a life of trouble with law enforcement agencies, and the lower-class youth who gets an academic scholarship might escape the negative effects of growing up in an under-privileged neighborhood.

Tittle's Control Balance Theory

Although Charles Tittle's control balance theory uses a number of other theories to present an integrated explanation of crime, it's important to note that this theory is not a combination of other perspectives, but is, rather, a new way of conceptualizing the central reasons why people break the law. Tittle contends that we control our lives to a certain extent. The control we have is mitigated by the control others have over us. In turn, we feel more in control when we have control of others. The optimum condition is when there is a healthy balance between the control we have over others and the control others (not necessarily the same others) have over us. When there is an imbalance of this control, deviant behavior is one way that we attempt to put the condition back into balance.[54]

If we have a deficit in the balance of control, we are likely to take actions that give us a sense of greater control. When we have a surplus of control, we commit deviant acts to extend that control or to take immediate advantage of our current situation. This is a very ambitious theory that seeks to explain a broad range of antisocial behavior by explicating the many ways in which individuals seek to redress their perceived imbalance of control. In language reminiscent of Merton's strain theory, Tittle lists a number of ways that a person might respond to being humiliated. First, a person might act in a conforming manner and simply endure the humiliation for the present and, over the long term, seek to address the alleged personal shortcoming and show the attacker, as well as everyone else, that he or she is a worthy individual and that the insult was inappropriate.

Second, the victim might respond immediately by attacking the attacker. This reaction is called *predation*, and although it has the advantage of immediate redress and satisfaction, it can cause more trouble than it's worth and cause the imbalance of control to become even greater. When we deal with people who have a great deal more power than we do, it's often necessary to defer our urge to strike back verbally or physically because they control the very resources we strive to accumulate. For instance, if you hit your boss, you could lose your job and the money that you're trying to earn.

A third way to respond according to Tittle's theory is to engage in an act of defiance, such as talking behind the attacker's back, giving him or her a bad job-performance evaluation, or showing contempt. Defiance can also have costs associated with it, so it isn't always the optimum option for attempting to restore the balance of control.

A person who feels especially helpless might engage in submission and not even attempt to redress the feelings of being in a control deficit. The victim accepts the attacker's view of the problem and doesn't challenge for control of power. With a bit of luck and some groveling, the attacker might spare the victim further humiliation.

If a victim's social location includes friends, family, or a position of power, he or she might engage in exploitation. The victim might get the attacker fired by arranging for others to boycott the business, hiring a private detective to uncover drug use or marital indiscretions, or hiring others to physically assault the attacker. If the victim is subtle, these activities won't be traced back to him or her, and the victim will get the inner satisfaction of correcting the imbalance of power.

Tittle's control balance theory is complicated because it attempts to do two useful things. First, it tries to explain a wide range of antisocial behavior. As an integrated theory, control balance accomplishes more than adding the sum of the parts of other theories. It adds an orientation that extends the range of the theory to become one of the most comprehensive explanations available. The second admirable task that Tittle has set is constructing the model in a way that can be empirically tested. As he and other criminologists provide the research to back up his ideas, control balance theory will likely become one of the leading integrated explanations of crime and delinquency. See Focus on Ethics 8.2 for a scenario involving control balance theory.

These three integrated theories represent different concepts of how criminological theories can be combined to form a more holistic picture of crime and delinquency. Although the authors of these theories are to be commended, they aren't without their critics. One perplexing problem in attempting to integrate theories is

---

8.2   FOCUS *on* ETHICS

KNOWING WHEN TO GIVE CHILDREN CONTROL

Your two children are both in trouble with the juvenile justice system, and you are at a loss to explain why. They are different in so many ways, yet here you are in the corridors of the juvenile court building having to deal with two youngsters who should be model citizens. The juvenile court judge is a veteran at turning troubled kids around, and she has called you and your spouse into her chambers to discuss your children's cases. You know that you will have to make some tough decisions, but you are surprised at how she diagnoses the issues underlying your children's behavior. The judge explains the cases by applying Charles Tittle's control balance theory and asks that you think about how to address the problems by restoring the balance of control in your children's lives.

Your daughter, a high-school junior, is a remarkable young woman who has suddenly strayed from the straight-and-narrow. She has been a straight-A student and a leader at her upper-middle-class high school. In addition to being captain of the cheerleading squad, she is on the math team and has had leading roles in the thespian society's plays. Everything seems to come easily for her, and she is used to getting what she wants. The judge believes that she hasn't been challenged enough at school or at home and that she's become bored. She now runs with a dangerous crowd. Instead of hanging out with other high-achieving students, she has several new and older friends from the local community college who are influencing her to neglect her old friends and her studies. She now wants to get body piercings and tattoos and talks not of going to college, but instead wants to open a health-food store. She seems bent on becoming someone very different than you and your spouse have imagined. She is before the juvenile court for possession of marijuana, which she claims is a legitimate medicine.

Your son is at the opposite end of the spectrum. As a ninth grader he thinks of nothing but sports, even though he isn't very athletic. He is a C- student and says the only reason he wants to go to school is to practice his basketball game and get a scholarship to college before he turns pro. When you point out to him that he barely made the junior varsity squad and that to get a scholarship he would need to be a star, he replies

that he is expecting a growth spurt and that Michael Jordan got cut from his high school team. Recently, he was arrested for shoplifting a Kobe Bryant jersey. You hope that your son will pick better role models as he gets older.

At home, your daughter has always ruled the roost, and your son has been the butt of her sarcastic wit and her friends' jokes. The judge explains that your children suffer from an imbalance of power and control. Your son has too little and your daughter too much. Your task is to work out with the judge some way in which to achieve some balance in the family dynamics and get your children headed in the right direction. The judge, your spouse, and you consider the following options to reorder the balance of power in the family.

What Should You Do?

1. Send your son to a military school where he will learn discipline and self-esteem. Your hope is that when he returns, he will be able to compete on a more equal basis with your daughter.

2. Send your daughter to live with her aunt in another state. The aunt is a college professor of psychology and can match wits with your daughter in ways that you and your spouse can't. With the daughter gone for two years, you think there will be room in the family dynamics for your son to grow.

3. Lay down the law and ground both of them. Have the judge put them on probation, and work with the probation officer(s) to ensure that your children straighten up. Tolerate no trouble from them, and insist that they behave appropriately, or you will have the judge place them somewhere where they will have little choice but to obey.

4. Get more involved in their lives and their goals. Help your daughter to set challenging goals, and support her when she tries new activities. Send your son to a summer basketball camp where the coaches also emphasize the importance of getting good grades.

5. Lighten up on your children. They are both going through a predictable phase, albeit in different ways. If left alone, they will outgrow their deviance.

that sometimes it's necessary to alter the original theory to make it compatible with other ideas. For instance, Elliott and Thornberry both employ Hirschi's social control theory, but they change key aspects of it to suit their purposes. Can it really be considered social control theory when it has been altered in such a way? Finally, the future of theory integration will almost certainly expand the range of types of theories considered. Like Terrie Moffitt, future criminologists will include biological, psychological, and sociological theories and connect the dots between them to provide new and expanded explanations of antisocial behavior.

SUMMARY

1. This chapter covers three types of theories: critical theories, life-course theories, and integrated theories.

2. Cullen and Agnew identify five central themes of critical theories: the concepts of inequality and power are integral to any understanding of crime and its control; crime is not a value-free concept but a political concept; the criminal justice system ultimately serves the interests of the capitalist class by enforcing laws in a discriminatory manner that favors the rich and hurts the impoverished; capitalism is a system of economics that causes a large degree of crime; the solution to crime, according to critical theories, is the creation of a more equitable society.

3. According to Bonger, who linked Marxism and crime, the impoverished in a capitalist state are stimulated to break the law for two reasons: to survive and because wealth is the measuring rod by which people are judged in a capitalist society.

4. Chambliss's Marxist theory of crime states that crime diverts the public's attention from the exploitive nature of capitalism and focuses it on the offenses of the impoverished.

5. Left realism contends that the idealism of Marxist criminology sacrifices the interests of impoverished people for the interests of lower-class offenders, who most victimize those who are in the same social class.

6. Critical-race theory, an extension of the field of critical legal studies, contends that race is a primary factor in how many legal systems dispense justice.

7. According to postmodern criminology, our concepts of justice, law, fairness, responsibility, and authority are all mediated by the context in which we live and therefore aren't absolute. According to Arrigo, three key issues inform the postmodern and

critical criminological enterprise: the centrality of language, partial knowledge and provisional truth, and deconstruction, difference, and possibility.

8. Cultural criminology considers the influence of media on the behavior of young people and observes how youngsters assign meaning to their behavior by using the media to portray symbols that are significant to them.

9. Peacemaking criminology presents a holistic view of the social and personal effects of crime and affixes responsibility not only to the individuals involved, but also to the social structure that accepts, enables, or encourages harm. The levels of the peacemaking pyramid are nonviolence, social justice, inclusion, correct means, ascertainable criteria, and categorical imperative.

10. Life-course theories examine crime in relationship to age. Most offenses are committed by people from their late teens to mid-20s.

11. Moffitt specifies two types of offenders who engage in antisocial behavior: life-course persistent offenders and adolescence-limited offenders. Life-course persistent offenders begin antisocial behavior at an early age and continue throughout their lives. Adolescence-limited offenders represent a larger group who engage in antisocial behavior for only a short period of time and only in certain situations.

12. Sampson and Laub's life-course theory considers how one's connection to conventional society changes over the life course and how these changes influence one's chances of offending. Pathways to crime might be interrupted by significant transitions or turning points.

13. Elliott draws on three leading theories of delinquency: strain, social control, and social learning. The three theories act on individuals in different ways, depending on factors such as social class and one's commitment to conventional society.

14. Thornberry draws on two types of delinquency theories to construct the interactional perspective: social control theory and social learning theory. Thornberry's model accommodates the interaction of youth with attachment to parents, commitment to school, belief in conventional values, and association with delinquent peers.

15. Tittle's control balance theory contends that we control our lives to a certain extent. The control we have is mitigated by the control others have over us. In turn, we feel more in control when we have control of others. The optimum condition is when the control we have over others and the control others have over us is balanced.

REVIEW QUESTIONS

1. How does Marxist theory relate to juvenile delinquency and crime?

2. How does left realism critique Marxist criminological theories?

3. What is false consciousness?

4. What are the primary concerns of left realism?

5. What are the levels of the peacemaking pyramid?

6. What is the primary issue that life-course theories examine in relationship to crime?

7. According to Terrie Moffitt, what is the difference between life-course persistent offenders and adolescence-limited offenders?

8. Why is it so difficult to integrate theories?

9. What three theories does Delbert Elliott draw on to formulate his integrated theory?

10. What two delinquency theories does Terence P. Thornberry use to construct the interactional perspective?

ADDITIONAL READINGS

Arrigo, Bruce A. *Criminal Justice–Social Justice: The Maturation of Critical Theory in Law, Crime, and Deviance.* Belmont, CA: Wadsworth, 1999.

Barak, Gregg. *Integrating Criminologies.* Boston: Allyn and Bacon, 1998.

Ferrell, Jeff, and Clinton R. Sanders. *Cultural Criminology.* Boston: Northeastern Press, 1995.

Fuller, John R. *Criminal Justice: A Peacemaking Perspective.* Boston: Allyn and Bacon, 1998.

Laub, John H., and Robert J. Sampson. *Shared Beginnings, Divergent Lives: Delinquent Boys to Age 70.* Cambridge, MA: Harvard University Press, 2003.

Piquero, Alex, and Paul Mazerolle. *Life-Course Criminology: Contemporary and Classic Readings.* Belmont, CA: Wadsworth, 2001.

ENDNOTES

1. Francis T. Cullen and Robert Agnew, *Criminological Theory: Past to Present* (Los Angeles: Roxbury, 2003), 333–336. Cullen and Agnew present a good description of what makes a theory a critical theory.

2. Ibid., 334–335.

3. David M. Gordon, "Capitalism, Class and Crime in America," *Crime and Delinquency* 19 (1973):163–186.

4. David F. Greenberg, ed., *Crime and Capitalism: Readings in Marxist Criminology* (Philadelphia: Temple University Press, 1993).

5. Karl Marx, *Selected Writings in Sociology and Social Philosophy,* trans. P. B. Bottomore (New York: McGraw-Hill, 1956).

6. Willem Bonger, *Crime and Economic Conditions,* abridged ed. (Bloomington: Indiana University Press, 1969). [Originally published 1916]

7. William B. Chambliss, "Policing the Ghetto Underclass: The Politics of Law and Law Enforcement," *Social Problems* 41(1994):177–194.

8. Raymond J. Michalowski, *Order, Law and Crime: An Introduction to Criminology* (New York: Random House, 1985).

9. Ronald L. Akers and Christine S. Sellers, *Criminological Theories: Introduction, Evaluations, and Application*, 4th ed. (Los Angeles: Roxbury, 2003), 210–213.

10. Jock Young and Roger Matthews, eds., *Rethinking Criminology: The Realist Debate* (New Park, CA: Sage, 1992).

11. Walter DeKeseredy, "Left Realism on Inner-City Violence," in Martin D. Schwartz and Suzanne E. Hatty, eds. *Controversies in Critical Criminology* (Cincinnati, OH: Anderson, 2003), 29–41.

12. Jock Young, "The Tasks of a Realist Criminology," *Contemporary Crisis* 12 (1987):337–356.

13. Walter DeKeseredy (see note 11), p. 37.

14. Shahid S. Alvi, Walter DeKeseredy, and Desmond Ellis, *Contemporary Social Problems in North America* (Toronto: Addison Wesley Longman, 2000).

15. Martin D. Schwartz and Walter DeKeseredy, "Left Realist Criminology: Strengths, Weaknesses, and the Feminist Critique," *Crime Law and Social Change* 15 (1991):51–72.

16. Katheryn K. Russell, "Critical Race Theory and Social Justice," in Bruce Arrigo, ed. *Social Justice–Criminal Justice* (Belmont, CA: Wadsworth, 1999), 178–187.

17. Katheryn K. Russell, "A Critical View from the Inside: An Application of Critical Legal Studies to Criminal Law," *Journal of Criminal Law and Criminology* 85 (1994):222–240.

18. In October 1994, Susan Smith strapped her 14-month-old and 3-year-old sons into their car seats and rolled the vehicle into a lake. She had originally told police that her car was stolen by a black male who drove off with the boys.

19. J. Floyd, "The Other Box: Intersectionality and the O. J. Simpson Trial," *Hastings Women's Law Journal* 6 (1995):241–274.

20. The O. J. Simpson Trial: *Opinion Polls*, www.law.umkc.edu/faculty/projects/ftrials/Simpson/polls.html.

21. bell hooks, "Misogyny Gangster Rap, and The Piano," *Z Magazine*, February 1994. Online at www.allaboutbell.com/misogyny.htm.

22. Bruce A. Arrigo, "Postmodern Justice and Critical Criminology: Positional, Relational, and Provisional Science," in Martin O. Schwartz and Suzanne E. Hatty, eds. *Controversies in Critical Criminology* (Cincinnati, OH: Anderson, 2003), 43–55.

23. Akers and Sellers (see note 9), p. 237.

24. Martin D. Schwartz and David O. Friedrichs, "Postmodern Thought and Criminological Discontent: New Metaphors for Understanding Violence," *Criminology* 32 (1994):221–246.

25. See *The Galileo Project: Copernican System* at galileo.rice.edu/sci/theories/copernican_system.html for a review.

26. Arrigo (see note 22), pp. 50–51.

27. Jeff Ferrell, "Cultural Criminology," in Martin O. Schwartz and Suzanne E. Hatty, eds. *Controversies in Critical Criminology* (Cincinnati, OH: Anderson, 2003), 71–84.

28. Ibid., 72.

29. Gregg Barak, *Media, Process, and the Social Construction of Crime: Studies in Newsmaking Criminology* (New York: Garland, 1994).

30. Gregg Barak, "Media, Crime, and Justice: A Case for Constitutive Criminology," in Jeff Ferrell and Clinton R. Sanders, eds. *Cultural Criminology* (Boston: Northeastern Press, 1995), 160.

31. Jody A. Miller, "Struggles over the Symbolic: Gang Style and the Meanings of Social Control," in Jeff Ferrell and Clinton R. Sanders, eds. *Cultural Criminology* (Boston: Northeastern Press, 1995), 213–234.

32. Ibid., 228.

33. Mark S. Hamm, "Hammer of the Gods Revisited: Neo-Nazi Skinheads, Domestic Terrorism, and the Rise of the New Protest Music," in Jeff Ferrell and Clinton R. Sanders, eds. *Cultural Criminology* (Boston: Northeastern Press, 1995), 190–212.

34. Kenneth D. Tunnell, "A Cultural Approach to Crime and Punishment, Bluegrass Style," in Jeff Ferrell and Clinton R. Sanders, eds. *Cultural Criminology* (Boston: Northeastern Press, 1995), 80–105.

35. Jeff Ferrell, *Crimes of Style: Urban Graffiti and the Politics of Criminality* (New York: Garland, 1993).

36. Harold E. Pepinsky and Richard Quinney, eds. *Criminology as Peacemaking* (Bloomington: Indiana University Press, 1991).

37. John R. Fuller, *Criminal Justice: A Peacemaking Perspective* (Boston: Allyn and Bacon, 1998).

38. Immanuel Kant, "The Categorical Imperative," in Daryl Close and Nicholas Meier, eds. *Morality in Criminal Justice: An Introduction to Ethics* (Belmont, CA: Wadsworth), 45–50.

39. Glen H. Elder, Jr., John Modell, and Ross Parke, eds. *Children in Time and Place: Developmental and Historical Insights* (New York: Cambridge University Press, 1993).

40. David I. Kertzer and Jennie Keith, *Age and Anthropologist Theory* (Ithaca, NY: Cornell University Press, 1984).

41. John Modell, *Into One's Own: From Youth to Adulthood in the United States, 1920–1975* (Berkeley: University of California Press, 1989).

42. Mark Warr, "Life-Course Transitions and Desistance from Crime," *Criminology* 36 (1998):369–388.

43. Terrie Moffitt, "Adolescent-Limited and Life-Course-Persistent Antisocial Behavior: A Developmental Taxonomy," *Psychological Review* 100 (1993):674–701.

44. Terrie E. Moffitt, "Pathways in the Life Course to Crime," in Francis T. Cullen and Robert Agnew, eds. *Criminological Theory: Past to Present* (Los Angeles: Roxbury, 2003), 452–457.

45. Ibid., 458–459.

46. Ibid., 460–465.

47. Ibid., 466–468.

48. Cullen and Agnew (see note 1), p. 470.

49. Robert J. Sampson and John H. Laub, *Crime in the Making: Pathways and Turning Points*

50. John H. Laub and Robert J. Sampson, *Shared Beginnings, Divergent Lives: Delinquent Boys to Age 70* (Cambridge, MA: Harvard University Press, 2003).

51. Robert J. Sampson and John H. Laub, "Crime and the Life Course," in Francis T. Cullen and Robert Agnew, eds. *Criminological Theory: Past to Present* (Los Angeles: Roxbury, 2003), 470–482.

52. Delbert S. Elliott, Suzanne Ageton, and Rachelle J. Canter, "An Integrated Theoretical Perspective on Delinquent Behavior," *Journal of Research in Crime and Delinquency*, 16 (1979):3–27.

53. Terence P. Thornberry, "Toward an Interactional Theory of Delinquency," *Criminology* 25 (1987):863–891.

54. Charles R. Tittle, *Control Balance: Toward a General Theory of Deviance* (Boulder, CO: Westview, 1995).

Through Life (Cambridge, MA: Harvard University Press, 1993).

PART THREE
Delinquency in Society

How is female delinquency different from male delinquency?

Why do females commit fewer offenses than males?

What explains how females are treated differentially in the juvenile justice system?

CHAPTER 9

Female Delinquency

Until recently, the popular view of juvenile delinquency was formed by looking at the antisocial behavior of males. As in other areas of social science and medicine, males have been considered the norm, and research on social problems such as delinquency has been done almost exclusively on males.[1] This neglect of females has distorted the level and breadth of knowledge of how just over half of the population is treated by society. The implicit assumption is that males are the standard by which issues are evaluated, and to the extent that females couldn't "measure up," they were found wanting. Men's issues were considered to be war, economics, and sports, and women's issues were considered to be child care, birth control, and shopping. Men were legally empowered and physically stronger, so it seemed only reasonable (to men that is) that they should be considered the standard by which all things are measured.[2]

This neglect of females has started to change over the past generation, and researchers are now recognizing that there is a gender dimension to just about every issue within society.[3] Women are quickly gaining ground in politics, professions, and the home. For the first half of the 20th century, it was rare to find a woman in law school or medical school. Now half of each class is female. Women are found in increasing numbers in Congress and in state legislatures across the country. Soon, it's predicted, the United States might have a female president. The adage that "a man's home is his castle" is no longer accurate for many households, because there is a sharing of power in marriage that is supported by the economic demands of family life as women work in professions.

Females break the law less often than males (see Figures 9-1 and 9-2), but it's still important to study female delinquency for three reasons. First, female crime and delinquency are changing in that both are on the rise (see Figures 9-3 and 9-4). Second, females are often the victims of crime and delinquency, and it's necessary to understand how and why they are in such close proximity to crime. Finally, much of male offending is a result of gender issues. As the social roles of men and women continue to evolve, it's interesting to observe how some men have a difficult time with the changing conceptions of manhood and with adjusting to the new power that women are demanding in relationships and in the workplace.[4]

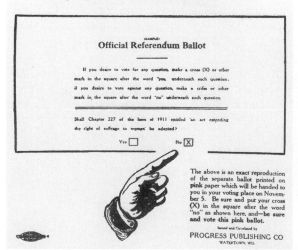

This political poster from 1911 warns that women should not be allowed to vote. Today, women are gaining ground in politics, professions, and the home. *(Courtesy Wisconsin Historical Society)*

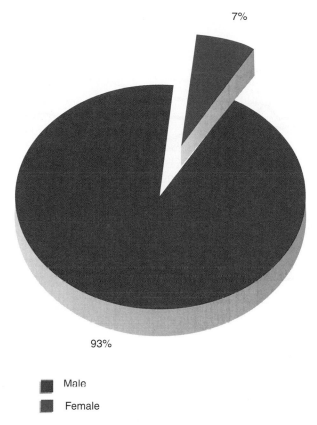

7%

93%

■ Male
■ Female

Figure 9-1   Inmates under the Jurisdiction of State or Federal Correctional Authorities by Sex, 2004
Source: Paige M. Harrison and Allen J. Beck, *Prisoners in 2004* (Washington, DC: U.S. Department of Justice Bureau of Justice Statistics, 2004), 4. Online at www.ojp.usdoj.gov/bjs/pub/pdf/p04.pdf.

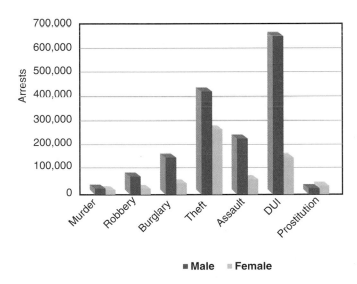

■ Male   ■ Female

Figure 9-2   Total Arrest Trends, Male and Female, All Ages, 2005 *Source:* Federal Bureau of Investigation, *Uniform Crime Reports, Crime in the United States*, Ten-Year Arrest Trends by Sex, 1996–2005, www.fbi.gov/ucr/05cius/data/table_33.html.

It is fair to say that we are in the midst of a gender revolution, and the proper roles for men and women and boys and girls are negotiated on a daily basis. (See Programs for Children 9.1 for a look at a typical girls' outreach program.) In Durkheim's ter-minology, it could be said that sex roles in the 21st century are experiencing a state of **anomie,** in which the norms are in flux. It is in this context of sex-role anomie that

**Instant Recall
from Chapter 7**
anomie
A condition in which a people or society undergoes a breakdown of social norms and values. Also, personal anxiety and isolation produced by rapidly shifting moral and cultural values.

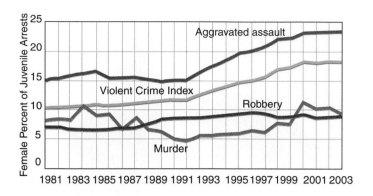

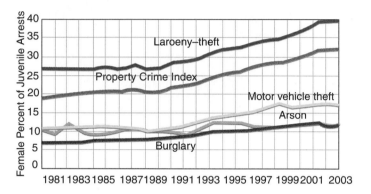

Figure 9-3   **The percentage of juvenile female violent-crime arrests increased between 1980 and 2003, with the main increase in aggravated assault arrests. (top)**

The percentage of juvenile female arrests increased between 1980 and 2003 for the four property-crime index offenses. (bottom) *Source:* Federal Bureau of Investigation, *Uniform Crime reports, 1980–2003* in Howard N. Snyder and Melissa Sickmund, *Juvenile Offenders and Victims: 2006 National Report* (Washington, DC: U.S. Department of Justice, Office of Justice Programs, Office of Juvenile Justice and Delinquency Prevention, 2006), 128. Online at www.ojjdp.ncjrs.org/ojstatbb/nr2006/downloads/NR2006.pdf.

this chapter examines female delinquency. Although it's also necessary to talk about male delinquency, especially the issue of masculinity, this is done primarily in contrast to female issues to tease out how gender influences crime.[5] The chapter is divided into five parts.

1. Girls to Women: A Developmental View
2. Gender and Delinquency
3. Theories of Female Delinquency
4. Feminist Theories of Female Delinquency
5. Gender and the Juvenile Justice System

When the student is finished with the chapter, it will be apparent that there is such a thing as gender roles and that they are changing rapidly. Additionally, it could be argued that the increase in women's power hasn't necessarily been at the expense of men. Although women have historically been constrained by their gender roles, so too have men. The empowerment of women has also allowed men to break out of the limited roles required by intense masculinity and to benefit from the ability to spend more time with children, look after their own health issues, and become more aware of their psychological well-being. Therefore, this chapter on female delinquency can also shed light on numerous issues that also can be applied to males.[6]

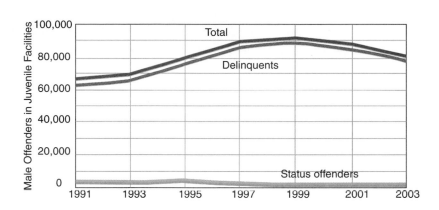

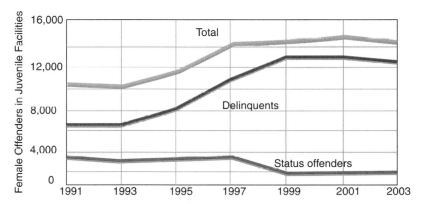

Figure 9-4   **Note that the number of female offenders in custody increased 52 percent from 1991 to 2003. Also, status offenders accounted for a greater share of female offenders than of male offenders.** *Source:* Howard N. Snyder and Melissa Sickmund, *Juvenile Offenders and Victims: 2006 National Report* (Washington, DC: U.S. Department of Justice, Office of Justice Programs, Office of Juvenile Justice and Delinquency Prevention, 2006), 206. Online at www.ojjdp.ncjrs.org/ojstatbb/nr2006/downloads/NR2006.pdf.

Girls break the law less often than boys, but the study of female delinquency is still important.

(Courtesy John Neubauer, PhotoEdit Inc.)

9.1   PROGRAMS *for* CHILDREN

GIRLS INC.

Formerly called the Girls Club of America, Girls Inc. is a nationwide program designed to empower girls to be strong, smart, and bold. Girls Inc. sponsors a number of programs designed to enable young women to develop their capacities in a broad range of fields. These include the following:

- *Operation Smart.* This program aims to increase the interest and abilities of girls in math, science, and technology. It specifically seeks to prevent girls who show talent in these areas from adopting an attitude that science and technology are male subjects and that girls can't excel in them.
- *Preventing adolescent pregnancy.* This program seeks to educate girls about the issues of sex and pregnancy. It is designed to address the concerns of girls at four age levels and to prepare them to be able to decide when they want to engage in sexual practices. The programs teach girls to say no to pressures for sex that come early in adolescence, as well as educate girls about sexual myths and the female anatomy. Additionally, girls are linked to public health organizations that can assist them in their health needs.
- *Media literacy.* This program teaches girls to think critically about the images of women as presented by the media—specifically, to focus on issues such as body image and the dysfunctional manner in which the media portray the female body as a sexual object.
- *Project Bold.* This program teaches girls about violence and its prevention. It teaches girls to resist violence at home and the school and shows them concrete examples of how to defend themselves.

- *Economic literacy.* This program teaches girls how to handle money. It presents the basic issues such as debt, interest rates, credit-card practices, and the value of savings and teaches girls to plan on controlling their own economic future.

These are but a few of the ways that Girls Inc. addresses the problems facing young women. Girls Inc. starts helping girls as young as age 6 and continues through adolescence. Its primary goal is to provide girls with a strong and healthy self-concept so that they can grow into women with confidence and competence. To that end, Girls Inc. has developed the Girls' Bill of Rights.

- Girls have the right to be themselves and to resist gender stereotypes.
- Girls have the right to express themselves with originality and enthusiasm.
- Girls have the right to take risks, to strive freely, and to take pride in success.
- Girls have the right to accept and appreciate their bodies.
- Girls have the right to have confidence in themselves and to be safe in the world.
- Girls have the right to prepare for interesting work and economic independence.

Girls Inc. provides a comprehensive program that helps girls build self-esteem and confidence. It aims to combat the many negative and limiting cultural messages prevalent in the media, schools, and family that perpetuate the second-class status of females in society.

Source: Girls Incorporated, www.girlsinc.org/.

GIRLS TO WOMEN: A DEVELOPMENTAL VIEW

sex

The biological designation of male or female.

gender

The characteristics attributed to and accorded to males and females by society and/or culture on the basis of sex.

Studying female development is risky because so much of what we thought were biologically and psychologically determined traits actually aren't. Here we must understand the difference between sex and gender. **Sex** is the biological designation of male or female. **Gender** refers to the characteristics attributed to and accorded to males and females by their societies and cultures on the basis of sex. Sex is determined by biology. Gender is determined by society. As we learn more about the effect of socialization and the potentials for development if given the right opportunities, we are finding that much of what was thought to be factual about females is turning out to be false. Take for example the old insult that "you throw like a girl." This phrase was used to put women down and to insult boys who weren't yet proficient in throwing a ball. One need only look at high school and college softball games to see women who don't "throw like a girl," but rather fling the ball as if it were "on a rope." What was once thought to be a female limitation has, in fact, turned out to be simply a limitation placed on females. Given the right coaching, females are proving to be adept at many skills thought to be specific to males. For example, until 1976, women weren't allowed to run the Olympic marathon. It was thought that women's bodies couldn't withstand the pounding of running for such a long period of time. In 2000, however, the winner of the women's Olympic marathon posted a time that would have won the men's Olympic marathon in 1956.[7]

Physical Development of Girls

Those who study child development look at the physical, cognitive, psychological, and sociological aspects of how children become adults.[8] Here we will detail how children make this journey, paying particular attention to females.

Unraveling the influence of physical and social development in females is difficult because of the rigid gender roles that societies enforce. We are able to observe very few systematic differences between infant boys and girls. They learn to walk, talk, and toilet train at about the same age. Although boys might gain weight a bit quicker, few physiological differences account for why boys and girls might become antisocial.[9]

The greatest differences in the maturation of girls and boys don't appear until adolescence. As we go through puberty, our bodies change rapidly, which influences our psychological self-esteem and our sociological interaction with others. One of the first differences between boys and girls is that girls experience a growth spurt in height at 14 years, while boys don't have theirs until about 16 years old.[10] Additionally, girls develop pubic hair, breasts, and begin menstruation before the age of 14, whereas boys lag until 16 before realizing any major physical changes. These changes affect the body image of both sexes as they react with horror and/or joy. Few adolescents are neutral about physical changes. In recent years, experts have noted that a growing number of girls are experiencing puberty early. See Kids in the News 9.1 for a look at the study of the relationship between early female puberty and delinquency.

According to Robert S. Feldman, girls in Western society used to react to the onset of menstruation with anxiety because of the negative aspects such as cramps. Now,

Much of what was once thought to be factual about females, such as their inability to withstand strenuous sports, is false. In 2004, the medalists for the Olympic women's marathon were (left to right) Catherine Nderba of Kenya (silver), Mizuki Noguchi of Japan (gold), and Deena Kastor of the United States (bronze). *(© Mike Blake/Reuters/CORBIS)*

The greatest differences in the maturation of girls and boys are not apparent until they reach adolescence. Here, an eighth-grade girl is able to lift her male classmate. *(Courtesy Bob Daemmrich, The Image Works)*

however, because menstruation is openly discussed, girls often welcome it as a rise in status and react with increased self-esteem and self-awareness.[11] The key to how one reacts to physical development is in the timing. An early- or late-developing body can cause anxiety. For boys, an early-developing body might mean they excel at sports sooner than their peers. They might also engage in delinquent acts sooner because they associate with older boys who are their size. For girls, early development might mean that older boys seek them out for dates. However, these girls often aren't socially mature and find these situations challenging.

Late-maturing bodies hold different problems for boys and girls. For boys, it means that they aren't as tall as their contemporaries and therefore are not considered to be as physically attractive. For girls, it means they might be overlooked in the dating scene and thus feel themselves to be undesirable. However, when they do finally mature later, they are better prepared to deal with dating and might experience fewer emotional problems.[12] Late-maturing girls are also more likely to fit the cultural ideal of being slender and to feel less pressure to diet.[13]

Cognitive Development of Girls

During adolescence, young people learn to think in more abstract ways and to understand both the physical and social world around them. More important, however, is that they learn more about their own psychology and begin to see themselves as they believe others see them. Young people develop their **metacognition,** or their own thinking processes, which allows them to have a better idea about how perceptive they are. One downfall of this increase in metacognition is that the adolescent might become particularly introspective and self-conscious.[14]

One observation that applies to many adolescents is that they are quick to find fault with authority figures, such as parents and teachers, and are unwilling to accept criticism. This age-related (but not age-exclusive) fault is a function of **adolescent egocentrism.** Adolescent egocentrism occurs when youths become so absorbed in

metacognition
The act of thinking about one's processes and means of thinking.

adolescent egocentrism
The belief common to many adolescents that they are the focus of attention in social situations.

Early Signs of Trouble

Girls are experiencing puberty earlier than their mothers or grandmothers. Experts give several reasons for this, but a primary factor appears to be weight. According to a 2005 study, girls who are overweight tend to get their first periods earlier.[1] Early puberty is typically defined as a first period before the age of 12; the average age for a girl's first period is about two and a half months earlier than it was 25 years ago.[2] Another study found that girls with a higher percentage of body fat at ages 5 and 7 and girls who experienced greater increases in body fat from age 5 to 9 were more likely to experience early puberty.[3]

Early puberty doesn't just mean that a girl (or boy) grows up sooner. Unfortunately, it's an indicator of increased juvenile delinquency, and females and males who experience early puberty are more likely to become both victims and offenders. Also, early-maturing girls have more trouble with depression and anxiety than girls who mature later.[4] A 2006 study found that children who go through puberty earlier also, for obvious reasons, tend to resemble adults at much earlier ages. This creates a social gap between those children and their later-developing peers. Therefore, the children who resemble adults look for friends who most resemble them physically and who also happen to be much older.

Girls who begin to resemble adults early on also appear attractive to boys who are much older. A 12- or 13-year-old girl might look and feel like she's ready to date a 16- or 17-year-old boy.[5] Because they are socializing with much older adolescents, and sometimes adults, the early maturers are at a much greater risk of being victimized or tempted into trouble. Early maturers might also seek more adultlike roles and might be more likely to associate with peers who engage in deviant or status offense–type behaviors, such as smoking, drinking alcohol, and staying out of school.[6]

The study points out that responsible adults, generally parents and teachers, might treat early-developing children differently. They might be less likely to protect early-maturing children from bullies and other aggressors and, in the case of parents, might restrict their activities less because of their adult appearances and attitudes.[7] Unfortunately, girls who have more male friends and spend more time with them are also at a greater risk for delinquency.[8] This leads to yet another male–female issue, that of romantic relationships. The younger girls, feeling pressure to maintain romantic relationships with older boys, might also be likely to commit deviant or status-offense acts to maintain these relationships.[9]

Think About It

1. Should more research be done into the connection between weight and early puberty? Should special precautions be taken to ensure that young girls don't become overweight during childhood?

2. How should girls who mature early be treated by other adults? Is it okay to let them seek out older friends and more mature experiences? Conversely, should more care be taken to protect them?

1. Aviva Must et al., "Childhood Overweight and Maturational Timing in the Development of Adult Overweight and Fatness: The Newton Girls Study and Its Follow-up," Pediatrics 116 (2005): 625.
2. Carla K. Johnson, "Study: Heavier Girls Hit Puberty Earlier," Associated Press, August 11, 2005.
3. Kirsten Krahnstoever Davison, Elizabeth J. Susman, and Leann Lipps Birch, "Percent Body Fat at Age 5 Predicts Earlier Pubertal Development among Girls at Age 9," Pediatrics 111, no. 4 (April 2003): 815.
4. Line Tremblay and Jean-Yves Frigon, "Precocious Puberty in Adolescent Girls: A Biomarker of Later Psychosocial adjustment problems," Child Psychiatry and Human Development, 36, no. 1 (Fall 2005). 73–94.
5. Jennifer Smith Richards, "Early Bloomers Found to Have Higher Crime Risk," Columbus Dispatch (OH), February 12, 2006.
6. Dana L. Haynie, "Contexts of Risk? Explaining the Link between Girls' Pubertal Development and Their Delinquency Involvement," Social Forces 82, no. 1 (2003): 355–397.
7. Dana L. Haynie and Alex R. Piquero, "Pubertal Development and Physical Victimization in Adolescence," Journal of Research in Crime & Delinquency 43, no. 1 (February 2006): 3 35.
8. Robert Agnew and Timothy Brezina, "Relational Problems with Peers, Gender and Delinquency," Youth and Society 29 (1997): 83–112.
9. Dana L. Haynie (see note 6).

their own lives that they are unable to view the world from other perspectives. They believe that everybody is scrutinizing them and finding all their real or imaginary faults. A new pimple that isn't noticed by others becomes a big problem for those who are so self-conscious and self-absorbed. Likewise, an offhand teasing remark by a popular football player can be the source of extreme embarrassment to the girl who isn't confident of her standing in the social order of her school. Adolescents tend to think in terms of an imaginary audience of real and fictitious others who pay attention to every detail of their lives. In reality, nobody is watching, or at least not to the detail and not with the mean-spirited intentions that the adolescent imagines.[15]

Because of the differences in the rates that males and females mature, girls can often participate on an equal level with boys in sports for several years until puberty occurs. This 10-year-old girl is suited up to play football. *(Courtesy Esbin/Anderson, Omni-Photo Communications, Inc.)*

Another cognitive concern of egocentrism is that many youths adopt the feeling that their problems are unique to themselves. As they endure the predictable crises of growing up, they personalize each event and respond as if no one else can possibly understand their trials and tribulations. This is especially true of their first broken heart or embarrassing faux pas in front of their peers. They tend to see their problems as separate from those of their peers. They do not believe they can get a sexually transmitted disease or a DUI because those things happen to other people, not to them. Their cognitive isolation allows them to become self-absorbed in their problems as if they were personal fables, and not the growing pains suffered by most adolescents.[16]

Psychological and Social Development of Girls

The healthy psychological and social development of young women has several aspects. Like young men, young women are concerned with establishing personal identity, fitting into their peer group, negotiating the pitfalls of dating and sexual activity, cutting the apron strings to parents, and establishing their independence. As young women negotiate these psychological and sociological passages, they are susceptible to feelings of inadequacy and inferiority. These feelings can result in depression and the contemplation of suicide if they can't be resolved in a positive way.[17] It is worth considering each of these concerns in more detail to appreciate the issues inherent in the change of status from girl to woman.

IDENTITY   It is common for youngsters to ask questions of themselves such as "Who am I?" and "Where do I belong in this world?" As they mature physically and cognitively, they see the world as a more complex place and their role in it as more complicated than it was when they were children. They understand that they will be pressured to perform adult activities, and they struggle to acquire a set of values, skills, and abilities in order to interact with others. Adolescents, especially girls, notice the dramatic changes in their bodies brought on by puberty and the fact that other people are reacting to them differently. These changes challenge their ability to have an accurate self-concept and, even more so, a healthy self-esteem.[18] As their lives become more intertwined with new activities and other people, they might find that they have a good idea of where they fit into society but not be very happy with how they see themselves.

According to Feldman, girls have a more difficult time with self-esteem than boys. This is primarily because girls are judged by their physical appearance much more so than boys. This becomes particularly problematic when one discovers that the cultural ideal for the appearance of young women isn't the cultural norm.[19] In fact, for most girls, obtaining the "perfect" female body that appears on the covers of magazines would require surgery in the form of breast implants, collagen injections, and liposuction. The social pressures to look a certain way are tremendous and can result in young women engaging in unhealthy and dangerous lifestyles or rejecting the ideal model and adopting a deviant identity.

FITTING IN AND BEING POPULAR   Another aspect of one's social development during adolescence is the forming of reference groups from which young people can gather information about the expectations of the adolescent role and be able to compare themselves with other young people. In high school, young people hang out with crowds or smaller cliques to establish their place in the social order. They label each other as a "jock" or "nerd" or "goth," and their position in the informal social order of the school is contingent on how they are perceived to fit into a variety of groups. Their social identity can be fluid as they move from one context (the classroom) to another (the dating scene or the athletic field). Some individuals have limited, rigid identities; others float from one group to another with little effort.[20] Young people can be overly concerned with their reputation and might allow peer pressure to get them into trouble. Young people have finely tuned antennae when it comes to determining who is popular and who isn't. Popularity becomes a goal for some teenagers, and it often proves to be a difficult one as events, styles, and friends change and those who were first become last in the struggle for acceptance.[21]

DATING AND SEX   The ideal function of dating is a practice of courtship that eventually leads to marriage. It gives adolescents an opportunity to get to know each other on a fairly risk-free basis in which the date is limited to a movie, dinner, or a party. Parents monitor the selection of a dating partner and set limits on the time, place, and activity of the date. In some cultures, all dating is done under the close watch of a chaperone. However, the reality of dating in the United States is very different from the ideal (see Focus on Ethics 9.1). Dating for adolescents has very little to do with finding a marriage partner. Instead, dating provides the functions of entertainment, establishing intimacy, and often prestige.[22] Being asked out by the football team captain or dating the prettiest cheerleader can consign a degree of status that is coveted by others.

Whether dating encourages intimacy is still an open question for those who are first starting out. Young people are so concerned with guarding their inner feelings that dating can take on a superficial atmosphere in which very little actual communication occurs. As adolescents get older, they are better able to handle their feelings, sometimes long after they have become physically intimate with a partner. As a source of entertainment, dating provides a major departure from family activities. Being outside the scope of adult supervision gives young people the opportunity to establish their identity in new ways, such as engaging in risk-taking behavior by driving fast or consuming alcohol or drugs.

In the 21st century, dating for teenagers has changed. Instead of a boy–girl date with an agreed-on activity, such as seeing a movie, young people now might engage in what amounts to group dating in what they call *hanging out*. Here several teens will meet at a friend's house or local mall to talk, shop, flirt, and engage in activities that traditional dating used to provide. It provides for risk-free emotional interaction during which teens can have fun, get to know each other, and establish their social hierarchy. Two teens might "hook up" and become emotionally or physically intimate, but this doesn't

FOCUS *on* ETHICS

9.1

SEX TALK

You are a single parent with 15-year-old twins. They are approaching the age and emotional maturity of youngsters who begin to think about the opposite sex, dating, and all the other issues you have neglected to consider because you really don't want to talk to them about adult topics. However, because you found a condom in your daughter's sock drawer, you know the time has come to have that "sex talk" with them.

As twins, your son and daughter are very much alike in some ways and very different in others. They are wonderful kids who do well in school, stay out of trouble, and provide you with emotional support since your spouse died four years ago. Until recently, they have been the best of friends and have always done things with the same group of peers.

Now, however, your daughter has started to attract the interest of older boys. She's streaking ahead of your son in her social and physical development, and this has started to concern you. Her 18-year-old boyfriend isn't someone you would have picked for her. Although he seems like a nice and respectful young man, his life's ambition is to be a drummer in a rock band. He already has all the tattoos, body piercings, and raggedy clothes that make him look the part, but he has a problem in not being able to keep a beat. His band kicked him out because of his poor playing, and now he sulks around your house all day. Your daughter has

fallen for his "woe is me" attitude and fancies herself as the only one who sees his hidden genius.

Your son has come to you and complained about how this "loser and leech" has brainwashed your daughter and how he wants him out of the house because he's eating everything in sight. Your son further informs you that the young man and your daughter spend a lot of time in her bedroom behind a locked door. Although you have known this day was going to come, you are uncertain about how to proceed.

What Should You Do?

1. Sit your daughter down and have that difficult talk about sex; you provide her with the scientific facts and make her aware of your expectations. Give your son the same talk about sex even though he seems to be a year or two from developing his own interest in girls.

2. Tell her to dump the boyfriend. Lay down the law of the house, and inform her she isn't to entertain males in her bedroom when you aren't home.

3. Do nothing and let her find her own way in the world. She is a good child, and you want to show her that you have confidence in her decisions.

4. Tell your son to stay out of your daughter's business.

---

necessarily mean that they are a couple. The intimacy is treated as entertainment and is attractive, because there is little in the way of a binding commitment, even for that evening, between them. The dating interaction gets more intense as the teenagers get older, especially when boys start driving and can escape the observation of others. Girls might begin dating older boys who have cars and money, which brings higher social status. Because boys physically and emotionally develop at a slower rate, girls often find themselves attracted to older boys who seem to be more worldly and sophisticated.[23]

Teenagers' first encounter with sex is most often by masturbation. About half of boys and a quarter of girls report sexual self-stimulation. Boys engage in masturbation early and then decrease its occurrence, while girls begin slowly in their early teens and reach a maximum later.[24] Sexual intercourse is a major milestone in the lives of most adolescents. It is usually preceded by other sexual activities such as petting, deep kissing, or oral sex. The age at which adolescents have their first sexual intercourse has been declining for the past 50 years. At least half of adolescents have had sex before age 18, and 80 percent by age 20. One important reason for the increase in the onset of sexual activity is the changing nature of the double standard that says sex is permissible for boys but not for girls. Today the double standard has been relaxed, and the new norm is called "permissiveness with affection." Here sexual activity is allowed to girls if it occurs in the context of a long-term, committed, or loving relationship.[25] This new standard isn't rigid, like abstinence, so the definition of what is long-term or loving can vary greatly, giving girls greater autonomy to engage in sex without loss of social status.

To deal with the issues of teenagers having sex, some groups have developed abstinence campaigns to encourage young teens to forgo sexual activity until marriage. Although these campaigns have been successful at getting many teens to take the pledge, the youths themselves have been less successful in maintaining their virginity (see Crosscurrents 9.1).

9.1

CrossCurrents

Saying the Pledge of Abstinence

In recent years, a social and legislative trend has arisen that seeks to encourage youths to abstain from sex until marriage. This is an interesting development. Only a few decades ago, it was assumed that adolescents didn't and wouldn't have sex until marriage, although many certainly did; therefore, the issue of adolescent sex wasn't discussed publicly or, it seems, privately. At the turn of the 21st century, however, the trend has flipped. Many parents, most of baby-boomer age, assume that their adolescents will have sex or be tempted to have sex and so have made adolescent sexuality a very public issue. The bar graphs show the percentages of high schoolers over the last couple of decades who claimed to have had sex and who claimed to be currently sexually active.

Generally, parents are worried about two issues concerning adolescent sexuality: pregnancy and sexually transmitted disease. Although teen pregnancy is certainly a worrisome issue, much of the emphasis on it might be cultural and, in part, emphasized by the media. The rate of births to females ages 15 to 19 has actually steadily decreased from its peak in the 1950s, with a slight spike in the early 1990s (see line graph).

Parents and adolescents now have a variety of programs and ceremonies, most of them religion based, that offer to assist in the endeavor toward sexual abstinence. For example, some teenagers wear "promise rings" to remind them of their "purity pledges." One program, Silver Ring Thing, which has received $1 million in federal funding, sells silver rings

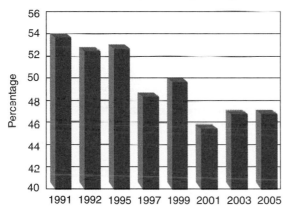

Percentage of Ninth to Twelfth Graders Who Have Had Sexual Intercourse, by Year

Source: National Center for Chronic Disease Prevention and Health Promotion, *The National Youth Risk Behavior Survey,* www.cdc.gov/HealthyYouth/yrbs/pdf/trends/2005_YRBS_Sexual_Behaviors.pdf.

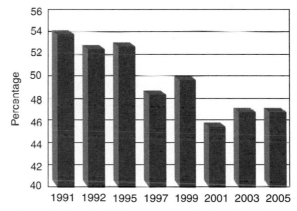

Percentage of Ninth to Twelfth Graders Currently Sexually Active

Source: National Center for Chronic Disease Prevention and Health Promotion, *National Youth Risk Behavior Survey,* www.cdc.gov/HealthyYouth/yrbs/pdf/trends/2005_YRBS_Sexual_Behaviors.pdf.

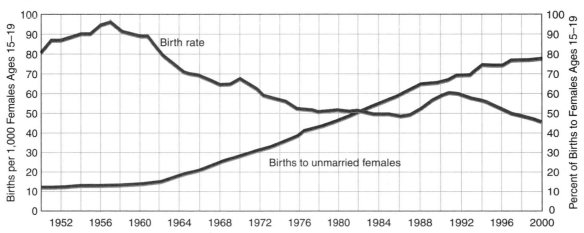

Births to Females Ages 15 to 19, 1952 to 2000

Source: Howard N. Snyder and Melissa Sickmund, *Juvenile Offenders and Victims: 2006 National Report* (Washington, DC: U.S. Department of Justice, Office of Justice Programs, Office of Juvenile Justice and Delinquency Prevention, 2006), 12. Online at www.ojjdp.ncjrs.org/ojstatbb/nr2006/downloads/NR2006.pdf.

(Continued)

(Continued)

inscribed with a Bible verse and a virginity symbol. On his or her wedding day, the wearer gives the ring to the new spouse. Programs that assist adolescents and parents with abstinence pledges include Passport to Purity, Purely Committed, Day of Purity, and True Love Waits.[1] Many programs involve ceremonies of varying involvement. More common, however, appear to be simple pledges in which teenagers of both sexes promise their parents that they won't have sex until marriage.

But do these pledges last? A National Longitudinal Study of Adolescent Health undertaken in 1995 and 1996 on 13,000 youths in grades 7 to 12 showed that abstinence pledges have more of an effect on adolescent veracity than on adolescent sexuality. That is, an adolescent is more likely to take the pledge, have sex, and recant the pledge, than not have sex. Also, those who take the pledge after having had sex are more likely to deny that they ever had sex at all. This phenomenon, called biased recall, is a normal human behavior. According to the study, regardless of age or gender, people are more likely when recalling past behavior to align the frequency of that behavior with their current behavior. For example, people who have stopped drinking alcohol altogether are more likely to underestimate how much alcohol they used to drink. The same goes for adolescents who have taken abstinence pledges after being sexually active. And adolescents who report having taken an abstinence pledge, then later report having sex, are more likely to deny ever having taken the pledge.[2]

The study also found that retracting or denying the pledge was most frequent among those adolescents who had just become sexually active or who were renouncing being born-again Christians. Conversely, those who claimed to be virgins after reporting on a prior survey that they had had sex tended to be those who had recently taken the pledge or had become a born-again Christian. In the study, 53 percent of the respondents retracted their abstinence pledge a year after reporting having taken it.[3]

Other studies have found that adolescents who take abstinence pledges contract sexually transmitted diseases at about the same rate as those who don't. What is interesting is that, although those who have pledged abstinence do have fewer sexual partners, they are less likely to use condoms and more likely to substitute anal or oral sex for vaginal sex.

Think About It

1. Would you ask your adolescent to take an abstinence pledge?
2. Do you agree with the results of the study?
3. Do you believe abstinence pledges work?

1. Ashley Fantz, "Teen Hot on Abstinence Rings (but Cool on Sex)," *Miami Herald*, May 24, 2005, Lifestyle section.
2. Janet E. Rosenbaum, "Reborn a Virgin: Adolescents' Retracting of Virginity Pledges and Sexual Histories," *American Journal of Public Health* 96, no. 6 (June 2006): 1098–1103.
3. Sandra G. Boodman, "Virginity Pledges Can't Be Taken on Faith," *Washington Post*, May 16, 2006, p. F04.

CUTTING THE STRINGS OF PARENTAL CONTROL   The final aspect of girls' healthy psychological and sociological development is the gradual disengagement of parental control that occurs during adolescence and young adulthood. This disengagement is more difficult for girls than it is for boys, because parents generally consider girls to be more fragile and vulnerable than boys, so they tend to try to exert control longer. Traditionally, boys are allowed more flexibility and autonomy at an earlier age than girls.[26] Boys are given later curfews, more access to cars, and less supervision than girls.

The struggle for girls typically begins at home with the mother. Predictably, the mother demands that the girl's room be clean and that the girl help with the domestic duties as preparation for the time when she has a family of her own. The girl might consider her room as the one location where she can establish her own domain and often keeps it messy as a way of proclaiming her independence from parental control. This conflict spreads to skipping religious services, choosing clothing styles, testing curfews, selecting friends, acquiring tattoos and body piercings, and selecting a college or career. Ideally, as the girl gets older, her parents give her graduated responsibilities and autonomy, but from the girl's point of view, this newfound freedom never comes fast enough.[27]

This overview of the development of young females has been necessarily brief. Each of the topics could have, and have had, books written about it. Our purpose here has been to alert the student to the major issues and concerns of development. For many of these issues, boys have the same concerns, and many boys find different ways of resolving the tasks of growing up. It is in light of these issues of differential female development that we now turn to the issue of female delinquency. The involvement of young females with crime, delinquency, and the juvenile justice system is very different from that of males. Girls commit less delinquency and less serious delinquent acts, are treated differently by justice officials, and, for the most part, are easier to put back on the right path. However, for a small number of girls, delinquency is a very serious issue because, either as perpetrator or victim, females have a vastly different experience with the criminal and juvenile justice systems than do males.

GENDER AND DELINQUENCY

The incidence of female delinquency is far less than that of males (see Figure 9-5). The reasons for females showing up in crime statistics at such a lower rate can be attributed to two factors. First, females commit fewer and different types of offenses and delinquency. Although this statement seems obvious, it's really very complicated. Why do females commit fewer offenses than males when they comprise half the population? What offenses do females commit? What types of delinquency do juvenile females commit? The second factor that accounts for why females don't show up in the crime statistics at the same rate as males is that the criminal and juvenile justice systems treat them differently.

Extent and Nature of Female Delinquency

Although females commit fewer offenses than males, female offending and delinquency are considered a serious problem. The pattern of female crime is different across age, geographic location, type, and seriousness. Here we will discuss the particular concerns of female delinquency, while recognizing that the discussion could be extended to female adult offending as well.[28] Of specific interest are the circumstances that lead to girls getting in trouble with the law. Therefore, we will concentrate on a few types of behaviors for which girls are subjected to the most attention from the juvenile justice system.

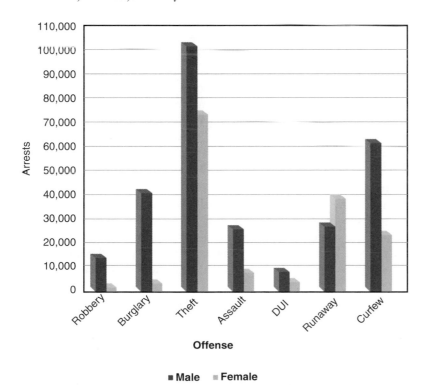

Figure 9-5   Arrest Trends, Male and Female, under 18, 2005

Note the arrest trends for runaways, which is the only category in which juvenile females out-offend juvenile males. *Source:* Federal Bureau of Investigation, *Uniform Crime Reports, Crime in the United States,* Ten-Year Arrest Trends by Sex, 1996–2005, www.fbi.gov/ucr/05cius/data/table_33.html.

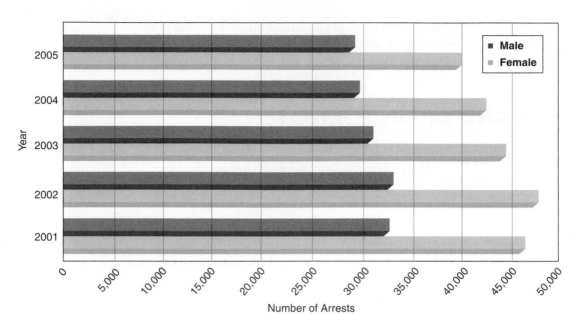

Figure 9-6   Runaways, Number of Males and Females Arrested by Year *Source:* Federal Bureau of Investigation, *Uniform Crime Reports, Crime in the United States,* Ten-Year Arrest Trends by Sex (Washington, DC: U.S. Government Printing Office, 2001, 2002, 2003, 2004, 2005).

Instant Recall from Chapter 1

status offense

An act considered to be a legal offense only when committed by a juvenile; it can be adjudicated only in a juvenile court.

- **Running away from home**   One of the few forms of delinquency that is committed more by girls than by boys is running away from home (see Figure 9-6). Running away is considered a **status offense** in that it's a violation of the law only because of age. Once a girl reaches the age of 18, the justice system, as with boys, is no longer concerned about her as a status offender. Why do girls run away from home at a greater rate than boys? There are two reasons for this pattern. First, girls might be running toward something. They might have an older boyfriend of whom the parents disapprove, and they might have to make a choice between the two. This is the classic Romeo and Juliet dilemma, in which the girl is caught up in the romantic passion of first love and in a battle with her parents, who consider her too young to make such decisions. The other reason girls run away from home at a greater rate than boys is because they are usually running from some sort of physical or psychological abuse. A father, stepfather, mother's boyfriend, uncle, or some other sexually abusing male can make life at home so unbearable that girls often feel forced to leave. Sometimes the boyfriend is used as a way to escape the abusing male in the home.[29]

- **Shoplifting**   Another form of delinquency that girls engage in at a high rate is shoplifting.[30] The social pressure on girls to wear the latest style in clothes and to buy expensive cosmetics is great, and for many young women the only way to acquire these items is to steal them. For some young women, shoplifting is a group activity. They enter shops in pairs or in groups and plan their actions, with some of the girls distracting the clerks, others serving as lookouts, and others committing the theft. Some girls are so proficient at shoplifting that they treat it as a form of job and steal to order. Others will tell the girl the exact item that they desire, including size, color, and accessories, and the girl will steal it for them for a fee. It isn't unusual for girls working in stores to allow their friends to shoplift. This type of delinquency is accessible to girls and is one that has little risk of physical injury.[31]

- **Fighting**   In her book *Odd Girl Out: The Hidden Culture of Aggression in Girls,* Rachel Simmons details the problems of young women dealing with each other in covertly aggressive ways.[32] Simmons explains the behavior in terms of relational aggression and contends that it starts as soon as girls form meaningful relationships. The aggression can take many forms. In its mildest form, relational

Teenage girls are often under intense pressure to wear fashionable and expensive clothes and cosmetics. However, the only way for many teenage girls to get these items is to steal them. *(Courtesy David Young-Wolff, Getty Images Inc.—Stone Allstock)*

aggression can be the silent treatment or the spreading of rumors. At its more extreme form, it leads to bullying and fighting. Girls, according to Simmons, aren't emotionally prepared to use physical violence in the same way that boys are, so fighting affects them more severely. Fighting is also an important feature of female gang activity. Jody Miller, in her book *One of the Guys: Girls, Gangs, and Gender,* describes how fighting is a form of resolving conflicts with rival gangs.[33] One interesting observation Miller makes is that females limit their violence to fighting, whereas male gang members will engage in deadly violence. Additionally, when there is a conflict with a female from a rival gang, the male gang members will tell the females to do the fighting. Miller points to this gendered nature of gang involvement and links it to the ways the society uses gender to assign status. Beating up a rival female gang member is beneath the male gang members. When they do engage in the rare event of violence against a female gang member, it includes rape, gang rape, or other sexualized violence.

These three types of delinquency that girls engage in are by no means exhaustive. In fact, girls will commit just about every antisocial act that boys will, but at a much reduced level. The examples provided here illustrate the range of female misbehavior and suggest that female delinquency can have a variety of causes, consequences, and challenges. What is important to remember is that when compared to boys' delinquency, the range, intensity, destructiveness, and frequency of girls' delinquency are much less. This isn't to discount female antisocial behavior but simply to place it in context.

THEORIES OF FEMALE DELINQUENCY

Scholars haven't devoted the time and energy to explaining female antisocial behavior that they have to explaining male antisocial behavior. Because girls and women don't break the criminal law or commit status offenses as often as males, female delinquency and criminal offending have not been considered a serious social problem. Further, there was an assumption that females broke the law for the same reasons as males, so all one had to do was extend the research findings on males to females. As we will see, this assumption was wrong. There are important distinctions between males and females that account for differences in motivation, technique, and social response. In considering these important differences, scholars have developed a number of biological, psychological, and sociological theories. Here we will briefly highlight the development of female criminality theories and then turn to recent scholarship on feminism.

Biological Theories

Cesare Lombroso set the foundation for much of the study of crime because of his attempts to use the scientific method. Although he made major errors in his science, his contribution to the study of criminology is fundamental, and many of his ideas still resonate today. His major concern was the physical differences between offenders and nonoffenders. Lombroso believed that criminal offenders weren't as highly evolved as other citizens. In adapting Charles Darwin's ideas about evolution, he suggested that offenders were a throwback to a less-developed human. The number of **atavisms** could evidence this lack of development.

In his book *The Female Offender*, written with William Ferrero, Lombroso explored reasons that women commit criminal offenses.[34] Lombroso found fewer atavisms in females than in males and essentially concluded that female offenders were very much like female nonoffenders. This isn't much of a compliment, because Lombroso believed that women in general were less intelligent than men and were weak, childlike, jealous, and vengeful. However, some females who committed serious offenses were deemed to be cunning, spiteful, deceitful, and capable of extreme cruelty. Those females who committed serious offenses were believed to possess extreme masculine traits, as well as the worst qualities of women. Lombroso believed female offending to be a result of the biological nature of women and, like many theorists who followed, linked it to sexual issues. A woman's sexuality and anatomy were believed to dictate her actions, and although this view is no longer prevalent today, Lombroso set the stage for its importance for a long time.[35] We will return to this theme after we examine some of the more recent biological explanations of female deviance.

Anthony Walsh contends that males and females engage in antisocial behavior in distinctly different patterns and that sociological theories don't fully account for these patterns. Walsh claims that the fundamental physiological differences between men and women dictate, to some extent, their prevalence in antisocial behavior. These differences have primarily to do with the production of testosterone and, without getting too technical, they are briefly presented here.[36]

- **Turner's syndrome**   Females with Turner's syndrome have either a missing X chromosome or an abnormal one and might possess exaggerated feminine traits that include passivity and high levels of nurturance and empathy. This syndrome, which points to the biological link between chromosomes and behavior, causes a variety of problems. Women with Turner's syndrome are unlikely to engage in antisocial behavior.

- **Androgen-insensitivity syndrome**   In this situation, male sex organs don't develop naturally. Consequently, these men don't have the masculinizing effects on the brain and, like women with Turner's syndrome, they develop exaggeratedly feminine behavior patterns.

- **Congenital adrenal hyperplasia**   This is a recessive trait that interferes with the synthesizing of cortisol from androgen. The result is increased sexual development in males and increased masculinity in females. In females, this condition increases male traits, such as having less interest in marriage and a lower maternal instinct. Because of their more masculine behavior, these females are more likely to engage in antisocial activities that are prohibited by the criminal justice system, while also having less interest in activities that would bond them

Instant Recall from Chapter 5
Cesare Lombroso
An Italian physician who developed a theory of criminal behavior based on offenders' physical charcteristics.

atavism
The appearance in a person of features thought to be from earlier stages of human evolution.

to the conventional roles of females and decrease their visibility to law enforcement officers.

- **Klinefelter's syndrome**   These males have two or more X chromosomes and one or more Y chromosomes and are generally taller than normal males. They also have small genitalia, form breasts at puberty, have low levels of sexual activity, and are passive. Their offenses are usually nonviolent or of a sexual nature.
- **XYY syndrome**   Men with XYY syndrome have an extra male chromosome and are more likely to be quick-tempered and impulsive. They are found in prisons and psychiatric hospitals at a greater rate than normal males. Although at one time it was thought that this chromosomal abnormality could explain a great deal of antisocial behavior, now it's simply considered to be an indication that biology does have some effect on behavior.

These physical conditions demonstrate that the relationship between androgen levels and masculinity can influence antisocial behavior. According to Walsh, social science can't explain the pattern of behavioral traits associated with biology. Consequently, the differences between male and female offending are attributable, at least in part, to the physiological differences between them.

Psychological Theories

In addition to being biologically different from males, females are also subjected to a range of pressures and stimulations that might make them respond in ways that males wouldn't. This is a tricky subject, because it's difficult to untangle the effects of biology and culture from the psychological makeup of individuals. Past efforts to do this can be faulted with the notion that men were considered the norm and that the behavior of females was considered deviant to the extent that it differed from that of males. Given the conventional wisdom at the time and the rigid sex roles that were in place, it isn't surprising to witness this assumed superiority of males. Today, however, it seems to many to be prejudicial.[37]

In his book *The Unadjusted Girl*, W. I. Thomas argued that girls had desires that weren't fulfilled by society. He said they had four categories of wishes: desires for new experiences, security, response, and recognition. In a society that limited their ability to realize these wishes, girls would use their sexuality as a sort of "capital" to accomplish their goals. In this way, they were propelled toward delinquent behavior unless they were successful at selling themselves only once through marriage, as upper-class women were able to do. Thomas claims that this arrangement was considered by girls as a way to get the things they wanted in life: attention, pretty clothes, and entertainment. In many ways, it was a deal with the devil because, by using her sexuality to fulfill immediate needs, she sacrificed her reputation and self-esteem and was punished later in the marriage market, where her value was considerably diminished by her sexual history. Thomas's solution to this problem was the juvenile court, where he believed the girls could be counseled to engage in more positive behaviors. As one of the **child-savers,** Thomas believed the court could compensate for the influence of a bad family and the psychological effects of demoralization that disadvantaged and unsuccessful girls struggled with.[38]

Another study that linked female crime to biological and psychological factors is Otto Pollak's *The Criminality of Women*. In this book, Pollak claimed that women have a precocious biological maturity that leads them to engage in sexual delinquency. He had a negative view of the overall character of women and contended that they are deceitful and manipulating because of the reduced opportunities they have in society. In addition to concealing sexual arousal, women hide their menstruation. This deceit is learned when girls are young and is a result of not having legitimate outlets for their natural aggression. Pollak's was a patriarchal view of female delinquency. He asserted that women actually break the law much more than is reported and that men excuse or overlook women's antisocial behavior to protect them. Pollak supports the view

Instant Recall from Chapter 2
child-savers

People at the end of the 19th century who were instrumental in creating special justice institutions to deal with juvenile delinquents and troubled youths.

that marriage should be a more one-sided affair, where men are allowed the dominant role and women should remain girls in their relationship with their husband, thus allowing a balance in the family power structure. In short, according to Pollak, the dominant culture's gender roles should be maintained to keep girls from going down the path of delinquency and crime.[39]

It is fair to say the history of research on the psychological nature of female delinquency has been flawed. For the most part, studies have viewed females in the traditional gender stereotype of weak, dependent, fragile beings. When strong females were encountered, it was suggested that they had a masculine characteristic that could explain their delinquency.[40]

We turn now to the traditional sociological theories of delinquency, most of which don't denigrate the character and motivation of females as much as simply neglect them. Most of these theories have been focused on lower-class males and have had little to say about females. Yet some would simply apply the theories to females with a caveat that only minor adjustments should be made to account for female delinquency.

Sociological Theories

The **social ecology** school of delinquency characterized by Shaw and McKay and Thrasher was concerned with explaining the geographic distribution of crime. They focused exclusively on male delinquents and illustrated crime patterns by making maps of the city and looking for patterns of offending. This work assumed that females were either prevented from offending because of custom and tradition, meaning the prevailing rigid sex roles of the time, or because they were more closely supervised by parents and teachers.

Strain theorists considered female delinquency differently. Although Merton and Cloward and Ohlin concentrated exclusively on male delinquents, they also applied the concept of strain to females, although in an offhand way. The central focus of **strain theory** was on men adapting to the culture by adopting roles in which they could achieve their success in a masculine manner. Antisocial women were assumed to want the same things as antisocial men. For the strain theorist, masculinity was at the core of delinquency, and the idea that females might experience other types of strain that propel them toward delinquent behavior wasn't considered.[41]

According to Meda Chesney-Lind and Randall Shelden, many early theorists were themselves locked into the gender roles of the time and explained any female delinquency as the inability of girls to adopt their natural role. For instance, Albert Cohen is quoted as saying that women want not only to excel, but to excel as a woman. The dominant gender roles of the 1950s are taken by Cohen as a given, and his sexism is therefore encoded in his view of delinquency.[42]

Other popular sociological theories, such as differential association and control theory, were also constructed and tested without females in mind. Although it's possible to retrofit these theories to include female delinquents, they simply assume that the premises behind the theories are applicable to females as well as males, and all that is required is to find a data set of female delinquency and apply the theory.

Still, other sociological theories have more to say about female delinquency. For instance, **labeling theory** has been used to explain a variety of concerns of female delinquency. **Primary deviance,** the label put on a youth by parents, teachers, peers, or the courts, tags a girl with the label of "tramp," "slut," or "thief," and consequently, others treat her that way. When the girl internalizes the label, which is **secondary deviance,** she believes it's an accurate description of her moral character and thus acts in the way she believes others see her.[43] Labeling theory, unlike many of the other sociological theories, can be used to explain a variety of criminal and status offenses and is able to account for the reaction of society to the girl's antisocial behavior.

Critical theories have also been applied to the explanation of female delinquency. When looking at social class as a reason for the disparity in opportunities afforded individuals in society, gender can be considered as one of the indicators of class.

social ecology
The study of the relationships among people, their behavior, their social groups, and their environment.

Instant Recall from Chapter 7
strain theory
The idea that juvenile delinquency is at least partially a result of being excluded from economic rewards.

Instant Recall from Chapter 7
labeling theory
A theory that describes how a label applied by society can affect an individual's self-perception and behavior.

Instant Recall from Chapter 7
primary deviance
A term from labeling theory that describes the label that society places on the offender.

Instant Recall from Chapter 7
secondary deviance
A term from labeling theory that describes the labels that individuals internalize and come to believe to be accurate.

Men have always held a privileged position in society, and it's axiomatic that lower-class women and children are the most affected by the inequitable distribution of wealth, power, and status. For instance, Chesney-Lind and Shelden state:

> Much of the "delinquent" behavior that girls engage in can be understood as an attempt by oppressed people to accommodate and resist the problems created by capitalist institutions, especially the family (since so many girls begin their "careers" in delinquency by running away from an oppressive family situation). Many of these girls adapt to their disadvantaged positions by their involvement in "accommodative" and "predatory" criminal behavior (e.g., shoplifting, prostitution, drug use).[44]

This accommodation to capitalist structures can be further exacerbated by the social conditions in which many females find themselves as a result of their overall social location. According to Chesney-Lind and Shelden, many females are at a fourfold disadvantage by being a person of color (race), young (age), a girl (gender), and impoverished (class). In this way, the critical theories speak to the issues of female delinquency but only as part of an overall pattern of discrimination by the powerful. Although sympathetic to the economic plight of women, most critical theories concern themselves with overall social justice and neglect explanations that cast females in a unique light. There are, however, theories that do focus on women and girls. Feminist theories of crime and delinquency are emerging to plug the gender gap in what we think we know about antisocial behavior.

FEMINIST THEORIES OF FEMALE DELINQUENCY

To appreciate the contributions made by feminist criminologists to the understanding of crime and delinquency, it's necessary to back up a bit and make sure that we are all considering the same concerns. Feminist scholarship refers to a specific way of looking at problems and does not indicate the physical sex of the scholar. Also, it would be a mistake to think of feminist criminology as solely the study of females and crime. Feminist criminology is more about approaching the serious study of how gender influences the reasons that people break the law and how the criminal and juvenile justice systems respond. Therefore, we find that criminologists who study masculinity are also considered to be feminist scholars. Feminist criminologists study sex and gender as ways of shaping the social world and, according to Kathleen Daly and Meda Chesney-Lind, their work can be differentiated from traditional criminology because it focuses on five features.

- Gender isn't a natural fact but is a complex social, historical, and cultural product; it's related to, but not simply derived from, biological and sex differences and reproductive capabilities.
- Gender and gender relations order social life and social institutions in fundamental ways.
- Gender relations and constructs of masculinity and femininity aren't symmetrical but are based on an organizing principle of men's superiority and social and political–economic dominance over women.
- Systems of knowledge reflect men's views of the natural and social world. The production of knowledge is gendered.
- Women should be at the center of intellectual inquiry, not peripheral, invisible, or appendages to men.[45]

Feminist scholars also recognize that the inequalities that women face are only part of their problems. Women who are members of racial minorities and are impoverished face additional and interlocking disadvantages. Therefore, let us proceed with the recognition that feminist criminology is more inclusive than we might first suspect. It is a complicated line of inquiry that sheds light on the criminal and juvenile justice systems in ways that traditional theories don't.[46]

Because knowledge is gendered, it's important to understand some of the obstacles faced by feminist criminology. By saying "knowledge is gendered," we mean that much of what we know about the world is a result of research that has focused on males and been generalized to females. This is a problem because of the marked differences in the experiences and makeup of males and females. Also, it's interesting that the research done on females isn't automatically applied to males. Males are considered the norm, and females, when they are considered, are treated as a subcategory of males. In criminology, because male offenders so outnumber female offenders, the study of female offending hasn't been in the mainstream.

In traditional criminology, according to Jody Miller and Christopher Mullins, women are considered as either an identical subcategory (the old "add women and stir" adage) of the crime problem, or they are seen as different only because of assumptions about how women differ from men.[47] These assumptions about the emotional character and physical makeup of women historically have been used to relegate them to second-class citizenship.

Not all feminist criminologists consider the problems of crime and justice in the same way. There are distinct differences in why feminist criminologists believe women commit the offenses that they do and in how they see the justice system dealing with female offenders. Further, feminists might disagree on what needs to be done to make the criminal and juvenile justice systems more equitable and effective. Daniel Curran and Claire Renzetti highlight three ways in which criminal offending can by understood from feminist perspectives.

1. **Liberal feminism**   Liberal feminists make two critiques about how gender influences crime and delinquency. The first argues that men control power and privilege in society. Men use that power to act in sexist ways to keep women "in their place" and to preserve the power and benefits of power for themselves. Liberal feminists have made strides toward breaking down the male-dominated and entrenched power structure but argue that much more needs to be accomplished before there is gender equity in society and in the juvenile justice system. The second critique concerns the way that boys and girls are socialized into adult roles. Given the highly gendered institutions in society where sex-role differences are systematically reinforced, it isn't surprising that more progress hasn't been made. The women's movement has broken down many barriers and has educated parents, teachers, and decision makers on the dysfunctional ways that boys and girls get socialized, but much remains to be done. It is important to add here that not everyone shares the goals of the liberal feminists, and there's considerable backlash in the form of maintaining distinct feminine and masculine sex roles.

2. **Radical feminism**   Radical feminists call for a major overhaul in the systems of gender relations in society. They would wipe out many of the patriarchal structures that put women at such a disadvantage in obtaining positions of power and in controlling their own destinies. For instance, in the military, the radical feminist would eliminate all job discrimination based on gender and allow women to engage in combat alongside men. This would give women the opportunity to gain the experiences that are used to decide promotion to a higher rank. In the criminal justice system, the radical feminist would argue that the traditional criminal justice system hasn't been responsive to women's needs. Crimes such as rape and domestic violence have historically been decided in ways that advantage male perpetrators. In recent decades, the feminist movement has corrected some of these injustices, but the radical feminist argues that justice is still gendered.

3. **Socialist feminism**   The combination of social class and gender is used as a "double-whammy" to deny women access to positions of power in society. Being

both female and impoverished has meant that women are perpetually kept from getting a decent education and job promotions, are saddled with the burdens of child care, and are denied control of important decisions affecting their lives by parents, boyfriends, husbands, and government authorities. Because impoverished women don't have access to power, their concerns are overlooked and neglected. Impoverished women who are also members of racial minorities experience an extra dimension of discrimination.[48]

In considering the problems of juvenile delinquency, the feminist perspective is poised to make major contributions to our understanding of how the juvenile justice system operates and how it affects girls even more negatively than it does boys. The juvenile justice system is similar to the family and the school in making assumptions about the basic nature of males and females and how society should treat them differently.

9.2   *CrossCurrents*

Liberation Hypothesis

Historically, women and girls have committed fewer offenses and different types of offenses than males. As such, they are not represented to the extent in the criminal and juvenile justice systems that males are, a fact that during the last few decades of intensive criminological research has been taken for granted. But why? Could the rigid gender roles that women have historically been forced to occupy have something to do with it? Do females commit fewer offenses and less serious offenses simply because they have had no opportunity to do so?

This was Freda Adler's hypothesis in her 1975 book *Sisters in Crime.* In her "liberation hypothesis," Adler speculated that as rights and opportunities for females increased, females would begin to commit more offenses that had been thought to be solely the domain of males, including violent offenses, such as assault, murder, and robbery. According to Adler, the delinquency gap between males and females would shrink, and the statistics would merge as females not only committed "male" offenses, but committed them more often.

On the surface, it seems that Adler's prediction is coming true. In the past decade, especially, the delinquency rate for girls has risen in comparison to that of boys, which has fallen. For example, the line graph shows juvenile violent crime arrest rates. And there is an increasing amount of anecdotal evidence.

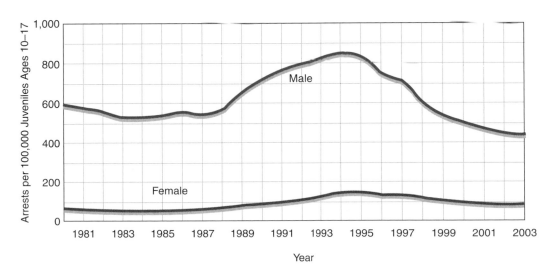

Juvenile Violent Crime Index Arrest Rates

Source: Howard N. Snyder and Melissa Sickmund, *Juvenile Offenders and Victims: 2006 National Report* (Washington, DC: National Center for Juvenile Justice, 2006), 132. Analyses of arrest data from the FBI and population data from the U.S. Census Bureau.

(Continued)

(Continued)

- In Boston, more than a dozen girls allegedly watched as four 15-year-old girls repeatedly kicked a 14-year-old girl in the head. A 13-year-old girl accused of attacking a classmate for wearing a short skirt bit her teacher and fought with police while being handcuffed.[1]

- In Los Angeles in 2004, a study found that girls committed about as many violent hate crimes as boys, with about 81 percent of girls' hate crimes being violent.[2]

- Local authorities are having trouble keeping up with the rise in girls' delinquency. One Illinois county official remarked that, although the methods for handling young female delinquents have not changed in years, the number of delinquents is rising beyond the system's capacity to deal with them.[3]

- An Idaho county official stated the courts there are increasingly seeing girls charged with battery, malicious injury, and assault.[4]

According to FBI data, the arrest rates of juvenile females rose from 2002 to 2003, with females under age 18 accounting for 29 percent of the arrest rate in 2003, up from 25 percent in 1995.[5] The arrest rate for juvenile males dropped about 3 percent during this same period.[6]

Why are more girls being arrested? Has the behavior of girls plummeted that badly, or are other factors at work? Some experts have blamed the media for girls' increased delinquency, with television, movies, and video games portraying violent, aggressive women. However, Meda Chesney-Lind disagrees with both Adler's liberation hypothesis and the media hypothesis. Chesney-Lind believes that girls aren't becoming more violent; it's just that now society is more willing to deal with their offenses formally, whereas in past decades it wasn't. The factors at work in the appearance of increased girls' delinquency are relabeling, rediscovery, and upcriming.

- *Relabeling.* Some status offenses are now being listed as violent offenses. Also, the mandatory arrest policies that some jurisdictions have for domestic violence have resulted in more arrests of females.

- *Rediscovery.* Girls have always been violent, but neither the public, obsessed with boys' violence, nor the juvenile justice system, geared toward boys, has noticed. Girls are now being arrested for behaviors that they wouldn't have been arrested for 10 or 20 years ago.

- *Upcriming.* Schools are now sending cases that would have been dealt with informally by school personnel to the police. More juveniles and more juvenile girls are being arrested and face more severe dispositions. For example, in 1986, a small pocketknife on a girl's key chain would have gone unnoticed in most schools. Now it can be grounds for arrest and expulsion from school.[7]

Whether girls are actually committing more offenses and more violent offenses or whether society has only recently become aware of female delinquency will continue to be debated. There is general agreement, however, that girls' motivation is markedly different from that of boys, with experts reporting that girls' violence is more controlled by their relationships with family, friends, and intimate partners.

Think About It

1. Is Adler's liberation hypothesis correct? How about Chesney-Lind's hypothesis that society is treating girls' delinquency more seriously?

2. Do you think girls are becoming more violent and more willing to break the law?

3. Should girls' delinquency be treated as seriously as that of boys?

1. Suzanne Smalley and Rick Kahn, "Violence Raging among Teen Girls," *Boston Globe*, June 20, 2005, 3rd edition, p. B1.
2. Troy Anderson, "Hate Crimes Drop but Get More Vicious; Attacks by Girls as Violent as Boys," *Daily News of Los Angeles*, Valley edition, December 17, 2004, p. N1.
3. Libby Sander, "Lake County Courts Try New Tack on Teen Girls," *Chicago Daily Law Bulletin*, July 20, 2004, p. 3.
4. Associated Press, "Counties Get Creative as More Teenage Girls Enter Court System," April 18, 2005.
5. Federal Bureau of Investigation, *Crime in the United States 1995*, (Washington, DC: U.S. Government Printing Office, 2004), 220–222. Online at www.fbi.gov/ucr/Cius_97/95CRIME/95crime4.pdf.
6. Federal Bureau of Investigation, *Crime in the United States 2003*, (Washington, DC: U.S. Government Printing Office, 2004), 282–284. Online at www.fbi.gov/ucr/cius_03/pdf/03sec4.pdf.
7. Meda Chesney-Lind, "Girls and Violence: Is the Gender Gap Closing?" VAWnet, August 2004. Online at www.vawnet.org/DomesticViolence/Research/VAWnetDocs/AR_GirlsViolence.pdf.

In 1975, criminologist Freda Adler advanced the theory that as females gained more power in society, they would break the law more often and commit the types of offenses believed to be the province of males. See Crosscurrents 9.2 for more on Adler's liberation hypothesis.

Drawing on the work of Daly and Chesney-Lind, Miller and Mullins laid out three ways in which feminist scholarship can inform how we consider the relationship between gender and offending.[49]

- **Gendered pathways to lawbreaking** Drawing on insights from the life-course theories of crime, feminist scholars have examined the individual histories of female offenders and found that their pathways to crime and delinquency are often very different than for males.[50] The remarkable thing is that many females become involved with the juvenile or criminal justice system for the first time as victims. There are "blurred boundaries" between offending and victimization. For instance, when a girl runs away from an abusive family situation, she commits a status offense, which could leave her fate in the hands of a justice system that might punish her for running away from home when that might be her best or only realistic choice. Mary Gilfus argues that many women start out as victims, then become survivors, and finally become perpetrators of street crime. Some young women must engage in prostitution or drug sales as a means to survive, and they are drawn into the justice system as offenders, although their behavior could be considered as something that victims or survivors have no choice but to engage in.[51] Victimization is but one pathway to crime for women. Drug and alcohol use, economic marginality, and experiences at school can also put girls in contact with the juvenile justice system. One other important pathway to delinquency for girls is association with a gang. This could be in the form of belonging to an all-girl gang or being involved with male gang members.

- **Gendered crime** Feminist scholars are interested in how offending is often organized by gender. When males and females offend together, are some aspects of the offense reserved for males and some for females? For instance, in cases in which the male customers of female prostitutes are robbed, the prostitutes tend to steal the money while their customers are asleep, while male pimps are more likely to use physical force. In a support role, such as lookout or getaway car driver, females are likely to remain in that task while males are allowed to move on to more instrumental tasks. Like the rest of society, the world of crime has some deeply entrenched ideas about which roles are appropriate for females. Even when girls rebel against the social order by breaking the law, they are still constrained by the social expectations of their male partners in the offense and often by the social expectations they learned as young girls.[52]

When involved in crime and delinquency with males, females often play support roles, such as lookout or getaway driver. Here a male gang member teaches a female member to aim a gun. *(Courtesy Doug Menuez, Getty Images, Inc.- Photodisc)*

- **Gendered lives** Finally, feminist scholars consider how gender is a factor in how men and women experience their lives. Because of the opportunities and limitations of gender roles, males and females are pressured in different ways that shape how they see themselves, their place in the world, and their relationship to the opposite sex. Girls and young women are more likely to be sheltered from many of the ways in which youngsters are recruited into delinquency. They are also initially more likely to be the victim of a street crime, rather than the perpetrator. This isn't to say that females don't choose to break the law. Although their victimization is real and harmful, there are also reasons to credit females with being active and creative in choosing delinquency. It is often a limited, poor, or contradictory choice based on circumstance, but it's a choice nevertheless.[53] Feminism isn't so narrowly focused on gender relations that it overlooks accountability for one's decisions. It does, however, explain how gender is a factor in many decisions and that a theoretical overview of crime and delinquency wouldn't be complete without considering how feminist criminology addresses the issues in ways that challenge the traditional and the customary.

GENDER AND THE JUVENILE JUSTICE SYSTEM

Does the juvenile justice system treat females differently than males? The answer isn't only yes, but also yes with a number of qualifications, explanations, and amplifications. Every institution of society treats females differently, so we shouldn't be surprised that the legal system reflects many of the same sex-role demands that are found throughout the culture.

Girls are treated differently for a structural reason. Because the juvenile justice system handles so many fewer girls than boys, the system has fewer alternatives for processing and sentencing girls. Municipalities have built intake and detention centers to accommodate all the male delinquents, and the facilities that deal with females are usually of a much lower quality. Policymakers might try to excuse the inferior facilities for girls by claiming that the crime problem is primarily a male problem and that there aren't enough females to justify the construction of separate facilities, but this tells only part of the story. The additional argument is that the lack of female facilities reflects the aversion society has to locking up girls and the willingness of officials to find alternative ways of handling girls' cases.[54]

One explanation for the differential treatment of girls in the juvenile justice system is the "chivalry hypothesis." This argument states that girls are treated more leniently than boys because officials consider girls to be weaker, helpless, and less threatening. Girls, when they are caught and processed in the system, don't appear to be physically dangerous.[55] Officials tend to consider them more as accessories or indirect victims of the offense, rather than as full-fledged perpetrators, and consequently give them lighter sentences. By treating them more like ladies, it's the intention of juvenile justice officials to diminish the effect of case processing on girls. Based in part on labeling theory and in part on lack of resources, the chivalry option looks beneficial for females but might not always be so. There is a fine distinction between chivalry and paternalism.

> Chivalry is associated with placing an individual on a pedestal and behaving gallantly toward that person, whereas paternalism involves taking care of the powerless and dependent. Both chivalry and paternalism, however, imply weakness and a need to protect another person or group, which can have dangerous repercussions when "protect" becomes "control." It's often difficult to tell whether preferential treatment of female defendants, when it occurs, is due to chivalry or paternalism, some combination of the two, or other factors.[56]

One interesting aspect of the chivalry hypothesis is that it isn't available to all females. It is mostly accorded to females who conform to traditional gender stereotypes. In a sense, then, a male authority extends chivalrous behavior to women who are deemed helpless, attractive, and harmless. Females who challenge established gender roles are more likely to be treated harshly and not have the benefits of chivalry offered to them.

There is a corollary to the chivalry hypothesis, the "evil-woman hypothesis," which is reserved for females who commit serious offenses. Because chivalrous treatment of murderers and child abusers would be deemed inappropriate for serious offenders and because females who commit these types of crimes quickly fall out of the traditional gender stereotype, the justice system treats them in a harsher manner.[57]

The point in the juvenile justice system at which sex discrimination occurs is an important concern for those who want to unravel how bias is subtly introduced into the process. Criminal and juvenile justice officials use discretion at many points in the system, and it's necessary to look at each point at which females are processed to see if there is differential handling of offenders based on gender. Here we will take a look at areas in which discretion is exercised.

- **Decisions made by law enforcement officers**   The police are the first contact a girl has with the juvenile justice system. She is likely to be treated differently than a boy in two ways. First, she is likely to be questioned about her sexual activities. Running away from home, incorrigibility, curfew violation, and such are considered status offenses, and girls who violate them are likely to be held to a different standard than boys.[58] Because a girl is more likely to be a victim of sexual offenses, she's dealt with more severely when she commits a status offense, such as running away, that could expose her to victimization. Although the police officer might mean well in the desire to protect the girl, the result is actually blaming and punishment. The second way in which a girl might be treated differently is the sexual exploitation and sexual abuse sometimes committed by police officers. According to Kraska and Kappeler, some police officers will exploit females when they follow them from a party or bar and offer to exchange overlooking a DUI or other offense for sexual favors.[59] The females most often confronted with such dilemmas are young and impoverished.[60]

- **Predisposition court decisions**   A number of decisions are made before a case goes before the judge. Many of these decisions can determine the outcome of the case. Other decisions, such as granting conditional release, reflect the attitudes and opinions of court workers toward the dangerousness and vulnerability of the juvenile. Girls are more likely to be released to their parents than boys are if the home is deemed to be a suitable place. However, some girls who display advanced sexual attitudes are more likely to be considered to need protective custody until a judge can render an appropriate disposition.[61] The important questions here are what policies are in the best interest of the young female defendant? Does it make sense to keep her at home with her family while evaluating how to proceed in her case, or is she in more danger at home than she would be in a detention facility? Because female juvenile delinquents have fewer pretrial resources, judges often have to make difficult decisions on what is the optimal short-term placement for the girl.

- **Disposition**   When girls are given a disposition by the judge, it's evident from a number of studies that they are treated in a chivalrous way. They are more likely to get probation, and boys are more likely to be sentenced to detention. The treatment is even better for white girls. Again, the extent to which girls project traditional gender roles influences their receiving better treatment from the juvenile court.[62] An important consideration at this point in the juvenile justice system is the cumulative effect of being female. If girls are treated differently than boys at each decision point, the additive effects of this small but mounting bias result in a very different quality of justice for girls as opposed to boys. Regardless of the well-meaning nature of this discriminatory treatment, the juvenile justice system must be constantly monitored to ensure that gender does not become a deciding variable in the detention decision. The bias might be almost invisible because it can happen in small increments at each stage in the process, but the resulting injustices are very real to those who end up being incarcerated or sent to detention.

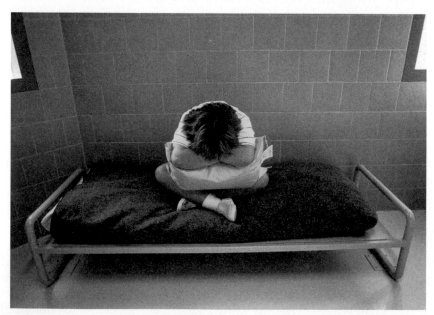

The reality of incarcerated girls and young women (bottom) is quite removed from the fantasies that have been portrayed in various exploitative movies. (Top: © Swim Inc 2, LLC / CORBIS. All Rights Reserved; bottom: *courtesy Bob Daemmrich, The Image Works*)

This disparity of treatment, it might be argued, is simply a reflection of society's values and the perception that girls are more vulnerable than boys and need greater protection. However, in a system in which the ideal is to be free of bias based on gender, race, and social class, this differential treatment is considered a serious problem. What is most remarkable here, however, is the idea that there are good reasons to treat delinquents differently according to gender. There are far fewer female delinquents than male, girls commit less serious delinquency than boys, and privacy concerns dictate that they have separate facilities. Feminist scholars strive to ensure that the differential treatment does not remain invisible and that the juvenile justice system operates in ways that don't simply reflect traditional gender roles but instead promote justice for females, the poor, and people of color.[63]

SUMMARY

1. Sex is the biological designation of male or female. Gender refers to the characteristics attributed to and accorded to males and females by their societies and cultures on the basis of sex.

2. The popular view of juvenile delinquency has been formed by looking at the antisocial behavior of males. The study of female crime has not been in the mainstream because male offenders so greatly outnumber female offenders.

3. The greatest physical differences between girls and boys don't appear until adolescence. Girls undergo the same issues during adolescence that boys do but in different ways and at different times.

4. The involvement of females with crime and the juvenile justice system is very different from that of males. Girls commit fewer and less serious delinquent acts, are treated differently by justice officials, and are typically easier to rehabilitate. When compared to male delinquency, the range, intensity, destructiveness, and frequency of female delinquency are much less.

5. Some physical conditions demonstrate that the relationship between androgen levels and masculinity influences antisocial behavior. These conditions include Turner's syndrome, XYY syndrome, Klinefelter's syndrome, congenital adrenal hyperplasia, and androgen-insensitivity syndrome.

6. Research has viewed females in the traditional gender stereotype of weak, dependent, fragile beings. It was suggested that strong females had a masculine characteristic that could explain their delinquency.

7. Unlike many other sociological theories, labeling theory can be used to explain a wide variety of female criminal and status offenses and can also account for society's reaction to female antisocial behavior. Critical theories have also been applied to the explanation of female delinquency because gender can be considered as one of the indicators of class.

8. Feminist criminologists study sex and gender as ways of shaping the social world, including crime and delinquency. Curran and Renzetti highlight three ways in which crime can by understood from feminist perspectives: liberal feminism, radical feminism, and socialist feminism.

9. Feminist scholars have examined the individual histories of female offenders and found that their pathways to crime and delinquency are often very different from those for males. Many women first become involved with the juvenile or criminal justice system as victims. Other ways include drug and alcohol use, economic marginality, and involvement with either a male or female gang.

10. The chivalry hypothesis can help explain the differential treatment of girls in the juvenile justice system. This argument states that girls are treated more leniently than boys because officials consider girls to be weaker, helpless, and less threatening.

REVIEW QUESTIONS

1. What is the difference between sex and gender?

2. What is adolescent egocentrism?

3. How might anomie affect gender norms?

4. What three behaviors get girls the most attention from the juvenile justice system?

5. Do the physical differences between males and females sometimes affect their behavior?

6. According to labeling theory, what are primary deviance and secondary deviance? How can these labels affect girls?

7. What is meant by the phrase "knowledge is gendered"?

8. By what pathway do females often first become involved with the criminal or juvenile justice system? What are some other ways?

9. What is the chivalry hypothesis?

10. What specific issues do girls face at the different discretion points in the juvenile justice system?

ADDITIONAL READINGS

Adler, Freda. *Sisters in Crime: The Rise of the New Female Criminal* (New York: McGraw-Hill, 1975).

Faith, Karlene. *Unruly Women: The Politics of Confinement and Resistance* (Vancouver, BC: Press Gang, 1993).

Faludi, Susan. *Backlash: The Undeclared War against Women* (Garden City, NY: Doubleday, 1991).

Kraska, Peter B, and Victor E. Kappeler. "To Serve and Preserve: Exploring Police Sexual Violence against Women." In Victor E. Kappeler, ed., *The Police and Society: Touchstone Readings* (Prospect Heights, IL: Waveland Press, 1999), 325–345.

Mann, Coramae Richey. *Female Crime and Delinquency* (Montgomery: University of Alabama Press, 1984).

Owen, Barbara. *In the Mix: Struggle and Survival in a Women's Prison* (Albany: State University of New York Press, 1998).

Richie, Beth E. *Compelled to Crime: The Gender Entrapment of Black Battered Women* (New York: Routledge, 1996).

ENDNOTES

1. Claire M. Renzetti, "On the Margins of the Mainstream (or They Still Don't Get It, Do They?): Feminist Analysis in Criminal Justice Education," *Journal of Criminal Justice Education* 4 (1993): 219–249.

2. Carol Travis, *The Mismeasure of Woman* (New York: Touchstone Books, 1992).

3. Roslyn Muraskin, "Ain't I a Woman?" in Roslyn Muraskin, ed., 2003. *It's a Crime: Women and Justice*, 3rd ed. (Upper Saddle River, NJ: Prentice Hall, 2003) 3–11.

4. Tony Jefferson and Pat Carden, eds., "Masculinities, Social Relations and Crime," *British Journal of Criminology* 36 (1996): 337–444.

5. James W. Messerschmidt, *Masculinities and Crime: Critique and Reconceptualization of Theory* (Lanham, MD: Rouman and Littlefield, 1993).

6. Judith Lorber, *Paradoxes of Gender* (New Haven, CT: Yale University Press, 1994).

7. On December 1, 1956, Alain Mimoun O'Kacha of France won the men's Olympic marathon in Melbourne, Australia, with a time of 2:25:00. On September 24, 2000, Naoko Takahashi of Japan won the women's Olympic marathon in Sydney, Australia, with a time of 2:23:14. See MarathonGuide.com at www.marathonguide.com/history/records/index.cfm.

8. Robert S. Feldman, *Child Development*, 3rd ed. (Upper Saddle River, NJ: Prentice Hall, 2004).

9. Ibid., 129–159.

10. Ibid., 413.

11. Jodee McCaw and Charlene Y. Senn, "Perception of Cues in Conflictual Dating Situations," *Violence Against Women* 4 (1998): 609–624.

12. A. C. Petersen, "Those Gangly Years," *Psychology Today* (September 1998): 28–34.

13. H. M. Wellman and S. A. Gelman, "Cognitive Development: Foundational Theories of Core Domains," *Annual Review of Psychology* 43 (1992): 337–375.

14. C. Lightfoot, *The Culture of Adolescent Risk-Taking* (New York: Guilford Press, 1997).

15. J. J. Arnett, "Adolescent Storm and Stress, Reconsidered," *American Psychologist* 54 (1999): 314–326.

16. R. H. Aseltine, Jr., S. Gore, and M. E. Colten, "Depression and the Social Developmental Context of Adolescence," *Journal of Personality and Social Psychology* 67 (1994): 252–263.

17. B. Byrne, "Relationships between Anxiety, Fear, Self-Esteem, and Coping Strategies in Adolescence," *Adolescence* 35 (2000): 201–215.

18. Feldman (see note 8), pp. 416–418.

19. Naomi Wolff, *The Beauty Myth: How Images of Beauty Are Used against Women* (New York: Random House, 1991).

20. Wayne Wooden and Randy Blazch, *Renegade Kids, Suburban Outlaws: From Youth Culture to Delinquency*, 2nd ed. (Belmont, CA: Wadsworth, 2000).

21. Thomas P. George and Donald P. Hartmann, "Friendship Networks of Unpopular, Average, and Popular Children," *Child Development* 67 (1996): 2301–2316.

22. J. K. Skipper and G. Nass, "Dating Behavior: A Framework of Analysis and an Illustration," *Journal of Marriage and Family* 28 (1966): 412–420.

23. Grace Palladino, *Teenagers: An American History* (New York: Basic Books, 1996).

24. I. M. Schwartz, "Sexual Activity Prior to Coital Inter-action: A Comparison between Males and Females," *Archives of Sexual Behavior* 28 (1999): 63–69.

25. J. S. Hyde, *Understanding Human Sexuality*, 5th ed. (New York: McGraw-Hill, 1994).

26. William Strauss and Neil Howe, *Generations: The History of America's Future, 1584–2069* (New York: Morrow, 1991).

27. J. G. Smetana, "Adolescents' and Parents' Reasoning about Actual Family Conflict," *Child Development* 60 (1989): 1052–1067.

28. Kimberly Kempf-Leonard and Paul. E. Tracy, "Gender Differences in Delinquency Career Types and the Transition to Adult Crime," in Roslyn Muraskin, ed. *It's a Crime: Women and Justice*, 3rd ed. (Upper Saddle River, NJ: Prentice Hall, 2003), 544–569.

29. Meda Chesney-Lind and Randall G. Shelden, *Girls, Delinquency and Juvenile Justice*, 3rd ed. (Belmont, CA: Wadsworth, 2004), 40–43.

30. Ronald Chilton and Susan K. Datesman, "Gender, Race, and Crime: An Analysis of Urban Trends," *Gender and Society* 1 (1987): 152–171.

31. However, it's important to note that the research shows that males shoplift more than females. See Chesney-Lind and Shelden (see note 29), p. 101.

32. Rachel Simmons, *Odd Girl Out: The Hidden Culture of Aggression in Girls* (New York: Harcourt, 2002).

33. Jody Miller, *One of the Guys: Girls, Gangs, and Gender* (New York: Oxford University Press, 2001).

34. Cesare Lombroso and William Ferrero, *The Female Offender* (London: Fisher Unwin, 1895).

35. Carol Smart, *Women, Crime and Criminology: A Feminist Critique* (London: Routledge and Kegan Paul, 1976).

36. Anthony Walsh, *Biosocial Criminology: Introduction and Integration* (Cincinnati, OH: Anderson, 2002), 210–212.

37. Christine Rasche, "The Female Offender as an Object of Criminological Research," in A. M. Brodsky, ed., *The Female Offender* (Beverly Hills, CA: Sage), 9–28.

38. W. I. Thomas, *The Unadjusted Girl* (New York: Harper and Row, 1967).

39. Otto Pollak, *The Criminality of Women* (Philadelphia: University of Pennsylvania Press, 1950).

40. Dorie Klein, "The Etiology of Female Crime: A Review of the Literature," in S. K. Datesman and F. R. Scarpitti, eds., *Women, Crime, and Justice* (New York: Oxford University Press, 1980), 70–105.

41. Joanne Belknap, *The Invisible Woman: Gender, Crime, and Justice* (Belmont, CA: Wadsworth, 2001), 4.

42. Chesney-Lind and Shelden (see note 29), pp. 107–118.

43. Edwin Schur, *Labeling Women Deviant* (New York: Random House, 1984).

44. Chesney-Lind and Shelden (see note 29), p. 119.

45. Kathleen Daly and Meda Chesney-Lind, "Feminism and Criminology," *Justice Quarterly* 5 (1984): 497–538.

46. Martin D. Schwartz and Dragan Milovanovic, *Race, Gender, and Class in Criminology: The Intersection* (New York: Garland, 1996).

47. Jody Miller and Christopher W. Mullins, "The States of Feminist Theories in Criminology," in Francis T. Cullen, John Paul Wright, and Kristie R. Blevins, eds. *Taking Stock: The Status of Criminological Theory* (New Brunswick, NJ: Transaction, 2006), 217–249.

48. Daniel J. Curran and Claire M. Renzetti, *Theories of Crime*, 2nd ed. (Boston: Allyn and Bacon, 2001), 209–228.

49. Miller and Mullins (see note 47), pp. 228–242.

50. Peggy Giordano, Stephen A. Cherkovich, and Jennifer Rudolf, "Gender, Crime, and Desistance: Toward a Theory of Cognitive Transformations," *American Journal of Sociology* 107 (2002): 990–1064.

51. Mary E. Gilfus, "From Victims to Survivors to Offenders: Women's Routes of Entry into Street Crime," *Women and Criminal Justice* 4 (1992): 63–89.

52. Sally Simpson and Lori Ellis, "Doing Gender: Sorting Out the Caste and Crime Conundrum," *Criminology* 33 (1995): 47–81.

53. Lisa Maher, *Sexed Work: Gender, Race, and Resistance in a Brooklyn Drug Market* (Oxford, UK: Clarendon Press, 1997).

54. Nguine Naffine, "Towards Justice for Girls: Rhetoric and Practice in the Treatment of Status Offenders," *Women and Criminal Justice* 1 (1989): 3–20.

55. Deborah Curran, "Judicial Discretion and Defendant's Sex," *Criminology* 21 (1983): 41–58.

56. Belknap (see note 41), p. 133.

57. Christy A. Visher, "Gender, Police Arrest Decisions, and Notions of Chivalry," *Criminology* 21 (1983). 5–28.

58. Ibid.

59. Peter Kraska and Victor Kappeler, "To Serve and Pursue: Exploring Police Sexual Violence Against Women," *Justice Quarterly* 12 (March 1995): 85–111.

60. Marvin Krohn, James P. Curry, and Shirley Nelson-Kilger, "Is Chivalry Dead? An Analysis of Changes in Police Dispositions of Males and Females," *Criminology* 21 (1983): 417–437.

61. Katherine S. Teilmann and Pierre H. Landry, "Gender Bias in Juvenile Justice," *Journal of Research in Crime and Delinquency* 18 (1981): 47–80.

62. Vernetta D. Young, "Gender Expectations and Their Impact on Black Female Offenders and Victims," *Justice Quarterly* 3 (1986): 305–328.

63. K. H. Federle and Meda Chesney-Lind, "Special Issues in Juvenile Justice; Gender, Race, and Ethnicity," in I. M. Schwartz, ed., *Juvenile Justice and Public Policy: Toward a National Agenda* (New York: Macmillan, 1992), 165–195.

How does the family influence delinquency?

What can families do to help prevent delinquency?

Why are abused or neglected children more likely to engage in delinquent behavior?

CHAPTER 10

The Family and Delinquency

The family is the most basic institution. Although the economic system and the types of school, religion, and government have varied greatly over the centuries, the family has remained the most stable institution. All societies and cultures have families, but the institution of the family has undergone some changes of its own. Today, we tend to idealize the family as a unit consisting of the biological parents and their immediate offspring. However, this isn't the dominant type of family in either the United States or the world.[1]

The type of family that we consider to be traditional is really a modern adaptation to the industrial age.[2] It requires that a married couple exclude extended family members and concentrate on themselves and their children. This structure is supported by the lifestyle of an era in which houses are built without extra rooms to accommodate the couple's parents, their siblings, the "spinster" aunt, or the "confirmed-bachelor" uncle. The three-bedroom home ensures that the family lives without all the supporting members of the extended family. However, it's interesting to note that the postmodern family, which includes a number of variations on the traditional theme, is replacing the traditional American family and differs significantly from it. Today, only 7 percent of families fit the idealized family model of a husband breadwinner, wife homemaker, and their biological children.[3] Instead, there is a proliferation of family types that include two-earner, single-parent, blended, gay, and cohabiting couples and couples without children. Actually, the number of married couples living with their children has dropped by nearly half since 1970 (see Figure 10-1). From 1970 to 2002, the total number of children living in two-parent households dropped from about 85 percent to less than 70 percent, with declines showing in all races (see Figure 10-2).

With all these variations, it is a wonder that the term *family* has any objective meaning. It might mean a wide variety of living arrangements with a range of individuals who might or might not be related by blood or legal contract. Other institutions have been forced to adjust to the family's changing nature. Schools must include

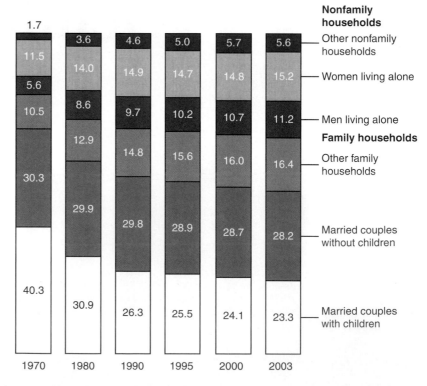

Figure 10-1   **Households by Type: 1970 to 2003 (by percent)** *Source:* U.S. Census Bureau, Current Population Survey, March and Annual Social and Economic Supplements: 1970 to 2003, in Jason Fields, ed., *America's Families and Living Arrangements: 2003* (Washington, DC: U.S. Census Bureau, 2004), 4. Online at www.census.gov/prod/2004pubs/p20-553.pdf.

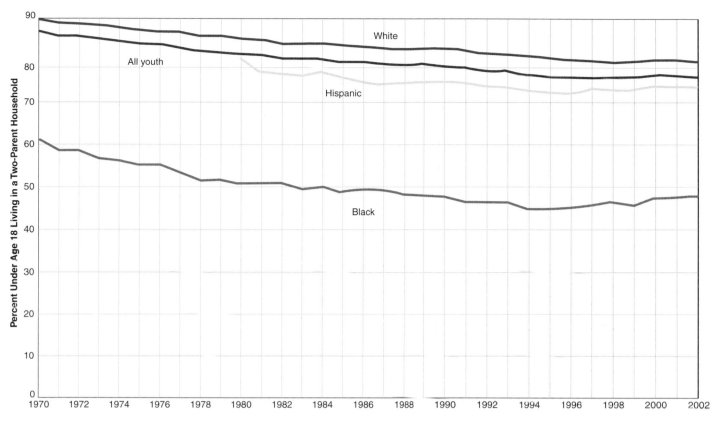

Figure 10-2 **Two-Parent Families Decline** *Source:* Adapted from U.S. Census Bureau, "Families and Living Arrangements, Historical Time Series," by Howard N. Snyder and Melissa Sickmund, *Juvenile Offenders and Victims: 2006 National Report* (Washington, DC: U.S. Department of Justice, Office of Justice Programs, Office of Juvenile Justice and Delinquency Prevention, 2006), 11. Online at www.ojjdp.ncjrs.org/ojstatbb/nr2006/downloads/NR2006.pdf.

The nuclear family is really a modern adaptation to the industrial age. The Cleavers from the television show *Leave It to Beaver* are considered in the popular imagination to be the classic nuclear family. Here the actors from the series pose for a promotional portrait: (clockwise, from left) Tony Dow, Hugh Beaumont, Jerry Mathers, and Barbara Billingsley. *(Courtesy Getty Images Inc. — Hulton Archive Photos)*

10.1 PROGRAMS *for* CHILDREN

HELPING IMMIGRANT FAMILIES

Sometimes families need help with issues concerning living and working in their communities, as well as raising children. Fortunately, hundreds of organizations throughout the country offer such help, many of which focus on ethnic minorities.

In New York City, the Coalition for Asian-American Children and Families (CACF) works to improve the health and quality of life for Asian- and Pacific-American children. Founded in 1986, CACF focuses on the children of New York City's East Asian, Southeast Asian, and South Asian communities to raise awareness of their health and social service needs. According to the CACF's website, Asian-Americans are twice as likely to be impoverished as non-Hispanic whites, and the Asian-American illiteracy rate is 5.3 times that of non-Hispanic whites.

The coalition's projects include the Child Welfare Advocacy Project, which works to reduce child abuse and neglect by educating immigrant families about the law and teaching social service providers about cultural differences. The CACF website provides both national and local directories of services, as well as a directory of resources for accessing government services and information about adoption, education, child health, and immigration.

The Committee for Hispanic Children and Families (CHCF) was originally founded in 1982 to serve Hispanic families in the foster care and adoption system but has since expanded its programs to assist low-income Hispanic families and children in youth development, child care, HIV/AIDS prevention and education, immigrant services, and public policy and advocacy.

The CHCF assists Hispanic children and families on the national, state, and local levels. Its Center for Advocacy and Community Building works on public policy and advocacy and building social service networks and also develops public and private partnerships in program development and policy research.

The organization provides a number of services for individual families, including child-care referral services for parents and training for those interested in becoming child-care providers. CHCF's Drop-out Prevention Program features afterschool programs, a family literacy project, and a family nutrition education program. According to CHCF, the Hispanic dropout rate is 28 percent, the highest of any group, while the dropout rate for foreign-born Hispanics is 44 percent.[1]

1 The Coalition for Asian-American Children and Families,www.cacf.org/index.html; the Committee for Hispanic Children and Families, www.chcfinc.org/.

---

afterschool programs for children who don't have a caregiver at home in the afternoon; many corporations provide health insurance for people who are only tangentially related, and the government must decide who can be legally married and enjoy the benefits of this legal status.

The family is significant to our study of delinquency because it is both a buffer against the influences that propel young people toward antisocial behavior and a source of antisocial behavior in its own right. The family is a place where young people can be both protected and victimized. Although we often talk in a romantic way about family values and the long-lasting positive influences of coming from a good home, the family can also be a place where young people are neglected, exploited, or abused.[4] Even for children who aren't victims of family violence, the context in which they grow up might contribute to their being antisocial and dysfunctional individuals. For example, racism, social inequality, poverty, and language barriers can all negatively affect children. (See Programs for Children 10.1 for a look at organizations that assist immigrant families and children.)

To fully understand delinquency, we must look at the history, structure, and function of the family and its relationship to delinquency.

FUNCTIONS OF THE FAMILY

Society invests important functions in the family. In fact, we might expect too much from families. In an age in which there is a tension between our freedoms and government intervention, a decided bias exists toward keeping government out of our lives and allowing individuals the chance to direct their own destinies. Historically, society has believed that "a man's home is his castle." This has meant that the husband and father has been the lord of the household with complete discretion in how he treats his family. Over time, this complete authority has been challenged, and the government has stepped in to correct abuses and ensure that women and children have rights and opportunities.

This government intervention is not complete, and dominant males still have a great deal of latitude to rule the household, but we have come to realize that there is more to being a family than simply allowing the husband and father to dictate the terms of family life.[5] Because the family is such a primary institution, it is expected to fulfill certain obligations in meeting its members' needs. When the family fails to do this, other institutions, including the juvenile justice system, must step in to ensure these functions are accomplished. The important functions of the family can be summarized by the following:

- **To raise children responsibly**   Human beings have a long period in their life cycle in which they are dependent on their parents and during which parents must pass on necessary skills and values. Unlike many species in the animal kingdom for whom parenthood ends at birth or shortly thereafter, human beings invest many years and considerable physical and emotional energy into preparing their young to survive on their own. The first task is to socialize the children into the culture's prescribed ways of doing the work of society and finding their role and identity in the world. During this socialization process, children must learn the values and skills that enable them to fit into their social context. For instance, a child must learn to share with others, pull his or her own weight in economic and social endeavors, and contribute to a variety of demands from the family, groups, and society. Another function the family must perform is to provide children with a set of moral values that is consistent with the norms and laws of society.[6] Ideally, children must learn the values of honesty, hard work, respect for others, and responsibility. Although it's true that the church, school, and other institutions contribute to children's acquisition of moral values, these values are first modeled and taught in families. Included in these moral values is the child's learning of the appropriate way of expressing sexual activity and engaging in the reproduction of the species. By the time a youth reaches age 18, the youth should be ready to engage in responsible sexual activity that will result in her or his own family.

- **To provide economic support**   At one time, this was the family's primary function. Long ago, in fact, the family was the sole unit of economic production in society and was essentially self-sufficient. It provided food, clothing, and shelter for its members and protected them from other groups. Today, family members support each other and pool their resources into shared household finances to provide for the necessities of life and to save for the future when they aren't so economically productive. Additionally, family members provide for each other when one gets sick and needs to be cared for or transported to the doctor. Therefore, it is the family that one generally first turns to for economic and material support. This support is shared, and it isn't a commodity as it might be with friends and acquaintances. An individual supports family members because they need it, not because he or she expects to be paid back.[7]

- **To provide emotional support**   As children struggle to find their place in the world, they turn to their families for the unconditional positive regard that enables them to weather the storms of life. Throughout childhood and adolescence, young people require the emotional support of family members when stiff competition, high obstacles, or life's disappointments challenge them. Ideally, family members can be counted on to stick by one another whether one is right or wrong, and, although there might be severe disagreements between family members, the family puts on a united face to the rest of the world. This is true to varying extents for most families. Certainly, family members can tire of the ne'er-do-well who continually takes advantage of the family's trust and resources. At times, stress within the family can sap more emotional energy than the family can support; but, for the most part, the family is a reliable provider of emotional support and love.

Can the family provide all these functions? The answer is yes, to some extent. Although there are wide variations in how well families live up to these expectations, it's assumed that all families attempt to fulfill these important roles. However, many families are prevented from being successful at these functions. For instance, some families have more economic and social resources than others to do this work. Also, there is an issue of changing gender roles in which husbands and wives, or parents and children, might not agree on the proper roles for males and females. Finally, there is the concern of family violence.[8] Instead of being the solution to that problem, the family might be the source.

It is important to realize that variations in social class, race, and ethnic identity can make families perform differently in attempting to accomplish these functions.[9] Again, we are faced with the illusion of the idealized family, and it is difficult but necessary to consider the vast differences in how families function. This leads to the issue of how families are structured. The number of individuals in the family and the roles they carve out for themselves can greatly influence the family's dynamics.

Challenges in Families Today

Many challenges that face families today differ from the problems that influenced family life in the past. Perhaps the most basic concern that confronts families today is the issue of structure and stability. In the past, there were limits on what one could do when faced with a family crisis. Marriage was considered a permanent union, and those who sought to dissolve the arrangement were met with negative sanctions by society. Divorce could mean the end of a promising career for men, social devaluation for women, and abject poverty for children. Couples would stay together because they believed it was in their children's best interests. Today, couples are much quicker to end an unsuccessful marriage and seek their happiness elsewhere. There is no longer a severe social cost to divorce, and society is generally more tolerant of alternative family structures. In lieu of the traditional intact nuclear family, today's families come in a wide assortment of structures.[10]

- **Single-parent families** Single-parent families can be either male-headed or female-headed. Male-headed single-parent families account for 2.1 percent of all households in the United States, while female-headed families account for 7.2 percent of all households.[11] In terms of children (recall that not all households have children), 23 percent of children live with their mother only, with 5 percent living with their father only (see Figure 10-3). These figures can be misleading, however, because they don't reflect the situation in which other adults might live in the home, such as grandparents or other relatives, or the common arrangement in which mothers or fathers live in another household. The reasons for a single-parent family are many, and we must be cautious about lumping them together. Some single-parent families are the result of a divorce. The divorce could have been traumatic and might have deeply scarred the parents and children, or it could have been amicable, with everyone adjusted well to the new living arrangement.[12] Divorce doesn't necessarily mean that the family suffered debilitating trauma. The single-parent family might be the result of a sexual union in which the father is unknown or has abandoned his responsibilities. The single-parent family might also be the result of the death of one of the parents, leaving the other to raise the children. Although a single-parent family departs from the nuclear-family ideal, it can't be automatically assumed that it's dysfunctional or an inferior type of family. Many single-parent families succeed in achieving the functions of family life. Although

Figure 10-3 **Household Relationship and Living Arrangements of Children under 18 Years, 2005**
These figures don't include other types of households, such as nonchild households or post-child-rearing married couples or people living alone. They also do not distinguish between married and unmarried partners. *Source:* U.S. Census Bureau, *America's Families and Living Arrangements: 2005*, Table C2, www.census. gov/population/www/socdemo/hh-fam/cps2005.html.

single parent families are found at all levels of economic class, those with sufficient wealth and income have a better time of overcoming the problems of having only one parent.[13] From a delinquency point of view, it is assumed that having both parents at home helps keep children out of trouble if both parents present positive role models and each spends time with the children.

- **Cohabitating parents** Some families include two adults who live together without being formally married.[14] These unions might contain the children of one or both of the partners from a previous relationship that might or might not have been a marriage. Often, this cohabitation is a prelude to a formal marriage, but the couple also might continue in the relationship for many years without being formally married.[15] Many issues confront those who cohabitate, including health insurance, tax issues, and legal matters. Some agencies or businesses have policies prohibiting cohabitation, but, for the most part, these policies are difficult to enforce.

- **Blended families** Blended families comprise adults who bring their children to the new marriage from a former marriage. These blended families face a number of adjustment issues, because the children must not only deal with a new adult in the home, but also with other children whom they haven't grown up with. There is nothing intrinsically negative about blended families, but there is always a period in which the new family dynamics must be worked out, something that children can find particularly stressful. Adjusting to a stepparent is one challenge, but accommodating the needs and desires of other children who are also under the stress of change is often difficult. One way in which children manifest this stress is through rebellion and delinquency.[16]

- **Gay and lesbian families** Gay and lesbian couples are families also. They might have children from previous heterosexual relationships, or they might adopt children or bear biological children by a surrogate. There is considerable debate about whether these families are suitable for raising children, but the reality is that they do raise children and that thousands of these families must

The postmodern family includes a number of variations on the traditional theme. In San Francisco, California, a gay couple shops for homes with their daughters. Each partner is the biological father of one of the girls and has adopted the other. *(Courtesy Rachel Epstein, The Image Works)*

confront the daily trials and tribulations of family life burdened with the negative attitudes of others.[17] Gay and lesbian families aren't immune from concerns such as family violence, and they have the additional problems of dealing with many in society who aren't sympathetic or are even hostile to their situations. Children in these families might experience problems at school that range from embarrassment to harassment. It should also be noted that many of these children experience few or no problems as a result of their family structure.

These alternative family structures make it difficult to discuss the typical family because counted together, these alternative structures outnumber traditional families. This makes for an interesting and difficult public policy debate. Should the school, church, and government devise policies based on the assumption that the family has a traditional structure? Does supporting families with these alternative structures encourage people to engage in relationships that deviate from the idealized family? Does society have an interest in shaping policies that benefit the traditional family structure and disadvantage alternative structures in an attempt to reduce divorce, make parents more responsible for the well-being of their children, and promote the idealized lifestyle? Regardless of how we answer these questions, the nature of the American family will continue to change, and the effect of family concerns on the delinquency of children will continue to be a challenge for those involved in schools, recreational programs, and the juvenile justice system.

Another major challenge to the family, in addition to the range of family structures, is concerned with parenting. A number of issues are of concern when discussing parents. The most fundamental issue is the entry barrier to becoming a parent. There is none. Anyone can become a parent regardless of his or her parenting skills, responsibility, maturity, sanity, motivation, criminal record, or economic resources. The right to reproduce is absolute, and society hasn't established a required educational program, fitness test, or maturity level that prospective parents must meet. The result is that there is great variation in the adequacy of parents.[18] Most are very good, but some are so incompetent, clueless, and dangerous that society has to take away their children to prevent injury or death.

Society establishes a threshold for driving a car, flying a plane, trading on the stock market, and becoming a teacher. Yet, adolescents who are barely children themselves are free to produce children whom they don't have the capability to nurture, support, or guide. This is the major challenge faced by the juvenile justice system. The family isn't always a decent and safe place for children to grow up in, and it can set the child off on a trajectory toward delinquency.[19]

What does it take to be a good parent? This is a complex question, because families have multiple goals for their children. For our purposes here, we will concentrate on how parents might keep their children from engaging in delinquent behavior. Sometimes, parents might go overboard in controlling their children (see Kids in the News 10.1). At the very least, good parenting requires the following tasks:

- **Providing a positive role model**   The parent's influence on the child's behavior is crucial. Although many parents lecture their children on being truthful, dependable, and law-abiding, the parents' behavior often paints a different picture. Children are quick to see the contradictions between what parents say

---

10.1    **K I D S** *in the* **N E W S**

Watching the Kids

Thanks to advances in technology, parents are now able to use a variety of devices to track their teenagers' movements. Meanwhile, teenagers, who are typically more comfortable with technology than their parents, complain about the invasion of their privacy.

Two popular adolescent surveillance devices include the ubiquitous cell phone and the "black boxes" on cars. These latter devices are capable of reporting to parents how fast the youth is driving; whether there have been any sudden stops, hard turns, or fast accelerations; the distance the car is being driven; and the date and time of each trip. Some devices even have an alarm to warn the driver if he or she is exceeding any preset limits. (It is interesting, however, that a National Institute of Child Health and Human Development study found that "a simple behavioral intervention"—the study used a newsletter and a parent–teenager driving agreement—was sufficient to control risky teenage driving behavior.)[1]

Another company offers cell phones equipped with the Global Positioning System so that parents can use the Internet to check the location and speed of their teen's car. Another service offers to e-mail or call parents if the car exceeds a certain speed or leaves a specified area. A similar service is available on cell phones to track a youth's movements regardless of whether the youth is on foot or in a vehicle.

Then there is the mountain of software available to track a youth's movements on the Internet, with systems for checking the youth's e-mail, instant messages, websites visited, and downloads. In many cases, when the design of the device or the software makes it possible, parents do not tell their children that they are being monitored. This is most often the case with computer-monitoring software, when parents wish to follow their children's online activities without being detected. Often, the reason is that parents fear their children will stop using the monitored computer to communicate with both friends and strangers.[2]

Think About It

1. Did your parents use technology to monitor you? Would you use technology to monitor your children?

2. Are parents who monitor their children's movements so closely invading their privacy?

3. When the technology becomes available, should parents have a chip implanted in their children to monitor not only their whereabouts, but their health and activities?

1 Bruce G. Simons-Morton et al., "Persistence of Effects of the Checkpoints Program on Parental Restrictions of Teen Driving Privileges," *American Journal of Public Health* 95, no. 3 (March 2005): 447–452. Summary online at www.ajph.org/cgi/content/abstract/95/3/447.
2 Janine DeFao, "Parents Turn to Tech Toys to Track Teens," *San Francisco Chronicle*, July 9, 2006; sfgate.com/cgi-bin/article.cgi?file=/c/a/2006/07/09/BIGMOTHER.TMP.

and what they do, and it's difficult for anyone to engage in entirely consistent positive behavior. Children get mixed messages when parents cheat, lie, or steal in some situations and not in others. In their efforts to teach their children how to survive in a competitive capitalist society, parents often inoculate their children with skills, values, and attitudes that test the boundaries of ethical and legal behavior.[20] There is no easy answer to dealing with matters of economic survival, and each parent struggles with striking a balance between making his or her children effective citizens and making them potential law violators.

- **Encouraging productive behavior**   One role of parents is to ensure that their children grow into responsible adults who will one day be self-sufficient and help to support other family members. During the productive working years between the ages of 21 and 65, society expects adults to support themselves, pay taxes, and provide leadership in civic activities. Parents gradually socialize their children to take on these adult roles by encouraging productive behavior starting at an early age. Requiring a 3-year-old to pick up her toys can take more work to enforce that it would for the parent to do it herself. However, keeping the child's room clean isn't as important as it is to instill in the child a sense of responsibility. This message is continued throughout childhood and can be a source of conflict between parents and children. During the adolescent years, young people must learn several crucial lessons before they are ready to engage in the full range of adult behavior. Adolescents must learn to make decisions on their own concerning activities such as driving a car, engaging in intimate relations, handling money, and solving problems and negotiating conflicts in ways that preserve and strengthen important relationships with family members, peers, and co-workers. Learning productive behavior as opposed to selfish, wasteful, or destructive behavior is a lifelong process that is shaped in early childhood by parents and adults who understand the value of teaching children responsibility, accountability, and the idea of serving others.[21]

- **Engaging in adequate supervision**   Encouraging responsible and productive behavior is pointless unless the parent is prepared to supervise and make corrections when the child falls short of the goal. Providing adequate supervision is tricky because, although heavy-handed oversight can make children follow directions, it fails to get them to think for themselves and to internalize the desired values of hard work, sacrifice, deferred gratification, and service. Having a child or employee who does good work only when there is a parent or boss standing around isn't effective. Although extensive supervision might be necessary early in a child's life when being responsible is a novel idea or when there is potential for harm, such as playing near a busy street, good supervision structures the situation so that the child is given the opportunity to apply the lessons learned.[22] Michel Foucault refers to the internalized grids of discipline that we unconsciously employ when we perform what we believe is the correct and appropriate behavior. According to Foucault, these grids of discipline can cause an oversocialization that can rob us of our creativity and humanity. For instance, when we criticize children for coloring outside the lines in an effort to teach them art skills, we also might be squeezing the artistic genius out of them and depriving society of the next Georgia O'Keeffe or Pablo Picasso.[23]

- **Instituting effective discipline**   Another task of parenting, and one that many parents don't do particularly well, is discipline. The problem with discipline is that if it's done poorly, it can actually do more harm than good.[24] Ineffective discipline can be counterproductive because it sends the wrong message to children, which can be manifested in later years in a variety of ways, including delinquency, crime, and other deviant behaviors. Discipline to many individuals is equated with spanking. This seems like a reasonable and responsible response to misbehavior, and it's administered by most parents with a sense of obligation and love. However, according to noted child authority Alice Miller, children don't experience spanking in the way that adults mean for them to; hitting children begins a cycle by which children learn that violence is the way that powerful people deal with the powerless.[25] Although we won't go into all the negative effects of spanking, it's worth noting here that some groups (see Kids in the News 10.2 for one example) have advocated against the corporal punishment of children. If spanking isn't a good way to discipline children, then what should a parent do? A number of strategies are more effective than corporal punishment in both the short and long term in shaping children's behavior.

10.2

Spoiling the Rod

Many philosophies govern the spanking of children. Some parents believe any sort of striking is permissible as along as the child isn't permanently harmed; others restrict striking to specific parts of the body. The choice of what to strike the child with is idiosyncratic, as well. Some parents believe it's only proper to strike a child with the bare hand; others believe a "neutral" item must be used for striking, such as flyswatters, belts, or wooden switches.

Until recently, parents who didn't want to use any of the above items for striking a child could purchase the Rod for $5. Manufactured by Slide's Manufacturing of Eufala, Oklahoma, the Rod was a 22-inch flexible nylon "whipping stick." The advertisement for the Rod described it as the "ideal tool for child training," "balanced and easy to use," with a "cushioned grip" and a "safety tip." The advertisement states, "Spoons are for cooking, belts are for holding up pants, hands for loving, Rods are for chastening."[1] The owner of Slide's Manufacturing, Clyde Bullock, told the *Boston Globe* that he had sold "a few a week" since 1999.[2]

Susan Lawrence, a Lutheran mother who is against corporal punishment, came across an advertisement for the Rod in the magazine *Home School Digest.* Deciding that Rods should be banned, Lawrence started a website called Stop the Rod, which features a copy of the Rod's advertisement and calls on the governor of Oklahoma to stop the sale and manufacture of the device. As of May 2005, the online petition, which has since been closed, collected over a thousand signatures.[3]

Although there has been no legal move to halt sales of the Rod, the owner of Slide's Manufacturing, Clyde Bullock, had to stop production anyway. The company that made the Rod's cushioned grip is no longer involved in the manufacture of the device. With the Rod out of production, Susan Lawrence has continued to crusade against spanking instruments. In May 2005, Stop the Rod started a petition against a company called Child Training Resources of Bakersfield, California, which sells a "chastening instrument," that, according to the company's website, "is made of premium grade polyurethane and measures 9" long, 1½" wide and 3/16" thick."

Think About It

1. Do you believe children should be spanked? If so, what with?
2. Were you spanked as a child? Who spanked you? What did they use?
3. Should sales of the Rod and similar devices be halted?

Many parents still prefer to use items such as belts, wooden switches, or flyswatters to spank their children. *(Courtesy Patrick Olear, PhotoEdit Inc.)*

1 Child Training Resources,www.biblicalchildtraining.com/index.htm.
2 Patricia Wen, "Sale of Spanking Tool Points Up Larger Issue," *Boston Globe,* January 10, 2005, www.boston.com/news/local/articles/2005/01/10/campaigner_targets_spanking_tools_sale/.
3 Stop the Rod,stoptherod.net/.

FOCUS on ETHICS

FACING DOWN A DRILL SERGEANT DAD
Jordan Riak

One prospective buyer for the old Winnebago I had advertised for sale was a couple with two small children—an infant and a boy of about 6 years. The dad was skilled in the building trades, and his plan was to pack his family in an RV and travel around the country, finding work where it was available. Thus, as he explained it to me, he'd mix earning a living with a bit of adventure. "I like to keep moving," he said, "and there's always plenty of work."

Immediately upon their arrival, I sensed there would be trouble. The dad's treatment of the boy was abominable. He didn't talk; he commanded. He shouted orders and warnings in a tone of voice that would scare a marine. "Michael! Get over here! Now I said! Do you hear me? Stand right here and don't you move, or you're gonna get it. I'm not telling you again." Clearly, the father wanted his son to be on his best behavior, but the boy seemed not to hear a word his father was saying. Curious and full of energy, he only wanted to break free and inspect everything. I pointed the parents to the Winnebago and told them to take their time. I then went into the house to get my weapon of choice for such occasions: the booklet Plain Talk about Spanking (www.nospank.net/pt2008.htm).

I returned and handed the man two booklets. "Here's something I think might be useful to you. You can have these. One for you, one the missus." He accepted the booklets, and I left him alone. As I walked to the front of the property, I saw the mom inside the Winnebago inspecting the equipment. I glanced back and saw the man examining one of the booklets

A short while later—probably no more than 5 minutes—I returned. I felt nervous, not sure how the father would react to having his private affairs criticized by a total stranger. One never knows. As I approached, he looked straight at me with a desperate, pleading expression. It was as though I possessed some vital secret that he needed to learn. "But how do I make that kid listen to me?" he asked, looking pathetic.

Here's what I told him:

"Look at it this way. Think about all the time in Michael's short lifetime that he has been on the receiving end of hollering, ordering, threats and spankings. Sure, he doesn't listen to you. To him, you're like the neighborhood barking dog that never shuts up. He just blocks out the noise. We all do that. It's normal. Now think about how little time you've spent listening to Michael. Is that fair? If you don't listen to him, why should he listen to you? Just because you're bigger? Try to remember this one thing—I call it the Golden Rule of Management: You get what you give; if you don't give it, don't expect to get it.

"Here's a practical suggestion for getting Michael to start listening to you. It might not work immediately, but if you keep at it, I think it will. The next time Michael is talking, this is what I want you to do. Listen. Don't say a word. Crouch down to his level so he faces you eye to eye, and keep listening until he has finished. Give this a rest (I pinched my lips together with two fingers), and put this to work (I cupped my ear with my hand). And when he is finished talking, you answer in a way that he knows you heard what he said. You're the daddy. You're the model. You want Michael to be a listener? Then you show him how to be a listener. And remember what I said about the Golden Rule of Management. It works."

About a week later, my wife received a call from the drill sergeant dad. She told him she was sorry, but the RV had been sold. He told her he was not calling about that—he had already decided on something else. He said, "Please tell your husband, thanks from the traveling carpenter. I took his advice and there's been a lot less shouting around this place lately."

Think About It

1. Did the author give the carpenter good advice? Or should he have minded his own business?

2. Is it really important to listen to children?

3. In your experience, does the Golden Rule of Management really apply to child raising?

Source: Jordan Riak, "Facing Down a Drill Sergeant Dad," Project NoSpank, December 6, 2001, www.nospank.net/riak89.htm.

* Jordan Riak is an internationally known expert on the discipline of children and is the founder and executive director of Parents and Teachers Against Violence in Education, Inc.

At the core of these alternative methods of discipline is the establishment of a safe, supportive, and loving home in which children are nourished and nurtured.[26] See Focus on Ethics 10.1 for a look at one father's efforts to bring positive change to another parent's relationship with his child.

Parenting is a complex task and everyone does it differently. Even within families, parents can treat one child differently than another depending on age, gender, level of maturity, or birth order. Sometimes parents supervise their first children to a much greater degree than those who follow because the parents have become more confident in their own abilities, less afraid of the natural ups and downs of childhood, and better able to predict how younger children will respond.

Parents also have different resources available to them for their parenting tasks. Poverty greatly restrains the ability of parents to meet all the physical, psychological, and social needs of their children. Families living in poverty are more likely to have only one parent, lack health insurance, and have a greater school dropout rate than other families. Problems caused by poverty have a cumulative effect on the family when the parents are required to work longer hours to support the children and thus deprive them of support and supervision.[27]

Impoverished families can be contrasted with those who are wealthy. Wealthy parents can purchase help in raising their children in the form of nannies, coaches, tutors, and baby-sitters. Instead of coming home to an empty apartment in what is sometimes a dangerous neighborhood, the children of wealthy parents might go to soccer practice one afternoon, violin lessons on another afternoon, a French tutor on a third afternoon, and yet other activities for the remaining days of the week. Although all this activity might be more beneficial than the circumstances of the impoverished child, it still might be problematic. Overscheduled children can lack the time to simply play with their friends. Additionally, children can be placed in positions where they must constantly perform, whether it's on the piano or the soccer field or in school.[28]

Although both impoverished and wealthy parents love their children, they aren't always available to love them. Work obligations or social duties might require the parents to leave the children alone or place them in day care, an afternoon recreational program, or with a baby-sitter. Unfortunately, some children's parents would rather be at the bar, country club, or racetrack having their own fun, rather than spending time with their children.

Challenges outside the family can also affect the likelihood of youths engaging in delinquency. Communities and neighborhoods can inadvertently pressure children into delinquency, or they can provide support and programs that shield children from the temptations of the street. In communities where drug sales flourish, youths are commonly employed as couriers because the juvenile justice system will penalize them less—or not at all if they are very young—if they are caught. Also, impoverished neighborhoods have fewer programs for children and more liquor stores, pornographic movie theaters, and street prostitution.[29]

Finally, challenges to the family have been increased over recent years by the reduction, or even removal, of the social safety net that the government provides for those who experience temporary difficulty. For instance, in 1997 the federal aid available under the Aid to Families with Dependent Children (AFDC) ended and was replaced by the Temporary Assistance for Needy Families (TANF) program. The features of the new legislation limited assistance to five years and required adults to begin working within two years. The intention was to get "welfare mothers" off public assistance and to decrease the number of female-headed households by removing the perceived incentive of receiving welfare for having children. However, research indicates that because of these women's lack of job skills and the lack of jobs in the community, the desired reform of welfare has yet to take place.[30]

Child Victimization in the Family

Because the family is such an important institution, it should not surprise us that it is also a place where bad things happen along with the good. As Tolstoy reminds us, a family can be dysfunctional in many ways, with devastating effects on children. All families are affected by outside forces, such as the quality of the neighborhood, the availability of jobs, and the availability of good schools. There are also sources of conflict within families that include its structure, problems of drug or alcohol abuse, and family violence. Here, we will look at two concerns that deeply influence children's quality of life.

First, we consider the issue of neglect. Some parents lack the parenting skills to meet their children's needs, and some parents simply do not place a priority on the welfare of their children because of problems of their own. Second, we look at the issue of family violence. Domestic violence is one of the greatest threats to the welfare and safety of children. It seems almost ironic that the family, the presumed source of love and nurturing for children, can also be one of the most dangerous places for them.

child neglect

According to criminologist Harvey Wallace, " The negligent treatment or maltreatment of a child by a parent or caretaker under circumstances indicating harm or threatened harm to the child's health or welfare."

CHILD NEGLECT   **Child neglect** is less visible than child abuse, so it is difficult to determine its exact prevalence in society. Although more child fatalities are caused by neglect only (see Figure 10-4), the common definition of child neglect isn't as well established as that of child abuse. One person might consider leaving a child alone at home after school to be neglect; another person might consider it a case of demonstrating to the child that he or she is trusted with personal responsibility. For our purposes here, we will adopt the definition used by criminologist Harvey Wallace, who states, "Child neglect is the negligent treatment or maltreatment of a child by a parent or caretaker under circumstances indicating harm or threatened harm to the child's health or welfare." This neglect, according to Wallace, runs a continuum from momentary inattention to gross action or inaction.[31] Although we typically think of poverty as the best indicator of neglect, economic resources are a misleading measure. Children from extremely impoverished families can be well cared for emotionally and supported in all their endeavors, while children of wealthy parents can be made to feel that, despite their material opulence, they are unloved and ignored by their busy parents.

How do parents who neglect their children differ from those who take good care of their children? Wallace suggests the following factors:

- **Inability to plan**   Some parents can't adequately plan for either the near- or long-term future. They don't establish goals, provide direction, or defer gratification. They lack a future orientation and live for the moment, which results in not having groceries for the week, clean clothes for school, or money for emergencies.

- **Lack of knowledge**   Many people have children when they are very young and have little knowledge of how to run a household and meet the family's needs. Their skills at cooking, nurturing, and housekeeping can be very limited.

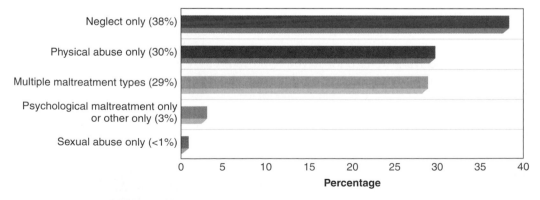

Figure 10-4   Child Abuse and Neglect Fatalities by Maltreatment Type, 2002

Fatal child abuse might involve repeated abuse over a period of time, or it might involve a single, impulsive incident. In cases of fatal neglect, the child's death results from a caregiver's failure to act. Like abuse, the neglect might be long-term, or it might be the result of a single incident. *Source: Child Maltreatment 2002* (Washington, DC: U.S. Department of Health and Human Services, 2004) as adapted from *Child Abuse and Neglect Fatalities: Statistics and Interventions* (Washington, DC: National Clearinghouse on Child Abuse and Neglect Information, 2004), 3. Online at www.childwelfare.gov/pubs/factsheets/fatality.pdf.

Having grown up eating fast food, they don't know how to cook a variety of nutritious foods and don't understand their children's emotional and psychological needs.

- **Lack of judgment** Parents who neglect their children sometimes lack the judgment to decide at what age the children should be given responsibilities to look after themselves. By not setting curfews for young children, giving fast cars to young adolescents, or overlooking and condoning drug or alcohol use, some parents allow their children to enter dangerous situations in which they might injure themselves or others. These parents might reason that children need to be entrusted with the responsibility of learning to take care of themselves, and although they might be partially right, they thrust this burden on children too early and without adequate supervision.

- **Lack of motivation** Some parents have given up on life themselves and have little interest in helping their children succeed. These parents might be more interested in their own drug or alcohol consumption, their favorite football team, or their own love life than they are in their children. At best, they might simply be clueless about their children's needs or, at worst, they might consider their children to be a drain on their time and finances and resent the fact that, as parents, they have a long-term responsibility.[32]

What is the difference between poor parenting and neglect? This is a difficult question to answer. Although parents might make poor decisions or be indifferent to their children's needs in some areas, they might be very attentive and supportive in others. The intentions of the parents might be honorable, but the execution of their plans might be haphazard, ineffective, and outright dangerous. Professionals who deal with children, such as teachers, school nurses, and recreational directors, constantly face judgment calls regarding their suspicions of child neglect.

Sometimes they notice subtle changes in the child's behavior, and sometimes it is clear that the child is not functioning at his or her full capacity. These professionals

Katrena Hunt, who is addicted to crack cocaine, lives on the streets of Jackson, Mississippi, with her young daughter.

look for a number of clues before reporting cases of child neglect. For instance, children who do not physically grow along with their peers might lack proper nutrition. Of course, this single indicator is problematic because children go through growth spurts at different stages in their lives, so it is necessary to check for other indicators of neglect. Is the child constantly hungry, or are there indications of malnutrition? Does the child have lice, body odor, or old and torn clothing? Other indicators of physical child neglect include listlessness or falling asleep in class and unattended medical needs, such as poor vision, dental problems, or lack of proper immunizations. If the child is left unattended for long periods of time or in situations of imminent danger, it might be a signal that the parents aren't adequately supervising the child.[33]

There are also a number of behavioral indicators of child neglect. The child might steal or beg for food because there aren't adequate meals at home. The child might be destructive to self or others and show extremes in behavior ranging from inactivity to aggressiveness. If the child assumes adult responsibilities for self or siblings, it might indicate a lack of responsible adult supervision at home. The child might exhibit hypochondria as a way of getting attention.[34] And, of course, delinquent behavior can be an indicator of child neglect. The following are some of the more common forms of child neglect:

Failure-to-Thrive Syndrome   Failure-to-thrive is a controversial issue. The symptoms might indicate a real medical problem rather than ineffective parenting. It is an identifiable medical diagnosis that classifies the child's physical development as deficient in relation to the established norms for children of that age. It might indicate a malfunction of one of the child's organs or a disease, or it might be the result of a nonorganic problem such as poor parenting. **Nonorganic failure-to-thrive** (NFTT) is indicated when the child is below the 20th percentile in both height and weight provided that the child was within the established norm at some point in her or his life. Children suffering from NFTT are physically emaciated, pale, and have little subcutaneous fat. Behaviorally, they appear listless and apathetic.

Still, a number of physical ailments might cause the same symptoms. Kidney disease, allergies, and congenital heart problems must be ruled out before NFTT can be diagnosed. The primary problem causing NFTT is lack of caloric intake, which can be reversed by adequate meals. School meal programs and policies such as replacing junk food in school vending machines with fruit are aimed at this problem. The problems originating from NFTT can be long-term even if it is eventually addressed and the symptoms disappear.[35] There are several types of neglect. The Study of National Incidence and Prevalence of Child Abuse and Neglect has sought to standardize the definitions of the various forms of neglect (see Table 10-1).

Emotional Neglect   **Emotional neglect** in children is extremely hard to detect and even harder to prove. It is defined as "acts or omissions of acts that are judged by community standards and professional expertise to be psychologically damaging to the child."[36] Because emotional neglect leaves no burn marks, scars, bruises, or broken bones, the problems can go unrecognized by authorities, the parents, and the child. The parents might believe they are simply arming their children with emotional toughness when they overly criticize or demean their children's character and behavior, but in reality, the parents might be doing severe emotional damage that prevents their children from establishing a positive and healthy sense of self-esteem.

Emotional neglect can take several forms. One such form is spurning or rejecting the child. Here the parent tells the child that he or she is stupid, worthless, and otherwise inadequate. Being compared unfavorably to siblings and having one's emotional needs ignored by parents can be extremely harmful to the child's sense of worth. A second type of emotional neglect consists of terrorizing the child with threats of violence, abandonment, or humiliation. Some children live in fear that their parents will expose their secrets or physically harm them. A third type of emotional abuse is isolating the child. Sometimes done as an alternative to physical punishment, isolating the child by

---

nonorganic failure-to-thrive

A medical term that describes an infant or child who has a measurable lag in height, head size, and/or development caused by environmental factors rather than an illness or disorder.

emotional neglect

From criminologist Harvey Wallace: "Acts or omissions of acts that are judged by community standards and professional expertise to be psychologically damaging to the child."

Table 10-1   **Various Forms of Neglect**

Physical Neglect	
Refusal of health care	Failure to provide or allow needed care in accord with recommendations of a competent health-care professional for a physical injury, illness, medical condition, or impairment.
Delay in health care	Failure to seek timely and appropriate medical care for a serious health problem that any reasonable layperson would have recognized as needing professional medical attention.
Abandonment	Desertion of a child without arranging for reasonable care and supervision. This category included cases in which children were not claimed within 2 days and when children were left by parents or substitutes who gave no (or false) information about their whereabouts.
Expulsion	Other blatant refusals of custody, such as permanent or indefinite expulsion of a child from the home without adequate arrangement for care by others or refusal to accept custody of a returned runaway.
Other custody issues	Custody-related forms of inattention to the child's needs other than those covered by abandonment or expulsion. For example, repeated shuttling of a child from one household to another due to apparent unwillingness to maintain custody or chronically and repeatedly leaving a child with others for days or weeks at a time.
Other physical neglect	Conspicuous inattention to avoidable hazards in the home; inadequate nutrition, clothing, or hygiene; and other forms of reckless disregard of the child's safety and welfare, such as driving with the child while intoxicated, leaving a young child unattended in a motor vehicle, and so forth.

Supervision	
Inadequate supervision	Child left unsupervised or inadequately supervised for extended periods of time or allowed to remain away from home overnight without the parent or substitute knowing (or attempting to determine) the child's whereabouts.

Emotional Neglect	
Inadequate nurturance or affection	Marked inattention to the child's needs for affection, emotional support, attention, or competence.
Chronic or extreme abuse or domestic violence	Chronic or extreme spouse abuse or other domestic violence in the child's presence.
Permitted drug or alcohol abuse	Encouraging or permitting drug or alcohol use by the child; cases of the child's drug or alcohol use were included here if it appeared that the parent or guardian had been informed of the problem and had not attempted to intervene.
Permitted other maladaptive behavior	Encouragement or permitting of other maladaptive behavior (e.g., severe assaultiveness, chronic delinquency) in circumstances in which the parent or guardian had reason to be aware of the existence and seriousness of the problem but did not attempt to intervene.
Refusal of psychological care	Refusal to allow needed and available treatment for a child's emotional or behavioral impairment or problem in accord with competent professional recommendation.
Delay in psychological care	Failure to seek or provide needed treatment for a child's emotional or behavioral impairment or problem that any reasonable layperson would have recognized as needing professional psychological attention (e.g., severe depression, suicide attempt).
Other emotional neglect	Other inattention to the child's developmental or emotional needs not classifiable under any of the above forms of emotional neglect (e.g., markedly overprotective restrictions that foster immaturity or emotional overdependence, chronically applying expectations clearly inappropriate in relation to the child's age or level of development, etc.)
Permitted chronic truancy	Habitual truancy averaging at least 5 days a month was classifiable under this form of maltreatment if the parent or guardian had been informed of the problem and had not attempted to intervene.

(Continued)

Table 10-1   (Continued)

Educational Neglect	
Failure to enroll or other truancy	Failure to register or enroll a child of mandatory school age, causing the school-age child to remain at home for nonlegitimate reasons (e.g., to work, to care for siblings, etc.) an average of at least 3 days a month.
Inattention to special education need	Refusal to allow or failure to obtain recommended remedial educational services or neglect in obtaining or following through with treatment for a child's diagnosed learning disorder or other special education need without reasonable cause.

Sources: U.S. Department of Health and Human Services, *Study of National Incidence and Prevalence of Child Abuse and Neglect,*www.childwelfare.gov/pubs/usermanuals/neglect/neglectb.cfm; U.S. Department of Health and Human Services, *Child Neglect: A Guide for Intervention*, 1993.

placing him or her in a closet, bedroom, or tool shed for long periods of time can be harmful. A fourth type of emotional neglect involves corrupting children by exploiting them. Some parents abuse their children sexually or allow others to touch, fondle, or film their children in sexual acts. This type of exploitation can have harmful and long-lasting effects on the children's emotional condition. Finally, emotional neglect can consist of denying the child's emotional responses. Parents who fail to talk to, touch, look at, or otherwise interact with their children can greatly harm their emotional development. Some parents believe their children should be "seen but not heard" and set up stringent rules concerning behavior in the home that prevent the children from playing, experimenting, or otherwise exploring their emotional boundaries.[37]

Unsafe Home Environment   Some children suffer from neglect by being raised in a home that is unfit because of filthy conditions, unsafe wiring, broken plumbing, or lice and rodents. Some homes are physically deteriorated and a real threat to the children's health and welfare. Parents who don't clean up animal feces, broken glass, or dirty dishes expose their children to injury and disease. Police officers, welfare workers, and teachers who make home visits are authorized to remove children from homes that are an immediate danger to children. The reasons that homes can be inadequate living quarters can range from the effects of poverty to neglectful landlords to parents who simply do not know how to keep a home clean and safe or understand how an unsafe home harms their children.

Drug and Alcohol Use   Parents and caretakers who use drugs and alcohol put their children at risk. The first serious problem of abuse and neglect related to drug and alcohol use is the transference of the substances from the parent to the fetus or newborn child. Although this problem has been overstated by some war-on-drugs publicity, no one seriously suggests that drug use by pregnant mothers is risk-free. The drugs pass through the placenta and affect the fragile fetus, and it is difficult, if not impossible, to gauge the actual effect on the child.

Most states now have legislation that mandates the reporting of newborns who have been exposed to drugs by the mothers and have established punishments that include removing the baby and placing it with family members or a foster home. The effect of alcohol on fetuses is better established than that of other drugs. **Fetal alcohol syndrome** (FAS) is suspected of being one of the primary causes of mental retardation. There is considerable debate about what to do with families in which the mother has used drugs or alcohol during pregnancy. Some would take the child away to be raised by others because of the likelihood of relapse by the mother. Others contend that treatment for new mothers can be effective because they are motivated to clean up their bodies in order to be allowed to keep the child.[38]

Medical Neglect   Sometimes parents fail to seek medical care for their children even when they are extremely ill. This should not be particularly surprising when we

fetal alcohol syndrome
The National Institutes of Health defines this condition as a pattern of mental and physical birth abnormalities found in some children of mothers who drank excessively during pregnancy.

Some children suffer from neglect by being raised in a dangerous environment. *(Courtesy Nathan Benn, CORBIS-NY)*

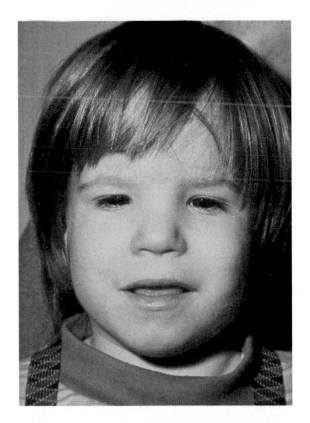

This child has fetal alcohol syndrome with symptomatic small, squinty eyes; flat, upturned *nose; and thin upper lip.* *(Streissguth, A.P., Landesman-Dwyer, S., Martin, J.C., & Smith, D.W. (1980). "Teratogenic effects of alcohol in humans and laboratory animals." Science, 209, 353–361)*

consider the inadequate system of medical insurance in this country. Medical care is expensive, and many can't utilize preventive services. Many parents take their child to a doctor only when the problem gets acute, and this is usually to a hospital emergency room. Children comprise the majority of those without insurance and suffer from a variety of ills that regular medical treatment and checkups could prevent.

Often, parents do not choose to neglect their children's medical needs but simply can't afford proper medical care. Other cases are more problematic. Some parents, for religious reasons, choose to forgo the advantages of advanced medicine in favor of letting their belief in supernatural forces decide the child's fate. A number of religions are suspicious of modern medicine or believe that illness and death are the will of God. Often these cases escape attention, and the children simply suffer and/or die because no one recognized or reported their plight to authorities. Other times, relatives, schools, or hospitals will become aware of the situation and implore the courts to intervene. The state will invoke its **parens patriae** authority and order medical treatment. The reasoning is that the child's well-being supersedes the parent's right to practice a religious doctrine that might result in grave illness or death.

Abandonment   A final form of child neglect is abandonment. Periodically, the media will report a case in which a newborn is found in a restroom or a trash bin. This is a clear case of abandonment, and the mother, if she is found, usually loses her parental rights. Sometimes, the case isn't so straightforward. A parent might leave the child in the care of a relative or a friend for an extended period of time, have no contact, and provide no material support and then show up years later wanting the child back. There have been cases in which a woman who is acting as a surrogate mother for a couple who is unable to conceive later decides that she really wants to keep the infant. In these cases, the court must decide on several important issues. The primary concern of what is best for the child must be balanced with the legal rights of the natural parents.

Child neglect is a substantial social problem in the United States. It is more prevalent than the actual physical abuse of children, although it is much less visible. The juvenile court, which we discuss in greater detail in Chapter 14, is vested with deciding how to deal with cases of neglect.

PHYSICAL CHILD ABUSE   The family is ideally a place of safety and comfort for its members. Increasingly, however, we are becoming aware that the family can also be a place where physical violence is perpetrated by one member of the family on another. Family violence takes several forms, but for our study of juvenile delinquency, we won't deal with family violence that doesn't directly affect children.[39] In this section, we cover the family abuse that might contribute to delinquency.[40] These forms of family violence include physical child abuse and sexual child abuse. Each form of family violence has its separate causes, solutions, and ramifications.

Our definition of **physical child abuse** is taken from Harvey Wallace's *Family Violence: Legal, Medical, and Social Perspectives*. Wallace defines physical child abuse as "any act that results in a nonaccidental physical injury by a person who has care, custody, or control of a child."[41] The distinguishing features of this definition are the aspects of physical injury and intent. A child slipping in the tub during a bath wouldn't qualify as physical child abuse. Although the child might be hurt in the accident, the parent did not intend to hurt the child, so the act might qualify as simply an accident instead of abuse.

The physical abuse of children has long been an established practice in human societies and, until recently, was actually institutionalized in some cultures. By that, we mean it was part of accepted social policy to kill or injure children. Many ancient societies, including those of Greece and Rome, accepted infanticide, most infamously by exposure, as a parental right. Infanticide might have served as a form of birth control, especially in times of scarcity.[42] In other societies, especially those that valued boys over girls, the killing of girl children might have been officially frowned on but was practiced anyway by parents who wished to have a boy instead.

The history of physical abuse of children must be put in context, however. It was once considered appropriate for parents to beat or even kill their children, but when we measure the behavior of older civilizations by our modern standards, we are guilty of what historians call **presentism**. Social conditions, value systems and ethics, and the economic feasibility of having large families have all changed over time, and what was considered necessary or appropriate in one era can be considered a crime in

physical child abuse

According to criminologist Harvey Wallace, "Any act that results in a nonaccidental physical injury by a person who has care, custody, or control of a child."

presentism

A belief that people of an earlier time should be accountable to the standards of the present time.

another.[43] Physical abuse of children can be likened to slavery or armies pillaging the lands they conquered. As despicable as these actions seem to us today, they were sanctioned and rewarded by the authorities of the time.

Parents are the most frequent physical abusers of children, far more than other relatives or caregivers (seeFigure 10-5), with mothers perpetrating the most fatalities (Figure 10-6). Physical child abuse is more obvious than neglect because the injury is visible. The problem becomes one of determining how the injury occurred. Because children injure themselves all the time, there is always the question as to whether the adult inflicted the injury or it happened as a result of an accident. There are a number of warning signs that abuse has occurred based on how the injury is explained.

- **Unexplained injury**   If the caretaker can't explain how the injury happened, there is a good chance that his or her was inflicted on the child. Especially if the child is too young to give his or her own account, the caregiver who abused the child might claim to have no knowledge. Certainly, there are times when a child is injured out of the adult's sight, and the caregiver's claim of having no knowledge is legitimate, but most caregivers are eager to tell medical personnel all they can about the circumstances of the injury.

- **Impossible explanations**   If the caretaker's story is inconsistent with the type and extent of the child's injury, it might be a sign that the caregiver is lying. A minor accident that is claimed by the caregiver shouldn't cause life-threatening injury. Common sense and good medical judgment can often alert professionals to the possibility of child abuse.

- **Different versions of the incident**   One tactic that police officers use to determine if child abuse has occurred is to talk to the parents separately and compare their versions of how the accident happened. Minor inconsistencies in which the parents did not get the details of their stories straight can lead to an unraveling of the explanation upon further investigation.

- **Different explanations**   When the caregiver must repeat the story of the incident to several different people at different times, the story might change.

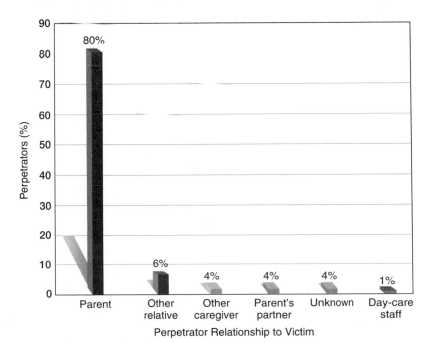

Figure 10-5   Parents Are the Most Frequent Child Abusers *Source:* Adapted from Walter R. McDonald and Associates, *Child Maltreatment 2003: Reports from the States to the National Child Abuse and Neglect Data System* (Washington, DC: U.S. Department of Health and Human Services, Children's Bureau, 2004) by Howard N. Snyder and Melissa Sickmund, *Juvenile Offenders and Victims: 2006 National Report* (Washington, DC: U.S. Department of Justice, Office of Justice Programs, Office of Juvenile Justice and Delinquency Prevention, 2006), 55. Online atwww.ojjdp.ncjrs.org/ojstatbb/nr2006/downloads/NR2006.pdf.

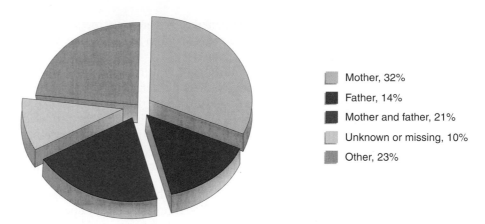

Figure 10-6 Perpetrator Relationships of Child Fatalities, 2004

Most child-abuse fatalities result from abuse by the mother. The Other category comprises abuse by mother, father, and other; mother and other; father and other; female relative; male relative; female foster parent nonrelative; male foster parent nonrelative; female day-care staff; male day-care staff; female partner of parent; male partner of parent; and male friend or neighbor. *Source: Child Maltreatment, 2004* (Washington, DC: U.S. Department of Health and Human Services, 2004). Online at www.acf.hhs.gov/programs/cb/pubs/cm04/table4_5.htm.

The circumstances of the truth never change, but when one must remember what lies were told, keeping the cover story consistent becomes difficult. As law enforcement officers talk with emergency room technicians and child protective service workers, they might find that on repeated explanations the story gets embellished and the facts become inconsistent or contradictory.

- **Delay in seeking medical attention**   Officials consider it a big red flag when someone who has a child with life-threatening injuries does not seek immediate medical attention. The person might hope the bump on the head or the sore ribs will heal with time, but this only puts the child in more pain and more danger. Concerned parents are more likely to err on the side of caution and overreaction than to delay getting the child to a doctor.[44]

Unfortunately, the youngest children, infants, bear the most physical abuse, with the numbers tapering off sharply once the youth advances into adolescence (see Figure 10-7). The types of physical child abuse are limited only by the imaginations of the abusers. Typically, however, the physical abuse fits into well-known categories because the abuse is spontaneous most of the time. According to Harvey Wallace, physical child abuse is normally associated with one or more of four types of injuries.

Bruises are the first common type of physical child abuse and the one that is hardest to distinguish from the normal bruises of an active child. The first thing that professionals look for on a bruised child is the injury's location. A child who falls off a swing, trips on the rug, or fights with his or her sibling will acquire bruises where there is little flesh. The shins, forehead, elbows, and knees are where normal bruising occurs. Bruises on the abdomen or buttocks, on the back of the arms or legs, or on the genitals might indicate injuries sustained when a child is being physically abused. Experts also look at the pattern of the bruising. Certain weapons such as belts, paddles, or cords leave distinctive marks, and a handprint on a child's face or bottom is a clue that the injury wasn't self-inflicted. Finally, bruises heal at a predictable rate and change color as they do so. This leaves a history of the trauma suffered by the child and shows the professional the recent history of the abuse.[45]

Another injury common to physical child abuse is burns. Some parents, as a way of punishing a child, use burns to punish by placing the child in a bowl of hot water or in some cases using a lighted cigarette. The seriousness of the burn is measured according to a scale that runs from first degree (looks like mild sunburn) to fourth

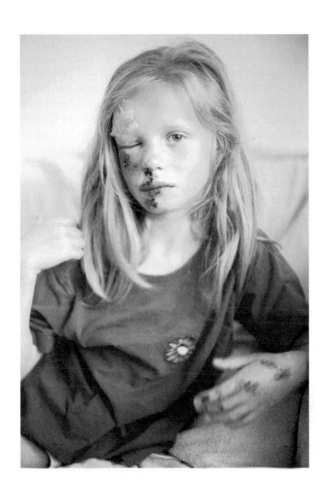

Young children are the most frequently abused. According to Harvey Wallace, physical child abuse is normally associated with bruises, burns, bone fractures, and internal injuries. *(© Hill Creek Pictures/Index Stock)*

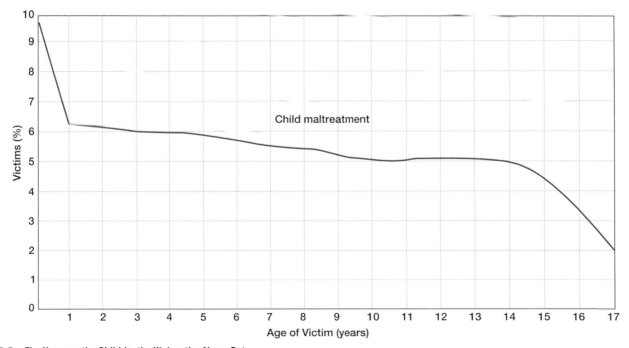

Child maltreatment

Figure 10-7   The Younger the Child Is, the Higher the Abuse Rate
The rate of maltreatment victimization is inversely related to age, with the youngest children enduring the highest rate of abuse. *Source:* Adapted from Walter R. McDonald and Associates, *Child Maltreatment 2003*, by Howard N. Snyder and Melissa Sickmund, *Juvenile Offenders and Victims: 2006 National Report* (Washington, DC: U.S. Department of Justice, Office of Justice Programs, Office of Juvenile Justice and Delinquency Prevention, 2006), 54. Online at www.ojjdp.ncjrs.org/ojstatbb/nr2006/downloads/NR2006.pdf.

degree (penetrates to the muscle or bone). Like bruises, burns leave a history of trauma on the child's skin that can alert professionals to the abuse.[46]

Bone fractures are another common result of physical abuse. The most common type of fracture indicating abuse is the spiral fracture in which the child's arm has been grabbed and twisted. In children who are young enough that their bones have not fully developed, a fracture is relatively rare. It takes a good deal of force to twist the arm to the extent that it breaks. Most likely, the adult didn't intend to break the child's bone but nevertheless exerted enough power to do this level of damage.

Finally, physical abuse can injure the head and internal organs, ranging from black eyes and skull fractures to kidney and liver damage. These injuries can occur when children are hit with a fist or weapon or when they are thrown into a wall or to the floor. These types of injuries can be the most life threatening and the hardest to prove that they were a result of child abuse.[47]

SEXUAL CHILD ABUSE   The sexual abuse of children is a subject that generates a lot of media attention these days. Whether it is a case in which a child is abducted, abused, and killed; a case in which members of the clergy or scouting organization take advantage of those under their care; or a case of incest, the media give a great deal of coverage to the sensational and lurid nature of these crimes. Part of the reason for this interest is the power relationship between children and adults. Children are not legally or emotionally capable of giving informed consent for the sexual encounter.[48]

10.1 A CLOSER LOOK at JUVENILE ISSUES

NOWHERE TO RUN, NOWHERE TO LIVE

Child sexual abuse is a serious problem that has become a popular issue among politicians and the public. Politicians vie to show their tough stances against sex offenders much as they did to show that they were "tough on crime" or "tough on drugs." As a result, new legislation has rewritten the definition of "child sexual abuser" and churned out whole new sets of rules controlling how those charged with child sexual abuse may live and work.

There are three levels of sex offenders: level 1 (low risk), level 2 (moderate risk), and level 3 (high risk). The majority of registered sex offenders are classified as level 1; that is, they are considered a low risk to re–offend and are probably first-time offenders. Many level 1 offenders were under the age of 20 at the time of the offense, although they might have been legally considered adults, with many offenders being adolescents who had sex with other adolescents. All 50 states require sex offenders to register as such, and all states have online sex-offender registries. The U.S. Department of Justice hosts the National Sex Offender Public Registry, from which all state sex-offender registries can be searched.[1]

States are becoming more strict in how they track sex offenders, especially those convicted of child sexual abuse. In 2006, the state of Georgia passed one of the harshest laws in the country, restricting registered sex offenders from living or working within 1,000 feet of a school bus stop, playground, school campus, child-care facility, church, or anywhere children must regularly gather. Registered sex offenders who break the law face at least 10 years in prison, and the law has no grandfather clause. That is, offenders who lived within 1,000 feet of a school bus stop prior to passage of the law had to move their residences. Although some states distinguish level 1 and level 2 offenders from level 3 offenders, the ones who are considered to be dangerous, Georgia doesn't, which meant that people convicted of statutory rape had to leave their homes as well. As of 2006, only 14 of Georgia's approximately 10,000 registered sex offenders were considered dangerous predators.

Sheriff's departments throughout Georgia attest that the law is practically unenforceable because they lack the resources to track down and force all the registered sex offenders in their counties to move. Also, experts in this area of the law worry that sex offenders will simply stop registering.[2]

Meanwhile, other states have found different solutions to keeping up with sex offenders. As of 2006, Illinois was planning a program to track its paroled sex offenders by the Global Positioning System (GPS). Missouri requires that some sex offenders be tracked by GPS for the rest of their lives as long as they live in the state.[3] Wisconsin mandates lifetime GPS tracking of those convicted of sexually assaulting children or committing violent sex crimes. Iowa's laws are so strict that many registered sex offenders are living at campgrounds in order to comply with state law. Some Iowa cities have banned offenders from living within 2,000 feet of swimming pools, libraries, parks, or trails.[4]

1 www.nsopr.gov/.
2 Jenny Jarvie, "Suit Targets Sex Offender Law," *Los Angeles Times*, July 2, 2006, p. A24, home edition.
3 Leah Thorsen, "State Is Set to Track Sex Offenders 24/7, New Law Calls for System Next Year, but Funding Remains a Question," *St. Louis Post-Dispatch*, July 6, 2006, p. B1, second edition.
4 Fox News/AP, "Iowa Residency Laws Pushing Sex Offenders to Live at Campgrounds," July 24, 2006, www.foxnews.com/story/0,2933,205255,00.html.

Although some abusers will claim the sex was loving in nature and agreed on by both parties, it is viewed by the courts, parents, and the public as one of the most despicable crimes in society.[49] Child sexual abuse is also an offense seized on by politicians to show that they are tough on crime (see A Closer Look at Juvenile Issues 10.1).

We typically think of the perpetrator as male and the victim as female. However, recent studies show that the incidence of male victims and female abusers is higher than originally thought.[50] There have been a few high-profile cases of female teachers having sexual affairs with male high school students, which has led people to question whether this type of behavior is as serious and detrimental as when the teacher is male and the victim female. Boys might not report sexual abuse as often as girls for a number of reasons. First, they are not questioned as closely as girls. They are given greater freedom to travel and stay out late, and parents do not automatically worry they might be taken advantage of sexually. The second reason boys might not report sexual abuse is because they are afraid of looking weak. Boys are taught to take care of themselves, and if they are seduced or forced into sex, they might endure more embarrassment than girls who realize immediately that they have been victimized.[51]

Younger children are more likely to be sexually victimized than older children. By age 4, children are sexually curious and can be manipulated by an adult, and by age 9 they have a desire to please and are willing to trust adults. Sexual abuse of children tapers off sharply at age 14, because the child is likely to either run away or threaten disclosure of the adult.[52]

Although sexual child abuse takes several forms, we are most concerned here with incest because of its connection to families and delinquency. Actually, statistics show that parents are less likely to commit sexual abuse than other adults the child knows. Nonparental relatives show the highest rate of sexual abuse with 30 percent of perpetrators, followed by day-care staff with 23 percent of perpetrators. Parents represented only 3 percent of sexual abuse perpetrators.[53]

The juvenile court is concerned with all types of juvenile victimization, but the crucial issue here is how family relations encourage or protect against delinquency. Incest involves sexual relations between blood relatives. Incest has an uneven history, because it was encouraged in some societies and outlawed in others. It is generally thought that incest is prohibited for biological reasons because of the strong possibility of passing along recessive genes that result in physical or mental disabilities. Most states have laws prohibiting marriage between relatives closer than first cousins.[54]

Incest is also prohibited for psychological reasons. When fathers dominate the family dynamics, daughters have little power to resist sexual advances either physically or emotionally. Therefore, a societal proscription against incest allows fathers to internalize a supportive and protective role and prevents them from viewing their daughters as potential sex partners. This incest taboo creates order and cooperation within the family unit and allows children to grow up trusting their parents and to later enter into intimate relationships with a member of a different family.[55] Because the incest taboo is so firmly entrenched in modern Western society, it is difficult for us to imagine it without being revolted. However, what we must realize is that the norms of society are socially constructed and that what is appropriate in one time and place might be inappropriate in another culture or century. However, in modern Western society, sexual relations with children are considered abuse and are likely a causative factor in delinquency. According to Andrea Sedlak and Diane Broadhurst, girls are sexually abused almost three times more often than boys.[56] The median age at which girls reported first becoming victims of sexual assault is 13.[57] Another study found that 92 percent of juvenile female offenders interviewed had experienced emotional, physical, and/or sexual abuse.[58]

FAMILIES AND DELINQUENCY

What is the link between the type and quality of the family and the likelihood that the children will engage in some type of delinquency? The quality of family life is clearly related to the victimization of children. This leads to the question of whether such victimization can propel the child toward victimizing others. It seems obvious that coming from a bad family where one is the victim of abuse or neglect would eventually result in further deviance, but the nexus is complicated and deserves close examination.[59]

To examine the dynamics of the relationship between the family and delinquency, we consider four areas that historically have been associated with this issue. First, we look at the effects of divorce on children. Second, we examine how well the family provides emotional and economic support to children. Third, we look at conflict within the family, and finally, we consider the influence of parental and sibling deviance on the delinquent behavior of children.

Divorce and Delinquency

More than half of marriages do not last "until death do us part." Divorce is such a prevalent feature of American family life today that it no longer carries the social stigma that it did in the past. Still, dissolving a marriage is no easy task. It has social, economic, and emotional costs that make adults put up with infidelity, emotional estrangement, public embarrassment, and feelings of betrayal and worthlessness. Although some might contend that a divorce is too easy to obtain, almost everyone who has endured one will attest that it is an unpleasant and heart-wrenching task.

Difficult as a divorce might be on the parents, it is the children who have the most difficulty adjusting to this monumental change in their family structure and living conditions. Many children react to divorce with the feeling that it is somehow their fault, and they experience a sense of misplaced guilt. Other children blame one of the parents and develop a sense of loyalty and protectiveness toward the other. Still other children see divorce as abandonment and feel as though the bonds of social control have been slackened and that they are free to engage in antisocial delinquent behavior.[60]

Not all children are affected in the same manner by divorce. The age and gender of children play an important role in how they adjust, and some studies suggest that boys are affected more than girls. With the male role model leaving the home, boys are more likely to test the mother's authority and to feel that they are now the "man of the house" and not subject to rules as they were when the father was at home.[61] With only one parent around to enforce discipline, discover deviance, and solve problems, it is not surprising that there is a clear relationship between divorce and delinquency. Research has shown that when the number of single-parent households goes up dramatically, so too does the incidence of status offenders and delinquents.[62] For example, one study found that 2 percent of female respondents who lived with both biological parents had been arrested in the last year as opposed to 5 percent of female respondents who lived in families with alternative structures. For males, the number was 4 percent (who lived with both biological parents) versus 10 percent (who lived in families with alternative structures). See Figure 10-8 for further comparisons.

Still, it is not wise to paint all divorces with the same brush. There is the concept of a "successful" divorce in which the partners and the children adjust and grow emotionally in their new living situations. The components of a successful divorce include both parents playing a positive role in their children's lives.[63]

Social Support in the Family and Delinquency

Each family environment is unique, and it can change over time depending on its structure, size, and economic conditions. When new children are added to the family, the dynamics are altered and the future changed as parents and siblings learn to accommodate the new members. Each family provides an endlessly broad range of support to every member, and this support greatly influences the chances that the child will not engage in delinquency.

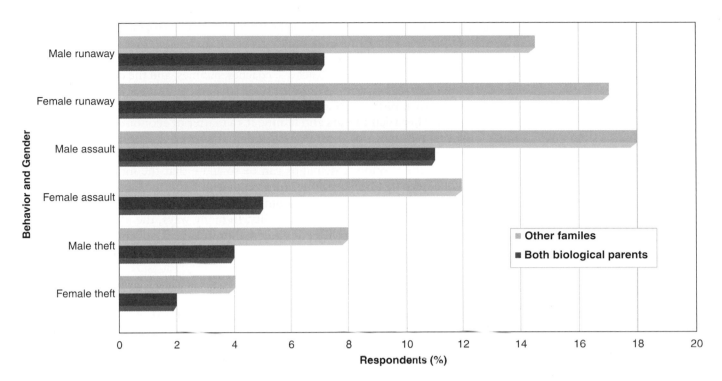

Figure 10-8   **The Relationship between Family Structure and Problem Behavior** *Source:* Adapted from C. McCurley and H. Snyder, *Risk, Protection, and Family Structure* (Washington, DC: U.S. Department of Justice, Office of Justice Programs, Office of Juvenile Justice and Delinquency Prevention, forthcoming) by Howard N. Snyder and Melissa Sickmund, *Juvenile Offenders and Victims: 2006 National Report* (Washington, DC: U.S. Department of Justice, Office of Justice Programs, Office of Juvenile Justice and Delinquency Prevention, 2006), 72. Online at www.ojjdp.ncjrs.org/ojstatbb/nr2006/downloads/NR2006.pdf.

The first issue dealing with social support revolves around the setting of rules and the enforcement of discipline. Human beings tend to behave better when they understand the boundaries of what is considered appropriate behavior for each social context. Many parents teach children that there is one volume of voice for recreation outside (the outside voice) and another for home, school, and church (the inside voice). We expect children who use the outside voice while inside to be corrected by the parent. It is the manner and nature of this correction that determines how the child will react in the future. If a child starts screaming in a restaurant, the parent might quietly tell the child to use the "inside voice," yell at the child to be quiet, strike the child, or remove the child by taking him or her outside. This circumstance, in which the parent shapes the behavior of the child, is repeated endlessly each day and forms a pattern of correction and discipline that both creates the self-esteem of the child and forms his or her future reactions to rules and rule violation.

Previously in this chapter, we covered the concerns of using physical punishment on children and, although that discussion is pertinent, we are concerned with the broader scope of support and discipline. Physical punishment can be a sign that the important lessons to be learned have already been lost. Children whose behavior can be corrected only with the infliction of pain can grow up to be problematic. One key to keeping children out of trouble is teaching them to evaluate and modify their own behavior. We all learn this at some point and to varying degrees, but those who engage in criminal offending are either unable to control their impulses or do not care if their behavior is inappropriate or harmful to others.

An issue related to family discipline is parents' availability to nurture and supervise children. Some parents work incredibly long hours to succeed in their careers. Their jobs require them to travel, bring work home at night and on the weekends, stay connected to the office through e-mail or cell phones, and to be on call and ready to drop family obligations to rush back to the office for an emergency. Although jobs like this might provide plenty of economic support to the children and model hard-working behavior, they are not without their own cost. This cost comes in the form of the parents' indulgence in their own careers at the expense of their children's needs. These parents miss school plays, soccer games, reading to their children, and countless other opportunities to form crucial relationships and provide positive supervision. Much of the work of being a parent is outsourced to teachers, coaches, nannies, and the computer.[64]

Other parents face the same issues of poor supervision but for different reasons. Some parents work more than one job to simply pay the bills. It is not a matter of making a choice between careers and family; it's a matter of economic survival. Their children spend long periods of time without adult supervision and might be influenced by older children to engage in antisocial or delinquent behavior.[65] Even in two-parent families, the economic demands can be so acute that the mother is forced to work instead of staying home with the children. It is difficult to blame families for the delinquency of children when the economic effects of globalization have disrupted the entire pattern of work and family stability. In many ways, the ideals of American family values are at odds with the economic realities of the 21st century.[66]

Conflict within the Family

Previously, we discussed child neglect and abuse in the context of children as victims of faulty parenting. Another dimension to this problem that bears further discussion is the effect of neglect and abuse on future delinquency. When there is a high degree of conflict within the family, it should not surprise us that children from such families end up having problems with school officials, community leaders, and the police. In environments where aggression and violence are rewarded, children learn that power and abusive behavior allow one to achieve goals. These are hard lessons for children to learn because children are often the recipients of the violent behavior. Such lessons are also difficult to correct later because, to children, they have become common sense.[67]

Children don't necessarily have to be physically abused themselves to learn that violence is a way to get what one wants. Witnessing the victimization of one parent at the hands of another demonstrates to a child that it is permissible to control and dominate by physical force. Family conflict can also teach a child impulsivity. When a parent "flies off the handle" for no apparent reason or resorts to violence with little provocation, children learn to be constantly on their guard and to be quick to react to real or imagined insults with violence. Additionally, these children have a difficult time learning to solve problems without turning to anger. Skills such as humor, physical and verbal support, and active listening are not part of the repertoire of children from families that suffer from a high level of conflict.

Children aren't always the recipient of family violence; sometimes they are the cause. Conflict might be a symptom of an underlying issue for children who are constantly creating problems and calling the family to the attention of authorities. For instance, if a daughter is sexually promiscuous and defying her parents, the family conflict might help to solve these concerns. Parents who are so disengaged that the daughter can do anything she wants are simply a different type of faulty parents. Many good parents struggle with adolescent children, and family conflict is necessary as children test their parents' will to enforce rules.

Families are dynamic institutions, and the many factors that influence family conflict are subject to change. For instance, younger siblings might find that their parents are tired of enforcing bedtimes, curfews, and chores. Older siblings can become resentful of how the younger children are given more flexibility and latitude. The reasons for this increased freedom are many. Sometimes, the economic status of the family has improved, and they live in a better, safer neighborhood where extremely close supervision is no longer required. Other times, the parents feel they can depend on the older siblings to assume some of the supervision and do not monitor the movements and behavior of the younger children as strictly as they did that of the older ones. Also, parents can become more confident in their judgment of when to intervene in their children's lives. Although parents once might have felt that they had to

Witnessing one parent victimize another teaches children that it is okay to control and dominate by physical force. *(© Tom & Dee Ann McCarthy / CORBIS. All Rights Reserved)*

know about every friend and activity of their older children, they now feel they can assess these things with much less information and intrusion into their younger children's affairs. This results in less family conflict and presumably happier children who don't manifest their anger and frustration in committing delinquent acts.

Parents, Siblings, and Delinquency

If parents engage in crime, it is reasonable to consider how this could influence their children's delinquency. Antisocial parents are poor role models for children. The children see the advantages of a quick gain with little corresponding work and are unlikely to look at police officers as trustworthy individuals. Exploring the link between law-breaking parents and delinquent youths raises a number of interesting issues. First, is the link between the antisocial behavior of the parent and the children genetic or sociological in nature? Are aggressive tendencies inherited or learned? Should delinquent children be returned to a home with a parent who has a criminal record?

These questions are difficult to answer, but some factors can shed light on intergenerational crime. Professionals who work with delinquent children consider the quality of parenting as a means to decipher the atmosphere in the home. For example, the home is viewed as a negative influence on youths who live with parents who are addicted to drugs or who sell drugs. Drug-using and drug-selling parents put their children at risk of falling into the same habits and attitudes, as well as exposing them to the dangers of the drug trade. Criminal justice authorities, including judges and law enforcement, are viewed as the enemy, and respect for any authority but the parent is discouraged.

The children of antisocial parents, even when they are good kids, are subjected to more scrutiny and surveillance from teachers, school administrators, and police. The old adage that "an acorn doesn't fall far from the tree" can become a self-fulfilling prophecy when youths whose parents have been identified as antisocial are subjected to greater supervision and given fewer breaks than children whose parents are not known to authorities.

A youth's siblings might also exert a negative influence. Older children can stay out later, range in a wider geographic circle, and engage in more risky behavior than younger children. When a boy runs around with his older brother, he might be exposed to deviant behavior at an early age before he has the emotional maturity and judgment to evaluate the effect it might have on his life (see Crosscurrents 10.1). Younger siblings are eager to gain the approval of older siblings and might break the law in order to be allowed to associate with the older crowd.[68] Because most youths eventually give up their delinquent ways as they become more involved in society, the age at which they began delinquent behavior is important. Youths who start their delinquent career early have more time to progress into serious crime and are likely to miss some of the positive aspects of childhood as they engage in antisocial behavior with their older siblings. In effect, they grow up fast and lose their innocence early, making it more likely that by the time they are ready to get married, start work, and enter into a respectable lifestyle, they already have the emotional and legal baggage of someone who has spent too much time in an antisocial lifestyle. It is not as easy for them to transition into respectable adulthood as it was for their older siblings who had a shorter delinquent period.[69]

10.1 CrossCurrents

Two of a Kind

Researchers have discovered that our siblings have an important effect on our behavior, both as children and as adults. It is our experiences with our siblings, they say, that do the most work in socializing us to deal with our peers. Siblings spend a great amount of time with each other. *TIME* magazine points to a 1996 Pennsylvania State University study that states that by age 11 siblings spend about 33 percent of their free time with brothers and sisters, which is more than with parents, friends, and teachers. And though siblings often pursue different life courses simply to be different—this is often the case when the siblings are close in age—siblings influence one another's choices.

TIME quotes Patricia East of the University of California, San Diego, as saying that a girl whose older teenage sister becomes pregnant or abuses drugs is four to six times as likely to follow the same path.[1] And, according to Abigail Fagan and Jake Najman, younger siblings are three to five times as likely to use tobacco and alcohol if their older siblings do it.[2]

Another study by Slomkowski and colleagues reported that for siblings of both genders, older siblings influenced their younger, same-sex siblings' entry into delinquency. Although this isn't really surprising, it is interesting that the researchers found that the relationship between the same-sex delinquent siblings was somewhat different. Although both sister–sister and brother–brother relationships displayed a high level of hostility, the relationship of the brother pairs also displayed a high level of warmth and support that the sister pairs did not.[3]

The number of siblings in a family might also affect delinquency. According to a much-cited study by D. J. West and D. P. Farrington, the more children a family has, the greater the risk of delinquency. Boys with four or more siblings by the age of 10 were twice as prone to delinquency, regardless of the family's socioeconomic status. This might mean that parents are not able to supervise larger sibling groups as closely as smaller sibling groups.[4]

Think About It

1. If you had an older brother or sister, did you feel compelled to try to do what they were doing or be "as grown up" as they were? If you had younger siblings, do you think you influenced their behavior?
2. Will the idea that larger families statistically have more delinquent siblings influence you to have a smaller family?
3. Do you have many siblings? How many of you got into trouble with the law?

1 Jeffrey Kluger, "The New Science of Siblings," *Time* 168, issue 2 (July 10, 2006):46.
2 Abigail A. Fagan and Jake M. Najman, "The Relative Contributions of Parental and Sibling Substance Use to Adolescent Tobacco, Alcohol, and Other Drug Use," *Journal of Drug Issues* 35, no. 4 (Fall 2005): 869–883.
3 Cheryl Slomkowski et al., "Sisters, Brothers, and Delinquency: Evaluating Social Influence During Early and Middle Adolescence," *Child Development* 72, no. 1 (February 2001): 280.
4 D. J. West and D. P. Farrington, *Who Becomes Delinquent?* (London: Heinemann, 1973).

SUMMARY

1. The family is the most basic institution. We tend to idealize the family as a nuclear unit consisting of the biological parents and their immediate offspring. However, this isn't the dominant type of family. Only 7 percent of families fit the idealized family model.

2. The word *family* might refer to a variety of living arrangements with a range of individuals who might or might not be related by blood or legal contract: single-parent families, cohabiting parents, blended families, and gay and lesbian families.

3. The important functions of the family are to raise children responsibly, provide economic support, and give emotional support. Good parenting requires the following: providing a positive role model, encouraging productive behavior, engaging in adequate supervision, and instituting effective discipline.

4. The quality of family life is related to the victimization of children. A basic concern that confronts families is structure and stability. Sources of conflict within families include its structure, problems of drug or alcohol abuse, and family violence.

5. Child neglect is less visible than physical abuse, so it's difficult to determine its prevalence. This neglect, according to Wallace, can range from momentary inattention to gross action or inaction. Child neglect is more common than the actual physical abuse of children.

6. Some of the more common forms of child neglect are failure-to-thrive syndrome, emotional neglect, unsafe home environment, drug and alcohol use, medical neglect, and abandonment.

7. Parents who neglect their children differ from those who don't by their inability to plan, lack of knowledge of parenting, lack of judgment, and lack of motivation.

8. According to Wallace, physical child abuse is normally associated with one or more of four types of injuries: bruises in specific places, burns, bone fractures, and internal damage.

9. Warning signs that physical abuse has occurred are based on how the injury is explained: unexplained injury, impossible explanations, different versions of the incident, different explanations, and delay in seeking medical attention.

10. Child sexual abuse has received a great amount of media attention. Younger children are more likely to be sexually victimized than older children.

11. Children's age and gender are important in how they adjust to divorce. Some studies suggest that boys are affected more than girls.

12. The first issue dealing with social support within families concerns the setting of rules and the enforcement of discipline. An issue related to family discipline is parents' availability to nurture and supervise children.

13. When there is a high degree of conflict within the family, children generally have problems with school officials, community leaders, and the police. Family conflict can also teach a child impulsivity. Sometimes children are the cause of family violence due to misbehavior.

14. The family can be a negative influence on youths who live with parents who engage in illegal activities. Criminal justice system authorities are viewed as the enemy, and respect for any authority but the parent is discouraged. The children of deviant parents are subjected to more scrutiny and surveillance from nonparental authority figures.

15. Siblings might also exert a negative influence. Older children can engage in more risky behavior than younger children and expose them to deviant behavior at an early age.

REVIEW QUESTIONS

1. What does the term *family* mean?

2. What are the important functions of the family?

3. What are the barriers of entry to becoming a parent?

4. What is the difference between child neglect and child abuse?

5. What are some of the more common forms of child neglect?

6. What are the warning signs of physical child abuse?

7. What four issues are related to the quality of family life and delinquency?

8. What effect do age and gender have on children whose parents divorce?

9. How might poor supervision be considered neglect?

10. How might family conflict affect a child's impulsivity?

ADDITIONAL READINGS

Currie, Janet. *The Invisible Safety Net: Protecting the Nation's Poor Children and Families* (Princeton, NJ: Princeton University Press, 2006).

Foucault, Michel. *Discipline and Punishment: The Birth of the Prison* (New York: Vintage, 1995).

Gosselin, Denise Kindschi. *Heavy Hands: An Introduction to the Crimes of Family Violence*, 3rd ed. (Upper Saddle River, NJ: Prentice Hall, 2005).

Halpern, Robert. *Fragile Families, Fragile Solutions: A History of Supportive Services for Families in Poverty*. (New York: Columbia University Press, 1999).

Popenoe, David. *Life without Father: Compelling Evidence That Fatherhood and Marriage Are Indispensable for the Good of Children and Society* (New York: Free Press, 1996).

Simons, Ronald, Leslie Simons, and Lora Wallace. *Families, Delinquency and Crime: Linking Society's Most Basic Institution to Antisocial Behavior* (Los Angeles: Roxbury, 2004).

Straus, Murray. *Beating the Devil Out of Them: Corporal Punishment in American Families and Its Effects on Children* (New Brunswick, NJ: Transaction, 2001).

ENDNOTES

1. Judith Stacey, *Brave New Families: Stories of Domestic Upheaval in Late Twentieth Century America* (New York: Basic Books, 1990).

2. Philip S. Gutis, "What Is a Family? Traditional Limits Are Being Redrawn," *New York Times*, August 31, 1989, C1.

3. U.S. Census Bureau 2000, p. 410, tables 655 and 656.

4. James Garbarino, Cynthia J. Schellenbach, and Janet M. Sebes, *Troubled Youth, Troubled Families: Understanding Families At-Risk for Adolescent Maltreatment* (New York: Aldine, 1986).

5. L. Gorden, *Heroes of Their Own Lives: The Politics and History of Family Violence: Boston 1880–1960* (New York: Viking, 1988).

6. Robert Coles, *The Moral Intelligence of Children* (New York: Random House, 1997).

7. Suzanne Bartholomae and Jonathan Fox, "Economic Stress and Families," in Patrick C. McKenry and Sharon J. Price, eds. *Families and Change: Coping with Stressful Events and Transitions*, 3rd ed. (Thousand Oaks, CA: Sage, 2005), 205–225.

8. Denise Kindschi Gosselin, *Heavy Hands: An Introduction to the Crimes of Family Violence* (Upper Saddle River, NJ: Prentice Hall, 2005).

9. Terri L. Orbuch and Sandra L. Eyster, "Division of Household Labor among Black Couples and White Couples," *Social Forces* 75 (1997):301–332.

10. Barbara Dafoe Whitehead, *The Divorce Culture* (New York: Knopf, 1997).

11. Mary Ann Lamanna and Agnes Riedmann, *Marriages and Families: Making Choices in a Diverse Society*, 8th ed. (Belmont, CA: Wadsworth, 2003), 8, Figure 1.1.

12. Constance R. Ahrons and Richard B. Miller, "The Effect of the Post-Divorce Relationship on Paternal Involvement: A Longitudinal Analysis," *American Journal of Orthopsychiatry* 63 (1993):462–479.

13. Joyce A. Arditti, "Women, Divorce and Economic Risk," *Family and Conciliation Courts Review* 35 (1997):79–92.

14. Jennifer Steinhauer, "No Marriage, No Apologies," *New York Times*, July 6, 1995, p. C1.

15. Judith Seltzer, "Families Formed Outside of Marriage," *Journal of Marriage and Family* 62 (2000):1247–1268.

16. Howard Wineberg and James McCarthy, "Living Arrangements after Divorce: Cohabitation Versus Remarriage," *Journal of Divorce and Remarriage* 29 (1998):131–146.

17. James Q. Wilson, "Against Homosexual Marriage," in Henry L. Tischler, ed. *Debating Points: Marriage and Family Issues* (Upper Saddle River, NJ: Prentice Hall, 2001), 123–127.

18. Lori Kowaleski-Jones and Frank L. Mott, "Sex, Contraception and Childbearing among High Risk Youth: Do Different Factors Influence Males and Females?" *Family Planning Perspectives* 30 (1998):163–169.

19. Marshall Jones and Donald Jones, "The Contagious Nature of Antisocial Behavior," *Criminology* 38 (2000):25–46.

20. Donald West and David Farrington, *Who Becomes Delinquent?* (London: Heinemann, 1973).

21. John Wright and Francis Cullen, "Parental Efficacy and Delinquent Behavior: Do Control and Support Matter?" *Criminology* 39 (2001):601–629.

22. Sung Jang and Carolyn Smith, "A Test of Reciprocal Causal Relationships among Parental Supervision, Affective Ties, and Delinquency," *Journal of Research in Crime and Delinquency* 34 (1997):307–336.

23. Michel Foucault, *Discipline and Punish: The Birth of the Prison* (New York: Pantheon, 1977).

24. Robert Brooks and Sam Goldstein, *Raising Resilient Children: Fostering Strength, Hope, and Optimism in Your Child* (New York: Contemporary, 2001).

25. Alice Miller, *For Your Own Good: Hidden Cruelty in Child-Rearing and the Roots of Violence* (New York: Farrar, Straus, and Giroux, 1983).

26. Murray A. Straus, *Beating the Devil Out of Them: Corporal Punishment in American Families and Its Effects on Children* (New Brunswick, NJ: Transaction, 2001).

27. William Julius Wilson, *The Truly Disadvantaged: The Inner City, the Underclass and Public Policy* (Chicago: University of Chicago Press, 1987).

28. Thomas J. Stanley and William D. Danko, *The Millionaire Next Door: The Surprising Secrets of America's Wealthy* (Atlanta, GA: Longstreet, 1996).

29. Elijah Anderson, *Code of the Street: Decency, Violence, and the Moral Life of the Inner City* (New York: Norton, 1999).

30. Janet M. Currie, *The Invisible Safety Net: Protecting the Nation's Poor Children and Families* (Princeton, NJ: Princeton University Press, 2006).

31. Harvey Wallace, *Family Violence: Legal, Medical, and Social Perspectives*, 4th ed. (Boston: Allyn and Bacon, 2005), 90–110.

32. Ibid., 94.

33. J. Myres, *Evidence in Child Abuse and Neglect*, 2nd ed. (New York: Wiley, 1992).

34. D. J. Hansen and V. M. MacMilan, "Behavioral Assessment of Child Abuse and Neglectful Families: Recent Developments and Current Issues," *Behavior Modification* 14 (1990):225–278.

35. I. W. Hutton and R. K. Oates, "Nonorganic Failure to Thrive: A Long Term Follow-up," *Pediatrics* 8 (1977):73–77.

36. Wallace (see note 30), p. 98.

37. S. N. Hart and M. Brassard, "Developing and Validating Operationally Defined Measures of Emotional Maltreatment: A Multimodal Study of the Relationships between Caretaker Behavior and Child Characteristics across Those Developmental Levels" (Washington, DC: Department of Health and Human Services, 1986).

38. D. Wiese and D. Daro, *Current Trends in Child Abuse Reporting and Fatalities: The Results of the 1994 Annual Fifty State Survey* (Chicago: National Committee to Prevent Child Abuse, 1995).

39. Although understanding forms of family violence such as spouse abuse, elder abuse, and abuse by gay and lesbian partners is important, they are only indirectly pertinent here. Students are advised to look elsewhere for a full discussion.

40. Timothy Ireland, Carolyn Smith, and Terence Thornberry, "Developmental Issues in the Impact of Child Abuse on Later Delinquency and Drug Use," *Criminology* 40 (2002):359–396.

41. Wallace (see note 30), p. 33.

42. W. V. Harris, "Child-Exposure in the Roman Empire," *Journal of Roman Studies* 84 (1994):1–22.

43. S. Radbill, "A History of Child Abuse and Infanticide," in R. Helfer and C. H. Kempe, eds. *The Battered Child*, 2nd ed. (Chicago: University of Chicago Press, 1974).

44. Wallace (see note 30), pp. 43–44.

45. H. Schmitt, "The Child with Nonaccidental Trauma," in R. Kempe and R. Helfer, eds. *The Battered Child*, 4th ed. (Chicago: University of Chicago Press, 1987).

46. J. Showers and K. M. Garrison, "Burn Abuse: A Four Year Study," *Journal of Trauma* 28 (1988):1581–1583.

47. John Longstaff and Tish Sleeper, *The National Center on Child Fatality Review* (Washington, DC: Office of Juvenile Justice and Delinquency Prevention, 2001), FS-200112.

48. David Finkelhor, *Sexually Victimized Children* (New York: Free Press, 1984).

49. B. Dermott, "The Pro-Incest Lobby," *Psychology Today* (March 1980):12.

50. Mic Hunter, *Abused Boys: The Neglected Victims of Sexual Abuse* (Lexington, MA: Lexington Books, 1990).

51. E. Porter, *Treating the Young Male Victims of Sexual Assault* (Syracuse, NY: Safer Society Press, 1986).

52. C. A. Courtios, "Studying and Counseling Women with Past Incest Experience," *Victimology: An International Journal* 5 (1980):322–324.

53. Adapted from Walter R. McDonald and Associates, *Child Maltreatment 2003: Reports from the States to the National Child Abuse and Neglect Data System* (Washington, DC: U.S. Department of Health and Human Services, Children's Bureau, 2004) by Howard N. Snyder and Melissa Sickmund, *Juvenile Offenders and Victims: 2006 National Report* (Washington, DC: U.S. Department of Justice, Office of Justice Programs, Office of Juvenile Justice and Delinquency Prevention, 2006), 55. Online atwww.ojjdp.ncjrs.org/ojstatbb/nr2006/downloads/NR2006.pdf.

54. B. Justice and R. Justice, *The Broken Taboo: Sex in the Family* (New York: Human Services Press, 1979).

55. G. Lindsey, "Some Remarks Concerning Incest, the Incest Taboo, and Psychoanalytic Theory," *American Psychologist* 22 (1967):1051–1059.

56. A. J. Sedlak and D. D. Broadhurst, *Executive Summary of the Third National Incidence Study of Child Abuse and Neglect* (Washington, DC: U.S. Department of Health and Human Services, Administration for Children and Families, 1996), 2.

57. Leslie Acoca, "Investing in Girls: A 21st Century Strategy," *Juvenile Justice* 6, no. 1 (October 1999):8. Online at www.ncjrs.gov/pdffiles1/ojjdp/178254.pdf.

58. L. Acoca and K. Dedel, *No Place to Hide: Understanding and Meeting the Needs of Girls in the California Juvenile Justice System* (San Francisco: National Council on Crime and Delinquency, 1998).

59. Ronald Simons, Leslie Simons, and Lora Wallace, *Families, Delinquency and Crime: Linking Society's Most Basic Institution to Antisocial Behavior* (Los Angeles: Roxbury, 2004).

60. Jackson Toby, "The Differential Impact of Family Disorganization," *American Sociological Review* 22 (1957):505–512.

61. Lawrence Rosen, "The Broken Home and Male Delinquency," in M. Wolfgang, L. Savitz, and N. Johnston, eds. *Sociology of Crime and Delinquency* (New York: Wiley, 1970), 489–795.

62. Edward Wells and Joseph Rankin, "Families and Delinquency: A Meta-Analysis of the Impact of Broken Homes," *Social Problems* 38 (1991):71–93.

63. Constance Ahrons, *The Good Divorce* (New York: Harper, 1995).

64. Susan Byrne, "Nobody Home," *Psychology Today* 10 (1977):40–47.

65. Lawrence Steinberg, "Latchkey Children and Susceptibility to Peer Pressure," *Developmental Psychology* 22 (1986):433–439.

66. Jody Miller, "Global Prostitution, Sex Tourism, and Trafficking," in Claire M. Renzetti, Lynne Goodstein, and Susan L. Miller, eds. *Rethinking Gender, Crime, and Justice, Feminist Readings* (Los Angeles: Roxbury, 2006), 139–154.

67. Carolyn Smith and David Farrington, "Continuities in Antisocial Behavior and Parenting across Three Generations," *Journal of Child Psychology and Psychiatry* 45 (2004):230–247.

68. David Rowe, Joseph Rogers, and Sylvia Meseck-Bushey, "Sibling Delinquency and the Family Environment: Shared and Unshared Influences," *Child Development* 63 (1992):59–67.

69. Marshall Jones and Donald Jones, "The Contagious Nature of Antisocial Behavior," *Criminology* 38 (2000):25–46.

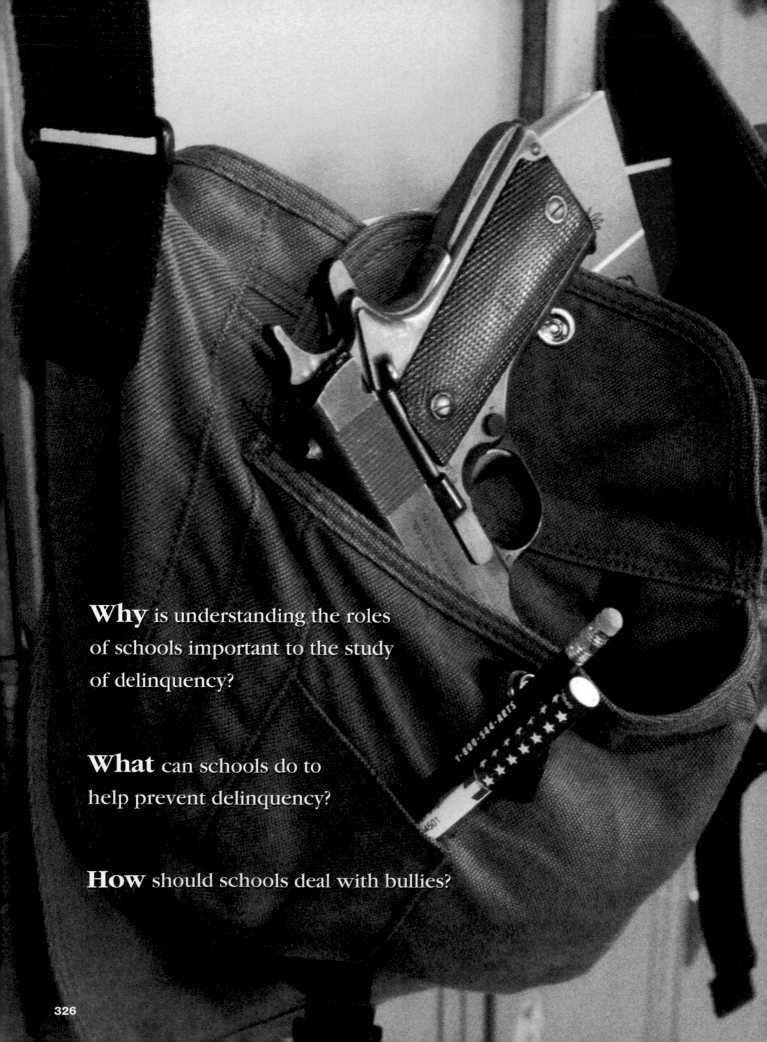

Why is understanding the roles of schools important to the study of delinquency?

What can schools do to help prevent delinquency?

How should schools deal with bullies?

CHAPTER 11

Schools
and
Delinquency

**Instant Recall
from Chapter 2**
socialization
*The process by which people learn
the norms, values, and culture of their
society.*

"Some teachers and principals say they can predict which youngsters will end up in prison. Recently a first-grade teacher in a city school pointed to two boys, both scheduled to be held back because of immature behavior and low skills. 'I know where they'll be in 10 years,' she told me. 'Sitting in a jail cell.'"[1]

School is a primary institution of **socialization** and the one that formally educates children. Besides the family, the school is where children spend the greatest amount of time and where they learn values and ideas that can protect them from becoming involved in delinquency. This also means that the school is where children can fall victim to other children, teachers, and outsiders. Parents are concerned with both the quality of education their children receive and with their children's safety.[2]

Society has set an ambitious role for schools, one that states and jurisdictions don't fulfill to the same degree. In fact, school quality is one of the most pressing social concerns facing the United States because it influences the extent and seriousness of delinquency.[3] Ineffective or inadequate schools don't serve students well, especially students who are marginal in terms of economic status, intellectual ability, maturity, or physical or mental health. These are the teenagers who are most likely to drop out of school or turn to delinquency, which is a serious problem for society. High school dropouts are three and a half times more likely to be arrested than high school graduates, and 82 percent of adult prison inmates are high-school dropouts.[4]

Let's begin by discussing how school affects the victimization of children and antisocial behavior.

WHAT SCHOOLS ARE SUPPOSED TO DO

Schools have a number of goals that affect delinquency. When schools accomplish these goals, that is, to educate and socialize children, we expect delinquency to decrease, and when schools fail to accomplish these goals, we shouldn't be surprised to see delinquency and victimization increase. The goals of schools can be roughly divided into the following categories:

- **Academic goals**   Schools strive to help students reach two academic goals. First is the attainment of basic skills such as reading, writing, and math, along with the skills to communicate ideas. The second set of academic goals concerns the abilities to think rationally, independently, and critically. Also, schools encourage students to be curious, accumulate knowledge, and solve problems. Students who succeed in attaining these goals are better equipped to make good decisions as adults and to compete in society for jobs of high social status and economic reward.

- **Vocational goals**   Schools are one of the training grounds where students acquire vocational skills. In addition to learning the academic skills that are necessary for almost all jobs, students are expected to learn appropriate work attitudes and habits and to select a career in which they can utilize their particular skills. It is generally accepted that adults who enter satisfying and meaningful careers are less tempted to engage in crime and antisocial behavior.

- **Social, civic, and cultural goals**   Schools also attempt to instill in students the ability to develop meaningful relationships, appreciate and contribute to the culture, and acquire important societal values. Schools encourage participation in citizenship activities, such as making informed choices in elections and voting, learning about representative government, contributing to the welfare of fellow citizens, and acting responsibly to preserve the environment. Ideally, schools also teach moral and ethical behavior. Schools encourage students to develop integrity and to evaluate their conduct in light of how it affects others.

- **Personal goals**   These goals include the development of physical and emotional well-being, including self-awareness, physical fitness, self-esteem, and coping skills. Additionally, schools teach students to explore their creativity and to appreciate it in others, as well as to tolerate new ideas. Finally, schools ask students to be responsible for their decisions, set reasonable personal goals, and continually evaluate their abilities and limitations.[5]

Clearly, not all students accomplish these goals to the same degree, and it is unrealistic to expect all students to benefit from their educational experiences in the same way. Several factors affect a student's level of academic and social accomplishment, including differences in mental abilities, economic opportunities, and simple desire and motivation. However, differences in attaining these goals become a major social issue when recurring problems based on race, social class, and gender appear generation after generation.[6] The reasons for such disparities in school quality are largely based on how they are funded.

School money comes from several sources and levels of government, but schools are mainly under local control. Local property taxes provide most school funding, and local school boards decide many school issues. One main idea behind local control is that the people closest to the schools get to have the most authority. Although local control is a deeply held value, it sometimes results in disparities in school quality.[7] For instance, prosperous communities have more money to spend on schools than impoverished communities, and schools in low-crime areas are likely to have fewer delinquency issues than schools in high-crime areas. These disparities directly affect the quality of education, which can be seen in standardized test scores and other indicators like school safety and rates of dropout and delinquency.[8] For an example, see Kids in the News 11.1 for a look at the troubling situation in the public schools of Baltimore, Maryland.

11.1   KIDS in the NEWS

Putting Out Fires

What comes first, bad schools or troubled kids? The situation in the public schools of Baltimore has many people wondering just that. The school system has some very disturbing problems. Schools in other states and districts report the same sorts of problems—gangs, out-of-control students, violence, theft—but not often with the same frequency or intensity. Here are some examples from recent school years.

- The *Baltimore Sun* reports that a 14-year-old girl went to the city's school board to ask for help at her middle school. "'During this present school year, there have been numerous incidents. . .food fights, fistfights, setting fires, pulling the fire alarm, smoking in the hallways and stairwells, group fights, robberies and parents attacking teachers. . . .The pupils are being influenced by gangs and are selling drugs and engaging in other violent activities.'"[1]
- In 2005, the state of Maryland designated Thurgood Marshall Middle School as "persistently dangerous" because of its high suspension rate for violent offenses. Another high school, Dr. Samuel L. Banks High School, is slated to move onto the campus that also contains Thurgood Marshall High School. PTA President Kenya Lee tells *the Baltimore Sun* that officials are ignoring a gang conflict between students from the two schools.[2]

- In 2006, a 12-year-old girl was stabbed by another girl with a steak knife for calling her names. In two earlier incidents, students were stabbed in the chest by other students.[3]
- Students at the Homeland Security Academy, the Liberal Arts Academy, and the Institute of Business and Entrepreneurship are locked in their classrooms for the rest of the afternoon after a teenager from yet another school is shot in the back nearby. The boy wasn't in school because he had been suspended.[4]
- Another school promises to enforce school uniform policies to prevent nonstudents from entering. Students are required to enter and leave through one entrance.
- Police Chief Antonio Williams says the fire-setting problem is improving. He points to 86 fires set at the schools at the midpoint of the 2006 school year, as opposed to 209 fires set during the same period in 2005. About 15 fires were set at Walbrook High School during the beginning of school year 2004–2005. As students evacuated for one of the fires, a gun was fired in front of the school. During the 2003–2004 school year, 168 fires were set.[5]

What's going on? Is Baltimore overrun with delinquent kids, or is there a bigger problem, one that has to do with money and leadership?

Thurgood Marshall Middle School in Baltimore, Maryland, November 2004.

(Courtesy Rachel Epstein, The Imageworks)

Are adults to blame as much as the students? According to Bebe Verdery, education director at the American Civil Liberties Union of Maryland, severe financial problems have led to increased class sizes, with 40 or more students to one classroom, and fewer teachers. In 2003, more than 1,000 staffers were cut, including 250 teachers. Verdery told the Associated Press in 2004, " 'When you combine that with the increased class sizes, the schools seem much less capable of controlling the violence and the fire-setting.' " Robert Balfanz, of the Johns Hopkins Center for Social Organization of Schools, points to reduced services for the students, many of whom are impoverished and have the greatest need for them.[6]

By 2006, conditions at least a couple of the schools improved with the arrival of new principals and building improvements. Calverton eighth grader Brandi Colbert, 14, told the *Baltimore Sun* that the fix was simple: New adults at the school showed the students that they care. " 'Since there are new things happening at the school—there's a new paint job and everything—we're like, 'Well, they really do care about us.' "[7]

Some critics of Baltimore's school system chalk up the drop in incidents to administrators not reporting them. According to a 2006 Baltimore Teachers Union's survey, 66 percent of the teachers who responded said incidents in their schools go unreported. Patricia Ferguson, chair of the union's safety committee, said schools are not reporting incidents for fear of being labeled "persistently dangerous" under the No Child Left Behind Act.

Think About It

1. Are poorly performing schools the result of too many troubled children?

2. What can schools in disadvantaged districts do to overcome the negative effects of poverty?

1 Sara Neufeld, "Few Deny Schools Need Change," *Baltimore Sun*, April 3, 2006, Section: State and Regional.
2 Ibid.
3 Foster Klug, "Dozens of Fires Burn at Struggling Baltimore Schools," Associated Press, November 9, 2004.
4 Ibid.
5 Ibid.
6 Ibid.
7 Neufeld and Jones (see note 1).

As the United States becomes more racially and ethnically diverse, schools struggle to maintain a level of quality and discipline that meets the needs of all students and keeps them in school and away from serious delinquency. A school or a school district might be unable to do this for many reasons, however.[9]

- **Inappropriate curricula and instruction**   Particularly diverse schools have students who don't speak English or don't speak it very well. There is a debate between those who advocate English-only classes as a means of rapid assimilation and those who believe foreign students need to be taught at least partly in their native languages. It is much easier for youths who don't speak English to give up on school and instead confine themselves to cultural and linguistic enclaves and possibly the youth gangs that inhabit them.

- **Differences between parental and school norms**   Children from ethnically diverse groups might not have absorbed American middle-class norms. This can cause problems ranging from children who study all the time and do little else to children who do not value education at all. Additionally, some parents have fixed ideas about the values they want schools to teach their children, and they resist efforts to teach subjects such as evolution and sexual health. Much like the language issues, this difference in norms can alienate students from their schools, separating them from a major socializing institution. Youths with little or no investment in society are more likely to rebel against it and its norms.

- **Lack of previous success in school**   Some students have trouble with difficult subjects because they missed important steps in earlier grades or failed those grades completely. Although rapid progress is possible, some students are discouraged and pessimistic about their chances of succeeding in school because they have failed in the past. Many of these youngsters drop out as soon as possible. Although a school dropout isn't automatically a delinquent, a young adult who doesn't have the diploma to pursue the many good jobs that require one is more likely to be attracted to crime. Figure 11-1 shows that most of the inmates in state prison, federal prison, and local jails didn't finish high school. Also, of all the inmates in state prisons, those with less education were more likely to have been sentenced as juveniles than those with more education.[10]

- **Teaching difficulties**   Lack of student preparation and effort frustrates teachers. This can be particularly acute if there is a language and/or cultural gap between teachers and students. Student behavioral problems often reflect these concerns.

- **Teacher perceptions and standards**   Teachers assigned to ethnically or economically diverse groups might not expect these students to do well. These perceptions might be based on the teacher's own experiences or on data that measure student success. The key is that a teacher's perception is important to how children learn. Teachers with low expectations might find that their students work only to that level, regardless of their economic or ethnic status. A teacher who isn't prepared for the diverse backgrounds of his or her students might have trouble keeping classroom order or keeping students in class at all.

- **Segregation**   Children from ethnically diverse backgrounds are likely to go to the same school if they live in the same jurisdiction. This means that patterns of learning and attitudes toward authority from the culture at home are likely to be altered as students attempt to fit into the school environment. Youngsters who do well in school might be ostracized by family and friends because they adopt new perspectives. This is especially true when gangs are prominent in the school.

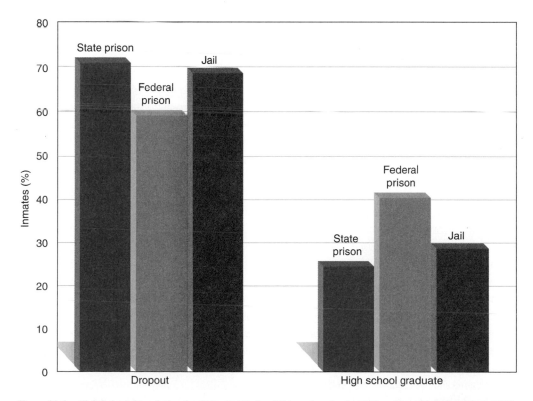

Figure 11-1   **High School Completion for State and Federal Prison Inmates in 1997 and Local Jail Inmates in 1996**

Source: Caroline Wolf Harlow, *Education and Correctional Populations* (Washington, DC: U.S. Department of Justice, Bureau of Justice Statistics, 2003), 3. Online at www.ojp.usdoj.gov/bjs/pub/pdf/ecp.pdf.

These issues are important to understanding how delinquency happens in schools and how schools encourage social environments that produce delinquency. As a pivotal social institution, the school is both the victim of and creator of the atmosphere that allows or encourages young people to engage in antisocial behavior and delinquency. However, blaming schools for delinquency is much like blaming the victim of a crime. When schools are overcrowded, underfunded, and burdened with multiple and conflicting mandates, they should not all be expected to function at the same high level.[11]

KEEPING CONTROL

The first and most obvious concern about schools is how they control students. Without some type of social order, maintaining any learning environment would be impossible, and delinquency would be rampant. Schools have different ways of establishing and maintaining social order, which helps them to keep their students safe. Children are taught very early that they must rein in their immature tendencies and start acting in a more adult manner when they enter school. In his influential essay "Kindergarten as Academic Boot Camp," sociologist Harry Gracey said that the purpose of kindergarten isn't to teach children how to write numbers and letters, but rather to establish the patterns of behavior that make learning possible. They learn to take their turn, share materials, not to talk while the teacher is talking, and many other forms of behavior that convert them from narcissistic 5-year-olds to well-behaved students. This is because social order in school is impossible without the cooperation of students.[12] Some experts on learning now believe that attending preschool before kindergarten improves a child's chances of not only doing well in public school, but also of avoiding delinquency and becoming a successful and productive adult (see A Closer Look at Juvenile Issues 11.1).

11.1 A CLOSER LOOK *at* JUVENILE ISSUES

THE SOONER THE BETTER

A youth who turns to delinquency is also likely to have problems in school, be they social or academic. In turn, school quality can affect which youths are troubled and what those troubles are. Delinquents and dropouts might have special needs that the school cannot meet, require special academic help, be bullied by their peers or even adults in the school, or suffer mental illness and depression.

States and school districts can institute a variety of practices, programs, and procedures to help troubled youths, but many experts say that one of the most important in terms of delinquency is getting children into school as early as possible. This used to mean kindergarten, which children typically begin at ages 5 and 6. Now some research shows that enrolling children in preschool as early as ages 3 and 4 can significantly affect not only their academic success, but also how well they avoid delinquency and the behaviors that lead to it.

Research on preschool has shown that people with at least one year of preschool are more likely to complete high school and go to college, less likely to be in special education classes or held back a grade, and less likely to become delinquent. A long-term University of Wisconsin study compared urban children who didn't attend preschool with those who did. The children who completed preschool had 41 percent fewer arrests for violent offenses and were 29 percent more likely to graduate from high school.[1]

A landmark study, the 1962 Perry Preschool Study, looked at 123 Michigan children, ages 3 and 4, who were at high risk of failing school.

Fifty-eight of the children went to preschool for two years, while the rest of the children didn't. Researchers met with the children annually until they were 11, then again at ages 14, 15, 19, 27, and 40. Of the preschoolers, 65 percent graduated from a regular high school, compared with 45 percent of the nonpreschoolers. In the late 1990s, researchers returned to the group, now age 40, to find that over 76 percent of the preschooled men had jobs, compared with 62 percent of the men from the control group. Those who hadn't attended preschool were more likely to be arrested for drug offenses, to be repeat offenders, and to have committed more than one violent felony.[2]

Preschool appears to affect delinquency and crime, but why? Some researchers say that teaching children as early as possible about things as simple as holding a book and how to wait turns encourages good behavior and gets children emotionally ready for school. The hypothesis is that as they grow up, youngsters with this increased confidence in school will be less likely to use drugs and alcohol and get involved with gangs or become delinquent, even if they are from places where crime and delinquency are common.

1 Brain Mattmiller, "Study: Early Intervention Cuts Crime, Dropout Rates," *University of Wisconsin–Madison News,* May 8, 2001, www.news.wisc.edu/6148.
2 High/Scope Perry Preschool Study Lifetime Effects, www.highscope.org/Content.asp?ContentID=219.

Although schools need a certain degree of structure, some people believe it comes with a social cost. Two important American values are individualism and creativity, and too much structure can snuff out these qualities, especially in impressionable young children. Schools encourage appropriate behavior by using tools and techniques to control students, many of which are criticized for sacrificing student welfare for social control. So how do schools balance the need for control with the desire to foster students' creativity? Here are a few of the more controversial measures.

- **School uniforms**   One problem that school districts face is the disparity in the income of students' families. In what sociologist Thorstein Veblen calls "conspicuous consumption," some students wear expensive clothes that other students' parents can't afford.[13] Some experts believe that this visible disparity in social class disrupts learning by creating an obvious caste system within the school. By requiring uniforms, the economic advantages of some families aren't broadcast by their children. An additional presumed benefit of uniforms in schools where gang activity is a problem is to prevent some youths from displaying gang affiliations. However, not everyone agrees. Research has shown that uniforms can have the opposite effect.[14]

- **Corporal punishment**   Spanking isn't confined to the family. Some schools have policies that specify that disruptive students can be struck with an object as a form of discipline. The object is usually a paddle, and the student is usually struck on the buttocks. The youth's pain and embarrassment are believed to deter future misbehavior. Many states and/or school districts have set up stringent guidelines on **corporal punishment**, while others have dispensed with the practice altogether. School paddling is less related to delinquency (serious juvenile delinquency is typically handled by the juvenile justice system, not by schools) than it is to what some experts criticize as the formalized victimization of children.[15] The concern is that victimization of this sort in a major socializing institution sends the message that "might makes right" and that it is acceptable

corporal punishment
The infliction of physical harm on a person who has broken a rule or committed an offense.

There is a long tradition in schools of striking children to make them behave. In this 19th-century illustration, a schoolmaster strikes a child with a wooden switch. *(Courtesy Corbis/Bettmann)*

**Instant Recall
from Chapter 1**
zero-tolerance policies
*School regulations that give teachers
and administrators little to no
discretion in dealing with rule
infractions.*

to assault people to make them do what you want. This has interesting implications in an institution whose major problems include bullying, fighting, and sometimes gang violence.

- **Zero-tolerance policies**   An extreme reaction to delinquency is **zero-tolerance policies**. For example, students who bring things to school that can be considered weapons or drugs face severe penalties. The penalties, which can include suspension and expulsion, do not give administrators a lot of discretion. For instance, some jurisdictions treat toy guns as they would firearms and aspirin as they would cocaine. The severe penalties for minor or technical rule infractions often make school districts and administrators look foolish. Whether zero-tolerance policies have actually stopped any extreme violence is questionable, but they do send the message that school administrators and teachers are concerned about student safety and that they are doing the best they can to ensure it.[16]

These policies are a response to what many consider to be deterioration in the social climate of the school. Many parents believe that schools were safer and more effective in their day than they are now. But adults might forget, or not realize, that their schools "back in the old days" might have been better funded or had fewer students in the classes. Each year, schools must deal with issues that past generations didn't have to contend with or even be aware of. The next two sections look at the internal constraints and external pressures that limit school effectiveness and contribute to behaviors associated with delinquency.

Preventing Delinquency in School

Children and teenagers spend a lot of time in school, which increases their chances of committing some types of delinquency on school property. For example, from 1992 to 2003, middle- and high-school students were more likely to be victims of theft at school and more likely to suffer serious violence or homicide elsewhere (see Figure 11-2).[17] Schools are also often the target of vandals, who strike on weekends or after school. They pick schools because of bad experiences in the classroom or rebellion against authority or because they wish to damage a rival's property. A great deal of resources have been devoted to making school a safe learning environment while addressing the needs of students who have the potential to commit a variety of delinquent acts. However, delinquency often consists of spontaneous acts committed against vulnerable targets. Teenagers are especially tempted to have some fun by breaking a window, spray painting a wall, or destroying classroom furniture. Recall from Chapter 7 that criminologist Albert Cohen referred to much of this activity as negativistic, malicious, and of no use, meaning that the reasons and motivations behind school vandalism are often unclear and inconsequential.[18]

target–hardening
*Making a focus of crime or
delinquency as difficult as possible
for potential offenders to access.*

Much of this kind of delinquency can be prevented by **target–hardening**, that is, making it more difficult for students to access the school after hours and by better monitoring of the property. Additionally, it is important during school hours to keep track of where children are and how they are being supervised. In 1999–2000, 75 percent of schools controlled access to buildings during school hours by locking or monitoring doors, and 34 percent controlled access to the grounds by locking or monitoring gates. During that same year period, 14 percent of primary schools, 20 percent of middle schools, and 39 percent of high schools used security cameras for monitoring.[19] Statistics suggest that at least some of these measures, plus increased attention to the prevention of bullying, have had a positive effect on the number of children who experience violence at school. The rate of violent-crime victimizations at school dropped from 48 per 1,000 students in 1992 to 28 per 1,000 students in 2003.[20]

Several common-sense steps can be taken to make vandalism and other forms of delinquency physically more difficult (see A Closer Look at Juvenile Issues 11.2).

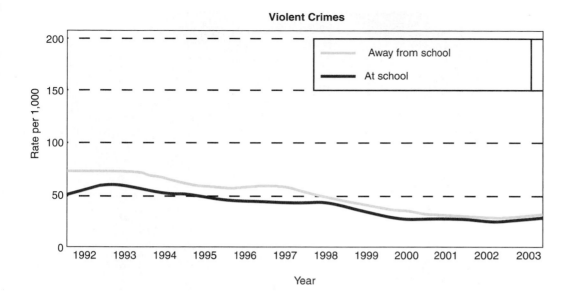

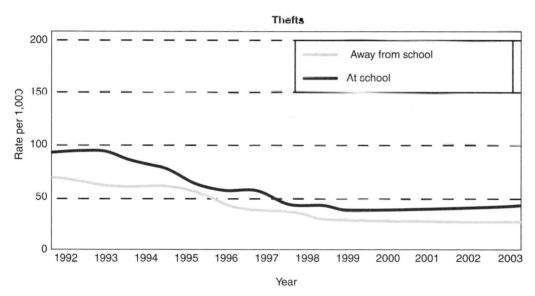

Figure 11-2   Student-Reported Nonfatal Offenses against Students Ages 12 to 18, 1992–2003 *Source:* Jill F. DeVoe et al., *Indicators of School Crime and Safety: 2005* (Washington, DC: U.S. Departments of Education and Justice, U.S. Government Printing Office, 2005), 11. Online at http://nces.ed.gov/pubs2006/2006001.pdf.

School safety goes beyond target–hardening, however. Well-trained staff and teachers who understand the need for safety and are willing to implement a security plan can significantly increase the students' sense of safety. School safety does not just happen. It has to be carefully planned and have plenty of resources allocated to it. Teachers and students who are not afraid of disruptive students or outside troublemakers can focus on teaching and learning. One study suggests that common-sense initiatives such as supportive leadership, dedicated teachers and administrators, behavior management for the entire school, and good academic instruction go a long way toward reducing the chances for delinquency.[21]

Another hypothesis that has shown some promise is that of **school bonding**, which is the connection that students have to their schools, their lives there, and their academic work. One study has found that high levels of school bonding might

school bonding
The connection that students have to school and their academic work.

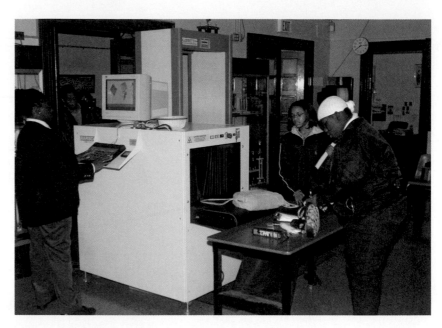

School safety goes beyond target-hardening. Here two teenage girls wait as a security guard x-rays their belongings at a Washington, DC, high school. *(Courtesy Cleve Bryant, PhotoEdit Inc.)*

11.2 A CLOSER LOOK *at* JUVENILE ISSUES

CAMPUS SECURITY

Ronald Stephens of the National School Safety Center makes the following recommendations to improve school safety.[1] This is only a partial list of the steps that schools can take to secure their grounds and classrooms. It is important to remember that policies have to address crime prevention at a number of levels.

- *Use good environmental design.* The first and perhaps easiest way to protect school campuses is through good environmental design. By making the campus less accessible to outsiders and having a plan for handling uninvited persons, the school can control its grounds, hallways, and classrooms.[2] A main principle of creating **defensible space** is making sure that it is subject to natural observation. People should be able to see playgrounds or ball fields from public areas. The school should define campus perimeters with appropriate landscaping and fencing and build wrought-iron fences instead of high concrete walls or chain-link fences, which provide ladders for people to enter school grounds.
- *Control campus access.* Closed campuses are safer than open campuses. School access should be controlled with monitored doors and gateways. This can be done with video cameras that can be checked later in the case of vandalism or some other delinquent activity. The number of roads into the campus should be controlled in order to supervise incoming and outgoing traffic. Parking lots should be fenced if possible.

- *Establish uniform visitor screening procedures.* It is dangerous for unidentified people to wander around the grounds. Specific plans should be made to direct visitors to the school office, where they must identify their business with the school and sign in. Visitors should be required to wear a pass that is visible to staff and teachers.
- *Post appropriate directional signs.* Stephens advises schools to place signs around the grounds that specify to students and visitors the kind of environment they are entering. For instance, signs stating that the school is a "drug-free zone" or that prohibit trespassing should be visible. Signs should also show the names of buildings, directions to important destinations, such as the principal's office, and directional flow of pedestrians and vehicle traffic.
- *Carefully manage and monitor hall passes.* During school hours, teachers should ensure that students are successfully supervised. Sometimes, individual students are let out of the classroom for a variety of reasons. A system should be established that records the student's name, date, time out, time in, destination, and purpose for any hall pass. These data can then be used to see which students were unsupervised if any crime or vandalism occurs.
- *Have adequate emergency communications.* Communication is a key element in providing a safe school. This means investing in technology that allows administrators to direct school personnel during emergencies. Each classroom should be linked to the main office, as well as to school security officers. Additionally, the school should have

immediate access to communications with outside safety agencies, such as fire and police departments, as well as to the school system's central office.

- *Identify and track repeat offenders.* Research has repeatedly demonstrated that most delinquency is committed by a small number of offenders. Disruptive students should be identified and monitored to ensure that they don't cause serious problems for other students. Ways of doing this include placing these students in the classrooms of more experienced teachers, preparing individualized lesson plans that address any specific educational difficulties the students are having, and assigning them lockers in places that are easily supervised and highly visible.

- *Develop a graffiti and community clean-up program.* Schools should work with community leaders to develop a plan that addresses quality-of-life issues such as graffiti and neighborhood blight. People who take ownership and pride in their surroundings are more likely to help prevent crime and delinquency. By working with the police to identify and shut down drug houses and discourage drug dealers, the school can help children avoid undesirable influences in the community.

- *Enhance multicultural understanding.* Many school problems can be prevented with an atmosphere of acceptance and tolerance. In many schools, students from different backgrounds and cultures are in conflict because they do not like how their differences are manifested in different clothes, speech patterns, and customs. By limiting the polarization of students, gang formation can be prevented, and educational programs that bring students together can be more successful.

- *Develop a school dress code.* Often, the social and economic differences among students are heightened by the way they dress. Those with wealthy parents can set standards that are impossible for other students to emulate. Dress can also be an issue of school safety when gangs sport symbols and signs that are considered an affront by other gangs. A dress code does not have to mandate school uniforms but need only specify the style and type of attire so that it is not a distinguishing feature of wealth or gang status.

- *Involve students in creating and enforcing the rules.* Students are more likely to become invested in preventing delinquency if they feel they have some input into school policies. Schools have long used organizations such as student councils to reinforce the lessons of democracy, and the same can be done to get students to help protect and enhance the school's social climate. A student court can also help establish the rules and the penalties for breaking them.

- *Establish a physical-restraint policy for staff.* Sometimes a teacher or staff member must use physical restraint with a student who is a danger to others. This policy should be written and communicated to students and parents. By knowing what the appropriate level of force is, the student, staff member, and parent are all better able to accept the necessity of such actions.

1 Ronald D. Stephens, "Recommended Practices for Safe Schools," in William L. Turk, ed., *School Crime and Policing* (Upper Saddle River, NJ: Prentice Hall, 2004), 63–83.
2 Timothy Crowe, *Crime Prevention Through Environmental Design*, 2nd ed. (New York: Butterworth-Heinomann, 2000).

decrease student use of drugs and alcohol. Major aspects of school bonding include the following:

1. Attachment to school (how much the student cares about the school)
2. Attachment to personnel (the quality of the student's connection with the teachers, staff, and administration)
3. School commitment (how much the student participates in school activities and how important these activities are for the student)

The bond that students have to their schools can affect drug and alcohol use, delinquency, antisocial behavior, academic performance, and self-esteem. Students who are more attached to their schools, according to research, enjoy better self-esteem and better grades. In turn, schools that are successful in bonding with their students often see less antisocial behavior among students, as well as lower levels of drug and alcohol use and delinquency.[22] Research on youth substance abuse found that students who were poorly bonded to school were less likely to believe that the use of drugs and/or alcohol would prevent them from achieving their life goals.[23]

What about the Teachers?

Teaching has long been considered an honorable profession that attracts talented individuals who are both intelligent and have a calling to serve others by doing an important job. However, several factors have greatly compromised the ability of teachers to teach according to their standards. These factors include pressure from administrators, parents, and government. Well-meaning programs, such as the federal government's **No Child Left Behind Act** initiative (see A Closer Look at

defensible space
The philosophy of creating living and working spaces that are secure by design.

No Child Left Behind Act of 2001
A federal law passed in January 2002 that seeks to improve the performance of K–12 schools.

11.3 A CLOSER LOOK *at* JUVENILE ISSUES

NO CHILD LEFT BEHIND

In January 2002, Congress passed President George W. Bush's No Child Left Behind Act of 2001 (Public Law 107-110), the stated purpose of which was "higher standards and greater accountability throughout the nation's school systems." The law requires that children take annual standardized tests in math and English and earn higher scores each successive year. For example, third graders in 2008 must earn higher test scores than third graders in 2007. A school that fails to meet these standards can be penalized or even closed. Students are also allowed to transfer to different schools, or the failing school's staff may be restructured.[1]

Critics of the law point out that many school districts are unable to meet what have been called unreasonable standards and that there is not enough federal funding for the schools to achieve the law's goals. In 2005, a federal judge in Michigan dismissed a challenge to No Child Left Behind, stating that the federal government could require states to spend their own money to comply with the law. Some states have complained that the law forces them to spend money they don't have.[2]

Another complaint is that the law doesn't recognize shifts in the population or improvements made by individual students. For example, one year's third graders are expected to exceed the test scores of the prior year's third graders, although they are not the same set of children. In response to some of these criticisms, some states in 2005 were allowed to modify how they measured student progress by tracking how student performance changed over time. Also, some states were allowed to use federal money to provide tutoring, while others were given more time to meet teacher-quality requirements. The law as originally intended provided no specific funding or assistance for schools troubled by gangs or delinquency, although it did request that parents become more involved in their children's schools:[3]

The following are some of the law's original requirements and provisions:

- School districts receive more federal money.
- Parents receive "report cards" rating the schools in their districts.
- Students may transfer away from schools that don't meet the law's standards.
- If a school is deemed to "need improvement" for at least two years, children may receive free tutoring.
- States must test children in reading and math annually in grades 3 to 8. Adolescents must be tested at least once in high school.

1 No Child Left Behind, www.ed.gov/nclb/landing.jhtml.
2 Michael Janofsky, "Judge Rejects Challenge to Bush Education Law," *New York Times*, November 24, 2005, A22.
3 Nick Anderson, "Bush Administration Grants Leeway on 'No Child' Rules," *Washington Post*, final edition, November 22, 2005, A01.

Juvenile Issues 11.3), have had unintended consequences that have made the job of teaching less attractive. Here are some other internal pressures when teaching school.

- **Standardization and regimentation**   Schools are required to account for the money they spend and the learning activities they present to students. Financially, this is a good idea, but unfortunately it limits teachers' discretion to design individualized lessons for students' specific needs. In an attempt to standardize the curricula, schools have adopted a one-size-fits-all philosophy that doesn't take advantage of the unique skills of individual teachers. One reason that teenagers drop out of school, often to become involved in gangs or delinquency, is because they are bored and don't believe the lessons are relevant to their everyday lives.

- **Standardized testing**   School systems, schools, administrators, and teachers are evaluated on how well students do on nationwide standardized tests. Schools that do not measure up can lose funding or even their accreditation. Critics of standardized testing say it ignores important factors such as the amount of resources and quality of funding that schools get and how well students are prepared (or aren't prepared).

tracking
Educational paths that schools use to group students into classes with other students who have similar needs.

- **Tracking**   Given the wide range of student abilities, interests, and motivations, many school districts group students with similar needs and abilities. **Tracking** youths with similar abilities and interests allows teachers to teach at a pace that is appropriate for everyone. Tracking has been criticized, however, for preventing some students from succeeding in school by forcing them into tracks that offer little academic challenge. Here, a bit of labeling theory can be applied. Although these tracks might have value-free titles, everyone in the school knows which tracks are for students who have special needs, have low IQs, are academically slow, or simply wish to prepare for a vocation rather than college.

Students in these tracks might meet with derision from their classmates and lower expectations from everyone else. This puts extra pressure on teachers to make sure these students do not lose faith in their schools and decide to drop out at the first opportunity, increasing their risk of delinquency.[24]

- **Limited teacher authority**   Despite being held responsible for what happens inside the classroom, teachers have limited authority to discipline students. Because of past abuses and society's increasingly litigious attitude, teachers must maintain classroom order without a great deal of formal authority. Formal procedures for dealing with problem students involve school administrators who are trained and mandated to dispense discipline. Unfortunately, teachers and administrators have only limited authority to deal with students who are disruptive or who commit minor delinquency, and much of the success of their disciplinary procedures depends on parental support. Severely disruptive or delinquent students might be referred to law enforcement.

These internal pressures make delinquency more likely because school officials often don't have the authority and resources necessary to maintain safe and effective schools. Teacher burnout can make an exemplary school mediocre and a poorly performing school dangerous.[25]

Schools must also respond to outside pressures that affect the way they handle students. These outside pressures have many sources, and it's difficult to tell if the threat is legitimate, significant, or potentially harmful. As an example, let's discuss the relationship between schools and parents. Parental involvement is important to school success. Schools work very hard to get parents to reinforce the educational mission and to keep them involved in the encouragement of their children's education. Not all parents, however, are equal to this task. Parents have a range of educational experiences of their own and possess different degrees of ability to appreciate the efforts of schools and teachers. Some parents are school dropouts and are limited in their ability to help their children prepare for and negotiate the challenges of school. Other parents are extremely well educated and have high expectations for their children's school, some of which might be unrealistic.[26]

Teachers sometimes find themselves dealing with parents who are clueless about what the school can and can't deliver in terms of a quality education. Affluent parents often abandon public schools and enroll their children in private schools. Although the property taxes of these parents still support the public school, their involvement is lost. Still other parents become deeply involved in their schools and communities. In the early 1990s, one woman's efforts to educate her son and defend her neighborhood from gang activity led to the creation of an award-winning tutoring program (see Programs for Children 11.1.)

The intent here is not to blame parents for the failure of the schools to provide a quality education, but rather to point out that schools get a variety of input from parents, not all of it positive. Sometimes, parents might refuse to recognize the limitations they have placed on their children with their own biases and lack of support. Some parents can turn a blind eye to the delinquent and criminal behavior of their children and refuse to allow the school to apply necessary corrective measures. In some instances, parents are confrontational or even violent with teachers or school administrators.[27]

Another external factor that affects the school's ability to educate is gangs. Schools aren't immune from community problems, and because they are where youngsters are legislated to be, a community's gang activity often follows. Chapter 12 deals with gangs in detail, but it is important here to understand that schools are not always equipped to handle serious gang problems and are often where gang issues are contested. The external stresses of drugs, violence, and rebellion that accompany gang life not only complicate the school's mission, but also might change the environment to the point where the school is more like an armed camp than a place of learning.[28]

11.1 PROGRAMS *for* CHILDREN

ROSIE'S GARAGE

When Rose Espinoza found that gangs had invaded her Los Angeles barrio, La Habra, she realized that the neighborhood's children, including her own son, needed a safe, quiet place to do their homework. So in 1991 she set up such a place in her home's garage.

At first, Espinoza, a medical-equipment designer, did all the tutoring herself. As the number of students seeking refuge from the streets grew, she hired teenage tutors and gave out packages of peanuts and candy to encourage the students to do their homework. According to Orange County Neighborhood Housing Services, recent evaluations showed that students tutored at Rosie's Garage increased their writing and math ability by at least two grade levels.[1]

After nearly two decades, although the garage's location has changed, Rose Espinoza's methods haven't. She runs the program much like a school study hall; the students arrive after school, spread out their books on a table, and start their homework. Those who have questions or need help can ask one of the tutors or Rosa herself, who attends the afterschool sessions whenever she is not at work. In 2003, Espinoza had to move the program from her garage after her dog bit a 6-year-old girl. Rosie's Garage is now located in a block of nearby city-owned offices that the program is allowed to use for free.[2]

The program has expanded to three other locations besides La Habra and is currently funded by donations and an annual 5-kilometer race. In addition to tutoring, Rosie's Garage also sponsors field trips to colleges, museums, and the theater.[3]

1 Neighborhood Housing Services of Orange County, www.nhsoc.org/community%20links/rosies.htm.
2 Agustin Gurza, "Rose Espinoza Nurtures a Little Flock," *Los Angeles Times*, Orange County edition, May 27, 2000, p. 3; Jennifer Mena, "Teaching a Lesson in Perseverance," *Los Angeles Times*, home edition, October 12, 2003, p. B5.
3 Rosie's Garage, rosiesgarage.org/.

Drugs, violence, and rebellion can change a school's environment to the point that it is operated more like an armed camp or a prison. *(Courtesy C. Lee, Getty Images, Inc. — PhotoDisc)*

SAFE AT SCHOOL

When parents send their children to school, they have every right to expect that their children will be safe from physical and psychological harm. Most schools meet this expectation. School officials and teachers work hard to provide students with a safe learning environment. There are, of course, exceptions. Some teachers harm students, some students harm teachers, and some students harm each other.

Fortunately, students are rarely seriously harmed at school. In fact, schools are one of the places where children are the safest. So why is the impression that the school is a dangerous place for children so widespread? Part of this impression comes from the way the media sensationalize school crime. Although these events are rare, school crime has been elevated from local news to national news. In many rather routine situations, the media have focused on linking unrelated cases in distant physical locations as if some sort of national trend were afoot. The most visible of these attempts is the coverage of school shootings.

School Shootings

Over the past two decades, there have been several well-publicized cases in which a student (or students) has murdered several other students and teachers in a blaze of spectacular violence.[29] School shootings in Littleton, Colorado; Red Lake, Minnesota; and Jonesboro, Arkansas, have affected the entire country. Each case represents different issues in terms of the motivation of the shooter(s), number of people killed, and effect on the community, and all are worth exploring in their own right. However, for our purposes, we will take a look at the case that has become the signature case of school shootings: Columbine High School in Littleton, Colorado.

On April 20, 1999, two high school seniors, Dylan Klebold and Eric Harris, walked into Columbine High School carrying two 20-pound propane bombs in duffel bags that they placed in the cafeteria. They set the timers and went outside to wait for the explosions. When the bombs didn't explode, they went back inside with an assortment of weapons and proceeded to shoot people indiscriminately. Over the next hour, they fired 188 rounds of ammunition and threw 76 bombs, 30 of which exploded. Klebold and Harris killed 13 people, then themselves.[30]

Two remarkable aspects of this case caused school administrators and law enforcement officials to develop new procedures for ensuring that schools will be

Eric Harris (left) and Dylan Klebold examine a sawed-off shotgun in this March 1999 video. About six weeks later, the pair killed 13 people at Columbine High School in Littleton, Colorado. Some of the weapons shown in the video were used in the shooting. *(Getty Images, Inc.)*

better protected from this type of attack. The first aspect is the apparent absence of any compelling motivations on the part of Klebold and Harris. No one saw this attack coming. The boys were well-behaved at school, and their parents didn't know they were making bombs in the garage. The second remarkable aspect of the case is the inadequate response of law enforcement. With no coordinated plan, law enforcement officers took a long time to fully comprehend the extent of the threat and to try to remove the attackers. Each of these aspects bears further examination in terms of how it has compelled authorities to plan for the prevention of and response to future incidents of extreme school violence.[31]

Were there warning signs that indicated that Klebold and Harris were capable of committing such a violent act? This question can never be fully answered. Klebold and Harris were unremarkable students who appeared to inhabit the fringes of several marginal groups. Much was made of the trench coats the boys wore to conceal their weapons and bombs. They were believed to be part of a clique called the "trench-coat mafia," and after the incident, others in this clique were questioned. In reality, the boys had given no indications that they were planning the attack. It is tempting to speculate that the boys were predisposed to violence because of their marginality and their preoccupation with video games and from being picked on by athletes in the school. But are these really substantial indicators of potential violence? Thousands of youths fit this profile, never harm anyone, and grow up to become normal and productive adults.

Robert Wooden and Randy Blazek deal with youth alienation in their book *Renegade Kids, Suburban Outlaws*. One central idea is that teenagers are alienated from society, especially the school, so they seek meaning in various subcultures that fulfill their need for identity, empowerment, and relationships with others similar to them. Much of youth culture exists in response to the feelings that teenagers have of being unconnected to the dominant culture.[32] For instance, body piercing and tattoos reflect attempts to express alienation with parents, schools, and society.

One problematic feature of this alienation that is related to delinquency is how the bar of deviance is continually raised. What used to shock people in the 1960s—bell-bottom pants, marijuana, long hair, and loud rock music—is now so common that it goes unnoticed. To attract attention and express the right amount of alienation, music has become more socially offensive; fashions and hairstyles have fragmented to the point where anything may be considered okay, and today's degree of scarring, branding, tattooing, and piercing was unimaginable in the 1960s.[33] So how does a youth filled with rage get attention in a society where nothing is shocking? Shooting one's schoolmates certainly fits the bill. More common, however, is membership in a particularly dangerous gang, petty theft, promiscuous sex, binge drinking, and dropping out of school altogether, all of which are hallmarks of juvenile delinquency.

This observation brings us back to Harris and Klebold. Writings of theirs that were released in 2006 reveal not a pair of psychotic adolescents, but young men who were in many ways normal teenagers. Both were intensely depressed: Harris because he felt that no one liked him and that everyone made fun of him and Klebold because of an unrequited crush on a girl and the fact that one of his friends now preferred spending time with a new girlfriend. These adolescent concerns are very typical, and most often they evaporate with adulthood. Why Klebold and Harris chose the path that they did, spectacular violence rather than typical rebellion or delinquency, and why millions of teenagers with the same problems go on to successful adulthoods will probably remain a mystery.[34]

Perhaps the most important thing to realize about school shootings is that they don't represent any typical aspect of juvenile delinquency. Like serial killers, young people angry enough to commit mass murder at school do exist, and school shootings have, of course, happened. However, they represent extreme exceptions within juvenile delinquency, just as serial killers represent the extreme exception among felons and even convicted murderers. This is one reason that law enforcement's response to Columbine was so inadequate. The officers had never faced anything like

A child smoking a cigarette is a far more typical act of delinquency than are school shootings. *(Courtesy Marc Grimberg, Getty Images Inc. — Image Bank)*

Andrew Golden, photographed in a soldier's uniform with a rifle. In 1998, at age 11, he and Mitchell Johnson, 13, planned a shooting ambush at their Jonesboro, Arkansas, school that ended in the deaths of four young girls and a teacher and wounded several others. Both boys were tried as juveniles. In 2005, Johnson was released from a Tennessee detention facility on his 21st birthday. Golden was released in 2007. *(Courtesy Corbis/Sygma)*

it before, and the incident was completely outside their training. Most law enforcement officers, most parents, and most children will never have to deal with a school shooting. Most of us will experience school shootings, if there ever are any more, only from our television sets in the form of hyperactive media coverage.[35]

The real issues of juvenile delinquency and schools are those that we hear about every day: gangs, status offenses, bullying, drug and alcohol use, and relatively minor delinquent behaviors such as theft and fighting. Behavior that leads to school violence, such as bringing a weapon to school, has actually declined in the past several years (see Figure 11-3), as has the number of youngsters who kill their acquaintances (see Figure 11-4, although youngsters still murder their acquaintances more than they do strangers or family members). And, as we learned in Chapter 10, most children who are murdered die at the hands of adults, not other children and not at school.

Bullying

bullying

The psychological or physical victimization of youths by other youths.

Although school shootings are rare, they have gotten a great deal of publicity, altered school safety policies, and generated fear in parents and children. An issue related to school safety that hasn't received the coverage of school shootings but is more prevalent and worthy of increased attention is **bullying**. Bullying is the victimization of

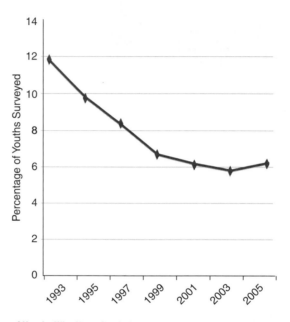

Figure 11-3   Percentage of Youths Who Have Carried a Weapon onto School Property, 1993–2005 *Source:* National Center for Chronic Disease Prevention and Health Promotion, *National Youth Risk Behavior Survey: 1991–2005, Trends in the Prevalence of Behaviors That Contribute to Violence on School Property*, www.cdc.gov/HealthyYouth/yrbs/pdf/trends/2005_YRBS_Violence_School.pdf.

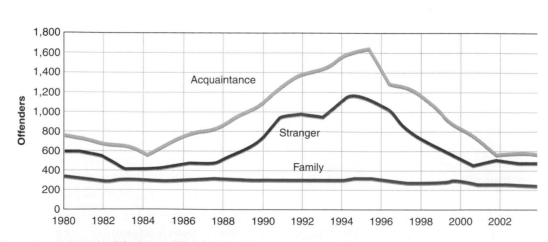

Figure 11-4   Known Juvenile Homicide Offenders and Their Relationship to Their Victims

Although juveniles tend to murder their acquaintances more than strangers or family members, the rate of juvenile acquaintance murder has fallen sharply since 1994. *Source:* Analysis of FBI Supplementary Homicide Reports, 1980–2002, by Howard N. Snyder and Melissa Sickmund, *Juvenile Offenders and Victims: 2006 National Report* (Washington, DC: U.S. Department of Justice, Office of Justice Programs, Office of Juvenile Justice and Delinquency Prevention, 2006), 68. Online at www.ojjdp.ncjrs.org/ojstatbb/nr2006/downloads/NR2006.pdf.

youths by their peers. It can range from verbal taunts, threats, and put-downs to deadly physical assaults. For some children, the experience of being bullied can result in severe trauma that affects them for many years.[36]

Bullying is nothing new. It has been part of the experience of school children in societies across the globe probably for as long as there have been schools and societies. Unfortunately, until very recently, bullying was considered a normal part of growing up and the way that youngsters establish social hierarchy. For the most part, scholars have considered bullying a relatively minor problem in schools and something that, although regrettable, is inevitable. This is changing, however. For a look at the new school response to bullying, see Crosscurrents 11.1.

11.1   *CrossCurrents*

Bullies

Bullying is a serious problem among children and in schools across the world. The Health Resources and Services Administration's antibullying website Stop Bullying Now! describes bullying as follows:

> when someone hurts or scares another person on purpose and the person being bullied has a hard time defending himself or herself. Usually, bullying happens over and over. Bullying is punching, shoving and other acts that hurt people physically; spreading bad rumors about people; keeping certain people out of a "group"; teasing people in a mean way; getting certain people to "gang up" on others."[1]

Although bullying can take both physical and psychological forms, experts say that physical bullying isn't as common as the psychological forms, such as exclusion, name calling, and gossip. Bullying respects no culture. International experts say that it happens in the same way in every school everywhere. Norway began its antibullying push relatively early, in 1982, after three adolescents committed suicide as a result of bullying. The country began a program of school interventions, including the establishment of classroom rules governing unacceptable behavior, teacher-development groups, and counseling for bullies, victims, and parents. In three years, school bullying was reported to have fallen by 50 percent.[2]

Several other countries have developed antibullying programs that use a variety of methods. Israel has had some success merely by increasing adult supervision. Studies there found—to little surprise, one hopes—that bullying happens most often when adults aren't around to stop it: in hallways and restrooms, on the playground, after school, and when the teacher has left the room. The U.S. government's Stop Bullying Now! website cites research stating that between 15 and 25 percent of students are frequently bullied and that 15 to 20 percent of students say that they frequently bully others.

Long assumed to be a normal part of growing up, bullying is now considered a serious problem among children and in schools throughout the world.

Although bullying itself might not constitute delinquency, the U.S. Department of Health and Human Services reports that delinquency and early criminal offending seem to be rooted in early childhood aggression, of which bullying is one aspect.[3] In response, antibullying programs are now becoming a trend in K–12 education. Perhaps the program that has garnered the most attention is the aforementioned initiative that was developed in Norway. Called the Olweus Bullying Prevention Program, it calls on elementary and middle-school teachers and staff to create a particularly caring and involved environment and to act as both authority figures and role models. The program calls for firm limits on disruptive behavior yet handles violations of the rules in a nonviolent manner.[4]

In some cases, however, bullying can be controlled merely by giving a problematic situation some specific attention. In one study, carried out in a very small rural school that consisted of one teacher and 28 students, acquaintances of the bully were asked to keep an eye on the bully and physically restrain the youth from further harassing the victim. The bully ceased the harassment thanks to the immediacy and intentionality

(Continued)

(Continued)

Of the response by the bully's peers. In other words, the bully knew why the other children were intervening and not just watching and that they expected the bully's behavior to stop.[5]

In the United States, the spate of school shootings in the last decade has brought new attention to the bullying behavior. In 2005, the House amended the Juvenile Accountability Block Grants program so that funds could be used to address school bullying prevention. Grants were also established so that school staffs could be trained to recognize violence and establish intervention policies.

An antibullying program that is becoming increasingly popular is the Peaceful Schools Project, developed by psychiatrists at the Menninger Clinic in Houston, Texas. The program considers the problem of bullying to involve three social roles, that of the bully, the victim, and the observer(s), with the idea that children typically engage in each of these roles at times. The Peaceful Schools Project operates from three perspectives, the first of which focuses on classrooms. There, disruptions are recognized and dealt with immediately, with the students asked to discuss and help develop solutions. Second, a sort of school public

relations campaign is developed that uses posters, buttons, and classroom stories to develop a positive climate. Last, a martial arts–based self-defense program helps children deal with situations in which they are physically harassed. The program also teaches methods of relaxation and how to identify emotions before acting on them.

Think About It

1. Why do some children become bullies?
2. Should bullying be left to the schools to deal with, or should these cases be brought into the juvenile justice system?
3. Have you ever been bullied? What did you do about it?

[1]Online at stopbullyingnow.hrsa.gov/index.asp?area=whatbullyingis.
[2]Marianne D. Hurst, "When It Comes to Bullying, There Are No Boundaries," *Education Week* 24, no. 22, (February 9, 2005):8.
[3]U.S. Department of Health and Human Services, *Youth Violence: A Report of the Surgeon General*, 2001, www.surgeongeneral.gov/library/youthviolence/toc.html.
[4]Paul R. Smokowski and Kelly Holland Kopasz, "Bullying in School: An Overview of Types, Effects, Family Characteristics, and Intervention Strategies," *Children & Schools* 27, no. 2 (April 2005): 101.
[5]Peter Edward Gill and Max Allan Stenlund, "Dealing with a Schoolyard Bully: A Case Study," *Journal of School Violence* 4, no. 4 (2005): 47.

We will deal with bullying in detail for two reasons. First, bullying, although not restricted to schools, is most common there and has the greatest effect there. The second reason is that bullying can deeply affect both the victim and the school's social environment. Bullying is related to delinquency because it often includes actual crimes and can influence the victim and/or the bully in terms of their becoming delinquent themselves.

Young people have a desperate need to belong. In school, especially, they establish cliques that share their viewpoints, social status, and biases. Youngsters work hard to establish identity by rigidly enforcing the in-group exclusiveness of their **clique**.[37] After all, how cool are you and your friends when anyone is allowed to join? A clique's initiation is usually informal and can range from mild to severe. Initiations usually entail mild forms of physical or psychological assault and can be recognized by anyone who has endured grade school. Here are a few ways that youngsters bully others and try to establish social dominance.

clique

Any small, exclusive group of people that controls how and if others may join.

- **Name calling**   Young people establish social hierarchy in a number of ways. One is to exclude others by designating them as undesirable based on some characteristic that they might or might not control. For instance, race is an obvious way that youths divide themselves. Despite the efforts of administrators and teachers, race continues to be a major sorting mechanism. Racial epithets are used to remind victims that they are outside a particular clique and that they are considered inferior regardless of their accomplishments. Name calling also singles out those with physical abnormalities or alternative lifestyles or who participate in specific activities. For instance, playing tuba in the band might be socially rewarded by some peers but derided by others. Name calling can be a cruel and debilitating experience and is used to terrorize those without much social capital.[38]

- **Practical jokes, shoving, and other forms of physical dominance**   Some youths bully others by making them the object of jokes or mild physical aggression. A boy who knocks the books out of another boy's hands when passing him in the hallway sends the message that the aggressor is dominant and that the victim dare not challenge the affront. Although it is tempting to dismiss this as typical "kids will be kids" behavior, it can have real consequences for the victim.

Humiliation in front of your peers can be devastating. Being a victim of such attacks can cause a child to lose focus on his or her schoolwork and avoid going to school. This type of bullying might even be learned by the victim and used on younger and weaker children. It is important to break the consistent cycle of bully–victim–bully.[39]

- **Assault**   This type of bullying worries adults the most. Some children are severely injured by beatings from older or bigger students. As with all types of bullying, this is not confined to boys but might also be common among some groups of girls. The beating usually isn't the first time the victim has been attacked. These incidences are often the result of a pattern of ever-increasing aggressive behavior against the victim. It is difficult to satisfy the committed bully because each day the victim reappears, and a new and more aggressive act is expected by the bully's friends. After a time, the bully has to physically harm the victim or risk losing his or her tough reputation. In the most extreme cases, this violent escalation can result in the victim's death.

A final consequence of bullying is, perhaps, suffered by the bully. Bullies who are allowed to continue their behavior and profit from it socially risk taking it with them into adulthood.[40] Bullying worked for them when they were young, why wouldn't it work as an adult? The bully might become accustomed to gaining social capital from the behavior and continue it in some form into adult life. Although some adult bullies stop physically tormenting others, they might continue to psychologically intimidate their spouses, co-workers, employees, and children. Depending on the personalities around them, these bullies can go on to lead successful and law-abiding adult lives, even while causing those who live and work with them a lot of stress. Adult bullies who never graduate from physical bullying invariably find themselves in trouble with the law. Or the bully may finally stumble on a more powerful person, perhaps another bully, who won't be pushed around. If the adult bully is particularly violent and has enough run-ins with the law, this meeting might happen in prison.[41]

DOES FAIL MEAN JAIL? SCHOOL FAILURE AND DELINQUENCY

Students who fail in school are more likely to have a difficult time for the rest of their lives, even if they never break the law. Academic failure, disciplinary practices such as suspension and expulsion, and dropping out are the important factors in the "school to prison pipeline."[42] A high school diploma or **GED** (general education diploma) is a vital requirement for a number of occupations, and those who don't have the necessary diploma, degree, or certificate can be automatically excluded from many jobs. Professions like medicine, law, architecture, and education cooperate with legislators to ensure that those who want to work in those professions meet certain standards.

Many tasks that require little in terms of advanced skill or education still require a high school diploma or GED. This requirement is assumed to ensure that the applicant can read instructions and has enough problem-solving skills to work independently. Although a diploma is not always a reliable indicator that someone will be a good employee or will find a good job—many people who haven't finished high school find well-paid, satisfying work—most employers require a high school diploma, which can be a barrier for many young people who drop out of school.

School failure can have severe consequences. A youngster who is identified as an academic failure can suffer troubling psychological and sociological problems. For instance, when a student does not meet the minimal standards to finish a grade and is made to repeat classes, go to summer school, or drop back a grade level, the student might be labeled by teachers and peers as "dumb." It is true that some students might not be very smart, but it is more likely that students who fall behind just are not able

GED

General education diploma. A certificate that certifies that a student has passed a high school equivalency test.

Instant Recall
from Chapter 7
labeling theory

A theory that describes how a label applied by society can affect an individual's self-perception and behavior.

to flourish under their school's conditions.[43] The psychological damage done to these youths, the not-very-smart and the smart-but-not-responding, can be devastating. In Chapter 7, we learned in the discussion of **labeling theory** that people treat deviants differently because of the label (primary deviance) and that the deviant will internalize the label and act as if it were true (secondary deviance).[44]

Students who have trouble in school experience primary deviance in several ways. First, the student might be placed in a classroom with other students who are not expected to succeed. This means that expectations for everyone are lowered, and when one of the students does learn something, he or she might be ignored or even picked on for exceeding the class norms or teacher expectations. It does not take too many times of being right but getting ignored or punished before the student will learn not to stick out in the class and become withdrawn or rebellious. This type of student is further labeled as problematic, and his or her every action is under supervision and review.

Secondary deviance is even more of an issue in delinquency. Youths who are labeled as failures often give up on their educations because they come to believe that they are not cut out for school. They might act out this behavior in delinquent acts aimed at the school or classmates, or they might simply withdraw from all school activities. Negative early school experiences can convince children who have learning disabilities or who are late bloomers that they will never be able to compete with those who do well in school early on. Whether these youths drop out of school or not, the ramifications of early failure can continually plague their self-esteem and prevent them from even trying to do well in school.[45]

Suspension and Expulsion

There is a special relationship between delinquency and the traditional school punishments of suspension and expulsion. A common outcome for misbehaving students is a series of suspensions that culminate in expulsion. Students who are suspended from school are often the least likely to have an adult at home to supervise them. According to the 2000 census, children from impoverished homes were more likely to have been suspended than children from homes at or above poverty level (see Figure 11-5).[46] Perhaps not coincidentally, youngsters who do the sort of things to get suspended or expelled—use drugs, commit delinquent acts, threaten or commit violence—aren't only poor but have been abused, are depressed, or are mentally ill. Between 70 and 87 percent of incarcerated juveniles have learning disabilities or emotional problems that affect their education.[47] These are the children who need an adult the most, or even professional help. Isolating them from their peers, friends, concerned adults, the culture of the school, and possibly any mental health professionals on staff who might be able to help is probably unlikely to correct the youth's behavior and might even make it worse.

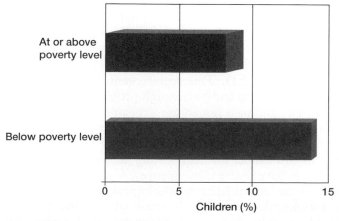

Figure 11-5 **Percentage of Children Ages 12 to 17 Years Who Have Been Suspended from School, by Level of Poverty** *Source:* Terry A. Lugaila, *A Child's Day: 2000 (Selected Indicators of Child Well-Being)* (Washington, DC: U.S. Census Bureau, 2003), 14. Online at www.census.gov/prod/2003pubs/p70-89.pdf.

This is especially important to the issue of delinquency because suspensions and expulsions separate the youngster with problems from the society he or she ultimately has to live in. The boy or girl who is increasingly estranged from socializing institutions, such as the school, might eventually see little point in trying to do what society expects and instead turn to delinquency. At this point, the next social institution the youngster is likely to encounter is law enforcement. Generally, a child or teenager who is home alone all day will find other things to do, and these things may include running with a gang or becoming involved in other kinds of delinquency.[48] According to a Centers for Disease Control and Prevention study, youths who aren't in school are more likely to get into fights, use drugs, smoke cigarettes, and carry weapons.[49]

Still, schools must have a way to deal with disruptive students and to protect and nurture students who aren't disruptive. Removing the problem student is often the easiest and most efficient way to do this. However, several school districts have dispensed with traditional suspension and expulsion. Some transfer problem students to supervised suspension areas or require a student's parents to attend school with him or her for part of the day. Others have the students do community service-type work at the school when classes aren't in session.[50]

Dropping Out

The dropout rate in the United States is remarkable because, given the national commitment to educating everyone, it's surprising that so many youngsters choose not to take advantage of a free education (see Figure 11-6 for a map of states with the highest dropout rates). In many other countries, passing up the opportunity for an education is almost unheard of. The reasons for dropping out of school cover a broad range of motivations, some the fault of the youth and the family and others attributable to the school climate and administrative procedures. Let's review some of the reasons that teenagers drop out of school and how these reasons are related to crime and delinquency.

- **Academic failure**   Many students drop out because they simply can't keep up. They are held back a grade while their friends advance. They find themselves in classrooms with children one or two years younger, and although they can compete on the playground or athletic fields, they are still unable to keep up in the classroom. This repeated and visible failure takes its toll on the student's self-concept and often results in a teenager dropping out the first chance he or she gets. Table 11-1 provides an interesting look at the earliest age that each state allows a student to quit school. Although some dropouts might eventually return to school and earn a GED, many never go back. For all practical purposes, their formal education is over, and their reading, math, and logic abilities are fixed. These limitations can decide what types of work they can get, making delinquency and crime attractive alternatives. Further, dropping out of school can be alienating and cause the youth to distrust authority and to scorn the American ethos of working hard, saving money, and planning for the future.[51]

- **Unmet special needs**   Schools sometimes miss the opportunity to recognize students' special needs. Those with learning disabilities and attention-deficit issues go undiagnosed, and their issues get attributed to low IQ or behavioral problems. For many of these youngsters, school is very frustrating. Without successful interventions, dropping out is an escape from a climate where they are the victim of forces beyond their control. It is often a short step to delinquency and crime for those whose special needs went unrecognized and unfulfilled. Sometimes the schools can diagnose the problem but don't have the facilities, staff, and/or programs to solve it. These youngsters can become bitter when they see resources going to athletes, cheerleaders, the band, and other extracurricular activities while their basic needs appear to be ignored.[52]

- **Cultural issues**   Often, schools can do little to prevent some students from dropping out. This is especially true when the students come from diverse

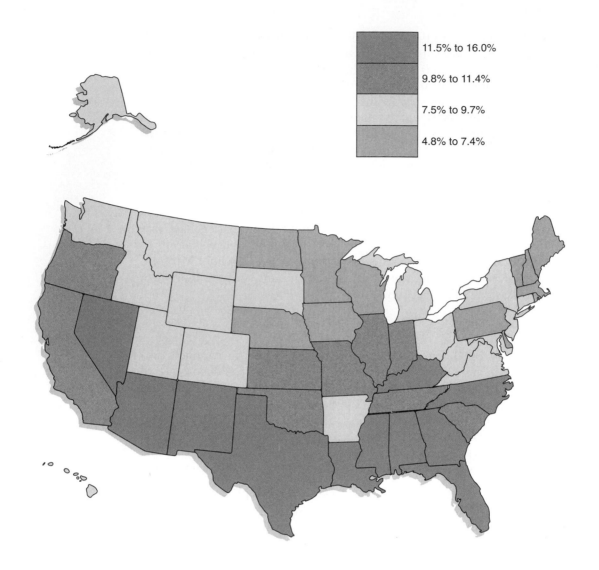

11.5% to 16.0%

9.8% to 11.4%

7.5% to 9.7%

4.8% to 7.4%

Figure 11-6 **High School Dropouts in 2000**

Percent of population, ages 16 to 19, who are not in school and haven't graduated from high school, by state. *Source:* Jennifer Cheeseman Day and Amie Jamieson, *School Enrollment: 2000, Census 2000 Brief* (Washington, DC: U.S. Census Bureau, 2003), 7. Online at www.census.gov/prod/2003pubs/c2kbr-26.pdf.

greedy institution

A formal or informal group or organization that demands undivided loyalty from its members.

social and cultural backgrounds. Although a school might try to foster a multicultural climate, sometimes the subculture of the student's family or peers is too strong to overcome. For instance, parents might require their children to quit school and work in the family business, or they might believe that daughters don't need as much education as sons and remove their daughters from school. Some parents just don't care if their children are in school or not. A youngster's involvement in gangs can also be a problem. The gang can be a **greedy institution** that demands time and loyalty from its members. Gangs generally don't value academic success, and the gang might be successful instead in coercing youngsters with a chance to succeed in school into deviant and antisocial behaviors. Dropping out of school and joining the local gang might seem like an obligation.[53] See Focus on Ethics 11.1 to explore a situation in which a teacher tries to keep a promising student out of a gang.

- **Boredom and questions of relevance** Many students find that school is not exciting enough to keep them interested. The school routine of classes, homework, sitting for an hour being lectured at, and taking tests is boring. Many

Table 11-1   Ages That School Attendance Is Required, by State

State	Required Attendance Ages		Exemptions
Alabama	7	16	Legally and regularly employed under child labor laws
Alaska	7	16	None
Arizona	6	16	14 with parental consent and gainfully employed
Arkansas	5	17*	*Must complete school year; otherwise no exceptions
California	6	18	None
Colorado	7	16	With current age and school certificate or work permit
Connecticut	5	18	16 with parental consent
Delaware	5	16	None
District of Columbia	5	18	None
Florida	6	17	16 with parental consent
Georgia	6	16	None
Hawaii	6	18	15
Idaho	7	16	None
Illinois	7	17	Employed and excused by school official
Indiana	7	18	16 with consent of parent and principal; 14 if parent agrees and state labor bureau issues certificate; must return to school within 5 days of termination of employment
Iowa	6	16	None
Kansas	7	18	17 or 16 with parental consent
Kentucky	6	16	None
Louisiana	7	18	17 with parental consent
Maine	7	17	15
Maryland	5	16	None
Massachusetts	6	16	14
Michigan	6	16	None
Minnesota	7	16	None
Mississippi	6	17	None
Missouri	7	16	14
Montana	7	16*	*Or completion of 8th grade, whichever is later; otherwise, no exceptions
Nebraska	7	18	14 and 16 with parental consent; special legislation for home schooling
Nevada	7	17	14 and excused by board of trustees; 14 if work is necessary for own or parents' support.
New Hampshire	6	16	None
New Jersey	6	16	None
New Mexico	5, or 8 if parents and school board agree	High school graduation	17 if excused by school board and gainfully employed or student is in alternative schooling with parental consent; otherwise no exceptions
New York	6	17*	*In cities with population of 4,500 or more and union-free school districts; 16 if approved by local school board; otherwise, no exceptions
North Carolina	7	16	None
North Dakota	7	16	Necessary to family support
Ohio	6	18	16 with parental and superintendent permission
Oklahoma	5	18	16 with written joint agreement

(Continued)

Table 11-1   **Ages That School Attendance Is Required, by State** (Continued)

State	Required Attendance Ages		Exemptions
Oregon	7	18	Or excused by district school board; 16 with school administration and parental consent
Pennsylvania	8	17	16 with certificate and regular employment; 15 in farm work or domestic service in private home with permit; 14, employed as above if completed elementary school with permit recommended by district superintendent or private school principal
Rhode Island	6	18	16 with written parental consent
South Carolina	5	17	16; further attendance is determined by court to be disruptive, unproductive, or not in child's best interest
South Dakota	6	16	Or completion of 8th grade if member of certain religious organizations; otherwise no exceptions
Tennessee	6	18	None
Texas	6	18	None
Utah	6	18	16 and 8th grade completed; home-schooled minors exempt from attendance
Vermont	6	16	15, completed 6th grade and needed for family support
Virginia	5	18	Exempt with parental consent along with that of principal or superintendent or a court ruling that the minor can't benefit from school
Washington	8	18	16 and parent agrees that child should not be required to attend, or child is emancipated, or child has certificate of competence
West Virginia	6	16	None
Wisconsin	6	18	None
Wyoming	7	16	None

Source: U.S. Department of Labor, *Employment Related Provisions in State Compulsory School Attendance Laws,* January 1, 2006, www.dol.gov/esa/programs/whd/state/schoolattend.htm.

youngsters feel alive only when outside the classroom, on the ball field, in some student club, or just hanging out with friends. They long for the time when they can have greater control of their daily schedule and don't have to adhere to the demands of teachers, administrators, and parents. The early signs of dropping out of school are truancy, behavioral problems in the classroom, refusing to do homework, not caring about grades, and taking shortcuts such as cheating and plagiarism. These youngsters are in danger of turning to delinquency as a response to the feeling that school can't give them what they want out of life and is, in fact, standing in the way. To them, school is just another opportunity for failure, and the sooner they can get out and on to something important, the better. Unfortunately, many of these youngsters have no realistic plan for something better. They are ill-equipped financially, emotionally, and intellectually to enter the work force with the skills and work habits it takes to succeed. Teenagers who drop out of school face two problems connected to delinquency. The first involves getting enough money to buy what they want. The second is what to do with their time. Dropouts can quickly get bored with hanging out with their friends in much the same way they were bored in school. They crave excitement and fun, as well as the money to buy it, which can lead them into taking law-breaking risks.[54]

- **Delinquency and crime**   Finally, many teenagers drop out or are thrown out of school because of criminal or delinquent acts. Schools are obligated to provide a safe learning environment, so they can't tolerate students who pose a

11.1 FOCUS on ETHICS

PUNISHING A POET

As a high school English teacher you have taught thousands of students over the past 20 years, but you have not yet had one with the talent of Carlos. Neither have you had a student who was wasting his talent like Carlos is. Carlos is a wonderful poet who can instantly understand the rhythm and the structure of any poem. When he reads Byron's *Prisoner of Chillon*, it is as if he is experiencing the pain of incarceration himself. Your fear is that he soon may actually be incarcerated because of his gang involvement, drug dealing, and attitude toward any type of authority.

Carlos has been your student for several years. When you moved from the middle school to the high school, he followed you and has taken every writing, literature, and poetry class you have taught. Although he is a mediocre student in other classes, he shines in English and literature and certainly is a good candidate to go to college. However, as much as he likes literature, the call of the streets is greater. He fancies himself as a romantic warrior struggling to achieve justice for his gang. He is completely wrapped up in the local turf wars with other gangs and is constantly in trouble for fighting, drinking, and being involved in dealing drugs.

You have a plan to save Carlos. You have convinced him that his talent for poetry can be used for many things. He likes rap music, and you have managed to hook him up with a record producer that your sister knows through a friend. This producer thinks Carlos has potential and is willing to help him make a demo record.

But there is a problem. Carlos has surrounded himself with an entourage of his gang members. They think they are all rebel artists and that they are entitled to the adulation that comes after someone is a big star, not before. To finance their rap star lifestyle, you have heard that they have been selling drugs at school. You have turned a blind eye to this possibility for some time because you were trying to wean Carlos away from the gang with music. Now it seems all your efforts have been in vain because you have heard about Carlos giving drugs to several sophomore girls.

You think that you might have made a mistake in getting too close to Carlos. Although you believe he is immensely talented, you realize that you have overestimated your influence on him. You thought that by presenting him with an alternative to gang life, you could divert him from delinquent and criminal activities. Now you are not so sure. The principal, who has had enough of Carlos and his gang buddies, has vowed to expel them if they get in serious trouble again. Without school and your small influence to add some structure to Carlos's life, you know that he will abandon his music, disappear into his gang, and probably end up dead or in prison. However, the principal says she can't allow Carlos and his gang to endanger the other students, and you have to agree.

What Do You Do?

1. Turn Carlos over to the school authorities. Your first obligation is to the school and all students to provide a safe learning environment. You have worked with Carlos and given him alternatives, but he likes gang life more.

2. Give Carlos another chance and try harder to convince him that he's in danger of losing his future.

3. Recognize that you can no longer make good judgments in this case. Carlos has become almost like a wayward son, and you have trouble distancing yourself emotionally. Additionally, you run the risk of angering his gang for telling Carlos to move on. You decide to seek professional guidance.

threat to other students or the school staff. The types of behaviors that lead to expulsion range from serious acts of delinquency to minor pranks. Depending on the school district, expulsion is the punishment for a wide range of behaviors. Clearly, criminal offenses such as murder, rape, and robbery are grounds for dismissal. Often, the school doesn't have to do anything with these types of cases because the juvenile court will take the delinquent out of school and place him or her in a secure detention facility. Other criminal offenses, such as drug use and drug sales, carrying a weapon to school, or making threats, are covered by school policies (usually zero-tolerance policies) and leave administrators little choice but to remove the student. Other offenses seem designed to rid schools of students even before they commit serious behaviors. Wearing clothes that violate the school dress code can result in suspension. For instance, in school districts with youth gang problems, a student wearing gang colors can be suspended or expelled. Although the necessity of such a punishment might be debated, the school must try to prevent disruptions. Students who are removed from school will find it difficult to return, at least to a regular school. Students are forced either to go to another school district or to attend an alternative school with other youths who had trouble with traditional school. Some alternative schools are excellent educational institutions that provide the specialized educational experiences and behavioral treatment that these students required in the first place. Unfortunately, other alternative schools are dumping grounds for youngsters who are **aging out** of the juvenile court system.[55]

aging out

In juvenile justice, reaching the age at which the system no longer serves a person, usually age 18.

Regardless of the specific cause, most dropouts will face challenges in entering the work force with the skills that will give them a reasonable chance to become self-supporting adults. Most schools employ a number of strategies to keep students in the classroom and provide them with the chance to earn the high school diploma that can mean the difference in getting a good job and a job that will not even pay the bills. Sometimes it can take a young person a year or two away from school to figure out the value of an education and develop the motivation to return to school with a positive attitude.

LEARNING THE WAY OUT OF DELINQUENCY

Many young people see getting an education as something they have to do to get a job. Then there are other youngsters who are so far into a delinquent career that they never have the opportunity to get an education, much less a job. Many of these youngsters are incarcerated in juvenile detention facilities where they cannot get traditional schooling. This is even more of a problem when the youth, who might even be a young adult, returns to society even further behind in his or her education. Getting a job at that point does not necessarily help, either. According to David Brown of the National Youth Employment Coalition, low-skill jobs don't prevent youngsters from becoming juvenile delinquents, nor do they reduce **recidivism**.[56]

Instant Recall from Chapter 5

recidivism

Continuing to commit delinquent or criminal offenses after being convicted and sentenced for prior offenses.

Recognizing this problem, some states have taken steps to help juvenile delinquents get some kind of education. Childhood and early adolescence are crucial points in the life course when people are best able to learn. Without this opportunity, youngsters face a trajectory of delinquency, crime, and further incarceration as an adult. Each state has a different way of educating juvenile delinquents. Here are some examples.

- **Delaware**   Delinquents attend school 35 days more each year than regular students.
- **Arizona**   Incarcerated youths are in school year-round.
- **California**   Juvenile court school is held every day, except for holidays and a few other excepted days.
- **Florida**   The education of incarcerated juveniles is left up to local school districts.[57]

Juvenile delinquents are more likely to miss getting an education than nondelinquent youngsters. The No Child Left Behind Act, which, as you will recall, mandates a series of reforms for the nation's school systems, includes the requirement that delinquents in juvenile justice schools get the same consideration as students in regular schools. The legislation provides additional money for educational programs that serve students in state institutions or community day programs and additional funding for school programs that cooperate with local correctional facilities. However, No Child Left Behind has yet to fulfill its promise in this respect. The act's limitations are, unfortunately, more pronounced for juvenile delinquents than for public school students.[58] For instance, in a study that compared 6,107 delinquent students with 5,187 nondelinquent students, the researchers concluded that

delinquent students do indeed suffer from a series of disproportionate educational deficiencies as compared to their nondelinquent counterparts.

Delinquent students were much more likely to attain lower GPAs, have poorer attendance records, be retained more often in the same grade, and receive more disciplinary actions. Moreover, these disproportionate educational deficiencies cannot be explained as a consequence of differences in such individual and school level variables as age, race, gender, socioeconomic status, exceptionality status or individual school. Consequently, it can be argued that these documented disproportional educational deficiencies may play an integral role in delinquency.[59]

If juvenile delinquents get an inferior education, should it be any surprise that they continue to break the law? A good education program can reduce delinquent recidivism rates by 20 percent or more.[60] Thomas Blomberg and George Pesta's study of 4,794 juveniles released from 113 Florida residential facilities shows that quality education programs "serve as a turning point in the life course" of many incarcerated juveniles. According to Richard Arum and Irenee Beattie:

- Juveniles in low- to moderate-risk programs who have high academic achievement and who attend regularly are more likely to return to school after being released and are less likely to be arrested again.

- Juveniles in high- to maximum-risk programs who get a high school diploma or GED while incarcerated are less likely to be arrested again.

- Juveniles with strong school attachment (see the prior discussion on school bonding) are more likely to return to school and not break the law again.[61]

The educational services provided to delinquents can be improved in a number of ways. These improvements require a rethinking of the role of education in rehabilitating juvenile delinquents, primarily by putting a greater emphasis on quality schooling early on in their difficulties.

- **Early identification and remediation**   It is important to identify students at the beginning of their educational difficulties and try to correct their problems immediately. The longer a student suffers declining grades and a sense of failure, the harder it will be to get him or her back on track. Additionally, the longer a student has this sense of failure, the more he or she is vulnerable to delinquency.

- **Instructional methods and classroom management**   Individualized instruction plans can quickly bring some delinquent students back into the norm. Teachers should be trained in how to deal with high-risk students by instituting classroom management techniques designed to keep the troublemaker's attention and get him or her involved in group activities.

- **School discipline**   Traditionally, the easiest way of dealing with a disruptive student has been to remove the student from the classroom. Although there will be incidents in which other students' safety is a primary concern, removal shouldn't be the only recourse. Sometimes removal better serves the teacher, rather than actual school safety. It might take more patience, understanding, and risk, but often the situation can be handled in such a way that the tension is reduced, and the delinquent or disruptive student is allowed to stay in class.[62]

Dealing with the educational problems of the juvenile delinquent is one of the most difficult issues facing schools and the juvenile justice system. Finding the right balance between safety and the needs of disruptive, abusive, or dangerous students can be incredibly challenging. Administrators and teachers must think about both what is good for the individual delinquent and what is good for all students in the school. Both parties have to be considered, and schools that sacrifice the delinquent for school safety might be missing the opportunity to prevent further delinquency and perhaps much more serious crime in the future.

SUMMARY

1. School is a primary institution of socialization that formally educates children. School quality is one of the most pressing social concerns facing the United States because it influences the extent and seriousness of delinquency.

2. The goals of schools can be roughly divided into the following categories: academic, vocational, social, civic, cultural, and personal.

3. Communities generally control their own schools, which can result in uneven school quality. Prosperous communities have more money to spend on schools than impoverished communities, and schools in low-crime areas tend to have fewer delinquency issues than schools in high-crime areas.

4. Issues important to understanding how delinquency happens in schools and how schools encourage social environments that produce delinquency are inappropriate curricula and instruction, differences between parental and school norms, lack of previous success in school, teaching difficulties, teacher perceptions and standards, and segregation.

5. Schools encourage appropriate behavior by using tools and techniques to control students, many of which are criticized for sacrificing student welfare for social control. Controversial measures include school uniforms, corporal punishment, and zero-tolerance policies.

6. Children and adolescents spend a lot of time in school, which increases their chances of committing delinquent acts on school property. Generally, middle and high school students are more likely to be victims of theft at school but less likely to suffer serious violence or homicide. Much of school vandalism can be prevented by target hardening.

7. School bonding is the connection that students have to their schools and their academic work. One study has found that high levels of school bonding might decrease student use of drugs and alcohol. Major aspects of school bonding include attachment to school, attachment to personnel, and school commitment.

8. Factors that have compromised teachers' personal standards include such internal pressures as standardization and regimentation, standardized testing, tracking, and limited teacher authority. Schools must also respond to outside pressures, including inadequate or counterproductive parental involvement and gangs.

9. Students are rarely seriously harmed at school. Over the past decade, school shootings have received a lot of attention from the media, giving the impression that all schools are unsafe. The real issues of juvenile delinquency are those that we hear about every day: gangs, status offenses, bullying, drug and alcohol use, theft, and fighting.

10. An issue related to school safety is bullying. A few ways that youngsters bully others and try to establish social dominance are name calling, practical jokes, shoving and other forms of physical dominance, and assault.

11. Students who fail in school are more likely to have a difficult time for the rest of their lives. A youngster who is identified as an academic failure can suffer from both primary and secondary deviance.

12. Schools sometimes use suspension and expulsion to control students. However, students who are suspended and/or expelled are often the ones who need the most help and are often the ones who become involved in delinquency.

13. The United States has a particularly high rate of school dropouts. Some of the reasons that teenagers drop out of school are academic failure, unmet special needs, cultural issues, boredom and questions of relevance, delinquency, and crime.

14. Incarcerated juvenile delinquents can't get traditional schooling and must be educated in some other way. Each state has a different way of doing this. Research has shown that a good education program can reduce delinquent recidivism rates.

REVIEW QUESTIONS

1. What is school an institution of?

2. What are the goals of schools?

3. How does local control of schools affect school quality and, in turn, delinquency?

4. What might prevent a school or school district from maintaining a high level of quality and discipline?

5. How do schools control and discipline students? What are some controversial measures?

6. What is target hardening? school bonding? How do these techniques affect delinquency?

7. What is No Child Left Behind? What effect does it have on the education of juvenile delinquents?

8. How do school shootings relate to general school safety?

9. How do youngsters try to establish social dominance?

10. How does labeling theory relate to failure in school and delinquency?

11. Why do some teenagers drop out of school?

ADDITIONAL READINGS

Arum, Richard. *Judging School Discipline: The Crisis of Moral Authority* (Cambridge, MA: Harvard University Press, 2003).

Ballantine, Jeanne H. *The Sociology of Education: A Systematic Analysis* (Upper Saddle River, NJ: Prentice Hall, 2001).

Gottfredson, Denise C. *Schools and Delinquency* (New York: Cambridge University Press, 2001).

McWhirter, J. Jeffries, Benedict T. McWhirter, Ellen Hawley McWhirter, and Robert J. McWhirter. *At Risk*

Youth: A Comprehensive Guide for Counselors, Teachers, Psychologists, and Human Service Professionals (Belmont, CA: Brooks/Cole, 2004).

Sanders, Cheryl E., and Gary D. Phye. *Bullying: Implications for the Classroom* (Boston: Elsevier, 2004).

Turk, William. *School Crime and Policing* (Upper Saddle River, NJ: Prentice Hall, 2003).

ENDNOTES

1. Susan Black, "Learning Behind Bars," *American School Board Journal* (September 2005): 51.

2. Carolyn S. Anderson, "The Search for School Climate: A Review of the Literature," *Review of Educational Research* 52 (1982): 368–420.

3. Adam Gamoran, "American Schooling and Educational Inequality: A Forecast for the 21st Century," in Jenne H. Ballantine and Joan Z. Spade, eds. *Schools and Society: A Sociological Approach to Education*, 2nd ed. (Belmont, CA: Wadsworth, 2004), 249–264.

4. Coalition for Juvenile Justice 2001 Annual Report Overview, *Abandoned in the Back Row: New Lessons in Education and Delinquency Prevention*, p. 2. Online at www.juvjustice.org/publications/overview2001.pdf.

5. Roberta M. Berns, *Child, Family, School, Community: Socialization and Support*, 6th ed. (Belmont, CA: Wadsworth, 2004), 213.

6. Jenne H. Ballantine, *The Sociology of Education: A Systematic Analysis* (Upper Saddle River, NJ: Prentice Hall, 2001). See especially Chapter 4, "Race, Class, and Gender: Attempts to Achieve Equality of Educational Opportunity."

7. Harold Wenglinsky, "How Money Matters: The Effect of School District Spending on Academic Achievement," in Jenne H. Ballantine and Joan Z. Spade, eds. *Schools and Society: A Sociological Approach to*

Education, 2nd ed. (Belmont, CA: Wadsworth, 2004), 213–219.

8. Martin Carnoy and Henry M. Levin, "Educational Reform and Class Conflict," *Journal of Education* 168 (1986): 35–46.

9. Myra P. Sadker and David M. Sadker, *Teachers, Schools, and Society* (New York: McGraw-Hill, 2003).

10. Caroline Wolf Harlow, *Education and Correctional Populations* (Washington, DC: U.S. Department of Justice, Bureau of Justice Statistics, 2003), 10. Online at www.ojp.usdoj.gov/bjs/pub/pdf/ecp.pdf.

11. Denise C. Gottfredson, "An Empirical Test of School-Based Environmental and Individual Interventions to Reduce the Risk of Delinquent Behavior," *Criminology* 24 (1986): 705–731.

12. Harry L. Gracey, "Learning the Student Role: Kindergarten as Academic Boot Camp," in Jenne H. Ballantine and Joan Z. Spade, eds. *Schools and Society: A Sociological Approach to Education*, 2nd ed. (Belmont, CA: Wadsworth, 2004), 144–148.

13. Thorstein Veblen, *The Theory of the Leisure Class* (New York: Penguin, 1994).

14. David L. Brunsma and Kelly A. Rockquemore, "The Effects of Student Uniforms on Attendance, Behavior Problems, Substance Abuse, and Academic Achievement," *Journal of Educational Research* 92 (1998): 53–62.

15. Murray A. Straus and Denise A. Donnelly, *Beating the Devil Out of Them* (San Francisco: Lexington Books, 1994).

16. Russell Skiba, *Zero Tolerance, Zero Effectiveness* (Bloomington: Indiana Education Policy Center, 2000).

17. DeVoe et al., *Indicators of School Crime and Safety: 2005* (Washington, DC: U.S. Departments of Education and Justice, U.S. Government Printing Office, 2005), iv. Online at nces.ed.gov/pubs2006/2006001.pdf.

18. Albert K. Cohen, *Delinquent Boys: The Culture of the Gang* (Glencoe, IL: Free Press, 1955).

19. DeVoe et al. (see note 17), vii. Online at nces.ed.gov/pubs2006/2006001.pdf.

20. Ibid., ix.

21. Christine A. Christle, Kristine Jolivette, and C. Michael Nelson, "Breaking the School to Prison Pipeline: Identifying School Risk and Protective Factors for Youth Delinquency," *Exceptionality* 13, no. 2 (2005): 69–88.

22. Samuel J. Maddox and Ronald, J. Prinz, "School Bonding in Children and Adolescents: Conceptualization, Assessment, and Associated Variables," *Clinical Child & Family Psychology Review* 6, no. 1 (March 2003): 31–49.

23. K. L. Henry, R. C. Swaim, and M. D. Slater, "Intraindividual Variability of School Bonding and Adolescents' Beliefs about the Effect of Substance Use on Future Aspirations," *Prevention Science* 6, no. 2, (2005): 101–112.

24. Delos Kelly, *Creating School Failure, Youth Crime, and Deviance* (Los Angeles: Trident Shop, 1982), 11.

25. Berns (see note 5), especially Chapter 7, "Ecology of Teaching," pp. 249–288.

26. J. L. Epstein, *School and Family Partnerships* (New York: Basic Books, 1996).

27. Robert J. Rubel and Peter D. Blauvelt, "How Safe Are Your Schools?" *American School Board Journal* 181 (1994): 28–31.

28. Daryl A. Hellman and Susan Beaton, "The Pattern of Violence in Urban Public Schools: The Influence of School and Community," *Journal of Research in Crime and Delinquency* 23 (1986): 102–127.

29. Katherine S. Newman et al., *Rampage: The Social Roots of School Shootings* (New York: Basic Books, 2004).

30. CNN, "One Year Later, Columbine Scars Remain," April 20, 2000, http://archives.cnn.com/2000/US/04/20/columbine.02/index.html.

31. Mary W. Green, "The Appropriate and Effective Use of Security Technologies in U.S. Schools: A Guide for Schools and Law Enforcement Agencies," in William L. Turk, ed. *School Crime and Policing* (Upper Saddle River, NJ: Prentice Hall, 2004), 173–201.

32. Wayne Wooden and Randy Blazek, *Renegade Kids, Suburban Outlaws: From Youth Culture to Delinquency* (Belmont, CA: Wadsworth, 2000).

33. Patricia Hersch, *A Tribe Apart: A Journey into the Heart of American Adolescence* (New York: Ballantine, 1999).

34. Susannah Meadows, "Murder on Their Minds: The Columbine Killers Left a Troubling Trail of Clues," *Newsweek* 148, no. 2 (July 17, 2006):28.

35. Ted Chiricos, Kathy Padgett, and Marc Gerty, "Fear, TV News, and the Reality of Crime," *Criminology* 38 (2000):755–785.

36. Cheryl E. Sanders, "What Is Bullying?" in Cheryl E. Sanders and Gary D. Phye, eds. *Bullying: Implications for the Classroom* (Boston: Elsevier), 2–19.

37. Maurissa Abecassis, "I Hate You Just the Way You Are: Exploring the Formation, Maintenance, and Need for Enemies," in Ernest V. E. Hodges and Noel A. Card, eds. *Enemies and the Darker Side of Peer Relations* (San Francisco: Jossey-Bass, 2003).

38. Diana Boxer and Florencia Cortés-Conde, "From Bonding to Biting: Conversational Joking and Identity Display," *Journal of Pragmatics* 27 (1997):275–294.

39. David S. J. Hawker and Michael J. Boulton, "Subtypes of Peer Harassment and Their Correlates: A Social Dominance Perspective," in Jaana Juvonen and Sandra Graham, eds. *Peer Harassment in School: The Plight of the Vulnerable and Victimized* (New York: Guilford Press, 2001), 378–397.

40. R. Loeber and D. Hay, "Key Issues in the Development of Aggression and Violence for Childhood to Early Adulthood," *Annual Review of Psychology* 48 (1997):371–410.

41. James Gilligan, *Violence: A Reflection on a National Epidemic* (New York: Viking, 1997).

42. Christle, Jolivette, and Nelson (see note 21), pp. 69–88.

43. Jonathon Konzal, *Savage Inequalities: Children in America's Schools* (New York: Crown, 1991).

44. Ross L. Matsueda, "Reflected Appraisals, Parental Labeling, and Delinquency: Specifying a Symbolic Interactionist Theory," *American Journal of Sociology* 6 (1992):1577–1611.

45. Delbert S. Elliott, "Delinquency, School Attendance, and School Dropout," *Social Problems* 13 (1966):307–314.

46. Terry A. Lugaila, *A Child's Day: 2000 (Selected Indicators of Child Well-Being)* (Washington, DC: U.S. Census Bureau, 2003), 14. Online at www.census.gov/prod/2003pubs/p70-89.pdf.

47. See note 4.

48. Howard L. Taras et al., "Out-of-School Suspension and Expulsion," *Pediatrics* 112, no. 5 (November 2003): 1206–1209.

49. Centers for Disease Control and Prevention, "Health Risk Behaviors among Adolescents Who Do and Do Not Attend School—United States, 1992," *Morbidity and Mortality Weekly Report* 43 (1994): 129–132. Online at www.cdc.gov/mmwr/preview/mmwrhtml/00025174.htm.

50. Jo Anne Grunbaum et al., "Youth Risk Behavior Surveillance—National Alternative High School Youth Risk Behavior Survey—United States, 1998," *Morbidity and Mortality Weekly Report* 48 (1999): 1–44. Online at www.cdc.gov/mmwr/preview/mmwrhtml/ss4807a1.htm.

51. Alan McEvoy and Robert Welker, "Antisocial Behavior, Academic Failure, and School Climate: A Critical Review," *Journal of Emotional and Behavioral Disorders* 8, no. 3 (Fall 2000): 130–140.

52. Aaron M. Pallas, Gary Natriello, and Edward L. McDill, "The Changing Nature of the Disadvantaged Population: Current Dimensions and Future Trends," *Educational Researcher* 5 (1989): 16–22.

53. Robert A. Peña, "Cultural Differences and the Construction of Meaning: Implications for the Leadership and Organizational Context of Schools," *Educational Policy Analysis Archives* 5, no. 10 (April 8, 1997). Online at epaa.asu.edu/epaa/v5n10.html.

54. James D. Raffini, "Student Apathy: A Motivational Dilemma," *Educational Leadership* 44, no. 1 (September 1986): 53–55.

55. Lawrence M. DeRidder, "How Suspension and Expulsion Contribute to Dropping Out," *Education Digest* 56, no. 6 (1991): 44–47.

56. David Brown et al., *Barriers and Promising Approaches to Workforce and Youth Development for Young Offenders* (Baltimore: Annie E. Casey Foundation, 2002), 5. Online at www.aecf.org/publications/pdfs/workforce.pdf.

57. Susan Black, "Learning Behind Bars," *American School Board Journal* (September 2005): 50.

58. Juvenile Justice Educational Enhancement Program, "No Child Left Behind and Its Implications for Schools Serving Florida's At-Risk and Delinquent Youths," in *2003 Annual Report to the Florida Department of Education: Juvenile Justice Educational Enhancement Program* (Tallahassee, FL: Juvenile Justice Educational Enhancement Program, 2003). Online at www.jjeep.org/annual2003.asp.

59. Ibid.

60. See note 4.

61. Richard Arum and Irenee R. Beattie, "High School Experience and the Risk of Adult Incarceration," *Criminology* 37 (1999): 515–540.

62. Xia Wang, Thomas G. Blomberg, and Spencer D. Li, "Comparison of the Educational Deficiencies of Delinquent and Nondelinquent Students," *Evaluation Review* 29, no. 4 (2005): 291–312.

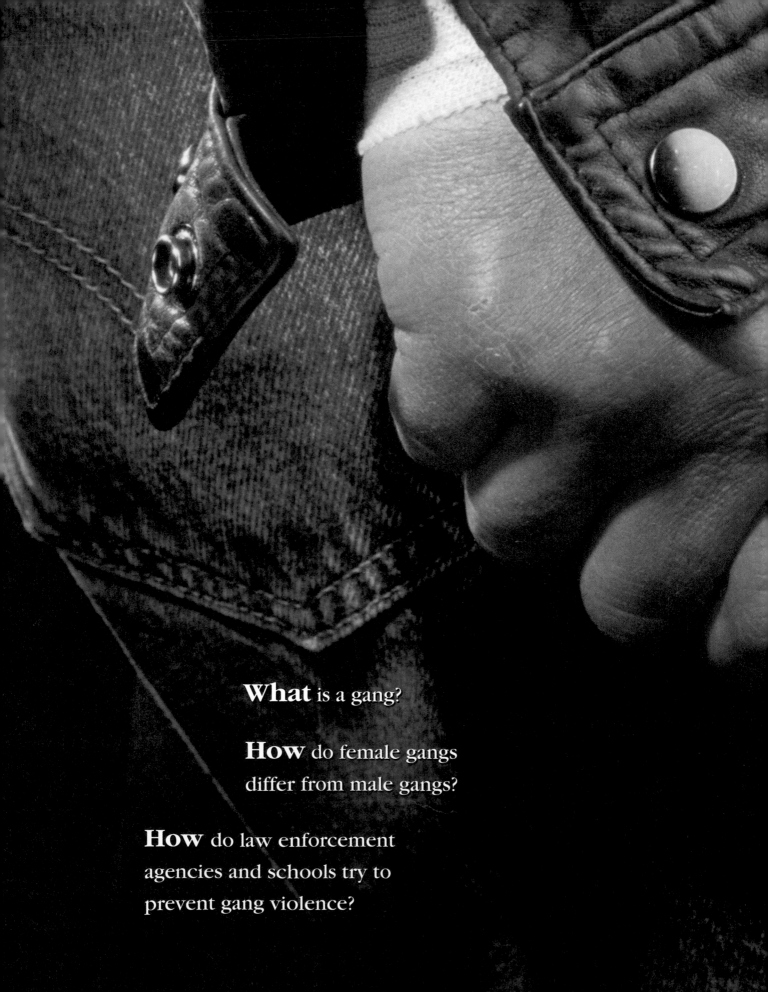

What is a gang?

How do female gangs differ from male gangs?

How do law enforcement agencies and schools try to prevent gang violence?

CHAPTER 12

Youth Gangs
and
Delinquency

Any discussion of juvenile delinquency must include the subject of youth gangs. Gangs present the juvenile justice system and law enforcement agencies with their most difficult challenges in limiting the harm done by youths to each other and to society.[1] Gang members are among the toughest offenders to rehabilitate, and juvenile gang members often mature into career offenders. Because the gang problem has been around for the past century, we might be tempted to think that we know how to deal with gangs. However, we would be mistaken. Despite extensive efforts by scholars, law enforcement, schools, and community groups, gangs are a major social problem not only in big cities, but also in smaller communities.[2] Although law enforcement reports of gangs have leveled off in recent years, the extent of the gang problem is still significant (see Figure 12-1).

Gang crime poses special challenges for criminal justice agencies for two reasons. The first concerns the motivation of juveniles to engage in gang activity. It is not enough to contend with the personal issues and shortcomings of the individual gang member; rather, the social context of group dynamics that involve gang membership must be addressed. This means not only must the educational, family, drug and alcohol, and psychological issues of the youth be treated, but also the network of gang peers must be severed and the youth introduced to a more supportive and positive social group. Breaking down the context for gang membership requires resources that are seldom available to criminal justice agencies, so unless or until communities develop comprehensive approaches to the problem of gang activity, the connection between delinquency and gangs will continue.[3]

A second reason that juvenile gang activity concerns criminal justice agencies is because, unless effective steps are taken to address gang crime while the juveniles are still juveniles, there is a good chance that they will continue to break the law when they become adults. In some gangs, members don't outgrow their involvement, developing other interests and leaving the gang. Some gangs are life-long organizations that include family members from several generations.[4]

This chapter is divided into six main sections. First, we present the problem of defining gangs. Although you might think this would be easy, there's considerable debate about just what constitutes a gang. Second, we will discuss the glue that holds gangs together, **peer relationships.** Gang loyalty depends on several complex factors, and these factors can be very different for various gangs. Third, we look at the structure of gangs. The size and level of commitment for individual gangs can be very different and have many implications. Fourth, we consider the different types of

peer relationships

The connections among those of equal standing within a group.

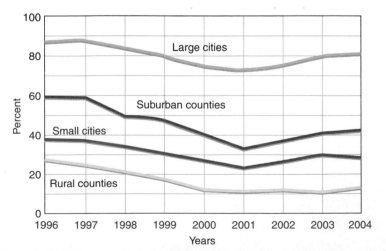

Figure 12-1   **Percent of Law Enforcement Agencies Reporting Gang Problems. Large cities have populations of 50,000 or more. Small cities have populations of 2,500 to 49,999.** *Source:* Arlen Egley, Jr., and Christina E. Ritz, *Highlights of the 2004 National Youth Gang Survey, OJJDP Fact Sheet,* in Howard N. Snyder and Melissa Sickmund, *Juvenile Offenders and Victims: 2006 National Report* (Washington, DC: U.S. Department of Justice, Office of Justice Programs, Office of Juvenile Justice and Delinquency Prevention, 2006), 82. Online at ojjdp.ncjrs.gov/ojstatbb/nr2006/downloads/NR2006.pdf.

gangs. Some gangs are based on race or ethnicity, some on the local neighborhood, and some on the type of illegal activity they pursue, if any. Fifth, we examine the nature and extent of gang criminality, as some gangs are more of a problem than others. Finally, we look at efforts to control gangs, focusing on the work of youth service workers, police, and the juvenile justice system to find strategies for resolving the issues that lead to gang activity.

DEFINING THE GANG: IT'S HARDER THAN YOU THINK

Criminologists have never agreed on exactly what constitutes a youth gang. Although most people think that they know a gang when they see one, the problems of measuring gang behavior require specifying the exact parameters of a number of characteristics. That is, before something can be measured, we have to know what it is. Because scholars can't agree on which characteristics to include in a definition and they can't agree on how the characteristics that they do agree on should be measured, a widely accepted definition remains elusive.[5] Therefore, we present one definition that includes many of the characteristics that we generally expect of gangs.

Walter Miller asked youth service agency workers, police officers, community outreach workers, judges, criminal justice planners, probation officers, prosecutors, public defenders, city council members, state legislators, ex-convicts, and past and present gang members about their definitions of a gang. The resulting list of characteristics was very long, but 85 percent of those surveyed agreed on the following six characteristics:

1. **A self-formed association of peers** This would exclude something like a football team or church group where there is adult supervision, financing, or other support. These peers choose to form gangs because of functions they believe the gang is able to provide that they can't get in their traditional relationships.

2. **Bound by mutual interests** These interests can be as simple as living on the same block of a street or being members of the same minority group. Gang members see their fellow gang members as interested in, influenced by, and having the same kinds of concerns that they do.

3. **Well-developed lines of authority and other organizational features** All gangs have some level of organization that includes leadership, division of labor, and lines of communication. Depending on the gang's size and complexity, the organization might have such roles as lookouts, drug couriers, drug sellers, money launderers, and street fighters. The leadership might be structured along military or corporate models.

4. **Acting together to achieve a specific purpose or purposes** For a gang to be successful, its members must work together to achieve their goals. This differs from a loose gathering of people who might, or might not, decide to participate in the group's activities.

5. **Involvement in illegal activity** This is one of the primary distinguishing features of a gang. Members engage in delinquent or criminal behaviors that range from drug sales to murder. The illegal activities are often oriented toward making money but are sometimes simply efforts to establish the gang's identity.

6. **Control over a particular territory, facility, or type of enterprise** Gangs usually protect some geographical area. It might be a section of their neighborhood, a shopping mall, school grounds, or even the exercise yard at a youth detention facility. Their goal is to preserve the integrity of their turf and to signal to others that they rule their limited domain. When gangs contest the ownership of a particular location, it can be a defining moment in the viability of their leadership and organization.[6]

These gang characteristics have a certain common-sense appeal. They include many of the features that anyone might use to identify a gang. If we asked a random selection of people to give us their definitions of a gang, their answers would vary.[7] However, Miller asked those who are intimately involved with gang behavior, which suggests a certain level of expert opinion. A couple of other elements could be added to the definition of a gang. Today, gangs use symbols to communicate their members' involvement. These symbols might be as simple as wearing certain colors (someone who is in the Bloods gang, for example, would wear red) or wearing the jerseys of a particular professional sports team. The flashing of gang signs also allows members to identify their loyalty to a gang, and graffiti can mark the boundaries of their turf or signify the gang's presence in public areas.[8]

Gangs can be defined in many other ways, but it's beyond the scope of this chapter to explore them all. However, there is concern that the definition of a gang depends on who is doing the defining.[9] The police might have one set of criteria that is useful to their mission of suppressing gang activity, and schools might have a different definition that is useful in targeting youths who are beginning to have academic and behavioral problems. Additionally, a youth detention facility might need to consider different criteria to separate potential gang members from each other or from the institution's general population. So, while recognizing its limitations, we will use Miller's definition because it contains information from across the juvenile justice system.

Studying Gangs

What we know about gangs really isn't very clear. A number of studies over the past 80 years have informed academics and criminal justice practitioners about the development and seriousness of gang activity. However, there is no collection of gang data that researchers use to update their knowledge of gangs. Researcher G. David Curry shared the popular misconception that the FBI or some other federal agency maintained a large database of information on gang members and gang-related activity. This isn't the case. According to Curry and Scott Decker, "Most of what we know about the national statistics on the gang problem is the product of a series of surveys conducted by different researchers over the past 25 years."[10]

What has the research on gangs concluded? The definition of a gang member has two aspects. The first aspect is involvement in crime.[11] Young people have a natural propensity to bond in friendship groups and cliques, but gang researchers are interested only in those groups who break the law. This is a crucial distinction that helps to differentiate gangs from other adolescent groups. In addition to violating the law, gang members show an affiliation with their gang through some cultural aspects that bond them with a family-like loyalty (see Crosscurrents 12.1). This bonding can be exemplified by the wearing of gang apparel, getting gang tattoos, or communicating with gang signs. Additionally, gang bonding includes spending time together in both criminal and noncriminal activities and swearing allegiance and loyalty to the gang. Members see the gang as what sociologists call a **primary group,** whereby the gang comes first in how members identify themselves and is a relationship that supersedes all others except for (in some cases) the family.[12]

primary group
A small social group whose members share personal, enduring relationships.

It is tempting to typify gangs based on ethnicity. This is because the membership of many gangs is racially and/or culturally homogeneous. For example, the Houston gangs discussed in the Kids in the News box later in the chapter are Hispanic, with roots in Mexico and Central America. However, in Table 12-1, researcher Malcolm Klein has developed a gang typology that he says is more useful than those based on ethnicity because it is based on gangs' activities and how they are formed, which he asserts is far more important and telling than the members' color and/or culture.

Varying levels of involvement in gang activities can complicate the definition of some youths as gang members. Some police agencies have claimed that they don't have a real gang problem but simply have some "wanna-bes" who like to dress in gang

The Grip of the Gang

Although not all gangs are alike, many have a powerful grip on their members. The loyalty some youngsters have toward their gang is truly remarkable, because the kids are willing to give up so much to be considered a respectable gang member. One might compare gangs to a football team or a Boy Scout troop considering the way members display loyalty, connectedness, and a common purpose. Gangs, however, transcend the commitment their members have to legitimate institutions. Gangs can be so encompassing that they could be compared to religion in how they involve their members. Although this analogy might seem extreme, a look at the sociology of religion shows that it's not far off the mark.

Looking at Emile Durkheim's *The Elementary Forms of Religious Life*, we can see how gangs perform many of the same functions for their members that religions do for their adherents. According to Durkheim, religion meets eight basic human needs. With a bit of imagination, we can apply five of these functions of religion to gangs.

- *Questions about ultimate meaning.* What is the purpose of life? Why are we here? Why do we have to suffer? These are the cosmic questions that religions answer for their followers. For gang members' questions such as "Why does society discriminate against me?" "How do I deal with being poor?" and "How do I act like a man?" gangs can supply the answers.
- *Emotional comfort.* Religion comforts people by providing support in times of sickness and death. Religious rituals are a great help to those suffering from traumatic events. For gang members, the rituals of the organization provide similar comfort. The loss of a gang member in gang warfare might be commemorated with graffiti or a tattoo. After the loss of a gang member's loved one, such as a parent or sibling who isn't involved in the gang, the gang can give the gang member an outlet for his or her grief and aggression.

- *Social solidarity.* Religious teachings and practices unite believers into a community that shares values and perspectives. Likewise, the activities of the gang bring its members closer together. Engaging in a street fight with another gang can illustrate to fellow gang members that "I got your back and you got mine."
- *Guidelines for everyday life.* Six of the Ten Commandments are instructions for living everyday life. The gang also has rules with how to interact with others, especially rival gang members. In some cities, a gang member who encounters a rival is almost always required to pick a fight to defend his gang's honor.
- *Social control.* Religion has a deep effect on groups by controlling the activities of its adherents and wider society if a majority of that society adheres to the religion. For example, in many parts of the United States blue laws restrict the sale of alcohol on Sundays and prevent the sale of alcohol within a certain distance of churches. Gangs are able to enforce rules of their own by claiming playgrounds or streets as territory and making others pay for the privilege of their use. Additionally, gangs can enforce a dress code that prohibits members of other gangs or nonaffiliated youths from wearing gang colors.

It is fair to say that the gang is the functional equivalent of religion for many gang members. Just as there is a range of religious involvement among citizens, there is a range of involvement among youths who claim to be in gangs. For those who are deeply committed to the gang culture, the symbols and signs take on an almost mystical meaning.

Think About It

1. Compare and contrast gangs with religions.
2. Are there positive aspects of gang membership?

Source: Emile Durkheim, *The Elementary Forms of Religious Life* (New York: Free Press, 1965; first published in 1912).

clothing and hang out looking like a gang. Curry and Decker don't like the wanna-be concept and contend that this designation obscures the fact that gangs have core members and fringe members. The fringe members might be young, emerging members and quite capable of committing violent offenses. By claiming they have only wanna-be gang members, police departments lose valuable time and intelligence in building a response to gang crime and violence.[13]

Once researchers identify gang members, they face the obstacle of gathering information. This can be precarious, because those involved in illegal behavior have good reasons for not talking about themselves and their activities. Researching gangs can be dangerous, too, as well as difficult. In addition to getting limited, inaccurate,

Table 12-1   **Characteristics of Five Street Gang Types**

According to Malcolm W. Klein, typing gangs by their ethnic or racial compositions is misleading, because what the group does and how it does it is far more important than its members' ethnicity.

Type	Subgroups	Size	Age Range	Duration	Territorial	Crime Versatility
Traditional	Yes	Average 180	Wide (20–30 years)	Long (>20 years)	Yes	Yes
Neotraditional	Yes	Average 75	No pattern	Short (<10 years)	Yes	Yes

Traditional and neotraditional gangs aren't the most common type of gang, but they are the largest, longest enduring, and most violent and commit the most offenses. These are large, inner-city gangs, such as the Crips, Bloods, and Mara Salvatrucha.

Type	Subgroups	Size	Age Range	Duration	Territorial	Crime Versatility
Compressed	No	Average 35	Narrow (<10 years)	Short (<10 years)	No pattern	Yes

Compressed gangs are mainly adolescent groups of 50 to 100 members. These are the most common and are found in both large and small cities.

Type	Subgroups	Size	Age Range	Duration	Territorial	Crime Versatility
Collective	No	Average 55	Medium wide (>10 years)	Medium (10–15 years)	No pattern	Yes

Collective gangs are the least common and are large but have little internal structure. They are sometimes bonded by loose neighborhood ties and extensive drug dealing.

Type	Subgroups	Size	Age Range	Duration	Territorial	Crime Versatility
Specialty	No	Average 25	Narrow (<10 years)	Short (<10 years)	Yes	No

Specialty is the smallest type but the most tightly structured. These gangs perpetrate a narrow pattern of offending and are devoted to certain types of crimes, such as robbery, burglary, car theft, or racial hate.

Source: Malcolm W. Klein, *Chasing after Street Gangs: A Forty-Year Journey* (Upper Saddle River, NJ: Prentice Hall, 2007), 55–56. Electronically reproduced by permission of Pearson Education, Inc., Upper Saddle River, New Jersey.

Young boys might be fringe members of gangs or not even members, but they are still capable of committing violence.
(Courtesy Lester Sloan, Woodfin Camp & Associates, Inc.)

and purposely slanted information from gang members, researchers might be exposed to intimidation or violence should the gang members not want to be studied or dislike the researchers' conclusions.[14]

Many research strategies can be employed to study gangs, but the two most common ones are to (1) examine records and talk to criminal justice administrators and/or schools and (2) talk directly to youths and gang members through surveys or interviews. Each strategy is useful for gathering information about gang activity and will yield different types of information. Researchers decide which to use depending on the issues they want to explore. For example, the question "Are there gangs in your city?" might get a vastly different response from the chief of police than it does from a gang member.

When researchers ask law enforcement officials about the prevalence and seriousness of gang activity in their cities, the researchers encounter some difficulties. The police might be reluctant to admit a gang problem. The police are vested with the responsibility to keep the community safe, and admitting a gang problem might be interpreted as admitting that the police department is failing. However, when money is available in the form of grants or other aid to fight gang activity, police agencies might claim to have gangs simply to become eligible for the funding.[15]

A more difficult problem for gang researchers involves determining how much crime is gang related. Law enforcement agencies don't always separate crime incidents according to whether they are gang related. Even more problematic is that it's usually impossible to determine whether a crime involves gang activity if there's no arrest. Drug sales, muggings, and larcenies are committed by gang members and nongang members alike.[16] Unless there was a witness capable of identifying gang monikers or colors or an actual arrest of a gang member, law enforcement can't attribute criminal activity to gangs. This makes law enforcement records unreliable for determining the level of gang-related crime. These records capture police activity better than they capture gang activity. Therefore, it's almost certain that law enforcement records will underreport the level and intensity of any gang problem.[17]

Field studies that interview or observe gang members offer a different perspective. Field studies aren't particularly well suited to collecting large amounts of data that can compare gangs between cities. Rather, they are useful for scholars concerned with the circumstances in gang members' lives, how the gang members interpret their circumstances, and how their behaviors and activities are shaped (see Kids in the News 12.1).[18]

12.1   Ⓚ Ⓘ Ⓓ Ⓢ in the Ⓝ Ⓔ Ⓦ Ⓢ

Life in MS-13

Much of what we know about gangs comes from journalists who go into the field and interview gang members. Like academic field studies, their reports are not really useful for determining how many gang members there are in a given city, what offenses they commit, and how often they commit them, nor is the information useful for comparing gang activities from city to city (see the discussion on generalizability later in the chapter). But broad inferences can be drawn from learning what goes on in the life of a particular gang member.

In December 2006, a reporter interviewed Alex, a member of Mara Salvatrucha or MS-13, a Hispanic gang in southwest Houston whose members typically have roots in Central America. Information about MS-13 gleaned from Alex's long life in the gang—he joined at age 11 and had been in the gang for almost 10 years at the time of the interview—can't be applied to other gangs in other cities, but it's useful for getting a feel for what gang life is like and why impoverished and alienated young people continue to join gangs.

MS-13 members in the National Penitentiary in Tamarac, Honduras, in December 2001. Members of MS-13 in the United States typically have roots in Central America. *(Courtesy Daniel LeClair, Corbis/Reuters America LLC)*

(Continued)

(Continued)

- Alex lives in what the Houston police call Gang Land, a group of apartment complexes that were built for single, young, working adults. In the early 1980s, as Houston's economy withered after the oil bust, the young singles moved away, and Hispanic immigrants moved in. Poverty, dense population, and alienation followed, along with the gangs.

- The gangs include the Southwest Cholos, La Primera, La Tercera Crips, Somos Pocos Pero Locos, and Mara Salvatrucha (MS-13). They typically wear T-shirts and pressed blue jeans or khaki pants, with their gang colors represented by long cloth belts, bandannas from their back pockets, and rosaries. MS-13's color is blue.

- Each gang is composed of cliques or smaller groups that claim streets, parts of streets, or apartment complexes. The cliques never have a mass meeting of any sort. Each clique operates independently, selling drugs, running prostitutes, charging rent to others who do those activities in their territories, or selling protection to local businesses.

- Alex is 20 years old. His parents arrived in Houston from El Salvador in 1985 just before he was born. Alex says he has been involved in 100 to 200 fistfights, knife fights, gun battles, and drive-by shootings. Among his tattoos is one on his left wrist: a triangle of three dots that is the symbol of *la vida loca,* or "the crazy life." The dots mean that if one continues to live *la vida loca,* he (or she) will end up in the hospital, in prison, or dead.

- Alex began gang life as a "boxer," which is slang for a street fighter. He was sent to detention at age 8 for beating up a kid who insulted him. Juvenile detention increased his gang contacts, and

a gang invited him to join after seeing him fight. After a second time in detention for attacking a man who hit his mother, he joined MS-13, or "clicked in" by allowing them to beat him for several minutes.

- Although Alex's juvenile record is long, his adult criminal record is not, with only three convictions for drug possession and one for assault.

- Houston police reports state that in the first half of 2006, gangs committed at least 298 assaults, 271 drug-related crimes, 130 robberies, and 32 murders. The "at least" part is important. Police officials say these statistics are too low because a state law checks law enforcement's ability to identify a suspect or a victim in a police report as a gang member.

- Since spring 2005, the Houston police have expanded their gang unit, set up a gang-murder task force, and allotted about $10.5 million in overtime pay to send more officers into high-crime areas. Houston law enforcement has also created the Violent Gang Initiative, comprising members of the department's gang unit, as well as agents from the FBI; the Bureau of Alcohol, Tobacco, Firearms, and Explosives; the DEA; and Immigrations and Customs Enforcement.

Think About It

1. Do you know anyone in a gang?

2. Will hiring more police help to control gangs? How about more and better economic opportunities?

Source: Skip Hollandsworth, "You Don't Want to Know What We Do after Dark," *Texas Monthly,* December 2006, p. 168.

This microlevel research provides the foundation for most of what we know about gangs. The long and informative history of ethnographic research done on American street gangs demonstrates the difficulties and pitfalls of doing research on deviant populations. Starting with Fredric Thrasher's seminal 1927 study of Chicago gangs and continuing through Jody Miller's significant study of female gangs in Columbus, Ohio, and St. Louis, Missouri, researchers have shown amazing ingenuity in discovering how gangs are structured and why they break the law.

Field researchers confront three problems when attempting to study gangs; the first is finding gang members who are willing to talk. Police officers, youth service workers, and teachers are able to identify gang members and sometimes have relationships with them that can help researchers talk to them. Once the trust of one key informant gang member is secured, this gang member can vouch for the researcher and introduce her or him to other gang members who can in turn provide further introductions. This method of finding research subjects, the **snowball sample,** is useful in getting into the gang subculture and targeting subjects who can provide relevant observations, opinions, and perspectives about gang activity. The crucial step in developing a snowball sample is gaining the trust and support of that first informant who will open doors into the gang and provide not only access, but also safety. Without this connection, the researcher would probably meet with suspicion, distrust, and resistance.[19]

A second concern of field research has to do with **generalizability.** When studying one particular gang, it's risky to attribute the findings to other gangs, especially in other places. Although the findings from studying a particular gang might be rich

snowball sample
A method of field research in which information is gathered by asking each person interviewed to suggest additional people for interviewing.

generalizability
The degree to which the results of an individual study and/or investigation sample can be applied to other studies and samples.

in detail and reveal intimate and fascinating insights, the likelihood that these findings can be transferred to other gangs in other cities is low. This doesn't mean that the research is flawed but only that it needs to be carefully considered before generalizations are made.

A third limitation of field studies has to do with the researcher's effect on the setting. Merely by being there and recording observations or interviews, the researcher can subtly influence the responses or behaviors of the subjects.[20] In sociology, this is called the **Hawthorne effect.** For example, the gang members might decide against a drive-by shooting or robbery because they think the researcher will report them to the police or, at the very least, record their behaviors in less-than-flattering terms.

We should be aware of the issues that are inherent in doing gang research, but we shouldn't be quick to dismiss the value of what has been reported about gangs. As gangs have become a very serious problem in many large and medium-sized cities, scholars have invested a great deal of time and attention into learning why gangs form and how they can be controlled.

Hawthorne effect
The tendency of research subjects not to act as they normally would as a result of their awareness of being studied.

Bad Influences: Delinquency, Peers, and Group Activity

By definition, gang delinquency is group behavior. To fully understand gangs, it is necessary to appreciate how and why juveniles pursue peer friendships and how nongang groups avoid becoming enmeshed in delinquent behavior.

American society is very much an age-graded society. This means that we mainly interact with others of our own age. This is particularly true during childhood, when schools group students into classes according to age. Occasionally, some students might advance a grade level or two because of exceptional ability, and other students who do not make satisfactory progress might fall behind and have to retake a grade. We see the same age grading among the elderly who move to retirement communities or nursing homes, where others around them share their concerns for medical care and safety.

For young people, this constant exposure to others who share their inexperience, immaturity, and long-term perspective means they might be occasionally tempted into delinquent behavior when adults are not around to supervise their decisions. As young people get opportunities through school and recreational activities to develop relationships outside the family, these peer bonds become extremely important to their emotional development. Part of growing up involves cutting the strings to our parents and finding new freedom to make decisions, be they good or bad.[21] Significantly, some research has shown that for youths who join gangs, stable membership—meaning that the youth joins the gang regularly and for good—typically occurs at age 13, exactly the time that puberty begins changing the child into an adult, and the child begins to seek separation from his or her parents.[22]

Generally, children and adolescents form cliques that center around activities, geography, or intimate feelings. For example, the eighth-grade basketball team, street-corner hustlers, computer club, or staff at a fast-food restaurant might find they have more in common with each other than they do with their families or classmates. These friendship groups establish norms that dictate appropriate styles of dress, how members should express themselves, and attitudes toward breaking the law. It is little wonder that parents are constantly concerned with their children's friends. Gradually, a child's friends play an increasing role in forming the child's values, and as parents lose control, they fear that their son or daughter will fall in with the wrong crowd.[23]

Teenagers in gangs are more likely to break the law than those who are not. Although this statement seems so obviously true that it's redundant to even make it, an important distinction should be considered. This distinction sets up a classic chicken-and-egg dilemma: Does delinquency make youths more likely to join a gang, or does gang membership tempt youths into delinquency?[24] The answers to these questions are yes and yes. Because juvenile delinquents often have codelinquents, they tend to develop close relationships that take on ganglike features. Loyalty to one another, rejection of conventional society, and increasing social isolation from schools

Figure 12-2 **Level of gang activity.**

and family mean that it is a short step for delinquent youths to become involved with existing gangs or to begin one of their own. Additionally, once in a gang, fighting, drug use, drug sales, motor vehicle theft, and larceny are all activities that youths are encouraged to commit to become respected members.[25]

There is evidence that boys who join gangs are more delinquent before they join than are boys who do not join gangs. Also, teenagers in gangs participate in more delinquency than those who are not in gangs. But just as delinquent acts increase significantly for boys who join a gang, they also decrease once the boy leaves the gang, dropping to the level prior to when the boy joined the gang.[26] The activity, then, looks a lot like Figure 12-2.

Basically, delinquent peers commit more delinquency together than apart. This is because young people, especially teenagers, have a desperate need to fit in with their peer groups. Those who participate in deviant behaviors, such as drug use and delinquency, seek out others who do the same to get a sense of belonging. One reason that gangs become so highly structured with symbols, signs, and rules is that the gang is replacing other institutions such as the family, school, and community. Belonging to a gang provides the youth with a sense of identity, a supportive network of friends, and a feeling of love and purpose. As some gang members get older and move into more conventional relationships, such as marriages and jobs, they replace the functions the gang plays in their lives, and eventually their involvement declines.[27] For those youths who have trouble finding these more conventional relationships, the possibility of a criminal career looms, especially if they have been periodically incarcerated and exposed to other, perhaps more serious delinquents.

One obvious strategy for helping young people avoid gangs is to ensure that they choose their friends wisely. Getting children involved in prosocial activities, such as sports, extracurricular activities, church groups, and employment, can take up their discretionary time and creative energies so that they have little opportunity or need to seek out delinquent friends.[28] Additionally, parental supervision can play an important role in helping youngsters make good choices in whom to hang out with. Parents can be instrumental in spotting early gang activity (see Figure 12-3). However, not all youths have equal support from parents and schools, and some are left on their own to occupy their time and choose their friends and activities. Those who live in disadvantaged neighborhoods without legitimate afterschool activities or whose parents are both working find more occasions to participate in delinquent behaviors than those youths with more conventionally structured lives.[29]

Some youths fail to find supportive friends in conventional society because their peers reject them. As children form cliques, they might adopt rigid rules about who and what is acceptable and cool, and those who are the slightest bit different might be left out. When a youth's family moves to a new town, a youth might have trouble

A Parent's Quick Reference Card
Recognizing and Preventing Gang Involvement

This quick reference guide provides common warning signs of gang involvement, but may not be all-encompassing. Parents should look for multiple signs to indicate possible gang involvement because some of these indicators alone, such as clothes or musical preferences, are also common among youth not involved in gangs. Parents are encouraged to familiarize themselves with local gang symbols, seek help early, and consider contacting school personnel, local law enforcement, faith leaders, and community organizations for additional assistance.

Warning Signs That Your Child May Be Involved with a Gang

- Admits to "hanging out" with kids in gangs

- Shows an unusual interest in one or two particular colors of clothing or a particular logo

- Has an unusual interest in gangster-influenced music, videos, movies, or websites.

- Uses unusual hand signals to communicate with friends

- Has specific drawings or gang symbols on school books, clothes, walls, or tattoos

- Comes home with unexplained physical injuries (fighting-related bruises, injuries to hand/knuckles)

- Has unexplained cash or goods, such as clothing or jewelry

- Carries a weapon

- Has been in trouble with the police

- Exhibits negative changes in behavior such as:

  * Withdrawing from family

  * Declining school attendance, performance, behavior

  * Staying out late without reason

  * Displaying an unusual desire for secrecy

  * Exhibiting signs of drug use

  * Breaking rules consistently

  * Speaking in gang-style slang

What Parents Can Do to Prevent Gang Involvement

- Spend quality time with your child

- Get involved in your child's school activities

- Be a positive role model and set the right example

- Know your child's friends and their families

- Encourage good study habits

- Teach your child how to cope with peer pressure

- Help your child develop good conflict/resolution skills (See www.safeyouth.org/scripts/teens/conflict.asp)

- Encourage your child to participate in positive afterschool activities with adult supervision (recreation centers, organized sports, youth groups)

- Take action in your neighborhood (create a neighborhood alliance, report and remove graffiti)

- Talk with your child about the dangers and consequences of gang involvement. Let your child know that you don't want to see him or her hurt or arrested. Explain to your child that he or she should NOT:

  * Associate with gang members

  * Attend parties or social events sponsored by gangs

  * Use hand signs, symbols, or language that is meaningful to gangs

  * Wear clothing, including specific colors, which may have meaning to gangs in your area

To obtain details on COPS programs, call the COPS Office Response Center at 800.421.6770

www.cops.usdoj.gov   www.fbi.gov   www.ojjdp.ncjrs.org

Figure 12-3   The Office of Community Oriented Policing Services produces these reference cards with tips for parents on how to recognize if their child is involved with a gang and how to prevent gang involvement.

Source: U.S. Department of Justice, Office of Community Oriented Policing Services, www.cops.usdoj.gov/Default.asp?Item=1383.

replacing the old set of friends and the niche he or she had carved out in the school's social structure.[30] New classmates might find the youth's clothing to be old-fashioned or speech to have a funny accent. Youths who experiment with body piercing or tattoos might discover that their new classmates consider such fashion statements to be silly or passé. Finding ways to fit into an entirely new social system can be overwhelming and propel the youth into seeking out others who don't fit in. Those who are socially rejected often use delinquent behaviors as a method of establishing and reinforcing their deviant status in school.[31]

Jumping-In: Joining the Gang

The reasons that young people join gangs can provide insight into how to find more conventional activities to replace the functions that gangs play in young people's lives. Not all gangs fill the same needs, and the range of youths who engage in gang activities spans the continuum of race, social class, sex, and age. Here, we discuss several reasons why a youth might join a gang with the understanding that no single reason is sufficient to describe all youths. Also, it's probable that some youngsters will have many reasons for joining a gang, which might be categorized as pushes and pulls. Some factors push a youth toward joining a gang, such as protection, friendship, and family tradition, while others pull the youth into the gang, such as status, money, and excitement.[32]

- **Pull: The gang as a buffer against poverty**   One of the most obvious features of gangs is that many of them comprise youths from disadvantaged neighborhoods. In a society where wealth and privilege are constantly celebrated, these youths find that they can't compete for status because of their families' social and economic situation. Rather than accept their circumstances, these youths join gangs to provide themselves with the things that their families can't. Gang activity gives the youths a certain status at school and in the community, because the gangs are seen as exclusive clubs that not everyone can join. In the view of gang members, gangs become elite organizations that only those with the right set of skills are allowed into. These skills might not be the types of skills that allow them to excel in school or get a job, but they are valued for gang activity. The willingness to fight, break the law, use drugs, and have an attitude that rejects the conventional society's values is useful for gang membership. The gang provides not only a sense of belonging and status, but also material items. Gangs that shoplift, commit robberies, or sell drugs can give the members the money, clothes, and other goods that allow them to feel on an economic par with their more conventional peers.[33]

- **Pull: The gang as a tribe**   The social organization of gangs suggests that they assuage a deep psychological need to belong to an extended group that provides meaning and a way of life. Anthropologists have noted how groups, clans, and tribes have rituals and ceremonies for young males to mark the passing from adolescent to adult.[34] These ceremonies or rituals might be formal rites of passage or simply a recognition that the youngster has done something significant and can now leave the mother and start hanging out with the tribe's adult males.[35] Although it might be a stretch of theory to contend that gangs are simply modern tribes, it's worth considering the social organization and rituals of gangs as such. One measure of a group is the types of symbols worn by members to denote status. Although there might be a very formal system of symbols akin to rank insignias in the military, some group members select their own accoutrements, and the very act of wearing the gang colors or getting a gang–related tattoo becomes a mark of status. Gangs might have elaborate or simple initiation rites that require newcomers to prove that they have what it takes to belong. These rites might be as simple as showing how much one is willing to sacrifice for membership by submitting to a "beat down," in which gang members beat up the inductee to gauge how much heart and fight he or she has.[36] Some gangs also have a generational component. In cities that have had gangs for many years, brothers, uncles, fathers, and sons are all members of a gang at one time or another. The gang in these neighborhoods acts like a community club (although somewhat more deviant) and provides its members with a sense of history, commitment, and belonging. Youngsters join gangs in these circumstances because they see it as being loyal to the family and wish to carry on the protection of the neighborhood, much like a child of a more conventional upbringing might join the military out of a sense of patriotism.

- **Push: Gangs as a response to social change** Sociologists use the term **anomie** to refer to the individual and societal feeling of aimlessness, alienation, or normlessness that occurs when there is rapid social change in a society. When change upsets the old rules and the old status systems, people look for new and emerging norms to guide them. Two good examples of this are found in the 19th–century gangs that existed in New York City and the gangs that emerged during the late 1960s. Both of these periods saw a tremendous amount of social upheaval. In New York City in the late 1800s, European immigrants were entering the United States by the shipload at Ellis Island, bringing with them the languages, habits, and customs of their homelands. In the late 1960s, it seemed that the young generation was bent on breaking, then rewriting, all the social rules that their parents had carefully constructed and followed. Both of these periods gave birth to gangs or ganglike institutions, some of which are still with us today, such as the Mafia, the Crips, and the Bloods (these last two are discussed later in the chapter). The attraction to joining a gang is that it provides young people a visible and seemingly viable way of negotiating life's challenges in times of stress and change. When suspended from school, kicked out of the home by a new stepparent, or confronted with moving to a new city, a young person can see gang involvement as an attractive way to find certainty and structure.[37]

- **Pull: Gangs as deviant "birds of a feather"** Some youngsters join gangs because that's where they can find others who share their deviant world view. Some research has found that aggressive children make friends with other, similarly aggressive children by the age of 10.[38] For those who are selfish, have few feelings of empathy or guilt, and prefer to manipulate others for their self–gain, the gang provides like-minded others who not only tolerate these behaviors, but share them. Many youths feel rejected by conventional society and suffer from limited life skills and low self-esteem. By participating in delinquent and criminal activities with fellow gang members, these youths can feel that they are in control of their situation and can define their behaviors as supportive of the subcultural goals of the gang, thus increasing their feelings of self-worth.[39]

- **Pull: Gangs as success** Failure in school, specifically the middle grades, when children are entering puberty, can be a warning of later gang involvement, especially when paired with peer rejection.[40] Or, more harshly, you are getting bad grades and no one likes you. These devastating things, especially when they are happening at such a vulnerable, malleable time as puberty, can lead to the aforementioned pull, or the grouping of deviant "birds of a feather." Children who are getting failing grades, who have behavior problems, who tend to be aggressive, and who have been rejected by the prosocial in-crowds will probably find each other and reinforce what they consider to be positive and exciting about each other. Not coincidentally, these are the things they consider to be positive and exciting about themselves.

- **Push: Gangs as a rational choice** Some youths feel at a disadvantage in conventional society because of their race, ethnicity, social class, or other variables beyond their control. They do not see life as a level playing field when they

Instant Recall from Chapter 7

anomie

A condition in which a people or society undergoes a breakdown of social norms and values. Also, personal anxiety and isolation produced by rapidly shifting moral and cultural values.

observe middle-class and affluent peers being able to take better advantage of legitimate opportunities. These youths think gang activity is an acceptable compensation for the discrimination they feel. Some gang members break the law with their eyes wide open and with the intention of profiting from it. The gang is simply a mechanism for doing better and more lucrative crimes. Gang membership provides the youths with a ready–made set of partners in crime to party with, as well as a way to find sexual liaisons with the gang's network of sisters, relatives, and neighbors. Gang members see this extended social network as something akin to a family, and the choice to join is considered rational. Gang life can be fun and exciting, prompting youths to seek out gang activity as a release from the boredom of living in disadvantaged neighborhoods where there is little to do. Additionally, some might make a choice to join a gang because they are victimized by other gangs in the area. Gang membership can provide physical security. This security can be especially important in female decisions to join a gang. Whether it is an all–girl gang or an ancillary of a male gang, membership can signal to others that messing with this young woman means messing with the gang.[41]

- **Push: Gangs as the only game in town**   Some youths don't have specific reasons for joining a gang. They don't even realize that they are choosing delinquent behavior. Like fish in water, they are clueless about alternative lifestyles. In many communities, gangs are such stable features of the institutional landscape that the question is not whether to join a gang, but which one. In communities where the governmental, educational, family, and religious leaders have failed to provide adequate education and recreational facilities, the gang becomes the one organization that speaks to the problems and needs of young, disenfranchised people.[42]

Instant Recall from Chapter 11
aging out

In juvenile justice, reaching the age at which the system no longer serves a person, usually age 18.

Gangs fill a perceived need in the lives of their members for a period of time. Eventually, most youths leave the gang environment. For the most part they are **aging out,** meaning, as they grow older, they find other activities that are more important than being in the gang. They find gainful employment, get married and have children, move to a new city, or simply tire of the gang lifestyle. With the exception of some intergenerational gangs, the gang culture is a young person's game.[43]

Types of Gangs

Gangs vary in a number of ways. Size, racial and ethnic makeup, criminal activity, organization, and geographic location are all factors that scholars use to differentiate among types of gangs. Although many gangs will demonstrate stability across these factors, some gangs change as circumstances change. For instance, a gang might allow females to participate at some level and then change its attitude and exclude them from gang status and allow them to participate only as girlfriends. Likewise, a gang might gradually move its geographic base as neighborhoods change in terms of racial composition or social class. As gang members get older, they might participate in more serious delinquent activities.[44]

With these dynamic changes in mind, let's now look at developing a typology of gangs based on race. Most gangs are racially homogeneous groups that are largely the result of urban geographic segregation. For example, ethnically defined neighborhoods such as San Francisco's Chinatown produce Asian gangs. The ethnic background of gangs has changed over time. Most of the Irish, German, and Italian youth gangs that were prevalent in the first half of the 20th century no longer exist in any quantity. These groups have largely been assimilated into American society and are no longer subject to the economic and racial discrimination that they previously experienced. Today, gangs comprise other groups that are readily identifiable by perceived racial and cultural characteristics.[45]

Two armed members of the Black Panther party stand outside the capitol building in Sacramento, California, in 1967 while a police officer checks a document. *(Courtesy Corbis/Bettmann)*

Black and Hispanic Gangs

There are black gangs in many cities in the United States; however, Los Angeles is home to the two largest and best known. Bitter rivals, the Crips and the Bloods have franchised their gangs to several other communities in California and beyond. It is difficult to know the exact size of these gangs, but because estimates of their combined membership exceed 30,000, they have been labeled as supergangs. Other gangs in large cities, such as the Folks in Chicago, are also included in the supergang category, but it is worth looking at each of these gangs separately to discern how they vary. It is also important to note that although these gangs aren't necessarily youth gangs, they recruit their members at very young ages, thus contributing to delinquency.

- **Crips**   The inspiration for the Crips was the 1960s Black Panther political party that became famous for their confrontations with authorities over a number of social issues. The Black Panthers transcended traditional street gangs and was able to promote itself as a prosocial group that defended disadvantaged people in the black community. Additionally, they provided a free breakfast program in some cities and generated a tremendous amount of goodwill from the community and the press, if not from the police. The party's Los Angeles chapter, established in 1968, was the model for several other gangs, such as the Avenues and Baby Avenues, who eventually became the Crips.[46] The exact origin of the name Crips is something of a mystery, but Tim Delaney suggests that it is either a mistake caused by the poor handwriting of one of its leaders, Stanley "Tookie" Williams, who was trying to write "Cribs," or a spelling mistake by another founder, Raymond Lee Washington.

  Currently, the Crips are involved in a number of illegal enterprises, such as murder, armed robbery, and the distribution of illegal drugs, and have been selling crack cocaine ever since it appeared in the 1980s. Stanley "Tookie" Williams sat on California's death row from 1981 to 2005, where he wrote a series of children's books. Williams publicly denounced his gang affiliation and was nominated for a Nobel peace prize but was executed in 2005 for the 1979 murders of four people during an armed robbery.[47]

The Eastside Crips arriving at the funeral of Stanley "Tookie" Williams in Los Angeles, December 2005. *(Courtesy Lucas Jackson, Landov LLC)*

There are fewer Bloods than Crips. Here Bloods members flash their gang signs. *(Courtesy Steve Starr, Corbis/Bettmann)*

According to Delaney, the Crips are the largest street gang in the world and have extended their reach from Los Angeles to every large U.S. city. Their organizational structure has become so unwieldy that the various Crips factions battle each other almost as much as they fight other gangs.[48]

- **Bloods** The Bloods originated in Compton, California, and have a severe disadvantage in numbers when compared to the Crips. There are three Crips to every Blood, but the Bloods are able to compete because they are so violent.[49] While primarily black, the Bloods, unlike the Crips, have accepted members from other racial groups, including Hispanic, white, and Asian. Like the Crips, the Bloods have spread nationwide. They are extremely strong in the Northeast, where they are affiliated with a gang based in Riker's Island Prison in New York called the United Blood Nation. In 2000, they had at least 500 members in New York City alone.[50]

The Bloods are known for their violence against other gangs, as well as against innocent civilians. To become a member, the individual must "blood in," which entails spilling someone else's blood. This is typically done by walking up to a stranger and slashing him or her across the face with a box cutter. In 1997 during a three-day sweep, the New York Police Department arrested 167 gang members and attributed 135 slashings to gang initiation rituals.[51]

The Bloods sell a variety of drugs, including heroin, LSD, PCP, and crack cocaine. The Bloods also commit other offenses, including robberies, car thefts, rapes, and murders. In addition to their presence on the streets of major cities, they are one of the most feared prison gangs in the United States. They take over the prison's underground economy and intimidate other inmates into joining the gang. In California, the Bloods and the Crips are routinely sent to different prisons because of the certainty of violence should they find themselves together on the prison yard or the cafeteria.[52] As the Bloods expand their territory into smaller cities, they bring their drug distribution enterprise and a reputation for backing it up with deadly violence. Because the Crips are expanding alongside the Bloods, drug- and gang-related violence will continue to be a problem in smaller cities as well as major ones.

- **The People, Latin Kings, and Vice Lords** Two large gangs based in the Midwest comprise what is loosely known as the People. The People Nation and the Folk Nation represent a different form of gang structure than found with the Bloods and Crips. First, People–style gangs are more racially heterogeneous than the California gangs. The People includes individuals from a variety of racial and ethnic backgrounds. Additionally, these supergangs comprise smaller gangs that have their own names and can change allegiance from one supergang to another. They are found in Chicago and Milwaukee primarily but have expanded to other cities, such as Detroit, Michigan; Cleveland, Ohio; and Columbus, Ohio.

The largest of the People-style subgangs is the Latin Kings. It is mainly composed of Hispanic youths, particularly Mexican and Puerto Rican, and is one of the oldest and most powerful gangs in the country. Originally based in Chicago, they formed alliances with other gangs such as the Vice Lords and grew to as many as 25,000 members in cities and states across the East and Midwest, including New York, Connecticut, New Jersey, Iowa, Indiana, Ohio, Florida, and Massachusetts. Of particular interest is the Latin Kings' well-formed organizational structure, which is patterned after the military. The hierarchical structures include foot soldiers and officers with titles such as lieutenant and sergeant. The Latin Kings have religious and mystical overtones that they mix with gang symbols and activities and a belief that God looks favorably on them because of their ethnic background. They are the most violent of the Hispanic gangs and participate in many criminal activities such as drug and weapons sales, assault, robbery, intimidation, and murder.[53]

The Vice Lords is another gang that fits under the People umbrella. The Vice Lords is a predominantly black gang that started in the 1960s in Chicago. Somewhat like the Black Panther party in California, the Vice Lords had overtones of a prosocial gang that attempted to eliminate crime and violence in the community and increase legitimate job opportunities in urban areas for disadvantaged youths. They even secured $1.4 million in federal antipoverty funds, which ultimately was channeled into illegal gang activities. The structure of the Vice Lords differs in some respects from that of other supergangs. Local leaders command the respect of members based on their power to persuade, rather than on violence. Consequently, leadership within the gang is always in flux, and power is based on how many followers a leader can point to at any one time.[54]

- **Folks** The Folks is a supergang that resulted from a coalition between the Simon City Royals, a white gang well known for burglary in Chicago, and the Black Gangster Disciples. The Folks are aligned with the Crips, while their rivals, the People, are loosely connected to the Bloods. Started in Chicago, the Black Gangster Disciples are estimated to have 30,000 members. Their founder, Larry Hoover, is serving a life sentence but is still considered to be the gang's leader. The Black Gangster Disciples are a sophisticated criminal organization that utilizes legitimate false-front businesses to conceal their drug distribution network. Stores and businesses such as car washes, music stores, barbershops, and apartment buildings are outlets for the drug enterprise or launder the money from criminal endeavors. In 1997, it was estimated that the gang's revenues were close to $100 million a year. When the revenues for all Chicago gangs are considered, the federal officials estimate the profits for drug sales exceed $1 billion.[55]

Asian Gangs

Traditionally, Asian gangs in the United States were confined to the various Chinatowns of the nation's largest cities. These gangs were derived from secret Chinese societies that formed in the 1600s. These Chinese triads or tongs were originally formed as patriotic and nationalistic organizations in China, but they were viewed by U.S. law enforcement as criminal organizations. Over 80,000 members of triad gangs are active in China, Taiwan, and the United States.[56] Because they are extremely secretive organizations, little is known about their actual numbers and activities. The criminal activities of the triads are widespread and include not only traditional gang activities, but also extend to more high-tech crimes, such as credit-card fraud, counterfeiting, software piracy, human smuggling, prostitution, loan sharking, and home-invasion robbery.[57] The most common crime committed by triads is the extortion of Asian businesses and

Four young Cambodian gang members in Long Beach, California, flash gang signs. *(Courtesy A. Ramey, PhotoEdit Inc.)*

other wealthy Asians. Triads are a juvenile delinquency problem because they recruit members as young as 13. Unlike many gangs in which members age out when they reach their 20s and get legitimate jobs and marry, those involved in triads stay in the gang until they are well into their 30s.

Tongs are Chinese social clubs that law enforcement officials suspect of being associated with illegal gambling, drug trafficking, extortion, and robbery. They started in places like San Francisco's Chinatown in the 1860s, where they ran gambling houses, opium dens, and brothels. They perform many positive functions for the Chinese community in the United States but are so secretive that it's difficult to judge the balance between their prosocial activities and their criminal and delinquent interests.[58]

One of the most interesting facets of contemporary Chinese gangs is the competition from the arrival of new immigrants. Those coming to U.S. shores in recent times have little in common with the members of old established gangs who speak English and who have access to legitimate employment opportunities and education. The newer Asian immigrants find much of American society, even Chinese–American society, closed to them, so they form gangs that don't honor decades-old agreements, protocols, and territorial claims. These contemporary Chinese gangs, which started to form in the late 1960s, borrowed their patterns of behavior from the traditional triads and from watching movies. This has given them an atmosphere based on clichés and stereotypes, rather than on necessity and tradition. Some new arrivals are able to enter the older gangs because of their willingness to provide the muscle for criminal enterprises that entail a high risk of violence or detection.

Some of the newer gangs have discarded the secrecy of traditional Chinese gangs and have developed styles of dress and tattoos that allow them to be readily identified as gang members. In New York, the American Eagles gang favors tight, straight-legged jeans and satin jackets, and its members bleach the tips of their hair blond. Although a relatively small gang, their visibility makes them appear more prevalent, and they are easier for victims to identify and for police officers to track. Chinese gang members have now adopted many of the accoutrements of the hip-hop culture and have their own rappers, who brag about being shot and about their run-ins with the law.[59]

Yakuza is the collective name for 2,500 Japanese gangs. These gangs have an estimated 200,000 members worldwide and are active in the United States, primarily on the West Coast and in Hawaii. The *Yakuza* are an exclusively male organization, preferring that women be wives and mothers rather than gang members. Its roots can be traced to the 14th century when outcasts banded together for protection from the authorities. *Yakuza* members are heavily involved in prostitution, including the smuggling of underaged girls for wealthy businessmen, and are deeply involved in weapons trafficking, particularly to Japan, where gun laws are extremely strict. The *Yakuza* invest their profits in legitimate businesses and have large holdings in several companies that are traded on the New York Stock Exchange. In the United States, they commit offenses generally within the Japanese–American community and are extremely secretive and difficult for law enforcement to infiltrate. Delaney relates an interesting way in which the *Yakuza* discipline those who violate the rules. Rather than killing violators, the *Yakuza* perform a ceremony called a *yubizume*, in which the offender cuts off his little finger and presents it to the insulted party as an apology. The offender is then kicked out of the gang forever.[60]

In the past 20 years, the Asian gang problem has shifted from those controlled by traditional Chinese and Japanese semilegitimate organizations to newer gangs comprising youths from Vietnam, Laos, and Cambodia. These youths are feeling the stress common in many recent immigrant groups for which there isn't a large enclave of fellow countrymen with established, stable ethnic subcultures. They experience problems in school and in the community because of language and cultural differences and turn to gangs to find protection, identity, and ways of coping with a new and strange society.

Asian youths are joining gangs in increasing numbers and engage in a variety of crimes but seem to specialize in home invasions. Home invasions entail breaking into the homes of wealthy families and terrorizing them until they produce money, jewelry, and other valuables. The perpetrators will beat the men and rape the female family members in crime sprees that can last for hours. The victims, who are also Asian, are reluctant to call the police, because in the countries they come from, the police are often corrupt and linked to criminal organizations.[61]

Vietnamese gangs are credited with being the most violent of the Asian gangs. Their main base of operation is in Orange County, California, which has a robust Vietnamese population. Vietnam does not have a history of organized criminal gangs, but Vietnamese who migrated to the United States after the Vietnam War were mostly linked to the South Vietnamese government, which was riddled with corruption, bribery, and violence. As new immigrants, the parents of gang members worked long hours to obtain an economic toehold in the United States, and the children were subjected to racial discrimination and hostility in the schools. Not surprisingly, these children coalesced into secretive and violent gangs that preyed on legitimate Vietnamese businesses and restaurants. The Vietnamese gangs, which are only loosely organized, sometimes form what is known as a "hasty gang" that is quickly put together for a brief crime spree and then disbands. This makes gathering intelligence on the gangs a difficult task for police gang units.[62]

Finally, there are a number of Filipino gangs on the West Coast and in Las Vegas. Large numbers of Filipinos were admitted to the United States because of their backgrounds in nursing or the military. Many Filipino men served in the U.S. Army during the Vietnam War and were rewarded with permission to move to the United States. Because of a shortage of nurses during the 1970s, immigration laws became more liberal for nurses, and many Filipino women took advantage of the economic and social opportunities available in U.S. hospitals. By 1988, 14 percent of all gang-related incidents in the United States involved Filipino youths, who committed robberies, drug sales, car theft, and drive-by shootings.[63]

As the Asian population in the United States grows, so does the gang problem. Although Asians have long been considered the "model minority" because of their commitment to working hard and achieving success, there is an underside to immigration in which some youths quickly shed the traditions of the old culture and adopt the behaviors of the street as a way to survive and protect themselves in circumstances in which they are continually victimized. As the more recent Asian immigrants are assimilated into American society, it is likely that the gang behavior will decrease. However, this does not mean that Asians, as well as youths from every other racial group in the country, will not participate in gang activity. At some point, gangs might not be organized according to race as they are now but will depend more on geography or a specific delinquent and criminal behavior.

White Gangs

White youths have traditionally joined gangs as a way to escape poverty or for protection from other gangs. White youths commonly join mixed-race gangs where they are in the minority. Although whites have an easier time being assimilated into the dominant culture and overcoming the effects of poverty by doing well in school or finding gainful employment, they often reject society and find meaning, satisfaction, and excitement in gang life. Three types of white gangs bear examination: skinheads, stoners, and taggers. Each of these types of gangs provides white youths with alternative ways of coping in a society where they are unable to find an outlet for their angry and violent behavior.

- **Skinheads**   Skinheads get their name because they shave their heads. They might also wear steel-toed boots and tight, straight-legged jeans. They pattern themselves after similar groups in Europe and commonly adhere to a racist agenda, claiming that minorities get preferential treatment in the United States and that whites should remain "racially pure" and not intermarry with other races. Although some skinhead gangs aren't racist, this concern with losing the numerical and social advantage that whites enjoy is a recurring theme in most skinhead gangs. They picture themselves as neo-Nazis and often use the swastika in their literature or as tattoos. Additionally, they look on Adolph Hitler as a visionary whose racism and anti-Semitic teachings are worthy of following. Skinhead music also celebrates the plight of working-class youth and is often racist, misogynistic, and violent. In areas with significant immigration from Hispanic and Asian countries, skinhead gangs often form in an attempt to protect what they see as a threatened white culture. In addition to being racist, most skinhead groups are homophobic and quick to use violence against gays and lesbians.[64]

- **Stoners** Stoners are youths who come from middle–class or upper–middle–class families and are unable to succeed in traditional ways. They are commonly high-school dropouts who exist on the fringes of conventional society. Funded by parents and minimum–wage jobs, stoners are loosely organized groups that are heavily into drugs and alcohol. Like other juveniles, they commit burglary, larceny, and sell drugs, and their drugs of choice are speed, LSD, rock cocaine, and PCP. Additionally, they are likely to inhale anything from glue to paint thinner. They might declare their independence and counter-culture attitudes by harming animals and committing ritual–style offenses, such as desecrating churches or graveyards. Their music and dress can have overtones of Satanism, and their purpose is to declare their rejection of traditional values. They don't compete with street gangs for territorial dominance and don't engage in high levels of violence. Rather, they congregate in smaller groups and are sometimes indistinguishable from other youths hanging out in the local mall. What makes stoners fall under the rubric of being a gang are the offenses they commit and the reliance on drugs and alcohol to define their worldview.[65]

A boy tags a building in Los Angeles.

(Courtesy Robert Yager, Getty Images Inc. — Stone Allstock)

- **Taggers** Taggers use graffiti to call attention to themselves. They use spray paint to deface road signs, walls, railroad cars, or sidewalks. Their goal is to leave their mark where other people can see it. Although most people are oblivious to the meanings of this graffiti, tagger crews have a highly structured symbolic language that allows them to recognize each other's work and appreciate the skill or risk it took to mark the surfaces. The tagger subculture in Southern California predominantly comprises young, white males. They range in age from 10 years old up to the early twenties, but most teenagers stop tagging at 15 or 16. An estimated 600 tagger crews with upward of about 30,000 youths live in Southern California. With numbers like this, it is impossible for police to keep track of all the taggers or to prevent their actions. The taggers' goal is to mark as many places as possible. Extra status is gained by putting graffiti in hard-to-reach, guarded, or dangerous places. Tagger crews will do battle with each other not by violence, but by attempting to outdo each other in putting their graffiti in more places. Some taggers carry weapons for protection from other tagger crews, but violence isn't the norm. Taggers are hard to identify because they aspire to a chameleon–like quality so that they can put their tags on surfaces and get away without being noticed. Like the stoners, taggers aren't particularly dangerous. Their delinquency is painting graffiti on public and private property, but they do not engage in gang warfare and drive-by shootings. Next to graffiti, their most common offense is larceny, whereby they steal a lot of spray paint. They have an almost inexhaustible appetite for paint, and many large retail stores have had to take special precautions to prevent taggers from wiping out their inventories.[66]

Female Gangs

Historically, gang activity has been considered a young man's game. Females were not considered full gang members and existed only in ancillary roles that served the male members' interests. This secondary gang status was thought to be primarily as a sex object, with limited participation in delinquent activities.

Little is known about female participation in gangs, but a number of surveys estimate that around 10 percent of gang activity can be attributed to girls and young women. Other studies put the figure closer to 30 percent. Female gangsters participate in criminal activities as part of male gangs and also can be found operating all-female gangs. Although we don't know the exact number of female gang members, we do know that they participate in a variety of ways and can be just as violent as male gang members.[67]

Females report a number of reasons for joining a gang. A primary reason is protection. Young women are often the victims of abuse by fathers or other family members, and joining a gang serves as a refuge from unwanted attention.[68] Often, female runaways can choose only between joining a gang and becoming the property of a pimp. The gang gives them higher status and more control over their sexual activities. Rebellious girls join gangs as a way to spite what they perceive to be overprotective parents. Sometimes the reason a young woman joins a gang is because her boyfriend is already a member, and she can either follow him into the gang or lose him to another female gang member. Finally, economic reality provides females with a reason to join a gang. By participating in gang behaviors such as shoplifting, drug sales, and larcenies, the girls can improve their marginal economic status and obtain the stylish clothes, fast food, and other items valued by teenagers. The females most likely to join a gang are those who suffer from low self-esteem, come from dysfunctional families, and have a history of victimization. Unlike males, who are often seeking thrills and action, females typically join gangs for defensive reasons.[69]

Females aren't recruited into gangs in the same way as males. They typically are not coerced or forced to join but do so because they have family ties in the gang or seek a buffer from poverty. At an age when many teenagers are experiencing major biological and physical changes, joining a gang gives girls a sense of commitment and belonging that is absent in other areas of their lives. There are three types of initiation rites for females who join gangs.

- **Jumped-in** This involves physical fighting. Sometimes the girl must fight other gang members, and because she is outnumbered, she inevitably gets beaten severely. The idea is to test her willingness and ability to fight. Sometimes being jumped–in means the girl has to commit some offense, such as assault on someone from a rival gang or a law enforcement authority. Drive–by shootings, face slashing, or muggings are ways females can show their willingness and toughness.[70]

- **Born-in** Because of family ties, a recruit might be admitted to the gang without having to prove her toughness. Sometimes with the blessing of established gang members, she can simply get some gang tattoos and verbally commit to the gang. Sometimes, these girls are second– or third–generation gang members who have been around the gang all their lives and are allowed to join as a matter of family status.

- **Trained–in or sexed–in** Here young women are required to have sex with several male gang members. The gang leaders have sex with her first, and others follow according to their rank. This is the least desirable way to become a gang member, and it carries a stigma. Girls who are trained-in seldom become fully accepted by other female gang members and might be continually abused by the males. It is certainly cause for a loss of respect, and these girls remain the most marginalized and exploited ones in the gang.[71]

Not every gang uses these methods of initiation, and the methods differ according to whether the individual is male or female. Female gang members fall into three categories: some are regular members of a mixed gang, some are members of independent female gangs, and some are auxiliaries to male gangs. These types of gang affiliation affect the type and seriousness of the female's delinquent or criminal behavior.[72]

With the exception of homicide, female gang members break the law at rates similar to that of males. Their offenses differ by type but not so much by frequency. For instance, Miller found that girl gangs in St. Louis, Missouri, and Columbus, Ohio, were as likely as boy gangs to commit larcenies, steal cars for joy riding, intimidate people, and commit vandalism. While they don't seek out violence in the same manner as boys, violence is part of gang life, and girls will use it to establish themselves within the gang culture and at school. Girls will sometimes be used by male gang members to help in fighting other gangs by seducing rival gang members in secluded areas so that the gang can jump them. Girls are also used to gather gang intelligence by sleeping with rival gang members.[73]

12.1 A CLOSER LOOK at JUVENILE ISSUES

OUTLAWING GANGS

Like many states, New Mexico has gang problems, with an estimated 310 gangs comprising about 8,000 members. Most of the gang members live in Bernalillo County, with some gangs going back four generations. To stem the rise of gang-related crime and violence, New Mexico considered (but did not pass) two new laws that were enacted in California.

- House Bill 60 would have made it a criminal offense to recruit others into a gang or for anyone to intimidate a member into staying in a gang.

- House Bill 65 added mandatory prison time of two to eight years to any felony sentence for an offender with a proven association with a gang.[1]

Law enforcement officials believe these laws would have helped fight gang activity and allowed them to put more gang members behind bars. The bills' detractors expressed concerns about civil liberties. After all, the First Amendment sets forth "the right of the people peaceably to assemble." Proving someone is recruiting for a gang is not easy, and it is even more difficult to determine if a group of people is assembling for bad purposes or not.

(Continued)

(Continued)

In Los Angeles, the public housing project Jordan Downs belongs to the Grape Street Crips, an established black gang. Jordan Downs has the highest rate of violent crime of Los Angeles's public housing projects, with 19 gang-related shootings and seven murders in January 2006. The Los Angeles Police Department has stepped up its antigang efforts with a 2005 injunction that allows the arrest of Grape Street Crips who are caught gathering in public.

The problem is that Jordan Downs is an old neighborhood, and the families there, as well as the gang, have coexisted for generations. As in any small town, everyone knows everyone else, and many of those people are in the gang, were in the gang, or know someone in the gang or who used to be in the gang.

As civil rights lawyer Connie Rice told the *Los Angeles Times*, "Anybody who's ever said hello to anybody in a gang is [considered] 'affiliated.'" The injunction can affect brothers riding together in their family's car or kids who walk to school together.

The original injunction applied to 16 gang members but allowed police to add others who met at least two of the nine "gang membership criteria," which include tattoos, nicknames, and style of dress. In nine months, the LAPD added nearly 300 names to the injunction and made 175 arrests for alleged violations, misdemeanors that can mean up to a $1,000 fine and a six-month jail term.[2]

The idea behind such injunctions is that the hassle of being arrested, getting booked, posting bail or being jailed, and returning to the street only to be arrested and sent through the process again will become too much trouble for gang members. The hope is that the gang members will simply lie low and stop breaking the law, leave the gang, or move on to where they are not hassled so much. So far, the third option seems to be the one many gang members are choosing. In La Mesa, California, the city council adopted an ordinance modeled on one in San Diego County that prohibits anyone from harassing a juvenile in or within 1,000 feet of parks, schools, and other public property. This is because police in La Mesa and nearby cities have said they are seeing increasing numbers of gang members who have been forced out of San Diego by court injunctions.[3]

Civil injunctions appear to be the most popular in California, a state that also has one of the worst gang problems.

- As of 2006, Fresno County, California, had three civil injunctions against specific gangs, including the Chankla Bulldogs, the Parkside Bulldogs, and the Modoc Boys. The most recent injunction has made it illegal for 21 members of the Modoc Boys to be together in public. Like the Los Angeles Jordan Downs injunction, the maximum penalty is a $1,000 fine and six months in jail. Police reported that the first injunction, against the Chankla Bulldogs, halved the crime rate in the gang's territory.[4]

The LAPD on Its Gang Injunctions

There are currently 29 active injunctions in the city involving 38 gangs. A gang injunction is a restraining order against a group. It is a civil suit that seeks a court order declaring the gang's public behavior a nuisance and asking for special rules directed toward its activity. Injunctions can address the neighborhood's gang problem before it reaches the level of felony crime activity.

Source: Los Angeles Police Department, www.lapdonline.org/gang_injunction/content_basic_SIEW/23424.

- In 2006, Anaheim, California, authorities got an injunction against the Boys from the Hood gang that prevented about 90 gang members from drinking in public, wearing gang clothing, associating in public with other gang members, and being out after 10 P.M.

- In 2006, a San Francisco judge extended an injunction against 22 alleged members of the Oakdale Mob that made it illegal for them to loiter in the Oakdale public housing area between midnight and 5:30 A.M. or to associate with each other there. The city attorney's lawsuit against the gang says about 50 members are suspects in at least 12 murders since 2003. Violations of the order could lead to up to five days in jail for each violation or a misdemeanor charge and six-month jail sentence.[5] The American Civil Liberties Union has sought to halt the injunction until the city notifies the alleged gang members and gives them a chance to challenge the order.[6]

Civil liberties concerns aside, a study by Cheryl Maxson, Karen Hennigan, and David Sloane offers three policy implications for gang injunctions.

- Injunctions might work in the short term, creating "modest immediate improvements in community safety and well-being."
- Police should be careful regarding the size of an injunction area and the type of gang targeted.
- An injunction might be more effective combined with efforts to improve neighborhood social organization and provide positive alternatives for gang members.[7]

1 Maggie Shepard, "A Void Filled by Danger," *Albuquerque Tribune*, February 11, 2006, p. A1.
2 Sandy Banks, "Injunction Has Community Feeling Handcuffed," *Los Angeles Times*, April 28, 2006, p. A1, Home Edition; David Reyes, "O. C. Judge Signs Injunction against Gang Members," *Los Angeles Times*, Home Edition, November 18, 2006, p. B4.
3 Liz Neely, "La Mesa Approves Law to Thwart Gang Activity," *San Diego Union-Tribune*, March 10, 2005, p. B1.
4 John Ellis, "Ruling to Keep Gang Members Apart," *Fresno Bee*, August 2, 2006, State and Regional News.
5 Jaxon Van Derbeken, "Judge to Extend Limits on Alleged Gang Members," *San Francisco Chronicle*, November 23, 2006, p. B1.
6 Jaxon Van Derbeken, "ACLU Works to Gang Injunction Plan," *San Francisco Chronicle*, October 27, 2006, p. B3.
7 Cheryl L. Maxson, Karen M. Hennigan, and David C. Sloane, "'It's Getting Crazy Out There: Can a Civil Gang Injunction Change a Community?" *Criminology and Public Policy* 4, no. 3 (2005): 577–605.

Drug sales and drug use are common features of gang life for many females. Girls sell drugs to get money to party, to buy clothes, and for personal use. When they break from home and live on their own or with a boyfriend, the drug sales might be the only stable source of income for rent and groceries. Selling drugs is a dangerous enterprise,

THE PROSOCIAL GANG

As the chief of police of a medium-sized city, you are concerned with the problem of spreading gangs. You have assigned two of your experienced officers to form a gang unit aimed at suppressing any emerging gang activity. These officers have come to you with an interesting problem, and you are unsure what to do about it. A local gang known as the Li'l Bad Boys has recently changed its focus of activities and now, instead of selling drugs and engaging in larcenies, they have appointed themselves as protectors of their downtrodden neighborhood.

It seems that one of the leaders has been recently released from prison, where he had an epiphany and now believes it is his mission in life to help those in need. He has convinced the members of the Li'l Bad Boys to clean up the crime and victimizations in the neighborhood. The gang now bullies both drug dealers and drug users and has unilaterally declared the neighborhood a drug–free zone.

While you agree with their goals, you cannot condone their tactics. They have beaten some youths severely and have committed home invasions on several residences they suspected of being crack houses. They have been wrong on at least two occasions. They made mistakes and broke into the houses of law-abiding citizens and did considerable damage and injured three people.

Overall, however, this gang has had a positive effect on the community. The level of crime is down, drug sales have moved to a nearby small town, and citizens are once again enjoying being on the streets and in the parks during the day and early evening hours.

Your two experienced gang officers are divided as to what to do with this gang. One claims they are cleaning up the area and are actually doing the work of the police. He is willing to tolerate a level of crime against drug dealers and says the few mistakes where law–abiding citizens are inconvenienced should just be considered collateral damage. In his view, it is better to have this gang working toward a safe neighborhood instead of against.

Your other gang officer has a different opinion. She says vigilante justice should not be condoned. The gang members break the law when they assault drug dealers and, although she has little sympathy for the victims, she says the police must investigate and respond appropriately to every law violation. Additionally, she is suspicious about the gang's motives and fears they might simply be trying to eliminate the competition under the guise of being a prosocial gang but will ultimately show their true colors and revert to traditional gang behavior. She urges you to target this gang for special surveillance.

What Should You Do?

1. Let the gang continue to clean up the community by victimizing criminals and drug dealers.
2. Crack down on the gang and require them to obey the law just like everyone else.
3. Call the leaders of the gang into a meeting and see if you can take advantage of their prosocial activities but channel them into appropriate methods. For instance, if the gang members know about drug activity, they are welcome to inform the police and help gather evidence.

---

and girls willing to undertake the risks must be tough and ready to use or respond to violence. They must protect their drugs, money, and lives by being aggressive and capable of convincing others that they will use deadly force to preserve their drug-dealing enterprise. Often, girls assist the drug-dealing of boy gang members.[74] The girls carry the drugs or weapons, so if they are stopped by police, the boys cannot be arrested. Girls will also work the streets or school to channel customers to the boys to buy drugs. The girls are useful because the police are less suspicious of them. Girls do not wear gang colors when dealing drugs to avoid police attention, and the fact that the girls can be arrested is considered to be the cost of doing business. The girls are considered less valuable than the boys. The girls' secondary citizenship in the gang reflects the patriarchal attitude of the lower-class population that provides the vast majority of gang membership. In addition to taking risks selling drugs and being used by male gang members as sexual objects, girl gang members cook, clean, and look after the children. Even at very young ages, girls are required to walk a fine line between being a violent gang member, a sex partner, and a maid.[75]

GANG PREVENTION

Although there is agreement that gangs are a problem and there are some broadly agreed-on strategies for dealing with gangs, the efforts to stem the growth of gangs and the damage they do to other young people and society have been largely unsuccessful.

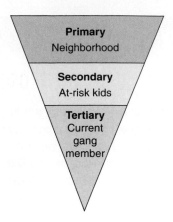

Figure 12-4   **Community Gang Prevention**

Police have reported limited success with one suppression effort that uses civil injunctions to prevent gang members from hanging out together in public (see A Closer Look at Juvenile Issues 12.1).

Nevertheless, gangs continue to plague large cities and appear to be spreading to smaller communities. For the rest of this chapter, we review some of the prevention, suppression, and treatment methods that have been used to deal with gangs. Although the success of these strategies is questionable, if they had the proper funding and support, they might have a greater effect. With this in mind, how might a prosocial gang affect the scene? Recall that the Crips has its roots in the prosocial activities of the 1960s-era Black Panthers. See Focus on Ethics 12.1.

Prevention, Suppression, and Treatment of Gangs

Community efforts to prevent the formation and sustainability of gangs fall into three categories: primary, secondary, and tertiary (see Figure 12-4). On a broad level, these categories are useful for examining the prevention of a wide variety of social and public health problems. By categorizing these community crime prevention efforts, we are able to appreciate how different levels of crime prevention are aimed at distinct target groups.

PRIMARY GANG PREVENTION   The idea behind primary gang prevention is to remove the factors from the community that are suspected to breed gang involvement. This is a broad strategy that is aimed at more than gang prevention. By improving schools, developing a healthy local economy and employment, and providing recreational opportunities, communities seek to improve the lives of all citizens. When meaningful communities meet the needs of children, gangs are not necessary to fill the gaps in identity, purpose, and protection. Much of what we call primary prevention of gangs is not really aimed at gangs at all but rather is designed to help all the children in the community. The idea is that, if successful, all children, including those who might join gangs, can get something from the programs.

It can be argued that primary prevention can be worthwhile even if these efforts don't prevent gangs because they provide so many other benefits. For instance, mandatory schooling until the age of 16 helps all children, even those who might join gangs. Later it will be easier to rehabilitate gang members if they have some skills that will help them to get a job.[76]

SECONDARY GANG PREVENTION   Secondary prevention of gangs involves focusing on potential gang members and intervening specifically to improve their attitudes toward conventional society and in the behaviors that might get them into trouble.

12.1   PROGRAMS *for* CHILDREN

The Jeopardy Program is the Los Angeles Police Department's gang prevention and intervention program for children ages 8 through 17 and their parents. The Jeopardy Program targets at-risk children and offers educational and physical projects, from academic tutoring to martial arts.

Source: Los Angeles Police Department, www.lapdonline.org/get_involved/content_basic_view/735.

Goals	Decrease truancy Improve grades Increase graduation rates Improve self-esteem Decrease the risk of gang involvement Improve conflict resolution and other life-affirming skills Improve and demonstrate goal-setting skills Improve reading and writing Decrease violent and other inappropriate behavior
Tasks	Identify the children that need help Notify their parents and hold a family interview Refer families to local community counseling agencies Hold monthly family seminars Offer alternative activities to be selected by each child Monitor the children monthly for at least one year
Community Involvement	Volunteer time as a tutor, sports coach, fund raiser, or class instructor Donate equipment, such as tables, chairs, chalkboards, art supplies, books, sports equipment, computers, printers, video games, televisions, pens and pencils, notebooks, paper, board games, and puzzles Offer a job to a young man or woman involved in the Jeopardy Program Contribute funding

One of the most effective secondary prevention programs is Head Start, a federally funded program for disadvantaged children. Head Start provides preschool education for children from needy families and is designed to get these children up to speed in social and academic development so that they can start the first grade with the same capabilities as children from more privileged families.

A number of other school–based programs target at–risk children, including interventions such as social–skills training, law–related education, classroom–management programs that focus on strengthening the bond between students and teachers, alternative schools, cooperative learning programs, and antidrug programs. One school–based program that is specifically designed to address the problems of gangs is the Gang Resistance Education and Training (GREAT) program. Patterned after the DARE (Drug Abuse Resistance Education) program, GREAT has uniformed police officers interact with children by providing community–based activities and classroom instruction. This nine-week program is intended to provide life skills that empower adolescents to resist the pressure to join gangs.[77] Another school–based program that has demonstrated some success is Broader Urban Involvement and Leadership (BUILD). This 12–week program distributes information on gang violence, substance abuse, gang recruitment strategies, and the consequences of gang membership. BUILD is used in Chicago middle schools that are in lower– and lower-middle-class neighborhoods. Youths who are considered at risk of joining a gang are enrolled in an additional afterschool program that provides recreational activities, job–training workshops, and educational assistance.[78] A third example of a secondary prevention program is the Los Angeles Police Department's Jeopardy program (see Programs for Children 12.1).

TERTIARY GANG PREVENTION   What can be done with youths who are already in gangs? Here we briefly review a couple of techniques, but the main material for answering this question is reserved for the following chapters, which deal with the juvenile justice system's response to crime and delinquency. Tertiary prevention involves convincing youths to give up their gang affiliation and become responsible members of the community. This is extremely difficult to do, because gangs can have a strong influence on adolescents and gang loyalty can be compared to religious conviction in the meaning it has for some young people. A committed gang member considers the gang to be the primary institution in his or her life, replacing even the family. To lure youths away from an organization that has such a strong grip on loyalty is difficult, and success is rare.

The juvenile justice system uses two approaches to stem gang activity: deterrence and treatment. Law enforcement agencies have developed specific gang units that gather intelligence on gang activities and attempt to arrest and convict gang members. The idea is that getting gang members off the street and punishing them for their criminal activities will deter others from joining gangs.

Although law enforcement authorities have been successful in incarcerating thousands of gang members, there is little evidence that this has stemmed the development of gangs. Once a gang member goes to prison, officials provide opportunities for education, job training, drug and alcohol counseling, and a variety of other rehabilitative efforts. However, there are two problems with this approach. First, effective treatment programs are expensive, and few states have allocated the money to provide comprehensive programs in all youth detention facilities and prisons.[79] These programs can sometimes be effective, but they simply do not have enough resources. The second problem with trying to rehabilitate gang members is that many youth detention facilities and prisons have highly organized gang subcultures that have a great deal of influence on inmates. Rehabilitation, then, takes a back seat to continued gang involvement. Often, young people become further involved in gangs as a result of incarceration, rather than receiving the treatment they need to break away.

To be truly effective, a comprehensive program that involves all three levels of prevention—primary, secondary, and tertiary—must be utilized in a thoughtful, coordinated, and well–funded approach. In cities with racially and ethnically diverse populations, the large disparities in income and wealth, large geographic areas, limited tax bases, and ineffective politicians affect the commitment to seriously address all three levels of crime and gang prevention.

SUMMARY

1. Gangs present difficult challenges in limiting the harm done by youths to each other and to society. Gang members are tough to rehabilitate, and juvenile members often mature into career offenders.

2. Criminologists don't agree on what a youth gang is, but most experts agree on six characteristics: a self-formed association of peers; bound together by mutual interests, well-developed lines of authority, and other organizational features; acting together to achieve a specific purpose or purposes; involved in illegal activity; and controlling a particular territory, facility, or type of enterprise.

3. The definition of a gang member has two aspects: (1) involvement in crime and (2) displaying gang affiliation through cultural aspects that bond them with a family–like loyalty.

4. Gathering information on gangs is difficult for researchers. Gang members are often reluctant to talk about themselves and their illegal activities, and researching gangs is dangerous because of their illegal and violent nature.

5. Many strategies can be employed to study gangs, but the two most common ones are to examine records and talk to criminal justice administrators

and/or schools and to talk directly to youths and gang members through surveys or interviews.

6. Police officials might be reluctant to admit a gang problem. A more difficult issue is determining how much crime is gang related. Law enforcement agencies do not always separate incidents according to whether they are gang related, and without an arrest, it's usually impossible to determine whether an offense involves gang activity. Most law enforcement records probably underreport the level and intensity of any gang problem.

7. Three more problems that field researchers confront when attempting to study gangs is finding gang members who are willing to talk, generalizability, and the researcher's effect on the gang's behavior.

8. Gang delinquency is group behavior. Teenagers in gangs are more likely to break the law than those who aren't. Because juvenile delinquents often have codelinquents, they tend to develop close relationships that take on ganglike features.

9. Once in a gang, fighting, drug use, drug sales, motor vehicle theft, and larceny are all activities that members are encouraged to commit to become respected.

10. Delinquent peers commit more delinquency together than apart. Young people, especially teenagers, have a desperate need to fit in with their peers. Those who participate in deviant behaviors seek out others who do the same to get a sense of belonging.

11. The reasons for joining a gang might be categorized as pushes and pulls. Some factors push a youth toward joining a gang, such as protection, friendship, and family tradition, while other factors pull the youth into the gang, such as status, money, and excitement.

12. Most youths age out of their gangs, meaning that they find other activities that are more important, such as getting married, having children, and/or moving to a new city. The exception is some intergenerational gangs.

13. Gangs vary by size, racial and ethnic makeup, criminal activity, organization, and geographic location.

14. Well-known black and mixed-race gangs include Crips, Bloods, People, Folks, Latin Kings, and Vice Lords.

15. Traditionally, Asian gangs in the United States, called triads or tongs, were confined to the various Chinatowns of large cities. Recent Asian immigrant gangs come from Vietnam, Laos, Cambodia, and the Philippines.

16. White youths join gangs to escape poverty or for protection from other gangs and commonly join mixed-race gangs where they are in the minority. Gangs that are primarily white include skinheads, stoners, and taggers.

17. Females join gangs for protection, status, rebellion, money, and/or to keep or impress a boyfriend.

18. Females are not recruited into gangs in the same way as males. Females can be jumped-in, born-in, or trained-in.

19. Community efforts to prevent the formation and sustainability of gangs fall into categories: primary gang prevention seeks to remove the factors from the community that are suspected to breed gang involvement, secondary prevention of gangs involves focusing on potential gang members and intervening to improve their attitudes and behaviors, and tertiary prevention involves convincing gang members to give up their gang affiliation.

REVIEW QUESTIONS

1. What holds gangs together?

2. What are the six commonly accepted characteristics of gangs?

3. What are the two aspects of the definition of a gang member?

4. What are the two most common research strategies used to study gangs?

5. Why might police officials be reluctant to admit they have a gang problem? Why might they overstate a gang problem?

6. Why is it difficult for researchers to determine how much crime is gang related?

7. How do generalizability and the Hawthorne effect interfere with researchers' efforts to study gangs?

8. How does peer rejection affect the formation of gangs?

9. What are the various pushes and pulls that can lead to a child joining a gang?

10. Why do gang members leave their gangs?

11. Why do girls join gangs? What are the three main ways that girls join gangs?

ADDITIONAL READINGS

Hamm, Mark S. *American Skinheads: The Criminology and Control of Hate Crimes* (Westport, CT: Praeger, 1993).

Huff, C. Ronald, ed. *Gangs in America*, 3rd ed. (Thousand Oaks, CA: Sage, 2002).

Klein, Malcolm W., and Cheryl L. Maxson. *Street Gang Patterns and Policies* (New York: Oxford University Press, 2006).

Sanders, William B. *Gangbangs and Drive-bys: Grounded Culture and Juvenile Gang Violence* (New York: de Gruyter, 1994).

Vigil, James D. *A Rainbow of Gangs: Street Cultures in the Megacity* (Austin: University of Texas Press, 2002).

Weisheit, Ralph A., and L. Edward Wells. "Youth Gangs in Rural America." *NIJ Journal* 251(2004):1–16.

ENDNOTES

1. Tom Hayden, *Street Wars: Gangs and the Future of Violence* (New York: New Press, 2004).

2. Ralph A. Weisheit and L. Edward Wells, "Youth Gangs in Rural America," *NIJ Journal* 5 (2004):2–6.

3. Finn-Aage Esbensen, *Evaluating G.R.E.A.T.: A School-Based Gang Prevention Program* (Washington, DC: National Institute of Justice, 2004).

4. Laura Caldwell and David Altschular, "Adolescents Leaving Gangs: An Analysis of Risk and Protective Factors, Resiliency and Desistance in a Developmental Context," *Journal of Gang Research* 8 (2001):21–34.

5. Richard A. Ball and G. David Curry, "The Logic of Definition in Criminology: The Purpose and Methods for Defining 'Gangs,'" in G. Larry Mays, ed., *Gangs and Gang Behavior* (Chicago: Nelson-Hall, 1997), 3–21.

6. Walter B. Miller, "Gangs, Groups and Serious Youth Crime," in David Schichor and Delos H. Helley, eds. *Critical Issues in Juvenile Delinquency* (Lexington, MA: D.C. Heath, 1980), 115–138.

7. Malcolm W. Klein and Cheryl L. Maxson, "Street Gang Violence," in Neil A. Weiner and Marvin E. Wolfgang, eds. *Violent Crime, Violent Criminals* (Newbury Park, CA: Sage, 1989), 198–234.

8. Tim Delaney, *American Street Gangs* (Upper Saddle River, NJ: Prentice Hall, 2006). See especially Chapter 6.

9. G. David Curry and Scott H. Decker, *Confronting Gangs: Crime and Community* (Los Angeles: Roxbury, 1998).

10. Ibid., p. 47.

11. Ibid., p. 13.

12. Martin Sanchey-Jankowski, *Islands in the Street: Gangs and American Society* (Berkeley: University of California Press, 1991).

13. C. Ronald Huff, "Youth Gangs and Public Policy," *Crime and Delinquency* 35 (1989):524–537.

14. Robert J. Bursik, Jr., and Harold G. Grasmick, "Defining and Researching Gangs," in Arlen Egley, Jr. et al., eds. *The Modern Gang Reader*, 3rd ed. (Los Angeles: Roxbury, 2006), 2–13.

15. Richard C. McCorkle and Terance D. Miethe, "The Political and Organization Response to Gangs: An Examination of a 'Moral Panic' in Nevada," *Justice Quarterly* 15 (1998):41–64.

16. Jerome H. Skolnick, "The Social Structure of a Street Drug Dealing," *American Journal of Police* 9 (1990):1–41.

17. G. David Curry, Richard A. Ball, and Scott H. Decker, *Estimating the National Scope of Gang Crime from Law Enforcement Data* (Washington, DC: National Institute of Justice, 1996).

18. George J. McCall, *Observing the Law: Field Methods in the Study of Crime and the Criminal Justice System* (New York: Free Press, 1978).

19. Frederic Thrasher, *The Gang: A Study of 1,313 Gangs in Chicago* (Chicago: University of Chicago Press, 1927); Jody Miller, *One of the Guys: Girls, Gangs, and Gender* (New York: Oxford University Press, 2001).

20. William F. Whyte, *Street Corner Society* (Chicago: University of Chicago, 1943). Although somewhat dated now, Whyte's appendix in this book detailing how his field research was done provides an excellent review of how to get access to and the trust of street youths.

21. Malcolm Klein, *Street Gangs and Street Workers* (Upper Saddle River, NJ: Prentice Hall, 1971), 151.

22. Wendy M. Craig et al., "The Road to Gang Membership: Characteristics of Male Gang and Nongang Members from Ages 10 to 14," *Social Development* 11, no. 1 (2002):53–68.

23. Albert Cohen, *Delinquent Boys: The Culture of the Gang* (Glencoe, IL: Free Press, 1955).

24. Kate Keenan et al., "The Influence of Deviant Peers on the Development of Boys' Disruptive and Delinquent Behavior: A Temporal Analysis," *Development and Psychopathology* 7 (1995):715–726.

25. Scott Decker, "Collective and Normative Features of Gang Violence," *Justice Quarterly* 13 (1996):243–264.

26. Rachel A. Gordon et al., "Antisocial Behavior and Youth Gang Membership: Selection and Socialization," *Criminology* 42, no. 1 (2004):55–88.

27. Scott H. Decker and Janet L. Lauritzen, "Leaving the Gang," in Arlen Egley et al., eds. *The Modern Gang Reader* (Los Angeles: Roxbury, 2006), 60–70.

28. Peggy Giordano, "The Wider Circle of Friends in Adolescence," *American Journal of Sociology* 101 (1995):661–697.

29. Thomas Vander Ven et al., "Home Alone: The Impact of Maternal Employment on Delinquency," *Social Problems* 48 (2001):236–257.

30. Penelope Eckert, *Jocks and Burnouts: Social Categories and Identity in the High School* (New York: Teachers College Press, 1989).

31. Daneen Deptula and Robert Cohen, "Aggressive, Rejected, and Delinquent Children and Adolescents: A Comparison of Their Friendships," *Aggression and Violent Behavior* 9 (2004):75–104.

32. Scott H. Decker and Barrick van Winkle, *Life in the Gang: Family, Friends, and Violence* (New York: Cambridge University Press, 1996).

33. Felix M. Padilla, *The Gang as an American Enterprise* (New Brunswick, NJ: Rutgers University Press, 1992).

34. Joseph F. Kett, *Rites of Passage: Adolescence in America 1790 to the Present* (New York: Basic Books, 1978).

35. Lowell Sheppard, *Boys Becoming Men: Creating Rites of Passage for the 21st Century* (New York: Authentic Media, 2003).

36. Curry and Decker (see note 9), pp. 65–67.

37. Tim Delaney (see note 8), pp. 145–148.

38. R. B. Cairns and B D. Cairns, "Social Cognition and Social Networks: A Developmental Perspective," in Debra J. Pepler and Kenneth H. Rubin, eds. *The Development and Treatment of Childhood Aggression* (Hillsdale, NJ: Erlbaum, 1991), 389–410.

39. Stephen W. Baron, "Self-Control, Social Consequences, and Criminal Behavior: Street Youth and the General Theory of Crime," *Journal of Research in Crime and Delinquency* 40 (2003):403–425.

40. Thomas J. Dishion, Sarah E. Nelson, and Miwa Yasui, "Predicting Early Adolescent Gang Involvement from Middle School Adaptation," *Journal of Clinical Child and Adolescent Psychology* 34, no. 1 (2005):62–73.

41. Karen Joe Laidler and Geoffrey Hunt, "Violence and Social Organization in Female Gangs," *Social Justice* 24 (1997):148–187.

42. Lawrence Rosenthal, "Gang Loitering and Race," *Journal of Criminal Law and Criminology* 91 (2000):99–160.

43. Decker and Lauritzen (see note 25), pp. 60–69.

44. Pamela Irving Jackson, "Crime, Youth Gangs, and Urban Transition: The Social Dislocations of Postindustrial Economic Development," *Justice Quarterly* 8 (1991):378–397.

45. Finn-Aage Esbensen and L. Thomas Winfree, Jr., "Race and Gender Differences Between Gang and Nongang Youths: Results from a Multi-Site Study", in Arlen Egley, Jr., et al., eds. *The Modern Gang Reader*, 3rd ed. (Los Angeles: Roxbury, 2006), 162–175.

46. Crips,www.gripe4rkids.org/crips.html.

47. Jennifer Warren and Dan Morain, "Crips Target of Prison Lockdown," *Los Angeles Times*, July 1, 2003, B1.

48. Delaney (see note 8), p. 184.

49. Randall G. Shelden, Sharon K. Tracy, and William Brown, *Youth Gangs in American Society* (Belmont, CA: Wadsworth, 2004), 54.

50. Howard Safir, *Security: Policing Your Homeland, Your City* (New York: St. Martin's Press, 2003).

51. Peg Tyre, "New York Turns Up the Heat on Crips, Bloods," *CNN Interactive*, Aug. 27, 1994.

52. John Irwin, *Prisons in Turmoil* (Boston: Little Brown, 1980).

53. John H. Richardson, "The Latin Kings Play Songs of Love," *New York* 30, no. 6 (February 17, 1997):28.

54. Delaney (see note 8), pp. 189–191.

55. Frank Main and Carlos Sadovi, "Gangs Channel River of Cash from Streets to Shops, Studios—Even Vegas," *Chicago Sun Times*, April 7, 2002, 6A-9A.

56. Gerald L. Posner, *Warlords of Crime: Chinese Societies— The New Mafia* (New York: McGraw-Hill, 1988).

57. Dennis J. Kenney and James O. Finckenauer, *Organized Crime in America* (Belmont, CA: Wadsworth, 1995).

58. J. Keene, "Asian Organized Crime," *FBI Law Enforcement Bulletin* 58 (1989):12–17.

59. Ko-Lin Chin, "Chinese Gangs and Extortion," in Arlen Egley, Jr., et al., eds. *The Modern Gang Reader* (Los Angeles: Roxbury, 2006).

60. Kenney and Finckenauer (see note 57).

61. Gregory Yee Mark, "Oakland Chinatown's First Youth Gang: The Suey Sing Boys," in Rebecca D. Peterson, ed. *Understanding Contemporary Gangs in America* (Upper Saddle River, NJ: Prentice Hall, 2004).

62. Illinois Police and Sheriff's News, Organized Crime & Political Corruption, Asian Street Gangs and Organized Crime in Focus: A Rising Threat from the Far East,www.ipsn.org/asg08107.html.

63. Bangele D. Alsaybar, "Deconstructing Deviance: Filipino Youth Gangs, 'Party Culture,' and Ethnic

Identity in Los Angeles," *Amerasia Journal* 25 (1999):116–138.

64. Mark Hamm, *American Skinheads* (Westport, CT: Praeger, 1994).

65. Wayne Wooden and Randy Blazak, *Renegade Kids, Suburban Outlaws: From Youth Culture to Delinquency* (Belmont, CA: Wadsworth, 2000).

66. Wayne S. Wooden, "Tagger Crews and Members of the Posse," in Malcolm W. Klein et al., eds. *The Modern Gang Reader* (Los Angeles: Roxbury, 1995), 65–68.

67. Finn-Aage Esbensen, Elizabeth Piper Deschenes, and L. Thomas Winfree, Jr., "Differences Between Gang Girls and Gang Boys," in Rebecca D. Peterson, ed., *Understanding Contemporary Gangs in America* (Upper Saddle River, NJ: Prentice Hall, 2003).

68. Joan Moore and John Hagedorn, *Female Gangs: A Focus on Research* (Washington, DC: U.S. Department of Justice, Office of Justice Programs, Office of Juvenile Justice and Delinquency Prevention, 2001). Online at www.ncjrs.gov/pdffiles1/ojjdp/186159.pdf.

69. Mary G. Harris, *Cholas: Latino Girls and Gangs* (New York: AMS Press, 1988).

70. Eduardo Luis Portillos, "Women, Men, and Gangs: The Social Construction of Gender in the Barrio," in Meda Chesney-Lind and John M. Hagedorn, eds.

Female Gangs in America (Chicago: Lake View Press, 1997).

71. Gini Sikes, "8 Ball Chicks: A Year in the Violent World of Girl Gangsters," in *Gangs* (New York: Thunder Mouth Press, 2001).

72. Jody Miller, *One of the Guys: Girls, Gangs, and Gender* (New York: Oxford University Press, 2001).

73. Ibid.

74. Mark D. Tatten, *Guys, Gangs, and Girlfriend Abuse* (Orchard Park, NY: Broadview, 2001).

75. Gini Sikes (see note 71), p. 244.

76. James C. Howell, "Promising Programs for Youth Gang Violence Prevention and Intervention," in Rebecca D. Petersen, ed. *Understanding Contemporary Gangs in America* (Upper Saddle River, NJ: Prentice Hall, 2004).

77. Finn-Aage Esbensen and D. Wayne Osgood, *National Evaluation of G.R.E.A.T.* (Washington, DC: Department of Justice, National Institute of Justice, 1988).

78. D. W. Thompson and L. A. Jason, "Street Gangs and Preventive Interventions," *Criminal Justice and Behavior* 15 (1988): 323–333.

79. John R. Fuller, *Criminal Justice: A Peacemaking Perspective* (Boston: Allyn and Bacon, 1998).

PART FOUR
Juvenile Justice System

How are police departments organized to respond to juvenile delinquency?

What special precautions must police officers take when dealing with juvenile offenders?

Why do some juveniles distrust police officers?

CHAPTER 13

The Police

Police officers have an uneasy relationship with juvenile delinquents. In many ways, the demands on the police are contradictory and confusing when dealing with children and adolescents who violate the law or are victims of abuse and neglect. Additionally, the job of the police in managing delinquency is complicated because they often don't know the age of the suspect until after they have had to take action. This can be dangerous for the police, because hesitating in a violent situation can result in injury or death. In this chapter, we will learn more about the ambiguous nature of the relationship between law enforcement and juveniles, with an eye toward appreciating the fine line that police officers walk between protecting society and acting in the best interests of young people.

The juvenile court revolutionized the legal processes for youths, but the police had no such revolution. Although many police departments have juvenile officers, there is no specialized juvenile police force, and police departments aren't required to have juvenile officers. Police management of juveniles is most often dictated by the courts, legislation, and the officers' own **discretion**.

The police are typically the first contact that young victims and delinquents have with the juvenile justice system. As with adults, law enforcement serves as the gatekeeper to the justice system. This is especially important, because this gatekeeper function often results in youths being labeled as delinquent, which can have profound consequences. The importance of a police officer's decision to introduce a child into the juvenile justice system can't be overemphasized.

Like the rest of the juvenile justice system, police must balance what is best for the youth with what is best for the community. However, unlike juvenile-oriented courts and corrections, the police have to function almost atypically because much of the treatment of juvenile delinquents has a social work aspect. Many police officers (and whole departments) prefer to focus on the justice aspects of police work: getting offenders off the streets, responding to emergencies, scoring big drug busts, and generally "catching the bad guys."[1] A situation involving a delinquent, however, is often complicated simply because the juvenile is considered to be a child and, as is currently accepted in our society, not completely responsible for his or her actions. The youngster might have an untenable home life involving abuse or maybe a single parent who

discretion

The power of a legal authority to decide what to do at any given point in the justice process.

A police officer circa 1940 holds a boy's arm while he speaks on the phone at a police call box. *(Courtesy Harold M. Lambert, Getty Images Inc. - Hulton Archive Photos)*

just can't cope; live in a neighborhood overrun by gangs; attend a poor school; have learning or behavioral issues; or all of the above. Whereas our society accepts that an adult is, in most cases, solely responsible for his or her actions, it also stipulates that a child or adolescent is not. This automatically brings in numerous other societal factors. The police must deal with some or all of the major socializing institutions—parents, families, schools, and neighborhoods—with nearly every juvenile arrest, whether the individual officers or departments are equipped to do so or not.

It is also important to keep in mind that much of law enforcement's interaction with young people concerns the maintenance of public order, such as controlling youths in public, rather than criminal law enforcement. This requires many low-visibility, discretion-based decisions from the police, which means that the police are almost a juvenile court unto themselves based on their powers of discretion.[2]

At this point, we should also discuss the word *juvenile*, a legalistic term that we have used throughout the book to refer to a person under the age of 18 (in most states). Parents with children never refer to the juveniles in their home, but the law does. So, in keeping with this custom, we will use *juvenile* to refer to young people who are involved in the juvenile justice system.

A SHORT HISTORY OF JUVENILE POLICING

The history of the police handling of juveniles delineates an important overall shift in juvenile justice, from the informal to the formal, from families to the police to the courts. In the early North American colonies, juvenile justice was handled by parents with the support of the local authorities, such as the constabulary, if any, or religious leaders. However, as the nation grew and became more diverse, it became necessary for a single authority to handle wayward and disruptive youths, especially in such large urban centers as New York City, Los Angeles, and Chicago. However, juvenile justice was formalized much more slowly than adult (criminal) justice. As covered in detail in Chapter 14, there was no juvenile court or even separate juvenile detention until the 20th century. Thus, in the formalization process, police served as the inter-mediate step between local institutions and the 20th-century juvenile court.

In the late 19th and early 20th centuries, the police dealt with youths in three general but very important ways:

1. The police decided which cases they would handle informally within their own departments and which to push to the (adult) courts. Only a small percentage ever made it to the courts.

2. The police used their discretion and power to round up youths for minor offens-es and attempt to scare them onto the "straight and narrow" and then release them on informal probation or even no probation at all.

3. The police made most detention decisions, using detention as a swift punishment for the youth, rather than for the protection of society or any long-term rehabil-itative effort.

During the early 20th century, the police resolved a large percentage of juvenile delinquency cases themselves without involving the juvenile court. Many depart-ments even supervised youths directly in a sort of informal probation. Sometimes the cases never hit the station house. The officers, using substantial discretion, would lecture and release the youth on the spot. For example, between 1930 and 1940, the juvenile bureau of the Los Angeles Police Department disposed of well over half of its cases within the department. Chicago's revolutionary juvenile court system saw only a small percentage of the city's delinquents, because the police resolved most of the cases themselves.

During the late 19th and early 20th centuries, juvenile policing was order-maintenance policing, with most arrests being for public-order violations and what we now call status offenses, such as running away and truancy. According to David Wolcott, "Arresting juvenile offenders was less a means of introducing them into the criminal justice system for punishment or rehabilitation, than of satisfying aggrieved citizens and of officially reprimanding disorderly youth."[3]

The police could also use their discretion to detain a juvenile for as long as they saw fit, with little court interference. Evidence points to the police using detention as a reprimand or a scare tactic. The detentions, which came prior to disposition or release to a juvenile court, typically lasted only days or weeks. In 1920s Chicago, despite overcrowding, "the police officers who controlled admission to the Juvenile Detention Home still used it as if it were a jail, holding youth there as a swift and secure form of punishment." In 1926, this detention home admitted 7,115 juveniles, but the court heard only 2,265 cases. Nearly half of the juveniles admitted were released within two days.[4]

After 1940, the police handling of juveniles shifted from the maintenance of order to ensuring that the law wasn't broken. This change in attitude resulted more from police professionalization than from the rehabilitative goals of the new juvenile courts. As a result, the police began arresting older juveniles and more juveniles who were suspected of felonies and sending them to the courts, rather than rounding up bands of 12-year-olds for petty thefts and letting them go after a couple days of detention.[5]

A final aspect of the order-maintenance function was social work. Much of police work, even today, involves helping people in difficult circumstances, such as refereeing explosive domestic situations, rescuing **dependent** children from bad homes, protecting the mentally ill from harming themselves and others, and preventing suicides.

A big part of law enforcement's work with juveniles includes protecting dependent and neglected children, not just delinquents. In the early 1900s, this social work with nondelinquent children and women was provided by "policewomen" trained in social work. According to Albert Roberts, "There is no evidence that policemen were assigned to perform social work functions during the first quarter of the 20th century. At that time social work was predominantly a female profession, and it's understandable that the first police social workers were women."[6] There was a division of labor in which male police officers rounded up delinquents, while female officers had the task of assisting neglected, abused, and dependent juveniles.[7]

Instant Recall from Chapter 1

dependent

A term describing the status of a child who needs court protection and assistance because his or her health or welfare is endangered due to the parent's or guardian's inability, through no fault of their own, to provide proper care and supervision.

LAW ENFORCEMENT: DEALING WITH JUVENILE DELINQUENTS AND VICTIMS

The manner in which police interact with youths presents a number of problematic issues. Perhaps the most pressing is the attitude the police have developed in the wars on crime and drugs, which have put delinquents in the position of being considered as dangerous as adult suspects and offenders. It is understandable that police are concerned for their safety as they confront juvenile delinquents. Youth who carry weapons are just as dangerous as adults, and some boys are so big and strong that they pose a physical challenge to the police officers who have to apprehend them. From the viewpoint of the police officer, age is an artificial criterion for determining danger. A 15-year-old can be as problematic as an adult, and until the encounter can be evaluated, the police must ensure their safety. From time to time, this might lead to a well-publicized case of excessive force, but that is a regrettable and all too frequently inherent part of the job. Thus, juveniles occupy a difficult and challenging place in police work for three reasons:

1. The police must deal with juveniles very often, especially teenagers.

2. Juveniles are more likely than adults to hold negative attitudes toward the police.

3. Juveniles commit a significant percentage of offenses.[8]

A major issue in the relationship between law enforcement and juveniles is *situational ambiguity*; that is, when juveniles encounter the law, the situation and what to do about it are often ill-defined. The opposite of this concept is *situational clarity*, when the situation and what to do about it are well-defined.

Sometimes no one, from the parents to the courts, is sure what's best for the child, or even more complicating, everyone is positive as to what's best for the child. Often, the status of the situation itself is unclear. For instance, a missing youth can be a runaway, abducted by a stranger or an acquaintance or abducted by a parent. In all three cases, the youth can be a victim, offender, or both. For instance, if a teenager runs away from home to escape an abusive parent and steals a car while doing so, the teenager is both an offender and a victim. In this case, the police must still act in the best interests of the youth.

In their interactions with juveniles, the police are guided by the mission of the juvenile justice system to rehabilitate delinquents and divert those on the path to delinquency. This directive is largely unofficial and indirect—after all, it's a philosophy rather than a law or a rule—but it's endorsed by juvenile court judges, many of whom would rather see disputes and complaints settled without referral.[9] The police are indirectly guided by the Juvenile Court Act, which states that juveniles are "taken into custody," not arrested. This is interpreted to mean the police's role is to salvage and rehabilitate youth, a role indirectly sanctioned by many judges.

Another issue when dealing with juveniles is that of determining if the subject is a juvenile. Often, juveniles in trouble will claim that they are adults, especially in the case of status offenses. Let's consider, for example, a group of teenagers drinking beer in a parking lot. The teens might claim to the inquiring officers that they are adults, hoping then that the only charge might be violation of an open-container ordinance and the issuance of a ticket, instead of being taken to the police station or driven home to their parents. Better yet, in some jurisdictions, there might be no charge at all for adults drinking alcohol in public. In either case, identifying themselves as juveniles only means more trouble.[10]

A final issue that requires consideration is the potential use of force by the police. The police are one of the few agencies that are sanctioned to use force. It can be said that police have a monopoly on the legitimate use of force, and this results in potentially coercive relationships in encounters between the police and lawbreakers. According to Kären Hess and Robert Drowns,

> Because the police have a monopoly on the *legitimate* use of force, they have the authority to impose themselves on conflicts as agents of social control. There-fore, police–violent youth encounters are *always* potentially coercive relationships. This is a particularly important contextual variable when considering the role of the police in controlling violent encounters.[11]

Specialized Juvenile Policing

Three units within police departments have the most contact with juveniles: special juvenile units (including gang units), juvenile officers, and patrol officers. Patrol officers cruise a regular beat and are the ones who will most often deal with status offenders and who will take juveniles into custody.[12]

The amount of special attention that juvenile delinquency gets from police departments depends a lot on the department's size. The smaller the department is, the fewer juvenile specialists it has. This is simply a function of the size of the department and jurisdiction and the department's budget. A small department might have only one or two juvenile officers; a large, urban department will have a whole juvenile unit, and many will have separate units for juvenile victims and missing children. The larger the department is, the greater the possibility it will have some officers who specialize in certain types of problems. Small police departments are unlikely to have juvenile officers assigned solely to motor vehicle theft, homicide, drugs, gangs, or juveniles. However, very large departments will have these special focus units and more. See Figure 13-1 for the distribution of youth-related units among local law enforcement agencies.

JUVENILE OFFICERS   Typically, juvenile officers are drawn from the ranks of the patrol staff. These officers might have little or no extra training in dealing with juvenile delinquency and might only repeat the lessons they learned as patrol officers. However, some of these officers are chosen because they have a special talent for dealing with juvenile delinquency. These officers might have backgrounds in social science, child psychology, adolescence, child–parent conflict, or sex offenses. Such officers can be extremely valuable in detecting, preventing, and treating delinquency and abuse cases. Often these officers do not enjoy high status in the department because they "work only juvie crimes." However, experienced juvenile officers are typically more skilled at classifying and dealing with juvenile delinquents than are regular police officers. Here is a summary of what juvenile officers do:

1. The juvenile officer is skilled at interrogating juveniles. Although a regular officer might have trouble categorizing a juvenile episode, the juvenile officer, because of his/her experience, usually does not.
2. The juvenile officer has many types of juvenile contacts, such as school officials, parents, neighbors, and victims.
3. The juvenile officer is experienced at handling difficult parents and dispositions, as well as a variety of juvenile delinquents and their situations.
4. Because of a knowledge of juvenile court procedures and dispositions, a juvenile officer is better able to handle juvenile interrogations. Given the same information from a juvenile about a situation, the juvenile officer might make an entirely different recommendation than a regular officer.[13]

JUVENILE UNITS   Large police departments have specialized units that respond to offenses that they suspect are committed by juveniles. Offenses such as bicycle theft, drug sales in the school, and fighting are investigated by juvenile-unit officers. Some officers might be assigned as school resource officers, where they maintain a presence in one or more schools and try to get to know the students in order to develop a positive relationship between youths and the police. The officers are also responsible for handling cases of abuse and neglect, as well as investigating offenses committed against juveniles. Working closely with the juvenile court and youth service workers,

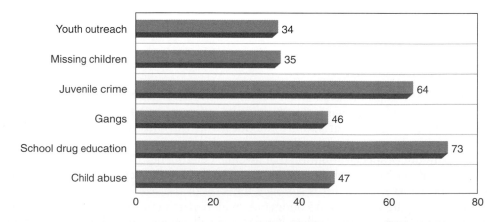

Figure 13-1   Percentage of Local Law Enforcement Agencies (County Police, Municipal Police, and Sheriff's Departments) That Have Special Juvenile Units with Full-Time Staff *Source:* Brian A. Reaves and Matthew J. Hickman, *Law Enforcement Management and Administrative Statistics, 2000: Data for Individual State and Local Agencies with 100 or More Officers* (Washington, DC: U.S. Department of Justice, Office of Justice Programs, Bureau of Justice Statistics, 2004), xvi. Online at www.ojp.usdoj. gov/bjs/pub/pdf/lemas00.pdf.

Most youths suspected of delinquency enter the juvenile justice system through contact with police. Here a police officer who has drawn his gun walks past a building spray painted with graffiti. *(Courtesy Jonathan Kirn, The Stock Connection)*

members of juvenile units typically attain a working knowledge of the problems of delinquency.[14]

Gang Units   In cities with gang problems, police departments may assign several officers to the gang unit, where they develop strategies to prevent and solve gang crime. By developing intelligence about the structure and behaviors of the gangs in their jurisdictions, gang-unit officers can provide other officers, schools, and the community with information for stemming the tide of gang activities. Additionally, these officers work gang-related cases and are in a much better position to understand gang graffiti, understand gang rivalries, and apprehend gang members than are regular police officers.[15]

PROCEDURE: WHAT THE POLICE DO

Most juvenile suspects enter the juvenile justice system through contact with police. Juveniles can be referred to the system in other ways, but police referral is the most common by far. In 2000, law enforcement sent 84 percent of all delinquency cases to juvenile court, with parents, victims, schools, and probation officers responsible for the rest of the referrals. This percentage seems high, but remember that police also divert many juveniles from the system altogether through the use of discretion.[16] Sometimes the police department deals with the juvenile's offense and then releases the juvenile, a process called **station adjustment**.

It is important to understand that police departments throughout the country manage juveniles under their supervision in a fairly uniform manner, with only the details differing from state to state. However, the juvenile's offense, victimization, and/or behavior will invoke specific procedures that are tailored to the situation. These situations can be broken into three broad categories: neglected and abused children, status offenders, and violent juveniles.

station adjustment
Handling and release of a juvenile delinquent within a police department.

Neglected and Abused Children

Although not all are juvenile delinquents, neglected and abused children often come into contact with the police. This is because police officers, who are first responders in times of crisis or emergency, are often the first officials to become aware of cases of child abuse or neglect. For example, during the arrest of some adults at their home for drug offenses, the police might discover their children living in squalid conditions. Or because the parents are going to jail, the police might have to deal with the children because the children have nowhere else to go. The role of the police officer in these situations is limited and predicated on doing what is best for the child. It might mean arresting a parent or guardian or removing the child from the home. These cases are quickly turned over to the office of child protective services, so police officers have only a tangential role as compared to their involvement with delinquency cases.

Status Offenders

Status offenders might be the easiest type of juvenile case for police because of the wide range of discretion and the situational clarity. A status offense, if you will recall, applies only to juveniles. Status-offense laws apply only to juveniles because they are the ones who are most frequently harmed by the activities these laws ban. Twelve–year–olds are prohibited from drinking beer because we believe they are harmed by inebriation and alcohol more than adults are. A police officer who catches a 12–year–old drinking beer has to do something about it but has a range of choices:

1. End the status offense (in this case, take the beer away), and release the youth.
2. Take the youth into custody with release to the parents; this can involve simply taking the youth home, with an explanation of what he or she was up to, or having the parents retrieve him or her from the station.
3. Take the youth into custody but with referral to counseling or other social service.
4. Take the youth into custody with formal charges and referral to juvenile court.

Police officers are likely to go easier on juveniles caught committing simple status offenses, because most status offenses are not very serious from a public safety perspective. Recall the prior example of teenagers drinking beer in a parking lot. Let's say the teenagers are out past the local curfew. The curfew and alcohol consumption violations are status offenses, but the teenagers, while they might be loud and obnoxious, are not endangering anyone with these activities alone. However, if one of the teens gets in a car and drives away while drunk, then the teen is a danger to public safety, but the offense has gone beyond being a simple status offense. Driving while drunk is illegal and dangerous for everyone, not just teenagers. At this point, the police have less discretion and must take the matter more seriously, with greater consequences for the drunk teenager.

Other status offenses, besides curfew violations and underage drinking, include underage driving, truancy (not being in school), and running away. Unless some other offense was committed, runaways generally don't incur much police involvement, other than locating the runaway and taking the child home. If abuse at home is obvious, then police are concerned with the abuser(s), not the runaway.

Violent Juveniles

Recall that police officers have a great amount of discretion, especially with status offenders, which generally leads to one of four outcomes. The first is doing nothing and ending the status offense, and the other three involve taking the juvenile into custody with (1) release to parents, (2) referral to an alternative social program, or (3) referral to juvenile court. A violent juvenile greatly curtails police discretion, however. If the violence is bad enough, the police have only the last option, referral to juvenile or criminal court, although the third option, referral to an alternative social program,

13.1   F O C U S *on* E T H I C S

SHOOT OR DON'T SHOOT?

As a police officer with over 12 years experience you have never had to fire your weapon in the line of duty. You qualify on the police pistol range every year and are proud that your abilities have allowed you to win the expert rank for the past 4 years.

Recently you have been distressed because the family of a young gang member who was shot during an armed robbery has sued a good friend who went through the police academy with you. The shooting review board ruled the killing as justified, but the publicity has made the police force wary. Your friend is taking the incident badly, because he wonders if he might have been able to handle the situation differently. He is depressed, has started drinking heavily, and has regular sessions with a psychologist who is trying to help him with his feelings of guilt.

All this is in the back of your mind on the night you are called to a domestic disturbance at the home of an immigrant family who does not speak English. As you and your partner forcibly subdue the intoxicated husband, the wife runs into the back bedroom screaming at an unknown number of children. You follow her down the hall, and out of the corner of your eye you see a gun being pointed at you from a side bedroom. As you draw your weapon, several things flash through your mind.

- The figure holding the gun is small and can only be a child.
- The gun could be a plastic toy pistol.
- In the darkened bedroom, you cannot be sure of the exact nature of the threat.
- If the gun is real and if the person pointing it at you is serious about shooting, you have but a split second to act without properly evaluating the degree of threat.
- If you shoot and it's a child with a toy gun, your career will be over. Regardless of what the shooting board rules, you won't be able to deal with shooting a child.
- A child with a gun can still kill you.

What Do You Do?

1. Shoot to kill. This is a predictable crisis that all police officers are trained to anticipate and trained in how to conduct themselves.

2. Shoot to wound. After all, you are an expert shot, and they do this on television all the time.

3. Don't shoot. As a firearms expert, you believe a responsible person shoots only when he or she knows exactly what he or she is shooting at. You are wearing a bulletproof vest, so you are willing to take your chances before pulling the trigger and making a big mistake.

---

might be possible in some circumstances. A violent juvenile will almost certainly be placed in detention.

Gun violence is a very troubling aspect of juvenile violence (see Focus on Ethics 13.1). As part of its guides for police, the Justice Department's Office of Community Oriented Policing Services (COPS) details police strategies for dealing with juvenile gun violence. The two types of strategies are offender-oriented responses and place-oriented responses (see Table 13-1 for details).

- **Offender-oriented responses**   The "pulling levers" deterrence strategy, which began in Boston as the Boston Gun Project/Operation Ceasefire, targets a small group of serious offenders with a very specific message that violence will not be tolerated. The strategy requires, in part, community support, effective communications, providing social services and opportunities, and searching for and seizing juveniles' guns.

- **Place-oriented responses**   Aside from community support, this strategy requires that police focus on "high–risk places at high–risk times." This strategy also involves intensive search and seizure of guns, as well as high contact with potential offenders, gang suppression, and gun buy-back programs.[17]

As of 2006, many jurisdictions reported an increase in juvenile violence that police and local authorities attributed to gangs. In some isolated situations, a simple increase in police patrols and arrest of gang members made some violence-prone areas safer. Other jurisdictions formed special task forces and juvenile units. See Kids in the News 13.1 for a look at how many jurisdictions handle spikes in juvenile violence.

Table 13-1   **COPS Summary of Responses to Gun Violence among Serious Young Offenders**

Response	How It Works	Works Best If	Considerations
Offender-oriented responses			
Enlisting community support	Helps community members to view police enforcement actions as legitimate	Police inform the community that gun violence is concentrated among groups of serious offenders and that they will focus their efforts on them.	Indiscriminate, highly aggressive law enforcement can undermine community support.
Developing an effective communication strategy	Warns potential offenders about the consequences of committing gun crimes	The message is direct and explicit, conveying clear cause and effect.	Nonviolent gangs and groups should be informed of what is happening to violent ones and why; probation and parole officers can require those under their supervision to attend forums, and social service providers and community members may be able to persuade gang members to do so.
Sending the initial message	Lets violent gangs and groups know that they are under close surveillance	Police immediately increase their presence and activities in areas.	Social service providers and community members should let would-be offenders know they support the police and offer help to those who want it.
Continuing communication	Reinforces the antigun violence message	Police make it clear to violent gangs and groups that they are focusing on them because of their involvement in gun crime.	Police agencies should be creative in communicating with offenders (e.g., by conducting forums with them).
Providing social services and opportunities	Diverts offenders from a violent lifestyle	Consequences for continued involvement in gun violence are severe enough to compel offenders to seek positive alternatives.	A variety of options should be available, such as substance abuse counseling and job skills training.
Searching for and seizing juveniles' guns	Reduces the opportunities for gun violence by eliminating the means	The affected community supports the initiative, parents or guardians trust police and prosecutors to keep their word about criminal prosecution and give signed consent for searches, and police base targeting on reliable intelligence about juveniles' gun involvement.	This is promising, but it has not yet proved effective in reducing gun violence.
Place-oriented responses			
Enlisting community support	Helps community members to view police enforcement actions as legitimate	Police managers meet with community members both before and during interventions and demonstrate effective leadership and supervision.	Communities with high rates of gun violence tend to support police intervention.
Training officers in appropriate search-and-seizure techniques	Ensures that officers conduct only legally warranted searches and seizures	Officers treat those they stop with respect and explain the reasons for stops.	Street searches of young male minorities may be viewed as police harassment.

Table 13-1   **COPS Summary of Responses to Gun Violence among Serious Young Offenders (Continued)**

Response	How It Works	Works Best If	Considerations
Increasing gun seizures	Reduces the opportunities for gun violence by eliminating the means	Police focus on high-risk places at high-risk times.	Research has shown that in some cases increases in gun seizures in targeted areas have resulted in decreases in gun crime there.
Increasing contacts with potential gun offenders	Subjects would-be offenders to increased police scrutiny	Police increase their visibility and contact with likely offenders within very small areas.	Both traffic stops and "stop and talk" contacts may be effective.
Suppressing gangs without providing programs and services to address the social conditions that contribute to gang affiliation	Reduces gun violence by identifying, tracking, and aggressively enforcing laws against known violent gang members	Based on a thorough understanding of the nature of gangs and gang violence problems in local jurisdictions and blended with social intervention, opportunity provision, and community mobilization activities.	Gangs and gang problems usually remain in the wake of these intensive operations; suppression programs may have the perverse effect of strengthening gang solidarity; gangs do not consider police threats to eliminate them credible; social intervention and prevention efforts are necessary complements to suppression efforts.
Implementing gun buy-back programs	Reduces the availability of guns that might be used in violent crimes by reducing the overall number of guns in the community		This has not proved effective in reducing gun violence. It fails to focus on the guns most likely to be used in violent crimes.

Source: Anthony A. Braga, *Problem-Specific Guides Series, No. 23: Gun Violence among Serious Young Offenders* (Washington, DC: U.S. Department of Justice, Office of Community Oriented Policing Services, 2004), 35–39. Online at www.cops.usdoj.gov/mime/open.pdf? Item=1078.

Females who commit serious acts of delinquency quickly fall out of the traditional gender stereotype. In 1992, Shannon Garrison (left) and Melissa Garrison of Gulfport, Mississippi, were charged with killing their mother, Betty Garrison.

(Courtesy Kevin Cooper, AP Wide World Photos)

13.1 KIDS in the NEWS

Violence Is In

In 2006, many communities across the United States reported an unusual increase in juvenile violence. Usually, local authorities and government statistics agree that property offenses are the sort that juveniles commit the most, which made the increased violence all that more mysterious and disturbing. Authorities tied the violent trend to a growing number of gangs, although other police departments also cited staff shortages, increases in the juvenile population, decreased parental involvement, and even the new focus on homeland security rather than "hometown security."[1] Here is what several jurisdictions reported in 2006.

- In Merced County, California, Jamari Lloyd-Patterson, 16, was shot several times and killed as he walked from a mall during his lunch break. Police arrested a 15-year-old and a 16-year-old in connection with the shooting. Jamari was the fifth person under the age of 20 killed in the county during 2006. From 2002 to 2005, the average age of a murder victim in the county was 33, but during 2006 the age dropped to 22. The Merced Police Department reported that the percentage of juveniles arrested for serious crimes jumped from 5 percent in the past four years to 7 percent in 2006.[2]

- In Houston, Texas, Cristian Ferman, 15, the fifth teen murder in less than three weeks was followed the next day by the sixth, the murder of a 14-year-old in the same neighborhood. A local official attributed the murders to a juvenile population boom and law enforcement's fading emphasis on gang control due to staff shortages. Other officials blamed a resurgence in gangs.[3]

- Hamilton County, Tennessee, noted a clear rise in juvenile violence. In 2005, juveniles charged with murder rose 700 percent, while juvenile rape charges rose 100 percent. A Chattanooga Police Department official attributed the rise in juvenile violent crime to parents and observed that juveniles were more easily provoked to violence now than in the past.[4]

- In Sacramento, California, police arrested a 14-year-old girl for allegedly shooting a pregnant woman. A 15-year-old boy was beaten to death in the middle of the day at an intersection by three

other boys who stole his backpack and fled in an SUV. In Sacramento County, the number of juvenile offenses involving weapons and violence rose 73 percent from 1981 to 2003. The number of juveniles arrested for crimes (not status offenses) increased 21 percent, while adult arrests rose only 8 percent. Local officials pointed to general population growth, as well as a boom in the juvenile population, gangs, and ganglike behavior. The Sacramento Police Department has launched a community policing–style youth unit comprising school resource officers, gang officers, and detectives focused on gang activity and violence.[5]

- An aggressive, problem–oriented policing response reduced gang–related juvenile violence in a Modesto, California, neighborhood park within a few months. Police arrested and evicted from nearby apartments gang members who hung around and committed offenses in the park by conducting multiagency parole and probation searches, making more arrests, and increasing patrols. The agencies participating in the crackdown included local police departments, the county gang task force, and the state's Alcoholic Beverage Control bureau.[6]

Think About It

1. Discuss the relationship between juvenile population explosions and juvenile violence.

2. Are gangs really a problem?

3. How can problem-oriented and community policing help communities control spikes in juvenile violence?

1 Mark K. Matthews and Willoughby Mariano, "Top Cops Take Aim at Halting Crime Rise," *Orlando Sentinel* (Flordia), August 31, 2006, State and Regional News, A1.
2 Leslie Albrecht, "Youth Violence Up, Solutions Remain Elusive," *Merced Sun-Star* (California), July 29, 2006, p. 01.
3 Allan Turner, Rosanna Ruiz, and Melanie Markley, "Answers Elusive in Youth Violence," *Houston Chronicle* (Texas), June 18, 2006, State and Regional News.
4 Brian Lazenby, "Juvenile Crime Is More Violent," *Chattanooga Times Free Press* (Tennessee), April 2, 2006, News, P. 1.
5 Christina Jewett, "City Police Form Unit to Tackle Youth Crime," *Sacramento Bee* (California), February 19, 2006, final edition, p. B1.
6 Melanie Turner, "Manteca Park Taken Back from Gang," *Modesto Bee* (California), December 6, 2005, first edition, p. B1.

Taking into Custody

Taking a juvenile into custody is an important decision for the police officer because it affects not only the juvenile's freedom, but also the justice system itself. Most juveniles taken into custody are referred to juvenile court (see Figure 13-2). About 2 percent are referred to a welfare agency or to another police agency.[18] The police can't take into custody every juvenile who is suspected of an offense because this would swamp the system with too many cases. In deciding to introduce the juvenile to the system, the custody must meet one of two standards:

1. **Probable cause**   **Probable cause** simply means that a reasonable person would conclude that there is a high probability that an offense is being or has been committed. One doesn't need absolute proof of guilt at this point but only a probability of over 50 percent that the juvenile is responsible.

2. **Reasonable suspicion**   **Reasonable suspicion** is a lower standard than probable cause. Here, the officer needs at least a 30 percent suspicion that an offense has been committed or that the youth needs supervision.[19]

Although police don't need probable cause or a warrant to take a juvenile into custody, many, if not most, departments notify the juvenile's parents after the fact. Many state laws require police to notify parents.[20] With this exception of notifying the parents, police follow the same procedures when taking a juvenile into custody as they do when arresting an adult. Two general classes of encounters are common in juvenile cases:

1. **Patrol**   Police who are on the street might be called to the scene by dispatchers passing on complaints from citizens, or they might witness infractions themselves that they view as suspicious.

2. **Investigations**   Juvenile officers make telephone or personal inquiries in the field or at the station when they investigate problems that are part of their caseload.[21]

In the case of situational ambiguity, the officer might arrest everyone involved for further interrogation or detention. Depending on the type and size of the department, a juvenile officer or detective might continue the investigation.[22]

Taking a juvenile into custody involves a decision to either send the matter further into the justice system or to divert the case, often into an alternative program. The police officer generally makes this decision after talking to the victim, the juvenile, and the parents and reviewing the juvenile's prior contacts with

probable cause
Sufficient reason for a police officer to believe an offense has been committed; probable cause must exist for an officer to arrest (or take into custody) without a warrant, search without a warrant, or seize property.

reasonable suspicion
Doubt that is based on specific facts or circumstances and that justifies stopping and sometimes searching an adult or juvenile thought to be involved in criminal activity or, in the case of a juvenile, a status offense.

- Handled by police
- Referred to juvenile court
- Other disposition
- Referred to criminal court

Figure 13-2   **Disposition of Arrested Juveniles, 2003** *Source:* Howard N. Snyder and Melissa Sickmund, *Juvenile Offenders and Victims: 2006 National Report* (Washington, DC: U.S. Department of Justice, Office of Justice Programs, Office of Juvenile Justice and Delinquency Prevention, 2006), 152.

Officers might arrest everyone suspected of delinquency until the situation can be sorted out. These Los Angeles police officers have detained members of the Crazy Street Boyz gang. (Courtesy A. Ramey, PhotoEdit Inc.)

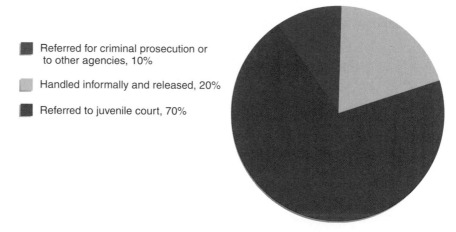

■ Referred for criminal prosecution or to other agencies, 10%

▢ Handled informally and released, 20%

■ Referred to juvenile court, 70%

Figure 13-3   Disposition of Juvenile Arrests

In 2003, in 20 percent of all juvenile arrests, police released the youths; in 70 percent of the arrests, the cases were referred to juvenile court. The remaining 10 percent of arrests were referred for criminal prosecution or to other agencies. *Source:* Howard N. Snyder and Melissa Sickmund, *Juvenile Offenders and Victims: 2006 National Report* (Washington, DC: U.S. Department of Justice, Office of Justice Programs, Office of Juvenile Justice and Delinquency Prevention, 2006), 14.

the juvenile justice system. Although each jurisdiction has different patterns for how these cases are handled and these patterns vary from year to year, the dispositions in 2003 are typical (see Figure 13-3).

Sometimes the police take into custody juveniles who aren't suspected of an offense, such as in cases of abuse, neglect, or dependency. This area does not have an analog in the adult legal system and illustrates why juveniles have a separate system, with slightly different rules and different terminology.

Booking

Once a juvenile has been taken into custody, the juvenile's case is evaluated in several stages and processed into the system. These activities differ from those of the criminal justice system in a few significant ways.

FINGERPRINTS AND PHOTOGRAPHS   Officers may fingerprint or photograph youths or collect their DNA under specific conditions. Until recently, juvenile law was very particular about how these records were handled, stating basically that they couldn't be kept or, in some states, even collected in a central database. Confidentiality has been considered crucial to juvenile system philosophy, with the idea that a stigmatized youth is more difficult to rehabilitate and that behavior changes significantly with age. Imagine being turned down for a job at age 36 because your potential employer finds out through a record check that you shoplifted a video game at age 13.

However, because some juveniles are being charged with increasingly serious and violent offenses, this attitude is changing. Several states have opened some juvenile court proceedings to the public, especially for serious offenses. Many states now retain juvenile records, not allowing them to be sealed, expunged, or destroyed, and some states now allow sealed records to be opened.[23] These records include evidence collected by the police, such as statements, fingerprints, photographs, and DNA samples. States' rules for collecting such information vary widely, with many specifying certain ages under which information such as fingerprints can't be collected at all. Local police must be well aware of their state laws concerning juveniles when collecting this information.

Search and Seizure

An officer may conduct a search without a warrant or probable cause if the subject, either a juvenile or adult, gives **consent**. There is no set age at which a juvenile is considered to be able to consent to a search, and simply being young or immature isn't necessarily enough to excuse juveniles from consent in states that allow juvenile searches. Courts evaluate a juvenile's ability to consent by considering whether the search was voluntary based on the **totality of circumstances**. This means that courts consider the juvenile's consent in light of a number of factors, including age and maturity level, intelligence, the type of offense, and whether the juvenile has had prior contact with the justice system. A 16–year–old who consents to a search that turns up marijuana and who has been taken into custody for the same offense before will probably be considered by the courts to be able to give consent. See Crosscurrents 13.1 for a particularly interesting twist on search and seizure.

If, for some reason, a court finds a juvenile's consent to be invalid, then all evidence turned up in the search will be thrown out. It is important to remember that juvenile searches and consent are yet another gray area in how police deal with juveniles and that the rules vary from state to state. Some states allow no juvenile searches, regardless of consent, while others allow them only when a parent or attorney is present.[24] Most states allow the consent of parents or guardians who give police permission to search the room and possessions of a juvenile who lives in their home without paying rent. If the child is paying for room and board—for instance, a 17-year-old who has a job—then courts usually require the teenager's consent. The difference isn't necessarily age but ownership of the property in question. Parents are considered to be the owners of their child's property, so the consent to search an 8–year-old's room must come through the parents. The 17-year–old, however, is considered to own the room he rents, even if it's from his parents.[25]

The other major special consideration of juvenile consent involves searches on school grounds. Basically, a juvenile may be searched while at school, including his or her possessions and locker, without a warrant, probable cause, or consent as long as administrators have reasonable grounds. The reason for this is that the safety of everyone else in the school outweighs the juvenile's right to privacy or consent.

consent
The voluntary agreement by a person of age or with requisite intelligence who is not under duress or coercion and who understands the proposition to which he or she is agreeing.

totality of circumstances
The consideration by the court of all the conditions surrounding an issue, such as police interrogation or juvenile consent to a search or interrogation.

13.1   CrossCurrents

Magic Bullet

The Fourth Amendment guarantees citizens "the right of the people to be secure in their persons, houses, papers, and effects, against unreasonable searches and seizures. . . . " A long trail of court cases applies this principle to the specific circumstances of cases. How far should the government be allowed to go in violating the privacy of citizens as it pursues suspected offenders? This is a slippery slope because as the court makes decisions on cases, these decisions become precedent for further interpretations of the law concerning search and seizures. One interesting case concerned that of 17–year–old Joshua Bush.

Bush was involved in the robbery of a used car lot and exchanged gunfire with the owner. When questioned a week later, he admitted taking part in the robbery but denied he had anything to do with the shooting. The police officers noticed one of his eyes was discolored and that he had a big knot on his forehead. Bush claimed he got hurt playing basketball, but when he went to the emergency room a few days later, claiming to have been struck by a stray bullet, the police wanted to investigate the case in greater detail.

A judge issued a search warrant allowing the police to schedule surgery to remove the bullet from Bush's forehead so that they could determine if it came from the gun of the car lot's owner. Bush has fought the surgery and, so far, the hospital has refused to do it because it claims that the medical profession should not be an arm of the state. The bullet is not life threatening and neither is the surgery, although it requires general anesthesia. The case presents several interesting legal issues. For example,

> Dr. Arthur Caplan, director of the Center for Bioethics at the University of Pennsylvania, predicted Bush's rights as a patient would trump the state's desire to get the bullet, and said authorities may have a hard time finding someone willing to extract the slug. "It truly is a moral quandary," Caplan said. "Doctors are caught between wanting to help solve crimes and their responsibility to patient's rights to refuse a procedure."[1]

This case also tests the constitutional right against unreasonable search. The government wants Bush to undergo surgery to gather evidence from his body that could help convict him of attempted murder. Presently, the government requires suspects to provide urine and blood samples and to submit to DNA collection, but these procedures are unobtrusive when compared to the Bush case. How far should the state be allowed to go in pursuing evidence?

Think About It

1. Should the Fourth Amendment protect citizens from getting unwanted procedures that would aid the police in making a criminal case?
2. Is the court qualified to make judgments that require medical procedures in criminal or delinquency cases?
3. Should Bush's age and delinquent status play any part in the decision to remove the bullet from his head?

1. Juan A. Lozano, "Teen Fights Removal of Bullet in Head," ABC News/AP, abcnews.go.com/US/print?id=2743894.

Interrogation

Miranda rights

The rules concerning arrest and police interrogation that stem from the 1966 criminal case *Miranda v. Arizona*.

Juveniles have the same **Miranda rights** as adults: the right to remain silent, the right to counsel, the right to know the specific charge, and the right to confront witnesses. Some states and the federal government even have "juvenile *Miranda*" requirements, which we will cover later. The rules regarding the interrogation of juveniles are much like those for adults, with a few key differences, such as ensuring that the youth understands the situation, the presence and concern of parents or guardians, and waiver of *Miranda* rights. This is part of the totality-of-circumstances test, in which courts consider all the circumstances of a case, including the juvenile's age, life experience, intelligence, maturity, and juvenile record, if any. The U.S. Supreme Court uses three amendments to regulate police interrogation (see A Closer Look at Juvenile Issues 13.1 for the full text of these amendments).

- **Fifth Amendment**   Privilege against self-incrimination
- **Sixth Amendment**   Right to counsel

13.1 A CLOSER LOOK at JUVENILE ISSUES

CONSTITUTIONAL AMENDMENTS REGULATING POLICE INTERROGATION

Fifth Amendment

No person shall be held to answer for a capital, or otherwise infamous crime, unless on a presentment or indictment of a grand jury, except in cases arising in the land or naval forces, or in the militia, when in actual service in time of war or public danger; nor shall any person be subject for the same offense to be twice put in jeopardy of life or limb; nor shall be compelled in any criminal case to be a witness against himself, nor be deprived of life, liberty, or property, without due process of law; nor shall private property be taken for public use, without just compensation.

Sixth Amendment

In all criminal prosecutions, the accused shall enjoy the right to a speedy and public trial, by an impartial jury of the state and district wherein the crime shall have been committed, which district shall have been previously ascertained by law, and to be informed of the nature and cause of the accusation; to be confronted with the witnesses against him; to have compulsory process for obtaining witnesses in his favor, and to have the assistance of counsel for his defense.

Fourteenth Amendment, Section 1

All persons born or naturalized in the United States, and subject to the jurisdiction thereof, are citizens of the United States and of the state wherein they reside. No state shall make or enforce any law which shall abridge the privileges or immunities of citizens of the United States; nor shall any state deprive any person of life, liberty, or property, without due process of law; nor deny to any person within its jurisdiction the equal protection of the laws.

- **Fourteenth Amendment**   Right to due process. This amendment received the most exercise up until the early 1960s. The Supreme Court's concern was that young age, maturity, and overall competence affected the ability to waive rights and give confessions, thus violating the juvenile's rights of due process and equal protection.[26]

Haley v. *Ohio* (see Case in Point 13.1), one of the seminal juvenile cases to reach the Supreme Court, set forth an important rule regarding coerced confessions.

MIRANDA AND JUVENILES   *Miranda* rights, which stem from the landmark case *Miranda v. Arizona,* apply to "custodial interrogation by law enforcement officers."[27] Everyone who is arrested (or taken into custody) must hear a *Miranda* warning (see A Closer Look at Juvenile Issues 13.2). These rights generally apply equally to juveniles and adults, with some exceptions (see the discussion of juvenile *Miranda* rights that follows). The key terminology here is *custodial* and *law enforcement officers.* The courts have found that *Miranda* rights do not apply if the subject is not in police custody (arrested) or the interrogator is not a law enforcement officer or acting as an instrument of the police (this would include some personnel who work with juveniles but aren't sworn police officers). *Miranda* rights do not apply in casual conversations with police officers or when the subject hasn't been arrested. They do not apply if the interrogator is not a police officer but is a parent, teacher, or school principal. In short, *Miranda* rights apply only to a narrow range of circumstances that still, according to some critics, have not been clearly defined.

For example, see Case in Point 13.2, *Yarborough v. Alvarado,* in which the police interviewed 17-year-old Michael Alvarado, who was not officially in custody. Alvarado confessed to the offense, and his statements to police were used to convict him. The U.S. Supreme Court ruled that the police were not required to read Alvarado his *Miranda* rights because he was never in custody. The dissent to the case pointed to the facts that Alvarado had been brought to the police station by his parents, the police had not allowed the parents to attend the interview, the interview continued for hours, and the police never told Alvarado, or his parents that they could leave at any time. From this point of view, the interview was custodial in all but name. The Supreme Court, however, following the totality-of-circumstances test, found in favor of the police.

13.1   CASE IN POINT

THE CASE	THE POINT
Haley v. Ohio, 332 U.S. 596 (1948).	*The U.S. Supreme Court rules that coerced confessions violate the due-process clause of the Fourteenth Amendment. This case is also the first time that the Supreme Court extended to juveniles the constitutional rights of adults, determining that juveniles must also receive due process.*

About midnight in 1945, William Karam of Canton, Ohio, was shot and killed in his store by either Alfred Parks, 16, or Willie Lowder, 17. John Haley, 15, was with both boys before they went into the store and was waiting for them outside when the shooting occurred. Five days later, Haley was arrested at his home just after midnight on Saturday and taken to the police station.

According to Haley and his mother, the police beat him. His mother testified that the clothes Haley wore when arrested, which she replaced two days later with clean ones that she brought to the jail, were torn and blood-stained. She also testified that when she first saw him five days after his arrest, he was bruised and skinned. The police denied beating Haley.

After arriving at the police station, police questioned Haley, alone, for about five hours in relays of one or two officers at a time. Haley confessed at around 5 A.M. Saturday morning, after being shown the alleged confessions of Lowder and Parks. The police never advised Haley of his right to see a lawyer, although the confession that the police typed began with a statement informing Haley of his constitutional rights.

Haley was jailed early Saturday morning. A newspaper photographer took Haley's picture after he confessed. Over the next few days, a lawyer that his mother had retained tried to see Haley twice but was refused by police. The police didn't allow Haley's mother to see him until Thursday. Haley didn't see a judge nor was he formally charged until three days after signing the confession.

Haley was convicted of first-degree murder and sentenced to life imprisonment. The Ohio Court of Appeals sustained the conviction over the objection that the admission of the confession at the trial violated the Fourteenth Amendment.

The U.S. Supreme Court reversed the decision, holding that "the Fourteenth Amendment prohibits the police from using the private, secret custody of either man or child as a device for wringing confessions from them."

13.2 A CLOSER LOOK *at* JUVENILE ISSUES

THE *MIRANDA* WARNING

This is the basic text of the *Miranda* warning. It might vary slightly by state.

You have the right to remain silent. Anything you say can and will be used against you in a court of law. You have the right to speak to an attorney and to have an attorney present during any questioning. If you cannot afford a lawyer, one will be provided for you at government expense.

The police must ensure that arrestees understand the warning. Some states have officers also say something like, "Do you understand these rights?" If the arrestee does not understand English, the warning and the arrestee's response must be translated. Also, an arrestee's silence doesn't constitute waiver of *Miranda* rights.

WAIVER OF MIRANDA RIGHTS   A juvenile may waive the *Miranda* rights, but this waiver must be intelligent and voluntary. The juvenile must understand what he or she is doing and what is at stake and must not have been coerced. Here most courts once again use the totality-of-circumstances test. Some states require courts to consider various other circumstances: whether parents are present, the length of the detention, and the offense for which the juvenile is being questioned.[28]

13.2 CASE IN POINT

THE CASE

Yarborough v. Alvarado 541 U.S. 652 (2004), 316 F.3d 841, reversed.

THE POINT

Only suspects who are in police custody require a Miranda *warning. Suspects who aren't in police custody don't require* Miranda, *although their statements to police may be held as evidence. The police aren't required to consider a suspect's age and experience. The circumstances that require a* Miranda *warning apply equally to adults and juveniles.*

In 1995, Michael Alvarado, 17, helped Paul Soto attempt to steal a truck. The owner of the truck was shot and killed, although Alvarado didn't pull the trigger. The Los Angeles police called Alvarado's mother, and she agreed to take him to the station for questioning. At this time, Alvarado was a high-school student with no arrest record.

Alvarado's parents took him to the station and asked to be present with their son during the interview but were denied. They waited in the lobby for two hours while Alvarado was questioned. Alvarado was interviewed by one detective in a small room in which only the two of them were present. The detective didn't advise Alvarado of his rights under *Miranda v. Arizona.*

Alvarado initially denied being present at the shooting but finally admitted that he helped Soto during the robbery and to hide the gun after the murder. The detective asked Alvarado if he needed a break twice during the interview. When the interview was over, Alvarado, who was never arrested, went home with his parents.

The state of California charged Alvarado with murder and attempted robbery. He was convicted of second-degree murder and attempted robbery in a state court. Although Alvarado didn't receive a *Miranda* warning, the court didn't allow Alvarado to suppress the statements he made in the interview. Alvarado sought a writ of habeas corpus, alleging that he was deprived of his Fifth Amendment rights in violation of *Miranda v. Arizona.*

The District Court of Appeal affirmed Alvarado's conviction, ruling that a *Miranda* warning was not required because Alvarado was not in custody during the interview and had been free to leave the station at any time, although the police had never advised him of this. The federal district court agreed with the state court, but the Ninth Circuit Court of Appeals reversed the decision, holding that the state court did not consider Alvarado's age and inexperience when evaluating whether a reasonable person would have felt free to leave the interview.

The U.S. Supreme Court reversed the Ninth Circuit decision in a 5–4 opinion, finding that the trial court had reached a reasonable conclusion in that Alvarado's interview didn't constitute custody and didn't require a *Miranda* warning and that age and experience made no difference in this matter.

A court will probably closely examine a juvenile waiver at some point, especially those given by young children and juveniles accused of serious offenses.[29] Also, both juveniles and adults must be very clear in refusing to waive *Miranda* rights, especially in states without strict requirements for juvenile waiver, such as *per se* or lawyer requirements. If the juvenile doesn't clearly assert *Miranda* rights, police can continue the interrogation, and the court will allow any evidence they collect.[30]

Apparently, most juveniles who do not have representation waive their *Miranda* rights. Studies have found that most children under the age of 15 simply don't understand the right to remain silent and to have a lawyer. They might feel like their counsel is working for the court and not them and that their right to silence might be later revoked in court.[31] Another reason could be related to the expectations of children from parents and teachers. They have no "right to remain silent" when being questioned for breaking a vase at home or cheating on a test at school, nor do they have the right to an attorney. So, from the child's viewpoint, why would they have these rights with police?

THE "JUVENILE MIRANDA"   The federal government and some states have rules that give arrested juveniles a bit more protection than adults. These juvenile *Miranda* rules, which vary by state, usually allow a juvenile to waive *Miranda* rights only after being informed of the right to consult with someone, such as a parent or guardian, who is interested in his or her welfare. Some rules allow extra protection only for very young juveniles, such as those under the age of 12. Some states require juveniles to consult with a parent, guardian, or "interested adult" before or during interrogation for a *Miranda* waiver to be valid. This is called a ***per se* requirement**, although it can be called an interested adult test, friendly adult test, or concerned adult test.[32] A few states require juveniles to consult with a lawyer before waiving their *Miranda* rights.[33]

The following is a summary of the guidelines for federal law enforcement officers to ensure that juvenile confessions aren't suppressed in court:

> Once a juvenile is in custody, the arresting officer must make a good faith effort to notify the juvenile's parents or guardian to tell them that the child has been taken into custody, what offense the child was accused of committing and the juvenile's *Miranda* rights. A juvenile's *Miranda* rights must be given in a language that the juvenile can understand. The confession must also be otherwise voluntary. If the juvenile requests an attorney or invokes his or her right to remain silent, the interrogation must stop immediately. The juvenile must appear before a magistrate "forthwith." If the juvenile is not afforded these due process rights, the confession may be suppressed.[34]

Basically, these are the same rights that adults have, with the exception of the requirement of notification of parents or guardians.

Custody

Police must treat juveniles in custody differently than adults in custody. In Chapter 15, we cover the punishment and treatment functions of juvenile incarceration, but first we must examine police detention. In reference to detention, the 2002 reauthorization of the Juvenile Justice and Delinquency Prevention Act holds that states must comply with four "core protections" to receive grants. These protections are the following:

- Deinstitutionalization of status offenders
- Separation of juveniles from adults in institutions (separation)
- Removal of juveniles from adult jails and lockups (jail removal)
- Reduction of disproportionate minority contact where it exists[35]

All these protections apply to state juvenile justice systems as a whole, but one, the separation of juveniles from adults in adult jails and lockups, applies specifically to police and the way they handle juveniles in custody.

> Federal regulations discourage holding juveniles in adult jails and lock-ups. If law enforcement must detain a juvenile in secure custody for a brief period to contact a parent or guardian or to arrange transportation to a juvenile detention facility, federal regulations require that the juvenile be securely detained for no longer than 6 hours and in an area that is not within sight or sound of adult inmates.[36]

A juvenile who is taken into custody is not necessarily "arrested." The juvenile might be placed under the state's control for his or her own protection. However, if the juvenile is suspected of unlawful behavior, he or she may be placed in **detention**.

per se *requirement*
The legal requirement that an arrested juvenile consult with a parent, guardian, or other "interested adult" before or during interrogation to waive Miranda rights.

detention
The temporary care of a child alleged to be delinquent who requires secure custody in physically restricting facilities pending court disposition or execution of a court order.

In 1980, Congress ordered that status offenders and nondelinquents (juveniles who are in custody because they are dependent, neglected, or abused) had to be removed from all secure facilities and that juvenile delinquents, status offenders, and nondelinquents could not be detained in adult jails and lockups. Basically, the rule for juveniles in custody is that they must be kept well separated from adult offenders, regardless of the facility.[37] There are two major reasons for keeping juveniles and adults separate (and this is true for prisons and other secure facilities, as well as jails and lockups). The first is to ensure the physical and psychological safety of the youths, and the second is so that secure facilities don't become crime schools.

Let's take a closer look at these two reasons. First, mixing juvenile delinquents with adults is not only traumatic, but dangerous for them. One study found that youths in adult facilities were sexually assaulted five times more often than those in juvenile facilities, as well as assaulted by staff twice as often and assaulted with a weapon 50 percent more often.[38] The second reason concerns the simple risk of adult offenders helping youths improve their crime skills, from, say, better ways to break and enter a residence to expanding a market for selling drugs. Basically, housing adult and juvenile delinquents together offends the philosophy of juvenile rehabilitation. These two problems are a risk at any confinement area, from a rural lockup, where the police are responsible, to a big state penitentiary at the corrections level. Remember, the juvenile justice system at all points in the system, including the police, is devoted to the protection and rehabilitation of juveniles.

DISCRETION: HOW THE POLICE DECIDE WHAT TO DO

The police don't take into custody every juvenile suspected of breaking the law. The police use a certain amount of professional judgment or discretion in deciding whom to arrest. When examining the factors that go into police discretion, it becomes clear that there is great variation in how the juvenile justice system processes cases. For the police officer, discretion can be divided into three types, based on the demands of the law, the situation, or bias.

Demands of the Law

The three legal factors that most influence taking a juvenile into custody are these:

1. **The seriousness of the offense**   This is the most important factor. Generally, as the seriousness of the offense increases, police discretion decreases, and custody becomes more likely.

2. **Frequency of offense**   If an officer sees a juvenile frequently in suspicious circumstances or if the juvenile is already known to be a frequent offender, the officer is more likely to take the juvenile into custody.

3. **Prior or current involvement with the juvenile justice system**   A juvenile with a history of custody and detentions or one who's under juvenile probation is more likely to be arrested if the officer suspects something.[39]

Demands of the Situation

A number of situational factors involving police discretion can influence whether an officer takes a juvenile into custody.

> The body motion, facial expressions, voice intonation, a known past record by the juveniles involved provide the officer with an initial basis for inferences, judgments, routinized evaluations as revealed in the language categories he employs.[40]

Different officers will use this discretion in different ways. Experience teaches them what to look for in the behavior of suspects and how the local juvenile justice system responds to particular issues and concerns. The situational factors the police officer takes into consideration when dealing with juveniles include these:

1. **Attitude**   A juvenile's attitude can make a big difference in police response depending on the offense. Serious or frequent offenders are more likely to be taken into custody regardless of their attitude toward the police, simply because the police have less discretion in the matter. But if the offense is not serious, such as certain status offenses, the amount of deference the youngster shows toward an officer can, in turn, affect the officer's attitude toward the youth and the decision to take him or her into custody.

2. **Family**   We have all seen movies or television shows, especially old ones, in which a police car pulls up to a house and the officer escorts a shame-faced boy or girl to the door and explains to a pair of very stern and displeased parents what the child has done. It is usually something minor or silly, like breaking a window or running away after a family spat. This scenario is not just something that happens on television. This is what officers do when the offense is minor enough and they can be relatively sure that the youth's family will discipline him or her. Such discretion is more likely in small jurisdictions or neighborhoods where the officers know the local residents and vice versa.

3. **Complaint**   If someone complains about a juvenile's behavior, especially if it is a victim, police are more likely to take the juvenile into custody. Most of the decisions that police make are invisible to the public, so they are free to use more discretion. However, a complaint or an obvious victim can throw a bright light on police discretion. If there is a complaint and no arrest, especially, say, if neighbors are standing around and watching, the officer risks the appearance of not doing his or her job, which can damage the department's relationship with the community.

4. **Style of policing**   In 1968, political scientist James Q. Wilson defined three policing styles: legalistic, watchman, and service. The legalistic style describes officers or departments who work strictly "by the book" and use little discretion. If a situation legally calls for an arrest, the officers arrest and follow the letter of the law. The watchman style is nearly the exact opposite. This style depends on discretion, and watchman–style officers act only on serious or very obvious offenses. If a watchman–style officer does not see trouble, then trouble is not there as long as public order is not disturbed. The last style, service style, is a combination of the other two. The service–style officer arrests (or takes into custody) offenders when it is called for but is also more likely to use alternative solutions or diversion, rather than sending the offender straight through the system. So, as you can see, a department's style can affect how officers treat juvenile delinquents. Consider a young teenager who is sitting outside a house drinking what appears to be a beer and smoking what might or might not be tobacco. A legalistic–style officer will attempt to take the status offender into custody, determine if she's smoking tobacco or marijuana, then proceed as the law specifies. A service–style officer might question the juvenile and determine where her parents are and what her juvenile status is (including her exact age, where she goes to school, where her home is, record of offending if any, etc.). The service–style officer will probably take the juvenile into custody but then might try to find the parents and/or refer her to an alternative program, rather than seek a formal disposition. The watchman–style officer will ensure that the neighborhood is calm and keep driving.

5. **Friends**   If a youngster is associating with known troublemakers, delinquents, or gang members, custody is more likely.

6. **Individual traits**   An officer might decide to pursue custody based on the youngster's age, physical appearance, and level of maturity. This also depends on the offense. A shoplifting 10–year–old might only be sent home to his parents with a stern warning, whereas a 16–year–old who commits the same offense might face more serious sanctions because he's closer to adulthood. On the other hand,

a bedraggled and frightened–looking 10–year–old at a bus station will most certainly be taken into custody for her own protection, whereas a 16–year–old with enough confidence and physical size might appear to be an adult and not be approached by the police at all.

7. **System characteristics**   These are extremely practical considerations. Custody is less likely, especially for a minor offense, if the police do not have a proper juvenile detention area or if this area is already crowded with more serious delinquents. If the community has few or no community referral programs and/or is having a problem with delinquency, even gangs, then custody and formal processing are more likely.

Discretion and Bias

Police officers dealing with delinquency must constantly operate on their best intuition. The law and departmental policy go only so far in guiding the police in doing a difficult job. At some point, officers must rely on their own judgment, background, and feelings. Although the great majority of officers do their jobs as objectively as possible, data suggest that a certain level of bias is inherent in the juvenile justice system, including the phase in which police officers interact with juveniles. This bias is both overt and unconscious on the part of the officers, and it can include racial, gender, and social class dimensions. It is overt in the sense that police officers participate in proactive policing in which they target specific neighborhoods, gangs, and offenses. It is unconscious because many police actions are predicated on issues that are, to a large degree, organized by race; therefore, racial bias is introduced into the activities of the police.

RACIAL DISCRIMINATION BY THE POLICE   Police officers will argue that illegal behavior, not race, is their motivation; however, a disproportionate number of minority juveniles are arrested. Officers will also argue that they are making that community safer when they target delinquents. Citizens demand that law enforcement officials provide adequate coverage to their neighborhoods and not let teenagers take over the streets. However, when police officers engage in racial profiling, their justifications for arresting greater proportions of minorities are suspect. Black youths complain of being stopped by police for "driving while black."[41] In other words, they believe they are specifically targeted because of their race and that white youths don't suffer the same level of suspicion even though they are engaged in similar activities.

Similarly, the actions of police officers have an unconscious dimension because of the societal bias against minorities. This principle can be demonstrated in two ways.

1. In his classic book *Justice without Trial*, Jerome Skolnick introduces the idea of **symbolic assailant**.[42] This is the mental picture that many people have of what criminals look like. To a disturbing degree, this symbolic assailant is a young, black male. People are so willing to accept this description of a criminal that when Susan Smith drowned her two children in South Carolina, she was successful for weeks at getting police officials to search for a black male who did not exist.

2. The unconscious bias against minorities is also demonstrated in a study cited by Everette Penn in his discussion of why race matters in juvenile justice. According to Penn, this study involved sending identical résumés to 1,300 places that advertised job openings. Some résumés had "white-sounding" names such as Brad, Matthew, Sarah, and Emily, while others had "black–sounding" names such as Rasheed, Tyrone, Jamal, and Lakisha. The "white" names had a 50 percent greater call–back rate than the "black" names, although the résumés bearing the black names showed superior qualifications, such as better schooling and more awards.[43]

Racial bias will become a constant theme in our discussion of the juvenile justice system throughout the remainder of this book. The effects of discrimination, which begin with law enforcement, compound throughout the system. According to Penn,

symbolic assailant
The mental picture that many people have of criminal offenders.

"Being Black" becomes a variable that explains the cumulative effect for black youths once they're inside the juvenile justice system. Discriminatory practices by individuals applied at various decision points throughout the system create insurmountable hurdles for black youths to overcome in order to exit it. In the end, these hurdles produce an invisible wall that in its current state cannot be fully seen, avoided, destroyed, or changed.[44]

The bias toward minority youths is not limited to black people. Youths of other ethnic and racial groups have also been treated differently by police. However, because of the way official records are collected, it is difficult to measure the amount of bias in the juvenile justice system. For instance, Myrna Cintrón lists reasons why Latinos are underreported in the juvenile justice system and why we know so little about how they are treated by criminal and juvenile justice agencies.

1. The criminal justice system lacks a uniform definition for the Latino group. Latino and Hispanic are used interchangeably, and many jurisdictions use terms of national origin (such as Puerto Rican and Cuban) for identification.

2. The system doesn't separate ethnicity from race. (Persons of Latino origin can be of any race.) As a result, counting Latinos as white inflates the proportion of whites in the criminal justice system while underreporting the proportion of Latinos in the system.

3. There is evidence that Latino youths are disproportionately arrested, detained, and tried in adult criminal courts. Their sentences are harsher, and their commitments are longer than those for white youths who have committed the same offenses. Latinos are significantly overrepresented in federal and state facilities, although arrest data are lacking or inconsistently collected across jurisdictions.

4. The juvenile justice system must recognize and address the challenge that the Latino population represents. The growth of the population, coupled with the effects of age, low educational attainment, immigration, acculturation, poverty, language, and discrimination, place Latino youths and their families at a greater risk for juvenile justice intervention.[45]

Cintrón's observations of the difficulties the juvenile justice system has in dealing with Latino or Hispanic youths reveal the problems of official definition and personal identity. The issues of terminology are magnified by the lack of attention given to the cultural uniqueness of each group of Latino youths. Youths whose families have been in the United States for generations find themselves stopped and questioned by police and immigration officers who suspect that they aren't legal citizens. Having a Spanish surname might single one out for suspicion and extra surveillance in schools and the juvenile justice system. The cultural lifestyle and dress preferences of Latino youths are sometimes interpreted by the police as signifying gang involvement.

GENDER DISCRIMINATION BY THE POLICE Girls aren't involved in nearly as much delinquency as boys. There are several reasons for this disparity, all of which are related to the biological differences and cultural experiences of growing up female in the United States. Generally, there are two aspects of the police treatment of juvenile girls. The first involves chivalry, and the second involves protection.

From the chivalry aspect, girls get more lenient treatment than boys because they are presumed to be less dangerous, and their delinquent behavior is assumed only to support boys. For instance, a girl who sells drugs is thought to be under the influence of a boyfriend, rather than simply working independently for a dealer. Therefore, the police are less likely to arrest her and to use her as an informant. Police officers act on their stereotypes of females and do not expect them to be serious delinquents and, therefore, do not proactively target them for arrest.[46]

The other side of gender discrimination concerns protection. This is most apparent with status offenses. Girls who commit status offenses are dealt with more harshly than boys. Running away from home is a status offense in which girls are arrested and referred to the juvenile court at a greater rate than boys. In the view of law enforcement and court officials, this is done for the girls' protection. Girls on the street are considered to be at a greater risk of victimization than boys. Being raped, recruited into prostitution, or otherwise victimized for sexual reasons is thought to be more likely for girls.

Researchers have confirmed that a double standard exists at many levels in the juvenile justice system whereby males are arrested more for delinquency, while girls are more likely to be processed for status offenses.[47] Like racial discrimination, gender discrimination is part of the discretion that police officers and other juvenile justice professionals introduce into the way they do their jobs. Whether overt or unconscious, this discretion results in young people being treated differentially by the system based on extralegal factors. This discretion might be limited or controlled in a number of ways.

Controlling Police Discretion

For the juvenile justice system to be applied fairly to the problems of delinquency, juveniles suspected of similar offenses and who have similar delinquent backgrounds should be treated in the same way. Although it is true that the juvenile justice system is more focused on treating each case on its individual merits, police discretion often results in practices that not only are racially or sexually biased, but also misspend resources on the wrong juveniles. By arresting, adjudicating, and incarcerating juveniles based on who they are rather than on what they have done, the system risks neglecting those who desperately need intervention and who may pose a real danger to society. What are the best ways to ensure that the juvenile justice system, especially police officers, exercises discretion in the most effective and fair way? At the very least, police should have clear guidelines that cover or include the following:

- **Restricting the law** One reason the police can use so much discretion in dealing with juvenile suspects is because youths are subjected to so many laws. In addition to the criminal code, juveniles also have the full range of status offenses that apply to them because of their age. These are well-meaning laws designed to protect youths from danger, but when used aggressively by police officers, they can result in greater surveillance and arrests. Instead of helping young people and channeling them toward the resources they need, the overreach of criminal and juvenile laws often suck them into the juvenile justice system. Some scholars have suggested that the best thing we can do for some delinquents is to ignore their behavior, because they will most likely grow out of their deviance as they grow older and become more integrated into society.

- **Written guidelines** Another way to control police discretion is to provide written guidelines on how to handle specific situations. Ideally, these guidelines are developed with the collaboration of juvenile court judges and youth service workers. By specifying the conditions under which a juvenile should be stopped, searched, or arrested, the guidelines would largely eliminate police discretion that focuses on gender, race, or ethnicity. The result would be a fairer pattern of police–juvenile interaction.

- **Training** Finally, police discretion could be controlled by properly training officers on the law, departmental procedures, and the youth development process. It is understandable that police officers consider juveniles to be as dangerous and intractable as adult suspects, but the police should be trained to use a certain amount of judgment and discretion in deciding which juveniles actually need intervention. There are behavioral reasons to bring the youth before the court that are independent of race, class, and gender. It is important to admit that discretion is inevitable and to train and educate officers in how it can best be applied to the problems of delinquency and the protection of children.[48]

The interaction between juveniles and police is problematic for several reasons. Although police might stop and question juveniles, their discretion is hard to keep track of until they take specific action and make a referral. The discretion used in deciding whom to stop, question, and refer rests on several factors.

First, youths who act suspiciously are most likely to attract the attention of the police. Additionally, youths loitering in or near high-crime areas will arouse police interest. Once stopped, youths who are polite and well–mannered will have an easier time than those who are impolite and challenge the officers' authority. The youth's style of dress, especially if it signifies gang involvement, could be deemed a sufficient reason for questioning, although no offense has been committed. Still, comparatively few youths are arrested when compared to the vast numbers who have street contact with the police. These stops are used as a filtering device, and the exact reasons for the stops and the arrests are hard to determine.[49]

PREVENTION: WHAT THE POLICE DO TO HELP

Generally, research shows that police are more successful in keeping the peace when they are closer to and more involved in the communities that they are policing. To this end, a number of philosophies, theories, and official programs seek to integrate officers into their communities in a variety of ways.

In traditional modern policing, officers are separate from their communities and react to situations. That is, they respond as offenses occur or are reported. Community policing-style programs and initiatives seek to make officers more proactive, trying to solve problems before they occur. Law enforcement agencies have long struggled to maintain order on the streets using a number of successful and not–so–successful approaches. Because a suspect's age isn't known until the time of police contact or arrest, these strategies are aimed broadly at both adult crime and juvenile delinquency.

A police officer gives a safety presentation to a kindergarten class at Thurgood Marshall Elementary School in Oakland, California. *(Courtesy Geri Engberg, Geri Engberg Photography)*

Here, we review three police strategies to address juvenile delinquency that are widely used, although with mixed results: community policing, problem-oriented policing, and zero-tolerance policing. These strategies involve very different patterns of interaction between the police and juveniles.

Community Policing

Law enforcement agencies struggle with the problems of gaining the community's trust and cooperation. This is especially true when dealing with juveniles who see police officers as authority figures with little tolerance for youthful behavior. As populations have grown larger in cities and technological advances, such as the patrol car, have put more social distance between the police and citizens, the bond between the police and the community has weakened. As the police have become more professionalized and bureaucratic, they have also lost close contact with their neighborhoods.[50]

Community policing is aimed at re-establishing the positive relationship between police and citizens. The idea is to get the police back on the streets where they can return to the roots of policing, the "neighborhood cop." Community policing covers a wide range of activities in which the police take an active part in the community. According to Samuel Walker and Charles Katz, community policing represents a major change in the role of police.

> While the police have traditionally defined their primary mission in terms of crime control, community policing seeks to broaden the police role to include such issues as fear of crime, order maintenance, conflict resolution, neighborhood decay, and social and physical disorder as basic responsibilities of the police.[51]

Community policing, then, is actually old rather than new. It represents what we expected of the police in the past before they became so focused on fighting crime and catching felons. The police are servants of the community, rather than an invading army, according to this perspective. Police scholar David Carter contends:

> It must be recognized that community policing is a philosophy, not a tactic. It is a proactive, decentralized approach to policing, designed to reduce crime, disorder, and fear of crime while responding to explicit needs and demands of the community.

Community policing seeks to establish the positive relationship between police and citizens. This officer is holding a little girl at an International Children's Day event in Central Park, New York City. *(© Brooklyn Museum / CORBIS All Rights Reserved)*

Community policing views police responsibilities in the aggregate, examining consistent problems, determining underlying causes of the problems, and developing solutions to those problems.[52]

On a daily basis, the work of the community police officer includes a variety of activities in addition to traditional law enforcement activities and responding to calls for service. These activities are concerned with making the officer a more integral part of the community and are designed to increase the interaction between the police and citizens. Many of the activities are aimed at crime prevention, while others are used to ensure that citizens have knowledge, confidence, and trust in the individual officers who are responsible for their community. According to Stephen Mastrofski, a community police officer's day includes the following:

- **Operating neighborhood substations**   One way that police departments have decentralized is by putting substations in neighborhoods, housing projects, and shopping malls. The idea is to have officers responsible for a consistent area, rather than having them roam throughout the city. This way the officers can become familiar with the people of the community, and citizens see a visible police presence in their neighborhood. In terms of juvenile justice, substations allow officers to become familiar with school personnel, youth service workers, and the youths who live in the neighborhood.

- **Meeting with community groups**   A range of community groups can assist the police in maintaining order in the community. Often, parents form groups that are concerned with their children's safety and welfare, and by including community police officers in their meetings, they are able to understand the concerns of law enforcement.

- **Working with citizens on crime-prevention programs**   The most notable of the crime-prevention programs is Neighborhood Watch. Here, officers help citizens "harden the target" by advising them on locking their homes, installing burglar alarms, and making sure they have emergency phone numbers handy. Additionally, police officers help neighbors establish procedures for looking after each other's homes when one is away.

- **Talking with students in schools**   There are a number of programs in which police officers enter schools in an attempt to become more effective in preventing and dealing with juvenile delinquency. These programs range from the traditional Officer Friendly school-resource officers to the DARE program. By maintaining a police presence in the schools, children are able to see at an early age that police officers are part of the social fabric of the school and community and will presumably be people whom they learn to trust and depend on.

- **Meeting with local merchants**   By maintaining close contact with local merchants, the police can gather a great deal of intelligence about what goes on in the community. Merchants are in their stores on a daily basis and are attuned to the patterns of interaction on the streets. Merchants depend on the police for timely responses to the problems of shoplifting and robbery, and forming a working relationship with the police is in their best interest. Even merchants who hire their own security guards find that a good relationship with the police is advantageous. Additionally, police officers who have intimate knowledge of those who work in the community are in a good position to see which liquor store owners, tavern keepers, or restaurant servers sell alcohol to underage youths.

- **Dealing with disorderly people**   Community police officers perform a number of order-maintenance functions. Rather than arresting every citizen who's teetering on the line between inappropriate behavior and violation of the law, community police officers attempt to settle disputes on the spot and channel disorderly people to agencies where they can get help.[53]

It is clear that community policing is aimed at more than the problems of juvenile delinquency. However, many of its activities affect juveniles who are delinquents or victims. Community policing is a broad philosophy aimed at building socially and physically healthy neighborhoods that can allow citizens to communicate effectively with the police. When specific problems are identified, community policing gives way to another type of police action, problem-oriented policing.

Problem-Oriented Policing

Problem-oriented policing, first developed by Herman Goldstein in 1979, is related to community policing but is different in substantial ways. The major difference lies in the proactive focus of problem-oriented policing. Rather than deal with improving relationships with the entire community to prevent crime, problem-oriented policing deals with specific recurring patterns of criminal or delinquent activity and addresses the underlying causes that promote law violations. For instance, in a downtown area that has a number of fights and muggings in the early–morning hours, the traditional police response would be to set up increased patrols to protect people from predators.

However, problem–oriented policing would take another approach. Looking at the patterns of fights and muggings surrounding several downtown bars, police would investigate to see if minors and obviously drunk patrons are being served and if closing times are being strictly observed. By conscientiously enforcing existing liquor laws, the problems of muggings and assaults can be addressed through problem–oriented policing, which focuses on the following principles:

- Focusing attention on substantive issues in the community
- A more analytical and empirical approach to the functions of the police
- Focusing on underlying problems instead of only individual incidents
- Employing a wider range of problem solutions instead of relying exclusively on the criminal law and its actual or threatened enforcement[54]

In dealing with juvenile delinquency, problem–oriented policing can be an effective strategy. Police have advised convenience–store operators and owners on methods to prevent teenagers from loitering in their parking lots. For example, by playing classical music on the loudspeakers outside the store instead of music generally preferred by teenagers, some store owners have discouraged them from hanging around. The attractive part of this tactic is that it did not result in interaction between youths and police. By altering the environment, the police and store owners were able to alter the conditions that led youths to engage in delinquent activity. The advantages of problem–oriented policing lie in the use of analyzing a problem and finding ways to resolve it without increased police resources or invoking the criminal law for minor delinquent acts.

Similar successes have been obtained when the police worked with other local and state officials to pressure landlords to bring their apartment buildings up to code and provide a clean, safe place for residents. As the housing improved, so did the overall quality of life in the neighborhood, making it more responsive to police efforts to address the problems of crime and drug sales. Problem–oriented policing encourages police departments to work with other government agencies as well as citizen groups to target hot spots where specific offenses occur because of underlying problems. By working on the causes of crime, problem-oriented policing can often prevent or greatly limit it.[55]

Zero-Tolerance Policing

Zero-tolerance policing is a form of community policing, but it is much more aggressive and proactive. The discretion that police use in zero–tolerance policing is aimed

Community policing is a broad philosophy aimed at building healthy, productive, and safe neighborhoods.

(Courtesy Myrleen Ferguson Cate, PhotoEdit Inc.)

at adults and juveniles suspected of minor offenses. Rather than handling these minor offenses informally, zero–tolerance policing uses discretion to invoke the full brunt of the law. By aggressively attacking minor offenses, it is presumed that delinquents and adult offenders won't have the motivation to commit major ones if they know that the minor ones are being dealt with so harshly.

Zero–tolerance policing is based on the "broken windows" theory developed by James Wilson and George Kelling.[56] Wilson and Kelling contend that run-down neighborhoods, that is, neighborhoods with broken windows, invite crime and delinquency. When people see that no one repairs the windows, they think that no one really cares about the property and that further vandalism will not be punished. By contrast, a neighborhood of well–kept homes signifies that the homes are occupied and cared about.

Wilson and Kelling apply the broken–windows analogy to public social interactions. This is where the theory becomes problematic and of interest in our discussion of the interaction between police officers and young people. Broken–windows theory suggests that streets populated with homeless people, con artists, and loitering youths are rife with minor crime and are unattractive places for law–abiding people to spend time. Streets and neighborhoods where socially marginal people are absent will be populated with families enjoying a walk outdoors and people window-shopping, and encourage an atmosphere of positive and socially connected exchanges between citizens.[57]

Broken–windows theory was the perspective behind the police efforts in New York City in the 1990s when Mayor Rudy Giuliani instituted a zero–tolerance policy. The police made misdemeanor arrests for offenses such as panhandling, public drunkenness, prostitution, jumping subway turnstiles, and public urination. By aggressively prosecuting these offenses, it was felt that many offenders would get the message that deviant behavior would not be tolerated. Additionally, this policy left a paper trail so that the police could keep track of those who committed minor infractions. The trail of arrest summonses and court hearings was useful for rounding up suspects when serious offenses occurred. This perspective has a certain logic, especially when crime rates decrease and citizens feel safe on the streets again. But there is reason to be cautious in judging its value.

Critics of the broken-windows perspective feel that it is biased against young people, the poor, and the socially marginal. By aggressively protecting the interests of the majority in the community, this perspective adversely affects the least powerful. In communities with few recreational activities for youths, does it make sense for the police to introduce them to the juvenile justice system when they commit minor offenses because they are alienated and bored? Constant police harassment can force youths to internalize the label of delinquent and make crime a self-fulfilling prophecy.[58]

A final concern with zero–tolerance policing that requires mentioning is **net-widening**, which refers to including increasing numbers of individuals under the control of the state. Under zero–tolerance policing, those who before were simply warned and released are now processed into the juvenile justice system and given some sort of minor sanction. A good deal of time, effort, and resources are devoted to dealing with offenses that are so inconsequential that they are often dismissed by a judge or diverted at the intake phase of the juvenile court.[59] As a police strategy, zero–tolerance policing alienates juveniles and provides them with reasons to distrust and hate the police. This is exactly the opposite of what community policing was envisioned to accomplish.

These various strategies that the police use to interact with juveniles produce different outcomes. With community policing, problem–oriented policing, and zero–tolerance policing, it is possible to see the range of approaches that can be used to attempt to prevent crime. Although these approaches are not specifically aimed at juveniles, they are important initiatives that greatly affect how police officers handle juvenile delinquency.

Instant Recall from Chapter 4
net-widening
Measures that bring more offenders and individuals into the criminal justice system or cause those already in the system to become more involved.

A police officer high-fives kids at a Boston school during gang resistance training. *(© Brooks Kraft / CORBIS)*

SUMMARY

1. The demands on the police are often contradictory and confusing when dealing with children and adolescents who violate the law or are victims of abuse and neglect.

2. The juvenile court revolutionized juvenile corrections, but the police had no such revolution. Although many police departments have juvenile officers, there is no specialized juvenile police force. Police management of juveniles is generally dictated by the courts, legislation, and officer discretion.

3. The step in the formalization process between local institutions and the 20th–century juvenile court was the police. During the early 20th century, the police resolved a large percentage of juvenile delinquency cases themselves without involving the courts.

4. Juveniles occupy a difficult and challenging place in police work for three reasons: the police must deal with juveniles often, especially adolescents; juveniles are more negative toward the police than adults; and juveniles commit a significant percentage of offenses.

5. A major issue in the relationship between law enforcement and juveniles is situational ambiguity; that is, when juveniles encounter the law, the situation and what to do about it are often ill-defined. The opposite of this concept is situational clarity.

6. Three units within police departments have the most contact with juveniles: special juvenile units (including gang units), juvenile officers, and patrol officers. The amount of special attention that juvenile delinquency gets from police departments depends on the department's size.

7. Patrol officers are the ones who most often deal with status offenders and take juveniles into custody. Larger departments have specialized juvenile units. In cities with gang problems, police departments have gang units.

8. Most juvenile delinquents enter the juvenile justice system through contact with police. A violent juvenile will almost certainly be detained after arrest. Cases involving neglected and/or abused children are turned over to child protective services.

9. Status offenders might be the easiest type of juvenile case for police because of the wide range of discretion they have. With status offenders, officers are likely to do nothing and end the status offense or take the juvenile into custody with (a) release to parents, (b) referral to an alternative social program, or (c) referral to juvenile court.

10. Violent juveniles curtail police discretion. If the violence is bad enough, the police have only the option of referral to court. Sometimes a third option, referral to an alternative social program, is possible.

11. Police do not need probable cause or a warrant to take a juvenile into custody, but many, if not most, departments notify the juvenile's parents after the fact. In deciding to introduce the juvenile to the system, the custody must meet one of two standards: probable cause and reasonable suspicion.

12. Once a juvenile has been taken into custody, the case is evaluated and processed into the system using a process called *booking*. Officers may fingerprint or photograph juveniles or collect their DNA under specific conditions. An officer may conduct a search without a warrant or probable cause if the subject consents.

13. Juveniles have the same *Miranda* rights as adults. The rules regarding the interrogation of juveniles are like those for adults, with a few differences, such as ensuring that the juvenile understands the situation, the presence and concern of parents or guardians, and waiver of *Miranda* rights.

14. A juvenile may waive *Miranda*, but this waiver must be intelligent and voluntary. These juvenile *Miranda* rules, which vary by state, usually allow a juvenile to waive *Miranda* only after being informed of the right to consult with someone, such as a parent or guardian, who is interested in his or her welfare.

15. Police must treat juveniles in custody differently from adults. Most important, juveniles must be kept well separated from adults when detained.

16. The three legal factors that most influence taking a juvenile into custody are the seriousness of the offense, frequency of the offense, and involvement with the juvenile justice system.

17. The situational factors the police officer considers when dealing with juveniles include attitude, family, complaint, style of policing, the juvenile's friends, individual traits, and system characteristics.

18. Generally, there are two aspects of the police treatment of girls: chivalry and protection. Girls get less police attention for serious offenses because they are thought to be less dangerous than boys or under the influence of boys. Girls get more police attention for status offenses because they are thought to need more protection.

19. Community policing-style programs and initiatives seek to make officers more proactive. Community

policing is aimed at re–establishing the positive relationship between police and citizens.

20. Problem–oriented policing deals with specific recurring patterns of criminal or delinquent activity and addresses the underlying causes that promote law violations.

21. Zero–tolerance policing is aggressive and proactive and uses discretion to invoke the full brunt of the law for even minor offenses.

REVIEW QUESTIONS

1. What is usually the first contact that young victims and offenders have with the juvenile justice system?

2. In the late 19th and early 20th centuries, how did the police deal with juveniles?

3. Which three police units have the most contact with juveniles?

4. How are the police most likely to handle status offenders?

5. What are police most likely to do with a violent juvenile?

6. What is probable cause? reasonable suspicion? Why are they important?

7. What are the special considerations involving taking a juvenile's fingerprints, photographs, and DNA?

8. What special conditions apply to juvenile waiver of *Miranda* rights? What is the "juvenile *Miranda*"?

9. What is detention?

10. What situational factors do police officers consider when dealing with juveniles?

11. What are the concerns of racial and gender discrimination by police?

ADDITIONAL READINGS

Bishop, Donna A., and Charles E. Frazier. "The Influence of Race in Juvenile Justice Processing." *Journal of Research in Crime and Delinquency* 25 (1998):242–261.

Braga, Anthony A., *Gun Violence among Serious Young Offenders* (Washington, DC: Office of Community Oriented Policing Services, U.S. Department of Justice, 2004).

Decker, Scott H. *Policing Gangs and Youth Violence* (Belmont, CA: Wadsworth, 2003).

Katz, Charles M. "The Establishment of a Police Gang Unit: An Examination of Organizational and Environmental Factors." *Criminology* 29 (2001):37–74.

Klinger, David A. "Demeanor or Crime? Why Hostile Citizens Are More Likely to Be Arrested." *Criminology* 32 (1994):475–493.

Pope, Carl, and Howard Snyder. *Race as a Factor in Juvenile Arrests* (Washington, DC: U. S. Department of Justice, Office of Juvenile Justice and Delinquency Prevention, 2003).

ENDNOTES

1. Samuel Walker and Charles M. Katz, *The Police in America: An Introduction*, 5th ed. (New York: McGraw-Hill, 2005), 253.

2. Barry C. Feld, *Juvenile Justice Administration in a Nutshell* (St. Paul, MN: West Group, 2003), 54–55.

3. David Wolcott, "'The Cop Will Get You': The Police and Discretionary Juvenile Justice, 1890–1940," *Journal of Social History* 35, no. 2 (Winter 2001):356.

4. Ibid., 359–360.

5. Ibid., 349–371.

6. Albert R. Roberts, "Police Social Workers: A History," *Social Work* 21, no. 4 (July 1976): 294.

7. Ibid., 294–299.

8. Walker and Katz (see note 1).

9. Kären M. Hess and Robert W. Drowns, *Juvenile Justice* (Belmont, CA: Wadsworth, 2004), 216.

10. Ibid., 219–220.

11. Ibid., 247.

12. Walker and Katz (see note 1), 254.

13. Aaron V. Cicourel, "Process and Structure in Juvenile Justice," in David L. Parry, ed., *Essential Readings in Juvenile Justice* (Upper Saddle River, NJ: Pearson Prentice Hall, 2005), 137. Appeared in *The Social Organization of Juvenile Justice* (New Brunswick, NJ: Transaction, 1968; first published by Heinemann Educational Books Ltd., 1968).

14. Walker and Katz (see note 1), p. 254.

15. Vincent J. Webb and Charles M. Katz, "Policing Gangs in an Era of Community Policing," in *Policing Gangs and Youth Violence* (Belmont, CA: Wadsworth, 2003).

16. Howard N. Snyder and Melissa Sickmund, *Juvenile Offenders and Victims: 2006 National Report* (Washington, DC: U.S. Department of Justice, Office of Justice Programs, Office of Juvenile Justice and Delinquency Prevention, 2006), 152.

17. Anthony A. Braga, *Problem-Specific Guides Series, No. 23: Gun Violence among Serious Young Offenders* (Washington, DC: U.S. Department of Justice, Office of Community Oriented Policing Services, 2004). Online at www.cops.usdoj.gov/mime/open .pdf?Item=1078.

18. Snyder and Sickmund (see note 16), 104.

19. Rolando V. del Carmen and Chad R. Trulson, *Juvenile Justice: The System, Process, and Law* (Belmont, CA: Thomson Wadsworth, 2006), 75.

20. Ibid., 73, 76.

21. Cicourel (see note 13), 137.

22. Ibid.

23. del Carmen and Trulson (see note 19), p. 102.

24. Ibid., 88–89.

25. Ibid., 89.

26. Feld (see note 2), 98.

27. Sarah H. Ramsey and Douglas E. Abrams, *Children and the Law* (St. Paul, MN: Thomson West, 2003), 527.

28. Feld (see note 2).

29. del Carmen and Trulson (see note 19), 101.

30. Ibid., 102.

31. Ramsey and Abrams (see note 27), 531–532.

32. Thomas Von Wald, "No Questions Asked! *State* v. *Horse*: A Proposition for a Per Se Rule When Interrogating Juveniles," *South Dakota Law Review* 48 (2003): 143–171.

33. del Carmen and Trulson (see note 19), 100.

34. Joey L. Caccarozzo, "Juvenile *Miranda* Rights" (Federal Law Enforcement Training Center, 2006), www.fletc.gov/training/programs/

legal-division/the-quarterly-review/research-by-subject/ 5th-amendment/juvenile*Mirandarights*.pdf/view.

35. Office of Juvenile Justice and Delinquency Prevention, *Guidance Manual for Monitoring Facilities under the Juvenile Justice and Delinquency Prevention Act of 2002* (Washington, DC: U.S. Department of Justice, Office of Justice Programs, 2003), 1. Online at ojjdp.ncjrs. org/compliance/guidancemanual.pdf.

36. Snyder and Sickmund (see note 18), 104.

37. Office of Juvenile Justice and Delinquency Prevention (see note 35),2.

38. Dale Parent et al., *Conditions of Confinement: Juvenile Detention and Corrections Facilities, Research Summary* (Office of Juvenile Justice and Delinquency Prevention, 1994); Martin Forst, Jeffrey Fagan, and T. Scott Vivona, "Youth in Prisons and Training Schools: Perceptions and Consequences of the Treatment-Custody Dichotomy," *Juvenile & Family Court Journal* 40, no. 1 (1989).

39. del Carmen and Trulson (see note 19), 77–78.

40. Cicourel (see note 13), 137.

41. Richard L. Lundman and Robert L. Kaufman, "Driving While Black: Effects of Race, Ethnicity, and Gender on Citizen Self-Reports of Traffic Stops and Police Actions," *Criminology* 41 (2003): 195–220.

42. Jerome Skolnick, *Justice without Trial: Law Enforcement in a Democratic Society*, 3rd ed. (New York: Macmillan, 1994).

43. Everette B. Penn, "Black Youth: Disproportionality and Delinquency," in Everette B. Penn et al., eds., *Race and Juvenile Justice* (Durham, NC: Carolina Academic Press, 2006), 47–64.

44. Ibid., 60.

45. Myrna Cintrón, "Latino Delinquency: Defining and Counting the Problem," in Everette B. Penn et al., eds., *Race and Juvenile Justice* (Durham, NC: Carolina Academic Press, 2006).

46. Christy A. Visher, "Gender, Police Arrest Decisions and Notions of Chivalry," *Criminology* 21 (1983):5–28.

47. Barry Krisberg, *Juvenile Justice: Redeeming Our Children* (Thousand Oaks, CA: Sage, 2005), 113–114. See especially Chapter 6, "Young Women and the Juvenile Justice System."

48. Samuel Walker, *Taming the System: The Control of Discretion in Criminal Justice 1950–1990* (New York: Oxford University Press, 1993).

49. David A. Klinger, "Demeanor on Crime: Why 'Hostile' Citizens Are More Likely to Be Arrested," *Criminology* 32 (1994): 475–493.

50. Robert C. Trojanowicz and Bonnie Bucqueroux, *Community Policing: A Contemporary Perspective* (Cincinnati, OH: Anderson, 1990).

51. Walker and Katz (see note 1), 205

52. David L. Carter, *The Police and the Community*, 7th ed. (Upper Saddle River, NJ: Prentice Hall, 2002), 49.

53. Stephen D. Mastrofski, "What Does Community Policing Mean for Daily Police Work?" in Willard M. Oliver, ed., *Community Policing: Classical Readings* (Upper Saddle River, NJ: Prentice Hall, 2000), 318–324.

54. Herman Goldstein, *Problem-Oriented Policing* (New York: McGraw–Hill, 1990).

55. Gordon Bazemore and Allen W. Cole, "Police in the 'Laboratory' of the Neighborhood: Evaluating Problem-Oriented Strategies in a Medium-Sized City," *American Journal of Police* 3 (1994): 119–147.

56. James Q. Wilson and George L. Kelling, "Broken Windows: Police and Neighborhood Safety," *Atlantic Monthly* 249, no. 3 (March 1982):29–38.

57. Robert Panzarella, "Bratton Reinvents, 'Harassment Model' of Policing," *Law Enforcement News* (June 1998): 13–15.

58. Lorraine Green, "Cleaning Up Drug Hot Spots in Oakland, California: The Displacement and Diffusion Effects," *Justice Quarterly* 12 (1995):737–754.

59. Thomas Blomberg, "Diversion and Accelerated Social Control," *Journal of Criminal Law and Criminology* 68 (1977):274–282.

How did the juvenile court develop into a separate system?

Why do juveniles have reduced due-process rights in the juvenile court?

What are the goals of the juvenile court judge?

CHAPTER 14

The Juvenile Court

The greatest differences between the criminal justice system and the juvenile justice system are apparent in the juvenile court. Although each system is charged with essentially the same task, dealing with violations of the law, the juvenile justice system has an even broader mandate. It also has a different operating philosophy, more complicated relationships with other institutions, and perhaps most important, the deep suspicion of many observers that it coddles young criminals and lets them get away with seriously bad behavior.[1] The juvenile court has a complex role, so we will focus not only on how it works, but also on some of its shortcomings and challenges. By gaining an appreciation of the juvenile court's difficult and ambiguous mission, you will better understand why it has always been a source of controversy in society's attempts to curb crime and delinquency.

ORGANIZATION AND JURISDICTION OF THE JUVENILE COURT

We covered the development of the juvenile court in Chapter 2, so we won't repeat it here. However, it's important to remember the reasoning behind the invention of the court and its proposed goals. The idea was that a juvenile court would deal with juvenile delinquency more effectively, as well as protect children from the dangers of being handled in parallel with adult offenders.[2] Additionally, it was presumed that having child specialists address juvenile delinquency and dependency would prevent the justice system from victimizing children. These goals still have not been fully accomplished despite the well-meaning activities of generations of juvenile court judges, youth service workers, and child advocates. Part of the difficulty of achieving effective and humane juvenile courts can be found in their organization and jurisdictional structure.[3]

The structure of juvenile courts varies widely. In some highly populated jurisdictions, they are part of a juvenile justice center that works in conjunction with other youth agencies. In other places, they are a specialized court that operates in a central courthouse along with the other courts. Usually, they are called *juvenile courts*, but in some places they are referred to as *family courts* or *magistrate courts*.

Juvenile courts are almost exclusively a state and county responsibility. The federal government specifies some of the rules and laws that apply to juvenile courts, especially in dealing with status offenders; but, for the most part, the federal government defers to the states on juvenile delinquency. For a discussion of the role of the federal government in adjudicating juvenile cases, see Crosscurrents 14.1.

It is difficult to discuss typical juvenile court structure because states vary so much in how they organize jurisdictional responsibilities. Del Carmen and Trulson illustrate this difficulty in their discussion of courts of specialized and limited jurisdiction:

> A characteristic of most juvenile courts is that they do not have jurisdiction in all matters involving juveniles. States in which courts are considered of specialized or limited jurisdiction may have one court for serious delinquency cases (the juvenile court), and another court for minor delinquency (limited jurisdiction juvenile court), anther court for related family matters such as divorce or child custody disputes (domestic relations court), and yet another court for cases involving status offending, dependency, and neglect (probate court). Family members with multiple legal problems may, under some state structures, find their cases being heard by different judges, at different times, and in different places.[4]

This fragmentation of juvenile court structure is a problem with two possible fixes. The first involves some sort of coordinating function in which the various judges dealing with the same family meet and discuss the case. This allows the judges to schedule the case in a way that permits the issues to be decided in a progressive fashion. For instance, it makes little sense for one judge to set up an

14.1

CrossCurrents

Being a Kid Isn't a Federal Offense

It is fair to say that the federal government isn't in the juvenile justice business. Most juvenile offenses fall under the jurisdiction of state juvenile courts. For certain offenses, such as the killing of a federal officer, offenses on a military or American Indian reservation, and violation of a federal law, the federal government might become involved. However, if the offense is also a violation of state law, federal officials will usually defer to the state juvenile court.

For a juvenile to be tried in the federal court system, certain conditions must be met to show that there is a *substantial federal interest.*

- The state has no jurisdiction or refuses jurisdiction.
- The state with jurisdiction doesn't have adequate programs or services for juvenile delinquents.
- The offense is a violent felony, a drug trafficking or importation offense, or a firearm offense.

For the most part, the federal government does not want to prosecute juveniles mainly because it does not have a juvenile court or a juvenile correctional system. If the juvenile has to be incarcerated, the federal government must make arrangements with a state-run juvenile correctional facility.

The federal government can also certify the juvenile as an adult, in which case the proceedings are held in federal court. In this case, the juvenile would be afforded all the rights of an adult in the federal court system, including a jury trial. According to del Carmen and Trulson, the federal courts take on only about 500 juvenile cases each year. Many of these cases involve American Indian juveniles who have committed serious offenses on reservations.

Sometimes, however, the federal government is eager to assert its jurisdiction over juveniles who break federal laws. The 2002 case of the DC Sniper involved an adult and a juvenile who shot and killed several people from ambush over a period of several weeks in several states. Also, one of the victims worked for the FBI, and because the case involved firearms, the federal government filed charges along with the states of Virginia and Maryland.

After the arrests of Lee Boyd Malvo, 17, and John Allen Muhammad, 44, U.S. Attorney General John Ashcroft ordered federal agents to transfer Malvo from federal custody to local authorities in Fairfax County, Virginia. Ashcroft said that it was imperative that the death penalty be an option. Neither federal nor Maryland state law allowed the death penalty for offenders who were juveniles at the time of their offense, but Virginia law did.[1] Although Malvo was not sentenced to death, this case still illustrates how the federal and state governments collaborate to handle juveniles who have committed offenses that fall under the jurisdiction of both levels of government.

Think About It

1. Should the federal government get more involved in juvenile justice and create a federal system to handle juvenile offenses?
2. Would the federal government do a better or worse job of dealing with juveniles?

Source: Rolando V. del Carmen and Chad R. Trulson, *Juvenile Justice: The System, Process, and Law* (Belmont, CA: Wadsworth, 2006).

[1] Amnesty International, Urgent Action Alert, October 8, 2003, http://web.amnesty.org/library/Index/ENGAMR511272003.

---

expensive family counseling program under the assumption that the juvenile will be returned to his or her parents, only to have another judge send the juvenile to a secure detention facility. Coordination would save resources, time, and duplication of services.

A second solution to the fragmented nature of the juvenile court is to institute a unified court system in which one judge handles all the issues and concerns of a case. This one-stop justice would ensure that the cases would be dealt with holistically, rather than piecemeal. Theoretically, this single judge would become familiar with the dynamics of the family and craft solutions to its various problems. By knowing the family's history, how the siblings influence each other, and the parents' capabilities, the judge could construct long-term programs for remediation. By having one judge responsible for all the problems faced by a family, that judge would presumably claim ownership for the results of the court's dispositions.[5]

If having a coordination council or a unified court would help solve the problems of fragmentation in the juvenile court, why don't more states institute such solutions? The answer to this question can be summarized by one word: politics. Court structures have evolved with state legislators determining the composition of the court system. Change in court structures is opposed by several groups for various reasons.[6]

- **Jobs** Streamlining and consolidating courts could take jobs from judges and court workers. Making the courts more efficient would require a prolonged look at how cases are processed and who provides needed and unneeded services.
- **Power** Having a coordinating counsel means that judges would have to agree on the best way to dispose of cases. Although this might be in the overall best interests of the juveniles and might save money for the government, not all judges will see things in the same way.
- **Philosophy** Some juvenile court judges believe that the fragmented nature of the court system, while inefficient, is desirable. Although a juvenile might exhibit a myriad of problems, a single judge or court isn't always equipped to deal with all the youth's issues. A family court judge might be very effective in determining which parent should receive custody in a divorce but might know little, and couldn't care less, about how to deal with a child who is addicted to drugs. Although only one family might be the focus, its problems can be the purview of several different courts, each of which believes it has the optimal philosophy, temperament, and skills to deal with individual concerns.

This discussion of the different ways the juvenile court is structured and the relative advantages of each type of configuration highlights some of the complexity of the juvenile court process.

KEY PLAYERS IN THE JUVENILE COURT

In addition to the organizational structure of the court, the various actors in the juvenile justice system can be different across jurisdictions. Let's take a look at the roles of those responsible for representing the interests of the parents, the state, and, most important of all, the youth, as well as at the cases that wind through the juvenile court.

The key players in the juvenile court represent varying interests but must work together to achieve the goals of ensuring justice, providing for the best interests of juveniles, and moving a high volume of cases through the system. The players in the juvenile court have a greatly reduced adversarial relationship when compared to their counterparts in the criminal justice system, but because of their elected or appointed positions, they might have vastly different ideas about how to proceed in specific cases.

Juvenile Court Judge

The nature of the work of the juvenile court judge varies greatly depending on the state and the organization of the court. However, all juvenile court judges have some things in common regardless of jurisdiction. First, the juvenile court judge has discretion in how to conduct the courtroom's business. Some judges are extremely formal and legalistic, emulating the criminal court, while other judges are informal and nonadversarial. Because judges are such key actors in the juvenile court, they set the tone of the proceedings. The judge embodies the principle of *parens patriae* in a way that no other participant in the court does.[7] This concept requires the judge to act as a surrogate parent for the juvenile to ensure that his or her best interests are addressed. In cases in which a juvenile's parents have failed in their duty to care for, protect, and control their child, the judge assumes the responsibility to take a holistic look at the case and make decisions that provide for the juvenile's welfare, even if it means removal from the home or placement in secure detention. See Focus on Ethics 14.1 for a look at the types of controversial decisions that juvenile court judges sometimes face.

Like the judge in the criminal court, the juvenile court judge has a number of responsibilities to ensure that juveniles receive due process. To this end, juvenile court judges rule on pretrial motions that challenge the circumstances of the arrest, interrogation, and search-and-seizure. The judge must also decide if the juvenile will be kept in custody while the case is processed or returned to the parents' supervision. Plea-bargain arrangements must be approved by the juvenile court judge, as well as trials or hearings concerning the facts of the case and the juvenile's **culpability**. Finally, the judge must decide on the disposition and be prepared for appeals. Sometimes, the judge has to ensure that the juvenile's best interests are guarded because the parents are absent or in conflict with their child. Here the judge may appoint a **guardian *ad litem*** who can advocate for the youth's best interests in custody or abuse cases.[8]

Qualifications to be a juvenile court judge vary by state, but the vast majority of states require the judge to have a law degree. Most juvenile court judges have experience in the court as defense lawyers, although some might be politically appointed with little or no juvenile justice experience or expertise.

culpability
Blameworthiness. The moral state of being wrong, improper, or injurious.

guardian ad litem
A person appointed by the court to take legal action on behalf of a juvenile or an adult who, because of minor age or infirmity, is unable to manage his or her own affairs.

14.1   FOCUS *on* ETHICS

WA(I)VE GOODBYE TO CHILDHOOD

As a juvenile court judge, you have seen it all. Over the years you have managed to do a lot of good by crafting creative, individualized sentences that have rehabilitated juveniles headed in the wrong direction. You have won awards for your forward–looking approach to justice and delinquency, and as you near retirement, you are proud of your reputation and accomplishments.

Now the case of your career is before you, and you are perplexed as to what to do. You have before you a 15–year–old boy, born in the United States of Syrian parents, who is accused of involvement in a terrorist plot. This boy, Samir, has lived in the United States his entire life but is mixed up in a suspicious venture involving his distant cousins who arrived from the Middle East six months ago.

Samir's cousins have been buying hundreds of cell phones from local electronics stores, giving Samir the cash to make the purchases. Samir's cousins told him they could sell the phones overseas at a 200 percent profit and that he would earn enough money to pay for college.

Samir and his cousins were arrested by local police and charged with conspiracy to commit terrorist acts. The police think the phones will be used to construct bombs that will be used overseas against U.S. citizens and troops. The government wants you to waive the case to federal court for Samir to stand trial along with his cousins. Before you do this, however, you have some questions.

- Is this simply a case of media and government hysteria over terrorism? The purchase of the cell phones is perfectly legal, and you have seen no evidence that the phones are intended to be used to make bombs.
- Even if the cousins were planning to make bombs, did Samir know? It is possible that Samir's cousins lied to him and that he acted in good faith that he was making money in a legal manner.
- Samir, unlike his cousins, is a U.S. citizen, and linking his involvement to theirs might be unfair. He might fare better if you retained jurisdiction in juvenile court and monitored his activities for the next two years. Not only has Samir had no contact with the law before this, but he is an excellent student and is involved in several extracurricular activities. You worry his promising life would be ruined if his case went to federal court.

You are under tremendous pressure to waive this case to federal court. The country is hungry for some news of a successful response to terrorism, and you are feeling the political heat.

What Should You Do?

1. Should you waive the case to the federal court? After all, you are not an expert on international terrorism, and the juvenile court is no place to deal with this threat. If Samir is tried as an adult in the federal court, he will get all the due–process rights guaranteed to U.S. citizens.

2. Should you maintain jurisdiction of the case in state juvenile court? As a juvenile court judge whose responsibility is to look out for the best interests of the child, you are suspicious that Samir is being railroaded for political purposes.

Juvenile court judges ensure that juvenile suspects receive due process. *(Courtesy John Neubauer, PhotoEdit Inc.)*

Prosecutor

The prosecutor represents the state's interests in juvenile court hearings. Historically, the juvenile court did not have prosecutors, and cases were presented directly by police officers, school officials, or caseworkers. After the due–process revolution in the 1960s, the prosecutor became a standard fixture in the juvenile court and has evolved into a key player who exercises important discretion.

As in the criminal court, the prosecutor is the gatekeeper in the juvenile court. As cases are referred to the prosecutor, she or he decides if there is enough evidence to proceed, if that evidence was gathered in a legal manner, and if the case is serious enough to warrant the court's attention. Sometimes the prosecutor will use discretion to divert the case to another agency to be handled in a nonlegal way. Because the prosecutor's power is so great, some states have taken steps to curtail or circumvent the decision–making authority of this key player. Especially in serious cases in which the juvenile could be waived to criminal court, legislators have indicated a lack of trust in the prosecutor's discretion and have passed laws requiring mandatory waiver for certain offenses. This is part of the get-tough-on-crime movement of the criminal court that has filtered into the juvenile court. This shift in discretion in the judicial and executive branches of the government is a direct result of sensational offenses committed by juveniles who are seen as literally "getting away with murder." Nevertheless, the prosecutor remains a key figure who is responsible for representing the state's interests, which are considerable, even though the juvenile court operates under a vastly different philosophy than the criminal court.[9]

Juvenile Defense Counsel

When juvenile courts were first instituted, defense counsel for juveniles was not considered necessary. The judge and caseworkers were assumed to be working for the juvenile's best interests. Still, the informality of the proceedings often resulted in due-process violations and troubling inconsistencies. In a series of cases decided by the Supreme

Court, due-process protections concerning standards of proof and the right to confront hostile witnesses required juveniles to be represented by competent counsel. Today, many jurisdictions have juvenile courts that mirror the adversarial proceedings found in the criminal court. Defense lawyers are serious about their mandate to protect juveniles from abuses resulting from well-meaning but punitive decisions by the state. Although many judges wish to maintain the juvenile court's informality, in cases in which serious offenses are at issue, it's almost always necessary for the juvenile to be represented by counsel.[10] The quality of the defense counsel for juveniles varies greatly both within and across juvenile courts. Like the criminal justice system, youths may be represented by either their own lawyer or by one appointed by the state.

PUBLIC DEFENDERS   Lawyers appointed by the state may be private lawyers who are appointed as part of a court rotation system, or they may be **public defenders**. Public defenders are full–time state employees who represent the interests of those who can't afford private counsel. Typically, public defenders work under conditions of oppressive caseloads and have little support staff. Public defenders often do not have the resources to take very many cases to trial and so often encourage their clients, especially if they are guilty, to plea bargain. Private lawyers appointed by the court work under many of the same constraints as public defenders. Their compensation might be set by the court, which discourages private lawyers from spending a great deal of time and resources on cases when the pay is substantially limited. Further, the type of private lawyer who seeks work from the court will often be new and inexperienced.

public defender
An elected or appointed attorney who regularly defends those accused of criminal offenses who cannot afford a private attorney

This haphazard system of supplying lawyers for juvenile cases means that often the lawyer is unaware of the juvenile court's specialized procedures or the various treatment and dispositional options available to the client. Finally, the public defender or court-appointed lawyer might have little knowledge or appreciation of the problems that young people have in communicating their concerns, constructing their self-image, or negotiating the challenges of schools, gang activity, or bad parenting. Although many public defenders and private court-appointed lawyers provide excellent representation for juveniles, there is no system to ensure a uniform level of expertise.[11]

Before moving on to the other key players in the juvenile court, we must consider the low level of prestige and status that goes with practicing law in the juvenile court. For many judges and lawyers, the juvenile court is the "low–rent district" of the criminal justice profession. It is where one goes to gain experience and techniques that will be useful later in the practice of criminal law. Because many of the cases are low-stakes propositions, there is a general belief that new and inexperienced judges and lawyers cut their teeth in juvenile court, where mistakes and poor judgment don't have the dire consequences that they do in criminal court. We can see evidence of this in the movement to waive serious felony cases to criminal court. This is unfortunate, because decisions made at the juvenile court level can profoundly affect the lives of juveniles, and those who practice law at this level should be committed to the process and the children.[12]

Juvenile Intake Officers

Juvenile intake officers occupy another important gateway in the juvenile justice system. When police officers, schools, nurses, or other individuals who have contact with children send cases to juvenile court, it is the juvenile intake officer who recommends to the judge whether the case should be moved to the juvenile justice system. In fact, more than half the cases are dismissed or diverted to other agencies at the intake stage. Several factors must be weighed in determining if the case should proceed. Issues such as the juvenile's personal safety, the risk of flight, and the risks to the public if the juvenile is released must be considered by the intake officer before deciding to place the juvenile in detention.[13]

Juvenile Probation Officers

Juvenile probation officers have two roles. One role is to craft supervised-treatment plans for juveniles placed on probation (this will be discussed in greater detail in Chapter 15). The other role is to act as an officer of the court by investigating juveniles' social backgrounds and making recommendations to the judge on appropriate dispositions. In some jurisdictions, probation officers might act as intake officers, or they might mediate out–of–court settlements between juvenile delinquents and victims of delinquency. In other instances, the probation officer will work with parents in cases of abuse or neglect to solve the problem before it gets to the point of official referral to the juvenile court.[14] These key players in the juvenile court are the ones who process the cases. The ideal is that each case gets careful attention, and the best interests of the juvenile are weighed against the protection of society. Unfortunately, the ideal is elusive, and decisions are often made based on expediency and available resources. These key players do not always agree on the outcome, and the juvenile court often has more adversarial interaction than was envisioned by its creators.

JUVENILE COURT PROCESS

Now let's look at the actual process of the court. We will trace the stages each case goes through and identify some of the issues and concerns that must be overcome. Although this process differs slightly from jurisdiction to jurisdiction, essentially the same functions are accomplished as cases move through the system (see Figure 14.1). The process might seem unwieldy and inefficient, and it is, but these stages are necessary to protect the rights of the juvenile and to allow the juvenile justice system the time and attention it needs to evaluate the case and options for disposition. The juvenile court process is similar in many respects to that of the criminal court, but there are also stark differences based on the core philosophies of each institution.

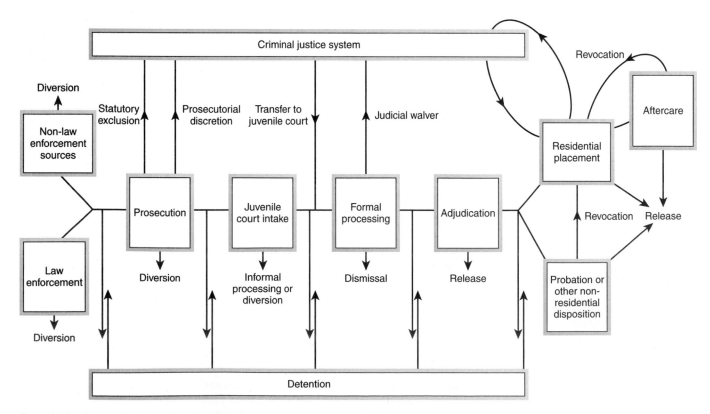

Figure 14-1   Stages of the Juvenile Justice System *Source:* Howard N. Snyder and Melissa Sickmund, *Juvenile Offenders and Victims: 2006 National Report* (Washington, DC: U.S. Department of Justice, Office of Justice Programs, Office of Juvenile Justice and Delinquency Prevention, 2006), 105.

Custody and Detention

As we learned in Chapter 13, taking a juvenile into custody is the equivalent of arresting an adult, with some minor qualifications. It is similar in that the juvenile may be taken into custody if the police officer sees a law being broken, if there is a court order, or if a complaint has been filed. Juveniles, but not adults, also may be taken into custody for their own protection in cases of abuse, neglect, or dependency.

Once in custody, the juvenile is subject to being held in detention until the intake officer and the juvenile court judge can evaluate the case to see if the youth should be returned to the care of parents or guardians until the hearing. If the juvenile is held in detention, the parents must be notified of the reasons for custody. Most juveniles are released to their parents, and only in circumstances in which the juvenile is in danger or a threat to others is detention preferred at this stage.[15]

Petitions and Summonses

Petition is the term used to refer to the filing of charges against a juvenile. Remember that there are additional reasons to file a petition besides actual delinquency. A petition may be filed to protect a child from harm if the parents are abusive or absent. A number of people, including police officers, teachers, parents, or nurses and doctors, may bring petitions to the court, but it is the court–appointed intake officer (often in consultation with the juvenile court judge) who decides to formally file a petition.

Once a petition is filed, a hearing date is set, and summonses, are issued for those concerned with the case. Typically, the summons is sent by registered mail, and failure to appear can result in a warrant from the judge.

Juvenile Court Hearings

The juvenile court has three types of hearings: the preliminary hearing, the adjudicatory hearing, and the dispositional hearing. Each state has its own rules on how

**Instant Recall
from Chapter 2**
petition
In juvenile court, a document that alleges that a juvenile is delinquent and that asks the court to assume jurisdiction over the juvenile, or asks that an alleged delinquent be waived to criminal court to be prosecuted as an adult.

The juvenile justice process resembles the criminal court process in many ways. However, there are some significant differences. *(Courtesy Mitch Wojnarowicz, The Image Works)*

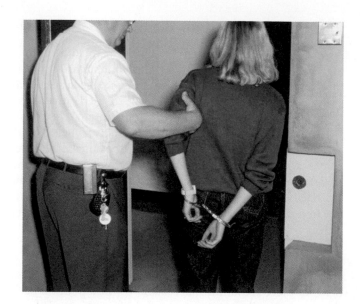

Juveniles who have committed serious offenses are typically held in secure detention facilities. This girl is being taken to a holding cell at a county jail. *(Courtesy James Shaffer, PhotoEdit Inc.)*

these hearings are conducted, each juvenile court judge will have a different standard of formality, and the lawyers will demonstrate varying levels of adversarial behavior.

preliminary hearing

The initial pre-adjudicatory hearing in which the judge explores the nature of the case and decides if it should be processed further.

PRELIMINARY HEARING   The **preliminary hearing** is the initial preadjudicatory hearing in which the judge explores the nature of the case and decides if it should be processed further. The judge reviews the intake officer's report and consults with the probation officer on the particulars of the case and the juvenile's social history and circumstances. The judge must determine that the parents and juvenile understand their rights, the nature of the charges, and whether the juvenile is likely to show up for further hearings. Additionally, the judge must decide if further detention is in order and, if so, in what type of facility the juvenile should be confined. For instance, juveniles who have committed serious offenses are typically sent to a secure detention facility similar to jail, and juveniles charged with status offenses or who need protection might go to foster homes. In large jurisdictions with heavy caseloads, the judge might be assisted by a court referee who will hear the less serious cases and make recommendations to the judge. At this stage in some cases, the judge will appoint a guardian *ad litem* to represent the juvenile's interests when there is conflict with the parents or if the parents aren't available.

adjudicatory hearing

The hearing in which a determination is made regarding whether the juvenile committed the offense with which he or she is charged.

ADJUDICATORY HEARING   The **adjudicatory hearing** is similar to a criminal trial with one major difference: there is no jury. Only in the rarest cases are juries used in juvenile court, and it is the judge who decides on the issue of culpability. Guilt and innocence aren't as important in juvenile court as they are in criminal court. The juvenile could be factually innocent of the charges, or the state might not present a convincing case, but the juvenile still may be placed in further detention. For example, in a case in which the judge decides the youth's home environment is dangerous or unsuitable or the youth is in danger of becoming a serious delinquent, the judge might decide not to wait until the youth commits a serious offense before intervening.

The judge has the latitude to craft solutions that are in the best interests of the juvenile and society regardless of what happens in the hearing.[16] However, the judge is concerned that the allegations be based on fact and will apply one of two standards of proof.

preponderance of evidence

The existence of enough evidence to be at least 50 percent convincing.

1. For status-offense cases, the judge will look for a **preponderance of evidence**. This is a fairly low standard that allows the judge to weigh the evidence and decide on the case if it is believed that the juvenile likely committed the offense or needs supervision.

The judge must find solutions that are in the best interests of the juvenile and society. Here a girl appears before the judge with her parents. *(© John Neubauer/PhotoEdit Inc.)*

2. In cases in which the juvenile is accused of a delinquent act that would be considered a criminal offense for an adult, the standard of proof is **beyond a reasonable doubt**. As in the criminal court, this standard ensures that there is convincing evidence that the juvenile committed the offense. The juvenile is given an opportunity to admit or deny the charges, and the juvenile's lawyer may engage in plea bargaining to get a reduced disposition. If the juvenile denies the charges, the judge will consider the facts of the case and render a finding of fact stating that the court believes that the juvenile committed the offense or is in need of supervision.

beyond a reasonable doubt
The state of being as convinced as possible of a fact.

Once the judge is convinced that a case is serious enough to warrant further processing, a **predispositional report** is ordered. The probation officer prepares this report to aid the judge in fashioning an appropriate disposition. Depending on the resources and the seriousness of the case, a great deal of information might be gathered and analyzed in the predispositional report, but basically two types of information are used.

predispositional report
A report prepared by a probation officer to assist the judge in designing an appropriate disposition.

1. **Legal** The probation officer will review the circumstances of the delinquency, such as what offenses were committed, the presence of codefendants, victim input, and any aggravating or mitigating circumstances. Also included in the legal section is a review of any past delinquency, including the type and seriousness of the behavior, the disposition of the case, and whether there is a pattern of increasing seriousness of delinquency.

2. **Social history and present circumstances** Information is collected on the parents, siblings, educational success and failure, use of alcohol or drugs, mental health problems, and housing situation. Depending on the case, the predispositional report will delve into every conceivable factor in order for the judge to get a clear picture of the juvenile so that problems can be corrected and a plan constructed that will allow the juvenile to thrive.[17]

DISPOSITIONAL HEARING   The **dispositional hearing** can take place weeks after the adjudicatory hearing while the probation officer prepares the predispositional report. In the dispositional hearing, the juvenile court specifies what should be done with the juvenile. In criminal court, the sentence details the offender's punishment, but in the juvenile court, the disposition is designed to help the juvenile. Although it's true that

dispositional hearing
The hearing in which the juvenile court renders judgment and specifies what should be done with the juvenile.

a delinquent who is sent to a secure detention facility will perceive the disposition as punishment, this isn't the intent. Sometimes it's believed that removing the youth from society and locking him or her up is the optimal way to correct the delinquency. However, the court's philosophy is to assist the juvenile in developing good behavior, not to punish bad behavior. Sometimes this distinction isn't appreciated by the juvenile who is behind bars.[18]

These three types of hearings in the juvenile court, preliminary, adjudicatory, and dispositional, are standard across jurisdictions. In some cases, the hearings may be combined. For instance, a judge who is familiar with the juvenile might combine the adjudicatory and dispositional hearings. The judge has no need of a new predispositional report if the juvenile has been before the court numerous times and the judge has already exhausted the available remedies short of secure detention.

Jury Trials and Plea Bargaining

plea bargaining
A negotiation in which the defendant agrees to plead guilty or no contest to some offenses in return for some accession to the defendant.

Jury trials and **plea bargaining** for juveniles are two procedures that account for how culpability is decided in the juvenile court. Juveniles don't have a constitutional right to a jury trial, but some states allow it under certain conditions. Plea bargaining can be considered a necessary evil because, although it sometimes appears to thwart justice, it helps to move a large number of cases through court.

JURY TRIAL   There are some good reasons to allow a juvenile a jury trial. The most significant one concerns the juvenile's potential loss of freedom if convicted of a serious felony. The Sixth Amendment (see A Closer Look at Juvenile Issues 14.1 for the amendment text) specifies that citizens charged with an offense be allowed an impartial jury. Although juveniles don't have all the rights of adults, contested cases may either be waived to criminal court for a jury trial or receive one in the juvenile court. In both cases, the juvenile's due-process rights are enhanced by the procedures inherent in a jury trial.[19] Some of the reasoning for a jury trial for juveniles is articulated in the dissenting opinion of Justice William Douglas in *McKeiver* v. *Pennsylvania* (see Case in Point 14.1):

- **Equal protection under the law should not exclude juveniles**   In cases of serious felonies in which the juvenile can be deprived of freedom, the court considers a jury trial to be part of equal protection.

- **Traumatic experiences**   One reason that juveniles have been denied jury trials is that it was presumed that it could be a traumatic experience. In a dissenting opinion, Justice Douglas remarked, "The fact is that the problems which are now followed in juvenile cases are far more traumatic than the potential experience of a jury trial. Who can say that a boy who is arrested and handcuffed, placed in a lineup, transported in vehicles designed to convey dangerous criminals, placed in the same kind of cell as an adult, deprived of his freedom by lodging him in an institution where he is subject to be transferred to the state's prison and in the 'hole' has not undergone a traumatic experience?"

14.1 A CLOSER LOOK *at* JUVENILE ISSUES

THE SIXTH AMENDMENT

In all criminal prosecutions, the accused shall enjoy the right to a speedy and public trial, by an impartial jury of the State and district wherein the crime shall have been committed, which district shall have been previously ascertained by law, and to be informed of the nature and cause of the accusation; to be confronted with the witnesses against him; to have compulsory process for obtaining witnesses in his favor; and to have the Assistance of Counsel for his defense.

14.1 CASE IN POINT

THE CASE

McKeiver v Pennsylvania,
403 U.S. 528 (1971)

THE POINT

Juveniles have no constitutional right to a jury trial during adjudication in a state juvenile court delinquency proceeding.

In May 1968, Joseph McKeiver, 16, was charged with robbery, larceny, and receiving stolen goods as acts of juvenile delinquency. McKeiver was represented by counsel during the adjudication hearing. The court denied his request for a jury trial, and McKeiver was adjudged a delinquent in juvenile court and placed on probation. The state superior court later affirmed the decision.

In January 1969, Edward Terry, 15, was charged with assault and battery on a police officer and conspiracy as acts of juvenile delinquency. As with McKeiver, the court denied Terry's request for a jury trial, and Terry was adjudged a delinquent. Terry was committed to a juvenile institution. The state superior court later affirmed the decision.

The two cases were consolidated for the purposes of appeal and for the consideration of the question of "whether there is a constitutional right to a jury trial in juvenile court."

The U.S. Supreme Court held that "trial by jury in the juvenile court's adjudicative stage is not a constitutional requirement."

- **Case backlog**   One reason that most states don't provide jury trials for juveniles is because it would hold up the flow of cases. Justice Douglas argued that "the very argument of expediency, suggesting 'supermarket' or 'assembly-line' justice is one of the most forceful arguments in favor of granting jury trials . . . It will provide a safeguard against the judge who may be prejudiced against a minority group or who may be prejudiced against the juvenile brought before him because of some past occurrence which was heard by the same judge."

- **Jury of peers**   A fair jury trial means that the jury comprises one's peers. But what, exactly, does a "jury of peers" mean? Should a juvenile have only other juveniles on the jury? Should a teenage female delinquent have only teenage females? Would a youth charged with delinquent behavior get a fair hearing from a 16-year-old who hasn't had a U.S. history class? Should juveniles be subject to jury duty just like adults? These are interesting questions that complicate the task of providing jury trials for juveniles. However, a *jury of peers* simply means that no one is systematically excluded. The local and federal jury pools are selected from the voting rolls, so anyone who votes is eligible to serve on a jury. In some cases, this might mean that the gender or racial composition of the jury doesn't reflect the local population, but as long as there is no systematic exclusion, this is permissible. In the case of juvenile delinquents, there is the potential for 18-year-old voters to be placed on the jury along with everyone else. For the purposes of jury selection, *peers* is defined simply as citizens, and no one has a right to a jury that looks like them, has had the same life experiences, or has the same political or religious tastes.

- **Public trial**   Juvenile proceedings are generally held in closed-door sessions for the juvenile's protection and privacy. Justice Douglas argued that juvenile proceedings are far from private. In fact, witnesses for both the prosecution and the defense, social workers, court reporters, students, police trainees, probation counselors, and sheriffs are present in the courtroom. Further, the police, armed forces, and the FBI have access to the court and police records. Having a public trial, therefore, wouldn't destroy confidentiality any more than the exceptions that already exist according to Justice Douglas.[20]

The Supreme Court has stopped short of requiring jury trials for all jurisdictions and allows the states to decide the matter. The state of California has set forth two main reasons for why the Supreme Court should resist making the juvenile court identical to the criminal court. First, the juvenile already has the right to waive his or her juvenile rights and go to criminal court and enjoy more procedural safeguards. Second, if the Supreme Court wanted to extend all due-process rights to juveniles, it would have to consider giving precise definitions to terms such as *neglect*, *abuse*, *dependent*, and *delinquent*. The discretion and informality enjoyed by the juvenile court can accommodate the vagueness in these terms, but they would become contentious in the criminal court. The state of California, therefore, has decided that how and when jury trials are used for juveniles should be encoded in state law rather than decided on a case-by-case basis by judges.[21]

PLEA BARGAINING   Although it would be preferable to give each case the time, attention, and resources required to bring it to a satisfying resolution, the sheer number of cases in both the criminal court and the juvenile court makes this goal impossible.[22] Other mechanisms must be found to control the vast number of cases that enter the system. One way might be to limit the scope of the criminal law and make permissible some currently illegal behaviors that don't constitute a threat to public safety. Drug laws are continually being placed under public scrutiny because of all the precious prison space being taken up by those who use or deal drugs but haven't actually hurt anyone. Other offenders in victimless crimes might also be handled by institutions other than the criminal or juvenile justice systems. But this solution to limit the scope of the law is a political one that would require legislative action. The juvenile justice system cannot unilaterally make the decision that it isn't going to respond to certain cases. Therefore, plea bargaining occurs at two points in the juvenile court.

- **Intake**   The intake officer has broad discretion in deciding what charges to bring against the juvenile. Because up to half of the cases brought to the court never make it past the intake officer, it is evident that important decisions are being made at this crucial stage of the process. In looking at the circumstances of the case, the intake officer is concerned with making a recommendation that fits the juvenile court's philosophy. The intake officer usually isn't qualified to determine the quality of the legal evidence against the juvenile and is more focused on deciding what interventions are best, rather than factual guilt or innocence. The intake officer can reduce the charges or divert the case to a community-based agency. This is the stage where drug treatment, restitution, or any of a number of other sanctions can be pressed on the juvenile and parents to avoid filing a petition. Parents who insist on pressing the facts of the case are warned that handling the case in a more formal manner could result in a more severe sanction. However, one study has shown that those who contest the charges actually end up with lighter sanctions than those who acquiesce to the intake officer.[23]

- **Adjudication and disposition**   Once a petition is filed and the case brought before the juvenile court judge, plea bargaining takes on a whole new and different urgency for the juvenile and parents. Defense lawyers are aware of how serious it is to have the juvenile adjudicated delinquent and will attempt to strike a deal with the prosecutor to reduce the charges and avoid the stigma.[24] For example, in cases involving sexual misconduct, the defense lawyer will try to get the prosecutor to agree to a plea bargain to charges that won't expose the youth to sex–offender laws that could affix a label that the youth might carry for life. Both the defense lawyer and the prosecutor have an interest in plea bargaining. The defense lawyer wants the most lenient sanction possible, while the prosecutor wants to impose a sanction that doesn't require a great deal of time or effort. The prosecutor must push a big caseload through the system, so as long as the case can be counted as a "win," the prosecutor isn't interested in holding out for the most severe sentence. Both the defense lawyer and the prosecutor are looking for ways to claim that they didn't lose a case, and the compromise inherent in the plea bargain allows each of them to claim this type of victory.[25]

Although the juvenile can gain a lot from a plea bargain in terms of reduced charges or reduced punishment, there is concern about this type of negotiated justice in the juvenile court. What gets lost in this activity is the *parens patriae* objective of looking out for the youth's best interests. When juvenile justice is reduced to a zero-sum game between the defense lawyer and the prosecutor, the most basic and underlying idea of the juvenile court is forfeited. As stated by one justice in *In re Gault* (see Case in Point 14.2), the child gets the worst of both the juvenile and the criminal justice systems. To compensate for the juvenile court's informality, reformers have concentrated on introducing more due process into the management of juvenile delinquents.

Due Process

Giving juveniles the constitutional right to due process is a controversial issue. Doing so changes the atmosphere and philosophy of the court from one in which juvenile justice officials collaborate in deciding how the juvenile might best be rehabilitated to one that is more adversarial. This treatment model is contrasted with the due process model, which results in often-contentious adversarial proceedings in which the judge sits as a neutral party while the prosecution and defense lawyers battle to win the case.

Juveniles enjoy due-process rights comparable to those of adults only in adjudicatory proceedings. Although many states do not provide for a trial by jury, other rights are expected in the juvenile court. For example, the prosecution must, if requested, share evidence with the defense lawyer that is favorable to the juvenile's case. Exculpatory evidence that shows the juvenile defendant wasn't at the scene of the offense or didn't have knowledge that codefendants were planning a robbery can't be hidden from the defense. Due process is concerned with fundamental fairness and stems from the Fourteenth Amendment.

The question for the juvenile justice system is how universal are due-process protections when dealing with juvenile delinquents? Juvenile rights are an evolving matter as the courts continually struggle with squaring the philosophies of the juvenile court with those of the Constitution. The court has left it to the states to

14.2 CASE IN POINT

THE CASE	THE POINT
In re Gault 387 U.S. 1, 87 S.Ct. 1428 (1967)	*The U.S. Supreme Court established juveniles' right to an attorney, the right to confront accusors, and protection from self-incrimination.*

In 1964, Gerald Gault, 15, and another boy were accused of making an obscene telephone call to a female neighbor. Gault was arrested without the knowledge of his parents, who were both at work, and questioned by police at the jail. He was held in detention for four or five days, then released to his parents. In the court proceedings, Gault was not allowed to cross-examine his accuser, who was never present, or to testify in his own behalf, nor was he advised of his rights. He was sentenced to the Arizona State Industrial School until he was 21. No appeal was permitted in juvenile cases in Arizona at that time. In 1967, the Supreme Court reversed the decision on appeal and established that juveniles have a right to an attorney, as well the right to confront accusers and protection from self-incrimination.

decide what level of due process is given to juveniles at many points in the proceedings of the juvenile justice system. Although juveniles are allowed many due-process rights in the adjudicatory hearing, there are other decision-making points in the system where their rights are less clear and subject to interpretation by judges and state legislatures. For example, in deciding the revocation of probation or a disciplinary action in a secure institution, the juvenile won't enjoy exactly the same due–process rights as an adult in a similar situation.

Until 1967, the U.S. Supreme Court maintained a hands-off policy toward the juvenile justice system. It wasn't until the landmark case *In re Gault* that the Supreme Court ruled that juveniles should have four constitutional rights if curtailment of their freedom was possible:

1. Right to a lawyer
2. Protection against self-incrimination
3. Right to notice of charges
4. Right to confront and cross-examine witnesses

In cases involving offenses where incarceration isn't likely, the Supreme Court has allowed the juvenile court to process cases without the juvenile having the benefit of these four due-process rights.

RIGHT TO A LAWYER   There is an old saying in legal circles that anyone who acts as his own lawyer is a fool. When one is a principal party in a case, one loses objectivity and can't make decisions in his or her own best interest. It is better to have a professional who not only knows the law, but can argue the case without seeming to be acting in his or her own self-interest. For example, when lawyers are accused of crimes or sued, they hire other lawyers to represent them. In the juvenile court, self–representation is also a concern. A juvenile does not have the legal training, the self–awareness, or the emotional temperament to provide an adequate defense. Additionally, parents lack objectivity and intimate knowledge of juvenile justice system

In cases of very serious delinquency, juveniles usually get a lawyer. In 1994, Eric Smith, 14, was accused of second-degree murder in the beating death of 4-year-old Derrick Robie. Smith, who was tried as an adult, was convicted and sentenced to nine years to life in prison. As of 2007, he remains in prison. *(AP/Wide World Photos)*

proceedings. To protect the juvenile's liberty, the Supreme Court has ruled in several cases that a lawyer may be retained to present the youth in the best possible light and to challenge the state's case.

However, there are some concerns with how the juvenile's right to a lawyer is applied.[26] The key issue is whether the juvenile could be incarcerated. In the case of very serious delinquency, a lawyer for the juvenile is fairly standard. In less serious cases in which the judge does not anticipate placing the youth in a detention facility, the proceedings might be conducted in a less adversarial manner without the juvenile being represented by counsel. However, some critics believe that abused and neglected children, especially in cases involving parental rights, need legal representation to ensure that their best interests are met. See Kids in the News 14.1 for a discussion of this situation.

The juvenile may also waive the right to a lawyer. Again, this happens in minor cases in which the intake officer or judge convinces the juvenile and parents that a less serious disposition is imminent and that securing a lawyer will delay the proceedings, cost money, and make the whole thing more adversarial. While stopping short of coercing the juvenile and parents with threats of more severe treatment by the court, the suggestion that a lawyer isn't needed can place subtle pressure on the juvenile and parents to waive this right. One study found that 80 to 90 percent of juveniles waive their right to counsel because they simply don't understand the consequences of waiving this right or even what the term *waive* means.[27]

The Supreme Court specified in *Gault* that juveniles have the right to be represented by a lawyer at the adjudicatory stage of the proceeding when there is a possibility of curtailed freedom. This leaves the juvenile's right to a lawyer greatly limited when compared to the rights of adults to be represented by a lawyer at "every critical stage of the case." For example, we have already discussed the substantial discretion enjoyed by the intake officer in deciding which cases are inserted into the juvenile justice system and which cases are adjusted or dismissed. This is a crucial stage of the proceedings that juveniles seldom benefit from, and they are often not made aware of their right to a lawyer. Because so many cases get informally plea bargained at intake, a lawyer can be of tremendous value to the juvenile at this critical point in the case.

Some parents can afford private lawyers, some private lawyers are appointed by the juvenile court judge based on a rotation system, and some larger jurisdictions have public defender offices that represent indigent clients. Juveniles without the financial resources to hire a lawyer are deemed to be indigent (poor) and can have a lawyer appointed by the court. However, all jurisdictions don't evaluate indigence in the same way. Judges consider many factors to determine if a juvenile or his or her family can afford to retain counsel. Does the family have a car? Are the parents employed? Do they own a house? What are the family's financial obligations? These considerations all go into the judge's decision on declaring a family indigent and thus having the state provide a lawyer.

Once the juvenile has a lawyer, the court proceedings might alter the traditional lawyer–client relationship. Although a lawyer is a zealous advocate for the client in the criminal court, the philosophy of the juvenile court alters the lawyer's role. There is a tendency to look out for the juvenile client's best interests, even when this might mean subjecting him or her to sanctions. For instance, when a juvenile needs drug rehabilitation, the defense lawyer might be persuaded to go along with this recommendation even though the state's case is weak. The defense lawyer is subtly influenced by the court to shift in occupational role from being a bulldog in defense of the juvenile's rights to being a surrogate family member or social worker involved in getting the youth into a physically and socially healthy environment.[28]

PROTECTION AGAINST SELF–INCRIMINATION   Another constitutional right guaranteed to adults is the right against self-incrimination. This means that a defendant doesn't have to answer questions that could be used as evidence against him or her in a criminal case. The protection against self-incrimination stems from language in the Fifth Amendment that states, "nor shall be compelled in any criminal case to be a

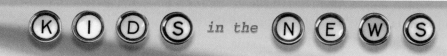

14.1

When Does a Child Need a Lawyer?

JoAnn and Kenneth Hamel of New Hampshire took into foster care a neglected 2-month-old boy, Damien. As usual, a judge named a trained volunteer to act as Damien's court-appointed special advocate. The Hamels and the volunteer, who wasn't a lawyer, tried for three years to reunite Damien with his parents, who had separated. Damien's mother, who had mental health problems, was unable to care for Damien, but his father wanted to keep Damien. However, he could not retain a job or an apartment, and he eventually stopped visiting the child.

The state set out to terminate the parental rights of Damien's father so that the Hamels could adopt the boy. Instead of using the court–appointed special advocate, the Hamels hired a lawyer for Damien. The judge ruled against the father, and the Hamels adopted Damien.

This sounds like a straightforward case, but it isn't. As we have noted earlier in this book, neglected and abused children present special challenges to the juvenile justice system. Children who are not accused of an offense have not, until recently, been considered to need a lawyer. They have not done anything wrong and are not at risk of being incarcerated or institutionalized. Such children need help from the judicial system and therefore fall under its care, but society does not need to be protected from them. In fact, they often need to be protected from society. However, the parties who typically have an interest in the child, such as parents, guardians, extended family, foster parents, and adoptive parents, are often at loggerheads. Unlike juveniles, adults have full constitutional rights, including the right to hire a lawyer, which complicates the issue. Let's break it down.

- *Child.* The child has a right not to be abused nor neglected and to have a nurturing home.
- *Juvenile justice system.* The system and its volunteers and child advocates wish to serve the child's best interests, but in a nonadversarial manner. This means, ideally, that everyone interested works out a solution.
- *Parents.* Parents have a right to raise their children as they see fit, as long as there is no neglect or abuse. It is very difficult for the

state to remove a child from his or her parents, even if the abuse is severe.

- *Guardians, foster parents, and adoptive parents.* Often, in cases of severe abuse, the child is placed with guardians or foster parents. Caretaking adults have an interest in the child, especially a very young child they have nursed back to health, and have constitutional rights as well. In many cases, the last two categories of caregivers are at odds. The parent wants the child back. The caretakers do not want to return the child to a harmful situation. Unfortunately, this scenario is inherently adversarial. However, the juvenile court, where the various parties are fighting it out, is not adversarial and seeks to avoid any competition that might damage the child's interests.

Federal law mandates guardians for all abused and neglected children, but the guardians do not have to be lawyers. The requirements vary by state.

- Illinois requires lawyers for children in counties with more than 3 million residents.
- California, as well as some other states, requires lawyers to represent children who are old enough to express their wishes. This means that children as young as 4 are appointed lawyers.
- New Hampshire and 18 other states do not guarantee lawyers for abused and neglected children.

Think About It

1. Should all neglected and abused children, regardless of age, be appointed a lawyer?
2. Should lawyers be banned from representing neglected and abused children?

Source: "States Vary on an Abused Kid's Right to a Lawyer," AP/CNN, December 26, 2006, www.cnn.com/2006/LAW/12/26/child.advocates.ap/index.html.

witness against himself." The Supreme Court extended this privilege to juveniles because it deems the protection to be unequivocal and without exception. Again, as in other rights granted to juveniles, the Supreme Court ruled that this protection against self–incrimination applies only to the adjudicatory stage of the juvenile court proceedings. The protection against self–incrimination protects both adults and juveniles in two ways.

1. **Privilege of the accused**   A person does not have to testify in a criminal case in which he or she is the defendant. Additionally, this choice not to testify cannot be used by the prosecution to impugn the defendant's integrity or motives. By this, we mean the prosecutor cannot say to the jury (or to the judge in a bench or juvenile trial), "If the defendant is truly innocent, why doesn't he take the stand and proclaim so? His silence betrays his guilt." If the juvenile does take the stand, however, he or she must answer questions truthfully, and the right against self-incrimination is forfeited. Further, by taking the stand and testifying on one's own behalf, the prosecution may then cross-examine the juvenile, who must answer hostile questions even if the answers are incriminating.

2. **Privilege of a witness**   Witnesses can be subpoenaed to appear before the court and required to answer questions from the prosecutor and the defense lawyer. However, if the answer to a question would implicate the witness in a criminal offense, he or she can refuse to testify. This protection against self-incrimination is extended to witnesses because they aren't the ones on trial and don't have the advantage of being prepared for the case and having a lawyer to look out for their rights. However, this protection is limited to criminal liability. The protection from self–incrimination doesn't apply to issues of civil liability or the possibility of shame or disgrace.[29] For instance, if a teenage boy is testifying as a friendly witness for a friend accused of an offense, the boy would have to admit that he'd snuck out of the house at night, even though he might get in trouble with his parents.

RIGHT TO NOTICE OF CHARGES   To properly defend yourself in a criminal case, you have to know what you are accused of. The right to notice of charges stipulates that the state has to provide you with written notice of the exact offenses or behaviors you are alleged to have committed. Further, this notice has to be provided far enough ahead of time so that you can prepare the case, research your alibi, and identify supporting witnesses.

For example, if the state accused me of stealing diamonds from a large department store in New York City at noon on December 21, 2006, I would need time to check my daily planner so I could show that at that particular time I was actually at home in another state writing these very words. Further, I might be able to produce the credit card statements showing I bought gasoline for my car, food for my cat, and a dozen new golf balls for the water hazards on my local golf course. Without the advanced written notice of the particular charges against me, I might not remember the events of this day or my whereabouts.

RIGHT TO CONFRONT AND CROSS-EXAMINE WITNESSES   The fourth due–process right extended to juveniles from *In re Gault* is the right to confront and cross-examine hostile witnesses. This means that the state must produce the witnesses in the courtroom, and they must testify to the facts of the case so that the juvenile and his or her lawyer can hear exactly how specific the testimony against the juvenile is. It is one thing to report misbehavior to the police and an entirely different experience to testify under oath in the courtroom about the particulars of what you have seen and heard concerning the juvenile's alleged misconduct. The certainty of one's beliefs and opinions is tested when testifying, and the state must rely on what is said in the courtroom, rather than interpret what is in the police report. As the prosecutor builds the case by questioning witnesses, the defense lawyer has the opportunity to ask questions that can show inconsistencies in the testimony, devious motivations of the witnesses, or the incompetence of expert witnesses. For example, when someone testifies as an expert witness, the defense lawyer, who wants to demonstrate the witness's lack of qualifications, often challenges the witness's credentials. It is considered a matter of basic fairness to subject accusatory witnesses to cross-examination. When witnesses are instructed to directly answer the prosecutor's questions and not to volunteer additional insights, it matters very much what questions are asked, how the questions are asked, and what questions aren't asked. The defense lawyer can give the court a

The right to confront and cross-examine witnesses extends to juveniles as well as adults. In 1996, Ray DeFord, 12, went to trial on arson charges in which he was accused of setting an apartment fire that killed eight people. *(Courtesy Don Ryan, AP Wide World Photos)*

better picture of the witness's believability by asking questions that can shed a more favorable light on the juvenile's activities.

PROTECTION AGAINST DOUBLE JEOPARDY   Protection against double jeopardy states that no one can be tried twice for the same offense. If a criminal defendant is accused of a serious offense and acquitted by a jury, then, even if further evidence is discovered, this person can't be brought to criminal trial again on the same charges. If this were the case, it would open the door for the state to keep trying the case until it won. The protection against double jeopardy doesn't mean the state can't appeal the case if there was some technical error or irregularities, but in doing so the state is limited to evidence and issues uncovered in the original case. This is why the prosecution must be very careful that they have a strong case before filing the charges.

In 1975, the Supreme Court extended the protection against double jeopardy to juveniles in *Breed* v. *Jones* (see Case in Point 14.3). In this case, a juvenile, Jones, was adjudicated delinquent in a juvenile court and detained. At his dispositional hearing, it was decided that Jones was not a good candidate for treatment as a juvenile, and the case was transferred to criminal court, where he was tried and found guilty of robbery.

Eventually, the Supreme Court found that the state had had its opportunity to contend the case and that sending him to criminal court to be tried as an adult violated the juvenile's Fifth Amendment protection against double jeopardy. The result of *Breed* v. *Jones* is that if the state wishes to prosecute a juvenile in criminal court, it must do so before the adjudicatory hearing.[30]

CONFIDENTIALITY AND ACCOUNTABILITY   As the juvenile justice system becomes more legalistic and adversarial, it is also becoming more open to public scrutiny (see A Closer Look at Juvenile Issues 14.2). This is further evidence of the strain on the traditional juvenile justice philosophy of *parens patriae*. Before the 1990s, juvenile

14.3 CASE IN POINT

THE CASE	THE POINT
Breed v. *Jones,* 421 U.S. 519 (1975)	*Trying a juvenile as an adult for an offense that has already been adjudicated in juvenile court constitutes double jeopardy.*

In February 1971, Jones, age 17, was accused of committing robbery while armed with a deadly weapon. A juvenile court found that Jones had violated a criminal statute and that he should be detained pending a hearing. At a March hearing, the juvenile court took testimony from two witnesses for the prosecution, as well as Jones himself, and determined that Jones had committed robbery with a deadly weapon.

At a subsequent hearing, the juvenile court determined that Jones was "unfit for treatment as a juvenile" and that he should be prosecuted as an adult. The Superior Court found Jones guilty of first-degree robbery and ordered him committed to the California Youth Authority. Jones, who had pled not guilty, argued that he had already been adjudicated in the juvenile court and that trial in the criminal court placed him in double jeopardy.

The case went to the Supreme Court, which ruled that Jones was indeed put in jeopardy at the juvenile court adjudicatory hearing, because the object of that hearing was to determine if Jones had committed acts that violated criminal law. The potential consequences of that finding included "the deprivation of liberty for many years."

The Supreme Court set forth that prosecution as an adult in criminal court after adjudication in the juvenile court for the same offense violates the Fifth Amendment double-jeopardy clause as applied to the states through the Fourteenth Amendment.

court proceedings were relatively closed, and the circumstances of cases kept from the public and the press. The idea, based on labeling theory (see Chapter 7), was to involve only those who had an interest in the case so that the juvenile's reputation wasn't damaged. The danger of this stigma, it was believed, was that it would become a self-fulfilling prophecy and that the youth would come to believe that the negative label accurately reflected his or her character. This philosophy guided the desires of court officials to keep the proceedings out of the public eye and the records sealed to protect the reputation and self-esteem of juvenile delinquents.

Under this philosophy, if an adult defendant had a juvenile record, this record wasn't available to the jury deciding the adult's case. So 18–year–olds with extensive juvenile delinquent histories were treated as first–time offenders upon their first adult arrest. Many criminal justice administrators and citizens objected to ignoring juvenile delinquent histories and moved to make the juveniles' contact with authorities more open and transparent.

In addition to making juvenile records more available to criminal justice officials, such as law enforcement officers, some states also open large portions of juveniles' official files to the public and press. Additionally, these records are open to insurance companies that are asked to pay for juvenile delinquents' mental health or drug treatment. Similarly, hearings are increasingly opened to the public and press. At issue is a balancing of values. The protection of the delinquent's privacy is weighed against the public's right to know. Accountability is considered desirable all across society's institutions, and the juvenile justice system is evaluated on how well it meets the needs of its charges and how it responds to delinquent behavior. Privacy is sacrificed for accountability, which might not be a bad thing. Openness allows scrutiny, which allows for reform. This is a path that U.S. society has taken for the past decade, and there is little likelihood that the juvenile court's secrecy and confidentiality will be reinstated any time in the foreseeable future.[31]

14.2 A CLOSER LOOK *at* JUVENILE ISSUES

WATCHING YOU: THE VANISHING PRIVACY OF JUVENILE COURT HEARINGS AND RECORDS

As the juvenile court moves from a philosophy of protecting the best interests of juveniles to one where juveniles have more due–process rights and the proceedings are more adversarial, the veil of secrecy is being lifted. As of 2004, the state of privacy for the juvenile court looked like the following:

- Delinquency hearings are open to the public in 14 states unless a judge orders them closed. The public's right to know is upheld unless the judge determines that there are good reasons to close the hearings.
- Access to delinquency hearings is limited in 21 states. These states have set criteria as to when a juvenile court hearing will be open to the public. Typically, open cases involve older juveniles who have a history with the court and/or are charged with serious offenses.
- Most states specify exceptions to juvenile court record confidentiality. Over the past decade, state legislatures have allowed more access to juvenile court records. All states allow one or more of the following parties the right to see at least portions of the record: prosecutors, law enforcement officials, social service agencies, victims, and members of the general public who have a "legitimate interest."
- All states allow certain juvenile delinquents to be fingerprinted and photographed, and most store the information. All states allow juveniles who have committed felonies or who have reached a certain age

to be photographed and fingerprinted. This information is not expunged after the juvenile leaves the court's jurisdiction.

- School–notification laws are common. Forty–four states have school–notification laws that specify that juveniles who have committed serious or violent offenses be reported to their schools.

The original intent of restricting information for the confidentiality of juvenile court hearings and records was to prevent the humiliation and demoralizing effects of publicity, which could affect rehabilitation. As the public demands more accountability of institutions, the juvenile court has been forced to open information about its proceedings.

Think About It

1. Should juvenile court hearings and records be kept confidential?
2. What are the benefits of allowing the press and the public to see what happens in the juvenile court?
3. Are open records and hearings the price juveniles must pay to be granted more due–process rights?

Source: Howard N. Snyder and Melissa Sickmund, *Juvenile Offenders and Victims: 2006 National Report* (Washington, DC: U.S. Department of Justice, Office of Justice Programs, Office of Juvenile Justice and Delinquency Prevention, 2006), 108–109.

TRIED AS AN ADULT: JUVENILES WAIVED TO CRIMINAL COURT

juvenile waiver
The process of sending a juvenile to be tried in criminal court.

Some juveniles commit such serious offenses that they are sent to criminal court instead of juvenile court. This process, **juvenile waiver**, exposes the youth to a more severe sanction but also allows for the full range of constitutional rights normally afforded to adult defendants. The process for waiving juveniles to criminal court is different from state to state, so there is no nationwide, uniform procedure. Basically, the discretion to waive the case to criminal court is vested in one of three places: the judge, the prosecutor, or the legislature. See A Closer Look at Juvenile Issues 14.3 for an explanation of the juvenile waiver provisions and Table 14.1 for the ways that each state may send a juvenile to criminal court.

Because each state has its own mechanisms for waiving the case to criminal court, blanket statements are difficult to make. However, some issues must be confronted. To give the jurisdiction to the criminal court, the juvenile court's responsibility must be terminated. This is done in many courts with a waiver hearing. The waiver hearing is typically requested by the prosecutor to show that there are good reasons for waiving the case to the criminal court. Basically, four issues must be decided to waive the case.

1. **Age** Most states have some lower age limit at which point the juvenile cannot be waived to criminal court. For instance, in Virginia, the juvenile must be 14 or older. Those under 14, regardless of the offense, will remain under the jurisdiction of the juvenile court. It is fair to say that the older the juvenile is, the more likely the case will be considered for waiver.

Table 14-1   Most States Have Several Ways to Send Juveniles to Criminal Court

	Judicial Waiver			Concurrent Jurisdiction	Statutory Exclusion	Once an Adult/ Always an Adult	Blended Sentencing	
	Discretionary	Presumptive	Mandatory				Juvenile	Criminal
Number of states	45	15	15	15	29	34	15	17
Alabama	•				•	•		
Alaska	•	•			•		•	
Arizona	•			•	•	•		
Arkansas	•			•			•	•
California	•	•		•		•		•
Colorado	•	•		•			•	•
Connecticut			•				•	
Delaware	•		•		•	•		
District of Columbia	•	•		•		•		
Florida	•			•	•	•		•
Georgia	•		•	•	•			
Hawaii	•					•		
Idaho	•				•	•		•
Illinois	•	•	•		•	•	•	•
Indiana	•				•	•		
Iowa	•				•	•		•
Kansas	•	•	•			•	•	
Kentucky	•							•
Louisiana	•			•	•			
Maine	•	•	•			•		
Maryland	•				•	•		
Massachusetts					•		•	•
Michigan	•			•		•	•	•
Minnesota	•	•	•		•	•	•	
Mississippi	•				•	•		
Missouri	•					•		•
Montana				•	•		•	
Nebraska				•				•
Nevada	•	•	•		•	•		
New Hampshire	•	•	•		•	•		
New Jersey	•	•	•					
New Mexico					•		•	•
New York					•			
North Carolina	•					•		
North Dakota	•	•	•			•		
Ohio	•		•			•	•	
Oklahoma	•			•	•	•		•
Oregon	•					•		
Pennsylvania	•	•			•	•		
Rhode Island	•	•	•			•	•	
South Carolina	•		•		•			
South Dakota	•				•	•		
Tennessee	•					•		
Texas	•					•	•	
Utah	•	•			•	•		

(Continued)

Table 14-1 **Most States Have Several Ways to Send Juveniles to Criminal Court (Continued)**

	Judicial Waiver			Concurrent Jurisdiction	Statutory Exclusion	Once an Adult/ Always an Adult	Blended Sentencing	
	Discretionary	Presumptive	Mandatory				Juvenile	Criminal
Vermont	•			•	•		•	
Virginia	•		•	•		•		•
Washington	•				•	•		
West Virginia	•		•					•
Wisconsin	•				•	•		•
Wyoming	•			•				

Source: Howard N. Snyder and Melissa Sickmund, *Juvenile Offenders and Victims: 2006 National Report* (Washington, DC: U.S. Department of Justice, Office of Justice Programs, Office of Juvenile Justice and Delinquency Prevention, 2006), 111.

Each state has its own procedures for waiving juvenile cases to criminal court. Here, Daphne Abdela stands next to her lawyer as she is arraigned in 1997 in New York. Abdela and her boyfriend, both 15, were accused of killing a man in Central Park.

2. **Seriousness of the offense**   Minor offenses are not sufficient reason to waive a juvenile's case to criminal court. The offense must be something that would be a major offense if committed by an adult. For this reason, status offenses are never transferred to criminal court. Similar offenses that are considered misdemeanors start under the jurisdiction of the juvenile court. Offenses such as homicide or rape may get waived to the criminal court and, usually, these must have some aggravating factor. In sensational cases, the prosecutor is under public scrutiny to show that the justice system is sufficiently tough on crime, regardless of the offender's age.

3. **Probable cause**   The standard of proof needed to waive a juvenile to criminal court is low. There need not be proof beyond a reasonable doubt to waive the case to criminal court, although this standard is required to convict. Because a waiver hearing doesn't qualify as a trial in which the juvenile could lose his or her freedom, the standard of proof is lowered to "preponderance of evidence" or "clear and convincing." Further, illegally seized evidence can be admitted into the hearing to waive the case to the criminal court although that evidence might not be admissible in a criminal trial.

14.3 A CLOSER LOOK *at* JUVENILE ISSUES

JUVENILE WAIVER

All states may try juveniles as adults. The three types of provisions for this are judicial waiver, direct filing, and statutory exclusion.

Judicial Waiver

A judge is responsible for sending the juvenile to adult court. The three types of judicial waiver are mandatory, presumptive, and discretionary.

- *Discretionary waiver.* Transfer of the juvenile to adult court is at the judge's discretion.
- *Mandatory waiver.* The youth's age and the seriousness of the offense invoke automatic transfer to criminal court.
- *Presumptive waiver.* The burden of proof shifts from the state to the juvenile, who must contest transferral to criminal court.

Direct Filing (Concurrent Jurisdiction)

- A prosecutor has the discretion to file charges in either juvenile or adult court.

Statutory Exclusion

- This is also called *legislative waiver*, because it comes from state legislatures and does not require a juvenile court hearing. Statutory exclusion automatically excludes from juvenile court juveniles who commit certain very serious offenses and sends them directly to criminal court. Offenses that might invoke statutory exclusion include murder and aggravated rape. Some states might also use statutory exclusion for minor violations such as traffic, fish-and-game, and some local ordinances.

4. **Amenability to treatment** In deciding whether to waive a serious case to the criminal court, the juvenile court judge will consider the likelihood that the juvenile would benefit from treatment in the juvenile justice setting. Because the youth's best interests are foremost in the juvenile court philosophy, a reasoned consideration as to whether the juvenile could benefit from one last chance at rehabilitation is appropriate. The judge must ask if all the resources of the juvenile justice system have been tried and whether there is good reason to suspect that the youth can be rehabilitated. However, the amenability–to–treatment consideration gets considered less seriously as the charge gets more severe. For some particularly heinous offenses, waiver to the criminal system is a foregone conclusion even if the juvenile is a first–time defendant. In states that don't have **statutory exclusion**, serious cases require a hearing. A prosecutor might examine the juvenile's delinquency record (if any) and make the argument that past treatment efforts have been unsuccessful and the only way to protect the public is to transfer the case to criminal court. In some cases in which the juvenile has had extensive involvement with the juvenile justice system, treatment programs might no longer be willing to take the case.

statutory exclusion
The legal requirement that certain offenses committed by juveniles automatically be waived to criminal court without a juvenile court hearing.

A juvenile whose case is transferred to criminal court faces serious implications. On the positive side is the certainty of receiving all the constitutional rights generally afforded to adults. This means the juvenile will receive a trial by jury in which the prosecutor must prove beyond a reasonable doubt that the juvenile committed the offense. However, along with constitutional rights comes the prospect of long-term incarceration in adult facilities. Although juvenile delinquents are separated from adult offenders, adult institutions are more focused on punishment than on treatment and rehabilitation. Until recently, having a serious case waived to criminal court has exposed the juvenile to the death penalty. (This issue will be considered in greater detail in Chapter 15.) Also, most states have "once an adult, always an adult" requirements. In over half of the states, juveniles who are tried and convicted as adults will continue to be tried as adults for subsequent offenses.[32]

See Table 14-1 for a listing of the methods the various states that use to send juveniles to a criminal court.

Blended Sentencing

A juvenile who is convicted in a criminal court is likely to receive an adult sentence, and a juvenile who receives a disposition in a juvenile court usually ends up with a

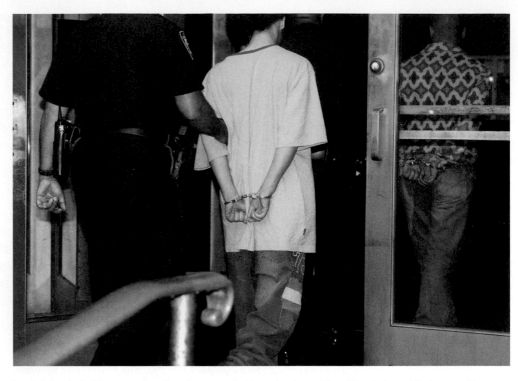

In more than half of the states, juveniles who are tried and convicted as adults will be tried as adults for any subsequent offenses regardless of their juvenile status. *(Courtesy Chet Gordon, The Image Works)*

blended sentencing

A sentence that combines a juvenile disposition with the possibility of a criminal sentence, or a criminal conviction with a "last chance" at a juvenile disposition and treatment.

juvenile sentence. However, in special cases, courts find it necessary to use **blended sentencing**, which has features of both. There are five types of blended sentences.

- **Juvenile exclusive**   The case is adjudicated in a juvenile court, but the court may impose a disposition involving either the juvenile or criminal correctional systems, but not both.
- **Juvenile inclusive**   The case is adjudged in a juvenile court, but the court has the authority to impose a disposition involving both the juvenile and criminal correctional systems. Usually, the criminal sentence is suspended pending the juvenile's successful completion of the juvenile disposition.
- **Juvenile contiguous**   The case is adjudged in a juvenile court, but delinquents must serve a juvenile sentence and then an adult sentence once they pass the age of the juvenile court's jurisdiction (usually age 17 or 18).
- **Criminal exclusive**   The case is tried in the criminal court, but the court may impose a sentence involving either the juvenile or criminal correctional systems, but not both.
- **Criminal inclusive**   The case is tried in the criminal court, but the court may impose a sentence involving both the juvenile *and* criminal correctional systems. Usually, the criminal sentence is suspended pending the juvenile's successful completion of a juvenile disposition.

Who Gets Waived to the Criminal Court?

The most recent data available demonstrate some interesting gender and racial patterns. In 2002, more male cases than female cases in each of the four general offense categories (person, property, drugs, and public order) were waived to criminal court. For example, males charged with person offenses were six times as likely as similarly charged females to get their cases waived to criminal court. Black youths were more likely than any other race to be waived to criminal court for drug offenses, while white youths were more likely than any other race to be waived to criminal court for property offenses. Youths of other races were more likely than either white or black youths to be waived for person offenses. And regardless of race, person offenses were more likely to be waived than other types of cases.[33]

There is considerable variation across jurisdictions in the patterns of who gets waived to the criminal court. Because so many factors are considered and because each case is judged on its merits in states that require waiver hearings, an attitude has developed that it would be more appropriate to remove discretion from the decision.

State legislatures have done this by specifying that certain types of offenses are waived to the criminal court without a waiver hearing. This mechanism, statutory exclusion, represents a major departure from the juvenile justice philosophy. The legislators dictate that all offenses that meet certain conditions will be heard by the criminal court regardless of the defendant's age. They want offenders to be held accountable for serious and heinous offenses. Also, legislators, who want to be re-elected, feel they must answer the public outcry when a juvenile commits a sensational offense. This public pressure introduces politics into the juvenile justice system and alters the ability of judges and prosecutors to decide what is in the best interests of the juvenile and of society.

Sometimes legislative intent has unanticipated and counterproductive consequences. For example, a few studies have shown that cases waived to criminal court actually receive less severe sanctions than if they had remained under juvenile court jurisdiction. Additionally, these cases don't benefit from the treatment options of the juvenile justice system. The result is that for some very serious offenses the juvenile escapes the punishment of the criminal court and misses the treatment of the juvenile court.

SUMMARY

1. The reasoning behind the invention of the juvenile court and its proposed goals was that such a court would deal with juvenile delinquency more effectively, as well as protect youths from the dangers of being handled in parallel with adult offenders.

2. The structure of juvenile courts varies widely. In some populous jurisdictions, they are part of a juvenile justice center that works with other youth agencies. In other places, they are a specialized court that operates in the courthouse along with the other courts. Juvenile courts might also be called *family courts* or *magistrate courts*.

3. Juvenile courts are almost exclusively a state and county responsibility. The federal government specifies some of the rules and laws that apply to juvenile courts, but the federal government generally defers to the states on juvenile delinquency.

4. This fragmentation of juvenile court structure is a problem with two possible fixes. The first involves a coordinating function in which the various judges dealing with the same family meet and discuss the case. The second solution is to institute a unified court system in which one judge handles all aspects of a case.

5. The key players in the juvenile court represent varying interests but must work together to ensure justice, provide for the best interests of juveniles, and move cases through the system. The key players are the juvenile court judge, the prosecutor, the juvenile defense counsel (including public defenders), juvenile intake officers, and juvenile probation officers.

6. The court process includes custody and detention, petitions and summonses, juvenile court hearings (preliminary hearings, adjudicatory hearings, and dispositional hearings), jury trials, and plea bargaining.

7. Giving juveniles the constitutional right to due process changes the atmosphere and philosophy of the juvenile court from one in which juvenile–justice officials collaborate in deciding how the juvenile might best be rehabilitated to one that is more adversarial.

8. Juveniles enjoy due-process rights comparable to those of adults only in adjudicatory proceedings.

9. In *In re Gault*, the Supreme Court ruled that juveniles should have four constitutional rights if curtailment of their freedom was possible: the right to a lawyer, the right against self-incrimination, the right to notice of charges, and the right to confront and cross-examine witnesses.

10. In 1975, the Supreme Court extended the protection against double jeopardy to juveniles in *Breed v. Jones*.

11. As the juvenile justice system becomes more legalistic and adversarial, it is also becoming more open to public scrutiny, and more juvenile records are being made public.

12. Some juveniles commit such serious offenses that they are sent to criminal court instead of juvenile court. Juvenile waiver exposes the youth to more severe sanctions but also allows for full constitutional rights.

13. Basically, four issues must be decided to waive a case to criminal court: age, seriousness of the offense, probable cause, and amenability to treatment.

14. Sometimes courts use blended sentencing, which uses features from both the juvenile and criminal courts. The five types of blended sentencing are juvenile exclusive, juvenile inclusive, juvenile contiguous, criminal exclusive, and criminal inclusive.

REVIEW QUESTIONS

1. Is the structure of juvenile courts the same in every state?

2. How does the federal government regard juvenile courts?

3. Why is juvenile court fragmentation bad? Why is it good?

4. Who are the key players in the juvenile court?

5. What do all juvenile court judges have in common regardless of jurisdiction?

6. Compare and contrast custody and arrest.

7. What are the three types of hearings?

8. What is the difference between preponderance of evidence and beyond a reasonable doubt?

9. What is plea bargaining? At what points does it occur in the juvenile court?

10. Why did Justice Douglas dissent in *McKeiver* v. *Pennsylvania*?

11. What juvenile rights came from *In re Gault*?

12. What are the five types of blended sentencing?

ADDITIONAL READINGS

Feld, Barry. *Bad Kids: Race and the Transformation of the Juvenile Court* (New York: Oxford University Press, 1999).

Krisberg, Barry. *Juvenile Justice: Redeeming Our Children* (Thousand Oaks, CA: Sage, 2005).

Penn, Everette B., Helen Taylor Greene, and Shaun L. Gabbidon, eds. *Race and Juvenile Justice* (Durham, NC: Carolina Academic Press, 2006).

Platt, Anthony. *The Child Savers: The Invention of Delinquency* (Chicago: University of Chicago Press, 1969).

Schwartz, Ira M. *Justice for Juveniles: Rethinking the Best Interests of the Child* (Lexington, MA: D. C. Heath, 1989).

Tanenhaus, David S. *Juvenile Justice in the Making* (New York: Oxford University Press, 2004).

ENDNOTES

1. Barry Krisberg, *Juvenile Justice: Redeeming Our Children* (Thousand Oaks, CA: Sage, 2005). See especially Chapter 2, "Juvenile Justice: Myths and Realities," pp. 1–8.

2. Anthony Platt, *The Child Savers: The Invention of Delinquency* (Chicago: University of Chicago Press, 1969).

3. National Conference of State Legislatures, *A Legislator's Guide to Comprehensive Juvenile Justice, Juvenile Detention, and Corrections* (Denver, CO: National Conference of State Legislatures, 1996).

4. Rolando V. del Carmen and Chad R. Trulson, *Juvenile Justice: The System, Process, and Law* (Belmont, CA: Thomson Wadsworth, 2006), 224–225.

5. Leonard P. Edwards, "The Future of the Juvenile Court: Promising New Directions," *The Future of Children* 6 (1996):143.

6. David S. Tanenhaus, *Juvenile Justice in the Making* (New York: Oxford University Press, 2004).

7. Leonard P. Edwards, "The Juvenile Court and the Role of the Juvenile Court Judge," *Juvenile and Family Court Journal* 43 (1992):3–45.

8. Chester Harhut, "An Expanded Role for the Guardian ad Litem," *Juvenile and Family Court Journal* 51 (2000):31–35.

9. James Shine and Dwight Price, "Prosecutor and Juvenile Justice: New Roles and Perspectives," in Ira Schwartz, ed. *Juvenile Justice and Public Policy* (New York: Lexington Books, 1992), 101–133.

10. American Bar Association, *A Call for Justice: An Assessment of Access to Counsel and Quality of Representation in Delinquency Proceedings* (Washington, DC: ABA Juvenile Justice Center, 1995).

11. George W. Burruss and Kimberly Kempf-Leonard, "The Questionable Advantage of Defense Counsel in Juvenile Court," *Justice Quarterly* 19 (2002):37–68.

12. Gus Martin, *Juvenile Justice: Process and Systems* (Thousand Oaks, CA: Sage, 2005), 207.

13. del Carmen and Trulson (see note 4), 181–183.

14. Patrick Griffin and Patricia Torbert, eds. *Desktop Guide to Good Juvenile Probation Practice* (Pittsburgh, PA: National Center for Juvenile Justice, 2002).

15. Ira M. Schwartz and William H. Barton, *Reforming Juvenile Detention—No More Hidden Closets* (Columbus: Ohio State University Press, 1994).

16. Roberto Hugh Potter and Suman Kakar, "The Diversion Decision-Making Process from the Juvenile Court Practitioners' Perspective," *Journal of Contemporary Criminal Justice* 18 (2002):20–36.

17. Joseph W. Rogers, "The Predisposition Report: Maintaining the Promise of Individualized Justice," *Federal Probation* 54 (1990):43–57.

18. Jeffrey Fagan and Martin Guggenheim, "Preventive Detention for Juveniles: A Natural Experiment," *Journal of Criminal Law and Criminology* 86 (1996):415–428.

19. Joseph B. Sanborn, Jr., "The Right to a Public Jury Trial—A Need for Today's Juvenile Court," *Judicature* 76 (1993):230–238.

20. *McKeiver* v. *Pennsylvania*, 403 U.S. 528 (1971).

21. Mary Clement, *The Juvenile Justice System: Law and Process* (Boston: Butterworth-Heinemann, 1997), 71.

22. Douglas Smith, "The Plea Bargaining Controversy," *Journal of Criminal Law and Criminology* 77 (1986):949–957.

23. R. Barry Ruback and Paula J. Vardaman, "Decision Making in Delinquency Cases: The Role of Race and Juveniles' Admission/Denial of the Crime," *Law and Human Behavior* 21, no. 1 (1997):47–69.

24. Joseph Sanborn, "Philosophical, Legal, and Systematic Aspects of Juvenile Court Plea Bargaining," *Crime and Delinquency* 39 (1993):509–527.

25. Albert W. Alschuler, "The Prosecutor's Role in Plea Bargaining," *University of Chicago Law Review* 36 (1968):50–112.

26. Tony Caeti, Craig Hemmens, and Velmer Burton, "Juvenile Right to Counsel: A National Comparison of State Legal Codes," *American Journal of Criminal Law* 23 (1996):

27. del Carmen and Trulson (see note 4), 254.

28. Barry Feld, "The Right to Counsel in Juvenile Court: An Empirical Study of When Lawyers Appear and the Difference They Make," *Journal of Criminal Law and Criminology* 79 (1989):611–632.

29. del Carmen and Trulson (see note 4), 256–257.

30. *Breed* v. *Jones*, 421 U.S. 519 (1975).

31. Howard N. Snyder and Melissa Sickmund, *Juvenile Offenders and Victims: 2006 National Report* (Washington, DC: U.S. Department of Justice, Office of Justice Programs, Office of Juvenile Justice and Delinquency Prevention, 2006), 109.

32. Ibid., 110.

33. Ibid., 187.

Why are detained or incarcerated juveniles separated from adult offenders?

How does the juvenile justice system attempt to rehabilitate juvenile delinquents?

What is shock incarceration?

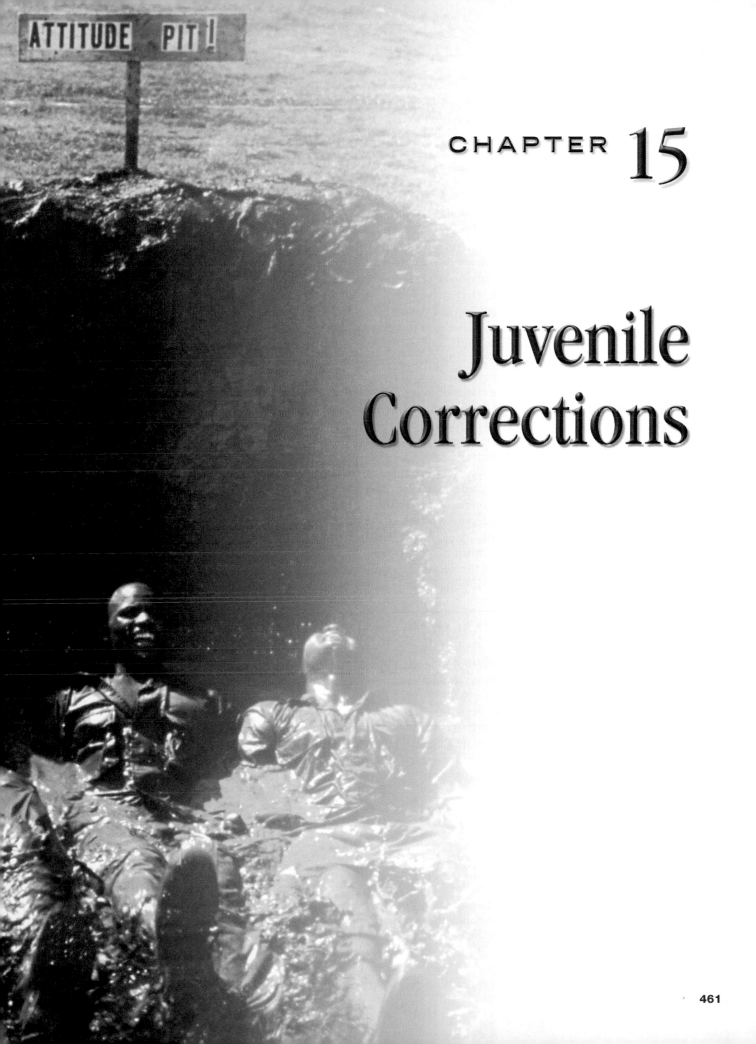

ATTITUDE PIT !

CHAPTER 15

Juvenile Corrections

Once the juvenile court judge has determined that a juvenile is delinquent, the question becomes "What do we do about it?" Juvenile justice isn't a one-size-fits-all enterprise and, depending on the resources available, there are a number of options. The goal of the juvenile justice system is to craft a disposition that is in the best interests of the youth while protecting society. But the "best interests of the juvenile" isn't necessarily the least restrictive sentence. For a youth with drug or alcohol problems, anger-management problems, or gang affiliations, release to the community on standard probation might not be the best option. To put the youth back on the street to deal with the same social problems without equipping him or her with the educational background, interpersonal skills, and character to resist temptation is asking for trouble. To succeed, youngsters need a supportive environment and individual attention. This is the job of juvenile corrections.

Before we delve too deeply into juvenile corrections, it is worth noting that some issues are beyond the mandate and abilities of the juvenile justice system. The social conditions that lead to delinquency, such as poverty, a sagging economy, drugs, inadequate schools, and ineffective families, are not things the juvenile justice system can fix. And yet, when these problems persist, they have a tremendous effect on the juvenile's chances of staying out of trouble. When families, the economy, schools, and communities fail to support youths in trouble, it is the juvenile justice system that gets blamed for high rates of recidivism. In previous chapters, we covered the issues and concerns of these other social institutions, so here we will simply acknowledge their importance and suggest ways that the juvenile justice system can use them to develop an atmosphere in which delinquent youths can thrive.

The particular emphasis of this chapter is individual treatment. What can be done to prepare delinquents to return to society? What does it take to turn around a life that seems to be destined for a career in crime? And, finally, what mistakes have been made and continue to be made in treating juvenile delinquents? To address these questions, we will look at community–based efforts for dealing with delinquency, as well as institutional programs. We cover the philosophy of juvenile correctional treatment and the vast array of programs to assess the successes and limitations of the current response to juvenile delinquency.

COMMUNITY CORRECTIONS

The traditional way to respond to juvenile delinquents is to provide the least restrictive treatment. The idea is not to harm the youth by placing him or her in a situation that does not allow for the positive personal growth envisioned by the court.[1] Placing juveniles in secure institutions is considered a last resort, and keeping them in the community so that they can live with their parents and attend their own schools is the optimal goal. To keep the juvenile in the community, the juvenile justice system has devised some programs and agencies to ensure that society is protected and that the juvenile gets the treatment and supervision needed for successful reintegration.

Standard Probation

Probation was developed in 1841 by John Augustus, a prosperous Boston shoemaker. Augustus bailed people out of jail, found work for them, allowed some to live temporarily in his home, and recommended dispositions to judges. In his 18 years of working with offenders, he reported that out of 2,000 cases only 10 jumped bail or probation and failed to appear in court.[2]

The concept of probation was very attractive to those involved in the emerging criminal justice system. When the first juvenile court was introduced in Cook County, Illinois, in 1899, probation was instituted as one of its cornerstones.[3] Currently, because of the large numbers of juveniles before contemporary juvenile courts, probation has become absolutely necessary.

Probation, the conditional release of juveniles to the custody of parents or guardians, has several presumed advantages. First, it reduces stigma. By not placing the youth in a secure detention facility, it is hoped that he or she won't adopt the self-image of a criminal. Staying at home and in the community allows youths to maintain their identities, for themselves and others, as good and decent persons. The second advantage of probation is that it encourages rehabilitation by employing community resources. Almost always, schools in the community are better at helping children than the schools available in juvenile correctional facilities.[4] Additionally, other community resources, such as mental health centers, recreational facilities, and churches, can help treat the youth. It is believed that rehabilitation and reintegration are more easily accomplished by maintaining the youth's bonds to the community.[5] The final suggested advantage of probation over incarceration is cost. It is very expensive to build and staff secure correctional facilities. Around–the–clock confinement means that the state must provide for three shifts of personnel, food, building costs, and therapy. On probation, most of these costs are the responsibility of the family, schools, and community. Detention space is a precious resource, and the juvenile justice system works hard to reserve it for only those delinquents who must be separated from society.[6]

The rules of probation require the youth to maintain contact with the probation officer. A variety of methods are used to maintain this contact, and these depend on the officer's caseload, the amount of trust in the youth, and technology. The youth might be required to report on a regular basis to the probation officer, the probation officer might visit the youth's home or school, or the youth might be required to submit monthly written reports attesting that he or she has met the conditions of probation.[7] Because so many people have cell phones, the officer must be wary of phone contact. Prior to cell phones, the officer could call the youth's home to check that curfews were being obeyed. Now the officer has to be aware of the opportunities for evasion by the youth.

Youths on probation must adhere to certain conditions. First, there are **standard conditions of probation** that apply to all probationers. Additionally, there are **special conditions of probation** that apply to the youth's particular needs. For instance, a youth with no history of drug or alcohol use is not required by the standard conditions of probation to submit to drug tests, while a client with a history of drug use or whose delinquent adjudication involved drugs or alcohol might find drug testing to be part of the special conditions. The conditions of probation are extensive and greatly limit the youth's freedom and privacy, leading some scholars to

probation
The conditional release of juveniles to the custody of parents or guardians.

standard conditions of probation
Requirements of probationers that apply to all probationers, regardless of individual needs or offense.

special conditions of probation
Requirements of a person on probation that apply specifically to that person.

A probation officer explains a form to a juvenile probationer. *(Courtesy James Shaffer, PhotoEdit Inc.)*

question the ability of a juvenile to fulfill all these requirements. For instance, Thomas Blomberg and Karol Lucken have compared the conditions of probation to a "stacked deck." So many demands are placed on the probationers that they are probably in some state of violation at any time.[8] This provides the probation officer with great latitude in supervising the case, because violations can be held against the youth.

Special conditions of probation are cause for further concern. The courts have ruled that these conditions cannot be arbitrary and must relate to the juvenile's offense or a reasonable treatment intervention.[9] Being on probation means that the youth waives certain rights as a condition of probation, such as allowing the probation officer to search his or her person, car, or home without a warrant. Further, the probation officer can require the juvenile to maintain a curfew, refrain from driving an automobile, and demonstrate a respectful demeanor and tone of voice to parents, teachers, and police officers.

How can the state restrict the freedom of those on probation to such a large extent? Because probation isn't a right but a privilege and is contingent on the juvenile agreeing to the conditions. As can be seen in A Closer Look at Juvenile Issues 15.1, the juvenile signs for the conditions under which the probation is granted and virtually waives away rights. The alternative is to be placed in secure detention, where all these rights and privileges are also forfeited. For the youth committed to correcting his or her delinquent behavior, probation is a reasonable price to pay for being allowed to live at home and proceed with a normal lifestyle. Youths who cannot abide by the conditions of probation find that their lives become more transparent, which makes the detection of additional delinquent behavior more likely.

Intensive-Supervision Probation

Probation was designed to give offenders the benefits of having a probation officer to help them negotiate the justice system and to provide emotional support and employment counseling, along with firm accountability for deviant behavior. When provided with enough resources, probation can be an effective alternative to incarceration. However, given the large numbers of juveniles on probation, the time and attention of probation officers are stretched so thin that many juveniles don't get the services they need. More importantly, many juveniles on probation aren't being supervised adequately and are committing additional offenses and abandoning their rehabilitative treatment plans.[10]

Traditionally, probation officers practiced a kind of triage by informally dividing their caseloads into three categories.

1. **Cases who will do well no matter what the officer does.** A great many juveniles on probation are good and decent people who got caught experimenting with relatively normal delinquent behavior. Juveniles go through a stage of testing the boundaries of appropriate behavior: they might drink alcohol, smoke marijuana, and drive fast and recklessly. Although these behaviors are against the law and juveniles need to be held accountable for them, many youngsters simply outgrow these things. Being taken into custody, processing through the juvenile court, and going on probation are a wake-up call for them. Aside from ensuring that juveniles are following the conditions of probation, the probation office spends little time and resources on supervision. In some jurisdictions, youths are placed on minimum–security caseloads and have very little contact with the probation officer. Typically, these juveniles successfully complete their terms of probation and go on to live productive and law-abiding lives, not because of anything the probation officer has done, but because they are relatively minor offenders who have adequate education, family support, and positive attitudes about life.

2. **Cases who will do poorly no matter what the officer does.** Some juveniles on probation really should be sent to institutions where they can be adequately supervised and treated. Because many state juvenile corrections facilities are so

crowded, the courts are forced to place some disturbed and even dangerous juveniles on probation. The probation officers realize that dealing with these serious delinquents requires extraordinary time and resources that simply are not available. Probation officers do the best they can under the circumstances, but given the demands of the other juveniles on their caseload, they realize the best they can do is to keep a close eye on the serious delinquents and revoke probation at the first sign of trouble.

15.1 A CLOSER LOOK *at* JUVENILE ISSUES

RULES OF PROBATION-SUPERVISED

WOOD COUNTY JUVENILE COURT
11120 EAST GYPSY LANE ROAD
BOWLING GREEN, OHIO 43402
(419) 352-3554, (419) 243-4223 EXT. 9205

NAME   DOB: CASE NO:

ADDRESS: PHONE: PROBATION NO.:

                                                          OFFENSE:

You have been placed on Probation on this date _____ by the Honorable David E. Woessner, Judge of the Wood County Juvenile Court. It is the Order of this Court that you shall abide by the following general and special conditions of Probation:

GENERAL CONDITIONS

1. You will obey all laws (Federal, State, and Local) and will report immediately to your Probation Officer if arrested or questioned by a law enforcement officer.
2. You will attend school daily, be on time, and obey all school regulations.
3. You will report for probation appointments as directed, being prompt to all such appointments. If, for any excusable reason, you are unable to report for an appointment, it is your responsibility to call your Probation Officer.
4. The use, possession or sale of alcohol or drugs of abuse is strictly forbidden unless prescribed by a licensed physician. You will submit to random urine screens and/or breathalyzer tests at the request of your Probation Officer. You will not be present where illegal drugs are used. Positive urine screens will result in a $5.00 fee. **You must produce a clean urine screen to be successfully terminated from probation.**
5. You shall not own or possess any deadly weapon or dangerous ordinance, as defined by the Ohio Revised Code.
6. You will not leave or remain away from your home without the permission of your parents. Your parents must have knowledge of your whereabouts at all times.
7. You will obey your parent(s), guardian(s,) school teachers, school authorities, law enforcement officers and Probation Officer and will treat, answer and address them with respect at all times. Should you be incarcerated at the Wood County Juvenile Detention Center, you will follow their Resident Rules of Conduct.
8. The maximum curfew hours are **p.m.** until **6:00 a.m.**, Sunday through Thursday, and **p.m.** until **6:00 a.m.** Friday and Saturday. Exceptions to these hours are when you are physically with your parent or guardian, or with the special permission of your Probation Officer. Your parents can establish curfew hours earlier than the Court, but not later.
9. You will submit your person and/or property to search and seizure by a Probation Officer, with probable cause, with or without a search warrant, at any time.
10. You will not leave the State of Ohio without the permission of your Probation Officer.
11. Any involvement with gang activity is strictly forbidden. This includes the wearing of colors or hats associated with gangs, writing or displaying graffiti, using gang signs, and associating with gang members.
12. You will abide by the advice of your Probation Officer and any other special conditions as established by the Court and/or your Probation Officer.
13. Any order of the Court requiring a fine, Court Costs, Supervision fee, urine screen fee, and/or restitution must be complied with strictly.
14. You are responsible for reporting any change of address, phone number, or school placement immediately to the Probation Department.

(Continued)

A CLOSER LOOK *at* JUVENILE ISSUES

SPECIAL CONDITIONS

Supervision Fee: $50.00   To be Paid by

Fine and Costs: To be Paid by

Restitution: To be Paid by

Community Service Work: **hours** to be completed by

Detention Time Ordered: days ordered to serve; days suspended

     Counseling as ordered by the Court

     Counseling as deemed appropriate by the Court

     Theft Offender Program on

     Parenting classes beginning

     Letter of Apology by

     Drug/Alcohol evaluation and complete recommended treatment

     House Arrest until

     Dr.'s excuse required for any school absence

     Driver's License/Right to Apply suspended until

     No Association with:

     Other:

The length of time that you remain on probation will depend on your attitude, behavior and successful completion of all Court orders (minimum six months). When you are terminated from probation, you will receive a judgment entry notifying you of the termination. Until that date, your probation status is active. If you violate your probation rules or any state or federal laws, you subject yourself to further Court action and possible incarceration. This is an opportunity for you to prove to yourself, and to the Court, that you can conduct yourself in a law-abiding manner and remain in your own home.

The above conditions have been explained to me by a Probation Officer. I understand them and agree to follow them. I will contact my Probation Officer if any questions arise. I also understand that the Court may revoke my probation, change the conditions of my probation, including the level of Probation Supervision, and extend the length of my probation. I also understand that my Probation Officer may arrest me without a warrant.

_____	_____	_____	_____
Probation Officer	Date	Probationer	Date

I, We understand that as the parent(s)/custodian(s) involved in this matter, I/We must notify the Probation Department concerning any probation violations that arise or subject myself/ourselves to another Court appearance. Further, I understand that I am responsible for the payment of counseling services, including assessments, as ordered by the Court.

_____	_____	_____	_____
Parent/Custodian	Date	Parent/Custodian	Date

(Courtesy of Wood County Juvenile Court, Bowling Green, OH.)

3. **Cases who can do well if the probation officer allocates time and resources.** This is the sweet spot that probation is designed to address. These juveniles are at a turning point in their lives, and if they receive the right guidance and support, they can succeed in getting on the right path. Probation officers who recognize these cases will work diligently to make sure that these youths get every possible means of support, including firm supervision and the threat of probation revocation. These cases can take up a disproportionate amount of the probation officer's time and energy, but the payoff in terms of helping a young person and protecting society can be immense.

Intensive-supervision probation is designed to allow the probation department to provide extended services to the juveniles who fall into category 2. It is a blunt reality that these are cases who, under better conditions, would go to a treatment center. Therefore, the probation department beefs up its supervision and tries to accomplish two goals. The first goal is to protect society by maintaining increased vigilance over these juveniles. The second goal is to provide treatment services that can affect the likelihood of turning these juveniles toward law-abiding behavior. Here the goal is to move the juvenile from a category 2 to a category 3 case. The risks are great, and the resources required are far beyond what standard probation has available, so intensive–supervision probation is designed to fill the gap between probation and incarceration in a secure facility.[11]

Intensive–supervision probation differs from standard probation in several ways. First, some jurisdictions don't use the normal caseload structure in which juveniles are assigned a single probation officer. Intensive–supervision probation programs often use a team approach in which a probation officer is supplemented by probation aides. By using teams, the probation department can be assured that someone is always available to respond to and monitor the juveniles' behavior. A second way in which intensive-supervision probation differs from standard probation is in the size of the caseloads. Instead of being responsible for over a hundred cases, the intensive–supervision officer, often along with a team of aides, is responsible for 30 or fewer juveniles. Finally, intensive-supervision probation activities are more highly structured. There are more offender accountability and more frequent checks by officers and aides. For example, a typical program structure for an intensive-probation supervision in Peoria, Illinois, has four phases that target juvenile delinquents on probation for gang-related behavior or substance-abuse offenses.

- **Phase 1: Planning and movement** This phase is designed to stabilize participants through intensive monitoring and movement control while allowing time to assess treatment needs. During this phase, juveniles are assessed for substance abuse and mental health treatment.

- **Phase 2: Counseling, treatment, and programming** This phase occurs within one week of phase 1. Youths begin outpatient treatment, intensive outpatient treatment, residential substance-abuse treatment, or some combination of these three. Intensive-supervision juvenile probation program officers attend group sessions as frequently as possible. Youths are referred to aftercare following completion of a treatment program. An antigang program is also offered at this time.

- **Phase 3: Community outreach** This phase requires the completion of a community service project or a report written and presented by the youth describing his or her experience in treatment.

- **Phase 4: Reassignment** This phase gradually reduces the frequency of contacts with the program officers to prepare youths for the transition to regular probation or probation termination. Throughout the first three phases, program officers make frequent contacts with program participants and their families, schools, and treatment providers. Parents are kept abreast of everything going on in their child's probation and are required to sign all case plans.[12]

As can be seen from this highly structured program, intensive–supervision probation includes many of the essential elements of standard probation but concentrates more on a few juveniles. For many of these youths, intensive–supervision probation is their "last, best hope" of turning their lives around before getting sent to a secure institution and losing daily contact with family members, friends, and schools, as well as their liberty. For those who can meet the requirements of intensive–supervision probation, the possibility of getting help to address treatment needs is high. For those who can't abide by the conditions and structure of intensive–supervision probation, the chance of getting caught in delinquent behavior again is virtually assured.

intensive-supervision probation
Close, controlled tracking of a probationer's activities by a probation officer or a team of officers.

Electronic Monitoring

electronic monitoring
The use of an electronic device, usually one that the offender wears, to monitor an offender's location and activities.

Another community-based corrections program often used in conjunction with probation, especially intensive–supervision probation, is electronic monitoring. **Electronic monitoring** can be thought of as a technological solution to a human problem. Given the size of probation caseloads and the geographic mobility of youth today, it is extremely difficult for probation officers to be confident of the whereabouts of their caseloads. It is time consuming for probation officers to drive to the home of each probationer on a regular basis. Also, once a probation officer has confirmed that the juvenile has complied with the curfew, it is always possible that the youth will slip out of the house after the probation officer has left and the parents have gone to bed.[13]

In an electronic-monitoring program, the probationer wears an electronic ankle bracelet or other device that is constantly monitored by a computer. A number of technologies are used to provide this type of electronic surveillance, and it is changing all the time.[14] One early technique put a monitor on the offender's home telephone that would send a signal to the probation office if the wearer of the ankle bracelet strayed too far from the phone. Soon it might be legal to implant a tracking chip in offenders' bodies. Probation officers could then use a computer to set certain geographic areas off limits to the probationer and activate an alert when these locations are visited.

The advantages of electronic monitoring are obvious. A single probation officer can monitor many more clients with a minimum of effort or expense, meaning that electronic devices will eventually pay for themselves in terms of reduced personnel costs.[15] Electronic monitoring also allows probationers to avoid incarceration and live at home with minimal supervision and interference from the probation officer. However, some critics of electronic monitoring liken it to an Orwellian 1984 scenario in which Big Brother is invading everyone's privacy and watching every move.[16] The invasion of privacy is a serious concern in a society with surveillance cameras in public spaces, computer monitoring by employers in the workplace, and identity theft. Critics of electronic monitoring say it violates the Fourth Amendment protections concerning

Electronic monitoring allows juveniles on probation to avoid incarceration and to live at home. This girl, who was known in her neighborhood as a gang member, was on probation for breaking-and-entering, possession of a concealed weapon, and assault and battery.

(Courtesy John M. Discher, Wide World Photos)

search and seizure. However, it needs to be remembered that, at least for now, no one is required to submit to an electronic-surveillance program. Probationers consent to be monitored to escape the more restrictive conditions of confinement in a secure detention facility. As the level of technology increases, however, legitimate privacy issues might arise in the future.

Another issue of electronic monitoring concerns tampering with technology. As our nation grows increasingly dependent on technology, it also grows increasingly vulnerable to hackers and system disruptions. For instance, a citywide electrical blackout can result in hundreds of probationers being "lost" for several hours. Similarly, people can hack into the probation office's monitoring system and manipulate the data. Some juveniles with sophisticated computer skills could introduce their own programs into the system to provide false information. So although this type of technology can be a useful supplement to probation, it cannot completely replace a well–trained probation officer.

The public might also be concerned that those on electronic-monitoring programs are not being punished enough. This criticism is especially pertinent to adult offenders but is less applicable to juveniles. Because the philosophy of the juvenile justice system is to act in the best interests of the youth, electronic monitoring can be treated as a less restrictive and more supportive treatment option than incarceration. Finally, electronic monitoring is limited in what it can provide in terms of community security. Although knowing the exact geographic locations of juvenile probationers is useful, electronic monitoring cannot tell the probation officer what the juvenile is doing. The juvenile could be selling stolen merchandise from home, using drugs, engaging in sexual activities, or playing illegal online poker.[17]

Home Confinement

Home confinement, or *house arrest* as it is sometimes called, restricts offenders and juvenile delinquents to their homes for large parts of the day. The idea behind home confinement for juveniles is to let them stay at home with their parents and attend school without disrupting their lives. It preserves the bond the youth has with family, school, and community while ensuring that the juvenile is not out causing trouble. Home confinement is often used in conjunction with intensive-supervision probation and electronic monitoring.[18] The major advantage of home confinement is cost. Keeping the juvenile at home means the parents pay for room and board, not the state. The type of punishment inherent in home confinement depends entirely on the parents' social and economic status. For some juveniles, who can maintain access to their video games, big-screen television, family swimming pool, and refrigerator full of junk food, home confinement might not seem to be much of an inconvenience. For other children, who come from disadvantaged homes, being made to stay inside except when they have legitimate reasons, such as school, might seem like a major imposition. Probation officers need to investigate the home to make sure it is a safe, positive environment in which to confine the youth.[19] Under some circumstances, the influence of a dysfunctional family might be the cause of the delinquency, and home confinement might be the wrong option.

home confinement
A sentence that requires that the offender be confined in and around the area of his or her home.

Fines and Victim Compensation

Sometimes, the court orders juvenile delinquents to pay fines or make **restitution.** These sanctions are accomplished in a number of ways, and the philosophy behind each is slightly different. The overall idea of fines and restitution is to make the juvenile accountable for his or her actions.[20] The big drawback to these sanctions is that not every youth is equally able to pay for her or his actions in monetary terms. Therefore, judges have invented creative ways for youths to "pay for their crimes."

restitution
Court-ordered compensation by the offender to the victim(s) for their psychological, physical, or financial losses resulting from an offense.

- **Fines** Fines may be imposed for any number of behaviors, such as speeding or vandalism. The problem with fines is that, for the most part, juveniles do not have their own money. Consequently, the parents end up paying the fine, and the sanction's message is lost on the youth unless the parents require him or her to somehow work off the payment. Additionally, fines affect economically disadvantaged families more than those with financial resources. This means fines can give the impression that the wealthy can buy their way out of trouble.

- **Victim restitution** Juveniles can be ordered to make monetary restitution to their victims, which can be accomplished in a number of ways. It can be as simple as paying the victim for damages. If a juvenile smashes the victim's car window and steals the stereo, it's relatively easy to determine the cost of replacement. If the amount is substantial, the court can order the payment to be made in installments. If the juvenile can't pay for the damages, the court may order the juvenile to provide victim–service restitution whereby the juvenile mows the victim's lawn or washes the car. This service is negotiated with the juvenile, the victim, and the court or probation officer to ensure that it is proportionate to the damage and the juvenile's culpability.[21]

- **Community service** Sometimes the victim doesn't want any further contact with the juvenile. It is understandable that victims would not want juvenile delinquents anywhere near them or their property. Often, the juvenile damages schools, parks, or other public property, so there is no individual victim to make restitution to. Under these circumstances, the court may order the juvenile to perform community service. This might be cleaning the sidewalks in the park or helping supervise children in an afterschool program (see Case in Point 15.1). Community-service programs have their drawbacks, however. To be effective, juveniles must be monitored to ensure that they show up, work the required hours, and do a good job. This monitoring is done by either the probation officer or program staff. Either way, the cost of training and paying those who supervise the work might be as great as the value of the work that is performed.

These types of victim–compensation programs provide delinquents an opportunity to right the damage they do. Whether restitution is made directly to the victim or to the community at large, the idea of holding the juvenile accountable for delinquent acts is presumed to help develop character.[22] But trouble arises in these types of programs

---

15.1 CASE IN POINT

THE CASE	THE POINT
M.J.W. v. *State of Georgia* 210 S.E. 2d 842 (1974 Ga App.)	*Community service for juveniles is considered to be "just restitution" and of rehabilitative value, not "involuntary servitude."*

M.J.W. was accused of throwing a match into a trash can in the school restroom that contained dry paper, which burst into flame. The school's assistant principal testified the damage amounted to less than $25.

M.J.W. was placed on probation for one year and required to "contribute 100 hours to the Parks and Recreation Department of DeKalb County." The youth's attorney objected, stating that the community service amounted to a fine and "that no statutory authority exists for imposing a monetary fine on a minor adjudged to be delinquent," and also that the community service constituted "involuntary servitude," thus violating the juvenile's constitutional rights.

The court ruled that community service work is restitution and not a monetary penalty and is also a regular part of probation and a helpful rehabilitative tool for "producing a good adult citizen."

when the juvenile fails to make adequate restitution. If the fine or restitution was predicated on the youth having a job, getting fired or laid off can land the youth back before the court. At times, broad social forces, such as a downturn in the employment rate, can result in a juvenile failing to have the means to make restitution, even when he or she is willing to do so.

Restitution programs can be instituted at different stages in the juvenile justice system. Often, they are added as a special condition of probation, and sometimes they are applied before the juvenile is adjudged as part of a diversion program. In this way, the juvenile can make restitution to the victim or community and avoid the stigma of being labeled a delinquent. However, restitution programs are susceptible to inequities in how they are administered. Juveniles who present the least threat to society, look clean–cut, have families who can provide transportation to community-service locations, and who have committed relatively minor offenses are more likely than others to succeed at restitution and community service. Without careful monitoring of these programs, it is likely that social class, race, and gender will become disproportionately important in who is selected for these programs and who receives a more severe penalty.

Residential Treatment Programs

For many youths, staying at home as part of a treatment plan is not a good option, because the parents might not have the interest or competence to ensure a good, supportive environment. In this case, judges are forced to look elsewhere for a positive living situation. Judges generally have two options: secure and nonsecure facilities.

Secure facilities are the counterpart of adult prisons and will be discussed in greater detail later in this chapter. Nonsecure facilities allow the juvenile to stay in the community in some sort of alternative living arrangement that has the advantage of maintaining access to schools, recreational programs, religious activities, and other community-based services. Additionally, many of the previously discussed sanctions, such as electronic monitoring and restitution programs, can be used with nonsecure detention. Often, **nonsecure detention** is used in conjunction with probation as part of a blended-sentencing program.[23] The overall intent of these programs is to provide services that compensate for the deficiencies, both social and personal, that resulted in the behaviors that landed the youth in front of a judge in the first place. Three of the more common types of nonsecure juvenile treatment settings are foster care, group homes and halfway houses, and alternative-experience programs.

nonsecure detention
Placement of a juvenile in a group home, foster care, or other program in which the juvenile may come and go with permission.

FOSTER CARE   Foster care is used when the court finds that a youth's parents are either unfit or unable to provide for his or her welfare. Social service agencies screen foster-care parents to weed out those who would exploit children. Foster-care parents might foster more than one youth in the home, and these children might come from different families. In addition, foster-care parents might have their own children in the home. The state pays these parents a stipend for the expenses of caring for the foster child, but it isn't a money–making proposition and, ideally, foster parents are motivated by a desire to help children in trouble, not to make money. Many of those placed in foster care are status offenders, and about half are delinquents.[24] Foster care can last from a very short period of weeks to a longer term of years. In some instances, the foster parents grow attached to the children and adopt them. Foster care can be an effective treatment strategy when all the youth needs is a stable and supportive environment. However, foster parents aren't trained social workers or psychologists and are usually ill–equipped to deal with children with serious emotional and behavioral problems.[25]

GROUP HOMES AND HALFWAY HOUSES   Group homes are different from foster care in that they accommodate more juveniles and are more structured. Although group homes vary widely, they typically hold 8 to 12 juveniles and have a professional staff that works shifts to ensure that there is always a responsible adult at the home. Group homes are usually large, single–family homes in residential neighborhoods that are indistinguishable from other homes. They are intended to provide an as-normal-as-possible living environment so that the youths can go to the same schools, recreational activities, and therapeutic services that are available to all children. Group homes also have strict rules. Juveniles are required to keep their rooms clean and orderly, maintain a curfew, attend school, and participate in therapeutic programs. Additionally, youths may be required to submit to drug testing or wear an electronic ankle bracelet.

Group homes and halfway houses are difficult to institutionalize because of high staff turnover, which diminishes the home's effectiveness. A well-trained and motivated staff is difficult to maintain. Because of low pay, the job is considered a steppingstone for many staff members who find that they need a more stable and better–paying job as they get older. Some group homes are run by a family, and as the family's circumstances change, the parents might find running a halfway house no longer desirable. Also, new staff members might not have developed a network with community and volunteer service agencies, including the trust of the juvenile court judges. Staff members get very little training, and most of what they learn is on the job, where mistakes in judgment can result in difficulties for themselves, the juveniles, and the halfway house. For instance, if a staff member gives a youth permission to stay out late and the youth commits a serious offense, the publicity can seriously harm the facility's reputation and bring calls to close it. Funding can also be problematic. Halfway houses are particularly vulnerable during times of scarce resources because they are easy to close. Often, the houses themselves are rented, so there is not a costly building that is unused when the halfway house ceases to exist.

ALTERNATIVE-EXPERIENCE PROGRAMS   A number of programs seek to provide juveniles with experiences that can help change their work habits, self-concepts, and ability to get along with others. These programs are typically conducted on ranches, in camps, or out in the wilderness. The idea behind such programs is to take the youths out of their regular surroundings and subject them to physical and mental stress in a carefully controlled way that ensures that they pass tests of their character. Successful completion of a difficult task is sometimes the first time the youths have been able to feel truly proud of themselves. The youths are required to learn new skills, such as working with animals, learning to climb mountains, or surviving in the wilderness. Many of the skills won't be particularly useful to youths who return to large cities, but the idea is not having the skills, but the process of learning the skills.[26] By learning to negotiate and work with others, persevere when extremely tired and uncomfortable, and follow directions in hazardous situations, it is believed that the youths will learn that they have capabilities of their own and can compete in legitimate ways with others.

Often, these camps, ranches, or wilderness programs provide youths with life–changing experiences that can arm them with the positive self–image they need to resist the temptations they find when returning to their neighborhoods. If done correctly, these alternative–experience programs can be extremely beneficial. However, if done wrong, these programs verge on child abuse. Untrained or incompetent staff members can ignore warning signs of mental and physical breakdown and push the juveniles into unsafe situations that can have lasting negative effects (see Crosscurrents 15.1).

ADVANTAGES OF RESIDENTIAL TREATMENT PROGRAMS   The first and most politically appealing advantage of residential treatment is that it's less expensive than placing the youth in secure confinement. The duration of residential treatment is much shorter than secure confinement. A residential treatment plan might last only 90 days, whereas incarceration often lasts longer than a year. So each treatment opening in a wilderness program, halfway house, or foster home will typically accommodate three to five juveniles a year, whereas secure confinement can deal with only one youth per opening. It is also cheaper to staff, feed, and supervise youths in nonsecure residential programs than in secure facilities.[27]

CrossCurrents

Rehabilitated to Death

In 2005 in Florida, Martin Lee Anderson, 14, took a joy ride in a Jeep Cherokee that his cousins stole from his grandmother and was sentenced to probation. Months later, he violated his probation by walking across school grounds to visit a friend. In 2006, about three hours after being admitted to Bay County Sheriff's Boot Camp, Anderson said he couldn't breathe while on a mandatory run. The staff thought he was being defiant and used "pain compliance" methods to shock him. The officers paused while a nurse examined Anderson and then allowed them to continue the "pain compliance" until he was unconscious. Anderson was taken to a hospital, where he died the next morning.[1] In 2007, a jury acquitted the guards and the nurse of aggravated manslaughter.[2]

Among the boot–camp prisons, wilderness adventure programs, and residential drug–treatment centers, there have been several well–publicized cases in which teenagers have died from inadequate supervision or punishment disguised as treatment. "Tough love" is a billion–dollar industry. Several hundred programs, both public and private, use the approach. Somewhere between 10,000 and 100,000 teenagers are currently held in treatment programs based on the belief that adolescents must be broken mentally (and often physically as well) before they can be fixed. No one keeps track of the number of kids in these programs, most of which are private. Most of the kids in boot-camp prison are sent there by a judge, while most in private wilderness programs are sent there by parents. Many private programs operate with no outside supervision and feature a combination of rigid rules, total isolation, emotional attacks, and physical punishment.[3]

There have been nearly three dozen deaths and thousands of reports of severe abuse in programs that use corporal punishment, emotional attacks, isolation, and physical restraint. In 1999, Gina Score, 14, died of heatstroke on a dirt road at a girls' boot camp. Guards left Score, who was in boot camp for shoplifting Beanie Babies, half–conscious in the sun for three hours after she collapsed during a morning run that she had to jog in while handcuffed and shackled.[4]

Although many see these programs as a good way to deal with stubborn and recalcitrant kids, there is a major flaw in how they select participants that scholars such as criminologist Thomas Blomberg calls "net–widening."[5] Many of the kids in these programs were never destined for secure detention. Their offenses were so minor that they normally would have been released to their parents' supervision. Criminologist Michael A. Hallett calls this focus on low–risk, nondangerous clients "creaming" or "skimming."[6] Private programs select clients who need little care and are likely to respond to any treatment. Unfortunately, this does little but widen the net of social control. When these programs are staffed by untrained, incompetent, and/or sadistic workers, abuses and tragedies are the result.

Think About It

1. Are boot camps and extreme wilderness programs still a good idea?
2. What changes in these programs would you suggest?
3. Are fatalities in any such program inevitable and rare, or are they evidence that these programs should be halted?

1 Carol Marbin Miller and Phil Long, "2nd Autopsy Rejects Natural Causes," *Miami Herald* (Florida), March 15, 2006, State and Regional News, p. 1A.
2 Tim Padgett, "What's Wrong with Florida's Prisons?" *TIME*, October 17, 2007, www.time.com/time/nation/article/0,8599,1672366,00.html?xid=rss-nation.
3 Maia Szalavitz, "The Trouble with Troubled Teen Programs," *Reason Online*, January 2007, www.reason.com/news/show/117088.html.
4 Alex Leary, "Boot Camps Losing Favor Nationally," *St. Petersburg Times* (Florida), March 5, 2006, p. 1B.
5 Thomas G. Blomberg, "Widening the Net: An Anomaly in the Evaluation of Diversion Programs," in Malcolm W. Klein and Katherine S. Teilmann, eds., *Handbook of Criminal Justice Evaluation* (Beverly Hills, CA: Sage, 1980), 571–592.
6 Michael A. Hallett, *Private Prisons in America: A Critical Race Perspective* (Urbana: University of Illinois Press, 2007).

The second major advantage of these programs is that they provide a less restrictive option. This type of residential option enables many juveniles to escape the negative consequences of being sent to a training school or other long-term correctional facility. To provide individualized treatment, these types of programs are necessary. The more quality programs that are available, the better the judge can match a juvenile who has particular problems with a treatment option that can successfully deal with them. But with fewer treatment programs, the judge is forced to send youths to programs that are neither appropriate nor effective.

Finally, these programs can limit the stigma placed on juvenile delinquents. Being sent to a wilderness survival program can prevent the youth from being considered a serious criminal both in the eyes of society and in his or her self–concept.[28] According to labeling theory, the further into the justice system juveniles go, the more difficult it becomes to reclaim them as productive citizens. So only the most serious cases who entail a danger to society are considered for secure confinement. Nonsecure treatment programs, if there are available options, can deal more effectively with the rest.

SECURE CONFINEMENT

Juveniles who have committed serious offenses or who have demonstrated that they are not amenable to community-based treatment options will often be sent to secure institutions. Much like an adult prison, secure institutions restrict the movements of the juveniles to the institution. Most juveniles in secure institutions have committed non–status offenses, that is, offenses that would be criminal if committed by adults. The Juvenile Justice and Delinquency Prevention Act of 2002 prohibits status offenders from being placed in secure facilities, although federal regulations have interpreted that to mean that accused status offenders can be held in secure juvenile facilities for up to 24 hours following initial contact with the police or the court.[29]

pains of imprisonment
Deprivations that define the punishment aspect of incarceration.

Secure confinement is a self–contained, closed environment that not only restricts freedom, but also features other **pains of imprisonment.** To appreciate the conditions of secure confinement, it is useful to consider the daily life and routine of inmates. In his classic book, *Society of Captives,* Gresham Sykes describes the five pains of imprisonment that adult offenders face. This concept is applicable to juveniles as well, because all secure institutions have these deprivations to some degree.[30]

- **Deprivation of liberty**   This is the most basic pain of imprisonment. Juveniles locked inside the institution can't leave to see friends and family. Additionally, they are confined within the institution and might even be restricted to their cells. The deprivation of liberty entails having to ask a staff member to unlock a door or gate and means the freedom to come and go is no longer a choice.

- **Deprivation of goods and services**   Juveniles are not free to acquire the things that many youths take for granted. Television, video games, and other activities are no longer freely available. Juveniles do not have the family refrigerator to snack from, and they cannot call their friends. They eat in an institutional dining room where there are no options and no menu. If the youth, for example, does not want to eat the liver and onions that are served, the alternative is to not eat. In most institutions, an underground economy of some sort develops in which some inmates will smuggle in cigarettes, drugs, or food and sell them for extravagant prices or trade them for services and favors.

institutionalization
The loss of the ability to make decisions for oneself because of the long period of time spent in a secure facility.

- **Deprivation of autonomy**   Here the juvenile loses the opportunity to make decisions. The staff, who make all the important and most of the trivial decisions, are concerned less about the inmates' comfort and happiness and more about institutional security. Long–term inmates might suffer **institutionalization,** meaning that they lose the capacity to make decisions and often have a difficult time returning to society.[31]

- **Deprivation of heterosexual relations**   For adult inmates, the deprivation of heterosexual relations means that they are separated from their spouses or girlfriends or boyfriends and no longer have normal releases for their sexual desires. This deprivation also affects female inmates. One would hope the deprivation of heterosexual relations would not be a major issue in juvenile institutions, but this simply is not the case. Adolescents have a highly developed interest in sexual relations, and life in a single–sex institution can give their behavior yet another sexual dimension. When heterosexual persons are denied social contact with members of the opposite sex, they must find other ways of expressing their sexual identities. In adult male prisons, homosexual rape is so common that it has become an expected part of the prison experience. In juvenile institutions, the inability to explore traditional sexual identities with members of the opposite sex can provide reasons for experimentation and exploitation.

- **Deprivation of security**   In any institution, the strong tend to take advantage of the weak, and those who are older, more experienced, and aggressive will attempt to dominate others through force. Juveniles might fashion homemade weapons to protect themselves, but there is little safety for anyone when juvenile gangs are active in an institution.[32]

These pains of imprisonment define life in an institution. They exist to varying degrees in every adult and juvenile institution and are an integral part of the incarceration experience. With the exception of deprivation of security, these pains of imprisonment are the foundation for making incarceration a deterrent. If they did not exist, prison would not be such a bad place. The deprivation of security, however, is unintended. Officials in adult and juvenile facilities are supposed to keep the inmates safe. The violence done behind bars is a direct result of the administration not having enough resources and options to keep inmates from fighting, raping, and killing each other. Security problems are doubled when juveniles are incarcerated. Not only is the rehabilitation mandate of the juvenile justice system violated, but juveniles are more mentally and physically vulnerable than adults. Juveniles in adult facilities under criminal jurisdiction have the right to mental health and medical care, education, due process, and access to their families and the courts. These rights also apply to juveniles in juvenile detention centers, training schools, jails and prisons, and other types of secure facilities.[33]

Jails

Jails and detention centers (discussed later) are the two basic short-term confinement options. Jail is the most troubling option, because jails also hold adult offenders and detainees. However, when juveniles must be detained for very short periods of time, they are generally sent to jails. Some youths who are confined in jails have actually been charged as adults and are waiting for criminal trials, and most juveniles who are held in jails are held as adults (see Figure 15-1). Juveniles who are being held as juveniles are sent to jails because they require secure confinement until they can be seen by a judge.

Federal law requires that jailed juveniles be held out of sight and sound of adults. Otherwise, the rules for young people in jail differ somewhat from state to state, with federal funding for each state depending on compliance with the "jail-removal" mandates

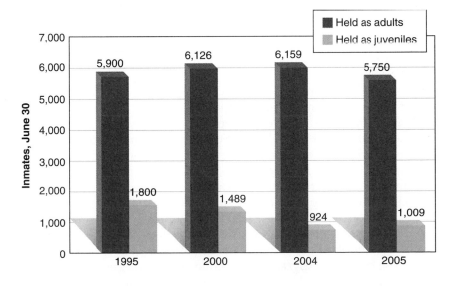

Figure 15-1   Average Daily Population of Juvenile Jail Inmates by Year *Source:* Paige M. Harrison and Allen J. Beck, *Prison and Jail Inmates at Midyear 2005* (Washington, DC: U.S. Department of Justice, Office of Justice Programs, Bureau of Justice Statistics, 2006), 8.

of the Juvenile Justice and Delinquency Prevention Act. The act specifies that juveniles who are detained in jails for non–status offenses can remain there for only a maximum of six hours while awaiting processing or release, transfer to a juvenile facility, or a court appearance. The act further specifies that juveniles awaiting a court appearance must be separated from adults and have access to someone who has been trained to work with juveniles. States do not uniformly comply with the act, however, the most common reason being that they lack the resources and facilities to provide jail alternatives for juveniles.

For example, in one 2006 case, a 16–year–old girl charged as an adult with murder in the District of Columbia was held in the women's wing of the DC jail and locked in her cell for 23 hours a day to minimize her contact with adults. Boys charged under similar circumstances were kept in a special wing out of sight and sound of adult inmates, but there was no such special wing for girls because the situation was so rare. There simply were not enough girls charged as adults with murder to warrant a special wing. In one of several hearings, the judge in the case admitted that the city was probably violating federal law.[34]

Detention Centers

Most states use secure detention facilities as sanctions, as well as to temporarily hold juveniles while their cases are processed. The use of detention varies by state. Some states use detention only for temporary holding, some states use it to sanction probation violators, while others use it as a disposition. Some states use secure detention for all three purposes. A judge will send a juvenile to detention if he or she thinks the youth presents a threat to the community, will be endangered by returning to the community, or will not show at a hearing. Juveniles also go to detention centers for diagnostic evaluation.

All states require that a detention hearing be held within a few days of custody. The judge will review the decision to detain the juvenile and either order a release or continued detention.[35] As of 2007, only nine states, Connecticut, Delaware, Kansas, Massachusetts, Missouri, New York, North Dakota, South Carolina, and Texas, used secure detention only for temporary holding.[36] Some jurisdictions have juvenile detention centers in the same locations with jails or lockups. These facilities must ensure that they provide separate and distinct facilities for juveniles.[37] Generally, each state does juvenile detention a little bit differently and approaches it with a different philosophy. See A Closer Look at Juvenile Issues 15.2 for an example of juvenile detention rules in the state of Florida in 2007.

Juvenile Correctional Facilities

Juvenile correctional facilities are called a variety of things depending on the state. In some states they are *training schools*, in others *reform schools*, and in still others *industrial schools* or *youth facilities*. Some states just call them juvenile correctional facilities. Regardless of the title, they all serve the same purpose: the extended, secure confinement of juvenile delinquents. So you can get a sense of the variety of titles, Table 15-1 lists a selection of states and what they call their long-term, secure juvenile facilities.

Whereas detention centers are local, juvenile correctional facilities are run by the state. Some secure facilities have reception and diagnostic centers that assess newly committed juveniles to determine their mental health, educational needs, and appropriate treatment. Some very large states, such as California, have specialized reception and diagnostic centers that run special programs for juveniles needing treatment for mental health or sex-offender issues. Some also have schools that are structured like regular high schools. These facilities offer a variety of programs and education, as well as substance-abuse programs and public-service programs. Some states have separate facilities for older adolescents and younger children. In 2002, there were more small juvenile facilities than large facilities, but the large facilities held nearly half of juvenile delinquents (see Figure 15-2).

15.2 A CLOSER LOOK at JUVENILE ISSUES

JUVENILE JUSTICE DETENTION

Youth under age 18 who are taken into custody by the police are evaluated immediately by the Florida Department of Juvenile Justice to determine if they should be detained under lock and key to protect the public. Youths taken into custody for minor offenses who are not considered a risk to public safety may be released into the custody of their parents or guardians. Otherwise, detention screening is performed at Juvenile Assessment Centers or by juvenile probation staff using a standardized Detention Risk Assessment Instrument.

Juvenile detention in Florida is a short-term temporary program. Delinquents who require long-term sanctions and rehabilitation are placed in nonresidential or residential correctional programs. Two types of detention are available: secure detention and home detention.

- Youths placed in secure detention have been assessed as risks to public safety and must remain in a physically secure detention center while awaiting court proceedings. They appear before the court within 24 hours of placement, at which time the juvenile judge decides whether there is a need for continued detention. Generally, there is a 21-day limit to secure detention, but those charged with serious offenses can be held up to 30 days. Serious delinquents also can be held in secure detention while awaiting placement in a residential corrections facility.

- Youths on home-detention status are released to their parents or guardians. Both youth and parents sign a home detention agreement. This agreement stipulates the conditions of home detention which the youth is to follow, i.e., mandatory school attendance and curfew.

- The Department operates 26 juvenile detention centers in 25 counties with a total of 2,057 beds. The detention centers provide custody, supervision, education and mental health/substance abuse services to juveniles statewide. Juvenile detention officers receive specialized training and certification.

Source: Florida Department of Juvenile Justice, www.djj.state.fl.us/Detention/index.html.

Table 15-1   A Selection of States and Their Long-Term, Secure Juvenile Facilities

State	Title of Facility
Georgia	Youth development campus
Colorado, District of Columbia, New Hampshire	Youth services center
Connecticut, Delaware, Iowa, Michigan, Mississippi, Nevada, New Mexico, Rhode Island, Texas, Washington, Wyoming	Training school
Illinois	Youth center
Iowa	Juvenile home (for girls)
Kentucky, Maine, North Carolina, Pennsylvania, Tennessee	Youth development center
West Virginia	Industrial home

Boot-Camp Prisons

Sometimes an idea that falls outside the traditional treatment realm becomes so popular that it gets funded and introduced into the juvenile justice system. One such idea was the melding of treatment with punishment in what became known as **boot-camp prison.** Sometimes it is difficult to distinguish between treatment and punishment. This is the case with shock incarceration programs such as juvenile boot camps, where inmates are considered not to need psychological services as much as they need to learn that deviant behavior can have negative consequences.

Juvenile boot camps are patterned after military basic-training programs. In the 1990s, they became the new panacea for dealing with juvenile delinquents. The programs last anywhere from 30 to 180 days and include strict discipline, physical training, and hard labor.[38] Juveniles are subjected to a highly regimented type of military structure that includes marching, being yelled at and insulted by correctional officers dressed as drill sergeants, and being forced to interact with military mannerisms, such as keeping the eyes looking straight forward, standing at attention, and responding to

**Instant Recall
from Chapter 15**
boot-camp prison
A short-term prison, usually for young offenders, that employs military boot-camp training and discipline techniques for rehabilitation.

questions and orders by yelling "Yes sir" or "No sir." However, some critics point out that the mandates of the military and juvenile corrections are considerably different.[39]

The military screens recruits to ensure that they are psychologically normal young men and women and then subjects them to physical and emotional stress in basic training to teach them military protocol and to follow orders without question. The goal of basic training is to ensure that these recruits are able to overcome their positive socialization and kill other human beings when ordered to do so.

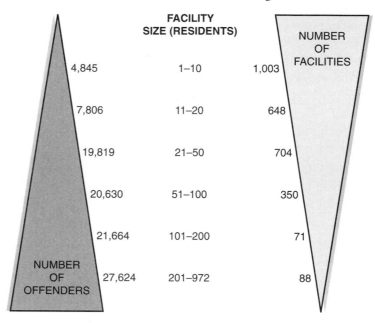

	FACILITY SIZE (RESIDENTS)		
4,845	1–10	1,003	
7,806	11–20	648	
19,819	21–50	704	
20,630	51–100	350	
21,664	101–200	71	
27,624	201–972	88	

NUMBER OF OFFENDERS

NUMBER OF FACILITIES

Figure 15-2 **Inverse Relationship between Facility Size and Number of Juveniles** *Source:* Howard N. Snyder and Melissa Sickmund, *Juvenile Offenders and Victims: 2006 National Report* (Washington, DC: U.S. Department of Justice, Office of Justice Programs, Office of Juvenile Justice and Delinquency Prevention, 2006), 222.

Juvenile boot-camp inmates march while carrying their mattresses at a Fort Lauderdale, Florida, jail in 2000.
(Getty Images, Inc.)

According to Gwynne Dyer, recruits come out of basic training a little bit crazy because it is such an artificial and stressful environment, and they are slightly traumatized by being treated in such a regimented and hostile manner. However, military boot camp is the beginning of military socialization, not the end. Recruits are then sent for further training under more normal conditions, and the negative effects of boot camp are gradually overcome by the discipline and pride they develop as valued members of military units. Further, the recruits stay in the military for years, and by the time they return to society, the negative effects of boot camp have disappeared.

The mission of juvenile corrections is very different from that of the military. The task is to take youths who have violated the law and teach them to think for themselves, evaluate their behavior, and not hurt other people. The military-style boot–camp prison is not suited to these tasks. Military boot camps take some aspects of recruits' positive socialization and replace it with military–style socialization and training. Boot–camp prisons take youths who have been negatively socialized and replace that with more negative socialization and little else. Also, there is no reintegration period for the juveniles once they are released. They are sent back into the same families, neighborhoods, and communities where they committed their offenses, armed not with new coping skills or educational experiences, but rather with the effects of being degraded, dehumanized, dominated, and traumatized. Some scholars suggest that boot–camp prisons are best suited to developing drug dealers and gang members who benefit from seeing others as enemies who can be killed without remorse.[40]

State Prisons

Most youths in adult prisons are 17 years old, male, and minority and have committed offenses against the person.[41] These youths arrive in state prisons, which are populated mostly by adult offenders, after having been charged as an adult and given a criminal trial. The conditions for the youths are the same as those for adults, except that, according to the Juvenile Justice and Delinquency Prevention Act, they must be kept out of sight and sound of adult inmates until they are of adult age themselves. See Figure 15-3 for a snapshot of the number of youths in state prisons.

An attorney talks to her young client in jail. *(Courtesy Shelley Gazin, Corbis/Bettmann)*

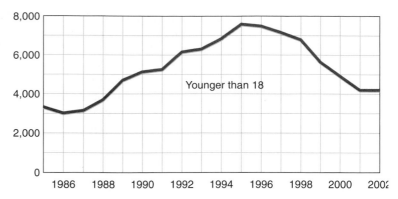

Figure 15-3   **New Admissions to State Prisons of Inmates Younger than 18.**

The number of new admissions of youths younger than 18 to state prisons fell 45 percent between 1996 and 2002. The decline in new admissions followed the decline in juvenile violent crime arrests over the same six years.

Source: Howard N. Snyder and Melissa Sickmund, *Juvenile Offenders and Victims: 2006 National Report* (Washington, DC: U.S. Department of Justice, Office of Justice Programs, Office of Juvenile Justice and Delinquency Prevention, 2006), 237.

The controversy regarding incarcerating such young people in state prison is closely connected to juvenile waiver. If these juveniles had not been tried as adults, they would not be in state prisons. See Kids in the News 15.1 for a look at how some states are finding that the extensive use of secure confinement doesn't work as well as planned and are giving rehabilitation another shot.

Overcrowding

A 1994 survey of 984 public and private juvenile detention and correctional facilities found overcrowding to be a major shortcoming. Too many youths are housed in facilities that are not designed to accommodate the population that is pressed into them. The result of overcrowding is "heightened stress, increased victimization and injury, more rapid spread of sickness and disease, and decreased security."[42] As the size of the facility increases, so too does the security. For institutions that hold 200 or more residents, the vast majority (86 percent) report that they lock the inmates in their sleeping rooms to confine them at least part of the time.[43]

Institutional overcrowding is a difficult problem for juvenile correctional administrators. Juvenile court judges decide who goes to a secure detention facility, and the administrators lack the discretion to refuse. In most states, the juvenile is sentenced for a fixed period of time, and the administrator can't grant an early release. Although building more juvenile facilities is possible, it is the legislature, not the juvenile justice bureau, that allocates the money and approves the construction of new facilities. This places the administrators in a difficult position as more and more juveniles are crowed into facilities.

In *Rhodes* v. *Chapman*, an adult case, the Supreme Court ruled that overcrowding itself is not unconstitutional. This ruling is considered to apply to juvenile institutions as well, except when the overcrowding leads to adverse conditions (see Case in Point 15.2). Consequently, as long as food is delivered, sanitation is adequate, inmates get medical care, and there is no increase in violence and victimization, overcrowding is something administrators and inmates must adjust to.[44]

Suicide Prevention

The adjustment to living in a secure detention facility is more than some juveniles can bear. Although successful suicides are rare, there were 122 suicide attempts in the year 2002.[45] These suicide attempts represented only 4 percent of the institutions surveyed, so it is fair to say that suicide attempts are also a relatively infrequent occurrence. Most institutions have developed screening procedures to identify those who might attempt to kill themselves. By being attuned to the warning signs of juveniles experiencing

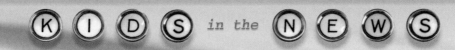

Rehabilitation Gets Another Chance

Several states are trying new approaches to juvenile justice other than incarceration. Throughout the 1990s, the "tough–on–crime" approach, augmented by the superpredator idea (see Chapter 3), became the popular way to deal with a rising tide of juvenile delinquents. The figure shows that violent victimizations by juvenile delinquents peaked in 1993 and dipped dramatically in the early 2000s. As juvenile delinquency has dropped off, it has become apparent to some state legislators that a tough, incarceration-based approach does little to prevent delinquency, rehabilitate delinquents, or stop them from becoming adult offenders.

In 1995, the *Chicago Tribune* called attention to the "filthy conditions" and "unqualified staff" of one local detention center where children would "languish . . . like warehoused animals." According to this article, the recidivism rate in Illinois as of 2006 was about 50 percent. About half of the juveniles whom the system "got tough on" came back for more.[1] Why?

Apparently, juveniles and adults perceive incarceration, punishment, and rehabilitation differently (see Chapter 6 for a discussion of the differences in adult and juvenile perceptions). What works for adults does not work for children, and vice versa. In 2002, *USA Today* described an interview with a 12–year-old boy who was serving time in a maximum–security prison. The boy had stolen a car, led police on a high–speed chase, and crashed into a roadblock. When the boy was asked whether he was sorry for what he had done now that he was incarcerated in a maximum–security adult prison, the boy said no, that the whole episode had been like *Smokey and the Bandit* and that it had been the "greatest day" of his life.[2]

Lately, several states have decided to pursue a more rehabilitative approach. In 2006, the MacArthur Foundation gave $10 million each to the states of Pennsylvania, Illinois, Louisiana, and Washington as a part of its Models for Change plan.[3] According to the foundation, the states plan a number of reforms.

- Illinois has created a new Juvenile Justice Department to treat youths differently from adult offenders.

- Before the grant, Louisiana had already separated its juvenile division from the adult corrections system. The state is also reducing secure confinement for juveniles. State facilities hold about one-fourth as many youths as they did in the 1990s.

- Pennsylvania is ensuring that services continue for juvenile delinquents who are returning to the community from secure facilities.

- Washington is using programs to reduce recidivism, such as Functional Family Therapy and Aggression Replacement Training.[4]

Think About It

1. Do you think juveniles really perceive punishment differently than adults?

2. Will the MacArthur initiative work, or does it amount to throwing money at a problem?

3. Will more states follow the lead of Illinois, Washington, Pennsylvania, and Louisiana? Should they?

1 Amanda Paulson, "New Tack on Teen Justice: A Push Away from Prisons," *Christian Science Monitor Online*, December 8, 2006, www.csmonitor.com/2006/1208/p02s02-usju.html.
2 J. Steven Smith, "Adult Prisons: No Place for Kids," *USA Today Magazine* 131, no. 2686, July 2002, pp. 34–35.
3 John D. and Catherine T. MacArthur Foundation, *Models for Change*, July 2006, http://modelsforchange.net/pdfs/Models%20for%20Change%20Overview.pdf.
4 Business Wire, "As Momentum for Juvenile Justice Reform Builds, MacArthur Foundation to Invest $100 Million," December 5, 2006.

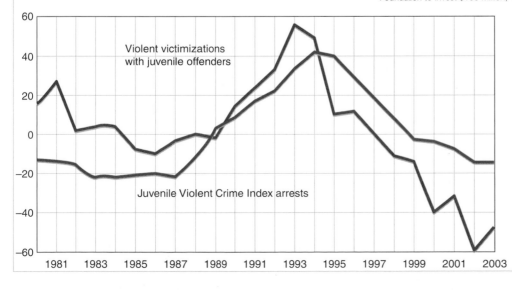

Source: Howard N. Snyder and Melissa Sickmund, *Juvenile Offenders and Victims: 2006 National Report* (Washington, DC: U.S. Department of Justice, Office of Justice Programs, Office of Juvenile Justice and Delinquency Prevention, 2006), 64.

15.2   CASE IN POINT

THE CASE

Nami v. Fauver, 82 F. 3d 63, 67 (3rd Cir. 1996)

THE POINT

Double-celling violates the Eighth Amendment under adverse conditions, such as poor ventilation, exposure to tobacco smoke, lack of exercise, not enough beds, and abuse from violent or psychologically disturbed cellmates.

In December 1994, Robert Nami, Maurice Thompson, Bart Fernandez, and Kenneth Thompson, who were in protective custody at the Administrative Close Supervision Unit at the Wagner Youth Correctional Facility in Bordentown, New Jersey, claimed that they were subjected to cruel and unusual punishment and denied access to the courts. Among other items, the plaintiffs alleged the following:

- Inmates in the protective custody unit were housed two to a single, small, one-bed cell, so that one inmate had to sleep on the floor by the toilet. The cells' solid doors and small windows made it difficult to call for help. Inmates often had to share cells with violent or mentally disturbed inmates. Nonsmokers were paired with smokers, and the ventilation system would shut down for very long periods. Double-celling allegedly led to increased rapes and other assaults. Inmates who wouldn't share a cell were punished with administrative segregation (solitary confinement) and loss of good time.
- Recreation was limited to one 2 1/2-hour period two days per week. Inmates were denied bathroom access during outdoor recreation, resulting in unsanitary conditions in the exercise yard.
- Access to drug and alcohol programs and to jobs and educational programs was restricted for protective custody inmates but not for the general population.
- When transported, protective custody inmates had to wear a "black box," a device so uncomfortable that it deterred inmates from seeking medical care.

A district court ordered the complaints dismissed, referring to the Supreme Court decision *Rhodes* v. *Chapman*, which set forth that double-celling alone doesn't violate the Eighth Amendment. However, the circuit court concluded that the district court finding, although the *Rhodes* decision stated that double-celling alone doesn't violate the Eighth Amendment, doesn't mean that double-celling *never* violates the Eighth Amendment. Reversed and remanded.

emotional stress when they are first brought to the institution, the staff can keep a close eye on them to ensure they make an adequate transition during the first days of incarceration. Most institutions screen juveniles the day they arrive, because that is when they experience the greatest stress (see Table 15-2).

What types of institutions have the most suicide attempts? In general, the more restrictive the institution is, the greater the threat of suicide. There are a few reasons for this.

Table 15-2   Screening of Juveniles for Suicide Risk, 2002

Time Frame for Suicide Risk Evaluation	Percent of Reporting Facilities			Percent of Juvenile Offenders in Reporting Facilities		
	Total	All Youth Evaluated	Some Youth Evaluated	Total	All Youth Evaluated	Some Youth Evaluated
Total	100%	80%	20%	100%	88%	12%
By end of day 1	66	61	5	74	70	4
Day 2 through end of week 1	15	11	4	12	10	2
After week 1	4	3	1	4	3	1
Other	15	6	9	10	5	6

Source: Howard N. Snyder and Melissa Sickmund, *Juvenile Offenders and Victims: 2006 National Report* (Washington, DC: U.S. Department of Justice, Office of Justice Programs, Office of Juvenile Justice and Delinquency Prevention, 2006), 228.

- **Type of juvenile resident** The residents of the most secure institutions are those who have committed the most serious offenses. A juvenile who has been adjudged of or convicted of homicide or rape and is looking at a long incarceration will probably experience a high level of stress. Additionally, juvenile residents who go to long–term, secure detention facilities are more likely than other delinquents to have significant drug or alcohol issues that add to their emotional instability.[46]

- **Isolation** Secure facilities are more likely to have rooms where disturbed residents are isolated from the rest of the institution's population. Although this isolation is often considered a security measure, it also can make the troubled youth even more depressed and out of touch with reality.[47] When separation is necessary, it is recommended that the rooms or cells be made suicide–proof. By having padded rooms and ensuring that the youths do not have belts or sheets to fashion into nooses, the staff can better protect suicidal inmates.

- **Trained staff** Often, security in an institution is inversely proportional to treatment. That is, the more secure an institution is, the less treatment is available. Security is paramount in facilities that house dangerous inmates. Because juvenile delinquents are also the most likely inmates to become violent, the staff must recognize that custody and treatment can be complementary.

A suicide in a detention center is a tragedy. When a 16–year–old kills himself while in custody, it is a signal that society has failed to protect the best interests of children. Fortunately, these occurrences are relatively rare.

Incarcerated Girls

Incarcerated girls have not received a great deal of attention because their numbers are relatively modest when compared with those of incarcerated boys. However, the problems of girls in secure confinement are often more acute. This is because most programs are modeled for boys' needs and not for the unique problems girls have when they are locked up.[48]

A law enforcement officer leans over a suicidal teenage boy who is in restraints. *(Courtesy Joanna B. Pinneo, Aurora & Quanta Productions Inc.)*

- Girls have higher rates of depression than boys throughout adolescence and are more likely to attempt suicide.
- The substance–abuse treatment needs of girls involved in the juvenile justice system are particularly acute.
- Adolescent girls who come into contact with the juvenile justice system report high levels of abuse and trauma.
- Adolescent female delinquents face significant challenges with parenting and other interpersonal relationships.[49]

These problems are even more serious for minority and impoverished girls. In a juvenile justice system based on middle-class values, those who come from disadvantaged circumstances are not as successful in taking advantage of the limited opportunities that female institutions offer. Minority girls are victims of the double discrimination of their gender and racial or ethnic statuses and do not get services for "their unique developmental, physiological, and emotional needs."[50]

In Chapter 9, we discussed the special concerns of female delinquents. Here, it is important to remember some of these concerns, because they continue to play a part in how female adolescents are handled when incarcerated. The chivalry hypothesis stated that the system treats girls more leniently than boys because they are viewed sympathetically by decision makers as being led into crime by their boyfriends. One indicator of the chivalry hypothesis at work is the vast disparity between the number of girls and boys who are arrested and processed. Although boys certainly commit more offenses than girls, girls get more consideration for diversion programs. The chivalry hypothesis has two exceptions, which shed some light on the difficulties of confined girls.[51]

1. **Status offenses**   Girls are more likely to be detained for status offenses, such as running away from home or engaging in sexual activities such as prostitution. Historically, juvenile justice officials have held the patriarchal attitude that girls' sexuality needs to be controlled more than that of boys. Because young girls can be physically victimized more readily than boys, who are stronger, and because adolescent girls risk becoming pregnant, the decision makers in the juvenile justice system have been more likely to lock the girls up "for their own protection." This double standard, even though it is applied with good intentions, has resulted in greater penalties for girls who violate sexual norms. This disparity is most noticeable in secure detention.[52]

2. **Lost causes**   Secure confinement for girls is a problem for another reason. Because the system excludes many nonserious female delinquents, those that sink far enough into the system that they wind up in secure detention are viewed as lost causes and lose much of the sympathy usually reserved for girls. This gender disparity is compounded when race is considered, and just as minority boys are disproportionately incarcerated, so are minority girls.[53]

The experience for incarcerated girls is very different than for boys. In the past, the treatment for girls has been to train them in the historically domestic roles of wife and homemaker. Boys received vocational education in subjects such as welding and small-engine repair, while girls were more likely to be schooled in cosmetology and food service. However, educational conditions are changing in some institutions because of personal computers. Most boys and girls are exposed to computers very early in their schooling, and many training schools and detention centers provide access to them. One promising avenue of education for incarcerated youths that diminishes the geographic limitations of confinement is online education. An impressive range of subjects is available, and as states invest more resources, it is likely that being locked up in a training home or detention center will no longer be a barrier to getting a decent education. For some youths, the online education might be superior to what they were getting in their own school.

Another important difference in the custody of female and male delinquents concerns how each gender deals with the pains of imprisonment. Although to protect themselves, males tend to develop extremely masculine roles that rely on strength, aggressiveness, and dominance, females tend to revert to traditionally feminine roles that emphasize family and connectedness. In both adult and juvenile female institutions, residents form **pseudofamilies** in which they act out the roles of father, mother, and children. The atmosphere is one of emotional involvement, companionship, and identity seeking. The females engage in courting behavior that is similar to that of traditional heterosexual relationships, and the intimacy is more emotional than sexual. They hold hands, touch, and kiss, but the homosexual relationships found in male institutions are largely absent. According to Coramae Mann, these pseudofamilies provide three functions for female inmates.[54]

pseudofamilies

The groups that females in adult and juvenile institutions form in response to the pains of imprisonment; they act out the roles of father, mother, and children.

1. **Affection and belonging.**   Young female inmates tend to bond in emotional and economic ways to compensate for being removed from their families and loved ones. Rather than retreating into a protective shell, these young women turn to each other for intimacy, emotional support, and the sharing of what limited goods and services are available in the institution.

2. **Protection.**   Pseudofamilies provide protection from attacks from other inmates. A resident who isn't connected to others is easy prey for those who would verbally harass or physically attack the weak. By belonging to a "family," the girl is insulated from being victimized by those who have mental problems or anger-management issues or are simply predatory.

3. **Social control.**   Pseudofamilies provide a stable social structure for the resident population. This is useful not only for the residents' well-being, but it helps maintain overall social control in the institution. As long as the residents have a well-defined, informal social structure, they all know where they fit in and are comfortable there. This situation can be contrasted with one that has a constant turnover of inmates, frequent roommate changes, and uncertain rules and regulations.

Correctional Programs

The primary mission of secure correctional institutions is to confine the residents so that they do not endanger society. Because virtually all delinquent inmates will eventually be released, institutions also have another extremely important mission. In an attempt to transform juvenile delinquents into self-sufficient, productive, and law-abiding citizens, juvenile detention facilities have instituted several programs to compensate for the social and vocational experiences that are normally provided to children in free society (see Crosscurrents 15.2). The four basic areas in which structured programs are available in juvenile institutions are education, vocational training, recreational programs, and counseling and treatment.

EDUCATION   Education in a juvenile institution presents many challenges that neighborhood schools normally do not have. Because so many juveniles who end up in secure detention facilities haven't had successful school experiences, detention facilities must offer the most basic remedial education. Many, if not most, of the juveniles are reading below their age and grade level, and some have not attended school for a substantial period of time. In addition to lacking basic literacy, many of these juveniles have histories of absenteeism, expulsion, and suspension from school.

Educating juveniles in secure detention presents additional issues. Many of these youths have learning disabilities (often undiagnosed) that might have contributed to their delinquency. Educational programs in training schools usually do not have the specialized teachers who can help these youths overcome their problems. In addition, and not surprisingly, those who end up in secure detention often have severe behavioral issues that make education difficult.

15.2

CrossCurrents

Real Hard Time

In 2005, Warren Messner and four other teenage boys beat to death a homeless man they found in the woods near Daytona Beach, Florida. The beating took place over several hours, and the boys returned three times to beat the man before they finally killed him. Messner, who was 15 at the time and weighed nearly 200 pounds, testified that he jumped on the man's chest several times.[1]

Messner, who was tried as an adult along with the other boys, pled to second-degree murder and was sentenced to 22 years in prison. Until eligible for prison, Messner has been held in juvenile detention. In December 2006, after being in detention for eight months, Messner asked a judge to reduce his sentence because prison was too difficult.[2] His mother told the judge that Messner wasn't "getting the mental health, the schooling. He is not getting anything, anything but locked in a cell all day long." Messner's attorney asked the court to sentence the teenager under Florida's youthful–offender law, which would call for a maximum of six years in prison. The judge said that deprivation of services and normal social contact were the purpose of prison and declined to reduce the sentence.[3]

Warren Messner (left), 17, speaks from the witness stand while Circuit Judge Joseph G. Will listens. Messner was 15 at the time of the crime. (Barbara V. Perez, *Orlando Sentinel*)

Although tried and sentenced as an adult, Messner was a juvenile at the time of his offense and, at the time of his hearing, would have been a juvenile for the next two years. His 22-year sentence will allow him back into society as a relatively young man in his late 30s. This case and the judge's response highlight some significant aspects of the juvenile and adult justice systems and how they work.

- Warren Messner was convicted of a heinous offense, one that would have earned an adult life in prison or capital punishment. Reportedly, when asked if he felt bad while jumping on his victim's chest, Messner said no.

- Although neither tried nor sentenced as a juvenile, Messner is still an adolescent. The goal of the juvenile system has always been rehabilitation and education for incarcerated juveniles.

- The judge's response, that denial of services and social contact is the purpose of prison, alludes to the possibility that Messner and the other boys will get little or no education, training, or psychological services while incarcerated for the next 20+ years.

- At age 15, Messner had not finished his formal education and is receiving no education or training while incarcerated. Upon his release, he is expected to hold a job until his early 60s and meet standards of probation for the rest of his life.

Think About It

1. Why was Warren Messner sentenced to a period of time that would allow him out of prison as a young man but allowed no rehabilitative or educational services?
2. Should he receive education and rehabilitative services?
3. What are Messner's chances of staying out of prison upon his release?

1 Ludmilla Lelis, "2 Teens Face Adult-Court Prosecution," *Orlando Sentinel* (Florida), June 15, 2005.

2 WFTV.com, "Teen Murderer Says Jail Is Too Hard, Appeals Sentence," December 4, 2006, www.wftv.com/news/10458584/detail.html.

3 Kristen Reed, "Judge Holds Firm on 22 Years for Teen," *Orlando Sentinel* (Florida), December 5, 2006.

The educational programs in a detention facility must provide a broad range of educational services from the most basic remedial reading programs to GED or high school diploma preparation. This is complicated by the fact that juveniles are in and out of the detention facility based on their legal issues, not educational ones. There is no semester or other school term to structure the instruction, so teachers must provide individualized instruction geared to each youth's specific needs and abilities.[55]

VOCATIONAL TRAINING   In addition to traditional education programs, many detention facilities provide vocational training aimed at providing youths with marketable skills that will enable them to get a job, support their future families, pay taxes, and, most important of all, stay out of trouble with the law. As the employment market changes, detention facilities have to change the types of programs they offer. For instance, mechanical drawing had always been considered a valuable skill. Today, this skill is essentially obsolete, as plans and blueprints are now drawn faster and better with computers. Therefore, detention facilities must be flexible and forward–looking in designing programs that can help youths find jobs.

This flexibility is especially important when gender is considered. As we noted earlier, the programs traditionally offered for females were food service, cosmetology, and secretarial training, while auto repair, woodworking, and drafting were aimed at males. Today, detention facilities don't attempt to track juveniles into these previously gender-related occupations but instead try to meet the needs and desires of youths in light of the limited resources that these training programs have.

RECREATIONAL PROGRAMS   Recreational activities can be an effective way to treat incarcerated juveniles. First, physical activity is a way for incarcerated youths to relieve stress. Playing basketball, running, or lifting weights can provide young people with beneficial exercise and relief from the tedium and boredom of institutional living. Engaging in competitive sports can give them team-building skills and teach them how to win and lose gracefully. However, there is also a negative side to relying too much on sports to mold character. This includes developing a win-at-all-costs attitude, the celebration of physical domination, and cheating. Recreational programs in detention facilities must be carefully planned and monitored to ensure that they achieve their goals without negative unintended consequences.[56]

COUNSELING AND TREATMENT   Can we systematically change the behavior of juvenile delinquents by counseling and treating them? Given the high rates of recidivism, do our correctional systems actually prevent crime? Certainly, most individuals who break the law don't adopt a criminal lifestyle, but is this because they have been successfully rehabilitated, or could it be that they didn't like incarceration and are deterred from further offending by the threat of punishment?

A drug prevention class at the Orange County Youth Guidance Center in Santa Ana, California. *(Courtesy Spencer Grant, PhotoEdit Inc.)*

Rehabilitation is a cornerstone of the correctional mission. Because nearly every inmate will eventually be released from the institution, it's considered essential to provide treatment and counseling so they can return to society. For a long time, no one argued with this ideal. However, in 1974 the rehabilitative philosophy came under attack because it was considered to be a practical failure. In his influential article "What Works? Questions and Answers about Prison Reform," Robert Martinson concluded that, although certain programs might work with certain offenders, no single approach would work for everyone.[57] This "what works" article was interpreted by politicians as "nothing works" and was used as a justification to dismantle rehabilitation programs and rely on punishment. Although prisons and youth detention centers have always maintained a treatment component, in many institutions it became only token treatment aimed at public relations and available to only a few offenders.[58]

Because juvenile justice system philosophy is so much more favorable than that of the criminal justice system to rehabilitation, more treatment programs are available. This is because society simply is not ready to give up on juvenile delinquents, and the juvenile detention facility is considered the last best chance that some of these youths have to turn around their lives. A vast number of counseling strategies have been used in correctional settings, ranging from the most traditional psychotherapies to New Age–style activities designed to provide inmates with greater insight. Let's review several types of treatments that have been used with adult offenders and juvenile delinquents.

Nondirective Counseling.   Nondirective counseling techniques are the least effective treatment methodology used in the juvenile justice system. We will review two nondirective techniques briefly, but they are seldom used with adult offenders and delinquents because they rely too much on clients' ability to discover their capabilities and find their own direction in life. In these two nondirective counseling techniques, psychoanalysis and client–centered therapy, the counselor plays a passive role and tries to allow the clients to discover their own values and solutions to problems.

- **Psychoanalysis**   Psychoanalysis is seldom used in correctional settings for many reasons. First, it is extremely involved, and practitioners require a time-consuming and expensive education to be certified. Second, its utility for dealing with criminal offenders and juvenile delinquents is questionable. Many people who break the law can control their emotions and feelings. They simply choose to do the offense, and investing in the expense of doing psychoanalysis with them is not necessary or useful because such offenders do not have personality problems or faulty views of reality. Finally, psychoanalysis is expensive and takes a long time to produce results. So why are we discussing psychoanalysis? The reason is that it is the theory from which all other counseling techniques evolved.[59] For those who counsel adult offenders and delinquents, the most useful ideas from psychoanalysis concern defense mechanisms. Defense mechanisms are what we all use to protect our self–concept from reality and what some people use to avoid responsibility for their behaviors (see Table 15-3).

- **Client–centered approach**   Client–centered therapy is used in the correctional setting under certain circumstances. Developed by Carl Rogers, it emphasizes the innate goodness in each person. The goal of the approach is to build a strong trust between the counselor and the client that allows the client to develop a healthy self–concept and to realize his or her capacity for self–actualization, which simply means reaching one's full potential as a human being. Rather than telling the client what to do, the counselor guides the client to positive values and behaviors by active listening and giving encouraging comments. The counselor portrays three important values that are at the heart of client-centered therapy. First, the counselor shows unconditional positive regard. This means the counselor shows full and genuine acceptance of the client in spite of the problems or shortcomings that led to unlawful behavior. The counselor adopts a nonjudgmental attitude, and while delinquency is not excused, the counselor doesn't criticize the client with negative comments. This encourages trust and allows the juvenile to

Table 15-3 **Defense Mechanism**

Defense mechanisms are unconscious and protect the self from a threatening reality by distorting it. Therapists must get through the mechanisms to help young offenders.

Denial	Offenders block out a part of reality that threatens them. This is particularly true of sexual feelings and activities.	
Rationalization	A pet defense mechanism of offenders is looking for and finding reasons for behaviors or experiences so that they can feel better about them. Offenders maintain an acceptable self-image by downplaying bad behavior and inadequacies and devaluing what they can't have ("sour grapes").	
Fixation	Many offenders are immobilized at an earlier stage of personality development because they are anxious about the further, more appropriate stage. Fear of the future.	
Displacement	Offenders might transfer feelings about someone or something onto someone else or an object because the original person or object is inaccessible or too powerful. Offenders often take out their anger on the innocent because they haven't learned to express their anger appropriately, so they choose safe targets.	
Intellectualization	Particularly intelligent or educated offenders use arguments to deflect blame by pointing out how others should be blamed. For example, a young vandal might point out how the government and corporations harm the environment.	
Projection	Offenders might attribute to others the feelings they refuse to recognize in themselves. The bad behavior of others often bothers us most when it's like our own repressed urges. For example, a young offender who thinks that no one likes her and is hostile is projecting onto others her own bad feelings about herself.	

Source: Anthony Walsh, *Correctional Assesment Casework & Counselling, 4th ed.* 4th ed. (Alexandria, VA: American Correctional Association, 2006), 175-176.

examine his or her behavior in a nonthreatening environment. The second value the counselor extends is genuineness. This means that the counselor is honest and revealing. There are no façades, gamesmanship, or "good cop/bad cop" routine. The third value is empathy, which involves considering the situation from the youth's point of view. However, true empathy is difficult simply because people have different backgrounds and life experiences, and the counselor's background is usually different from the inmate's. A middle–class, female, white college student might have difficulty truly appreciating the circumstances of a street–wise, young, male gang member who is illiterate and addicted to drugs.[60]

These nondirective counseling techniques are very popular in society but have some drawbacks when used with correctional clients. Although developing positive relationships with inmates is useful and important, there is always a conditional nature to the degree of acceptance the counselor can have with delinquents. Because counselors work for the institution, they must be concerned with the safety of society, the institution's rules and regulations, and the inmate's potential for dishonesty. The counselor must promote positive behavior and reject lawbreaking attitudes. For these reasons, nondirective counseling isn't well suited to dealing with juvenile delinquents.

Directive Counseling Directive counseling techniques require the client and the counselor to be actively involved. Instead of passively trying to guide the inmate to develop insights into his or her reasons for breaking the law, the directive counselor challenges the inmate to identify and deal with problems quickly and to use reason rather than emotion to evaluate behavior. Transactional analysis and reality therapy place the burden of understanding squarely on the inmate's shoulders and, if done right, empower the inmate to understand and change his or her own behavior.

- **Transactional analysis** Transactional analysis was developed by Eric Berne in his books *Games People Play* and *I'm OK, You're OK*. It is sometimes called the "poor man's Freud" because it splits the personality into three parts: child, adult, and parent. Transactional analysis focuses on the interaction between individuals and contends that people communicate best when they employ the "parent" part of the personality. The theory is relatively easy to understand, so the goal is to help offenders analyze how they communicate with others. Transactional analysis is useful for correctional counselors because it provides insight into inmates' manipulative behavior. However, the use of transactional analysis by inexperienced counselors can raise some problems. It is easy to get caught up in terminology (parent, child, adult, games, scripts) and treat counseling as an intellectual exercise. By focusing on the theory's analogies, it is easy to lose sight of the inmate as a person and to treat him or her as a puzzle to be solved or a game to be won. Also, many adult offenders and juvenile delinquents are verbally adept and can use transactional analysis not to reveal themselves, but to hide.[61]

- **Reality therapy** William Glasser developed reality therapy from experiences dealing with troubled youth at the Ventura School for Delinquent Girls. Instead of analyzing feelings, reality therapy focuses on behavior. It does not have a fancy vocabulary like transactional analysis and is easier to teach the client. It is particularly useful with juvenile delinquents because it requires them to define their actions as either responsible or irresponsible. Reality therapy does not dwell on the past. Regardless of one's reasons or excuses for irresponsible behavior, reality therapy focuses on constructing a plan for responsible behavior. The plan is important, because it forces the inmate to take responsibility for his or her behavior. Clients are not punished for failing to execute a given plan; they are taught to analyze it to see where they went wrong and to make a new plan. For example, many clients make unrealistic or vague plans. If the goal is to get a job, the counselor helps the inmate identify specific steps that will lead to employment. For example, a first step might be to write a résumé. If the inmate has trouble with this step, the counselor will break down the task and help the inmate decide what to put in the résumé, what format to use, where to have it typed up and copied, and where to send it. The idea is to break the plan into parts that can be accomplished. To most college students, this seems like common sense, but Glasser argues that common sense isn't so common, especially for juveniles.[62]

- **Rational–emotive behavioral therapy** Albert Ellis developed rational–emotive behavioral therapy as a way to help inmates understand how the way they think about events can sometimes result in bad behavior. For instance, a youth might blame his behavior problems on his parents because they are divorced. Ellis would say it is not the divorce that caused the problems, but the way the boy thinks about it. Because the marriage failed, he might harbor feelings of abandonment, misplaced guilt, or anger. In rational–emotive behavioral therapy, the counselor doesn't allow the inmate to hide behind defense mechanisms or to leisurely find her or his own solutions; rather, the counselor challenges the inmate's thinking patterns to uncover irrational reasoning. This approach can be confrontational. Although it shouldn't be done in a dogmatic or condescending manner, rational–emotive behavioral therapy strips away the inmate's self-defeating ideas by challenging him or her to reinterpret negative thinking patterns and defense mechanisms.[63]

The advantage of directive–counseling techniques over nondirective ones lies in their appropriateness for the types of clients found in the juvenile justice system. Psychoanalysis and client–centered therapy require extensive training for the counselor and a certain level of insight on the part of the inmate. Additionally, they can take months or years to show results and can be very expensive. Directive–counseling

15.3 A CLOSER LOOK at JUVENILE ISSUES

CRIME COUNSELING

My first job after I graduated from college was as a probation and parole officer for the Florida Probation and Parole Commission in Fort Lauderdale. We had 34 officers and supervisors, and I got to know many of them well. They quickly taught me how to deal with offenders, and after getting lied to several times, I tried not to become cynical about the truthfulness, integrity, and honor of the 100+ felons on my caseload.

One day my supervisor said to me, "John, why are you so surprised that murderers, rapists, and armed robbers turn out to be liars? They'll tell you what they think you want to hear. You have the power to send them back to prison, so don't think you can be their friend. Make sure you verify everything they tell you."

Although I understood what my supervisor said, I believed I was a great judge of character and could help some of my clients become productive citizens. Many of the department's old-timers told me I was kidding myself, but one other new hire, Paul, had the same goal as I: to help make people better.

Paul and I discovered that we had several young probationers with the same circumstances. Between us, we had over a dozen 18- and 19-year-old clients who were on probation for minor drug violations, breaking-and-entering, and motor vehicle theft. We thought they were basically good kids going through the transition from adolescence to adulthood and that, if properly guided, they would turn out all right. We entered them in GED and vocational training programs, and they seemed to be adjusting well to probation.

So Paul and I decided to form a group to meet with the young men on a biweekly basis. Without really knowing what we were doing, we developed what we thought were dynamic, positive group–counseling sessions. Anywhere from 8 to 12 clients showed up for each session, and the discussions were lively and interesting. Paul and I were delighted at how the group developed an instant cohesion in which everyone liked and respected one another. We bragged to the rest of the office about how successful we were in counseling these young men, and we decided that if we got graduate degrees, we could become professional counselors. We obviously had a knack for it.

After a year, I left the department and began my graduate education at Florida State University's School of Criminology. Paul stayed in Fort Lauderdale and continued the group. After about four months, he called to tell me that six of the group members had been caught sawing through the roof of a convenience store.

Our group, which we were so proud of, had formed a burglary ring and had been committing crimes after each group session, which they had been doing since the third time the group had met. Apparently, the reason they showed up so consistently and got along so well was that they indeed had something in common. They all loved to break the law.

What did I learn from this? First, probation officers must ensure that their perceptions of reality can be corroborated by tangible evidence. Second, group counseling is difficult. Offenders must be carefully screened and monitored. Paul and I thought that just because the group seemed to be successful, all was well. It was a classic case of putting rotten apples together and being surprised at the stink.

---

techniques are better suited for the correctional setting. They provide inmates with expectations of appropriate behavior and expect them to evaluate the morality of their actions and make positive changes. Directive–counseling techniques are easy to understand and have the potential to allow both adult offenders and juvenile delinquents to become emotionally self-sufficient and no longer require contact with the counselor.[64]

Group Counseling   Group counseling is used in correctional settings out of necessity. There are simply too many inmates to provide one–on–one counseling services for everyone. Group counseling in a correctional setting takes advantage of having all the clients in one place, and incarcerated juveniles don't have the demands of family and jobs to hinder their treatment.[65] In fact, group therapy might be attractive as a way of breaking up the monotony of institutional living. Group therapy in juvenile detention facilities has a number of advantages and disadvantages.[66]

- **Advantages**   Group therapy can provide a prosocial outlet for juveniles who want to improve their situation. In many institutions, cliques or gangs set an atmosphere of negativity and are counterproductive. An inmate code develops that works against those who want to explore the reasons that they are delinquent. The dynamics of group counseling help inmates to share their problems and learn alternative coping skills. Group counseling can lead to a sense of community and teach juveniles to work together to solve problems. Many of these youths have a difficult time relating to others, and learning to communicate respectfully within a group of juvenile delinquents is an effective way of learning to deal with others. Finally, group counseling does not have the authoritarian relationship that's present in individual counseling. There might be a trained leader who is a member of the institution's staff, but the real work of the session is done by the juveniles who are equal members of the group and can exert peer pressure or challenge irrational reasoning.

- **Disadvantages**   Many juveniles aren't comfortable sharing their problems, concerns, and feelings with their peers. The group counseling session can intimidate those who are, for example, shy, physically small, or homosexual. To push these youths to reveal their vulnerabilities in front of more verbally aggressive and judgmental peers can be damaging. It is easy to get off topic in group counseling sessions, and the group leader does not know where the discussion is going until it spins out of control. What might look like promising avenues of inquiry can end up wasting time and diverting the group from dealing with the important rehabilitation issues. Also, the session's dynamics might have some unintended consequences. Despite the group leader's efforts, the group members might actually learn more negative attitudes from each other than positive attitudes. Selecting the right members for the group is important, as well as recognizing that some members can emerge as leaders with bad intentions (see A Closer Look at Juvenile Issues 15.3). Finally, it's easy for the group to confuse activity with results. Although there might be a great deal of discussion about a topic, the time will be wasted if the group leader cannot connect the discussion to the goals of developing insights and positive attitudes and reforming behavior. Group therapy should not be a freewheeling discussion but should have structure, purpose, and realistic goals.

Treatment and rehabilitation are important goals in the juvenile justice system. Society cannot afford to give up on all the youths who get into trouble with the law. By providing timely and effective interventions, the state can correct the wayward course of many delinquents. These interventions can occur in a variety of community-based or institutional settings and can include a wide array of services.

SUMMARY

1. Providing the least restrictive treatment is the traditional way to respond to juvenile delinquents. Placing juveniles in secure institutions is considered a last resort.

2. Probation, the conditional release of juveniles to the custody of parents or guardians, has several presumed advantages. It reduces stigma, encourages rehabilitation by employing community resources, and is relatively inexpensive when compared to secure alternatives.

3. Youths on probation must adhere to certain conditions. Standard conditions of probation apply to all probationers, and special conditions of probation apply to a specific youth's particular needs.

4. Traditionally, probation officers informally divide their caseloads into three categories: cases who will do well no matter what the officer does, cases who will do poorly no matter what the officer does, and cases who can do well if the probation officer allocates enough time and resources.

5. Intensive-supervision probation allows the probation department to provide extended services

to the cases who can do well if the probation officer can allocate time and resources.

6. Intensive-supervision probation differs from standard probation in several ways: use of a team approach, the reduced size of the caseloads, and more highly structured activities.

7. Electronic monitoring is a community-based corrections program often used in conjunction with probation. Home confinement, or house arrest, restricts juvenile delinquents to their homes so that they can remain with their parents and attend school without disrupting their lives. Sometimes, the court orders juvenile delinquents to pay fines, make restitution, or do community service.

8. Secure facilities are the counterpart of adult prisons. Nonsecure facilities allow the juvenile to stay in the community in some sort of alternative living arrangement that has the advantage of maintaining access to schools, recreational programs, religious activities, and other community-based services.

9. Three common types of nonsecure juvenile treatment settings are foster care, group homes and

halfway houses, and alternative–experience programs.

10. Juveniles who have committed serious offenses or who are not amenable to community–based treatment options will often be sent to secure institutions. These include jails, detention centers, juvenile correction facilities (often called training schools), boot-camp prisons, and state prisons.

11. Secure confinement, even for juveniles, features the pains of imprisonment: deprivation of liberty, of goods and services, of autonomy, of heterosexual relations, and of security.

12. Overcrowding is a major shortcoming of juvenile correctional centers. In *Rhodes* v. *Chapman* the Supreme Court ruled that overcrowding itself is not unconstitutional.

13. The majority of institutions screen juveniles for suicide on the day of arrival because they experience the greatest stress then. The more restrictive the institution is, the greater the threat of suicide.

14. The problems of girls in secure confinement are often more acute, because most programs are modeled for boys' needs and not for the unique problems of girls.

15. An important difference in the custody of female and male delinquents concerns how each gender deals with the pains of imprisonment. Males tend to develop extremely masculine roles that rely on strength, aggressiveness, and dominance. Females revert to traditionally feminine roles that emphasize family and connectedness and often form pseudofamilies.

16. The four basic areas in which structured programs are available in juvenile institutions are education, vocational training, recreational programs, and counseling and treatment.

17. Nondirective counseling techniques, which include psychoanalysis and the client–centered approach, are the least effective treatment methodologies used in the juvenile justice system. Directive counseling techniques require the client and the counselor to be actively involved. These techniques include transactional analysis, reality therapy, and rational–emotive behavioral therapy.

18. Group counseling is used because there are too many inmates to provide one-on-one counseling services. Group counseling in a correctional setting takes advantage of having all the clients in one place, and incarcerated juveniles don't have the demands of family and jobs to hinder their treatment.

REVIEW QUESTIONS

1. What are the presumed advantages of probation for juveniles?

2. What are standard conditions of probation? What are special conditions of probation?

3. How is intensive–supervision probation different from standard probation?

4. What are the advantages and disadvantages of electronic monitoring? home confinement?

5. How are fines, victim restitution, and community service different?

6. What are three of the more common types of nonsecure juvenile treatment settings?

7. What are the advantages of residential treatment?

8. What are the five pains of imprisonment?

9. Why is incarcerating youths in boot-camp prisons and state prisons controversial?

10. Why is overcrowding in juvenile facilities a problem?

11. What are some of the special problems incarcerated girls and incarcerated minority girls encounter?

12. What are the four basic areas in which structured programs are available in juvenile institutions?

13. Compare and contrast nondirective counseling with directive counseling.

ADDITIONAL READINGS

Bilchik, Shay. *A Juvenile Justice System for the 21st Century* (Washington, DC: Office of Juvenile Justice and Delinquency Prevention, 1998).

Feld, Barry C. *Race and the Transformation of the Juvenile Court* (New York: Oxford University Press, 1999).

Miller, Jerome. *Last One over the Wall: The Massachusetts Experiment in Closing Reform Schools* (Columbus, OH: Ohio State University Press, 1991).

National Institute of Justice, *Correctional Boot Camps: Lessons from a Decade of Research* (Washington, DC: National Institute of Justice, 2003).

Schwartz, Ira. *Juvenile Justice and Public Policy* (New York: Lexington Books, 1992).

Walsh, Anthony. *Correctional Assessment, Casework, & Counseling*, 4th ed. (Alexandria, VA: American Correctional Association, 2006).

ENDNOTES

1. Anthony Platt, *The Child Savers: The Invention of Delinquency* (Chicago: University of Chicago Press, 1969).

2. Kären M. Hess and Robert W. Drowns, *Juvenile Justice* (Belmont, CA: Wadsworth, 2004), 369.

3. Platt (see note 1).

4. Bruce I. Wolford, *Juvenile Justice Educating: "Who Is Educating the Youth,"* (Richmond, KY: Council for Educators of At-Risk Youth, 2000).

5. Randy Borum, "Managing At-Risk Offenders in the Community," *Journal of Contemporary Criminal Justice* (2003):114–137.

6. Angela A. Robertson, Paul W. Grimes, and Kevin E. Rogers, "A Short-Run Cost-Benefit Analysis of Community-Based Interventions for Juvenile Offenders," *Crime and Delinquency* 47 (2001):265–284.

7. Robert A. Shearer, "Probation Strategies of Juvenile and Adult Pre-Service Trainees," *Federal Probation* 66 (2002):33–42.

8. Thomas G. Blomberg and Karol Lucken, "Stacking the Deck by Piling up Sanctions: Is Intermediate Punishment Designed to Fail?" *Howard Journal of Criminal Justice* 1 (1994):62–80.

9. *In re J.G.* 692 N.E. 2d 1226 (Ill. App. 1998).

10. Richard G. Wiebush, "Juvenile Intensive Supervision: The Impact on Felony Offenders Diverted from Institutional Placement," *Crime and Delinquency* 39 (1993):68–89.

11. Kim English, Suzanne Pullen, and Susan M. Chadwick, *Comparison of Intensive Supervision Probation and Community Corrections Clientele* (Denver: Colorado Division of Criminal Justice, 1996).

12. Intensive Supervision Juvenile Probation Program, http://guide.helpingamericasyouth.gov/program detail.cfm?id=598.

13. Wendy Johnston, "An Innovative Solution to the Problem of Juvenile Offenders in Missouri," *Journal of Offender Monitoring* 13 (2000):18–38.

14. Timothy P. Cadigan, "PACTS," *Federal Probation* 65 (2001):25–30.

15. David Listug, "Wisconsin Sheriff's Office Saves Money and Resources," *American Jails* 10 (1996):85–86.

16. Julie M. Houk, "Electronic Monitoring of Probationers: A Step toward Big Brother?" *Golden Gate University Law Review* 14 (1984):431–446.

17. Alvin W. Cohn, "Electronic Monitoring and Graduated Sanctions," *Journal of Offender Monitoring* 13 (2000):19–20.

18. Terry L. Baumer, Michael G. Maxfield, and Robert Mendelsohn, "A Comparative Analysis of Three Electronically Monitored Home Detention Programs," *Justice Quarterly* 10 (1993):121–142.

19. Ronald Ball, Ronald Huff, and Robert Lilly, *House Arrest and Correctional Policy: Doing Time at Home* (Newbury Park, CA: Sage, 1988).

20. William Staples, "Restitution as a Sanction in Juvenile Court," *Crime and Delinquency* 32, no. 2 (1986):177–185.

21. Sudpito Ray, "Juvenile Restitution and Recidivism in a Midwestern County," *Federal Probation* 59 (1995):55–62.

22. Anthony Walsh, *Correctional Assessment, Casework, and Counseling*, 4th ed. (Alexandria, VA: American Correctional Association, 2006), 408.

23. Patricia Torbet and Linda Szymanski, *State Legislative Responses to Violent Juvenile Crime* (Washington, DC: U.S. Department of Justice, 1998).

24. Dean Champion, *The Juvenile Justice System: Delinquency, Processing, and the Law* (Upper Saddle River, NJ: Prentice Hall, 2004), 479.

25. Burt Galaway et al., "Specialist Foster Care for Delinquent Youth," *Federal Probation* 59 (1995): 19–27.

26. Thomas Castellano and Irina Soderstrom, "Therapeutic Wilderness Programs and Juvenile Recidivism: A Program Evaluation," *Journal of Offender Rehabilitation* 17 (1992):19–46.

27. Angela R. Gover and Doris Layton MacKenzie, "Importation and Deprivation Explanations of Juveniles' Adjustment to Correctional Facilities," *International Journal of Offender Therapy and Comparative Criminology* 44 (2000):450–467.

28. Jon Gunnar Bernburg and Marvin Krohn, "Labeling, Life Changes, and Adult Crime: The Direct and Indirect Effects of Official Intervention in Adolescence on Crime in Early Adulthood," *Criminology* 41 (2003):1287–1318.

29. Melissa Sickmund, *Juveniles in Corrections* (Washington, DC: U.S. Department of Justice, Office of Justice Programs, Office of Juvenile Justice and Delinquency Prevention, 2004), 17. Online at www.ncjrs.gov/pdf-files1/ojjdp/202885.pdf.

30. Gresham M. Sykes, *The Society of Captives: A Study of a Maximum Security Prison* (Princeton, NJ: Princeton University Press, 1971).

31. Erving Goffman, *Asylums: Essays on the Social Situation of Mental Patients and Other Inmates* (Garden City, NY: Doubleday, 1961).

32. Matthew Silberman, *A World of Violence: Corrections in America* (Belmont, CA: Wadsworth, 1995).

33. James Austin, Kelly Dedel Johnson, and Maria Gregoriou, *Juveniles in Adult Prisons and Jails: A National*

Assessment (Washington, DC: U.S. Department of Justice, Office of Justice Programs, Bureau of Justice Assistance, 2000). Online at www.ncjrs.gov/pdffiles1/bja/182503.pdf.

34. Henri E. Cauvin, "Girl's Jailing Likely Breaks Federal Law, Judge Says," *Washington Post*, September 16, 2006, p. B4.

35. *OJJDP Statistical Briefing Book, 2003*, http://ojjdp.ncjrs.gov/ojstatbb/corrections/qa08605.asp?qaDate=20030212.

36. Patrick Griffin and Melanie King, *State Juvenile Justice Profiles* (Pittsburgh, PA: National Center for Juvenile Justice, 2006). Online at www.ncjj.org/stateprofiles/overviews/faq13t.asp#disp.

37. Sickmund (see note 29), 18.

38. Roberta C. Cronin, *Boot Camp Prisons for Adult and Juvenile Offenders: Overview and Update* (Washington, DC: U.S. Government Printing Office, 1994).

39. Margaret Bezer, "Juvenile Boot Camps Don't Make Sense," *American Bar Association Journal of Criminal Justice* 10 (1996):20–21.

40. Malcolm Feeley and Jonathon Simon, "The New Penology: Notes on the Emerging Strategy of Corrections and Its Implications," *Criminology* 30 (1992):449–474.

41. Sickmund (see note 29), 19. Online at www.ncjrs.gov/pdffiles1/ojjdp/202885.pdf.

42. Dale G. Parent et al., *Conditions of Confinement: Juvenile Detention and Corrections Facilities* (Washington, DC: U.S. Department of Justice, Office of Juvenile Justice and Delinquency Prevention, 1994).

43. Sickmund (see note 29), p. 222.

44. *Rhodes* v. *Chapman*, 452 U.S. 337 (1981).

45. Snyder and Sickmund (see note 43), 228.

46. P. Rohde, J. R. Seeley, and D. E. Mace, "Correlates of Suicidal Behavior in a Juvenile Detention Population," *Suicide and Life-Threatening Behavior* 27 (1997):164–175.

47. Craig Haney, "Infamous Punishment: The Psychological Consequences of Isolation," in Edward J. Latessa et al., eds. *Correctional Contexts: Contemporary and Classical Readings*, 2nd ed. (Los Angeles: Roxbury, 2005), 172.

48. American Bar Association and National Bar Association, *Justice by Gender: The Lack of Appropriate Prevention, Diversion and Treatment Alternatives for Girls in the Juvenile Justice System*, (Washington, DC: The Associations, 2001).

49. National Mental Health Association, *Mental Health and Adolescent Girls in the Justice System*, www1.nmha.org/children/justjuv/girlsjj.cfm.

50. *Justice by Gender* (see note 48).

51. E. A. Anderson, "The Chivalrous Treatment of the Female Offender in the Arms of the Criminal Justice System: A Review of the Literature," *Social Problems* 23 (1976):350–357.

52. Meda Chesney-Lind, "Juvenile Delinquency: The Sexualization of Female Crime," *Psychology Today* 19 (1974):43–46.

53. Michael J. Leiber, "Disproportionate Minority Confinement (DMC) of Youth: An Analysis of State and Federal Efforts to Address the Issue," in Everette B. Penn et al., eds., *Race and Juvenile Justice* (Durham, NC: Carolina Academic Press), 141–185.

54. Coramae Mann, *Female Crime and Delinquency* (Tuscaloosa: University of Alabama Press, 1984), 188–189.

55. Bruce I. Wolford, "Youth Education in the Juvenile Justice System," *Corrections Today* 62, no. 5 (2000):128–130.

56. Brenda Robinson, "Leisure Education as a Rehabilitative Tool for Youth in Incarceration," *Journal of Leisurability* 27 (2000):27–34.

57. Robert Martinson, "What Works? Questions and Answers about Prison Reform," *Public Interest* 35 (1974):22–54.

58. James B. Jacobs, *Stateville: The Penitentiary in Mass Society* (Chicago: University of Chicago Press, 1977).

59. R. Fine, "Psychoanalysis," in R. Corsini, ed., *Current Psychotherapies* (Itasca, IL: Peacock, 1973).

60. D. Kinsit, "Rogerian Theory: A Critique of the Effectiveness of Pure Client-Centered Therapy," *Counseling Psychology Quarterly* 13 (2000):345–531.

61. Anthony Walsh (see note 22), 193–200.

62. William Glasser, *Reality Therapy: A New Approach to Psychiatry* (New York: Harper, 1975).

63. Albert Ellis, *A New Guide to Rational Living* (Hollywood, CA: Wiltshire, 1975).

64. B. Sharp, *Changing Criminal Thinking: A Treatment Program* (Lanham, MD: American Correctional Association, 2006).

65. David Lester, "Group and Milieu Therapy," in P. Van Voorhis, M. Braswell, and D. Lester, eds. *Correctional Counseling and Rehabilitation* (Cincinnati, OH: Anderson, 2000).

66. For a comprehensive list of advantages and disadvantages of group counseling, see Walsh (note 22), p. 253.

What are the emerging trends in the juvenile justice system?

How can other institutions reduce delinquency?

Why is there reason to be optimistic that juvenile delinquency will wane?

The Future of Delinquency and Juvenile Justice

Juvenile delinquency is a rapidly changing field of study. However, it doesn't change in a linear fashion, meaning that it isn't all progress or regress. In some ways, we could say that the more the field of juvenile delinquency changes, the more it stays the same. Attitudes and practices of what to do about juvenile delinquency and dependency fluctuate between extremes of getting tough on young people and helping them.

So what lies ahead for delinquent and needy children and the juvenile justice system? Can we expect more delinquency in terms of frequency and seriousness? Is it still a good idea to have a separate juvenile justice system, or is it time to make adolescents and children fully accountable for their behaviors and treat them as adults and accord them full constitutional rights?

In this concluding chapter, we will explore these questions in light of some encouraging and alarming trends that are appearing in society and the juvenile justice system. The bottom line is that the future of delinquency and juvenile justice is uncertain. There are reasons to be optimistic that society will fulfill its obligations to provide every child with a good education, decent health care, and a safe, nurturing home. In contrast, however, there are legitimate concerns that those who most need positive intervention will instead be met with a get-tough approach that will doom many young people to a life of crime, despair, and institutionalization.[1] As we turn to specific issues, it is important to understand that opinions on what the best policies are vary widely depending on a number of sociological and economic factors. Whereas

CASE IN POINT

16.1

THE CASE	THE POINT
Roper v. *Simmons*, 543 U.S. 551 (2005) 112 S. W. 3d 397, affirmed.	The Eighth and Fourteenth Amendments forbid the execution of offenders who were under the age of 18 at the time of their offense.

In 1993 in Missouri, Christopher Simmons, a 17-year-old high school junior, conspired with two friends to commit a burglary and murder. Simmons told the boys that they would break into a home, tie up a victim, and throw the victim off a bridge. Simmons said they could "get away with it" because they were minors.

The three boys met at about 2:00 A.M. on September 9, but one boy dropped out. Simmons and the other boy broke into the home of Shirley Crook. The boys covered her eyes and mouth with duct tape and bound her hands. They drove her in her minivan to a state park, where they covered her head with more duct tape and threw her off a railroad trestle into the Meramec River. That afternoon, Shirley Crook's husband, Steven, returned home from an overnight trip and reported his wife missing. Later in the afternoon fishermen recovered Shirley Crook's body from the river.

Simmons bragged about the murder, and the next day police arrested him at school and read him his *Miranda* rights. Simmons waived his right to an attorney and agreed to answer questions. Simmons confessed and later re-enacted the murder at the crime scene.

The state charged Simmons with burglary, kidnapping, stealing, and first-degree murder. At the time of his offense, Simmons was 17 and outside the criminal jurisdiction of Missouri's juvenile court system. About nine months later, after he turned 18, Simmons was tried as an adult, convicted, and sentenced to death.

Simmons's appeals were rejected. Meanwhile, the U.S. Supreme Court held in *Atkins* v. *Virginia* that the Eighth Amendment, applicable to the states through the Fourteenth Amendment, prohibits the execution of a mentally retarded person.

Simmons argued that *Atkins* established that the Constitution prohibits the execution of a juvenile who was under 18 at the time of his offense. The Missouri Supreme Court agreed and set aside Simmons's death sentence in exchange for life imprisonment without release. The U.S. Supreme Court affirmed the decision.

one person might support a policy, another person will be vehemently opposed. It is not up to us to decide the best solutions for these issues, but only to be aware of why these concerns are contested and that good and well-meaning individuals can have legitimate differences of opinion about how to deal with problem children.

CAPITAL PUNISHMENT

In 2006, the Supreme Court ruled in *Roper* v. *Simmons* (see Case in Point 16.1) that offenders who committed their offenses as juveniles would no longer be subject to the **death penalty**. Actually, states were not executing juveniles but adults who had committed serious offenses while they were under 18. The time between conviction and execution stretched for years, and some offenders were twice as old at the time of execution as they were when they committed their offense (see A Closer Look at Juvenile Issues 16.1). This long delay in implementing the death penalty is similar to what happens in the adult criminal justice system, but it raises some interesting questions for the practice of capital punishment for juveniles.

death penalty
A punishment in which the offender is sentenced to death. Also called capital punishment.

- At what point should society give up on redeeming an offender? It is understandable that hardened offenders with long records of crime and hurting people receive little sympathy from society and are viewed as evildoers who should be put to death for the protection of all. Even the most vocal opponents of capital punishment agree that some offenders are so dangerous and have committed such heinous offenses that they should never be released. However, there is a big difference between a 44-year-old career offender and a 16-year-old juvenile who commits one very serious offense. Given the right treatment and provided adequate support and supervision, most youths, no matter how serious their offenses, are amenable to rehabilitation. They haven't yet been immersed in the criminal lifestyle long enough to be completely antisocial and beyond redemption.[2]

- By the time the sentence is carried out, the individual is a very different person. Young people are extremely malleable. They are amenable to dramatic changes in their personalities and world view. After spending years behind bars, they have had time to reflect on their behavior, and many of them are safe to be released. Being separated from the dysfunctional family, violent gang, or grinding poverty has provided these youths with the opportunities to seek employment skills, religious perspectives, and interpersonal tools that can make them a substantially different type of person from the one who committed the offense.

- It is questionable that young people are fully capable of realizing the gravity and consequences of their actions. In a society where a juvenile is not allowed to drink alcohol, vote, or enter into legally binding contracts, is it reasonable to require them to pay the ultimate price for poor judgment? It can be argued that, without all the rights and privileges of adults, juveniles shouldn't be held accountable to the same degree.

There are a number of other reasons for opposing capital punishment for juveniles and adults, such as issues concerning fairness, deterrence, and morality, but the distinction here concerns the age at which society can expect a person to be fully responsible for his or her behavior.[3] Proponents of capital punishment argue that certain behaviors and offenses are so egregious that the offenders deserve to pay with their lives. Another argument is that a 16- or 17-year-old gang member is fully capable of realizing the seriousness of homicide and chooses to kill.

Capital punishment for juvenile delinquents probably will not return in the foreseeable future. However, as with many issues of crime and delinquency, political and social forces influence public opinion and the law. It is conceivable that a few well-publicized cases of sensational juvenile homicide or terrorism can elicit new demands

EXECUTING THE YOUNG

Between 1985 and 2003, 22 offenders were executed for offenses they committed when they were younger than 18 (Table A). The states of Georgia, Louisiana, Missouri, South Carolina, and Texas limit juvenile court jurisdiction to age 16 and younger, so 18 of the offenders who were younger than 18 when they committed their offenses were considered adults in their states.

Many of the offenders spent almost half of their lives on death row. The average age at the time of offense was 17, while the average age at the time of execution was 29 (see Figure A). The oldest offender to be executed, Joseph John Cannon, actually spent more time on death row than in society.

Table A   Offenders Executed for Offenses Committed When They Were under Age 18

Name	Year of Execution	State	Age at Offense	Age at Execution	Race or Ethnicity
Charles Rumbaugh	1985	TX	17	28	White
James Terry Roach	1986	SC	17	25	White
Jay Kelly Pinkerton	1986	TX	17	24	White
Dalton Prejean	1990	LA	17	30	Black
Johnny Frank Garrett	1992	TX	17	28	White
Curtis Paul Harris	1993	TX	17	31	Black
Frederick Lashley	1993	MO	17	29	Black
Ruben Montoya Cantu	1993	TX	17	26	Hispanic
Christopher Burger	1993	GA	17	33	White
Joseph John Cannon	1998	TX	17	38	White
Robert Anthony Carter	1998	TX	17	34	Black
Dwayne A. Wright	1998	VA	17	26	Black
Sean R. Sellers	1999	OK	16	29	White
Douglas Christopher Thomas	2000	VA	17	26	Black
Steve E. Roach	2000	VA	17	23	White
Glen Charles McGinnis	2000	TX	17	27	Black
Gary Graham (Shaka Sankofa)	2000	TX	17	36	Black
Gerald L. Mitchell	2001	TX	17	33	Black
Napoleon Beazley	2002	TX	17	25	Black
T. J. Jones	2002	TX	17	25	Black
Toronto Patterson	2002	TX	17	27	Black
Scott A. Hain	2003	OK	17	32	White

Source: Courtesy of National Center for Juvenile Justice.

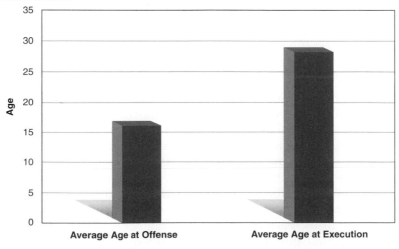

Figure A   Average Age of Offenders at Time of Offense and Execution

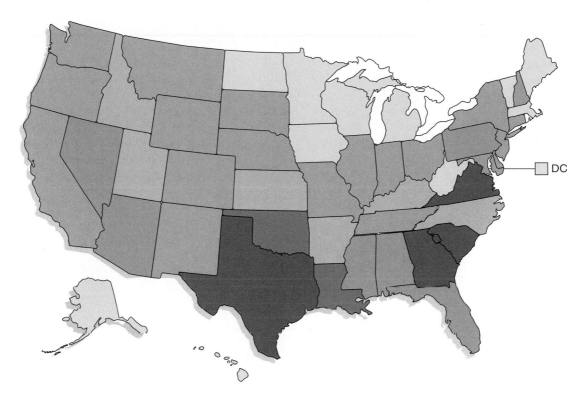

Application of death penalty for crimes committed at age 17 or younger:

☐ No death penalty for any age

☐ No death penalty for juveniles

☐ No executions since 1976, no current death row inmates

☐ No executions since 1976, some current death row inmates

☐ Execution(s) since 1976, no current death row inmates

■ Execution(s) since 1976, some current death row inmates

Figure 16-1   Who Had the Death Penalty for Juveniles?

While *Roper* v. *Simmons* was being decided, 30 states and the District of Columbia had no death penalty for offenders age 17 or younger. Since 1976, only four states have executed those who have committed offenses at age 17 or younger. It was these four states, Georgia, South Carolina, Texas, and Virginia, that had young offenders on death row during *Roper* v. *Simmons*.

Source: Death Penalty Information Center, "Emerging National Consensus on the Juvenile Death Penalty," in Howard N. Snyder and Melissa Sickmund. *Juvenile Offenders and Victims: National Report* (Washington, DC: U.S. Department of Justice, Office of Justice Programs, Office of Juvenile Justice and Delinquency Prevention, 2006), 240.

for capital punishment for juvenile delinquents. See Figure 16-1 for a look at which states had no death penalty for juvenile delinquents and which ones had juveniles on death row prior to *Roper* v. *Simmons*.

TECHNOLOGY, JUVENILE DELINQUENCY, AND VICTIMIZATION

Technology is changing so fast it's hard to know how it will ultimately affect society. Technology is making work more efficient, inexpensive, and, in many cases, radically different. Many offices no longer have typing pools where workers sit before electric typewriters cranking out documents for the few bosses. Now many bosses produce their own documents with computers. People have more control of their output and are able to accomplish more in a single day than they previously could in a week. This new technology has been embraced by children who are exposed to it in elementary school and

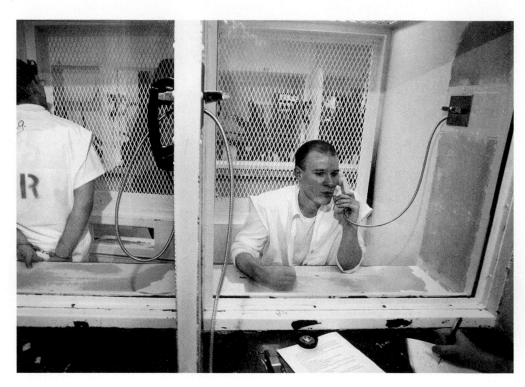

Leo Little (right) on Texas's death row. Little was 17 when he was sentenced for shooting a carjacking victim in 1998.

(© Bob Owen/San Antonio Express/ZUMA/ CORBIS. All Rights Reserved)

white-collar crime

Offenses committed by people who typically work in office and professional environments.

Instant Recall from Chapter 15

electronic monitoring

The use of an electronic device, usually one that the offender wears, to monitor an offender's location and activities.

at home, and they quickly adapt to each new gadget and improvement. Emerging technologies affect the types of offenses committed by juveniles, as well as the methods used by the juvenile justice system to deal with delinquents. The influences of technology can be seen in the following areas:

- **Computer crime**   Computer technology is changing the face of juvenile delinquency. Young people now have opportunities to engage in a wide variety of **white-collar crime** that previously had been the purview of adults or simply not even possible. For instance, computer gambling has allowed teenagers to bet money without having to deal with bookies or enter casinos. Additionally, youngsters can stalk others, or be stalked by others, view online pornography, and download illegal content. Young people can hack into computer systems, write viruses, embezzle money, or steal trade secrets. The juvenile justice system now has to deal with a new type of sophisticated delinquent.

- **Surveillance**   Technology not only allows juveniles to engage in a broader array of offenses, but also allows the state to keep a closer eye on offenders. In Chapter 15, we discussed **electronic monitoring** as a solution for restricting the movements of probationers and parolees. The future holds many other technological tools that will be useful for keeping tabs on delinquents. For instance, improved drug-testing techniques can uncover drug use that occurred months ago by examining the offender's hair follicles. Computer chips that allow satellite tracking could be implanted in offenders' bodies. Pharmaceutical advances will make controlling violent behavior more feasible than it is presently. Although these technological advances are possible, Americans must decide if they are desirable. Ethical questions will challenge us to find ways of preserving human dignity while controlling deviant behavior (see Crosscurrents 16.1).

- **Victims of technology**   Technology also makes children and adolescents potential victims in ways never before imagined. A most worrisome issue for

Parents can use software that blocks Internet access to user-specified content, such as pornography or hate speech.

(© Andrew Holbrooke / CORBIS. All Rights Reserved)

16.1   *CrossCurrents*

1984, Technology, Surveillance, and the Future

In 1948, George Orwell wrote the classic and disturbing novel *1984,* in which he envisioned a future where a totalitarian government monitors the lives of the populace to ensure unswerving loyalty through surveillance, propaganda, and brainwashing. The most memorable aspect of the novel is the omnipresent telescreens, which are two-way interactive televisions that allow the government to watch the citizens. These screens are always on, even in the bedroom, and individuals never know if their behavior is being watched or recorded.

The term *1984* has become a shorthand way of implying that the government has intruded on the privacy of citizens. Now video surveillance is everywhere. Cameras record public life in stores, on city streets, and at the entrances of government buildings. A person in the public space must act as if someone is always watching. Also, the fear of terrorism has made Americans more willing to allow the government to intrude into their bank records, telephone calls, and business dealings. All this would have been unthinkable in 1948, or even 1984.

Children and teenagers are the most vulnerable to privacy invasions. Their possessions may be searched at will by schools and law enforcement, and police need only the permission of parents to search children's rooms at home. Many parents are using their children's cell phones to keep tabs on their whereabouts, which has given rise to the term *helicopter parent.* Implanting chips in children might not be far off, as this is technologically possible now with automobiles and pets. Sometimes these invasions of privacy are voluntary. Children, teenagers, and young adults post videos and webcam streams of their private lives on the Internet, something that Orwell didn't forsee.

Society has legitimate reasons to be concerned about the safety of children and the behavior of adult offenders and delinquents. However, even with these groups, the power of the state is not absolute, and constitutional guarantees must be observed or changed. This balance between privacy and safety is a hotly contested issue, and it's wise for students to keep abreast of where the law draws and redraws the line of freedom and privacy.

Think About It

1. Should children have any expectation of privacy?
2. Should delinquents and adult offenders have any expectation of privacy?
3. Which constitutional amendments speak to privacy issues?
4. How much privacy are you willing to sacrifice for personal security?

parents is the sexual exploitation of their children through the Internet, which has opened a vast new market for child pornography. Without going into graphic detail, it is important to emphasize that there is a thriving market for pictures of children being used in sexual ways. These pictures and movies can be found by even a casual Internet search and are sold on numerous sites that attract pedophiles. Because of easy accessibility and inexpensive photo and video technology, outlets for child pornography have proliferated; consequently, more children are drawn into the clutches of those who want to use children for sex or make money selling them for sex. Efforts to regulate the child pornography industry tend to be ineffective. Internet sites change quickly, and it is difficult for law enforcement authorities to track down offenders, many of whom are overseas. Additionally, it's impossible to determine the true age of children in the pictures and movies, so sites that claim to show only adult pornography sometimes purvey child pornography, or vice versa. The Internet has also made it easier for pedophiles to directly contact children. Those who exploit children prowl chat rooms and other websites, passing themselves off as other children. They arrange meetings with potential victims where they sexually molest, kidnap, or even kill their young victims. It is difficult for parents to monitor all their children's online friends, and sometimes the parents' computer skills are so inferior to their children's that they are completely unaware of the danger.[4]

In the future, technology will continue to provide new avenues for both juvenile delinquency and juvenile victimization, although probably more for juvenile victimization. Although strides are being made in keeping children safe, providing them with innovative methods of education, and helping them maintain good health, technology will also expose them to unforeseen dangers and temptations.

WARS ON CRIME, DRUGS, AND CHILDREN

The future of delinquency and juvenile justice will also be affected by the ongoing war mentality that Americans have toward crime. War is used as a metaphor for public policy toward crime, and although it is an attractive metaphor, it's also a misleading one that causes a substantial number of unintended consequences.[5] It is worth considering how the war metaphor is used in the efforts to control crime and how it negatively affects young people.

- **The idea of "the enemy"**   To fight a war, it's necessary to have an enemy. Things can be done to enemies that we would never do to our friends, such as killing them. The enemy is demonized to the point that future civil relationships are nearly impossible. The problem with using the war metaphor in the criminal and juvenile justice systems is that our own citizens and our own children become the enemy. This places society in an "us versus them" relationship with youths who enter the jurisdiction of the juvenile court. The war–on–crime approach against youth directly conflicts with the juvenile justice system's guiding principle of acting in the best interests of children and sometimes affects juveniles in unintended ways. See A Closer Look at Juvenile Issues 16.2 for a review of how the pursuit of adult child molesters and the social compulsion to protect teenagers and children from sex have ruined some young people's lives.

- **Idea of sacrifice**   War is an inappropriate metaphor from which to view juvenile delinquency because we aren't willing to sacrifice our own comforts to effectively provide children the tools to become productive citizens. The use of the war metaphor conjures up images of World War II, in which citizens on the home front sacrificed comfort, money, and sons in order to vanquish the enemy. There is no willingness to make such sacrifices in the **war on crime**. Citizens are constantly calling for smaller government and fewer taxes to the point that the juvenile justice system is underfunded and understaffed. Further, the institutions that deal with children, such as schools and community programs, don't have the resources to effectively prevent crime. In this way, the war metaphor rings hollow when applied to issues of crime.[6]

- **Idea of winning**   The war metaphor implies that the problems of juvenile delinquency will one day be over. However, each new generation brings its own problems of socialization and adjustment. In many ways, juvenile delinquency is a symptom of more serious and systemic challenges, such as poverty, racism, and globalization. We can't "win" the war on crime because we aren't at war but simply dealing with the problems of developing

war on crime

The philosophy that the prevention of crime and treatment of offenders should be fought as a nation would fight a war, with similar tactics and strategies, and with the idea of an enemy.

16.2 A CLOSER LOOK *at* JUVENILE ISSUES

DO AS I SAY, NOT AS I DO

In January 2004, Genarlow Wilson, a 17–year–old high school senior, was arrested during class with five other boys at his Georgia school. Several nights before, at a New Year's Eve party at a local hotel, they had sex with at least two girls who were classmates. One of the girls, who was 17, reported that she had been raped. Another girl, a 15–year–old, who had engaged in oral sex with several of the boys, including Wilson, made no complaint. The sexual acts were recorded on videotape.

Five of the boys, all of whom had juvenile records, accepted plea deals, while Wilson, an honor student, homecoming king, and star athlete, did not, asserting that he had done nothing wrong and that he had only engaged in consensual sex. Wilson was charged with raping the 17–year–old. Because the girl with whom he had oral sex was 15 and the age of consent in Georgia is 16, he was also charged with aggravated child molestation.

Wilson was acquitted of the rape at his February 2005 trial. However, the jury, following the letter of the law, convicted Wilson of aggravated child molestation, only later learning that the charge carried a mandatory 10–year prison sentence and that Wilson would have to register as a sex offender for the rest of his life.[1] In October 2007, the Georgia Supreme Court, in a 4–3 ruling, ordered Wilson's release from prison, stating that the sentence was cruel and unusual punishment.[2]

Age–of–consent laws, which can be traced back 800 years to England, were originally designed to protect the virginity of girls, who were considered to be their fathers' property. Modern underage–sex laws seek to protect children from adult predators, but several states have Romeo and Juliet laws, which reduce or remove the penalties for teenage sex.

In the Genarlow Wilson case, the author of the law that put Wilson in prison said that the law was supposed to protect children from adult sexual predators, not to punish sexually active teenagers. A confounding issue is separating juveniles with severe problems and who are potentially adult predators from those who are merely participating in normal sexual activity or sex play. Here are two examples:

- Fourteen–year–old Joshua Wade was sent to a juvenile home for sexually assaulting then 8–year–old Amie Zyla. As an adult, Wade commit-

ted another sexually related offense and is now serving 25 years for assaulting children. Zyla, now age 18, argued that had Wade's name been on a sex-offender list and not sealed with his juvenile record, he might have been prevented from offending again.

- At 10 years old, Leah DuBuc play–acted sex with her stepbrothers, then ages 8 and 5. At age 12, she pled guilty to charges of criminal sexual conduct and spent 18 months in a residential treatment program. DuBuc was added to her state's sex–offender registry at age 18 and will be on it until she's 37. Because her name is on the list, DuBuc, now a college student, has been turned down for jobs and internships.[3]

In 2006, Georgia's new Romeo and Juliet law went into effect for teenagers who engage in consensual sex. According to the law, no teenager prosecuted for consensual oral sex can be incarcerated for more than 12 months or be required to register as a sex offender.

Think About It

1. Should teenagers be prosecuted for having sex with teenagers within a few years of their own age? What would have happened if these laws had applied to our parents? our grandparents?

2. If you were a state legislator, could you write better laws that protect children and teenagers from adult predators but refrain from punishing teenagers and children for engaging in normal sexual activity?

1 ABC News, "Outrage after Teen Gets 10 Years for Oral Sex with Girl," February 7, 2006. Online at http://abcnews.go.com/Primetime/LegalCenter/story?id= 1693362&page=1; Chandra R. Thomas, "Why Is Genarlow Wilson in Prison?" *Atlanta Magazine*, www.atlantamagazine.com/article.php?id=158; CNN, "Court orders Wilson freed in teen sex case," October 26, 2007, www.cnn.com/2007/US/ law/10/26/Wilson.freed/index.html.

2 CNN, "Court Orders Wilson Freed in Teen Sex Case," Oct. 26, 2007, www.cnn.com/2007/US/law/10/26/wilson.freed/index.html

3 Martha T. Moore, "Sex Crimes Break the Lock on Juvenile Records," *USA Today*, July 10, 2006, www.usatoday.com/news/nation/2006-07-10-juvenile-offenders_x.htm.

meaningful communities in a time of rapid change. Society's response to deviant behavior is contingent on how deviance is defined, who has the power to get their values encoded into the law, and who controls the criminal and juvenile justice systems.[7] These issues can be observed in how Americans think about drug use. For example, in the 1960s, drugs were a prominent feature of the youth culture, and many states reduced the penalties for using marijuana. Later, as the baby boomers grew into adulthood, they led the move to recriminalize marijuana as part of the war on drugs to prevent their children from experiencing drug-using behavior.

- **Idea of being right**   The war metaphor also includes the notion that those who pass the laws are gifted with the insight to know how to best respond to crime, delinquency, drug use, and terrorism. Politicians invoke tradition, religion, history, and their version of common sense to justify laws that restrict the freedoms and liberties of children and adults. Although no one is in favor of increased crime and delinquency, sincere critics contend that waging a war on deviant behavior is counterproductive and filled with unintended consequences. However, it's difficult to champion alternatives to the war metaphor without being branded as soft on crime. Effective ways to deal with the underlying causes of drugs and crime require a more sophisticated response than locking up people or executing them.

In many ways, it is understandable why the war metaphor is used to respond to crime. The harm done by delinquency, drugs, and predatory crime is significant, and law-abiding citizens want to be protected. However, the war metaphor is a simplistic concept of the nature of the crime problem and a harmful model on which to base a response. If it continues to be employed in the rhetoric about delinquency and the paradigm for reacting to juvenile delinquency, the future will continue to ignore some of the more promising approaches to helping adolescents make the transition from dependency to adulthood.

The philosophy of the juvenile court is often criticized as being too easy on serious juvenile delinquents.
(© Don Murray/ZUMA/CORBIS. All Rights Reserved)

Generational Conflict

Juvenile delinquency is, by definition, an age–determined concern. The laws covering delinquency apply only to juveniles who will eventually get older and fall under the protections and control of the criminal justice system. Children are involved in a sort of legal trade-off in which their constitutional protections are sacrificed for a philosophy that focuses more on their best interests. Although some critics suggest that youths would be better served by having their cases handled by the criminal justice system, others contend that what is needed is more resources and attention.[8]

The United States, along with other advanced industrialized countries such as Japan, the United Kingdom, France, and Germany, is undergoing a major demographic transition that will affect the ability of society to deal with children's social and educational concerns. The populations of these countries are aging, meaning that the ratio between the number of young people and the number of older people is shrinking. As health care improves and allows people to live longer and families continue to have fewer children, the burden of caring for society's needs falls on fewer and fewer people. This demographic shift is most noticeable as the baby boomers begin to reach retirement age and shift from work to leisure and retirement. See Figure 16-2 for a look at the U.S. population and the position of the baby boomers within it.

This means that another generational conflict is about to engulf the United States. Age will be an important political factor that could work against children's interests. It has long been a stable feature of American politics that older people vote at a greater rate than younger people. The baby-boom generation, because of its greater numbers, will be, as it always has been, a powerful advocate for its own interests. There will be a major transfer of wealth from working families to retirees, and Social Security benefits, health care, and other concerns important to older people might deplete the government's coffers and require higher taxes. Rather than putting money into schools, recreational facilities, and employment training for youth, the country will be forced to care for an increasingly older population that has the power to demand that politicians pay attention to their concerns.[9]

This shift of resources won't affect everyone in the same way. The sons and daughters of those financially well-off families won't be affected in the negative ways that the children of the lower middle–class and the disadvantaged will be. Wealthy children will be increasingly enrolled in private schools, private sporting activities, and exclusive social clubs. Communities might abandon programs such as Little League baseball, afterschool sports, and school arts programs. Families who are unable to provide private instruction and experiences for their children will find little support from local, state, and federal governments that are catering to the demands of an older population that votes, pressures, lobbies, and coerces politicians.[10]

How will this shift in the nation's demographics affect delinquency and the juvenile justice system? The prospects are not encouraging. We can expect a greater proportion of children to become involved in delinquency as there are fewer social programs, less money devoted to education, and a greater willingness to ignore the concerns of youth in favor of dealing with the demands of the aged. With fewer young people to do the work necessary to keep the country moving forward, there will be a demand for immigrant laborers, who will send their earnings back to their home countries rather than spend or invest it in the United States. This will further exacerbate the downward spiral of the opportunities for poor children and stimulate even greater pressures to engage in delinquent behavior.

The juvenile justice system can expect more clients and fewer resources. Juvenile court judges will have fewer sentencing alternatives, and detention facilities will be crowded, staffed with underpaid workers, and lack adequate rehabilitation programs. The coming demographic changes in the United States have the potential to cripple the ability of the juvenile justice system to prevent and respond to delinquency.

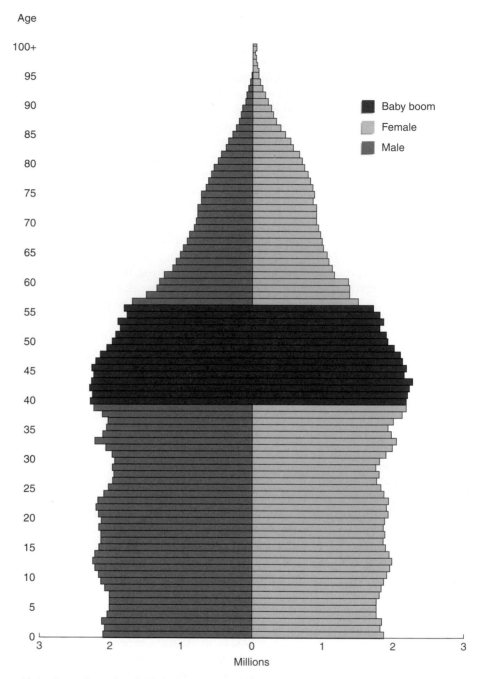

Figure 16-2   United States Population by Age and Sex, 2003 *Source:* Wan He et al., *65+ in the United States: 2005, U.S. Census Bureau Current Population Reports* (Washington, DC: U.S. Government Printing Office, 2005), 5. Online at www.census.gov/prod/2006pubs/p23-209.pdf.

But this pessimistic scenario is not destiny. Although it might come to pass if nothing is done to improve conditions for young people, democracy responds to the demands of citizens. Only the most cynical among us believe that older people are so self-centered and selfish that they will greedily spend all the nation's resources on themselves and let the country's children grow into adulthood without the education, social tools, and motivation to take the reins of society. It would be self-defeating for the aged to deny the young the things they need to become economic producers. There is a symbiotic relationship between the generations that helps to ensure a smooth and healthy transition of power and privilege. The demographic

What Restorative Justice Does

Restorative justice has been practiced for up to 20 years in several states, Europe, and Australia. It is especially well suited for juvenile justice cases, because these are usually situations in which rehabilitation is the goal, rather than punishment.

In Illinois courts, the approach, known as "balanced and restorative justice," has strong support among prosecutors. In 1995, Cook County prosecutors filed more than 21,000 juvenile cases, but in 2005, thanks to new diversion programs, they filed just over 8,000. More than 5,000 potential cases were diverted to community agencies, and thousands more were resolved without court intervention. Juveniles are diverted to community agencies by prosecutors who believe the offender, who might be a minor or first offender, would be a good fit. Since 2000, the institute has held more than 3,000 juvenile conferences with offenders whose cases were diverted there directly by police.[1]

Albuquerque (New Mexico) High School is using a restorative justice–style program for high school students who get into fights. Formerly, the students were arrested, suspended, or expelled from school and waited months at home for a court date, often without adult supervision. Often, if the students returned to school, according to the school's assistant principal, the fighting continued because the original disagreement hadn't been settled. Under the new program, offending students without extensive histories of violence are suspended for only three days, meet with a community accountability board comprising community leaders, probation officers, students, members of the religious community, teachers, and school administrators, and the person they fought with. The board's job is to ensure that the students repair any damage and harm.[2]

The personal meeting is currently the most extensively tested restorative justice model. However, questions still remain about whether restorative justice prevents recidivism or how consistently it does so, if at all. For example, in one study, violent offenders recidivated less with restorative justice approaches than with traditional approaches, but property offenders appeared not to be affected at all. In another study, the property offenders recidivated less under restorative justice programs, but it was violent offenders who recidivated at the same rate.[3]

So far, the only consistent results that have been measured are those concerning victims, who apparently thrive under restorative justice. Studies have shown that although victims often say they want retribution and punishment, what they really want is to feel better and to receive an apology. Research has shown that restorative justice reduces victims' fear, desire for revenge, anger, and even posttraumatic stress.

Think About It

1. If you were a crime victim, would you be willing to participate in restorative justice with the offender?

2. What do you think of the results produced so far by restorative justice approaches? Are they confined only to special cases, like juveniles? Do you think they could be successfully used with adults or more serious offenders?

1. Libby Sander, "Restorative Justice: Giving Kids a Second Chance," *Chicago Lawyer*, April 2006, p. 8.

2. Leann Holt, "Prudent Punishment," *Albuquerque Journal*, August 27, 2005, p. E2.

3. Heather Strang, Charlotte Gill, and Lawrence Sherman, "Confronting the Perpetrators," *New Statesman*, August 1, 2005

challenges must be recognized, and the aged (and aging) must be willing to lay the foundation for youth-serving programs and policies. Currently, the growing economic and political concerns of the baby-boom generation are getting a great deal of attention. However, what needs to be more fully appreciated and planned for are the needs of children. Precisely because they are a smaller and more vulnerable proportion of the population, their education and social development are going to be needed more than at any other time in the country's history.

RESTORATIVE JUSTICE

Not all the lessons of the over-100 years of the juvenile court have been lost on those whose responsibility it is to deal with delinquency. Although powerful social forces,

restorative justice

An alternative justice model that uses community programs to repair the harm done by crime and attempts to craft long-lasting and satisfying solutions to the problems of crime.

such as poverty, racism, changing gender roles, and globalization, are affecting the lives and opportunities of youngsters, there is also a growing body of literature about why delinquency happens and what to do about it. Some promising strategies have emerged that build on the knowledge gained from so many years of dealing with crime, drugs, gangs, and indifference to the problems and challenges of youth. One of these strategies is **restorative justice**.

Restorative justice offers a very different approach to solving the problems of deviant behavior (see Kids in the News 16.1).[11] Instead of pitting the offender against the state and the victim as the traditional justice system does, restorative justice requires these parties to work together to repair the harm. Instead of blaming the offender, restorative justice takes a more holistic look at the causes and conditions of the community in which crime regularly occurs and attempts to craft solutions that not only respond to the offense, but also repair the community so that crime is prevented. Restorative justice works toward the creation of meaningful communities, as well as the reduction of crime, alienation, selfishness, and disenfranchisement.

One foundation of restorative justice is the realization that crime is basically a violation of relationships. Because a lot of crime is committed by offenders who will continue to have some kind of relationship with the victim(s), the present method of punishment and revenge does little to prevent future crime and, in many ways, actually encourages continuing conflict between people who know each other, are related, or otherwise must pursue mutual interests. Restorative justice seeks to repair relationships by bringing the affected parties together to talk about the offense and find a solution that can satisfy everyone.

To illustrate how restorative justice works, let's consider the following example. Two 16–year–old boys who are having academic and social problems are caught late at night in a stolen car. They have vandalized a local church and its graveyard and were involved in a high–speed chase with police. Additionally, several items of stolen property were traced back to the homes of three of their female classmates who are high-achieving students and members of the cheerleading squad. Under the traditional juvenile justice system, the boys would face the following charges:

- Motor vehicle theft
- Numerous traffic violations resulting from the high-speed chase
- Resisting arrest
- Destruction of property
- Three counts of burglary

The juvenile court judge would consider the case after the boys' attorneys sought to exclude evidence, question police procedures, and suggest that the girls encouraged the boys as part of a school–based system of social hierarchy. The boys would be adjudicated delinquent and sent to a detention center. After a certain period of time, they would return to the community under the surveillance of a probation officer in some type of graduated early-release program. As a condition of their release, they would be sent to different schools, told not to have any contact with the girls, forbidden to go near the church they vandalized, and not allowed to have a driver's license for at least one year. The boys would have a juvenile record, lose valuable time from school, and have been exposed to hard-core delinquents in the detention center. The prospects for the successful reintegration of the boys into a healthy and law-abiding lifestyle would be dim. This one mistake (a serious one to be sure) could become a turning point in their lives that accelerates them into a life of crime and antisocial behavior.

The process of dealing with this case would look very different under a restorative justice program. Instead of going to the juvenile court and having the case dealt with in a quasi-adversarial manner, the boys would have the opportunity to face everyone whom they had injured, and they would be held morally, psychologically, and socially accountable for their actions and given the chance to make amends to each party. Additionally, each of the affected parties would be given the chance to explain their point of view and suggest ways that the boys could repair the harm they did. The process might be similar to the following scenario:

- A conference would be held in which the boys, their parents, the girls, their parents, representatives from the church, the police, the prosecutor's office, the probation office, the insurance company, and the school would gather to discuss the case.

- The boys' academic issues would be discussed and a plan made to address them. This plan could include testing for learning problems, the provision of extra tutoring to get them up to their grade's academic standards, or placement in an alternative school. This incident might be the first indication that the boys have school-based concerns that must be addressed.

- Representatives of the church could explain to the boys how their vandalism affected others. Not only have the church and its insurance company been financially harmed, but the families of those whose gravestones were destroyed were psychologically distressed. The representatives from the church can put a human face on the victims of the vandalism and impress on the boys that their prank had serious consequences.

- The girls and their parents can explain to the boys what it feels like to have one's home invaded by thieves and to lose valuable possessions. Questions can be asked as to why these particular girls were chosen as targets, and the girls can express how they were made to feel violated, afraid, and embarrassed.

- The police can explain how the boys put the lives of innocent people at risk with the high-speed chase through the city's streets. The long list of offenses the boys committed can be enumerated and shown to be a public danger that could have ended up with more serious consequences.

- The boys' parents can explain how they see the case. They can both defend their children by assuring everyone that they are basically good kids, at the same time demonstrating to the boys that their unlawful behavior has embarrassed them.

- The boys are the biggest benefactors from this conference. Not only do they get to see the consequences of their actions, but they are also able to gauge the full effect of the harm they caused to the many victims of their offenses. Most importantly, they have the opportunity to apologize for the harm they caused. In an adversarial setting, the defendants can come to think of themselves as victims of the justice system and avoid taking responsibility for their actions. By looking the victims in the eye and making a sincere apology, the boys can take a big step toward not only repairing relationships, but also dealing with their own feelings of guilt and shame.

One more dimension to restorative justice bears mentioning. In addition to being an alternative way of handling cases in the juvenile justice and criminal justice systems, it also has the potential to assist in building community. In many ways, restorative justice, when viewed broadly, fits in nicely with community and problem-oriented policing. Criminologists Gordon Bazemore and Mara Schiff have extended conventional restorative justice practices and shown how they can become a new basis for thinking about the relationship between crime and the community. In their book *Restorative Community Justice: Repairing Harm and Transforming Communities*, Bazemore and Schiff envision a future justice system that is humane, effective, and positive.[12]

RIGHT TO TREATMENT

In the future, the juvenile justice system will have to do a better job of ensuring that all youths get the treatment they need to deal with their individual problems and deficiencies. Although a certain amount of blame for crime and delinquency can be placed on impoverished schools, disadvantaged neighborhoods, and lack of employment opportunities, many children's problems stem from their inability to deal with frustration, disappointment, and substandard intellectual abilities. These children are susceptible to well-planned and adequately funded treatment programs.[13] Unfortunately, not all jurisdictions have the programs to effectively deal with all the youths who need psychological intervention, drug treatment, or anger-management and life–skills programs (see Crosscurrents 15.2 on page 486).

The right-to-treatment issue is being marginalized by the increasing propensity to waive juveniles to the criminal justice system.[14] In essence, this says that some juveniles are so dangerous and beyond redemption that their cases should be treated with the full range of constitutional rights and punishment options. With the exception of the death penalty, those who commit serious felonies as juveniles are subject to life sentences with little hope of getting any type of effective rehabilitation. In the future, it can be expected that this dichotomy between those treated in the juvenile justice system and those punished in the criminal justice system will grow.

GLOBALIZATION

globalization

Extensive economic relationships among nations.

One broad social force that will affect delinquency and juvenile justice during the 21st century is **globalization**. The ongoing shift from an industrial economy to a service economy is profoundly affecting employment patterns in North America. As high-paying technical jobs move offshore to Mexico, India, and China, American

Developing countries often put children to work in factories to manufacture inexpensive exports for the U.S. market. *(© JP Laffont/Sygma/CORBIS)*

youths will find their employment options dwindling and realize that having a decent education will be even more important than it is today. Those without the skills demanded by the new economy will find themselves relegated to boring, low–paying jobs that have few benefits. Those who have the right combination of skills and can adjust to changes in technology will find they are in high demand.[15]

One aspect of globalization that is stressing the juvenile justice system, as well as every other social service agency, is immigration. The United States is absorbing millions of immigrants, many of them without the legal papers that allow them to fully assimilate into the economy and social network of schools, communities, and work force.[16] Globalization will also affect the nation's ability to respond to crime. With fewer tax dollars to allocate to competing social programs, the prevention and treatment of juvenile delinquency might take a back seat to more pressing criminal justice concerns, such as hiring more police officers and judges and building more prisons and juvenile detention centers.

ON PREDICTING THE FUTURE

How these trends will affect the future, or whether they will even continue, is, of course, unknowable. Building a society where young people can grow and prosper without resorting to delinquency will not happen by accident. To prepare for the generations that follow, it's necessary that much care, thought, and resources be allocated to planning and correcting some of the dysfunctional ways in which we now raise our youth. This class in juvenile delinquency should be instrumental in alerting students to the problems and possibilities of effectively creating a safe, supportive society. At the same time, it's wise to believe there will always be young people who need more guidance, support, and discipline than their families and communities provide. After taking this class and reading this text, we hope each student, regardless of the profession he or she chooses, will always take a special interest in the problems of delinquency. Our children deserve it.

SUMMARY

1. The Supreme Court ruled in *Roper* v. *Simmons* (2006) that adult offenders who committed their offenses as juveniles would no longer be subject to the death penalty.

2. The influences of technology on juvenile delinquency and victimization are or will be seen in computer crime and surveillance. In the future, technology will continue to provide new avenues for both delinquency and juvenile victimization.

3. The future of delinquency and juvenile justice will be affected by the American war mentality toward crime and criminal offenders.

4. The United States, along with other advanced, industrialized nations, is undergoing a major demographic transition that will affect society's ability to deal with children's social and educational concerns as the populations of these countries age.

5. Restorative justice is a promising crime-control strategy. Instead of pitting the offender against the state and the victim, restorative justice requires these parties to cooperate to repair the harm.

6. The increasing propensity to waive juveniles to the criminal justice system is marginalizing juvenile delinquents' right to treatment.

7. One aspect of globalization that is stressing the juvenile justice system is immigration. Globalization will also affect the nation's ability to respond to crime. With fewer tax dollars to allocate to competing social programs, the prevention and treatment of juvenile delinquency might take a back seat to more pressing criminal justice concerns.

REVIEW QUESTIONS

1. What is the significance of *Roper* v. *Simmons*?

2. Speculate about the role of technology in future juvenile delinquency and victimization. What is more likely to be affected, offending or victimization?

3. What is the war on crime? How does it affect juveniles?

4. How will a shift in U.S. demographics affect delinquency and the juvenile justice system?

5. What is restorative justice?

6. How could globalization affect juvenile delinquency?

ADDITIONAL READINGS

Bazemore, Gordon, and Mara Schiff. *Restorative Community Justice: Repairing Harm and Transforming Communities* (Cincinnati, OH: Anderson, 2001).

Feld, Barry C. *Bad Kids: Race and the Transformation of the Juvenile Court* (New York: Oxford University Press, 1999).

Krisberg, Barry. *Juvenile Justice: Redeeming Our Children* (Thousand Oaks, CA: Sage, 2005).

Males, Mike A. *The Scapegoat Generation: America's War on Adolescents* (Monroe, ME: Common Courage Press, 1996).

Penn, Everette B., Helen Taylor Green, and Shaun L. Gabbidon. *Race and Juvenile Justice* (Durham, NC: Carolina Academic Press, 2006).

Van Ness, Daniel W., and Karen Heetderks Strong. *Restoring Justice: An Introduction to Restorative Justice*, 2nd ed. (Cincinnati, OH: Anderson, 2006).

ENDNOTES

1. Mike A. Males, *The Scapegoat Generation: America's War on Adolescents* (Monroe, ME: Common Courage Press, 1996).

2. This statement is open to debate. We say "most" juveniles are redeemable but understand how people, especially victims of violent crime, might feel strongly about this issue.

3. For a good review of the argument for and against capital punishment, see Robert M. Bohm, *Deathquest II: An Introduction to the Theory and Practice of Capital Punishment in the United States*, 2nd ed. (Cincinnati, OH: Anderson, 2003).

4. The number of people engaging in online exploitation of children is so high that news programs on television set up sting operations where the predators are drawn to a home and then confronted by an investigative journalist and arrested. These programs receive high viewer ratings and serve as a perverse form of entertainment. One could question the ethics of the news agencies almost as much as those of the pedophiles.

5. Eugene Czaikoski, "Drugs and the Warlike Administration of Justice," *Journal of Drug Issues* 20 (1990): 125–129.

6. Eva Bertram et al., *Drug War Politics: The Price of Denial* (Berkeley: University of California Press, 1996).

7. For a good discussion on this point, see "The Problematic Meaning of Deviance: What (Who) is Deviant," in Jack D. Douglas, *The Sociology of Deviance* (Boston: Allyn and Bacon, 1984), 13–14.

8. Barry C. Feld, *Bad Kids: Race and the Transformation of the Juvenile Court* (New York: Oxford University Press, 1999). See especially Chapter 8, "Abolishing the Juvenile Court: Sentencing Policy When the Child Is a Criminal and the Criminal Is a Child," 287–330.

9. Males (see note 1), especially Chapter 9, "Generation Y," 255–292.

10. Jay Coakley, *Sports in Society*, 9th ed. (New York: McGraw-Hill, 2007). See "The Privatization of Organized Programs," 125–127.

11. Daniel W. Van Ness and Karen Heetderks Strong, *Restoring Justice: An Introduction to Restorative Justice*, 3rd ed. (Cincinnati, OH: Anderson, 2006).

12. Gordon Bazemore and Mara Schiff, *Restorative Community Justice: Repairing Harm and Transforming Communities* (Cincinnati, OH: Anderson, 2001).

13. Morton Birnbaum, "The Right to Treatment," *American Bar Association Journal* 46 (1960):499.

14. Dale Parent et al., *Transferring Serious Juvenile Offenders to Adult Courts* (Washington, DC: U.S. Department of Justice, National Institute of Justice, 1997).

15. Kathy Koch, "High-Tech Labor Shortage," *CQ Researcher* 8 (1998):361–384.

16. Dianne Schmidley, *The Foreign-Born Population in the United States* (Washington, DC: U.S. Bureau of Census, 2002).

Glossary

A

adjudicate The act of arriving at a judicial decision. To pass judgment.

adjudicatory hearing The hearing in which a determination is made regarding whether the juvenile committed the offense with which he or she is charged.

adolescence The period between puberty and adulthood in human development that typically falls between the ages of 13 and 19.

adolescence-limited offender In life-course criminological theory, youths who engage in antisocial and deviant behavior for only a short period of time and only in certain situations.

adolescent egocentrism The belief common to many adolescents that they are the focus of attention in social situations.

aging out In juvenile justice, reaching the age at which the system no longer serves a person, usually age 18.

androgen A general term for male hormones.

anomie A condition in which a people or society undergo a breakdown of social norms and values. Also, personal anxiety and isolation produced by rapidly shifting moral and cultural values.

apartheid An official policy of racial segregation involving political, legal, and economic discrimination against non-whites.

arrest rate The number of arrests made in a given year divided by population, to produce a measure that can be compared to other jurisdictions.

ascertainable criteria In peacemaking criminology, the concept that the language and procedures used to pursue justice must be made clear to all.

atavism The appearance in a person of features thought to be from earlier stages of human evolution.

B

behaviorism A field of psychology that focuses on the study of behavior that is observed.

beyond a reasonable doubt The state of being as convinced as possible of a fact.

biosocial theory The study of the effects of Darwinian evolution on brain structure and human behavior.

blended sentencing A sentence that combines a juvenile disposition with the possibility of a criminal sentence, or a criminal conviction with a "last chance" at a juvenile disposition and treatment.

boot-camp prison A short-term prison, usually for young offenders, that employs military boot-camp training and discipline techniques for rehabilitation.

bourgeoisie In Marxist theory, those who own property and the means of production.

bullying The psychological or physical victimization of youths by other youths.

C

capitalism An economic system characterized by the private or corporate ownership of production and distribution; the prices and production of goods are determined by competition in a market.

categorical imperative In peacemaking criminology, the concept that a system of justice must treat cases with similar characteristics consistently if the system is to be perceived as fair and impartial.

Cesare Lombroso An Italian physician who developed a theory of criminal behavior based on offenders' physical characteristics.

child neglect According to criminologist Harvey Wallace: "The negligent treatment or maltreatment of a child by a parent or caretaker under circumstances indicating harm or threatened harm to the child's health or welfare."

child-savers People at the end of the 19th century who were instrumental in creating special justice institutions to deal with juvenile delinquents and troubled youths.

classical school of criminology A school of thought that employs the idea of free will to explain criminal behavior.

clearance by exceptional means A special condition used by law enforcement to generate a clearance in the case of an offender who cannot be formally charged and prosecuted.

clearance rate The number of offenses cleared or "solved" by at least one offender being arrested, charged, and prosecuted.

clique Any small, exclusive group of people that controls how and if others may join.

cohort A set of people who share a particular statistical or demographic characteristic.

collective efficacy A group's shared belief of the extent to which the group can successfully complete a task.

communism A system of social organization in which the ownership of property is ascribed to the community or to the state.

consent The voluntary agreement by a person of age or with requisite intelligence who is not under duress or coercion and who understands the proposition to which he or she is agreeing.

corporal punishment The infliction of physical harm on a person who has broken a rule or committed an offense.

correct means In peacemaking criminology, the concept that the process of arriving at justice must be done in a just manner.

crime A violation of a law in which a person or persons are harmed.

critical-race theory A theory that asserts that race is central to law and social justice issues.

culpability Blameworthiness. The moral state of being wrong, improper, or injurious.

cultural criminology A theory that explores the relationships among culture, media institutions, crime, and social control.

D

dark figure of crime   A term used to describe crime that goes unreported to police and criminal justice officials and is never quantified.

death penalty   A punishment in which the offender is sentenced to death. Also called *capital punishment*.

defensible space   The philosophy of creating living and working spaces that are secure by design.

delinquent   See *juvenile delinquent*.

demographics   The study of the characteristics of human populations and population segments.

dependent   A term describing the status of a child who needs court protection and assistance because his or her health or welfare is endangered due to the parent's or guardian's inability, through no fault of their own, to provide proper care and supervision.

detention   The temporary care of a child alleged to be delinquent who requires secure custody in physically restricting facilities pending court disposition or execution of a court order.

determinism   The philosophical doctrine that human action is determined by external forces and is not a result of free will.

deterrence   The control of behavior through the fear of consequences.

differential association theory   A theory by Edwin Sutherland that states that crime is learned.

differential reinforcement   The rewarding of one behavior and not another or the rewarding of one behavior and punishment of another.

discretion   The power of a legal authority to decide what to do at any particular point in the justice process.

disposition   The final determination of a case or other matter by a court or other judicial entity.

dispositional hearing   The hearing in which the juvenile court renders judgment and specifies what should be done with the juvenile.

DNA (deoxyribonucleic acid)   The substance inside a cell nucleus that carries the instructions for making living organisms.

E

ego   In Sigmund Freud's theory of the human psyche, the ego is the conscious part of the personality, which one typically identifies as "self," that mediates between the pleasurable drives of the id and the moral demands of the superego.

electronic monitoring   The use of an electronic device, usually one that the offender wears, to monitor an offender's location and activities.

emotional neglect   From criminologist Harvey Wallace: "Acts or omissions of acts that are judged by community standards and professional expertise to be psychologically damaging to the child."

ethnocentrism   The belief in the natural superiority of one's particular ethnic group or culture.

eugenics   The idea that humans can be improved by strictly controlled breeding.

evolution   A gradual process in which the genetic composition of a population changes over many generations as natural selection acts on the genes of individuals.

F

false consciousness   In Marxist theory, the belief that the arrangement of the bourgeoisie owning the means of production and the proletariat working for the interests of the bourgeoisie is legitimate.

fetal alcohol syndrome   The National Institutes of Health defines this condition as a pattern of mental and physical birth abnormalities found in some children of mothers who drank excessively during pregnancy.

fraternal twins   Siblings produced by the simultaneous fertilization of two egg cells; the twins are only as genetically similar as regular siblings.

free will   The ability or discretion to make choices that are unaffected by agencies such as fate or divine will.

G

GED (general education diploma)   A certificate that certifies that a student has passed a high school equivalency test.

gender   The characteristics attributed to and accorded to males and females by society and/or culture on the basis of sex.

general deterrence   A method of control in which the punishment of a single offender sets an example for the rest of society.

generalizability   The degree to which the results of an individual study and/or investigation sample can be applied to other studies and samples.

genes   Short lengths of DNA that determine the inherited characteristics that distinguish individuals.

globalism   The philosophy or act of placing the interests of the world above those of individual nations.

globalization   Extensive economic relationships among nations.

greedy institution   A formal or informal group or organization that demands undivided loyalty from its members.

guardian *ad litem*   A person appointed by the court to take legal action on behalf of a juvenile or an adult who, because of minor age or infirmity, is unable to manage his or her own affairs.

H

Hawthorne effect   The tendency of research subjects to act differently than they normally would as a result of their awareness of being studied.

hearing   A session that takes place without a jury before a judge or magistrate in which evidence and/or argument is presented to determine some factual or legal issue.

hedonistic calculus   The idea that potential offenders plan their actions in order to maximize pleasure and minimize pain.

heredity   The handing down of traits from parents to their offspring.

heterogeneity   Consisting of dissimilar elements or parts.

home confinement   A sentence that requires that the offender be confined in and around the area of his or her home.

house of refuge   An early form of the reformatory during the mid- to late-19th century that housed impoverished and delinquent children and status offenders.

hypothesis   An untested idea that is set forth to explain a given fact or phenomenon. An educated guess.

I

id   In Sigmund Freud's theory of the human psyche, the id represents the most primitive, irrational instincts and is controlled by the pleasure principle.

identical twins   Siblings produced by the division of a single fertilized egg cell who are genetically identical.

impulsivity   The tendency to act quickly without considering the consequences.

indictment   A formal written statement that charges a person or persons with a serious offense, usually a felony.

institutionalization   The loss of the ability to make decisions for oneself because of the long period of time spent in a secure facility.

intelligence quotient (IQ)   A measure of intellectual functioning indicated by an intelligence test, usually the ratio of mental age to chronological age.

intensive-supervision probation   Close, controlled tracking of a probationer's activities by a probation officer or team of officers.

J

juvenile   An age-related status that has legal ramifications. The United States legal system generally considers anyone under 18 years of age a juvenile.

juvenile delinquency   A legal term describing the behavior of a youth that is marked by violation of the law and antisocial behavior.

juvenile delinquent   A person, usually under the age of 18, who is determined to have broken the law or committed a status offense in states in which a minor is declared to lack responsibility and may not be sentenced as an adult.

juvenile waiver   The process of sending a juvenile to be tried in criminal court.

L

labeling theory   A theory that describes how a label applied by society can affect an individual's self-perception and behavior.

left realism   A theory that considers mainstream criminology to underestimate the victimization of the poor and women and is concerned with why the poor commit offenses mainly against one another.

lex talionis   The law of retribution and/or retaliation drawn from the book of Leviticus.

life-course persistent offender   In life course criminological theory, an offender who begins inappropriate behavior at an early age and continues to commit antisocial and deviant acts.

longitudinal study   A type of study or survey in which the same subjects are observed over a usually long period of time.

M

metacognition   The act of thinking about one's processes and means of thinking.

Miranda rights   The rules concerning arrest and police interrogation that stem from the 1966 criminal case *Miranda* v. *Arizona*.

N

National Incident-Based Reporting System   A crime reporting system in which each separate offense in a crime is described, including data describing the offender(s), victim(s), and property.

negative reinforcement   Avoidance of painful or stressful conditions or events.

net-widening   Measures that bring more offenders and individuals into the criminal justice system or cause those already in the system to become more involved.

neurotransmitter   A chemical that transmits information between neurons.

No Child Left Behind Act of 2001   A federal law passed in January 2002 that seeks to improve the performance of K-12 schools.

nonorganic failure-to-thrive   A medical term that describes an infant or child who has a measurable lag in height, head size, and/or development caused by environmental factors rather than an illness or disorder.

nonsecure detention   Placement of a juvenile in a group home, foster care, or other program in which the juvenile may come and go with permission.

O

operant conditioning   A form of learning based on the positive or negative consequences of an action.

orphan trains   A term that encompasses the practice of 19th- and early 20th-century child-welfare societies of placing orphans, impoverished children, and young adults on trains to less populated parts of the United States, primarily the West.

P

pains of imprisonment   Deprivations that define the punishment aspect of incarceration.

parens patriae   Latin for "father of his country." Refers to the philosophy that the government is the ultimate guardian of all children and disabled adults.

patriarchy   A social system in which males have authority and fathers are considered the absolute head of the family.

peacemaking criminology   A branch of criminology that considers the social and personal effect of crime as a whole: not only the offender and victim, but also the social structure that accepts, enables, or encourages the offense.

peer relationships   The connections among those of equal standing within a group.

per se **requirement**   The legal requirement that an arrested juvenile consult with a parent, guardian, or other "interested adult" before or during interrogation in order to waive Miranda rights.

petition   In juvenile court, a document that alleges that a juvenile is delinquent and that asks the court to assume jurisdiction over the juvenile, or asks that an alleged delinquent be waived to criminal court to be prosecuted as an adult.

phrenology   The outdated study of the skull as an indicator of personality.

physical child abuse   According to criminologist Harvey Wallace: "Any act that results in a nonaccidental physical injury by a person who has care, custody, or control of a child."

plea bargain   A negotiation in which the defendant agrees to plead guilty or no contest to some offenses in return for some accession to the defendant.

positivist school of criminology   A school of thought that considers the causes of crime and delinquency to be external to the offender and uses scientific techniques to study crime.

postmodern criminology   In criminology, a theory that considers justice, law, fairness, responsibility, and authority not to be absolute, but to be mediated by personal contexts.

predispositional report   A report prepared by a probation officer to assist the judge in designing an appropriate disposition.

preliminary hearing   The initial pre-adjudicatory hearing in which the judge explores the nature of the case and decides if it should be processed further.

preponderance of evidence   The existence of sufficient evidence to be at least 50 percent convincing.

presentism   A belief that people of an earlier time should be accountable to the standards of the present time.

primary deviance   A term from labeling theory that describes the label that society places on the offender.

primary group   A small social group whose members share personal, enduring relationships.

primogeniture   A system of inheritance in which the oldest son receives the entire estate.

probable cause   Sufficient reason for a police officer to believe an offense has been committed; probable cause must exist for an officer to arrest (or take into custody) without a warrant, search without a warrant, or seize property.

probation   The conditional release of juveniles to the custody of parents or guardians.

proletariat   In Marxist theory, the working class.

pseudofamilies   The groups that females in adult and juvenile institutions form in response to the pains of imprisonment; they act out the roles of father, mother, and children.

psychopath   A person with a personality disorder who behaves without remorse or caring for others. Often used interchangeably with *sociopath*.

public defender An elected or appointed attorney who regularly defends those accused of criminal offenses who cannot afford a private attorney.

R

rational choice theory A theory that holds that people consciously choose criminal behavior.

reasonable suspicion Doubt that is based on specific facts or circumstances and that justifies stopping and sometimes searching an adult or juvenile thought to be involved in criminal activity or, in the case of a juvenile, a status offense.

recidivism Continuing to commit delinquent or criminal offenses after being convicted and sentenced for prior offenses.

reintegrative shaming A form of justice in which an offender is confronted and dealt with by those in his or her social network.

restitution Court-ordered compensation by the offender to the victim(s) for their psychological, physical, or financial losses resulting from an offense.

restorative justice An alternative justice model that uses community programs to repair the harm done by crime and attempts to craft long-lasting and satisfying solutions to the problems of crime.

rites of passage Ceremonies that serve to mark the passage from one stage of life to another, especially the entry of a youth into adulthood.

routine activities theory A theory that states that three conditions must be addressed in order to eliminate crime: motivated offenders, targets of opportunity, and ineffective guardianship.

S

school bonding The connection that students have to school and their academic work.

secondary deviance A term from labeling theory that describes the labels that individuals internalize and come to believe as accurate.

sex The biological designation of male or female.

shaming The act of applying a mark or stigma on disgraced individuals.

shock deterrence The practice of subjecting minor offenders, often juveniles, to an alarming experience with the justice system in order to convince them to obey the law.

shock incarceration The practice of sentencing offenders to a long period of incarceration and then granting them probation after a short time without their prior knowledge.

snowball sample A method of field research in which information is gathered by asking each person interviewed to suggest additional people for interviewing.

social cohesion A condition in which the majority of a given society's citizens respect the law and are committed to social order.

social control The framework of rules and customs that a society collectively applies to the individuals within it to maintain order.

social ecology The study of the relationships among people, their behavior, their social groups, and their environment.

socialization The process by which people learn the norms, values, and culture of their society.

social learning theory The idea that people learn behaviors by watching other people and mimicking interactions that are rewarded and avoiding those that are punished.

sociological imagination The idea that one must look beyond the obvious to evaluate how social location influences how one considers society.

sociopath A person with a personality disorder who behaves without remorse or caring for others and who often has a history of criminal behavior. Often used interchangeably with the term *psychopath*.

special conditions of probation Requirements of a person on probation that apply specifically to that person.

specific deterrence A method of control in which an offender is prevented from committing additional offenses by either incarceration or death.

spiritual explanations Explanations for crime and deviance that stem from religious belief.

standard conditions of probation Requirements of probationers that apply to all probationers, regardless of individual needs or offense.

station adjustment Handling and release of a juvenile delinquent within a police department.

status offense An act considered to be a legal offense only when committed by a juvenile; it can be adjudicated only in a juvenile court.

statutory exclusion The legal requirement that certain offenses committed by juveniles automatically be waived to criminal court without a juvenile court hearing.

strain theory The idea that juvenile delinquency is at least partially a result of being excluded from economic rewards.

superego In Sigmund Freud's theory of the human psyche, the superego internalizes the values and standards of society and represents morality.

superpredator A term coined by John Dilulio in 1995 to describe a cohort of children who were supposed to grow up to be particularly violent juvenile offenders because of poverty, maternal drug abuse, and other factors.

symbolic assailant The mental picture that many people have of what criminals look like.

T

target-hardening Making a focus of crime or delinquency as difficult as possible for potential offenders to access.

techniques of neutralization A theory that describes how some youths who break the law use rationalizations to explain away their deviant behavior.

theory A set of interconnected statements or propositions that explain how two or more events or factors are related to one another. (Daniel J. Curran and Claire M. Renzetti, *Theories of Crime,* 2nd ed., Boston: Allyn and Bacon, 2001, p. 2.)

totality of circumstances The consideration by the court of all the conditions surrounding an issue, such as police interrogation or juvenile consent to a search or interrogation.

tracking Educational paths that schools use to group students into classes with other students who have similar needs.

typology A systematic classification of types.

U–Z

Uniform Crime Reports An annual publication by the Federal Bureau of Investigation that uses data from all participating U.S. law enforcement agencies to summarize the incidence and rate of reported crime.

victim precipitation A situation in which a crime victim plays an active role in initiating a crime or escalating it.

war on crime The philosophy that the prevention of crime and treatment of offenders should be fought as a nation would fight a war, with similar tactics and strategies, and the idea of an enemy.

white-collar crime Offenses committed by people who typically work in office and professional environments.

zero-tolerance policies School regulations that give teachers and administrators little to no discretion in dealing with rule infractions.

Name Index

Subject Index

Page numbers in italic type refer to display material. Entries in bold type are key terms.